S0-AZU-401

THE INSIDERS' GUIDE TO
Tampa Bay

THE INSIDERS'® GUIDE TO

Tampa Bay

by
Suzy Dixon
and
Paula Stahel

Insiders' Publishing
105 Budleigh St.
P.O. Box 2057
Manteo, NC 27954
(252) 473-6100
www.insiders.com

Sales and Marketing:
Falcon Publishing, Inc.
P.O. Box 1718
Helena, MT 59624
(800) 582-2665
www.falconguide.com

•

THIRD EDITION
1st printing

•

Copyright ©1998
by Falcon Publishing, Inc.

•

Printed in the United States
of America

•

All rights reserved. No part of this
book may be reproduced in any form
without permission, in writing, from
the publisher, except by a reviewer
who wishes to quote brief passages
in connection with a review in a
magazine or newspaper.

Publications from The Insiders' Guide®
series are available at special discounts
for bulk purchases for sales promotions,
premiums or fundraisings. Special
editions, including personalized covers,
can be created in large quantities for
special needs. For more information,
please write to Karen Bachman, Insiders'
Publishing, P.O. Box 2057, Manteo, NC
27954, or call (800) 765-2665 Ext. 241.

ISBN 1-57380-080-5

Insiders' Publishing

Publisher/Editor-in-Chief

Beth P. Storie

Vice President/
New Business Development

Michael McOwen

Creative Services Director

Deborah Carlen

Art Director

David Haynes

Managing Editor

Dave McCarter

Production Manager

Jeanne Reilly

Project Editor

Lorraine Morton

Project Artist

Carolyn McClees

Insiders' Publishing
An imprint of Falcon Publishing Inc.
A Landmark Communications company.

Preface

When we were first approached about writing the definitive guide to the Tampa Bay area, our right brains took over immediately. We would wow you with our intimate knowledge of the area, from restaurants to attractions to little-known places for a romantic sunset rendezvous. We fantasized how we would simultaneously become the local experts on fishing and boating, and yes golf, too. We visualized how we would give painless birth to hundreds of pages of melodic prose filled with breathtaking insight and laced with award-winning humor. We mentally soared with the prospect of unfolding Tampa Bay's magnificent panorama like film processing in developing solution.

Then it happened. Our left brains kicked in.

We were struck by the weighty responsibility of representing our region — every conceivable nook and cranny of our region — in a manner that would convey to you, our reader, our humble appreciation and awesome respect for this land called the Tampa Bay region. It was then that we realized how very, very much there actually is to see and do here, far beyond what any human being could accomplish in a mere lifetime. It was then that we knew we had to do that one critical thing that was the one and only way to put us on the trajectory to our goal. Start writing.

And write we did. About the glorious, white powder beaches of the Gulf that suddenly became broader and more beautiful through our investigative eyes. About the neighborhoods, alive and vigorous with the spirit of community, which reflected in a new light the pride we all take in our homes and our area. About the previously undiscovered passion people feel about their leisure sports, about their favorite places to eat and about the care and pride they take in raising and educating their children. About the diversity of cultures that are reflected in our language, our cuisine and our marketplaces. About our thriving business environment and those gleaming facilities where our medical community stands ready to heal us when we're sick and to help bring a new generation of Floridians into the world. And about the rich history that is the soul of Tampa Bay, and those pioneering visionaries who came before us to carve out a better place to live.

What you now hold in your hands is the result of our two brain halves coming together for a singular purpose to tell you, Insider, newcomer or visitor, about the journey of new discovery that waits for you, too. We sincerely hope that you will use this book as a trusted friend in your exploration of all that is great about Tampa Bay.

Let the adventure begin!

About the Authors

Suzy Dixon

Suzy Dixon left her native Virginia for Tampa Bay four years ago and since has perfected the kamikaze driving posture that entitles her to true Tampa citizenship. Even though she faced a monthly commute between Virginia and Florida for more than two years, the genuine hospitality of Floridians made her feel like a native in very short order.

The owner of an advertising and public relations firm specializing in real estate marketing, Suzy now enjoys the company of clients in both the Hampton Roads region of Virginia and around Tampa Bay. A previous co-author of The Insiders' Guide® to the Chesapeake Bay, she has been a frequent contributor to several lifestyle magazines and is the former editor of the CommunityNews family of newspapers in Tampa Bay.

Suzy and husband Rick, a senior advertising executive, are proud to claim the title of empty nesters. They have just successfully lived through the birth of their second granddaughter, Payton, who joins Griffin in helping son Scott perfect the fine art of diaper changing in the home he shares with his wife, Monique, in Virginia Beach, Virginia. Daughter Lisa, a resident of Largo, has diligently served as deep throat for many of the Generation X Insiders' activities in the greater Tampa Bay marketplace. In their leisure time, Suzy and Rick thoroughly enjoy exploring Tampa Bay neighborhoods, taste-testing restaurants, maintaining year-round tans and calling friends back home in midwinter to inquire about their weather.

Paula L. Stahel

A firmly rooted transplant to Florida, Paula L. Stahel has made Tampa her home for nearly 20 years — long enough to look proudly on much of the area's growth, and long enough to lament the passing and changing of places and events beloved by all local Insiders.

This Michigan native adores the year-round summer climate and has even reached the point where she again enjoys West Central Florida's version of winter weather — when the temperatures actually drop below 70 for periodic three-day cold snaps, and everyone dresses like Nanuck of the North, except tourists who still think it's beach weather.

An independent writer for nearly as long as she's lived in Tampa, Paula's experience ranges from newspaper and magazine work, to an extensive list of regional and national business clients and several books.

Fully entrenched "SOK" (Insider shorthand for South of Kennedy Boulevard), Paula and her family reside in the SoHo area of Hyde Park, with a menagerie including parrots, canaries, a dog, cats and a pond lovingly known as Little Lizard Lake & Toad Refuge.

Acknowledgments

Suzy ...

So many new-found Tampa Bay friends helped steer me through the complexities of this invigorating marketplace. First thanks go to my husband, Rick, for turning the humble Weber into the primary cooking utensil during the writing of this saga. Grateful appreciation to my son and daughter-in-law, Scott and Monique, for believing Mom could do it, to daughter Lisa, who used her own Insider's savvy to steer me in the right direction, and to my mother, Eleanor, who constantly suggested that staying off the beach and hovering over the keyboard would be the smartest move to making timely deadlines.

More thanks to Connie Murphy of Intermedia Communications for her cheerleader support and guidance to the right resources for research information; Jerry King of Smith & Associates and Sarah Hand for their child care and kidstuff investigative efforts; Denny Antram of the GTE Suncoast Classic for his insights into Tampa Bay's golfing world; Janet Greene, former Director of Development for the Crisis Center of Hillsborough County Inc., for sharing her vast knowledge of the community and public agencies; and all the committed people from both Hillsborough and Pinellas counties' government agencies that provided volumes of research materials for our use. And, a most special and heartfelt thanks to Paula, who kept me informed, updated and laughing through the tears of the whole writing process.

Paula ...

There's no way to begin listing all the people and resources who contributed and helped, over both the writing of this book and the nearly two decades I've spent becoming an Insider. There are so many, from the county government employees worth far more than our taxes pay them to the wit of a bar patron in Nashville, Tennessee, who's bathroom wall graffiti is now my favorite water conservation mantra. (It's in The Natural World chapter.) But Jan, I really have to single you out for all your incredible help.

Thanks is certainly due to everyone who made and makes our area what it is — from the political escapees who long ago created Ybor City and the Crackers who settled despite the mosquitoes, to the movers and shakers who continue to lead us into the future. We're fun people with serious senses of mission and are diverse and wonderful — from the man who tutored Stevie Wonder as a teenager and now quietly helps other blind people find their places in life, to a transplanted Broadway/movie star who brings some of theater's greatest dancers here to teach clinics for local kids. Even without knowing it, they've contributed to this book, because they've contributed so much to our region.

Still, a few people deserve to be thanked by name. Suzy, once again it was a pleasure sharing this adventure with you (and commiserating over looming deadlines!). And Jan, have I mentioned how much I appreciate what you've done for my sanity? Lastly, to the honeys in my life, HJ and T, for your patience, your pride and your constant suggestions of "Here's something interesting for the book ...." I always thought so, and I hope you, dear reader, will too.

Photo: St. Petersburg/Clearwater Convention & Visitors Bureau

Collecting treasures from the sea is an age-old beach tradition.

Table of Contents

Directory of Maps

Tampa Bay Area

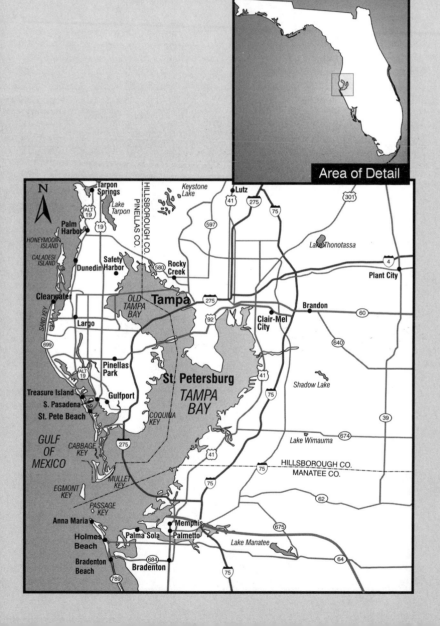

Tampa

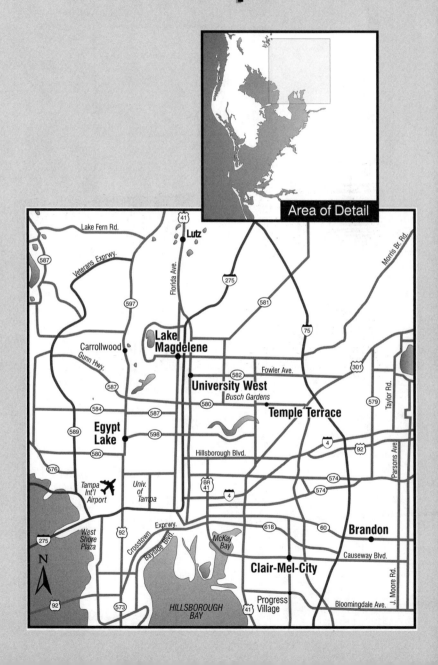

Area of Detail

St. Petersburg

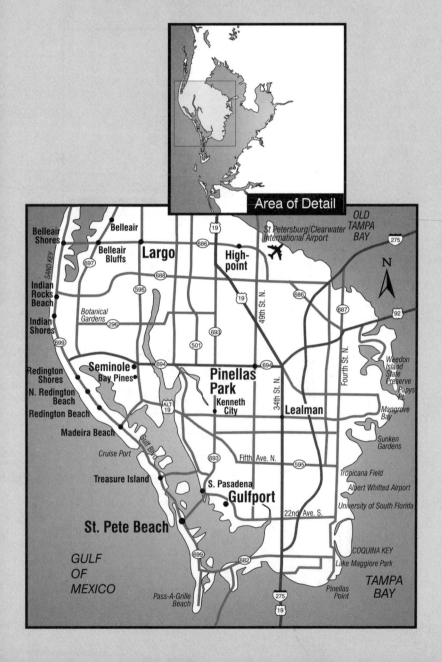

Area of Detail

How to Use
This Book

Now that you've briskly thumbed forward and back through this Insiders' Guide®, absorbing a surface grasp of all there is to know about our area, we'd like to offer you some tips for zeroing in on exactly the information you need.

Since the Tampa Bay region is so vast, within each chapter you'll find sections for Hillsborough County (which includes Tampa, Brandon, Temple Terrace and Plant City) and Pinellas County (covering St. Petersburg, Clearwater, Dunedin, Palm Harbor and all the Gulf beaches).

After a quick peek at our handy maps, you can easily see the two counties are held apart by the waters of Tampa Bay. But if your passion is for hunting antiques, shopping or museums, don't let the visual boundaries stop you from whisking from one side of Tampa

Bay to the other. A quick study of the Getting Here, Getting Around chapter will guide you easily.

It is because of the easy access from one side of the water to the other that we have broken our own organizational rule and designed our Restaurants chapter by specific cuisine, then take the county-by-county approach within each taste area.

For listings in practically every chapter (such as Attractions, Accommodations, The Arts, etc.), there is no special order, least of all alphabetical, nor are they listed in order of preference or importance in the Tampa Bay scheme of things. This is primarily because everyone's likes are so different — why, even we two coauthors couldn't manage to similarly rank any category! We'll just give you our best inside scoop and let you enjoy the

www.insiders.com

See this and many other Insiders' Guide® destinations online — in their entirety.

Visit us today!

Florida's Keys • Golf in the Caro
ving
Civil
hmond • Chesapeake Bay •
C's Central Coast • Bermu
• Relocation • Boca Rato
olina's • NC's Mountains •
gton • Cincinnati • Madiso
s • SW Utah • Salt Lake Ci
Civil War Sites • The Poco
an
es
Florida's Keys • Golf in the Caro

Photo: St. Petersburg/Clearwater Area Convention & Visitors Bureau

St. Petersburg/Clearwater area beaches stretch for 35 miles along the beautiful Gulf of Mexico. Treasure Island (shown here) claims the whitest beach on Florida's west coast.

spirit of discovery for yourself. Entries for our most popular destinations and attractions will probably be included in several different chapters. If you want to have all the background on one special item, the best place to begin is in the index at the back of the book. It will guide you to references throughout the many chapters. Insiders' Tips — those only-the-locals-know tidbits — are scattered throughout the chapters, as are special Close-ups on really important stuff such as Busch Gardens, the Tampa Theatre and Ybor City.

A note here: While you might slide right by the History chapter and feverishly flip to Nightlife, please do us the honor of taking the time to read about our rich heritage. Florida was not discovered by spring-breakers, but by stalwart, fascinating visionaries who gave this region its diversity and unwavering pride.

And lastly, because this guide is updated annually, we need to hear from you. If we missed exiting the interstate to your favorite spot or neglected to mention something you feel is important to share about Tampa Bay, tell us so we can include it in the next edition. Just drop us a note at *The Insiders' Guide to Tampa Bay*, P.O. Box 2057, Manteo, North Carolina 27954. Or visit *The Insiders' Guide®* *to Tampa Bay* online at www.insiders.com; there's a comment form on the site.

What had been a sleepy little Cracker town suddenly coped with an influx of new residents whose accents identified New York, Wisconsin, Ohio, Indiana and other chilly birthplaces.

History

The late James Michener made his winter home in St. Petersburg during many years of his life. Had he told the story of Tampa Bay's history, it probably would have begun, "Thirty million years ago …."

He would intimately guide us through the process of how this land rose from the ocean and how the Gulf of Mexico came to be. We would see the jellyfish emerge from single-cell ancestors. We would view a Paleo-Indian family from around 10,000 B.C., gathering food from the land, and furrow our brows as the father stalked a saber-toothed tiger, waiting until the exact second to thwart its lunge that would surely kill his girl child. We would watch the mammoths roam, then disappear from the land around 6500 B.C.

Michener would have shown us the rivers develop and the dwellers adapt. We would see other peoples come from the Mississippi Valley to trade and share knowledge. We would watch artistry grow as an intricate design formed beneath a young man's hands as he created a ceramic pot while on the shore at Weedon Island watching the sunrise.

We would see villages grow and the animals of the sea become the food staple, and trade missions expand between the tribes of Florida, Georgia and Alabama. As time moved closer to the Western delineation date of Christ's birth, we would see the bow and arrow rise as tools of choice in settling territorial disputes. Finally, we would watch Europeans arrive, bringing new plants such as citrus from the Orient and animals such as cattle and horses, and diseases and animosity that would annihilate and displace the natives.

But this Insider prefers to tell you the Yamasee legend that is Florida's history.

Princess of the Sea was the adored and beautiful daughter of Big Chief of the Sea. Prince of the Sun was a courageous and handsome suitor who won the princess's heart. Big Chief of the Sea so delighted in their love that he wanted to bestow upon them a special gift to honor their marriage. From the depths of himself, the sea, his magical powers brought forth a new kingdom to be their home. This new land was covered with glorious flowers, reflecting his daughter's beauty. Treasures glimmered everywhere, echoing the shimmering strength of his new son-in-law, and rivers flowed throughout, so Big Chief of the Sea could swim to visit the couple wherever they might be.

The New World Takes Hold

This peninsula, beloved for its lush beauty and myths of gold, finally settled into "mainstream America" on March 3, 1845, as the 27th member of the United States. For more than 50 years, it's been the American dream to live well, prosper and retire to Florida, but it was nearly 500 years ago that Florida first became a mecca to European explorers in search of their own riches.

Charlotte Harbor, to the south of Tampa Bay, is where Juan Ponce de Leon landed in 1521 in search of that still-elusive Fountain of Youth. Unfortunately, much like some of today's Floridians, the locals — the giantlike Calusas Indians — weren't keen on transplants increasing the area's population with the New World's very first settlement, and de Leon lost his life to an arrow wound.

Still, Ponce de Leon's death and the settlement's abandonment did nothing to diminish other Spaniards' dreams of gathering glory and gold. What they didn't know was that the small amount of gold that had been found by natives had actually washed ashore from wrecked Spanish galleons and pirate ships. It was de Leon, though, who introduced what would eventually become another form of gold to this state: It's believed that six heifers and a bull, abandoned by his settlement, became the progenitors of this state's rich cattle industry.

Next, Spain's King Charles II tapped explorer Panfilo de Narvaez in 1527 to seek El Dorado on the "island" of La Florida. Tossed off course by a hurricane, de Narvaez's expedition finally made its way to shore on April 12, 1528. The landing point on Boca Ciega Bay is commemorated on Park Street N. in St. Petersburg. Like de Leon, however, de Narvaez met his death at the hands of natives.

Another decade passed before Hernando de Soto took up King Charles' quest for riches. While he also failed to discover "The City of Gold," de Soto did realize that Florida was a peninsula, not an island as had been thought.

Reaching Tampa Bay in 1539, de Soto's group found five mineral springs near a large native village. Sick members of the party seemed miraculously cured after drinking and bathing in the springs, so de Soto called the waters *Espiritu Santo*, or "holy spirit." Native legend had long held that the waters were magical, and these springs still flow at the Safety Harbor Spa and Health Club on the edge of Tampa Bay, east of Clearwater.

Spain's rule gave way to British colonization in 1763, after the English captured Havana and returned it to Spain in exchange for all the Florida peninsula. Because of an alliance between the British and the Creek Indians in Georgia, an offshoot of Florida's then-dominant Seminole tribe, white settlers initially fared well. The territory remained loyal to England during the 1776 American Revolution. It was the British's loss in that war that made Florida a pawn to be traded back to the Spanish in the 1783 Treaty of Paris.

British settlers departed for the Bahamas and the West Indies and were replaced by the new Americans, whom Spain welcomed. Disputes, however, continually arose between the American settlers and Spain, and Florida finally became a United States possession in 1821.

Three years later Fort Brooke was created, in what is now downtown Tampa, as an outpost to protect the Bay and a few white settlers. Ten years after that, in 1834, the Territory of Florida established Hillsborough County, named after the British lord. Virtually all of central Florida — 5 million acres — comprised the county. Boundaries ran along the Gulf of Mexico from what is now Sarasota County north into Hernando County, then inland and north through Citrus and Marion counties, southward through Lake, Seminole, Orange, Osceola, Brevard, Indian River, St. Lucie and Martin counties and west at Lake Okeechobee through Glades and Charlotte counties, and back to the Gulf again. Fewer than 100 people — all white settlers since the Seminoles had been driven out — inhabited this vast region.

Among that group was the family of Dr. Odet Philippe. As a surgeon in Napoleon's French navy, Philippe was captured in the Battle of Trafalgar and imprisoned in the Bahamas. He later emigrated to South Carolina, where he married, fathered four daughters, then settled with his family on Florida's east coast. Warned by friendly Indians of an impending attack, the Philippe family sailed around the peninsula coast to the magical waters of *Espiritu Santo* they'd heard about. This first family of white settlers on the Pinellas peninsula is today honored at Safety Harbor's Philippe Park. But the doctor's legacy extends far beyond the Tampa Bay area: He adapted grapefruit to the Florida environment.

www.insiders.com

See this and many other **Insiders' Guide®** destinations online — in their entirety.

Visit us today!

INSIDERS' TIP

Courtesy of Eagle Scout Kip Zwolenski, there's now a Tampa Historical Trail you can follow. The trail meanders from Ybor Square through downtown, over to Harbour Island, along Bayshore Boulevard and back to Ybor. For trail directions, call the Tampa Historical Society at (813) 259-1111.

Photo: St. Petersburg/Clearwater Area Convention & Visitors Bureau

Docents in period costumes bring the history of Pinellas
County to the present at Heritage Village in Largo.

Before his death in 1849, Philippe greeted several more white settlers and saw considerable growth. Philippe died in 1849 after greeting more white settlers and seeing considerable growth. For example, Antonio Maximo Hernandez, who had received a land grant for fighting in the Second Seminole War, established a fish camp in 1843 near what is now St. Petersburg's Maximo Point. In 1845, Col. Robert E. Lee and troops surveyed islets in Tampa Bay, leading to the 1848 installation of the first lighthouse on Egmont Key.

During the Civil War, Florida was the third state to secede from the Union. Few battles were fought in the state, although Tampa Bay was blockaded by a contingent of Union soldiers encamped on Egmont Key.

The Reconstruction Period attracted new attention to west central Florida. Dunedin, a word meaning "peaceful nest" in Gaelic, was settled by Scottish merchants in the 1870s, and that national flavor still prevails there. Fort Harrison was established at about the same time in what was then called Clearwater and home to only 50 families.

A Union veteran became Passe-a-Grille's first resident around 1884. The next year, at the meeting of the American Medical Association in New Orleans, Pinellas' peninsula was hailed by Dr. W.C. Van Bibber for its beaches, fresh air and climate. In fact, he recommended that a world health city be established in St. Petersburg.

One deterrent to growth existed, however, and it was transportation. Travel from Gainesville, less than 200 miles away from the Pinellas coast, was a month-long trip. It took the railroads to open up Florida, and it took rivals Henry Bradley Plant and Peter Demens to bring the railroads here.

Demens extended the Orange Belt Railway from Sanford, where he owned a lumber mill, to the Gulf of Mexico on the Pinellas peninsula. H.B. Plant, who had built railroads along the state's east coast, brought trains to Tampa in 1884 — three years before the

Ybor City

It's part of Tampa, but Ybor City is a world unto itself, and it's a place that played an important role in world history.

Don Vincente Martinez Ybor and Ignacio Haya, two already prosperous cigar manufacturers, were attracted to the area in the late 1800s by a mutual friend, Gavino Gutierrez, who thought to build a guava processing plant here before he recognized a greater opportunity. The climate was much like Havana, where regulations were forcing out the cigar-making factories. Hundreds of skilled cigar workers had fled to Key West and could be easily lured. Railroads were opening the region to agricultural product transportation. Ybor and Haya saw the same future as Gutierrez and purchased a 40-acre tract of land outside Tampa.

Close-up

Don Vincente built the first cigar factory, but it was Haya who was first into production on April 13, 1886. Ybor had made the ill-fated move of hiring a fellow Spaniard as a cigar worker, and nationalistic passions led the Cubans to strike on the company's very first day of operation.

More than 20,000 skilled tradesmen hand-rolled pure Cuban tobacco leaf during the heyday of the "Cigar Capital of the World." Only a few women were employed, but those who were received fully equal rights, including the same pay and privileges as the men and the right to vote on union affairs.

At Gutierrez's first visit, Tampa was a village of only 700 people. By 1891— just five years later — Ybor City alone boasted 15,000 residents. Italians joined the Cubans, learned the Spanish language and worked in the cigar factories. Extolling the virtues of the area to friends and family back home, more Italian immigrants brought their farming and merchandising skills to the area.

Nearly every factory worker was illiterate, but they were among the best-informed people in the nation. The reason? Each contributed 25¢ a week to pay "El Lector," a highly respected person who read aloud in Spanish from a loft above their work-tables as they toiled almost silently for 10 hours each day.

The readers kept the people current on literature and news, especially conditions in their native Cuba where political unrest was growing. Written dissension was best articulated by Dr. Jose Marti, a teacher and a writer born in 1853, who led an uprising against the Spanish rulers of his homeland. Until Marti left Cuba for Ybor City, however, the revolution was a poorly organized, guerrilla affair.

Marti was a political outlaw, a wanted man in Cuba. Guarded closely by compatriots, he arrived in Ybor City in 1891. His hosts, the Pedroso family, found their home at the corner of Eighth Avenue and 13th

A bust of Jose Marti, the patron saint of Cuba's independence from Spain, graces the exterior of the Cuban Club in Ybor City.

Photo: Courtesy of Ybor City Chamber of Commerce

— continued on next page

Street transformed into a revered site among the cigar workers who stood nightly vigil outside.

Newspapers reported that more than 10,000 Cuban *émigrés* listened as Marti delivered his most memorable speech from the steps of Don Vincente's factory, now Ybor Square, in 1893. Marti called for their aid in winning Cuba's independence, eliciting roars of "Cuba libre!" again and again from the crowd. His eloquence aroused such a pitch of patriotism that workers in every Ybor factory pledged a day's pay each week to the revolutionary fund. Hundreds of men formed infantry groups to accompany Marti on the quest to create the Republica de Cuba. But in the Insurrection of 1895, at the age of 42, Dr. Marti lost his life at Dos Rios, Cuba, never to see the country freed.

Retaliation was swift. Cuba's captain general embargoed tobacco in an attempt to destroy Ybor City's economy and cut off the revolutionaries' financial backing. Ybor City manufacturers learned of the plan and approached railroad baron Henry Plant, who immediately sent his fastest two ships to Havana. Tobacco growers packed them to the hilt, staterooms and all, with the largest cargoes of tobacco ever exported from the island. It was enough to supply the cigar factories for a full year, while the Cuban's struggle for independence from Spain continued.

Historians today are divided on what actually precipitated the Spanish-American War, but when the battleship *Maine* exploded in 1898 in Havana Harbor, Ybor City reached its crescendo of rage against Spain. Lt. Col. Teddy Roosevelt and his Rough Riders were welcomed as heroes even before they embarked to fight that war. After Cuba was released from Spain's control, many Yborcitenos returned to their native land, but many more remained, keeping alive the language, the foods and the customs Tampa is so proud of today.

city incorporated. It was another endeavor — the 1891 opening of the Tampa Bay Hotel on the Hillsborough River, across from the original site of Fort Brooke — that gained him immortal fame, though. Plant invested the then-unbelievable cost of $3.5 million to create and elegantly furnish the Alahambra-style hotel with its 13 silver minarets. The hotel, now part of the University of Tampa, attracted crowned heads and tycoons from the world over.

When the Spanish-American War broke out in 1897, Plant was busy building the Belleview Hotel (now the Belleview Biltmore Resort & Spa) in Clearwater. His Tampa Bay Hotel became debarkation headquarters for Teddy Roosevelt and his Rough Riders, who trained on the hotel grounds before sailing to Cuba. In anticipation of the war's escalation, Fort De Soto went up on Mullet Key, across from Egmont Key. The munitions were, however, never needed — the war ended before the fort was completed.

Flight Into History

Getting between Tampa and St. Petersburg — a quick trip these days — was difficult at the turn of the century. St. Petersburg, incorporated in 1903, was a two-hour boat ride from the county seat of Tampa. The train from Tampa was a 64-mile, 12-hour ride. That dis-

INSIDERS' TIP

Rail baron Peter Demens, born Petrovich Demenscheff in St. Petersburg, Russia, and Gen. John C. Williams, who settled 1,700 acres of waterfront on the Gulf, flipped a coin in 1888 to see who would name the city they created. Demens won and honored the city where he was born. Williams' consolation was to name the town's first hotel after his hometown — Detroit, Michigan.

Photo: HLA Advertising and Public Relations

Tony Jannus flew the world's first commercial flight — between St. Petersburg and Tampa — in 1914.

tance fueled St. Petersburg residents' desire to break away from Hillsborough County. By a landslide vote in 1911, Pinellas County became a separate government entity, with Clearwater as the county seat.

St. Petersburg residents Tom Benoist and Percival E. Fansler were men of vision beyond even what the Wright Brothers foresaw. By 1912 Benoist was known for his School of Aviation outside of St. Louis, Missouri, and for building biplanes. Fansler, a marine diesel engine salesman, became intrigued by the idea of "flying boats" after racing hydroplanes. When the two men connected and found a city ready to "fly into the future" — St. Petersburg — commercial aviation was born.

With the backing of local businessmen, the St. Petersburg-Tampa Airboat Line was created, and famed pilot Tony Jannus was tapped to fly the new "airboat" route. In 1912, Jannus had flown the plane from which the world's first parachutist jumped. Then, he and his mechanic had set a 1,900-mile, over-the-water flight record along the Missouri

and Mississippi rivers, from Omaha to New Orleans.

On New Year's Day in 1914, more than 3,000 people gathered at a St. Petersburg waterfront hangar. Following a parade, Jannus fired up the airboat at 9:59 AM and skimmed off 15 feet above the harbor. Engine problems developed, so he set the plane down in the middle of Tampa Bay, fixed the problem and took off again.

At 10:26 AM, Jannus's airboat landed in Tampa. On hand to greet him was J.M. Lassiter, who'd made the three-hour steamer trip from St. Petersburg the night before. It took Jannus and his passenger only 23 minutes to cover the same distance. The return flight departed Tampa at 11 AM sharp and then settled down to routine flights.

Eleven days later, the budding airline again made history. A shipment of four hams and three sides of bacon from Swift & Company in Tampa to Hefner Grocery Company in St. Petersburg became the first commercial air cargo delivery. It took a scant 17 minutes. By the end of the month, an entire industry was born, launching competitors and routes that ranged from Manatee, Bradenton, Sarasota, Pass-A-Grille nd Tarpon Springs. Within two years, however, strapped by financial woes, the St. Petersburg-Tampa Airboat Line closed.

Tony Jannus died in October 1916, while testing a single-engine Curtiss K boat over the Black Sea. Today, his achievements are recognized with the annual Jannus Awards, sponsored by the Greater Tampa Chamber of Commerce. Among its recipients are such aviation pioneers as Chuck Yeager, former astronaut Frank Borman and war hero Lt. Gen. James H. Doolittle.

Greek Flavor on the Gulf

Dodecanese Boulevard doesn't seem to fit with the Indian and Latin heritage displayed elsewhere throughout the Tampa Bay area. Instead of the aromas of Spanish bean soup or grouper on the grill come the scents of moussaka and baklava. Greek music, from melodies to conversing voices, surround visitors. This is Tarpon Springs, named by Mary Ormond Boyer in 1880, for the abundant tarpon fish in the Gulf and the nearby freshwater springs.

In 1936 Tarpon Springs was the largest sponge center in the world. More than 2,000 Greeks had relocated here from the Dodecanese Islands to dive for sponges and then sell them to brokers who came from around the world to buy them. In the 1940s, though, marine bacteria destroyed most of the sponge beds, and sponge divers turned to fishing, shrimping and other businesses. Today, tourism is the city's No. 1 industry, but Tarpon Springs is once again the largest provider of natural sponges in the United States. During the summer months, weekly sponge auctions draw buyers from around the world.

Once called the "Wall Street for Sponges," the waterfront Sponge Exchange is now a shopping and dining district.

The Greek influence extends throughout the community. St. Nicholas Greek Orthodox Cathedral on N. Pinellas Avenue, a replica of St. Sophia's in Istanbul, is an outstanding example of neo-Byzantine architecture. Grecian marble in the cathedral came from the Greek pavilion at the 1939 New York World's Fair.

The War Years

Under the War Powers Act of 1942, both the Gandy Bridge and the Davis Causeway (now the Courtney Campbell Causeway) became government property. The tolls their private owners had charged were banished in an effort to speed travel by military personnel stationed at Drew Army Air Force Base. Today, this site is home to Tampa International Airport and MacDill Field as well as Naval Aviation cadets in training at St. Petersburg's Alfred Whitted Municipal Airport.

Since 1939, MacDill has been an important part of life here. Flyers trained here for duty in World War II and Korea, thus bringing thousands of families and jobs into the area. Just two years before the missile crisis, Congress began plans to substantially reduce staffing at MacDill. Castro and the Cold War changed that. Instead, MacDill's importance grew. The United States Strike Command was established here, joining all branches of the military into a fighting force capable of responding to crises anywhere in the world. That readiness was tested in the Gulf War, as our own Gen. Norman Schwarzkopf proved to the entire world.

Anyone living in Tampa during the Cuban Missile Crisis will go to their grave remember-

INSIDERS' TIP

Looking to research family roots? The Tampa Family History Center, 4106 E. Fletcher Avenue, is the place to start. This extension of the Mormon's Genealogical Society of Utah offers access to the world's largest collection of information on family lineage. Call (813) 971-2869 to schedule the necessary orientation class, then delve to your heart's content Monday through Thursday from 9 AM until 5 PM and on Tuesdays and Thursdays from 7 until 9 PM.

ing images of military tanks streaming down Dale Mabry Highway. There were rumors of Russian missiles based in Cuba that were aimed at certain strategic locations in the United States. Tampa was a prime target because of MacDill Air Force Base.

In 1993, we heard the last of the locally based F-16s roar away to a new home, ending 52 years of Air Force flying operations in Tampa. But as it has for 30 years, MacDill continues to provide a home base of operations for unified commands and training of leaders. A recent contribution to national appointment was the naming of Command Sgt. Major Robert Hall to sergeant major of the United States Army, the highest rank any enlisted soldier can achieve.

Coming Into the Cold

Like other Florida locales, the Tampa Bay area remained primarily a winter destination for travelers until air conditioning became affordable in the late 1950s. In 1971, two almost simultaneous, yet independent, developments thrust Central Florida into national limelight: Walt Disney World opened near Orlando, and Tampa International Airport led off a frenzy of economic development in the Bay area.

Continually ranked as one of the world's three top airports, Tampa International attracted corporate relocations and expansions. What had been a sleepy little Cracker town suddenly coped with an influx of new residents whose accents identified New York, Wisconsin, Ohio, Indiana and other chilly birthplaces. Fortune 500 firms opened offices. Tampa became even more attractive when John Naisbitt named it as one of the nation's 10 great cities for the 1990s in his book *Megatrends*.

Today, the most significant businesses in the Tampa Bay region are tourism and conventions, agribusiness, health/biomedical, information/high technology, business/financial services, distribution and light manufacturing. We've earned the nickname "Technology Bay" for a concentration of high-tech manufacturing and research facilities.

Still, entertaining folks, whether on vacation or in their homes, remains our greatest attraction — and the No. 1 draw is definitely sports.

Sporting Good Business

Since the days when Babe Ruth signed his first baseball contract at the Tampa Bay Hotel, our area has enjoyed the glamour of pro sports. Recently, the list of professional teams here

Photo: Florida's Pinellas Suncoast

Fill your buckets with fun on Gulf Coast beaches.

has exploded like the population. Lots of Major League teams come to our area for spring training, including The New York Yankees. In fact, the team has a new ballpark just across from Raymond James Stadium, Legends Field. Tourists and competitors flock for such annual events as the New Year's Day Hall of Fame Bowl, the Gasparilla Distance Classic and the St. Anthony's Triathlon. We also see competition on the national tours of the Senior PGA, women legends of tennis, equestrian show jumping, beach volleyball and probably a lot more we're forgetting to mention.

The National Football League awarded the Tampa Bay Buccaneers' franchise in 1974, which eventually attracted national attention from Super Bowls XVIII and XXV, and another Super Bowl in 2001. Sports have been steady throughout the decades and the persistance has culminated in a su-premely historical achievement — the AL East's newest Major League Baseball expansion team, The Tampa Bay Devil Rays! Local pride in having hometown hero Fred "The Dawg" McGriff on the team and our Pewter Power winners, the Tampa Bay Buccaneers, is running so high everyone's popping their buttons with pride to say "I'm from Tampa Bay!"

With the expansion of Major League baseball to St. Petersburg, acclaimed performances hosted at such venues as the Tampa Bay Performing Arts Center, Ruth Eckerd Hall and the Bayfront Center/Mahaffey Theater complexes, and international attention drawn to exhibits offered by museums that include the Salvador Dali Museum and the Florida International Museum, the Tampa Bay area has stepped across the threshold of a new chapter in its history. Visit often and stay tuned.

Both Tampa and
St. Petersburg are laid
out in your basic grid
pattern, with major
roads and highways
obligingly crossing each
other in a sensible
cross-hatch.

Getting Here, Getting Around

AGetting Around Tampa Bay Primer: Dale Mabry Highway, Interstate 275, U.S. Highway 19. End of story.

Actually, if you constantly get that urge to merge, getting around either Hillsborough (Tampa) or Pinellas (St. Petersburg/ Clearwater) counties is not so difficult. As long as you can memorize north and south, east and west, you and any white-knuckled passengers have got it made. Both Tampa and St. Petersburg are laid out in your basic grid pattern, with major roads and highways obligingly crossing each other in a sensible crosshatch. As you stop-go, stop-go through Tampa, most directions will advise you on exits from I-275 or cross-street references from Dale Mabry Highway.

In St. Petersburg and Clearwater, you'll zip east or west off U.S. 19. Central Avenue is the north-south dividing line in St. Petersburg. Fans of the one-way system will love this city. For the most part, south of Central Avenue, even-numbered avenues go west and odd-numbered avenues go east. North of Central Avenue, even-numbered avenues go east and odd-numbered avenues go west. Streets, you ask? Most even-numbered streets go south and odd-numbered streets go north. Got it?

For Gulf Beaches, it's a piece of cake. Gulf Boulevard is the only way to traverse that crooked finger of land. It runs north and south, with crossing avenues extending as far as the landmass itself allows, matching Gulf Boulevard addresses with avenue numbers. For example, if 5500 shows up on a Gulf Boulevard address, lay your bets on it being at 55th Avenue.

Getting to the heart of the matter in Tampa, standing at the corner of Kennedy Boulevard and Florida Avenue will literally put you in the center of the city. Kennedy Boulevard (Fla. Highway 60) is the east-west dividing line of the city, splitting the city north and south. Florida Avenue, running north and south, separates east side from west. The most heavily traveled, shopping-stripped and restaurant-laden roadway is Dale Mabry, called N. Dale Mabry above Kennedy and S. Dale Mabry below, territorially referred to as N.O.K. (north of Kennedy) and S.O.K. (south of Kennedy). If you must know the truth, real Insiders know how to get from one tip of the city to the other without laying wheel one on this wild and wacky strip of asphalt, where the rules of the road are in a foreign language for everyone except those road warriors who have steered through a California freeway or the streets of Manhattan.

In St. Petersburg/Clearwater, U.S. 19 can claim the same infamy — note the bumper stickers that read "Pray For Me. I Drive 19." Because most drivers know exactly where they're going and need to get there in a dreadful hurry, our advice is to take a moment to carefully chart your course and locate the correct exit to get you to your destination. Then, get in the proper exit lane miles before you think you need to. The same holds true for I-275 in both cities. Posted speed limits don't seem to be worth the metal they're painted on. If you're unsure of where you are, stay to the right, stay cool and stay out of harm's way.

If you're feeling really comfortable about driving around, we need to point out one spot in Tampa, lovingly referred to as Malfunction Junction, where I-275 slaps up to I-4 on the east side of town, which, in turn, swings you to I-75, the major north-south route in and out of our region. Shall we just say that an armored tank couldn't provide more protection than your own keen attention to the merging traffic in this area. While courtesy spills out of normal people when their feet are on solid ground, place a little round wheel in their hands and there's just something about this intersection that stimulates the Jekyll-Hyde syndrome. Be warned. Be careful. And, as long as you're on treacherous "merge alert," also keep your eyes wide open at I-275 and Bearss Avenue, I-275 at Busch Boulevard and the Courtney Campbell Causeway at Fla. 60. These have been deemed the most notorious of the accident-prone intersections by the Florida Department of Transportation.

Now that we have those car keys rattling uncontrollably in your hand, we'll point out some good stuff. All major roadways and interstates are unusually well-marked for most popular destinations, giving you adequate advance warning that a lane change might be necessary.

Insiders with correct directions are everywhere and helpful, usually giving you excellent landmark references to get you to where you want to be — don't hesitate to pull off the road and ask for help. Maps of both counties are plentiful and free, and most clearly illustrate popular points of interest. Grab a bunch and use them.

If you must traverse Tampa from north to south, may we suggest the $332 million lifesaver — the Veterans Expressway. Running for 15 miles, from the northern part of Hillsborough County to the Courtney Campbell Causeway and connecting to I-275, the Veterans most times appears to be an undiscovered wasteland because traffic has been so light since its opening at the end of 1994. Perhaps it's because it's a toll road, costing $1.25 to run its full length, but a very small price to pay to avoid the kamikaze mentality of drivers on N. Dale Mabry Highway. While the map may be the easiest way to locate entry points to the expressway, signs that specifically say "Veterans Expressway" are clearly posted.

Even with the trillions of cars on the road with passengers on their way to who knows where, parking isn't all that difficult a feat in Tampa or St. Pete. All attractions and shopping areas have adequately paved the way for your parking convenience, and, even in downtown areas, you should be able to find a close-by garage, lot or metered on-street parking. Along the beaches, metered parking is the rule, though there are some mini-lots along Gulf Boulevard if you know where to look and are early enough to snag a space. Clearwater Beach has two large lots available, but do arrive early to secure your position. In almost every case where there is a charge for parking, the fee is nominal and clearly posted. Now, having said that, do be aware that if it's New Year's Eve, a Bucs, Devil Rays or Lightning game night or any other major event, leave yourself a little extra time — and change — to stash your vehicle.

As for the basic rules of the road, we'll refresh your memory:

Wear your seat belts and restrain children younger than the age of 5.

Turning right on red is permitted after a full stop and allowing other vehicles and pedestrians the right of way.

Then, there are the special Tampa Bay rules:

Do not tailgate. You're most liable to wind up in the other car's backseat.

www.insiders.com

See this and many other **Insiders' Guide®** destinations online — in their entirety.

Visit us today!

INSIDERS' TIP

Alert for teens behind the wheel! A new law bans 17-year-olds from driving between 1 and 5 AM and 16-year-olds from driving between 11 PM and 6 AM. The only exceptions are for teens going to or from work, or if they are accompanied by a driver who is at least 21 years old.

Saltwater anglers can snag more than 300 varieties of fish from the Gulf.

A light sprinkle can be as dangerous as a blinding thunderstorm as our roadways become surprisingly slick at the first spit of rain. Unless you're trained for stuntman wheelies, take extra precaution when storm clouds gather.

Although most drivers, presumably assuming you have ESP, do not bother to use a turn signal when changing lanes, use yours in last-ditch self-defense.

And lastly, even if you're in our fair cities to party, party, party, do not even think of attempting to operate a vehicle under the influence of alcohol. Call a cab, instead, and live to enjoy the remainder of your vacation.

Bridging the Gap

Going from Point A: Tampa, to Point B: St. Petersburg/Clearwater and the beaches, requires either a watercraft or a bridge. Starting from the top (north) down, you can select your bridge du jour, beginning with the Courtney Campbell Causeway, a narrow strip that runs just west of the airport in Tampa and takes you to Clearwater. All along its length you'll see small pockets of beachgoers and anglers splashing and casting into Old Tampa Bay. Except in peak rush hours, it's the most pleasant of crossings, coasting along this palm-lined connector that will drop you on Fla. 60 for your trek to U.S. 19 or the Gulf beaches.

A stone's throw south of the Courtney Campbell is the Howard Frankland Bridge, part of the I-275 system. If speed is of the essence (except, again, in the peak rush-hour frenzy), the Howard Frankenstein — a popular nickname — is a superb choice with its two bridges of four lanes each. Otherwise, we'd opt for the more scenic route every time.

Lastly, there's the Gandy Bridge, exiting the southernmost part of Tampa just north of MacDill Air Force Base and shooting you to St. Petersburg. Having just completed a $31 million facelift for a new westbound span, the good old Gandy is once again a commuter's favorite crossing.

Preparing for Bridge Overload

Once you've gotten from Tampa to St. Petersburg or Clearwater, you've yet to catch a glimpse of the Gulf of Mexico. Here are a few choices to get from here to there, again north to south.

The Memorial Causeway links downtown Clearwater with Clearwater Beach. It's just a short hop, and you'll see the cruise boats, the Clearwater Marina and beautiful waterfront homes in the distance as you descend onto official Clearwater Beach territory. On route to the causeway, don't panic when you're faced with the choice of Fla. 60 Business or Bypass; both will get you back to the same point. Just try to keep your eyes on the road.

Clearwater Beach Pass, the cherished antique bridge that connected the southern tip of Clearwater Beach to Sand Key, was recently demolished to give breathing space to the new 74-foot-high span that has replaced it. If you're new to our area, you might hear talk about the old days when crossing from one shore to the other meant driving on the rickety old span at a maximum speed of 15 mph.

Belleair Causeway links lucky residents of Belleair Shore, Belleair Beach and Sand Key

Tampa International Airport — One Of The World's Best

Tampa Bay area residents are rightfully proud of Tampa International Airport: even though it's passed its quarter-century mark, it's still considered one of the top airports in the world and is consistently rated as the best in America.

When it opened in 1971, it revolutionized airport design because so much attention is paid to traveler convenience and pleasure. And that focus has never been lost.

What makes TIA unique?

First, its overall design. TIA is made up of a central facility called the Landside terminal. In this three-level building are ticketing, baggage, car rental agencies, shops, restaurants, a bank, a foreign currency exchange, duty-free shops, a Marriott hotel and other amenities. Multi-level short-term and long-term parking facilities are above and immediately adjacent to the Landside.

Extending from the Landside hub are six satellite terminals called Airsides. Visitors move between the Landside and the Airsides via automated shuttles. Passengers are never more than a few steps away from escalators, elevators or people-movers. In fact,  you never have to walk more than 700 steps, even on your way to the most remote gate. (Just try that at Atlanta's Hartsfield or Chicago's O'Hare!) At each Airside, travelers find more shops, restaurants and lounges.

CK's Restaurant offers an incredible view of the Tampa Bay area. Set atop the Marriott, CK's spins 360 degrees each hour, providing a panoramic scope of downtown Tampa's skyline, Old Tampa Bay and the bridges to St. Petersburg and Clearwater. This is a great place to celebrate an achievement or anniversary, or just have a drink and watch the spectacular sunset.

Shopping at the airport ranges from expected Florida souvenirs to the truly unusual. A completely redesigned shopping arena at the center of Landside opened in the summer of 1998, filled with the entire array of cosmopolitan selections one would find in a unique village. Shoppers find everything from daily necessities to the pampering of aroma therapy, from a vast selection of fresh Florida produce to the jolt of Starbucks'

— continued on next page

Photo: HLA Advertising and Public Relations

Travelers worldwide agree — TIA is one of the best airports.

java, and a glimpse into area attractions, a step into the fantasy of flight and museum-quality art.

You'll find art in numerous places throughout TIA. Individually sculpted bronze birds and porpoises float high above escalators and stand watch throughout the ticketing area. If you're connecting with traveling companions or guests, the perfect place to suggest is "The Meeting Place," a sculpted tree filled with bronze pelicans centered at Landside.

Our favorite TIA art is in the baggage claim area. Here, take notice of the enormous, gorgeous wall tapestries depicting Florida scenes. Each is hand-woven, using an ancient African method and done by women who came to America for two years to create their art exclusively for our airport.

Tampa International Airport has another unique element — the group which governs it. The Hillsborough County Aviation Authority (HCAA) was created more than 50 years ago by our State Legislature as a "Public Body Corporate." This authority was one of the first in the nation to combine the revenue-generating ability of private enterprise with the public accountability of a governmental institution. At first, the HCAA received a limited property tax levy for operating income. But for the past quarter-century, it's been financially self-sufficient. Today, the value of county airport property exceeds $1 billion.

Since its opening, TIA has earned an unbroken string of No. 1 rankings in surveys conducted by such groups as the U.S. Travel and Tourism Administration, the International Passengers Association and the readers of *Conde Nast Traveler* magazine. The travelers prove it with their love of the Tampa Bay area — nearly 14 million passengers passed through the airport in 1997. And by the end of this decade, TIA expects to serve more than 20 million travelers.

We hope you're among them!

Beach with Largo and Belleair Bluffs. Indian Rocks Bridge is passageway for Indian Rocks Beach and Largo, and Park Boulevard Causeway connects Indian Shores with Pinellas Park/Seminole (north of St. Petersburg). Next is Tom Stewart Causeway, which ties Madeira Beach to St. Petersburg, and then the Treasure Island Causeway, which costs 50¢ to get to St. Petersburg. St. Petersburg Causeway is the main connector between St. Petersburg and St. Pete Beach and, lastly, Pinellas Bayway requests 50¢ to do a similar St. Petersburg/St. Pete Beach connection.

So, How Do We Get There?

In typical Tampa Bay cart-before-the-horse fashion, we really should get you here first.

By Car

By car, I-75 is the ticket, entering Hillsborough County from the north, and picking up to the south via the Skyway Bridge from St. Petersburg. Extending from South Florida to Georgia and on to the Midwest, I-75 is scheduled to be widened to six lanes north through Atlanta within the next three years.

By Air

Tampa International Airport
Tampa • (813) 870-8770

Arriving by air is a real traveler's treat, especially if you fly into the one and only Tampa International Airport. Bragging rights are totally in order for this exceptional facility, served by nearly every major United States airline and a number of international carriers. Please do us the pleasure of reading this chapter's Close-up about our award-winning airport, of which we are exceedingly and justifiably proud.

With high hopes of landing in the middle of a huge fare war, you may contact the following airlines who serve our market: Air Canada, America West, American, Cayman Airlines, Continental, Delta, Midwest Express, TWA, United, USAirways and the Insiders' favorite TIA resident, Southwest Airlines. Our advice is to start with a competent travel agent who can let his or her computer fly through the myriad of options to secure your most direct route and lowest fare.

St. Petersburg/Clearwater Airport
Roosevelt Blvd., Clearwater
• **(727) 535-7600**

You can opt to fly directly into the St. Petersburg side of Tampa Bay through the St. Petersburg/Clearwater Airport, which served nearly a million passengers in 1997. A full-service facility, the airport is also a favorite for corporate jets and private aircraft. The real plus here is the free parking, almost unheard of these days.

Albert Whitted Municipal Airport
108 Eighth Ave. S.E., St. Petersburg
• **(727) 893-7654**

In St. Pete is the Albert Whitted Municipal Airport, along the downtown waterfront. Service here is geared toward corporate aircraft, helicopters, private pilots and instructors, air ambulances and other medically related transportation.

Car Rentals

Departing either TIA or St. Petersburg/Clearwater airports is almost as simple as flying in. Rental-car companies have the drill down to a science, and we bet you'll be most pleasantly surprised with their superior speed and service. Advance booking for your rental car is a given, however, so be certain to contact any of the major rental-car companies to secure your wheels of choice prior to your departure. (May we sug-

---

INSIDERS' TIP

An Orangecycle? If you spot a bright orange bicycle along a downtown Tampa street, hop on for a free ride. It's one of 50 "orangecycles" — stolen or lost bikes that were never claimed from police — painted our favorite Florida color for free public use.

gest a sporty convertible? It's the only way to go!)

A few car-rental recommendations:
Alamo, (800) 327-9633;
Avis, (800) 331-1212;
Budget, (800) 527-0700;
Dollar, (800) 800-4000;
Enterprise, (800) 325-8007;
Hertz, (800) 654-3131;
Thrifty, (800)368-2277;
Value, (800) 468-2583.

Taxis

Taxis are another option if your plans do not include do-it-yourself driving or complimentary hotel transportation. If headed to the Gulf beaches, plan on spending $12 to $35 from TIA and $10 to $25 from St. Petersburg/Clearwater Airport, depending on your carrier. Check the fare before you load your inner tube in the trunk. For around town jaunts, you can expect to pay fares that range from 95¢ to $1.50 a mile.

In Tampa:
Tampa Bay Cab Co., (813) 251-5555;
Taxi Plus, (813) 228-7587;
United Cab, (813) 253-2424;
Yellow Cab, (813) 253-0121.
In St. Petersburg and on the Beaches:
AAA Taxi and Limo, (727) 392-1978;
ABC All Beaches Taxi, (727) 398-7620;
BATS Taxi Company, (727) 367-3702;
Beach Taxi and Airport Service,
(727) 797-2230;
Clearwater Yellow Cab, (727) 799-2222;
St. Pete Taxi, (727) 327-3600;
Suncoast Yellow Cab, (727) 821-7777.

Limousines

For more decadent travelers:
Alpha Limousine Inc., (813) 247-6190;
The Limo Inc., (813) 572-1111;
Red Line Limo Inc., (813) 535-3391.

By Train

Amtrak
601 Nebraska Ave. N., Tampa
• (800) 872-7245

If you're headed to our cities from northern points, Amtrak says "All aboard!" Journeys on either the *Silver Star* or *Silver Meteor*

trains terminate at the brilliantly restored Tampa Amtrak Station on Nebraska Avenue in Tampa, (813) 221-7600. If your final destination is St. Petersburg, you'll be shuttled to the St. Petersburg Amtrak Station at Pinellas Square Mall in Pinellas Park. If Clearwater is your final destination, you'll be shuttle-bused to the Holiday Inn Suites at 20967 U.S. 19 N.

If you're planning to stay a while, or at least until it warms up in your own hometown, you might want to check out Amtrak's Auto Train. While you won't be transported directly into the Tampa Bay area, you'll have just a short trip from the Auto Train's Sanford depot, about an hour northeast of Orlando. Both you and your vehicle can board the train in Lorton, Virginia, about an hour south of Washington, D.C. You'll be wined and dined on the overnight trip, with your auto or van comfortably stowed in a secure car carrier. For current rate and schedule information, call Amtrak toll-free at (800) 872-7245.

By Bus

Greyhound/Trailways
610 Polk St., Tampa • (813) 229-2112
180 Ninth St. N., St Petersburg
• (800) 231-2222

Greyhound/Trailways buses arrive every day from departure points all across the country. Polite drivers drop Tampa-bound passengers on Polk Street, and St. Pete riders at the carrier's downtown depot on Ninth Street N.

By Boat

If, when sailing the Gulf, you perchance want to buzz by and check out the sights, several marinas are ready to toss you a docking rope. Do be forewarned, however, that the most popular marinas have waiting lists and docking limits, so be certain to make your arrangements in advance, lest you be cast off to drift asea.

In Tampa:
Harbour Island Marina, (813) 229-5324.

In St. Pete:
St. Petersburg Municipal Marina,
(727) 893-7329;
Harborage at Bayboro, (727) 821-6347;
Maximo Moorings, (727) 867-1102.

What's in a Name?

If you're wondering how the streets in Tampa got their names, we're here to save the day with a few little tidbits of history. Many of the streets in early Tampa were named for presidents, including Washington, Jefferson, Tyler, Pierce, Jackson and Polk. In Ybor City, streets were originally named for states, but since early immigrants just couldn't pronounce the names, they were changed to numbers. Only the street named Nebraska survived the transformation. Other byways got their monikers from early residents and developers, politicians and pioneers of the day. Here are just a few street names you might recognize and the people who inspired them:

Ashley Drive — Named for the city's first city clerk and a warden for Port of Tampa, William Ashley (1804-1873).

Armenia Avenue — Named, some believe, for the daughter of the founder of Armina Cigar Company. Others believe it was named after the country of Armenia, which was under attack by the Turks during the time the street was originally named.

Busch Boulevard — Not such a toughie. It was named for August A. Busch Jr., who brought us Busch Gardens.

Fowler Avenue — Named after Maud C. Fowler (1874-1941), a successful real estate operator and developer of Temple Terrace.

Florida Avenue — This one got its start as Monroe Street, after President James Monroe.

Howard Frankland Bridge — Named for William Howard Frankland (1901-1980), the president of First National Bank and inventor of the tandem bicycle.

Gandy Bridge, Gandy Boulevard — Named for the builder of the bridge, George S. Gandy (1851-1946).

Henderson Boulevard — Tampa's most diagonal road was the result of a cattle route used by William Henderson (1839-1909). He was also the president of the Bank of West Tampa and co-owned Tampa Steamship Company.

Himes Avenue — In 1915, William F. Himes (1879-1949) sponsored a bill that created the State Road Department, father of today's Department of Transportation.

Hyde Park — Named by developer O.H. Platt for his hometown of Hyde Park, Illinois.

Linebaugh Avenue — This one is in tribute to Henry T. Linebaugh (1865-1943), who came to Tampa on a wagon train, labored as a Ybor City cigar worker and organized the YMCA.

Dale Mabry Highway — Dale Mabry (1891-1922) was a World War I pilot killed when airship *Roma* crashed during a test run in Norfolk, Virginia.

Plant Avenue — This one's for the man who brought the railroad to Tampa. Henry B. Plant (1819-1899) also built the Tampa Bay Hotel, which is now part of the University of Tampa.

— continued on next page

Whiting Street — Maj. Levi Whiting (17??-1852) became commanding officer of the 1st artillery at Fort Brooke following his enlistment in 1812.

Zack Street — Because he knew John Jackson, who named most of the downtown streets, President Zachary Taylor (1784-1850) can claim the honor. He also oversaw Fort Brooke during the Seminole Indian War.

Getting Around Town by Land and by Sea

Other than rental car, taxi, limo and flip-flops, there are more ways to cruise through and around our region. Public transportation — read: The Bus — is one option. Schedules and days of operation do vary, and a phone call may help avoid much frustration and delay. Buses in outlying communities offer local transit as well as connections to the Pinellas Suncoast Transit Authority (PSTA).

Public Transportation

The Hillsborough Area Regional Transit Authority/HARTline
Tampa • (813) 254-HART

It costs $1.15 for local service and $1.50 for express routes along the 1,000-mile HARTline system. If you're a biker, you might want to check out BOB, the affectionate name for the Bikes on Buses Program. Almost every HARTline bus has a special bike rack attached in front to accommodate two bicycles. This means that even if you pedal out with Tour de France fervor, good old HARTline has a backup plan in place to get you back home. If you're curious about who uses this innovative service, here are some stats: most are between 30 and 50 years of age, use BOB at least three times a month and are

headed to the downtown area. If you want to join the 4,000 people who take advantage of BOB every month, you will be required to get a special permit. All you need to do, however, is watch a brief safety film and go through a short educational session to receive your permit that resembles a driver's license, complete with your mugshot.

The Pinellas Suncoast Transit Authority/PSTA
St. Petersburg/Clearwater
• **(727) 530-9911**

One of the most difficult things about taking a bus is figuring out which one to take. PSTA makes it simple with their Infoline, (727) 530-9911, that can help you chart your route seven days a week. The basic fare is $1; one-day, seven-day and monthly passes can be purchased at reduced rates.

For people with disabilities, PSTA offers a special door-to-door transportation service called DART (Dial-A-Ride Transit). Vehicles in this fleet are equipped with wheelchair lifts. For complete information, call (727) 530-9921.

BATS City Transit
St. Pete Beach • (727) 367-3086

The fare is $1 for this small line that serves St. Pete Beach. It runs seven days a week from Pass-A-Grille north on Gulf Boulevard and loops from St. Pete Beach Causeway to the South Pasadena Shopping Center. BATS also connects with PSTA buses that run to downtown St. Petersburg.

INSIDERS' TIP

Ready to get your Florida driver's license? To get your assigned number, the Florida Department of Motor Vehicles uses the Soundex system to scramble your name, date of birth and sex to produce your own personal number. A tiebreaker number is also thrown in just in case someone else shares the same information.

Treasure Island Transit System
Treasure Island • (727) 360-0811

Again, $1 is the fare and you can connect with PSTA routes. The buses run hourly within the boundaries of Treasure Island.

Jolley Trolley
Clearwater Beach • (727) 530-9911

Insiders who favor Clearwater Beach vote for the Jolley Trolley, operated by PSTA, which offers a free lift along Mandalay Avenue, Gulf Boulevard and S. Gulfview Boulevard. It runs every day of the week from 10 AM until midnight, and even if you have a rental car you ought to give the Trolley a run. It's pretty much a loosy-goosey sort of transportation. Just flag it down at any point along the route.

People Mover
Downtown Tampa • (813) 202-1930

If in downtown Tampa with a hankering to visit Harbour Island, do what all bona fide Insiders do — try the People Mover. It's a motorized tram that whisks you from the Fort Brooke Parking Garage on Whiting Street between Franklin and Florida. Although rumor has it that the People Mover will be scrapped in favor of a rubber-tired trolley, as of this writing you can still turn in your quarter for a token to travel Monday through Saturday from 7 AM until 2 AM and Sunday from 8 AM until 11 PM.

Westshore Shuttle
Tampa

This great service for the popular Westshore area helps alleviate gridlock when the noontime bell rings. Four buses circulate along a popular 3-mile route every five minutes between 11 AM and 2 PM, Monday through Friday. Just 25¢ will get you to Westshore Plaza and back in a blink of the eye.

Tampa–Ybor Trolley
Tampa • (813) 254-4278, (813) 623-9988

Clang! Clang! Clang! Here comes the Tampa-Ybor Trolley, rolling from downtown Tampa to Garrison Seaport to the Florida Aquarium to Ybor City. The antique green diesel-powered trolley cars are Tampa Bay's version of the San Francisco cable cars and are as warmly greeted by people on the move. There are 18 convenient stops along the Trolley's full route that runs from 9 AM until 4 PM. Between the hours of 7:30 and 9 AM and 4 and 5:30 PM, the Trolley takes on five popular stops: Marion Street at Fort Brooke Station, Franklin Street at Whiting Street, Tampa Bay Convention Center, Harbor Island and the Florida Aquarium. Hop on board for the 25¢ one-way fare.

Clearwater Express
Drew St. Dock, Clearwater
• (727) 422-RIDE

For a different twist on taxi service, try out the Clearwater Express, a water-taxi service that connects downtown Clearwater with Clearwater Beach. The fare is $2, and ferries operate Tuesday through Sunday, but schedules do vary according to whim. Call for current crossing schedules.

Tampa Water Taxi
Tampa • (813) 223-1522

Not to be outdone, Tampa also has its own version of the water taxi, the Tampa Water Taxi, which makes waves along the downtown waterfront. The precious green-and-white flat-bottomed vessels are jet-driven, not propeller-driven, to protect manatees and other sea life. From its base on a floating barge at the northeast end of the Florida Aquarium's waterfront, the ferry stops at Tampa Bay Convention Center, Tampa Museum of Art, Henry B. Plant Museum, Quality Hotel Riverside, Tampa Bay Performing Arts Center, Tampa General Hospital, Bayshore Marina and Marjorie Park Marina on Davis Islands. Half-hour cruises cost $6 a round trip for adults, $5 for seniors and $4 for students. Children younger than 6 travel at no charge on the Water Taxi that runs daily from 11 AM until 5 PM.

And if you want to take a cruise to nowhere, do we have options to surprise and confuse you! Fast-forward to the Attractions chapter for the whole rundown of options.

Tourist Information

For maps and miscellaneous volumes of visitors propaganda to study prior to your visit, these are the organizations to contact:

Tampa/Hillsborough Convention & Visitor Association Inc., Visitor Information Center, 111 Madison Street, Suite 1010, Tampa, FL 33602, (813) 223-2752, (800) 44-TAMPA;

Tampa Bay Visitor Information Center, 3601 E. Busch Boulevard, Tampa, FL 33612, (813) 985-3601;

St. Petersburg/Clearwater Area Convention & Visitors Bureau, 4905 34th Street S., #333, St. Petersburg, FL 33711, (727) 345-6710, (800) 951-1111; Canadian Office, 102 Bloor Street W., Suite 460, Toronto, ON M5S 1M8 Canada, (416) 927-1505.

For more in-depth information on our region, please contact:

Greater Tampa Chamber of Commerce, 401 E. Jackson Street, Tampa, FL 33602, (813) 228-7777;

Sun City Center Chamber of Commerce, 1651 Sun City Center Plaza, Sun City Center, FL 33573, (813) 634-5111;

Ybor City Chamber of Commerce, 1800 E. Eighth Avenue, Tampa, FL 33605, (813) 248-3712;

St. Petersburg Area Chamber of Commerce, 100 Second Avenue N., St. Petersburg, FL 33731, (727) 821-4069;

Chamber of Commerce of Largo, 395 First Avenue S.W., Largo, FL 34640, (727) 584-2321;

Greater Clearwater Chamber of Commerce, 128 Osceola Avenue N., Clearwater, FL 34615, (727) 461-0011;

Gulf Beaches on Sand Key Chamber of Commerce, 105 Fifth Avenue, Indian Rocks Beach, FL 34635, (727) 595-4575 and 501 150th Avenue, Madeira Beach, FL 33708, (727) 391-7373;

Dunedin Chamber of Commerce, 301 Main Street, Dunedin, FL 34698, (727) 755-3197;

Greater Palm Harbor Area Chamber of Commerce, 33451 U.S. Highway 19 N., Palm Harbor, FL 34684, (727) 784-4387;

Palm Harbor Area Chamber of Commerce, 33451 U.S. 19 N., Palm Harbor, FL 34684, (727) 784-4387;

Pinellas Park Chamber of Commerce, 5851 Park Boulevard N., Pinellas Park, FL 33781, (727) 544-4777;

Safety Harbor Chamber of Commerce, 200 Main Street, Safety Harbor, FL 34698, (727) 726-2890;

St. Pete Beach Chamber of Commerce, 6990 Gulf Boulevard, St. Pete Beach, FL 33736, (727) 360-6957;

Tarpon Springs Chamber of Commerce, 210 S. Pinellas Avenue, Tarpon Springs, FL 34689, (813) 937-6109;

Treasure Island Chamber of Commerce, 152 108th Avenue, Treasure Island, FL 33706, (727) 367-4529.

Depending on whether
you plan to wear a tie or
flip-flops, there's
a sleep-tight place
just your style.

Accommodations

You're pooped. You need a comfy bed and a plump pillow. Well, you've certainly come to the right place.

Whether your destination is Hillsborough or Pinellas County, and you're on a business trip or a vacation, we can offer a full menu of accommodation choices that run the gamut from drop-dead gorgeous, upscale resorts to pin-striped executive hotels to down-home friendly mom 'n' pop beach cottages. So, depending on whether you plan to wear a tie or flip-flops, there's a sleep-tight place just your style.

A few room rules here. First, if you plan to visit during the high season (that's December through April), don't even think about heading our way without an advance reservation. Especially along the Gulf beaches, the "No Vacancy" signs flash nonstop during that time of year, likewise for Tampa properties that are favored by the convention and meeting crowd. Also be aware that there may be minimum-stay requirements at most hotels on the beaches; make certain you're aware of these minimums as well as the respective cancellation policies as well.

In Tampa (with the exception of the hotels clustered around Busch Gardens) and downtown St. Petersburg, you can expect weekend rates to be considerably lower than weekday rates when the rooms are usually filled with business types. And if you can plan your vacation during May, September or October, you can expect to save up to 50 percent off the high-season rates along the popular Gulf beaches.

Around these parts, nothing's guaranteed except sunburn and taxes. If you stay in Tampa, you'll pay an extra 10.5 percent tax on the price of your room (6.5 percent for Florida sales tax and 4 percent for city and resort tax). In St. Pete, count on 10 percent tax (7 percent for Florida state and county taxes and a 3 percent resort tax). When it comes to tipping, that will be at your own discretion if daily maid service is provided.

Note: Each establishment sets its own policy concerning pets. If you plan to travel with a four-legged friend, we suggest you check with your hotel of choice as to its specific pet policies.

There are, however, a few places that actually roll out the red carpet wide enough for four legs and encourage you to bark for room service. First, there's the All Pets Inn, 5340 66th Street N., St. Petersburg, (727) 546-1108, a pooch-pampering experience for your pet to vacation on his or her own. Actually it's a kennel with a twist — private rooms, "home-cooked" gourmet food and a staff vet who will minister to your animal's every desire for affection.

Price Code

What follows is a brief overview of the accommodation possibilities and just a sampling of the wide spectrum of alternatives that await your reservation. We provide you with a nifty little price code, too. These dollar signs represent the average rate for double occupancy, and you can expect these rates to fluctuate from high season to low. Please confirm the current going rates when making your reservations. While practically all hotels listed here accept major credit cards, please confirm the plastic of your choice when you call.

$	Less than $50
$$	$50 to $95
$$$	$96 to $130
$$$$	More than $130

If you want to share every lovely minute of your holiday with your special pet, book into the Lorelei Resort, 10273 Gulf Boulevard, Treasure Island, (727) 360-4351, (800) 35-GO-DOG. Every room comes equipped with a pet bed, and the sundeck and waterfront patio are enclosed to avoid any mischievous wandering away ... but why would they? They not only have their own swimming platform, but a groommobile for that bath and haircut, and even a photographer ready to snap that winning tail wag. Just in case, there's a vet on call 24 hours a day. Now, who says Tampa Bay isn't all things to all people — and pets, too!

www.insiders.com

See this and many other **Insiders' Guide®** destinations online — in their entirety.

Visit us today!

Hotels, Motels and Resorts

Tampa

Downtown/Harbour Island

Hyatt Regency Tampa
$$$$ • 211 N. Tampa St., Tampa
• (813) 225-1234, (800) 233-1234
In the heart of downtown at the Tampa City Center is 17 stories of mirrored glass known as the Hyatt Regency. Tampa's largest hotel and a popular meeting site for conventions, you know you're in for a luxurious treat from the first sight of the eight-story atrium lobby with a two-story waterfall. The rooms are plush, with the pale woods and pastel colors so popular in Florida. If budget allows, the Regency Club on the top two floors will not only offer you a spectacular view of Hillsborough Bay, but also a concierge, a private elevator and a complimentary breakfast and afternoon cocktails. On the lobby level, you can lunch at Saltwaters Bar and Grille, or head to Pralines, a cafe with both indoor and outdoor seating. For an adult beverage and a little keyboard magic, try Breeze's Lounge on the second floor of the atrium. For exercise, you'll find an outdoor heated pool on the rooftop and a health club.

Wyndham Harbour Island Hotel
$$$$ • 725 S. Harbour Island, Tampa
• (813) 229-5000, (800) 996-3426
This is one gorgeous hotel, rising 12 stories above its foundation on Harbour Island and

surrounded by Hillsborough Bay. Just two minutes from the bustle of downtown Tampa, it's part of the Harbor Island complex, with a broad concrete boardwalk overlooking the water to the city skyline. If you stay here, you'll have all the privileges of the Harbour Island Athletic Club, including its 20 tennis courts plus racquetball and squash courts. The rooms are naturally plush, with rich floral fabrics and elegant dark woods. You'll have a coffee maker and work area in regular rooms, and a wet bar is included in many of the suites. Outside, you'll enjoy a heated swimming pool (complete with underwater music!) and boat slips for 50 vessels.

Radisson Riverwalk Hotel
$$$-$$$$ • 200 Ashley Dr., Tampa
• (813) 223-2222, (800) 333-3333
Formerly the Tampa Hilton and then a Quality Inn property, a $7 million renovation has once again made this downtown grand dame a popular stop for the Tampa business community. Just two blocks from the convention center, its facade wraps around the Hillsborough River and boasts totally refurbished rooms with private balconies that overlook the water. The bathrooms are especially nice, with hair dryers, makeup mirrors and phones. The renovated rooms are outfitted with coffee pots, irons and telephones with voice mail and data ports. For a quick lunch, you can grab a bite in The River Deli, toast the evening at The Lounge and dine at the newly opened Ashley Street Grill. You'll also find an outdoor heated pool and an exercise room. If you are feeling especially frisky, why not request the suite where Vice President Al Gore recently stayed. It boasts a $4,000 wood-frame bed, satellite television with 100 channels, a built-in wet bar and a 30-foot balcony with a view that extends to St. Petersburg.

Holiday Inn–Ashley Plaza
$$ • 111 W. Fortune St., Tampa
• (813) 223-1351, (800) HOLIDAY
Next door to the Tampa Bay Performing Arts Center along the Hillsborough River, this 14-story Holiday Inn is a longtime favorite for

www.insiders.com

See this and
many other
Insiders' Guide®
destinations online
— in their entirety.

Visit us today!

downtown stay-overs. The guest rooms are especially spacious and well-decorated, including full-length wall mirrors. If you'll be staying a while, you might request one of the 22 rooms that are equipped with kitchenettes, and absolutely request a room with a view of the river. You'll find an outdoor heated swimming pool, a fitness room and coin-operated laundry, too. For food and drinks, there are three choices on the lobby level: The Backstage Restaurant, with its theatrical decor; The Deli, for a quick sandwich; and the Encore Lounge for drinks. A nice note, here: This is the only major hotel in downtown Tampa with free on-site parking.

West Shore/Rocky Point

Sheraton Grand Hotel
$$$ • 4860 W. Kennedy Blvd., Tampa • (813) 286-4400, (800) 325-3535

Part of Urban Center, a financial office complex in the heart of the Westshore business district, the Sheraton Grand is a showstopper along Kennedy Boulevard — a real beauty, all sleek with rounded glass. From the glass elevators and atriums packed with natural greenery and waterfalls, to the well-appointed guest rooms, it is a true star of the Westshore district. We like the built-in armoires and full-length mirrors as well as the easy chairs and writing desks in every room. The restaurants here attract a lot more people than those just staying at the hotel. Try J. Fitzgerald's on the lobby level, or the Courtyard Cafe. There's piano music seven days a week in the Atrium Lobby Lounge, and the Grand Slam Sports Bar is a rowdy place to grab a brew. Best of all, check out Shula's Steak House (see our Restaurants chapter) for a manly-manly evening feast. You can soothe your muscles in the outdoor heated swimming pool that overlooks Tampa Bay, and follow your dip in the pool with a treat from the 24-hour room service. The West Shore Plaza Mall (see details in our Shopping chapter) is just across the street.

Holiday Inn Crowne Plaza
$$$ • 700 N. Westshore Blvd., Tampa • (813) 289-8200, (800) 465-4329

If a European atmosphere suits your fancy, the Holiday Inn Crowne Plaza, part of the Austin Center South, is for you. The skylit lobby is all marble, mirrors and palms, and even the spacious guest rooms pamper you with all the right amenities, including hair dryers in the bathrooms. The 11th floor is the executive level, with its own private lounge, concierge and extra guest-room goodies, such as telephones in the bathrooms. Restaurant-wise there's Seasons, known for its regional cuisine and local seafood, with a popular lounge connected at the hip. Work out in the fitness room, or do a few laps in the heated outdoor swimming pool.

Embassy Suites Hotel
**$$$-$$$$ • 555 N. Westshore Blvd.,
Tampa • (813) 875-1555, (800) EMBASSY**

If you're here for a long stretch, the 16-story Embassy Suites should fill the bill. With its arched corridors and Florida seabird art decorating the walls, it has a real tropical ambiance right in the heart of the Westshore business action. Each suite has a separate living area and bedroom in addition to a fully equipped kitchen. Some two-bedroom units are available, too. Check out the heated outdoor pool and the sundeck as well as the exercise room, sauna and library.

Doubletree Suites
Tampa Westshore
**$$$ • 4500 W. Cypress St., Tampa
• (813) 879-4800, (800) 222-8733**

This is the salmon-colored eight-story building you see as you're whipping down I-275 from the airport. Inside it's light and bright, with a plant-laden atrium, waterfalls and a garden courtyard that's all tropical and lush. The suites are delightful, especially for a longer stay. Each has a separate living area and bedroom and is equipped with a microwave, coffee maker and wet bar. For exercise, you'll find an indoor swimming pool, sauna and steam room.

Courtyard by Marriott
**$-$$ • 3805 W. Cypress St., Tampa
• (813) 874-0555, (800) 321-2211**

As do all courtyards, this four-story complex features guest rooms that surround a lush central courtyard and gazebo. You have your choice of a room with a king-sized bed or two doubles, and every room has a coffee maker. Also offered are a whirlpool, outdoor pool, exercise room and laundry facilities.

Tampa Airport Hilton
at Metrocenter
**$$-$$$ • 2225 N. Lois Ave., Tampa
• (813) 877-6688, (800) HILTONS**

Right between the airport and downtown Tampa is the 12-story Hilton. The rooms here are tastefully decorated with pale walls and carpeting, and the bathrooms all have a separate vanity area. Nonsmokers will appreciate the eighth floor, totally dedicated to nonsmokers, and the top two floors feature concierge-type rooms with balconies.

Crowne Plaza Tampa–Westshore
**$$-$$$ • 700 N. Westshore Blvd., Tampa
• (813) 289-8200, (800) 227-6963**

At the corner of Westshore Boulevard and Cypress Street await 272 primo guest rooms just longing for your reservation. Recently renovated with everything from new carpet and drapes to bedspreads and televisions, the Crowne Plaza pampers its guests with a fully equipped exercise room, outdoor pool and a whirlpool for the bone-weary traveler. The popular Maxwell's Restaurant and Lounge is right on the premises. Might we suggest you request the Crowne's executive-level accommodations, one full concierge floor where you'll be spoiled with breakfast in the morning and drinks and hors d'oeuvres every afternoon.

Rocky Point Area

Hyatt Regency Westshore
**$$$$ • 6200 Courtney Campbell Cswy.,
Tampa • (813) 874-1234, (800) 233-1234**

Plunked in the center of a 35-acre mangrove preserve overlooking Tampa Bay, the Hyatt Regency is a spectacular establishment, with its imported marble floors and hand-painted ceilings. The rooms are equally as lush, all light and Florida pastels, with balconies overlooking the Bay. Outdoors, there are two swimming pools, two lighted tennis courts, nature walks and jogging trails. On the 14th floor, you'll find the wonderfully romantic Armani's, a rooftop restaurant with the most divine Italian offerings. Just behind the hotel is Oystercatchers (check out our Restaurants chapter), a very popular indoor-outdoor Key West-style eatery.

Radisson Bay Harbor Inn
**$$$ • 7700 Courtney Campbell Cswy.,
Tampa • (813) 281-8900, (800) 777-7800**

Every room with a view. That's the Radisson, a six-story hotel that not only overlooks Old Tampa Bay, but also has its own sandy beach to boot. The rooms are designed with art-deco flavor and pastels, and you'll enjoy a heated outdoor pool, two lighted tennis courts and an

Photo: Tampa Bay Magazine

The Renaissance Vinoy Resort in St. Petersburg is all Florida graciousness. An amazing $93 million facelift has brought this grand dame back to life.

exercise room. You'll also have wonderful views of the water from Damon's, a delightful restaurant that's part of the hotel complex.

Residence Inn by Marriott

$$$-$$$$ • 3075 N. Rocky Point Dr., Tampa • (813) 281-5677, (800) 331-3131

It looks like a residential complex and, judging from the numbers of long-term guests, it might as well be. Overlooking the Bay with its own fishing pier and boat dock, the hotel's suites include a living area, bedroom and fully equipped kitchen with microwave, coffee maker and even a dishwasher. You can select from a studio suite or two-story penthouse suite, all with a private balcony or patio and exceptional closet space. Larger units have two bedrooms, and most have wood-burning fireplaces, too. With typical Marriott hospitality, you can enjoy a daily, complimentary continental breakfast as well as hospitality hour with hors d'oeuvres from 5 until 7 PM every day.

Days Inn Rocky Point

$$-$$$ • 7627 Courtney Campbell Cswy., Tampa • (813) 281-0000, (800) DAYS-INN

Six two-story wings spoke out from the outdoor swimming pool at Days Inn, which includes its own private beach that slides down into Tampa Bay. The rooms are fine for the price,

but the real benefit is the activity along the beach with WaveRunner and paddleboat rentals. There are also two tennis courts, a volleyball court, a children's playground and spaces for shuffleboard, badminton and horseshoes.

Sailport Resort

$$-$$$ • 2506 Rocky Point Dr., Tampa • (813) 281-9599, (800) 255-9599

More space. Less filling. Sailport offers stretch-out suites for the price of a regular room. Each has one or two bedrooms, a fully equipped kitchen, a balcony overlooking Tampa Bay and a stereo system. The furnishings are comfy, and you'll even find a medicine chest in the bathroom. For recreation, you can head outdoors to the fishing pier and tennis courts, or lounge around the outdoor pool. There's no lobby per se, but there's a 24-hour grocery store for last-minute pickups.

Busch Gardens Area

Crown Sterling Suites Hotel–USF/Busch Gardens

$$$ • 11310 N. 30th St., Tampa • (813) 971-7690, (800) 433-4600

From the inventors of the "all-suite" concept, comes this 129-suite hotel just a mile north of Busch Gardens. It has a Southern mansion look to it, with its veranda-style outdoor corridors complete with hanging plants and wrought-iron trim. The suites offer a living area, separate bedroom, wet bar, microwave, fridge and coffee maker. There's courtesy shuttle service to Busch Gardens, and you can relax in the outdoor heated pool after your African adventure.

Holiday Inn Tampa/Busch Gardens
$$-$$$ • 2701 E. Fowler Ave., Tampa
• (813) 971-4710, (800) HOLIDAY

Opposite the campus of the University of South Florida, this is the largest hotel in the Busch Gardens area with 395 guest rooms, and it's just a mile north of the theme park. Most of the guest rooms face a central courtyard with tropical gardens and mini-waterfalls surrounding the fantastic free-form pool and gazebo. There's a T.G.I. Fridays here, so you know you won't go hungry.

Quality Suites
Hotel–USF/Busch Gardens
$$ • 3001 University Center Dr., Tampa
• (813) 971-8930, (800) 228-5151

This is a traveler's delight, not only for the location (it sits adjacent to Busch Gardens), but also for the great value it offers both vacationers and business travelers. Starting out with a free breakfast every morning, you won't need to use the microwave that's in every suite, but the coffee maker will come in handy for an early morning pick-me-up. There's also a living/dining room with sofa bed, wet bar and stereo/VCR unit to complement the separate bedroom. Real treats for you business types are the voice-message and computer hookup capabilities in each suite. An outdoor swimming pool, naturally, and coin-operated laundry are also on the property.

Days Inn–Busch Gardens/Maingate
$ • 2901 E. Busch Blvd., Tampa
• (813) 933-6471, (800) DAYS-INN

This is a favorite for families who make the journey to visit Busch Gardens. The rooms are (thank goodness) off the major highway and surround an outdoor swimming pool. The children's playground is a great spot for any little people not already exhausted from their daytime adventures. Rooms are pretty standard, but the price is right.

Econo Lodge
$ • 1701 E. Busch Blvd., Tampa
• (813) 933-7681, (800) 553-2666

Big families love this place because of the availability of connecting units. The decor is Busch Gardens chic, with wildlife art to get you in the mood. About a mile west of the theme park, the Econo Lodge has a swimming pool and restaurant.

Red Roof Inn
$ • 2307 E. Busch Blvd., Tampa
• (813) 932-0073, (800) THE-ROOF

The rooms are bright and decorated in lively colors, the outdoor pool and whirlpool are soothing, and the whole place is set back far enough from busy Busch Boulevard to guarantee a peaceful night's sleep. The landscaping on the property is remarkably well-planned and well-maintained for this value price.

Travel Lodge at Busch Gardens
$ • 9202 N. 30th St., Tampa
• (813) 933-3958, (800) 578-7878

One of the closest hotels to the Busch Gardens entrance, Travel Lodge is actually a quite attractive building with its mirrored facade. You'll either love or hate the room decor — some rooms are jungle-fever brown and others are bright pink and purple. After a day of fun at Busch Gardens, you can escape to the hotel's outdoor pool that's planted in a tropical garden setting or ship the kids off to the game room.

Howard Johnson Main Gate
$ • 4139 E. Busch Blvd., Tampa
• (813) 988-9191, (800) GO-HOJO

The HoJo decorators stayed a bit too long in the jungle and brought back wildlife prints and jungle-patterned bedspreads that might give your little ones nightmares. No, not really, but if you want to "live" Busch Gardens Tampa Bay, this is the place to stay. If you do, check to see if any of the rooms with king-sized beds, wet bars and refrigerators are available — they're the best of the lot.

Sheraton Inn Tampa

$$$ • 7401 E. Hillsborough Ave., Tampa • (813) 626-0999, (800) 325-3535

While not really in the exact Busch Gardens area — you'll be about 10 minutes away — the Sheraton Inn is a 276-room masterpiece of cordial hospitality. It's actually close to the State Fair Grounds and makes a perfect launch pad if you're planning a daytrip to Orlando. The rooms are generously sized, and many overlook the central landscaped courtyard. Touches of brass and mirrored closets are nice amenities, as are the balconies and patios, outdoor heated swimming pool and the health club.

Pinellas County

Safety Harbor

Safety Harbor Resort

$$$$ • 105 N. Bayshore Dr., Safety Harbor • (727) 726-1161, (800) 237-0155

Did we hear you whining for a little pampering? You can do no better than the world-famous Safety Harbor Resort, founded in 1926 and built around five natural, sulphur-filled springs reputed to have been discovered in 1539 by Hernando de Soto. Completely renovated in the late 1980s, the resort offers programs of up to 35 different activities, and the knowledgeable staff will happily put you through your paces as you attack swimming, tennis, rowing, walking, golf and bicycling, not to mention water aerobics, stretch classes and weight training. Since you'll be almost too exhausted to notice, we'll point out that the rooms are delightful. They're furnished tropical-style with original artwork, rattan furniture and bright, happy colors.

The fare is not your typical bland spa cuisine and is prepared by some of the finest chefs in the world. For those in need of a beauty makeover, the Clarins Institut de Beaut is on the spa's grounds. In July 1995, the spa became part of the South Seas Resorts Co., the state's largest owner and operator of beachfront resorts. The proud new owners have committed to invest more than $2 million in improvements to the property, already listed among the top-10 spas in the United States in the latest Zagat hotel survey.

Downtown St. Petersburg

Renaissance Vinoy Resort

$$$$ • 501 Fifth Ave. N.E., St. Petersburg • (727) 894-1000, (800) HOTELS-1

An amazing $93 million has brought this cherished grande dame back to life. Sprawling along the Bayfront between Beach and Bay Shore drives, the Mediterranean-style peach facade is all Florida graciousness, welcoming its guests to superb accommodations, most of which overlook the Bay waters. The celebrated landmark is named on the National Register of Historic Places and is a member of the exclusive Historic Hotels of America. Your first step into the grand lobby with its soaring, arched ceilings, glittering chandeliers and sconces and magnificent Oriental carpets will undoubtedly make you catch your breath.

Yes, prepare to be pampered. The rooms are luxury personified, with three phones, a TV in the bathroom and hair dryers. The newer rooms even boast private Jacuzzis and spacious balconies or patios. When it comes to dining, you'll not find a better choice than Marchand's Grille, a waterfront dining experience named after the original Vinoy's first chef, Henri Marchand. The main dining room is The Terrace Room, and there's also the gazebo-style AlFresco for casual lunches near one of the two swimming pools. For outdoor activity, there is no equal, as the Vinoy is Florida's only west coast resort that can boast a private marina, an 18-hole championship golf course and a 16-court tennis complex, not to mention two heated pools, waterfall included, three outdoor spas and a 5,000-square-foot, state-of-the-art fitness center. After a round of croquet, take a peek at the Grand Ballroom, an eye-popping 6,000 square feet of refined elegance.

St. Petersburg Bayfront Hilton and Towers

$$$ • 333 First St. S., St. Petersburg • (727) 894-5000, (800) 445-8667

Just across from the Bayfront Center, the 15-story St. Petersburg Hilton welcomes you with its lobby filled with handsome antiques and art, marble, crystal and gleaming tile. Even if you don't opt for the 15th-floor concierge level, you'll be pleasantly surprised at the spaciousness of the guest rooms, which are decorated in restrained art deco and flooded with natural light from extra-wide windows. Along with an outdoor heated pool and Jacuzzi, you'll find great American cuisine at Charmette's and great steaks at Eli's. If you're in a party mood, check out Wings, a happening bar with a real biplane suspended from the ceiling.

The Heritage/Holiday Inn
$$-$$$ • 234 Third Ave. N., St. Petersburg • (727) 822-4814, (800) 283-7829

If you need to be close to downtown, but want to escape the commercial environment, head for The Heritage. Dating back to the 1920s, it sits in a quiet residential neighborhood and is very Southern-like with its inviting veranda, French doors, fountains and lush, tropical courtyard. Completely restored in the late 1980s (it was called the Martha Washington in its previous lifetime), the hotel's rooms are charming and include period antiques and brass beds mixed in with modern conveniences. You'll have the best of both worlds. Sitting in a quiet center courtyard surrounded by the coral-shuttered facility and meticulous plantings, the pool is absolutely delightful. And while we usually offer modest recommendations for restaurants that are part of a hotel, this is truly an exception. Dining at the Heritage Grille (see our Restaurants chapter) is a culinary dream. Do plan to stay "home" one night to take advantage of the gourmet magic. Call (727) 823-6382 for reservations.

St. Petersburg South

Holiday Inn–St. Petersburg
$$ • 4601 34th St. S., St. Petersburg • (727) 867-3131, (800) HOLIDAY

Unpack your bags here, midway between downtown St. Pete and the Sunshine Skyway Bridge. Even though you're a hair's breadth away from busy U.S. Highway 19, the two-story motel is set back off the road right across from a marina. Rooms are suitable, but the real goodie is Leverock's (see our Restaurants chapter) right there at Maximo Moorings.

Howard Johnson Hotel
$$ • 3600 34th St. S., St. Petersburg • (813) 867-6070, (800) 446-4656

It looks like the sister of the Coliseum with its huge columns at the entry ramp. The decor is delightful, all wicker and Florida pastels with loads of well-tended hanging plants. There's live music in the Celebrity Lounge, and the Tiki Bar out by the pool is a great afternoon hangout.

Days Inn Marina Beach Resort
$$$ • 6800 34th St. S., St. Petersburg • (727) 867-1151, (800) DAYS-INN

This is the year-round base of the world-famous Annapolis Sailing School, so we guess you can figure out that it's right on Tampa Bay. In fact, it rests in the center of 14 lush, tropical acres along the shoreline just north of the Skyway Bridge. You can go for the regular rooms or request a one-, two- or three-bedroom lodge. Either way, you'll have two outdoor pools, seven tennis courts, a pier, a marina and watersports rentals easily available.

Clearwater

Belleview Biltmore Resort
$$$$ • 25 Belleview Blvd., Clearwater • (727) 442-6171, (800) 237-8947

Very posh indeed. Opened in 1897 by railroad magnate Henry Plant, it immediately became a magnet for industrial types and royalty like the Duke of Windsor. The largest occupied wooden structure in the world, and rightfully listed on the National Register of Historic Places, the "Queen of the Gulf" is perched high on a bluff overlooking Clearwater Bay. It's surrounded by an amazing variety of natural foliage such as water oaks, cabbage palms, citrus trees, orchids and palmettos.

The structure itself is a massive, white-clapboard Victorian beauty — multi-gabled and grass-green-roofed, it looks like it just fell off the pages of a romance novel. Tiffany stained-glass windows, crystal chandeliers and spit-polished brass fixtures adorn the lobby. The rooms are equally as elegant, with high ceilings, Queen Anne decor and four-poster beds. Recreation is likewise superb, including the resort's 18-hole championship golf course, four clay tennis courts, indoor and outdoor pools,

Photo: Bradenton Herald

Thousands of accommodations choices are offered along the Gulf beach strip.

Swiss showers, jogging trails and a private Cabana Club on the Gulf of Mexico.

Comfort Inn
$$ • 3580 Ulmerton Rd., Clearwater
• (727) 573-1171, (800) 228-5150

This is a popular spot for business travelers to the Clearwater area. It stands out from the crowd because of its modern-looking glass elevators and geometric design. Rooms are sleek, with light woods and modern art, and most have balconies or patios that overlook the central courtyard.

Courtyard by Marriott
$$ • 3131 Executive Dr., Clearwater
• (727) 572-8484, (800) 321-2211

You know the layout — rooms that surround a central courtyard. The news about this particular hotel is that it's one of the newest along this Clearwater corridor. Suites with refrigerators are available, along with the standard single or double rooms. What's especially nice is that it's

exceptionally quiet here, even though you're right in the middle of a very busy area of town.

Hampton Inn Clearwater
$$ • 3655 Hospitality Ln., Clearwater
• (727) 577-9200, (800) HAMPTON

Sitting right next to a Holiday Inn, Hampton Inn does what it does best — offers a clean, comfy room for a great price. It doesn't have many frills, but it does have an outdoor heated swimming pool, whirlpool, sauna, lighted tennis court and exercise room. Plus, you're right next to a municipal golf course in case you need to sneak in a quick 18.

La Quinta Inn
$$ • 3301 Ulmerton Rd., Clearwater
• (727) 572-7222, (800) 572-0076

It's got that Southwestern feeling as do all the properties in this chain. Rooms are fairly spacious, and outdoors you have a heated swimming pool, sauna and exercise room. Its real claim to fame is its proximity to the studios of the Home Shopping Network.

The Gulf Beaches

You'd never live long enough to stay in the zillions of hotels and motels that stretch along the Gulf beach strip, let alone have room to write about them. What we will do is highlight the most popular — or most unique — properties in each area, starting our pillow talk from the north in Tarpon Springs and coming to a final rest at the southern end at Pass-A-Grille.

Tarpon Springs

Quality Inn Resort
$$ • 38724 U.S. Hwy. 19 N., Tarpon Springs • (813) 934-5781, (800) 228-5151

Just a few minutes from the famous sponge docks, this Quality Inn was opened in 1990. You can choose from a standard room or spread out in one of the 34 fully appointed suites. While it's not directly on the beach, the hotel does have an outdoor pool, whirlpool and sauna. A game room is available for those not-so-sunny days.

Best Western Tahitian Resort
$ • 2337 U.S. Hwy. 19 N., Tarpon Springs • (813) 937-4121, (800) 528-1234

Your small pet is welcome here at the Best Western, and the hotel even has foreign language interpreters for worldwide traveling guests. There's a beautifully landscaped, heated swimming pool, and both tennis and golf are very close by.

Westin Innisbrook Resort
$$$$ • 36750 U.S. Hwy. 19 N., Tarpon Springs • (813) 942-2000, (800) 456-2000

Absolutely primo. Whether you come for the exceptional, world-class golf (the Copperhead Course is rated as one of America's Greatest, and the Island Course is ranked in the Top-50 Resort Courses by *Golf Digest* magazine) or the tennis (can you say 15 courts?), Innisbrook is in a class by itself when it comes to getting away from it all. Sprawling across 1,000 acres of rolling hills, there's a

serenity that's impossible to duplicate and even harder to describe.

Accommodations are absolutely first-class, including rooms in 28 three-story lodges scattered along the resort's three golf courses. Each unit has a balcony or patio, a fully equipped kitchen and a living area. In addition to golf and tennis, there are six outdoor pools for lounging, jogging tracks and nature trails for wandering and a variety of restaurant facilities for dining. And, not to worry about getting around the complex, complimentary on-site tram service and beach-shuttle service are available, so you never have to get behind the wheel until it's time to depart.

Dunedin

Best Western Jamaica Inn
$$ • 150 Marina Plz., Dunedin • (727) 733-4121

Sitting adjacent to Dunedin Marina, this waterfront resort overlooks St. Joseph Sound. All the rooms have balconies or patios with a view of the water. Most rooms also offer kitchen facilities, which can come in handy for a quick snack before hitting the beach or the outdoor pool. Some of Europe's finest chefs perform nightly in the acclaimed Bon Appetit Restaurant and even take their masterpieces out to sea on the *S.S. Bon Appetit*, a 61-foot yacht that sails from the Inn.

Clearwater Beach

Adam's Mark Caribbean Gulf Resort
$$$ • 430 S. Gulfview Blvd., Clearwater Beach • (727) 443-5714, (800) 444-ADAM

This was where we stayed on our very first trip to the Tampa Bay area. The hospitality of the staff, wonderful weather and round-the-clock activity convinced us that this was the area we wanted to come to put down new roots. Sitting just to the south of fabulous Clearwater Beach, the design is interesting — lobby and lounges on the ground floor, parking on three levels above that and then the rooms on the upper floors, each with a balcony that overlooks the Gulf waters. Calico Jack's is a bustling place for a Caribbean-style dinner, but our favorite place was out on the huge waterfront deck with the live Jimmy Buffet-beat music and a mean burger and a pink frozen delight.

Doubletree Suites Surfside

$$$ • 400 Mandalay Ave., Clearwater Beach • (727) 461-3222, (800) 222-8733

On the north end of Clearwater Beach sits the Doubletree Suites Surfside, a nine-story beauty on 10 acres of prize beachfront. All the rooms have balconies to take in those breathtaking sunsets, and it's a real hub of activity when it comes to watersports rentals (windsurfers and the like), volleyball tournaments and spontaneous beach events. It rocks at night, too, especially at the Surf Club, a multilevel state-of-the-art disco.

Clearwater Beach Hotel

$$$ • 500 Mandalay Ave., Clearwater Beach • (727) 441-2425, (800) 292-2295

This is one of the most picturesque places on any of the Gulf beaches as far as we're concerned. Its history goes back more than 80 years, but recent renovations have brought back the spit and polish that this grande dame deserves. The main building is six stories high and decorated in the gracious Southern style that makes you want to wear a smoking jacket and talk in a low whisper. There are also two smaller wings that spread out around the pool (with food and beverage service) and perfectly manicured grounds. The rooms are beautifully decorated in light woods and sophisticated florals, and many have small kitchens and balconies. If you're looking for a lazy vacation with a decided touch of class, this is definitely the place for you. Even if you don't stay here, you should plan at least one evening meal in their romantic dining room. For reservations, call (813) 443-2180.

Radisson Suite Resort

$$$ • 1201 Gulf Blvd., Clearwater Beach • (727) 596-1100, (800) 333-3333

Spreading over seven acres on Clearwater Harbor, the Radisson sits right next to the Shoppes at Sand Key (see our Shopping chapter) with its chic shops and world famous Columbia Restaurant (see our Restaurants chapter). Opened in 1990, this $40 million property offers suites, each with a separate bedroom and balcony, living area with a sofa bed, a microwave, a coffee maker and a video entertainment unit.

The pool is really neat — a free-form job with 35-foot cascading waterfalls and surrounded by a wonderful deck and tropical plants. You'll also find a waterfront boardwalk and a marina with 60 slips. The Radisson offers a variety of innovative travel packages. The one we like best is the "Suite and Convertible," where you not only get a luxury suite, but also a wind-in-your-hair vehicle to cruise the strip.

Sheraton Sand Key Resort

$$$ • 1160 Gulf Blvd., Clearwater Beach • (727) 595-1611, (800) 325-3535

If you love your watersports, the 650-foot beach that spreads out in back of the Sheraton is just your cup of saltwater. Sitting on 32 Gulf-front acres, it's at Sand Key Island's northern tip, and all the rooms have balconies with views of either the Gulf or Clearwater Harbor. You'll discover an outdoor, heated freshwater pool (with the Gazebo Bar ready to serve!), three lighted tennis courts, a children's playground, a pool and a volleyball court.

Belleair Beach

Belleair Beach Resort Hotel

$$ • 2040 Gulf Blvd., Belleair Beach • (727) 595-1696, (800) 780-1696

Once you get to this area of the beach, you lose the slammed-together hotel landscape and come into a more residential atmosphere. It's here that you'll find the Belleair Beach, discreetly shaded by tropical foliage and opening directly to some of the most pris-

---

INSIDERS' TIP

There are more than 24,000 hotel and motel rooms just along the Gulf beaches and thousands more in the remaining sections of Pinellas County and throughout Hillsborough County.

tine beach on the Gulf. Many of the units are equipped with kitchens, and all face either the central courtyard and pool or the Gulf.

Indian Rocks Beach

Alpaugh's Gulf Beach Motel Apartments

$$ • 1912 Gulf Blvd., Indian Rocks Beach • (727) 595-9421
68 Gulf Blvd., Indian Rocks Beach • (727) 595-2589

Family-owned and operated with that "glad-to-see-ya" feeling that's hard to find in the super-hotels, Alpaugh's is a longtime tradition in Indian Rocks Beach. Both properties are right on the beach with central courtyards and fountains, lawn games, picnic tables and shuffleboard. Rooms are the good-old homey motel variety, but they do offer kitchenettes and dining areas. Cute little one-bedroom cottages are available at the 1912 Gulf Boulevard site.

Pelican East & West

$$ • 108 21st Ave., Indian Rocks Beach • (727) 595-9741

Guess it's the rule that family-owned motels operate in at least two locations in Indian Rocks. For more than 25 years, Mike and Carol McGlauglin have thrown out the red carpet to those who come to stay at either Pelican East (on the Bay side of the road) or Pelican West (right on the Gulf). Both offer just four units each. The units include a separate bedroom and kitchen. You'll be living like the natives in this peaceful beachy community.

North Redington Beach

North Redington Beach Hilton

$$$ • 17120 Gulf Blvd., North Redington Beach • (727) 391-4000, (800) HILTONS

We figure that this new establishment was built in this lovely community largely to accommodate lingering houseguests in the adjacent residences. Well, not really, but the property offers rooms that could easily pass as a guest room at your swinging Aunt Martha's — extra-large with stocked mini-bars, custom-de-

signed armoires with TVs, full-length mirrors, separate dressing areas and super-big bathrooms. The hotel sits on 250 feet of beachfront, and every room has a spectacular view of either the Gulf or Boca Ciega Bay. The multilevel Jasmine's Steak House is a very popular place for the last meal of the day.

Anglers Cove

$$$ • 7450 Gulf Blvd., N. Redington Beach • (727) 526-1234, (800) 535-7776

If you want a beach home away from home, here's the place. Anglers Cove is a 48-unit condominium complex that offers three-bedroom, three-bath condos that are fully equipped, including full-sized kitchens with all the appliances, to linens and soap. Master bedrooms have a queen bed, and the other two bedrooms have two full beds each. The complex is right on the Gulf and also has an outdoor heated pool, Jacuzzi and outdoor tiki bar.

Madeira Beach

Holiday Inn

$$$ • 15208 Gulf Blvd., Madeira Beach • (727) 392-2275, (800) HOLIDAY

Perched at the north end of the Madeira strip, this four-story Holiday Inn covers 600 feet of Gulf beach, and every room has a balcony to take advantage of the spectacular views. Rooms are relatively good-sized, with either two double beds or a king-sized bed. Try the Tiki Bar that's right next to the outdoor heated pool for a snack and cool tropical drink, then trot off to the lighted tennis court for some love-action. They'll be pleased to rent you a cabana, beach chairs, assorted watersports equipment and even a babysitter so you can take a night off.

Treasure Island

Bilmar Beach Resort Hotel

$$$ • 10650 Gulf Blvd., Treasure Island • (727) 360-5531, (800) 826-9724

You can't miss this mega-resort spread out along 500 feet of beachfront on the TI strip. It's a lush complex of three-, four- and eight-story buildings that hold 168 rooms and

Photo: The Don CeSar Beach Resort & Spa

The Don CeSar, a.k.a. the Pink Palace, is without a doubt the crown jewel of Florida's Gulf Coast.

four super suites. Most rooms have balconies or patios and come with kitchenettes for your basic food needs. There are two outdoor heated pools, and the Beach Bar Cafe is ready to mix up your favorite frozen concoction. For an evening meal, the Grog Shoppe Restaurant is a charming place that's quite unbeachy — both the decor (deep-wood paneling and plaid carpeting) and the menu are decidedly Old English.

Buccaneer Beach Resort Motel
$$ • 10800 Gulf Blvd., Treasure Island • (727) 367-1908, (800) 826-2120

Ahoy matey! Plant yourself here at the Buccaneer, right on the powdery shores of the Gulf of Mexico. The "treasure" of Treasure Island, you can go for a charming motel room, fully furnished efficiency or a one- or two-bedroom courtyard apartment — every one comes equipped with a refrigerator. Brother and sister proprietors, Jim and Gordie, have made extensive renovations to this popular Gulf destination. You'll find it just

steps from charter fishing boats, tennis courts, golf and shopping.

Captain's Quarters Inn
$$ • 10035 Gulf Blvd., Treasure Island • (727) 360-1659, (800) 526-9547

This is a mini-place, run by Ron and Mickey McCaughan in a down-home friendly manner. The six efficiencies (with brand new mini-kitchens) and three units (with a separate bedroom and full kitchen) share 100 yards of Gulf beachfront. Also offered are an outdoor pool, boat dock on the Bay and some pretty lively guest barbecues.

Ramada Inn of Treasure Island
$$ • 12000 Gulf Blvd., Treasure Island • (727) 360-7051, (800) 228-2828

If you're more comfortable with a name-brand sleepover place, try this Ramada Inn. It's typical of the chain and includes clean, comfy rooms and loads of sandy beachfront. Tennis, golf and fishing are nearby, if you can pull yourself away from the Gulf and the heated outdoor pool.

Tahitian Resort

$$ • 11300 Gulf Blvd., Treasure Island • (727) 360-6264

Five years ago, when Bob and Alice Siepak had had enough of Chicago winters, they packed up and aimed toward Treasure Island to become the proud hosts of the Tahitian Resort that rests along the Gulf shore. With 53 efficiencies, all offering kitchens complete with everything from refrigerators to coffee makers and toasters, the Tahitian Resort is a grand place to kick off your winter boots and just take it easy. Whether you stroll to shopping or restaurants or lounge at the outdoor pool or beach, the Siepak's hospitality will surely make your stay a memorable one.

St. Pete Beach

The Don CeSar Beach Resort & Spa

$$$$ • 3400 Gulf Blvd., St. Pete Beach • (727) 360-1881, (800) 282-1116

If you were to die and go to resort heaven, you might just wake up in the Pink Palace also known as The Don CeSar. When you approach it, you are dumbfounded by the sight — it's a mammoth structure with a fairy-tale blend of Moorish and Mediterranean architecture sprouting imperial turrets and bell towers and painted the most amazing flamingo pink. Builder Thomas Rowe named the hotel for his hero, Don Caesar de Bazan, an English opera character. It's included on the National Register of Historic Places and is, without a doubt, the crown jewel of Florida's Gulf Coast.

The circa 1928 masterpiece was rehabilitated in the late 1980s to the tune of a reputed $15 million and was once again updated in 1994. As you walk quietly by classic high windows and archways and stare at the amazing Italian crystal chandeliers, French candelabra, English Exminster carpets, marble floors and original works of prized European art, you might just catch a glimpse of the ghosts of former guests such as Babe Ruth and Lou Gehrig, who called the Don home during New York Yankees spring training in the 1930s. F. Scott Fitzgerald was also a frequent visitor.

The guest rooms are equally as impressive, with silky-white Italian marble bathrooms, traditional furnishings and high ceilings. If you're in a lavish kind of spending-spree mood, request one of the two penthouse suites. They are decidedly spectacular, both in size and luxury and have private terraces poised to catch the sunset over the Gulf.

Along with the magnificent beach, you'll also find an outdoor pool, two lighted tennis courts, a fully equipped exercise room and a professional masseuse. Dining is extraordinary, whether it be in The King Charles Room, recipient of the prestigious Trans Culinaire Five Star Award, or "underwater" dining in The Maritana Grille (see our Restaurants chapter) surrounded by 1,500 gallons of salt water and indigenous Florida fish. Or you can choose the more casual Beachcomber bar or Poolside Grille for your midday repast, along with Andy's Ice Cream Parlor and the Lobby Bar.

Tradewinds

$$$$ • 5500 Gulf Blvd., St. Pete Beach • (727) 367-6461, (800) 808-9822

What would you say if we suggested that you jump aboard a gondola and glide around the hotel grounds? You'd say it must be the Tradewinds, a one-of-a-kind 18-acre beachfront paradise with an amazing 840 rooms. Rambling waterways punctuate the tropically lush grounds, and hammocks welcome you for an afternoon nap on the white powder beach. Three heated outdoor pools and one indoor swimming pool, four tennis courts, a fitness center, watersports rentals and a video game room — what more could you ask for? OK, maybe you'd ask for an evening stroll on the wooden footpaths to one of the charming Victorian gazebos. That is, if you ever want to leave your spacious room, complete with kitchen or kitchenette and balcony.

For dining, the favorite is the Palm Court, an Italian bistro (see our Restaurants chapter). You may also choose from the Flying Bridge, a beachside, floating, Florida crackerhouse restaurant, or Bermuda's, which offers casual family dining. Catch the live entertainment at B.R. Cuda's, or order up a frosty beverage at Salty's Beach Bar. There's no doubt you'll have a blast here at one of the largest hotel complexes on St. Pete Beach!

Radisson Sandpiper Beach Resort
$$$ • 6000 Gulf Blvd., St. Pete Beach • (727) 360-5551, (800) 333-3333

You could go with the older wing of the Sandpiper that sits right on the beach, or you could choose the newer wing and have your own private balcony. Whichever you choose, you'll be pleasantly surprised by the tropical decor, including rattan, light woods and a pale tropical palette. Along with the beachfront pool, you'll find another enclosed heated pool, exercise room, activities for the kids and two air-conditioned courts for racquetball, handball and squash. You can dine inside or out at Piper's Patio or head over to Tucson's Family Grill for a hearty supper.

Holiday Inn SunSpree Resort
$$$ • 5250 Gulf Blvd., St. Pete Beach • (727) 360-1811, (800) HOLIDAY

It's like a zippy 11-story piece of art, with its circular facade, glass-walled elevator and revolving rooftop lounge, Bali Hai, where you can soak up the sunsets from every angle. In its former 20-year lifespan as a Hilton, the facility was well-known for its upscale appeal. Now under the Holiday Inn banner, the property will try to put on more of a family face, all the way to incorporating a separate check-in desk just for kids (they'll be given their own list of scheduled activities). Every spacious room has a private balcony with a view of either the Gulf or Boca Ciega Bay. Amenities include an outdoor heated pool, whirlpool, game rooms and beach rentals for parasailing and other watersports. Do check out the buffet at C.C. Chan's on the lobby level, or go super casual at Schooner's Beach Bar and Grill that serves poolside.

The Inn on The Beach
$$ • 1401 Gulf Way, St. Pete Beach • (727) 360-8844

There are only 16 units, and they sit in a mostly residential area at the southern tip of St. Pete Beach. But, the pastel exterior and lush landscaping scream old-Florida charm. Each unit at The Inn on The Beach is more charming than the next, with ceramic tile floors, wicker furniture and an antique here and there. Each one also has a kitchen, and most have private decks or courtyards. Help yourself to beach chairs, umbrellas, bicycles and the gas grill — they're all there free for the asking.

Bon-Aire Resort Motel
$$ • 4350 Gulf Blvd., St. Pete Beach • (727) 360-5596

Pick one: a single or double room, a half- or full efficiency with kitchenette, or a full apartment with a separate bedroom and living room. There are two outdoor heated pools, four shuffleboard courts, barbecue grills and Sandbar Bill's Bar and Grille for a casual meal.

A Pronunciation Gazetteer

Local language is heavily influenced by Spanish, Cuban, Italian and Indian contributions. This isn't Alabama, so don't lay on a thick "y'all" to fit in. The correct pronunciation of certain words makes you an Insider faster.

Alafia AL-uh-fy
Bearss (Avenue) Bierce (as in Pierce)
Caladesi (Island) CAL-uh-dee-see
Ciega See-AY-gah
Coquina Coe-KEE-na
Dunedin Done-EE-din
El Pasaje (Plaza) El PAH-sigh
Kissimmee Kuh-SIMM-mee
Lutz LOOts
Maggiore MAJ-ee-yore
Masaryktown Mah-sah-rick-town
Micanopy MICK-uh-no-pee
Okeechobee O-kuh-CHOE-bee
Ozona Oh-zone-uh
Pinellas some say PINE-ell-us
            others say PINN-ell-us
Withalacoochee WITH-la-coo-chee
Ybor EE-boar

Bed and Breakfast Inns

For a stay with a twist, there are several bed and breakfast alternatives that provide a more homey atmosphere for your stress-relieving overnights. We'll point out a few of the most popular destinations, but if you want to explore every possible option, we'll point you to a delightful book by Herbert L. Hiller called *Guide to the Small and Historic Lodgings of Florida*. If bed and breakfast inns are just your style, we implore you to make your reservations well in advance; most of these special properties have limited guest rooms. For details on all our bed and breakfast inns, you might want to call the B&B Suncoast Accommodations of Florida at (813) 360-1753.

The Lighthouse Bed & Breakfast
$$ • 13355 Second St. E., Madeira Beach • (727) 391-0015

Open only during the high season, this Key West-style bed and breakfast is built around a private courtyard with palm trees and a gazebo for relaxing or dining. Most of the studio and one-bedroom units can accommodate as many as four people, and there's a three-bedroom cottage for larger groups. A gas grill in the courtyard and a spacious sundeck for napping under the sun are available for you to use.

Island's End Resort
$$ • 1 Pass-A-Grille Way, St. Pete Beach • (727) 360-5023

Six charming cottages with one to three bedrooms await you here. All are quite well-appointed and have fully equipped kitchens. There's a fishing dock on the grounds, but the highlight is the continental breakfast of fresh-squeezed orange juice, croissants, cakes and coffee served three times a week in the gazebo.

J.O. Douglas House
$$$ • 209 Scotland St., Dunedin • (727) 735-9006

In the first home ever built in Dunedin by the town's founder, Ogilvie Douglas, innkeepers Jeffrey and Sherril Melio have created a wonderful Victorian retreat listed on the Historic Register of Homes. Perched on the Gulf of Mexico, the Douglas House also overlooks the Pinellas Trail where you can easily rent skates (bicycles are available at the house). Outside is a throwback in time, with hammocks in the large shaded yard perfect for that little nap after a dip in the pool or hot tub. Inside, find five charming rooms where you're guaranteed a grand night's sleep. Awaken to a leisurely breakfast in the colonial dining room, and then enjoy a daily afternoon tea complete with light snacks. And best of all, you can pack away your car keys. The town of Dunedin with its galleries, shops and gourmet restaurants is just a short stroll away, as is the Dunedin Marina, farmers market and Blue Jays Baseball Stadium.

Bayboro House
$$ • 1719 Beach Dr. S.E., St. Petersburg • (727) 823-4955

Bayboro House is a lovely three-story historic home with antiques and elegant furnishings. In its former lifetime, it has served as a bank, merchant's venue and even the winter home to north Florida cattle ranchers. Every room offers an individual decor and theme, the constant being the antique beds and armoires and elegant fine linens and quilts. A favorite pastime here is relaxing in the swing or rocking chairs on the wide veranda and watching sailboats and seabirds sail past the sandy beach of Old Tampa Bay.

Mansion House Bed & Breakfast
$$ • 105 Fifth Ave. N.E., St. Petersburg • (727) 821-9391

Find Welsh hospitality from your hosts Alan and Susan Lucas within the walls of this 1904

INSIDERS' TIP

For decades, St. Petersburg was famous for green benches along its sidewalks, but the first 50 benches, installed by Realtor Noel Mitchell around the turn of the century, were actually orange.

Photo: St. Petersburg/Clearwater Area Convention & Visitors Bureau

Resorts in the Tampa Bay area are perfect for romantic getaways.

Southern home. Within easy walking distance of the Pier, museums, beach and restaurants, you might opt to stay "at home" in the lounge, TV/library room, indoor sitting porch and outside covered screen porch. Reputed to have been the home of the first mayor of St. Petersburg, we bet he would have thoroughly enjoyed the sumptuous English-style breakfast served every morning. Mansion House is the proud recipient of both the 1993 St. Petersburg Beautification Award and the 1994 Chamber of Commerce Building Enhancement Award.

Bay Gables
$$ • 136 Fourth Ave. N.E., St. Petersburg • (727) 822-0044

Truly reminiscent of an era gone by, Bay Gables not only offers nine beautifully appointed rooms, but also the all-important afternoon tea. A Key West-style property, the Victorian beauty is also open for lunch inside or on the gracious wraparound porch. The lovely garden area is a favorite place for local weddings and receptions.

Condominiums

Even with all the suite hotels available, many of you would rather create your vacation comfort zone in a real home-type place. That translates to condominium, and there are plenty to be found along the Gulf beaches. Every condominium rental offers you a fully equipped and furnished home away from home, many with rates that are less than their hotel neighbors. Most will have swimming pools and Gulf beaches, but you won't have the on-site restaurants and other amenities offered by the resort hotels. For an extended stay, or a very private "let's be a local" getaway, we suggest you contact the following.

Suncoast Resort Rentals Inc.
16401 Gulf Blvd., Redington Beach • (727) 393-3425, (800) 237-6586, Canada: (800) 338-5945

Suncoast offers a variety of condo options, from one-bedroom apartments for two

St. Pete Beach offers a beautiful stretch of powdery, snow-white sand along the Gulf of Mexico.

Photo: St. Petersburg/Clearwater Area Convention & Visitors Bureau

people to three-bedroom condos that can accommodate as many as six. Price ranges vary according to size and season. Suncoast offers a full-service, front-desk operation complete with central switchboard, housekeeping staff and maintenance personnel.

JC Resort Management
17200 Gulf Blvd. N., Redington Beach
• (727) 397-0441, (800) 535-7776,
Canada: (800) 421-6663

JC Resort Management handles a wide variety of Gulf-front properties in both Redington and Indian Shores. Units can accommodate from two to six happy campers, who will have fully furnished and equipped accommodations, all the way to linens. Weekly maid service and a full maintenance staff are at your service.

Florida Resort Condominiums/Jack Collins Inc.
20001 Gulf Blvd., Indian Shores
• (727) 595-2001, USA/Canada:
(800) 237-9831

Pick your size, pick your locale — Indian Shores, Indian Rocks, Redington Shores, Madeira Beach. The portfolio of Florida Resort Condominium properties is a who's who of luxury Gulf and Intracoastal-front places, all offering a broad spectrum of views, sizes and price ranges. Typical accommodations include all the amenities of home, such as washers and dryers and fully equipped kitchens with icemakers. Most are exceptionally tastefully furnished, too, which can really make a difference in your comfort level.

From rowdy,
casual beach cafes
to romantic, candlelit
dining rooms, from
regional Southern
seafood specialties to
pizza, pasta and pai
fan, the Tampa Bay
area's got your tummy
growls covered.

Restaurants

The gods de la cuisine looked down upon Tampa Bay and made their gastronomic plan. They watched while we swung our hearts out for 18 holes, shopped 'til we dropped, backstroked through the crystal blue Gulf and tromped through every available attraction in our path. And then they saw that we were … starving! … crazed for food and lots of it! Tasty, piled high and reasonably priced! And they opened the floodgates for restaurant after restaurant, serving seafood, beef, Oriental, Cuban — you name it. And so we came, oh yes, even waited in line, to get inside each and every one. And it was good. Real good.

And so it came to be that on every corner, and many times in between, you'll find a place that satisfies your hunger, no matter what flavor your taste buds are crying for. If you've got a yearning, we've got just the spot to quench it. From rowdy, casual beach cafes to romantic, candlelit dining rooms, from regional Southern seafood specialties to pizza, pasta and pai fan, the Tampa Bay area's got your tummy growls covered.

Now, thinking about all that luscious food is one thing. Actually getting in and being seated is quite another. While some of the more elegant restaurants insist on, or at least encourage, reservations, most follow the first-come, first-served policy. In high season, that might mean a fairly extended wait, but if that's the case, you can usually expect a magnificent meal at the other end. Larger restaurants, and even many smaller ones, have an indoor or outdoor bar area to make your wait more enjoyable. Our suggestion is always leave for your restaurant of choice prior to getting to the point of starvation, and turn the evening into an experience, rather than just running out for a bite to eat. If you're the impatient type and don't mind an early dinner, check around for early-bird specials, usually from 4 until 6 PM. They're plentiful at any time of year, there's

rarely a long wait, and prices are surprisingly reasonable. Also note that while we have given you basic hours of operation for most of the eateries listed here, the hours of many change with the crowds and the seasons. Be certain to call ahead before you go, especially at lunchtime.

Price Code

We'll help in the money department by using our dollar-sign codes to alert you to the tab you can expect at the end of your evening meal. The codes represent the price for a reasonable dinner for two, sans cocktails or wine. Tax and gratuity are not included in our price code either. Cash, traveler's checks and most major credit cards are the norm for payment — no personal checks, please. If you're concerned about which credit cards are accepted, just call ahead to check the restaurant's current plastic policy. Unless otherwise noted, you can expect your credit card to be accepted at all the restaurants listed.

$	Less than $25
$$	$25 to $40
$$$	$41 to $55
$$$$	More than $55

To help guide you through the Bay area restaurants, we'll take you through the different categories of cuisine, breaking them down to Hillsborough and Pinellas counties. We've come to realize that sometimes it's the food and service that's most important to locals and visitors, not necessarily the proximity to their front doors. While the categories of flavor are listed alphabetically, the restaurants themselves are in no particular order.

You won't find among the listings the national chains of Bennigan's, Chili's, Olive Garden, Pizza Huts and the like. There's not much we can tell you about these that you don't already know and, while they all are excellent places to grab a familiar meal, we'd much prefer to steer you to some local favorites with that singular Tampa Bay charm. We will, however, take just a short commercial break to advise you that Outback Steakhouse started right here in Tampa Bay (the one-and-only original is at 3403 Henderson Boulevard), and the owners are now repeating their success with a chain of Italian grills called Carrabba's.

American/Continental

Hillsborough County

CK's Revolving Restaurant
$$$ • Tampa Airport Marriott, Tampa • (813) 878-6500

Watch the city's nighttime skyline spin beneath you as you dine in Tampa's only revolving rooftop restaurant. True, you're at the airport, but once seated, with the aroma of grilled, marinated quail with pear brandy sauce making your taste buds squeal with delight, you could pretend you're anywhere on earth. The grilled sliced rack of lamb with rosemary dijon sauce never disappoints, but our hands-down favorite is the veal Lemuel, sauteed with lobster, white asparagus and hollandaise sauce. Simply divine. Pay special attention to the marvelous sauces. All are enhanced with herbs from the chef's personal herb garden. CK's is open for dinner Sunday through Thursday from 5 until 10 PM and Friday and Saturday from 5 until 11 PM. A sinful Sunday brunch awaits you on Sunday from 10:30 AM until 2:30 PM.

The Wine Exchange
$$ • 1611 W. Swann Ave., Tampa • (813) 254-9463

So, so trendy, this European-style bistro is in Old Hyde Park Village. We adore the smoked chicken ravioli, and the grilled Delmonico with roasted garlic will send those taste buds to the moon. Best of all, the restaurant has an exceptional number of fine wines available by the glass, just to help you better savor the creative food offerings. The Wine Exchange serves dinner nightly beginning at 5:30.

The Castaway
$$ • 7720 Courtney Campbell Cswy., Tampa • (813) 281-0770

Billed as the only beachfront restaurant in Tampa, The Castaway sits on stilts leaning over Old Tampa Bay. Needless to say, the views are spectacular, and the food follows suit. Seafood brochettes, coconut shrimp, Hawaiian chicken and shrimp curry are just a few temptations from the menu with a decided Polynesian influence. The bouillabaisse is some of the best around, and even your meat lover will be pleased with the generous prime rib portions. If you can't make it at supper time (dinner is served nightly beginning at 5:30), don't miss the Sunsational Champagne Sunday Brunch. And don't fight over those Belgian waffles — there are plenty to go around.

Circles
$$ • 14362 N. Dale Mabry Hwy., Tampa • (813) 960-2007

Don't allow the strip center facade to turn you away. You won't regret a short wait to be seated in this casual metro bistro, with its amazing duck, veal, Thai-style chicken and poached fillet of fresh fish. Whether you order one of the pastas, entrees or Circle sandwiches (served with toasted pita bread, naturally) we assure you that your lunch, served Monday through Saturday beginning at 11:30 AM, or dinner, served nightly from 5:30, will be one of your more exceptional taste treats in town.

BuddyFreddy's
$ • I-4 at Exit 11, Plant City • (813) 754-5120
134 S. Gornto Lake Rd., Brandon • (813) 661-6005

Y'all come back, ya hear? If you just whisper that you're headed for BuddyFreddys for

www.insiders.com
See this and many other **Insiders' Guide®** destinations online — in their entirety.
Visit us today!

Dining options in the Tampa Bay area range from romantic, candlelit dining rooms to rowdy, casual beach cafes.

Photo: St. Petersburg/Clearwater Area Convention & Visitors Bureau

lunch or dinner, you'll find the car packed with hungry souls looking for a ride. We are talking eats with a capital E — the BuddyFreddy's Buffet with pot roast, fried chicken, fresh fish, collard greens, black-eyed peas, baked ham with raisin sauce, sweet potato souffle and, oh make them stop! We're so stuffed we can't move! OK, maybe just a tiny little space for that red velvet cake. then just roll us out to the rocking chairs on the wraparound porch and let us take a nap. Prepare for your BuddyFreddy's feast every day of the week beginning at 11 AM.

Jesse's

$ • 524 W. Brandon Blvd., Brandon
• (813) 685-2381
Fowler Ave. at 56th St., Temple Terrace
• (813) 980-3686
551 Gulf Blvd., Clearwater Beach
• (727) 443-6210

Named by owner Frank D'Amico for his daughter Jessica, Jesse's is a local favorite for Black Angus beef and seafood. (Go

ahead and order the infamous golden Texas fries — you can count calories tomorrow.) The fireplaces, aquariums and solid wood bars give these restaurants that warm, inviting feeling, as does the most obliging staff. The restaurants serve lunch and dinner daily, and if you get the hungries very late at night, Jesse's in Brandon is the place to head. From midnight until 2:30 AM, the most divine night-owl breakfast of steak and eggs is served. To note: Jesse's Clearwater Beach location will be remembered by old-timers as the Flagship.

Pinellas County

Bob Heilman's Beachcomber
$$$ • 447 Mandalay Ave., Clearwater Beach • (727) 442-4144

You know how sometimes you can just look at a place and know your meal's going to be the best? Things like a warm, inviting entry and a packed parking lot? You've just spotted Bob Heilman's Beachcomber. Now, it's not on the water, but that doesn't make any difference. Inside, it's all tropical plants and striking murals, and the food is phenomenal! Beef lovers will be forced to order prime rib, or maybe break the mold and go for Everglade's frog legs or a Maine lobster. We'll just stick by the "back-to-the-farm" fried chicken created from the original 1926 receipe and noted as one of the most popular menu items. No evening would be complete without either an aperitif or after-dinner cordial at the bar, and don't neglect a peek at the new 25,000-bottle wine cellar. The restaurant's open for dinner only, beginning at 5 PM.

Heritage Grille
$$$ • 256 Second St. N., St. Petersburg • (727) 823-6382

With all the charm of a true country inn, you'll find the Heritage Grille inside the Heritage Hotel/ Holiday Inn, tucked in a residential neighborhood moments from downtown (see our Accommodations chapter). The French doors, local art and ornate wood carvings set the scene for a delightful dining experience in one of the four main dining areas. Whether you choose to be seated inside or out, the roasted-walnut dijon-crusted rack of lamb with mint pesto should be high on your list, but we can also recommend the crab cakes with andouille, spinach and Creole mustard Bearnaise sauce. Heritage Grille is open every day for lunch and dinner beginning at 11 AM.

Apropos
$$ • 200 Second Ave. N.E., St. Petersburg • (727) 823-8934

Right on the corner at the marina by The Pier, Apropos is all art-deco chic, with a menu that benefits from the chef's use of fresh herbs and light sauces. The rosemary chicken and lamb chops are superb, and if you're in a seafood kind of mood, ask about the lobster. This is a trendy place for noontime or evening repast, and whether you sit indoors or on the patio, the water views are grand. With the advent of the Devil Rays playing right down the street at Tropicana

Field, the place gets quite busy on game day. Plan accordingly.

Captain Kosmakos
$$ • 9610 Gulf Blvd., Treasure Island • (727) 367-3743

Here's what you'll see: a big glass building on concrete stilts. If you look up to the top, you'll know where you're headed — to a noisy, popular eatery with fantastic views of the waters between St. Pete Beach and Treasure Island. If you're the hungry-man type, this place will make you happy. The portions are huge, whether you go for seafood such as grouper or crab cakes, or the chicken cacciatore, veal Marsala or shish kabob. Come hungry for lunch or dinner, starting at 11 AM.

Sunset Beach Cafe
$$ • 9701 First St. E., Treasure Island • (727) 367-3359

If you want to bring a little Continental spirit into your lunch or dinner dining experience, try the Sunset Beach Cafe on the southern tip of TI. On the wall space left between the wraparound windows, there are Renoir and Monet reproductions in this family-owned and -operated bistro. Indulge in scallops scampi, fried chicken or coconut shrimp. Just make sure you save room for some of the best Key lime pie on the strip.

94th Aero Squadron
$$ • 94 Fairchild Dr., Clearwater • (727) 524-4155

Every time we've mentioned Boatyard Village in this guide, we've tried to point out the 94th. Housed in a look-alike World War II French farmhouse, you're greeted on the front lawn by an authentic 1917 Sopwith Camel, and inside you'll be surrounded by sandbag walls, old pictures and war posters, military artifacts of every description and four fireplaces flanked by antique bottles and books. OK, so you can also sit in the part of the restaurant that overlooks the water. No matter where you sit, you're certain to enjoy the Colorado lamb, stir-fry dishes, pastas, local seafood or our favorite blue crab quesadilla. For dessert, there's no other choice but the 94th's signature Belgium chocolate truffle torte. Dinner is served daily from 5 PM. Don't fly by it.

Alley Cat's Cafe

$$ • 2721 Gulf Blvd., Indian Rocks
• (727) 595-7877
2475-M, McMullen Booth Rd.,
Clearwater • (727) 797-5555

If you're dying for a dish that will "singe your whiskers," head straight for a Back Alley Burger with chili and melted cheddar. For the meek, stick with Nachos ... la Cat or the baked chicken. Pasta lovers should not pass up a chance for their specialty Black Cat Pasta, black (yes, black!) angel-hair pasta with lobster sauce and jumbo shrimp. For closers, indulge in an Alley Cat Cafe with Kahlua, Creme de Cacao and Grand Marnier. Meow! A purr-fect place for lunch through late-night dining (until 2 AM Monday through Saturday and until midnight on Sunday) beginning at 11:30 AM Monday through Saturday and 12:30 PM on Sunday.

Dave & Bubba's

$$ • 34980 U.S. Hwy. 19 N., Palm Harbor • (727) 786-0077

Hubba bubba, this is one wacky place! It starts with the menu. One side says Supper with Bubba; the other, Dinner with Dave. Not to mention its wine list — every bottle is priced an outrageously low $1 more than cost. (The fine print says "Bubba made a big mistake. Order it before he notices.") As for the food, look out taste buds, here it comes! Beef lovers will be in heaven, especially with the Carpetbagger Filet Mignon that's stuffed with red onion and sauteed Portobello mushrooms, then drizzled with a demiglace. Seafood lovers better be plenty hungry when they order Bubba's Maryland Crabcakes — they're the size of baseballs with hardly any filler. And then there's the primo dessert, Dottie's Coca-Cola Cake, smothered in hot fudge and ice cream. We venture to say that you'll be so stuffed after your meal, you might feel just like the life-size blow-up of Bubba, posing as Edvard Munch's The Scream! Dave & Bubba's serves dinner only, beginning at 5 PM.

Keegan's Beach Birds Cafe

$$ • 1412 Gulf Blvd., Indian Rocks Beach • (727) 593-3578

American goodies all the way — big, fat buffalo shrimp; fried, stuffed jalapenos; cold, smoked prime rib; baked grouper with mushroom deluxes; a fine bouillabaisse — all hearty, tasty and reasonably priced. If you want to rub shoulders with a casual, local crowd, Keegan's is the place to do it. The restaurant opens at 11 AM for lunch and dinner.

Wine Cellar

$$$ • 17307 Gulf Blvd. N., Redington Beach • (727) 393-3491

Every six months the menu changes, but you can always count on a melt-in-your-mouth beef Wellington, rack of baby lamb and the ever popular Ted's Souse Shrimp. Along with an extensive wine list — an 800-bottle, 47-wine selection — it also has one of the most extensive selections of appetizers with its star, Swiss cheese soup. For dessert, you must save room for the black Russian pie or the Black Forest cherry torte. Open Tuesday through Sunday for dinner only beginning at 4:30 PM, the award-winning Wine Cellar with its seven delectably different dining rooms has been a continental favorite since 1976. A note on dress is in order here. Unlike most of the casual eateries along the beach strip, this is one place that expects you to dress "smartly casual" for your dining adventure.

Coffeehouses

Although most coffeehouses are open from early morning until late evening and we have given specific times, do call ahead because the hours seem to change daily.

Hillsborough County

Joffrey's

$ • 1468 N. Dale Mabry Hwy., Tampa
• (813) 264-1649
1628 W. Snow Cir., Hyde Park, Tampa
• (813) 251-3315
Eastlake Woodlands Plz., Palm Harbor
• (727) 789-4464
1616 E. Seventh Ave., Ybor City
• (813) 248-5282

Forget Starbucks ... Joffrey's is here! The aroma (need we mention) is enough to get your nostrils flaring, even in the heat of summer. Along with the specialty coffees (a must is the Mochachino Cooler, a divine concoction made with espresso, sugar, chocolate and whipped cream), don't pass up the opportunity to dive into the sumptuous gourmet desserts and bakery goods. As we see it, the caffeine will get your system going fast enough to burn off any excess calories. Trivia buffs will appreciate this little tidbit: Joffrey's roasts all the coffees it sells in its stores, almost 17,500 pounds a month!

Cafe Kaldi Ybor City

$ • 1725 E. 7th Ave., Ybor City
• (813) 241-BEAN

Beam me up some cyberjava! Ybor's first Internet Cafe, here's the place where you can nibble on a fresh-baked pastry, sip on a house specialty like Razz Matazz, Rocky Road or Almond Joy and surf the Net at the same time. You can get connected for $6 an hour, plus you can even take a free Internet class on Thursday nights from 8 until 9 PM. If you've got a hunger for something a little different, you ought to try the Veggie Big Mac, a seven-grain bakery bun piled high with sliced tomatoes, buffalo mozzarella, roasted red peppers, fresh basil and sprouts. The cafe's open seven days a week; Friday and Saturday nights until 3 AM.

SideBern's

$ • S. Howard at Morrison, Tampa
• (813) 258-CAFE

If caffeine and people-watching go together in your book, here's the place. You'll see the young and hip in this dessert cafe that bears the name of its famous father, Bern's Steakhouse. You'll enjoy the same sinfully rich desserts, fresh roasted coffees, ports, wines and single-malt scotches, but here you can enjoy a much more casual atmosphere. You'll even find a cigar lounge and a delightful outside patio. Drop by on Tuesday through Thursday from 6 until 11 PM and until 1 AM on Friday and Saturday.

Cool Mo's

$ • 10322 N. Dale Mabry Hwy., Tampa
1218 W. Fletcher Ave., Tampa
• (813) 968-2541

Well, Cool Mo's isn't exactly a coffee-

house, it's actually a double-decker bus/drive-through for java fiends on the road. If this sounds a bit silly, just take a gander at the line-up waiting to pull through for that morning jolt and a mini-blueberry muffin or bagel on any given workday morning. While self-billed as bad, slow, expensive and inconvenient, it's still one of the hottest places to grab an espresso in north Tampa, beginning around 6:30 AM.

Bean There ... A Travelers Coffeehouse

$ • 3202 Bay to Bay Blvd., Tampa
• (813) 837-7022

Where you "bean," baby? That and so many other answers to mindless questions are answered daily by the devout regulars at Bean There, voted "Best Coffeehouse" by the *South Tampa News*. Along with fabulous iced coffee drinks, you can also order up your favorite wine or beer along with a light breakfast or lunch. It's open 7 AM until 3 PM Monday through Friday, 8 AM until 3 PM on Saturday and from 8 AM until 2 PM on Sunday.

Sacred Ground

$ • 11118 30th St. N., Tampa
• (813) 972-5344

The coffeehouse your Momma warned you about is close to the University of South Florida, just south of Fowler Avenue. Along with monthly poetry jams, you can order up your favorite coffees, teas, milkshakes and bagels and snacks. Check out all the action Tuesday through Saturday from 5:30 PM until "late," and Sunday from 6:30 PM until midnight.

Whistle Stop

$ • 110 N. Montclair Ave., Brandon
• (813) 685-0038

At the front counter, you can select from a "library of coffee." The garden backyard is the setting for charming gazebos where you can order up an espresso from the coffee bar. It's a homey, neighborhood kind of place, especially on Saturday mornings when locals pedal their bikes over for the luscious, soon-to-be-famous, cinnamon rolls. Count on that first brewed cup by 7 AM Monday through Friday and by 8 AM on Saturdays.

Pinellas County

Ethnic

East of Java
$ • 2551 Drew St., Clearwater
• (727) 799-3788

Drink it here or take it home by the pound. One of Clearwater's most popular coffee cafes can satisfy the java lover in all of us, and backs it up with the freshest pastries and desserts.You can track it down by following the scent of brewing nirvana at the Campus Walk Shopping Center starting at 7 AM Monday through Saturday. If you're just not in the mood for a hot cup of anything, request one of those killer shakes! The cafe's open until 10:30 PM Monday through Thursday and until midnight on Friday and Saturday.

Sweet Sage Coffee
$ • 16725 Gulf Blvd. N., Redington Beach
• (727) 391-0453

Part of the Grey Fox Art Gallery, Sweet Sage is a popular place for the chic and hungry to gather in the afternoon to sip a specialty java or tea (in a real china cup!) and munch on a light lunch or all-natural dessert. You are cordially welcome each day beginning at 11:30 AM.

Spiritual Wings
$ • 1248 S. Highland, Clearwater
• (727) 446-5678

Open your senses … and your mind. In this metaphysical bookstore and cafe, you can reach out to the beyond while sipping on the famous-flavored Cappuccinos, Lattes or exotic teas. Psychic readings are available every day, and there's even karaoke every Wednesday, Friday and Saturday from 8 until 11 PM. This coffeehouse opens daily at noon.

Cafe Nepenthe
$ • 777 Dodacanese Blvd., Tarpon Springs • (813) 938-0079

Sip on some delightful specialty brews in this Euro-style coffeehouse that sits right at the famous Sponge Docks in Tarpon Springs. A true sidewalk cafe, it's a great place to just hang out and taste-test a coffee drink, microbrew, wine or soft drink. Light fare and desserts round out the menu.

Hillsborough County

Ali Baba's Pakistani Indian Restaurant
$$ • 13145 N. Dale Mabry Hwy., Tampa
• (813) 968-7575

Hearty appetites and adventurous first-timers are encouraged to visit on Sunday night — that's when the grand buffet is laden with lamb, beef curries, lentils and soups. Thursday night, the buffet is strictly vegetarian and delicious enough to satisfy even the most diehard meat lovers. Special cooking requests, from spice intensity to no oil or salt, are welcomed, so don't hesitate to state your preferences. The atmosphere here is soothing and quiet, making it all the easier to savor the meal and those sharing it with you. The restaurant is closed Mondays, but dinner is served all other days from 5:50 to 10 PM.

Bombay Masala
$$ • 4023 W. Waters Ave., Tampa
• (813) 880-7511

Its modest storefront location in the Northwest Plaza almost hides the fact that this is one of the area's most well-known ethnic restaurants. For lunch and dinner, an incredibly varied array of authentic Indian foods is available here, ranging from the highly spiced to flavors sublime. Though flowers grace the eight booths and six tables, the atmosphere is fairly casual — probably because the emphasis is on pleasing your palate instead of feeding the owner's ego. The owner's satisfaction comes from hearing diners rave over such offerings as Goan shrimp curry, with a zesty combination of spices and soothing ground coconut. Beer and wine are offered. It's closed Mondays, but lunch is served Tuesday through Friday and on Sunday between 11:30 AM and 2:30 PM. Dinner hours are 5 until 10 six nights a week.

Cafe Creole
$$-$$$ • 1330 E. Ninth Ave., Ybor City
• (813) 247-6283

N'Awlins meets Cuba in this extremely popular nightspot where jazzy music attracts locals by the droves. While the atmosphere in the lounge — with its bird's-eye view of people parading through the streets of Ybor— can get lively, Cafe Creole lends a sense of Victorian charm and elegance to every dining experience. The old red-brick, wood and glass building sets a tone of comfort that's enhanced by the friendly and efficient waiters. The topnotch menu includes seafood and steaks, yet proves why gumbo and beans and rice must surely be the food of the gods. Hours for lunch are 11:30 AM till 4 PM Monday through Friday, with dinner till 10 PM Monday through Thursday, till 11:30 PM on Friday and from 5 to 11:30 PM on Saturday.

Rumplemayer's
$ • 4812 E. Busch Blvd., Tampa
• (813) 989-9563

This place is much more than a restaurant, it's a festival — or, more accurately, a festhaus! Start with a selection from the many wines or scores of international beers. Plunge into a platter of assorted wurst or swoon over the zigeuner Schnitzel, with veal and Bavarian ham in paprika sauce. Laugh and clap along with the accordion-backed entertainment that starts most nights at 6, and get out there on the dance floor yourself. You'll never again think Germans are somber, and you'll leave making plans for another dinner visit soon. Open for lunch and dinner seven days a week, Rumplemayer's serves from 11 AM till 11 PM.

Sam Oh Jung
$ • 602 N. Dale Mabry Hwy., Tampa
• (813) 871-3233

Korean cuisine combines artful Oriental presentation with unique flavors in dishes ranging from puckery hot kim chee to delicately flavored fish. Personalize your entrees with a flavorful assortment of condiments. The adventurous will certainly want to sample the Korean fare and variety of sushi choices, but aficionados of Chinese cuisine will also be pleased. The sushi selection here is truly extensive, including such delicacies as flying-fish roe. Those who prefer their fish cooked should give "Tampa" makimono a try — it's deep-fried grouper rolled sushi-style in rice and seaweed that is oh, so delicious. Sam Oh Jung is open for lunch and dinner from 11 AM until 10 PM weekdays and from noon till 11 PM on Saturdays and Sundays.

Star of India
$ • 11154 N. 30th St., Tampa
• (813) 977-7827

India was the star of the British Empire, and the Star of India returns the compliment, serving up such mouthwatering delicacies as garlic and mushroom chicken in a sparkling British setting. Smokers — either dine elsewhere or leave your cigarettes or cigars outside, because this is a no-smoking establishment. A full menu is offered, but the real treat is the evening buffet, served nightly from 5 till 10. And vegetarians won't be limited to salad by the sizable selection of non-meat dishes. Beer and wine are available with lunch and dinner. Noon-time dining is from 11:30 AM till 2:30 PM. The Star of India is closed on Mondays.

Sukhothai
$$ • 8201 N. Dale Mabry Hwy., Tampa
• (813) 933-7990

Its name means "dawn of happiness," which is an apt description of what happens to your taste buds when they meet the true Thai cuisine here. Sukhothai has long been a favorite with Bay area Insiders, certainly for the food but also for the friendly, casual atmosphere. Diners may choose seating either at round tables with chairs or on brightly colored cushions on the Khan-toke room's shiny hardwood floor, traditional to Thai hospitality. The pineapple lobster will delight seafood lovers — it's topped with shrimp and pineapple curry sauce. Beer and wine are offered to accompany the cuisine. On weekdays, service begins at 11 AM and ends at 11 PM. On Saturday and Sunday, only dinner is served, from 5 till 11 PM.

Pinellas County

Ai-Mei Thai Restaurant
$ • 4200 34th St. S., St. Petersburg
• (727) 867-0965

Take heart — there's no MSG used here, and Thai fare is traditionally low in cholesterol. But the food's as spicy as you please, because you get to choose mild, hot or really spiced. Ai-Mei is regarded as the only true Thai restaurant in St. Petersburg. One of the most popular menu choices is the Three Buddies, a platter combining deep-fried duck, shrimp and chicken. Beer and wine are available at this bright and cheerful establishment. Ai-Mei serves lunch from 11 AM until 3 PM weekdays and dinner every night from 5 until 10.

Cajun Cafe on the Bayou
$ • 8285 Park Blvd., Pinellas Park
• (727) 546-6732

For sand, seafood and steaks, you can't beat this Cajun home-like cafe on Cross Bayou. Po' Boys are a staple, as are mudbugs during season (more refined diners call these crawfish). Adding a touch of Florida to the fare is Gator Jumbalaya Gumbo. Beer or wine may accompany your meal. Lunch and dinner are served Tuesday through Sunday from 11:30 AM till 10 PM. On Friday, Saturday and Sunday, Cajun and Blues rock the joint.

Gumbo's
$ • 250 75th Ave., St. Pete Beach
• (727) 367-7363

The colorful, merry Mardi Gras atmosphere is an ideal accompaniment to the spicy Cajun/Creole menu. Of course, you've got to try the gumbo — either seafood or chicken will more than satisfy. One thing this place offers that no one else does is crawfish cornbread — ooh-eee! The kitchen's open from 11 AM till 1 AM every day except Sunday, when the doors open at 4 PM, and Saturday, when they open at noon. Sunday night's the night to show up for the Blues Jam, which starts at 8.

Kasba
$$ • 1200 Eighth Ave. S.W., Largo
• (727) 581-2055

With a golf-course view, this Persian restaurant creates a country-club mood, but please remember that no shorts or sandals are allowed. Even non-adventurous palates will be pleased by the subtle taste combinations presented in such specialties as lamb shank, saffron rice or Continental-style scampi or grouper. At the other end of the savory spectrum are Persian delicacies, including gheimeh, which is beef with yellow lentils and citrus zest, or duck with pomegranate sauce, which must be ordered a day ahead. Dinner is served nightly, except Sunday, from 5:30. Monday through Thursday the kitchen is open until 9 PM and on Friday and Saturday till 9:30 PM, and it's a good idea to call ahead for a reservation.

Madkof's Restaurant & Bar
$ • 1280 Main St., Dunedin
• (727) 738-0022

Don't shy away because of the gaudy exterior. Inside, you'll find richly appointed decor and impressive art, and you'll feel as if you're being served in Austrian owner/chef Eric Madkof's home. Middle- and Eastern-European specialties beckon hearty diners, with Old World treats such as Hungarian goulash, Bulgarian borscht, escargot jardiniere, suckling pig, beef Stroganoff and warm apple strudel. Since Madkof's is set so close to the Gulf, seafood gets the continental treatment, too. Try the Portuguese grouper that is steamed in white wine with peppers and onions. Madkof's is open for lunch and dinner daily from 11:30 AM till 10 PM.

Siam Garden II
$ • 21338 U.S. Hwy. 19 N., Clearwater
• (727) 822-0613

A must for tastes that run to Thai, Siam Garden II is well known by Insiders as one of the best ethnic restaurants in the Bay area for either lunch or dinner. You can tell a lot about a restaurant's atmosphere by the length of its menu — tony places tend to limit your choices, but here you have three score plus four items to select from, as well as beer and wine. There's simply nothing we wouldn't recommend. But if the choices are just too confusing, we suggest the chili garlic grouper — an entire fish covered with red bell pepper and garlic. It's a flavorful favorite. Lunch is served Monday through Saturday from 11 AM till 3 PM and dinner from 5 till 10 PM. On Sunday, dinner is served from 4 till 10 PM.

French

Hillsborough County

Le Bordeaux
$$ 1502 S. Howard Ave., Tampa
• (813) 254-4387

Just one block off Bayshore Boulevard, Le Bordeaux sits in a bungalow-turned-bistro with its two dining rooms saturated with the divine aromas of exquisite French cuisine. French-born chef and owner Gordon Davis changes his menu nightly, usually offering you at least 10 choices, including veal with wild mushrooms, pot au feu, salmon en croute, beef au Roquefort, homemade pâtés and pastries. Do have your highball before you arrive; only beer and wine are available. Only dinner is served, beginning at 5 PM.

Cafe by the Bay
$$ • 1350 S. Howard Ave., Tampa
• (813) 251-6659

For years, Sunday morning in Hyde Park meant grabbing a newspaper and heading over to Cafe by the Bay. Not any more! Today, this charmer of a restaurant is totally French, almost a Le Bordeaux clone right down to a few of the waiters. The menu changes weekly, but you can always count on being greeted by the dizzying aroma of fresh bread wedges. From there, go on to try the herb-crusted salmon, rack of lamb with delicate fig sauce or pan-seared Jumbo Shrimp and Crab Cake. And you must save room for the Cappuccino Cake to fill that last little space in your stomach. A must-do for dinner, it's open Tuesday through Saturday from 5:30 until 10:30 PM.

Monte Carlo
$$ • 3940 W. Cypress, Tampa
• (813) 879-6245

Oui! Oui! A member of *Who's Who in American Restaurants* and honored as America's Finest, Best Chef and Best Restaurant in the National Registry, Mildred Lancaster and Romeo Berranini have never rested on their laurels. Instead, they continue to produce amazing power lunches and dinners, including their most popular beef Wellington, Chateaubriand Bearnaise for two, Veal Valentino or rack of lamb. Adventurous souls must give the duck with fig sauce a go. A divine dining experience ... la Francaise in a wonderfully dark and romantic French country house. Join them for lunch Monday through Friday from 11:30 AM until 2 PM and for dinner Monday through Thursday from 6 until 10 PM and Friday and Saturday from 6 until 11 PM.

Pinellas County

Le Grande Cafe
$$$ • 247 Central Ave., St. Petersburg
• (727) 821-6992

Selected as one of Florida's top-200 restaurants by *Florida Trend Magazine* in 1993 and 1994, Le Grande serves two different three-course meals every day at a fixed price, along with its regular menu. The chefs are masters with tenderloin of lamb and veal, but the escargot (with chopped mushrooms in garlic and herbs in a dome of puff pastry) is to die for. New and not to be missed is the Courtyard, a relaxing, contemporary setting that begs for port wine and a cigar, an appetizer or dessert and good conversation. Plan on a delightful dining experience Monday through Saturday beginning at 5:30 PM.

The Anchor Room
$$$ • 800 Mandalay Ave., Clearwater Beach • (727) 461-7079

Bouillabaisse, veal, poultry and seafood cooked the French way — this is the only French restaurant operated by a French family on Clearwater Beach, and its cozy atmosphere and divine entrees make it a favorite for locals and visitors alike. If you're staying along Clearwater Beach or Sand Key and have a hankering for a romantic evening of French cuisine, call the Anchor Room. The staff will arrange for free transportation to and from your hotel. The restaurant serves lunch from 11:30 AM every day except Monday and Tuesday. Dinner is served every night except Monday.

La Tour Eiffel
$$$ • 796 Indian Rocks Rd., Belleair
• (727) 581-6530

This is as authentic a French restaurant as you can find. In the finest French manner, La Tour Eiffel not only delights the palate but also the heart. In addition to the specialties of the house such as salmon en croute with its unique lobster sauce, filet au poivre with creamy pepper and brandy sauce and brilliant lamb shanks, you can order from "The Lites of Paris," a menu of lighter dishes created with the assistance of top dieticians from Morton Plant Hospital. Before your entree, you'll relish the cold cucumber soup. A must is saving room for chocolate mousse prepared with the best Belgian chocolate and Grand Marnier. Chef/owner Marcel and his wife, Anne Marie, greet guests for lunch and dinner beginning at 11:30 AM every day except Monday when the restaurant is closed. No dinner is served on Sunday.

Cafe Largo
$$$ • 12551 Indian Rocks Beach Rd., Largo • (727) 596-6282

From the moment the roasted rack of lamb with mustard sauce is set before you, you'll know you may have to swear off burgers forever. At Cafe Largo, you can delight in traditional French cuisine served in a most romantic atmosphere. To begin with, do try the escargot bourguignonne, and for the finale, sample a treat from the tantalizing selection of homemade French pastries. Better yet, order the cafe's trademark souffles au choix, made with orange liqueur, chocolate, Frangelico and fruit. The service is impeccable, whether you come for lunch or dinner. The restaurant is open daily beginning at 11:30 AM.

La Brasserie
$$$ • 200 E. Tarpon Ave., Tarpon Springs • (813) 942-3011

Under the scrutiny of owners Eric and Marie Pierre, both classically trained in Europe, La Brasserie not only delights with its authentic French offerings, it's also the inplace to see and be seen in downtown Tarpon Springs for either lunch or dinner Monday through Saturday. If you can hold back from ordering the traditional escargot for an appetizer, try La Flamiche, an onion tart made from a recipe that originated in the northwest area of France. A seafood favorite is the Crepe Imperiale, loaded with crab, shrimp and scallops in a Normandy sauce. The filet of beef sauteed in bourbon, served on a bordelaise sauce and topped with Roquefort cheese will satisfy any beef lover. And please do not miss the creme caramel — it's the ultimate dessert after a most marvelous meal.

Greek

Pinellas County

Dino's Restaurant & Taverna
$$ • 604 Athens St., Tarpon Springs • (813) 938-9082

Just off the sponge docks sits this homey little restaurant that amply proves why Greek food is so popular. Start off with an appetizer platter that includes selections of tzatzike, taramosalata, skordalia, feta cheese, olives, vegetables and pita bread. Then choose from traditional entrees such as the very affordable moussaka, shrimp corfu over pasta or the baby back ribs in a spicy sauce, or go for the house specialty, octopus. Dino's is a great place to round out a day of sightseeing and soaking up the Old World charm of Tarpon Springs. In other words, the staff wants you to be impressed by the food, instead of them being impressed by what you're wearing. Dino's is open Sunday through Wednesday from 11 AM until 11 PM. On Friday and Saturday it's open from 11 AM till 2 AM, and you'll enjoy live music and Greek folk dancing.

Hellas
$ • 784 Dodecanese Blvd., Tarpon Springs • (813) 943-2400

Since it's a Greek community, Tarpon Springs is studded with little Greek restaurants. And this delightful, casual choice is definitely among the best for a midday or evening meal. Feta aficionados will swoon over the feta Greek salad. Too full to order dessert after that delicious saganaki? Stop in at its famous next-door bakery and pick out a sweet reminder of your visit. Open daily from 11 AM till 10 PM, outside dining is also offered.

George Pappas Restaurant
$$ • 607 Clearwater/Largo Rd., Largo • (727) 584-6235

Rose lovers will especially delight in the ambiance of the Victorian garden in full bloom. But whether you're coming for lunch from the office or dinner during a weekend on the beach, there's much more to tempt you than traditional Greek foods at Pappas — prime rib prepared German-style, roast lamb and crab cakes. The Greek salads are zesty and the gyros so succulent. A full bar is available, and if you've never tried ouzo, do so here. Pappas is open from 11 AM every day and closes at 9 PM Sunday through Thursday and at 10 PM Friday and Saturday.

Italian

Hillsborough County

Bernini
$$$ • 1702 E. Seventh Ave., Tampa
• (813) 248-0099

Imagine innovative Italian food served up in surroundings filled with replicas of 17th-century Baroque sculptor Giovanni Bernini. It conjures up romance and elegance, doesn't it? This is the sort of place that reminds you of fine restaurants in New York City. Lunch, served from 11:30 AM till 2 PM Monday through Friday, is certainly casual, with butcher block paper covering the tables. The dinner atmosphere, beginning at 5:30 PM, is definitely jazzed — literally — with the sounds of acid jazz wafting in the background. You'll find an open dining room plus mezzanine dining in the cigar/martini bar upstairs. The menu changes daily, but don't miss the appetizer of calamari and bruschetta. The restaurant's closed on Sundays, and no dinner is served Monday nights. Dinner is served Tuesday, Wednesday and Thursday until 10 PM and Friday and Saturday till 11 PM.

CDB Italian Restaurant
$-$$ • 5104 E. Fowler Ave., Tampa
• (813) 985-1336
5929 Memorial Hwy., Tampa
• (813) 886-0875
5303 W. Erlich Rd., Tampa
• (813) 962-1221

CDB's is famous for those times you're craving outstanding pizza or have a big hunger for excellent Italian food in a casual setting. And it's a popular lunch and dinner gathering spot for all types, from the after-the-ballgame crowd to romancing couples. This is a great place to take the kids because the menu is vast enough to satisfy every preference. Everything from linguine with artichoke hearts to good old American cheeseburgers is on the menu. But one taste of the fresh ravioli and the kids will never be satisfied with Chef Boyardee again. Lunch is served seven days a week from 11 AM till 3 PM. Dinner then runs from 3 PM till midnight, except on Sunday when it closes at 11 PM.

Caffe Alberto Pizzeria & Ristorante
$$ • 13949 W. Hillsborough Ave., Tampa
• (813) 854-5546

The cozy, casual setting of this small eatery belies the creations produced in the kitchen. Sure, pizza lovers won't be disappointed — choose from regular, Sicilian, stuffed or double-decked. But the gustatory delights extend to the gourmet, with choices such as an award-winning veal scaloppini, pollo rosso or Grandma Rose's meatballs in a rich Bolognese sauce. Alberto's offers spicy Southern Italian fare, and the fra diavolo, fiery mussels in marinara sauce, makes a devilishly delicious appetizer. Caffe Alberto serves diners from 11 AM till 10 PM Monday through Saturday and from 5 to 10 PM on Sunday.

Caffe Amaretto
$$$ • 5915 Memorial Hwy., Tampa
• (813) 885-4700

Elaborate and elegant, this is ideal for a romantic evening for two or a joyous night of celebration. Let yourself be pampered all the way: first by waiters serving your selections from the antipasto table, and then with a rich, well-cheesed Caesar salad prepared at your table. That feeling of wealth continues with such beautifully presented entrees as rack of lamb with rosemary sauce, the tortellini luna (stuffed with ricotta and Parmesan cheeses and spinach in pesto and cream sauce), penne alla vodka or cannelloni stuffed with veal. Then let the romance of your evening build as you linger over coffee and strawberry cake, watching to see if you can spot Tampa's mayor, members of the Bucs or any other celebrities. The restaurant is closed Sundays. Weekday lunches are offered from 11:30 AM till 2:30 PM. Dinner begins at 5:30 and ends at 10 PM Monday though Thursday and at 11 PM Friday and Saturday.

Caffe Italia
$$ • 3114 Bay to Bay Blvd., Tampa
• (813) 831-0600

Enchantment, elegance and romance add to the true tastes of Tuscany served at Caffe Italia. Though reservations are recommended, you'll want to arrive early enough to linger over a drink and enjoy people-watching in the bar. Nibble on the antipasto misto, a combination of homemade mozzarella cheese, tomatoes, roasted peppers and marinated eggplant. Seafood lovers will not be disappointed with unique presentations of three fish-of-the-day choices. If you dine on an evening when gnocchi with gorgonzola cream sauce is offered, throw fat-caution to the wind and indulge — word has it you'll never find better. Dining begins every day except Sunday at 5:30 PM. Service continues until 10:30 PM Monday through Thursday. On Friday and Saturday, when there's live piano music, service ends at 11:30 PM.

Caffe Firenze
$$ • 719 N. Franklin St., Tampa
• (813) 228-9200

Downtown dining in Tampa isn't plentiful after dark, which makes Caffe Firenze a real find for Insiders. Owners Stelvio and Lisa Pacchini came to Tampa directly from Florence, Italy, and have created a lovely garden cafe near Tampa Theatre. There are more than a dozen pasta dishes on the menu, and the linguine con scampi and penne alla Siciliana are well-recommended choices. Lunch is always busy here on weekdays, but daytime hustle and bustle gives way to romantic leisure and tableside music for dinner, from 5 till 10 PM Monday through Thursday and till 11 PM on Friday and Saturday. Caffee Firenze is closed on Sundays.

Ciccio & Tony's Ristorante
$$$ • 1015 S. Howard Ave., Tampa
• (813) 251-8406

A bit of Miami's South Beach atmosphere is now part of Tampa's SoHo row, including a fountain sparkling up the patio dining area here. The menu sports 15 pasta dishes — a great time to try them out is Sunday, Monday or Tuesday evenings when the Pasta Festivali offers an all-you-can-eat sampling for $11.95. Be sure to save room for the Italian cheesecake that is rich with ricotta. Lunch is offered weekdays from 11:30 AM till 2:30 PM, and dinner begins at 5:30 PM. Dinner service continues until 9:30 PM Sunday through Tuesday, 10:30 PM Wednesday and Thurday and 11:30 PM Friday and Saturday.

Donatello
$$$$ • 232 N. Dale Mabry Hwy., Tampa
• (813) 875-6660

Tuxedoed waiters. A rose for the lady. China, crystal, silver and subdued lighting. And look — is that George Steinbrenner din-

Photo: Bradenton Herald

Treat yourself to gourmet dining in the Tampa Bay area.

ing with longtime friend and sports writer Tom McEwen? Truly a special evening, but don't overlook this place for romantic or power lunches. The Northern Italian cuisine is as elegantly prepared and presented as the atmosphere and service. Every one of the veal dishes is superb and so is the pasta. Plan for a pleasurably long and leisurely meal that's a true example of a rich dining experience. This is definitely not a place for the children, unless your youngster just won the Van Cliburn competition. Reservations are absolutely necessary for dinner. Weekday lunch service runs from 11:30 AM till 2:30 PM, and dinner is served every night from 6 till 11.

Lauro Ristorante

$$ • 3915 Henderson Blvd., Tampa
• (813) 281-2100

Chef/owner Lauro Medaglia proudly put his name on the sign when he opened his restaurant more than a decade ago, and it's a name that means outstanding Northern Italian cuisine to Tampa. Well-trained in Italy and Europe before coming here more than 20 years ago, Medaglia's specialties are delightful for weekday lunches or dinner any night. The capellini crab and the lobster linguine are two of the most popular choices. The agnolopti (fresh pasta with ricotta and portabella mushrooms) is another. And you'll find just the right wine from an extensive list to add that special touch to a special evening on the town. Closed Sundays, Lauro's serves weekday lunches from 11:30 AM until 2 PM. Dinner is served Monday through Saturday from 5 till 10 PM.

Malio's

$$ • 301 S. Dale Mabry Hwy., Tampa
• (813) 879-3233

Malio's south entrance, for private club members only, is where the Who's Who of Tampa wine, dine and deal. (The food's so good that Los Angeles' Tommy Lasorda doesn't even think about dieting when he comes to town.) Next door, through the north entrance, everyone's welcome at the casual Malio's Cafe. The atmosphere is cozy — dim lighting for a romantic date, but enough of a sports decor to make this a good place to

party after the game. Lunch and dinner run the gamut from sandwiches and fries to prime rib and lobster, with a hearty dollop of Italian specialties rounding out the fare. Monday through Friday, lunch is available from 11:30 AM till 2:30 PM, and dinner begins at 5 PM. It's served till 10:30 PM Monday through Thursday and till 11 PM Friday and Saturday. Malio's is closed Sundays.

Ristorante Francesco

$ • 1441 E. Fletcher Ave., Tampa
• (813) 971-3649

Whether you're looking for a noonday escape or an elegant evening, "Frankie's Place" should be at the top of your list. This intimate restaurant is stashed in a strip center along busy Fletcher Avenue and is distinguished by an unusual, white circular sign. Owner Francesco Marchesini will undoubtedly stop by your table to make sure you're happy, while chef Jay Lanier works his magic on such dishes as scaloppini Marsala, medaglioni di manzo or the star of the menu, Mamma Lucia's tris di pasta. A buon appetito experience, especially with musical accompaniment every evening. Sunday hours are 5 till 9:30 PM. Lunch is served weekdays from 11:30 AM till 2 PM, and dinner is served Monday through Saturday from 5:30 till 9 or 10 PM.

Tuscan Oven

$$ • 808 S. Howard Ave., Tampa
• (813) 251-0619

Red-sauce lovers will adore this warmly casual, farm-style restaurant with outside seating in Tampa's So Ho district. The menu ranges from hearty pizzas and pastas to delectable lamb shank and scallops Tuscany. A family place, kids are catered to here, and so are parent's budgets: the youngsters eat free on Sundays. A unique service provided by the Tuscan Oven is a shuttle for downtown Tampa diners who are on tight lunch schedules. Reservations aren't necessary unless there are six or more in your party. The restaurant is open every day and lunch is served from 11:30 am till closing. The dinner menu is offered from 4 PM Sunday through Saturday with the doors closing at midnight except on Friday and Saturday when they close at 1 AM.

Spaghetti Warehouse

$ • 1911 13th St., Ybor City
• (813) 248-1720

Twirl away in this popular, antique setting in one of the city's old cigar factories. That's twirl as in pasta on your fork. The platters come heaping, whether with spaghetti and gargantuan meatballs or a slab of 15-layer lasagna. You'll also find a variety of seafood entrees, such as seafood Alfredo with shrimp, scallops, whitefish and cheeses. Don't worry about all the sinful calories — after lunch or dinner, stroll them off with a walk through the adjacent shops at Ybor Square. Lunch is served from 11 AM till 3 PM, then dinner lasts till 10 PM every night except Friday and Saturday when it's served until 11 PM.

Pinellas County

Bella Roma

$ • 13980 W. Hillsborough, Oldsmar
• (813) 854-3888

Chef Nagy is known for the elegance of his tortellini Michelangelo and the earthiness of pasta e fagioli (best pronounced pasta fazool, so it rhymes with drool — taste it once and you'll know why). This is the sort of place to go when your body and soul want comfort food and a delicious wine or cool beer. The atmosphere is casual enough to embrace the whole family or nurture a budding romance. Lunch is served Tuesday through Friday from 11:30 AM until 2:30 PM. Dinner is offered from 5 till 10 PM Tuesday, Wednesday and Thursday, until 11 PM on Friday, from 4 to 10 PM on Saturday and from 4 to 9 PM on Sunday.

Bertoni

$$ • 16 Second St. N., St. Petersburg
• (727) 822-5503

Set in the old ballroom of the Detroit Hotel, St. Petersburg's oldest building, Bertoni dishes up delicious dishes such as Osso Buco DiVitello, slow-braised veal in sauce, or linguine in a rich, garlicky clam sauce. Bertoni's is designed for casual dining, but no tank tops or shorts are allowed in the evening. Beer and wine are offered with the weekday lunch and dinner menus. On Sunday, Bertoni's is closed. It's open from 11:30

AM until around 9 PM Monday through Friday, and only dinner is served on Saturday, from 5:30 to 10 PM. For your added dining pleasure, a guitar soloist performs Monday through Thursday from 6 to 9 PM. Plan on a wait, especially weekends, unless you call ahead for reservations.

Brunello Ristorante

$$$ • 3861 Gulf Blvd., St. Pete Beach
• (727) 367-1851

As expected from its name, the choice of wines is impressive at this gracious and casually elegant dinner restaurant. The seafood is impressive, too, prepared with a distinct flair that expands on traditional Italian. One of the best appetizers on the menu is crab cakes topped with roasted-pepper remoulade. Risotto lovers will especially appreciate the creamy rice dish here; a different one is featured daily. Our entree suggestions: pan sautéed tuna loin or Ossobuco. Don't feel you have to leave the kids out of this smartly casual dining experience — half-portions are just one of the reasons this place is "kid friendly." Open Tuesday through Sunday, dinner is served from 6 until 10 PM.

Campanella's

$$ • 7420 49th St. N., Pinellas Park
• (727) 544-7388

Fresh, homegrown herbs add just the right zest to lovingly prepared foods here, and more than 60 different wines are offered. Insiders know that owners Ralph and Rita Campanella can be persuaded to make special orders not listed on the menu. The veal velvet is as delightful as its name, and steaks and seafood also benefit from the kitchen's special touch. Tucked into the Park Plaza Shopping Center, the informal Roman atmosphere makes for relaxing, family dining for lunch or dinner. Service begins at 11 AM and runs till 11 PM Monday through Saturday.

Domenic's Capri

$$ • 4111 Mandalay Ave., Clearwater Beach • (727) 441-1111

Affordable, casual and delicious — what more can you want? Domenic's is known as the place with the wine-barrel entrance, and once you step inside, the only thing you'll want is a bigger tummy to match those big eyes when it comes to homemade pastas, breads and desserts. Nearly all the fresh seasonings are homegrown by the master himself, who insists that only vine-ripened tomatoes grace his dishes. Steak lovers will appreciate the grilled filet mignon, slathered with fresh mushrooms and wine sauce. For Italian gourmets, we suggest the veal pizzaiola in a tomato sauce seasoned with garlic, oregano and sherry. Beer and wine are also available. Dinner is served nightly from 5 to 10:30, but the restaurant is closed on Tuesdays.

El Gordo's

$$ • 7815 Blind Pass Rd., St. Pete Beach • (727) 360-5947

First known for a Mexican menu that included Drunken Chicken, El Gordo's now sports an Italian theme and offers thick, rich lasagna and succulent steaks that make your mouth water. Although the atmosphere is casual, the first floor Garden Room adds candlelight for a touch of romance. Upstairs, you'll find the piano bar and dance floor. Dinner is served daily from 5 PM till 2 AM. Wednesday through Saturday, classical sounds from the piano fill the air from 6 till 9 PM, when the joint starts jumpin'. Dying to see Elvis? This is where to do it, Thursday through Saturday nights.

Emm & Cee Pasta-Seafood Grill

$ • 4401 Gulf Blvd., St. Pete Beach • (727) 367-5656

What's not to like about a brightly decorated place that lets you scribble all over the paper tablecloth with crayons and then follows up with fresh, delicious fare? The choices are varied enough to make this a great place for a special evening out. The bread here is superb, or maybe it's the garlic, herbs and pepper in the dipping sauce that makes it so hard to resist. You don't have to worry about trying to figure out what's in a lot of fancy dishes, because this is the simple food that's made Italy famous — spaghetti and meatballs, rigatoni, tortellini. Or try the shrimp (a full dozen of them) over linguine, tossed with fresh tomatoes and spinach. Dinner is served daily, except Tuesday, from 5 PM, and reservations are accepted.

G. Bellini's Brick Oven & Rotisserie

$$ • 2544 McMullen Booth Rd., Clearwater • (727) 724-5716

You'll find Bellini's in the shopping center of Northwood Plaza, but step inside and the atmosphere transports you to Northern Italy. Here, the description "rustic" translates into oh-so-comfortable and gives a new meaning to the term comfort food. There is a variety of regional pastas to choose from, or try the salmon or roast duck. Or try the Tuscany pizza, very different from our Americanized version, and only one of the 10 specialty pizzas offered from the homey brick oven. Then indulge in a classic Italian dessert to sweeten your cup of espresso. Kids especially enjoy Italian sodas, and early bird specials from 4:30 to 6 PM make for excellent budgeting. Closed on Sundays, Bellini's serves lunch from 11:30 AM until 2 PM and dinner from 4:30 until 9:30 PM (10:30 on Friday and Saturday).

Italian Pavilion Cafe

$ • 11002 Fourth St. N., St. Petersburg • (727) 577-7738

For cozy dinners or lunch buffet feasts, the Italian Pavilion Cafe has been keeping locals happy for the past couple of decades. The atmosphere is comfy and casual, designed to let you concentrate on all the delicious menu selections instead of worrying about dipping cuff links in the sauce. Don't miss the grouper Monte Carlo, broiled in garlic lemon butter and served with jumbo prawns and pimento. Friday and Saturday nights, a small band livens up the atmosphere. Lunch is served weekdays from 11 AM until 2:30 PM. Dinner is served from 5 till 10 PM Monday through Thursday and till 10:30 PM Friday and Saturday.

Julio's

$$ • 6218 66th St. N., Pinellas Park • (727) 546-6287

Julio's started as a deli more than 20 years ago, but the cuisine became so popular that it grew into a revered, fine restaurant. The atmosphere's still casual, though, even if it is far more polished than any deli diner. Three years ago Julio Pereiro turned the kitchen over to his son, who added more creative American dishes to the Italian specialties developed by his mother, Joyce (who, by the way, whips up all the desserts with her professional baker daughter, Julianne). There's a mouth-watering linguine you should definitely try — chicken sauteed in olive oil and garlic with tomatoes, spinach, prosciutto and cannellini beans. But it's dessert that's to die for here. Joyce's tiramisu draws raves even from Italians visiting the area. And the chocolate torte! How good is it? Well, one regular brought John Travolta in expressly for it, and the late Sergio Franci insisted on having an entire cake whenever he dined here, and he never shared it with anyone! Still, Julio's remains a friendly family place that serves dinner every evening beginning at 4. The restaurant only closes on Sundays between June and October.

La Trattoria Restaurant da Gaetano
$$$ • 2152 Main St., Dunedin
• (727) 733-5664

Like a good family meal served at home by a happy uncle, owner Gaetano Pamieri decides what he feels like serving each day instead of offering a set cuisine. That means you can expect an adventure in dining as well as a pleased palate. Servers in this tiny establishment first present a tray of the day's featured appetizers for you to choose from. Next comes a bowl filled with salad to serve the table family-style, plus a loaf of crusty Italian bread fresh from the oven. Instead of a printed menu, waiters describe in detail the evening's entrees, such as Portobello mushrooms in wine sauce or penne pasta with sausage and roasted peppers. Plus, you have a good selection of wines and beers to choose from. On Sunday, dinner is served from 4 till 8 PM. On Monday through Thursday, it's served from 5 till 9 PM and on Friday and Saturday from 5 till 10 PM.

Nick's On The Water
$-$$$ • 800 Second Ave. N.E., St. Petersburg • (727) 898-5800

As abundant as water is in our area, it's not so easy to find restaurants — especially excellent ones — on the water. Set near The Pier, Nick's is one of those places with a great view, doubling the delight of seafood lovers. When the weather's balmy, choose an outdoor table. Selections run the gamut from casual meatball hoagies at noon to elegant Maine lobster at market price for dinner. Nick's opens for lunch seven days a week at 11:30 AM. Sunday through Thursday, dinner is served till 10 PM and on Friday and Saturday until 11 PM. This is an excellent spot to grab a bite before a Spring Training baseball game or nibble on tiramisu after a show at the Bayfront Center.

Mulberry Street Ristorante
$$ • 28530 U.S. Hwy. 19 N., Clearwater
• (727) 791-0881

Want to sample a variety of Italian wines at house wine prices? Then this "quainty" place is where to dine — often. The house wine changes several times each month. But even better, there are so many excellent menu items to choose from that you'll want to try them all. Don't worry if it takes a lot of time to make your choice — it just means you'll have more time to enjoy the strolling violinist and romantic, very casual atmosphere. Delicious pastas compete for your taste buds against fork-tender veal, stuffed crepes and succulent seafood. Whatever you decide, start off with the excellent Caesar salad, prepared right at your table. For dessert, you don't want to miss the tiramisu, cannoli and cheesecakes. Lunch is served from 11 AM till 2 PM Tuesday through Friday, and dinner is served nightly from 5 until 10. Reservations are suggested at this popular spot for Northern Italian cuisine.

Palm Court
$$ • 5500 Gulf Blvd., St. Pete Beach
• (727) 367-6461 Ext. 404

The Tradewinds Resort is one of those places Insiders choose when they want a close-to-home beach break. And it's Palm Court that gives us an excuse to take a dinner vacation as often as possible. The bistro atmosphere, where white linens grace the tables, is airy and delightful, and the beach location is perfect for shelling after lunch or strolling in the moonlight after dinner. Try the grilled salmon lasagna — it's different and really delicious. Or opt for shrimp, red peppers and pesto over angel hair pasta. Except for the brunch that is served from 10 AM until 2 PM, the Palm Court is closed on Sundays. All other days of the week, lunch is served from 11:30 AM till 2 PM and dinner from 5 till 10 PM.

Mexican

Hillsborough County

Cactus Club
$$ • 1601 Snow Ave., Tampa
• (813) 251-4089

Patio dining is hot here when the weather's warm, so arrive early or linger in the bar while awaiting an umbrella-covered table. People-watching is mucho popular, both indoors and out at lunch, dinner or after a movie. The atmosphere is casual, but in trendy Hyde Park that usually means that a Brooks Brothers blazer tops off a pair of walking shorts. While the decor is decidedly Southwestern, the menu is a wide-open range that even includes a touch of Szechwan and Caribbean. Veggie lovers will want to try the pesto veggie pizza topped with broccoli, mushrooms, red onion, jack cheese and herbs. And bring the kiddies — the children's menu is a bargain with all items priced at just $1.95. The Cactus Club is open every day from 11 AM till 11:30 PM.

Miguel's
$ • 3035 W. Kennedy Blvd., Tampa
• (813) 876-2587

Owner Miguel Rodriguez comes from a famous family of restaurateurs — his Aunt Consuelo owned the much-missed Tampa restaurant which bore her name; another aunt, Consuelo's sister, is famed throughout Texas for her chain, Ninfa's. Now, Miguel and his wife expand the family legacy with their personal spin on Mexican dishes, such as shrimp and sea scallops topped with jack cheese, and jalepeños stuffed with shrimp. The decor's as casual and vibrant as you'd expect — the passing traffic makes for a fun distraction as you sip beer or wine and linger over spicy nibbles and satisfying portions at lunch or dinner. There are three all-you-can-eat dinner specials after 5 PM. On Monday, it's bronzed lobster tails. Tuesday, the choice is fajitas and Wednesday it's Alaskan and snow crab. Weekdays, lunch is served from 11 AM until noon and on Saturday and Sunday, the hours are extended till 3 PM. Then the dinner menu kicks in and continues until 9:30 or 10:30 PM, depending on the crowds.

Tex Mex Cantina
$ • 6415 Courtney Campbell Cswy., Tampa • (813) 637-8880

Fun is definitely on the menu here and at no extra cost. This is a great, very casual spot for groups looking to imbibe in large portions of Mexican favorites, including South of the Border beers or Margaritas by the pitcher-full. The bar is one of the most popular around town for happy-hour gatherings. But couples, kids and extended families all fit right in and are drawn back for lunch or dinner by the zesty chili rellenos and mouth-watering enchiladas. Lunch starts every day at 11 AM, and dinner's served till 10:30 PM Sunday through Thursday and until 11:30 PM Friday and Saturday. The bar, however, is open much later.

Pinellas County

Caramba's Restaurante Mexicano
$$ • 1840 Drew St., Clearwater • (727) 446-7469

A serving of salsa deeper and darker than you've ever seen starts things off, letting you know right away that you're in for an unusually sumptuous experience. While salsas, sauces and moles are the staples of any good Mexican dinner, here you get a variety of selections most restaurants ignore. Generous portions get extra help from beans that are good enough to enjoy as a meal on their own. You'll also find a delicious choice of grouper entrees at this casual, "very Mexican" little restaurant with red, white and green awnings and bark paintings on the walls. Offering beer and wine, Caramba's serves lunch and dinner Monday through Saturday from 11:30 AM till 10 PM. Sunday, it's dinner only, from 4 until 10 PM.

Red Mesa
$$$ • 4912 Fourth St. N., St. Petersburg • (727) 527-8728

When you're looking for a good Mexican dinner for a special night out, here's a casual and upscale place to try. Diners are truly

Photo: St. Petersburg/Clearwater Area Convention & Visitors Bureau

Downtown Clearwater offers several restaurants,
art galleries and shopping opportunities.

guests — the first thing you're asked is where you'd like to sit; you're not just steered to the nearest open table. Selecting fare from this truly large menu is a harder choice than seat preference, though. That's OK, take your time. You'll not be hurried in Red Mesa's comfortable, subdued atmosphere. Southwestern standards such as chilaquiles, empanadas and pozole are offered, but so are more unusual entrees made with fish and beef. Beer and wine are on tap to accompany lunch and dinner. On weekdays, lunch is served from 11:30 AM till 2 PM. Dinner is served Sunday from 5 till 9 PM, Monday through Thursday from 5 till 10 PM and Friday and Saturday from 5 till 11 PM.

Aunt Chilada's Cantina
$ • 34718 U.S. Hwy. 19 N., Palm Harbor
• (727) 789-4979
   Just enough of the spice that makes Mexican food really fun in a brightly festive atmo-

sphere also turns your noon or evening into a party. Things are lively here on Tuesday nights, with strolling mariachi players sizzling along with the sounds of fajitas on hot iron. The chimichangas are well worth pretending you don't know a gram of fat from a frijole — besides, you won't care, since this place proclaims the best cheese sauce in town! Beer drinkers have nearly a dozen Mexican brews to sample, plus there are 21 different tequilas — just don't try them all the same evening! There's a band Saturday evening, and kids eat dinner free Monday through Thursday. Hours are noon to 9:30 PM on Sunday, 11:30 AM to 9:30 PM Monday through Thursday and 11:30 AM to 11 PM on Friday and Saturday.

Casa Tina Mexican Grill
$ • 369 Main St., Dunedin
• (727) 734-9226
   When on vacation, your choice in vegetables is too often restricted to french fries; not so at

this cozy, very casual and authentic Mexican cafe. There's wonderful vegetarian fare to accompany authentic and meaty delicacies, all prepared by Javier and Tina Avila, who learned their skills in native Guadalajara. Try the fish with Veracruz salsa for a unique seafood treatment, or go traditional with the delicious tomatillo enchiladas. This is a great place to get a zingy start on weekends, when traditional Mexican breakfasts are served (huevos con chorizos — yum!). Casa Tina serves lunch daily from 11 AM to 3 PM. Dinner is offered Friday and Saturday till 11 PM and Sunday till 10 PM.

Nouvelle American

Hillsborough County

Mise en Place
$$ • 442 W. Kennedy Blvd., Tampa • (813) 254-5373

Directly opposite the University of Tampa, this cutting-edge bistro is known for its innovative American cuisine that takes great advantage of the freshest local ingredients. Every day brings a new menu, but lamb, roast duck and seafood can usually be found among the daily offerings. When Mediterranean spiced, free-range chicken or South Carolina saltimbocca veal scallopine is offered, jump on it. For dessert, you must try the white chocolate rice pudding ... fantastic! Lunch is grand, too, with curried chicken and chutney, along with specialty omelets leading the favorite's list. Hours for lunch are Monday through Friday from 11 AM; dinner is served Monday through Saturday from 5:30 PM. If you enjoy your meal, don't neglect a trip to the Mise en Place Market, 2616 S. MacDill Avenue, Tampa,

(813) 839-3939. It's packed to the rafters with ready to heat-and-eat entrees, bakery goods, side dishes and wines in the delectable Mise en Place tradition of out-of-this-world gourmet.

Spoto's
$$ • 13079 Park Blvd., Seminole • (813) 545-9481

For almost a half-century, Spoto's Supper Club has been the magnet for food aficionados who adore being pampered with exceptional service. Scan the menu for duck Montmorency with black cherry sauce, a delicate ravioli Cardinale or linguini and salmon. If you must eat with your fingers, go straight to the baby back ribs, those hickory-smoked and barbecued morsels created from Spoto's original recipe. Open for dinner only Monday through Saturday from 5:30 PM, you'll want to dress your best to be seen at this elegant restaurant. It's closed on Sundays.

Pinellas County

Maritana Grille
$$$ • Don CeSar Hotel, 3400 Gulf Blvd., St. Pete Beach • (727) 360-1882

Why let only the Don's guests have all the pleasure? March right up and make yourself at home, surrounded by the 1,500-gallon tank of native Floridians with fins. Just don't look them in the eye as you order the grille's signature Dover Sole. Formerly the King Charles, Maritana has retained all its glamour and even added a full selection of healthful and vegetarian dishes to complement the resort's new spa (see our Accommodations chapter for all the details). Featuring Tampa Bay's only Chef's Table, Maritana Grille serves dinner every day beginning at 5 PM.

INSIDERS' TIP

Too tired to cook or even go out for dinner? Tampa residents have no need to just go hungry. Dine-One-One delivers restaurant meals from MacDill Air Force Base south to Tampa Palms north and all points in between. From a single dinner entree to lunch for 20 or more, it's on the way; you can even charge it. Quarterly catalogs listing all the participating restaurants are available at area eateries, or ask them to send you one. For emergencies of the palate, call (813) 870-FOOD.

Sea Porch Cafe

$$ • Don CeSar Resort, 3400 Gulf Blvd., St. Pete Beach • (727) 360-1884

Again, the nod goes to the Don for transforming the old (and somewhat dowdy) Zelda's into a trendy hot spot for fine cuisine. Leave it to Chef Eric to come up with entrees such as steamed tiger prawns with papaya mustard and stone pizza with sweet red peppers and ricotta. If you're a soup lover, order the roasted wild mushroom and garlic soup. Whether you come for lunch or dinner, we guarantee you'll rave about it for months. The cafe opens daily at 11 AM.

Seafood

Hillsborough County

Shells

$$ • 202 S. Dale Mabry Hwy., Tampa
• (813) 875-3467
14380 N. Dale Mabry Hwy., Tampa
• (813) 968-6686
11010 N. 30th St., Tampa
• (813) 977-8456

This is a local institution. No frills, no reservations, no big dinner tab. Nothing but peanut shells on the floor and sumptuous seafood on the tables. Founded in 1985, you can today find Shell's clones in 20 places across Florida and as far away as Atlanta and Nashville. Just yell over the laughter of happy campers and order Alaskan king crab legs, scallops, shrimp or grouper. Or go upscale and request shrimp Fra Diablo or seafood Newberg. And always pay attention to the nightly specials ... they can turn out to be the biggest taste splash of the menu. Shells is open for dinner nightly beginning at 4:30.

Crabby Tom's

$$ • 3120 W. Hillsborough Ave., Tampa
• (813) 870-1652
14404 N. Dale Mabry Hwy., Tampa
• (813) 961-3499
1414 W. Brandon Blvd., Brandon
• (813) 651-3499

When you talk seafood around these parts, the name "Crabby" comes up a lot. A cousin of Crabby Bill's in Pinellas County, Crabby Tom's offers the same, no-frills, picnic bench, wild and crazy atmosphere — the perfect background for slamming your fingers into a spicy bowl of steamed shrimp, ripping apart some snow crab legs or strapping on a bib for a lobster from the 140-gallon tank. This is really casual, this is really affordable, this is seafood at its most fun for lunch or dinner. Read the hand-scrawled posters on the walls — you'll see specials not normally listed on the paper placemat menus. Food service begins at 11 AM Monday through Saturday and at noon on Sunday.

Crab Shack

$$ • 11400 Gandy Blvd., Tampa
• (813) 576-7813

Built in 1946, the venerable old Crab Shack certainly looks like no one's changed a thing since it opened. But don't be put off by the restaurant's ramshackle appearance. Inside you'll find the best blue crabs anywhere in town. Also on the must-try list are the Snapper Corvina, based on an authentic Costa Rican recipe, and the signature, spicy Cajun Creole Soup. Pop by for lunch or dinner Monday through Saturday beginning at 11 AM and Sunday at 1 PM.

AJ Catfish

$$ • 8751 N. Himes Ave., Tampa
• (813) 932-3474

Umm, let's see if we can all guess the specialty at AJ Catfish! Yup, it's catfish. Grilled, blackened, cajun, fried — however you want it, you got it good and plentiful at this hopping, popular eatery nestled in the trees on N. Himes Avenue, just one block east of N. Dale Mabry Highway. Of course, there are all sorts of other grand seafood served here, along with pastas, beef and chicken. Not to miss are the jalapeno hush puppies, fresh-from-the-farm greens and delectable, homemade cole slaw. The atmosphere is lively here, too, and it's an Insider's favorite place that draws good friends and family together to celebrate a birthday or other special occasion. It's open for lunch and dinner Tuesday through Saturday at 11:30 AM. AJ's offers only dinner on Sundays and is closed on Mondays.

Rusty Pelican
$$ • 2425 Rocky Point Dr., Tampa
• (813) 281-1943

Just like neighbors Crawdaddy's and Whiskey Joe's, the Rusty Pelican is the place to be at sunset. Perched on Tampa Bay at the south end of Rocky Point Drive, you just can't let the view interfere with the marvelous shrimp Chardonnay, scallops with linguine or the ever-popular Florida mixed grill: shrimp, lobster and tuna over pasta. Non-seafood eaters vote for the chicken Jack Daniels and the charbroiled lamb chops. Either way, you'll love the ceiling-high potted trees, two huge stone fireplaces and fine crystal that makes this eatery so special. It opens for lunch and dinner at 11:30 AM Monday through Saturday. Sundays are reserved for a fabulous brunch.

Oystercatchers
$$$ • 6200 Courtney Campbell Cswy., Tampa • (813) 281-9116

In a Key West-style building connected by a 250-foot boardwalk to the Hyatt Regency Westshore complex, Oystercatchers is all pale blue and sea-foam green. White patio furniture can be angled to get a great view out of the wide windows overlooking Old Tampa Bay. At dinnertime, your best bet is usually the catch of the day. It's the absolute freshest served, and you can choose to have it mesquite-grilled, blackened, sauteed or poached. We always find it hard not to order the rock shrimp, maybe because it's served with snail butter. Those who say no to seafood will be more than satisfied with the rack of lamb, steak or duck. Oystercatchers is a sure bet for a delicious lunch or dinner — beginning at 11:30 AM Monday through Saturday — or for a divine Sunday brunch.

Crawdaddy's
$$ • 2500 Rocky Point Dr., Tampa
• (813) 281-0407

Named after Beauregard "Crawdaddy" Belvedere, a roaring '20s tycoon, Crawdaddy's is one of the three musketeers that cluster on Old Tampa Bay. (Rusty Pelican and Whiskey Joe's complete the trio.) It's three levels with seven dining rooms — all chockablock with Victorian furnishings, books, pictures and collectibles — and serves the most delectable beer-battered shrimp, fried grouper and the most unusual jalapeno hushpuppies. This is real down-home eatin', day or night, even if you decide on the jambalaya or one of the many stir-fry dishes. Service begins Monday through Saturday at 11:30 AM and on Sunday at noon.

Seabreeze
$ • 3409 22nd St., Tampa
• (813) 247-2103

For more than 66 years, the Seabreeze shrimp boats have been bringing in the catch that has made Seabreeze the place for seafood lovers. Whether you opt for dining inside or out on the broad deck in full view of a magnificent sunset over Tampa Bay, the menu presents you with the same challenge — which entree to choose. For a first visit, you must at least sample the world-famous deviled crabs. And if you think you'll have room, go for the Neptune Platter, piled high with succulent scallops, shrimp, fresh fish fillet and stuffed crab. Seabreeze serves lunch and dinner every day except Monday beginning at 11 AM.

Pinellas County

Johnny Leverock's Seafood House
$$ • 4801 37th St. S., St. Petersburg
• (727) 864-3883
7000 U.S. Hwy. 19 at Park Blvd., Pinellas Park • (727) 526-9188
10 Corey Ave., St. Pete Beach
• (727) 367-4588
565 150th St., Madeira Beach
• (727) 393-0459
551 Gulf Blvd., Clearwater Beach
• (727) 446-5884

Can you say fresh? Dating back to 1948, Leverocks has spread its fins throughout Pinellas County with the most divine seafood and down-home service, and the restaurants are currently undergoing a face-lift to the tune of about $300,000 a restaurant. Whether you come for a late lunch (that means Leverock's version of the traditional, club sandwich stuffed with Bay shrimp) or for supper (which to us translates to the Captain's Platter with its shrimp, scallops, fish, crab legs and petite lobster tails), you can probably expect a wait. Just get in line and chill out in the bar. It's the price you have to pay for these magnificently prepared delicacies from the sea. The doors to all the Leverocks open daily at 11 AM.

Hurricane Seafood Restaurant
$ • 807 Gulf Way, St. Pete Beach
• (727) 360-9558

Try to imagine serving more than 5,000 pounds of grouper in an average week. Grouper Parmesan, grouper Florentine, grouper Oscar, grouper au gratin. We assume you've gotten the hint that if you're a big fan of grouper, and especially if you've never tried it before, the Hurricane is the place to head every day of the week beginning at 11 AM. Overlooking Pass-A-Grille Beach, this informal three-story eatery is always packed for lunch and dinner, but the best time to be there is at sunset. This is what Florida's all about.

Crabby Bill's
$ • 5100 Gulf Blvd., St. Pete Beach
• (727) 360-8858
401 Gulf Blvd., Indian Rocks Beach
• (727) 595-4825

We are now talking a seafood restaurant with an attitude. Like, sure you're going to wait forever … what's your rush? Like, what's a tablecloth? … just slide your bottom on that picnic table bench. Like, you want it good, we got it the best, and you are going to want to eat until you're so stuffed you can't move. We'll just also mention that you can get about anything that formerly lived underwater here, from steamed blue crabs and garlic crabs to catfish and mahimahi, oysters, clams and mussels to shrimp, stone crab and crab cakes. Our bottom line definition of Crabby Bill's is this: If you want great food at a great price, this is the place to come for lunch or dinner Monday through Saturday starting at 11 AM and Sunday at noon. Just don't try to call it Happy Bill's. Just doesn't have the same ring to it. A note about the St. Pete Beach Crabby Bill's. It suffered a disastrous fire in the spring of 1998. Plans to reopen are sketchy as of this writing, but we've decided to leave in this location just in case of a miraculous and welcome rebirth!

Friendly Fisherman
$ • 565 150th St., Madeira Beach
• (727) 391-6025

It all started with a busy fishing business anchored at John's Pass Village. The natural evolution led to the Friendly Fisherman, named after Capt. Wilson Hubbard, whose good humor, fast smile and hearty laugh we lost in 1995. His tradition of hospitality continues here at the restaurant he loved, and the seafood is still brought in fresh daily by his fleet of boats that set sail every day in search of amberjack, stone crabs, shrimp, grouper, snapper and flounder. For lunch or dinner, you can eat inside or out on the deck; either way you'll have gorgeous views of the Gulf. Get ready to pig out Monday through Saturday at 11 AM and Sunday at noon.

Fourth St. Shrimp Store
$$ • 106 Fourth St., St. Petersburg
• (727) 822-0325

Any restaurant that is packed to the rafters every night of the week has got to be good. And Fourth St. is that. Everything is prepared fresh and fast — and at remarkably reasonable prices. The jumbo fried shrimp are legendary, and if you love clam chowder, you'll rave about it here. It's not real fancy, but it certainly is the place to see what the locals order when they're in the mood for seafood. It's open for lunch and dinner daily beginning at 11:30 AM.

Lobster Pot
$$$ • 17814 Gulf Blvd., Redington Shores • (727) 391-8592

From the outside you'd never know that just inside those rustic doors awaits a lobster lover's nirvana, topped off with fine linens, crystal and candlelight. Here you can order from 22 varieties of lobster dishes, all sold at market prices. Select tails or whole, as is or under sauce, from Denmark, Maine, Florida or South Africa. Other seafood dishes present much the same ordering dilemma. You'll choose from shrimp, scallops, grouper, swordfish and even Dover sole, all prepared to your pleasure. To take a break from the super-casual, eat-and-run beachy eateries, the Lobster Pot is a superb dinnertime alternative. It's wise to dress up a bit for your dining experience that begins Monday through Saturday at 4:30 PM and Sunday at 4 PM.

Guppy's on the Beach
**$ • 1701 Gulf Blvd., Indian Rocks Beach
• (727) 593-2032**

Eat inside if you must, but we always gravitate to the patio to sit under the pastel umbrellas. This is a happening place, a favorite local hangout, and the seafood is always excellent, no matter what you choose to order. For lunch or dinner, you can have your favorite fish or shellfish anyway you want, but we'd suggest you be more adventurous and try the Upper Potato Crust Salmon with a creamy leek and garlic sauce or the fried shrimp with pineapple jalapeno salsa. For starters, try their signature Santa Fe salad with corn, black beans, red peppers and zucchini. Yummy. The taste temptations begin every day of the week at 11:30 AM.

Seafood & Sunsets at Julie's
$ • 351 S. Gulfview Blvd., Clearwater Beach • (727) 441-2548

On the main drag across from Clearwater Beach is a charming beach house that posts the time of sunset on a blackboard every day just so you won't miss it. You can pack inside, or join us on the patio at the umbrella-shaded tables. (This is also an excellent spot for people-watching!) Julie Nichols is usually around, making certain that your order of stone crabs, conch, grouper and every other variety of fish is cooked to your satisfaction. We say just forget your manners and dig your hands in a big basket of peel-'em-yourself shrimp. We won't say a word as you drag them through that hot melted butter. The restaurant serves lunch and dinner daily beginning at 11:30 AM.

Frenchy's Rockaway Grill & Beach Club
$ • 7 Rockaway St., Clearwater Beach • (727) 446-4844

If you must have real, live local color, you must have Frenchy's. Spilling right out onto the beach, you can eat indoors where it's cool, or plant yourself for a feast out on the beachfront deck. Order anything you want; it's all great, especially the seafood, because Frenchy picks up the seafood in his own boats. The grouper sandwich is reputed to be the best on the beach. We prefer the stone crabs, especially when they're served up hot and steaming right at sunset. At lunchtime, the "crabby shrimp" sand-

wich is your only order. You'll find other Frenchy's along the beaches. The original Frenchy's Cafe is at 41 Baymont Street, (727) 446-3607; Frenchy's Saltwater Cafe is at 419 Poinsettia, (727) 461-6295; and the newest restaurant child is the Mandalay Seafood Company at 455 Mandalay Avenue in Clearwater Beach. All are open for lunch and dinner every day of the week beginning at 11:30 AM.

Jessie's Dockside
$$ • 345 Causeway Blvd., Dunedin • (727) 736-2611

Let's just see if we can tempt you. Baked mushrooms stuffed with crabmeat, lobster bisque or seafood gumbo. Can't you just smell it all steaming right in front of you? You should, along with all the locals who know that Jessie's is one fantastic place to go when you must have seafood and have it hot, fresh and now! Lucky for us, it's open for lunch and dinner Monday through Saturday beginning at 11:30 AM and Sunday at noon.

Sea Sea Riders
$$ • 221 Main St., Dunedin • (727) 734-1445

In a rustic, real 1920s old Florida Cracker-style home that sits right at the entrance to Dunedin's quaint downtown area, Sea Sea Riders is one of those places that just smells great as soon as you push through the front door. Family-owned and -operated, it also serves up the freshest catches of the day in the most marvelous and innovative homemade sauces, or plain, if you prefer. The Coco Cabana fried shrimp in coconut is one of our menu favorites, but the black bean chili comes in a very close second place. Sea Sea Riders serves both lunch and dinner beginning at 11:30 AM Monday through Saturday and at noon on Sunday.

Sea Grill
$$ • 3255 S.R. 584 (Tampa Rd.), Palm Harbor • (727) 787-6129

Seafood with a twist and a delicious one at that. To understand what we mean, how does Scallops Sebastian delicately flavored with raspberries sound to you? Or the grouper piccata or grouper courte boullion, poached in Creole sauce and laced with honey and orange? The Sea Grill is elegant and casual at the same

Photo: The Don CeSar Beach Resort & Spa

Tempt your tastebuds with a wonderful Gulf-side lunch in St. Pete Beach.

time, and those who just are not in the mood for seafood will thoroughly enjoy the Black Angus beef offerings. Caesar salad comes with all entrees, which will always win our hearts in the restaurant game. To fill that last little crevice in your tummy, order the peanut butter, chocolate chip truffle cake. You won't be disappointed when you choose the Sea Grill restaurant for dinner. Daily service begins at 5 PM.

Spanish and Cuban

Hillsborough County

Cafe Pepe
$$ • 2006 W. Kennedy Blvd., Tampa
• (813) 253-6501

A spacious, tiled lobby belies the cozy atmosphere found in the various small dining areas at Cafe Pepe. This is a popular gathering spot for business meals, roman-

tic dates and family gatherings. The Spanish Bean soup is wonderfully filling even as a meal, or try the stuffed shrimp a la Pepe or the filet Salteado for a unique taste of seafood and beef. Cafe Pepe is open weekdays for lunch and dinner from 11 AM till 10 PM, and on Saturday, dinner only is served from 5 until 10 PM. The restaurant is closed on Sundays.

Castillo's Cafe
$ • 1832 E. Seventh Ave., Tampa
• (813) 248-1306

A true, family-style Cuban restaurant, this is where to start your day with a hearty breakfast served daily from 7:30 till 10:30 AM. It's definitely the generous portions of tasty food and low prices that attracts Insiders to this cafeteria, which prides itself on not catering to a yuppie crowd. The pressed Cuban sandwiches are prepared the way they're meant to be, and the ropa vieja (shredded beef) is oh-so-tender. Daily lunch runs from 11 AM till 4

PM, and dinner continues well into the night — as late as 3 AM on Fridays and Saturdays. The cafe's closed on Sundays.

Carmine's Seventh Avenue
$, no credit cards • 1802 E. Seventh Ave., Ybor City • (813) 248-3834

During the day, Carmine's is popular with casual lunch crowds. At night, its bar and patio nightclub draw the eclectic party clientele. Try a deviled crab roll, Cuban sandwich or chicken and yellow rice and you'll be tasting history — this is the food that satisfied Ybor City cigar workers for decades. You'll love it, too. For more fun, enjoy weekend entertainment on the patio and in the nightclub upstairs. Carmine's opens daily at 11 AM. Dining service runs till 11 PM Monday through Thursday and till 3 AM on Friday and Saturday, but things close up early — at 6 PM — on Sunday.

Columbia Restaurant
$$ • 2117 E. Seventh Ave., Tampa
• (813) 248-4961
800 Second Ave. N.E., St. Petersburg
• (727) 822-8000
1241 Gulf Blvd., Clearwater
• (727) 596-8400

The top of the Spanish elegance spectrum, Columbia's flamenco dancers charm diners in this world-renowned and cigar-friendly establishment. Opened in 1905, the Ybor City location is the oldest restaurant in the entire state of Florida. And with 11 rooms to accommodate 1,660 diners, it's also the world's largest Spanish restaurant. With a copy of the Columbia Restaurant cookbook, you can try your hand at cooking such popular dinner items as paella a la Valenciana. We've even included the restaurant's recipe for black beans and rice as a Close-up in this chapter. The Columbia is open on Sunday from noon until 9 PM, Monday through Thursday from 11 AM till 10 PM and Friday and Saturday from 11 AM to 11 PM.

Ceviche
$$$ • 2109 Bayshore Blvd., Tampa
• (813) 250-0203

Start off with tapas and a pitcher of sangria. Relax in the cozy, candlelit atmosphere. And vegetarians? You won't want to miss this place at Bayshore Boulevard and Howard Avenue — Ceviche proves that more than meat makes for fine dining. Ceviche is actually a fresh fish or seafood marinated in spicy lime juice, and as this Insider will attest, is heavenly both on the tongue and between the teeth. Dinner is served from 5 PM till midnight Tuesday through Saturday, but the restaurant's bar stays open till 3 AM on Friday and Saturday. Wednesday and Thursday nights, the entertainment is electric violin. On Friday and Saturday, a guitar duo serenades the crowd with Spanish music.

La Teresita
$ • 3248 W. Columbus Dr., Tampa
• (813) 879-4909
8218 Hanley Rd., Tampa
• (813) 888-9017
902 E. Brandon Blvd., Brandon
• (813) 662-9333
7101 66th St., Pinellas Park
• (727) 546-5785

A very casual place, La Teresita serves breakfast, lunch and dinner in a friendly, family atmosphere. One of the hallmarks of Tampa's Spanish restaurants, La Teresita has expanded its affordably delicious meals around the Bay. You simply can't go wrong with yellow rice and chicken with fried plantains on the side. Or jump-start your day with a potent cup of cafe con leche and a delicious slab of Cuban toast with cheese. Cafeteria-style service starts at 8 AM and lasts till 10 PM, except on Friday and Saturday when it's 11 PM.

The Lincoln Spanish Restaurant
$ • 3247 W. Columbus Dr., Tampa
• (813) 354-8335

Now this is homey — simple, white tablecloths, paper placemats, baskets of warm Cuban bread and mounds and mounds of mouth-watering food on your plate. We've never met a bowl of Spanish bean soup we didn't like, but here you'll find one of the best. And the steak Salteado is so filling you'll definitely ask for a to-go box. Open Monday through Saturday from 9 AM to 9 PM, you really won't get breakfast if you stop by early … just coffee and that delicious bread.

Latam at The Centro
$-$$ • 1913 Nebraska Ave., Tampa
• (813) 223-7338

The 80-year-old building that houses Latam sports the world's largest onyx and marble bar. From the simple yet deliciously filling entrees to specials such as Key West lobster or Chateaubriand, everyone from kids to business associates will leave satisfied. Lunch is served Monday through Friday from 11 AM until 2 PM, and dinner is offered on Thursday from 5 until 10 PM and on Friday and Saturday from 5 till 11 PM. It's best to call ahead for reservations because the Latam does a lot of private parties, and on those nights the restaurant is closed to the public.

Valencia Garden
$$ • 811 W. Kennedy Blvd., Tampa
• (813) 253-3773

The Valencia holds several distinctions in Tampa. Since opening more than 70 years ago, it's remained under the operation of the original owner. This is definitely the place for business and government power brokers to dine. And never will you see a waiter write down your order — it's a mark of pride that Spanish waiters memorize which member of your party chooses paella, trout a la Russa, chicken and yellow rice, or any of the other delicious concoctions offered by the kitchen. The Valencia serves lunch Monday through Friday from 11 AM until 2:30 PM and dinner Monday through Saturday from 5 until 10 PM. It's closed on Sundays.

Cafe Don Jose
$$ • 11009 56th St., Temple Terrace
• (813) 985-2392

More than just Spanish, Cafe Don Jose serves an eclectic selection of Mediterranean, continental and Tampa-American cuisine in an atmosphere as comfortably elegant as its entrees. If you've been hearing about the flavor of heart-healthy ostrich meat (it's got 40 percent less fat than beef), here's a place where you can try it, served as medallions sauteed with olive oil, dry sherry, thyme and mushrooms. If you're more interested in fins than feathers, don't pass up the cazuela de Marisco — lobster, shrimp and grouper in sauce and served over yellow rice. The restaurant, which is closed on Sundays and Mondays, serves lunch Tuesday through Friday from 11:30 AM till 4:30 PM and dinner from 5 till 10 PM. Friday and Saturday evenings, the atmosphere takes on a romantic mood with music performed at the grand piano from 6 PM till closing.

Pinellas County

Chateau Madrid
$$$ • 19519 Gulf Blvd., Indian Shores
• (727) 596-9100

A little bit dressier than shorts and sandals, but not so fancy you've got to dress up, Chateau Madrid spans the spectrum of Spanish, Continental and American. Naturally, there's a wonderful selection of fresh seafood. But if you're not sure what you want to fill up on, order an appetizer and tell your tummy to pipe down so you can concentrate on the menu. It's three pages long and chock full of delectable descriptions for everything from paella to rack of lamb. Voted the best Spanish restaurant in the area by a local magazine, Chateau Madrid serves dinner only, from 4 till 10 PM Sunday through Thursday and till 11 PM Friday and Saturday.

Hilda La Tropicana
$ • 320 First Ave. N., St. Petersburg
• (727) 898-9810

Cuban-tropical is the setting here at one of the new restaurants attracted to the Tropicana Field neighborhood of St. Petersburg. When

---

INSIDERS' TIP

Got a hankering for a tube steak? Then hightail it to Mel's Hot Dogs at 4126 E. Busch Boulevard in Tampa, (813) 985-8000. This is the Insiders' favorite for all-beef, kosher franks from the Chicago Vienna Beef Company, bratwurst with sauerkraut or Polish sausage under grilled onions. The menu also offers chicken breast and Italian sausage sandwiches, plus a veggie burger.

Arroz con Frijoles Negros (Black Beans with Rice)

Once you've feasted on black beans and rice — which The Columbia Restaurant also calls "Moors & Christians" — you'll want to add them to your menu at home. Not only is this dish delicious, it's a wonderful meal to offer a crowd. And it's so easy to prepare! This recipe is reprinted from The Columbia Spanish Restaurant Cookbook, which is filled to the brim with other wonderful recipes and lots of the history that gives Ybor City its own special flavor.

1 qt. cooked black beans
2 bay leaves
2 c. long-grain white rice, uncooked
1 tsp. oregano
½ tsp. ground cumin
4 c. water
¼ c. extra-virgin olive oil
1 large onion, chopped
Salt and pepper to taste
1 large green pepper, cut in strips
1 tsp. hot sauce
1 T. vinegar
1 tsp. finely chopped garlic

In a large casserole, saute onion and green pepper in olive oil. When onions are transparent, add garlic, oregano, bay leaves, salt, pepper and cumin. Stir well. Add rice, water, black beans, hot sauce and vinegar. Stir. Bring to a boil. Lower heat, cover and cook for approximately 20 minutes. Test rice for doneness. Fluff rice with a large two-tined fork. Serves 6 to 8.

Photo: Paula Stahel

The Columbia Restaurant Spanish Cookbook dishes up Ybor City with delicious recipes and stories.

the breeze is cool, opt for a table on the patio for even more tropical flair as you sip your wine or beer. If you have a hard time deciding what to choose, go for the roast pork. Delicately seasoned, it flakes at the touch of your fork. On Friday and Saturday, music livens things up from 7 PM till closing. Open every day, lunch service begins at 11 AM. Dinner hours are until 9 PM Monday through Thursday and till 10 on weekend nights.

Pepe Restaurant & Tapas Bar
$$ • 3665 Ulmerton Rd., Clearwater
• (727) 573-3363

Tapas are delicious little appetizers and, as the name suggests, you can stop in for a selection with drinks or settle in for a sumptuous repast. Doesn't it just make your mouth water to think of mussels sauteed in wine, butter and garlic? Or how about duck, chicken livers and truffles in mousse? Those two delicacies are just two of the long list of tapas. When it comes to full entrees for dinner or lunch, among the most popular choices are grouper la Russa, paella Valenciana or a full-pound Maine lobster. This is a great place to introduce youngsters to Spanish cuisine; they eat for half-price. Downstairs the atmosphere is casual, while upstairs is more upscale. And the sculpture and paintings around you are as pleasing to the eye as the food is to the palate. Pepe is closed on Sundays. On Saturday, dinner is served from 5 till 11 PM, and other days of the week, from 11 AM until midnight.

Tio Pepe Restaurant
$$ • 2930 Gulf-to-Bay Blvd., Clearwater
• (727) 799-3082

The Golden Spoon Award is highly prized by Florida restaurants because it means the food is really, really good. And Tio Pepe is justifiably proud to have earned that award for several years in a row. But that doesn't mean this place is stuffy — the casual atmosphere, enhanced with lovely Spanish antiques, is especially popular with couples. Wine lovers will be particularly intrigued with the large wine room, and anyone who enjoys a good loaf of bread will be delighted by what comes out of the restaurant's own bakery ovens. Top choices here include paella, rack of lamb and shrimp a la Pepe. Lunch is served Tuesday through Friday from 11 AM until 2:30 PM. Dinner is served from 5 till 11 PM Tuesday through Saturday and from 4 till 10 PM Sunday. The restaurant is closed on Mondays.

Sports Bars and Pubs

Hillsborough

Goodfellas
$ • 4802 Gunn Hwy., Tampa
• (813) 969-0550
15363 Amberly Dr., Tampa Palms
• (813) 977-8543

Food, fun and sports combined for the triple play that led to two locations for this popular place for dinner. Both the atmosphere and the solid portions are designed for the macho with hearty interests and appetites. For example,

there's a burger called "Minnesota Fats" and then there's the "Bucs Deluxe Platter." You'll also find a lot to attract light eaters, such as shrimp pasta or the chunky Hawaiian chicken salad (at only 326 calories). There's live music on Fridays and Saturdays and karaoke on Thursdays. Good Fellas is open till 3 AM seven days a week and starts serving at noon on Sunday and at 11 AM all other days.

Proud Lion Pub
$ • 124 W. Fletcher Ave., Tampa
• (813) 915-1101

The Proud Lion is a popular on-the-way-home stop for folks who live in north Tampa. Although it's billed as a pub, this place is really a full-service restaurant with a very casual flair. More than a dozen appetizers are offered for those with the munchies. From there, the menu ranges from pasta, steak, ribs and burgers to gourmet sandwich platters and a lot of meal-sized salads. One nice choice offered as an alternative to french fries is the zesty Cajun dirty rice. Although there's no set kid's menu, there is a choice of inexpensive selections for the young set. Proud Lion serves lunch and dinner and opens every day at 11 AM. It closes Sunday at 11 PM, Monday through Thursday at midnight and Friday and Saturday at 1 AM.

Beef 'O' Brady's
$ • 210 S. Kings Ave., Brandon
• (813) 681-3428

Actually, there are a dozen Beef 'O' Brady's sports bars throughout Tampa, but the Brandon location is where it all started. No question beer and bouts go hand-in-hand here. But at each of the Bay area locations, the casual flavor's definitely designed to attract families as well as sports buddies. The children's menu offers standbys sure to please, and the selection of burgers and deli sandwiches is large enough to satisfy the heartiest appetite. This is the sort of place where you'll feel right at home wearing that team tank top and your biking shorts. It's open for lunch and dinner every day from 11 AM until 11 PM.

L.A. Sports Grill
$ • 18421 U.S. Hwy. 41 N., Lutz
• (813) 948-3686

We don't want to hear any complaints that

you can't see the TV. L.A. Sports Grill sports 15 of them, so the viewing is always easy. If you're not glued to the action on the set, let your mind wander through sports history brought back by more than 300 photos and pieces of paraphernalia. When you belly up to the solid mahogany bar, think of all the other sports addicts who've leaned against it since it was built in 1902. Games are broadcast on 15 TVs, but no games are played with the food here — just delicious straightforward fare such as burgers, ribs, chicken, chops and steaks. Tucked in a shopping plaza at Sunset and U.S. 41, L.A. Sports Grill serves lunch and dinner. Open at 11 AM every day, the menu continues till 10 PM Sunday through Thursday, and till 11 or later on Friday and Saturday.

Pinellas County

Babalu
$ • 9246 Fourth St. N., St. Petersburg
• (727) 576-7414

Fist-full portions for man-sized hunger, plus daily lunch and dinner specials make this place popular with Insider jocks. You've got more than two dozen burgers to choose from, but the grouper sandwich always draws raves. The casual eatery makes you feel like Mom's in the kitchen cooking up the meat loaf, chili and those savory slabs of ribs. Definitely a place to go when you're looking for a large night on a light pocketbook (it costs just a buck-fifty to feed the kiddies). Babalu is open Sunday from 1 till 9 PM. The rest of the week, it opens at 11 AM and closes at 10 PM, except Friday and Saturday when closing is at 11 PM.

Bleachers Sports Bar & Restaurant
$ • 10478 Roosevelt Blvd., St. Petersburg • (727) 576-2216

Readers of the *St. Petersburg Times* rate this as the top sports restaurant in town. One reason is that no matter where you sit, the view is great — not only because of the suspended monitors, but because every single booth has its own TV. Natch, the atmosphere's casual, but also a bit on the upscale side, so you won't be embarrassed taking either your buddies or your honey here. When the game gets intense, send the kiddies off to the game room so you

can concentrate. And don't forget to pay attention to the good food, from simple sandwiches to filet and stir-fry. Hungry? Go for the Bleacher Burger, all half-pound of it! Bleachers is open 11 AM until 2 AM six days a week and from noon till 9 PM on Sunday.

El Cap
$ • 3500 Fourth St. N., St. Petersburg
• (727) 521-1314

The granddaddy of all area sports bars, El Cap is to St. Pete what Sloppy Joe's is to Key West — a must stop; especially for the burger, which is big and beefy and flavorful. Daily specials accompany the regular menu at this casual, sports memorabilia-packed eatery. Within walking distance of the Devil Rays' "Fruit Dome," this is a great place to meet before a game or to gather afterward while the traffic clears. Open for more than 30 years and sporting 13 TVs, El Cap serves lunch and dinner from 11 AM till 11 PM seven days a week.

The Extra Inning Ballpark Cafe
$ • 1850 Central Ave., St. Petersburg
• (727) 896-9872

"Proper dress," as you'd expect, is casual at this sports bar near the Devil Rays' home. But there's more than just baseball showing here. With 20 TV's — seven of which are big screens — pool tables, darts and a video game room you won't get easily bored. While your staples of sandwiches and pizza are on the menu, it's likely you'll never run out of something new to try; there are 70 items to choose from, as well as six levels of seating! A cigar bar is open Friday through Monday after 5 PM. Lunch and dinner are served seven days a week from 11 AM till midnight. On Sunday, you can also fill up on a hearty breakfast before the game du jour gets started.

Flanagan's Hunt Irish Pub
$$ • 465 Main St., Dunedin
• (727) 736-4994

The Irish and the Scots should always merge so well as they do here in Dunedin. At Flanagan's, lunch and dinner fare are served up via Erin and the United States, with imported draft beers or wine to wash it all down. Live Scottish folk songs mix with the music of those wearin' the green on Wednesday through Sunday. And like any good pub, the regulars come from all generations and all walks of life, making for a comfortable mix of new friends. On Sunday, the pub serves dinner from 5 till 10 PM. Every other day, lunch service begins at 11 AM with the pub closing at midnight Monday through Thursday and at 1 AM on Friday and Saturday.

Steak Houses

Hillsborough County

Armani's
$$$$ • 6200 Courtney Campbell Cswy., Tampa • (813) 281-9166

Words like superb, impeccable, extravagant, elegant and very formal just naturally seem to attach themselves to Armani's. Set high atop the Hyatt Regency Westshore on the edge of Old Tampa Bay, the view is as spectacular as the food and service. The menu provides a well-balanced selection of pastas, seafood and poultry to accompany the beef, but the signature entree here is the veal Armani. This makes for a dining experience to be remembered long after the charge card is paid off. Get out that sharp suit, slip into that little black dress and go for dinner, but never without a reservation. Dining is 6 until 10 PM Monday through Thursday and 5:30 till 11 PM Friday and Saturday.

Bern's
$$$$ • 1208 S. Howard Ave., Tampa • (813) 251-2421

"Art in steaks" is host Bern Laxer's motto at the restaurant he made world-famous for succulent, aged steaks ordered by the inch. Al-

most as famous as the steak is the wine list. But don't let anything about your meal here intimidate you — the impeccably trained staff wants to ensure your pleasure, not scowl over your choice of forks. In fact, the Laxers are so concerned with quality they raise all their vegetables on a private farm. Reservations are a must for dinner, served every night except Christmas from 5 till 11 PM. After dinner, slip up the street to SideBern's, the restaurant's newest addition, for a sweet treat. Bern's upstairs dessert room at the restaurant became so popular that a two-hour wait wasn't unusual, so SideBern's was built to meet the demand and offer a selection of specialty wines for purchase. It's just down the block from Bern's, at 1002 S. Howard Avenue; phone (813) 258-2233 for reservations.

Iavarone's Steak House
$$ • 3617 W. Humphrey St., Tampa • (813) 932-5241

Tired of steak staked on a theme? Iavarone's serves it up straight, plain and proud. Generous, tender cuts come to your table on those simple metal-and-black platters that were found in any reputable restaurant kitchen from the '50s through the '70s. But this place isn't stuck on steak — also on the menu are a delicious angel hair pasta with crab, ribs, chicken and plenty of fresh seafood. Lighter portions might be just your style at lunch, served 11:30 AM till 4 PM weekdays. Dinner is then served till 10 PM Monday through Thursday and until 11 PM on Saturday.

Outback Steakhouse
$$ • 3403 Henderson Blvd., Tampa • (813) 875-4329

OK, we said we wouldn't include chains in this chapter. But this, we can't ignore. The

---

INSIDERS' TIP

Sooner or later your timetable, pocketbook or taste buds will demand a quick burger. Pass right on by the fast-food names you see back home and pull up for service at a Checkers Drive-In Restaurant. You don't have to travel far to find their distinctive red, white and black shiny-chrome buildings. Since opening, this fast-growing Clearwater-based chain has won "best burger" in every local contest. They're good, juicy, hot and cheap. But it's the uniquely seasoned fries that are truly addictive. It's strictly a get-and-go establishment, but a walk-up window and three or four patio tables are available if you want to dine outside your car.

Henderson Boulevard location is the daddy of all the Outbacks — the very first location in a chain that's gone virtually nationwide. It wasn't supposed to be that way. All the three owners wanted was a couple of places to keep them busy when they weren't playing golf. Instead, they created an Aussie phenomenon. The interior is woody and warm, which somehow makes it a perfect place to take the grandparents or a new date. The portions are so huge you don't need an appetizer, but it's hard to pass up the Bloomin' Onion (which other restaurants have tried to imitate). If there's a better house salad anywhere, we haven't tasted it yet. (We once spotted a diner pretending to lick out his bowl.) Steaks are wonderfully seasoned, and the fresh catch of the day is always choice. You can expect a wait at any of the popular chain's locations. But once you taste the food, you'll know it was worth it. All Outback locations serve dinner only, except for the one on Henderson Avenue, which still serves lunch on weekdays.

Shula's Steak House
$$$$ • 4860 W. Kennedy Blvd., Tampa • (813) 286-4366

Yes, it's that Don Shula whose name is on the door. And you can bet the legendary football coach delivers a winning experience when you're out to show off the best of everything, whether wooing a sweetheart over dinner or dealing business at lunch. Of course the menu is big on beef — take, if you can, the 48-ounce porterhouse! But seafood and chicken rack up kudos here, too. Meat, however, isn't all you pay for; absolutely everything, from salad to potatoes, vegetables and desserts, is priced separately. Still, with a phalanx of service staff constantly at attention, you and your palate are in for the kind of pampering star athletes are used to. Reservations are a good idea. Shula's serves lunch Monday through Friday from 11 AM to 2:30 PM. Dinner begins at 5:30 PM and ends at 10 PM Sunday through Thursday and 11 PM on Friday and Saturday.

Yellow Rose Steak House & Saloon
$$ • 5915 Memorial Hwy., Tampa • (813) 888-7673

Wild West heroes and heroines are honored here with their names on terrific steaks.

And Southwestern cuisine gets a tip of the 10-gallon hat with a choice of Tex-Mex appetizers to start things off. But don't feel you've got to be in jeans and boots to be comfortable. You'll see folks in everything from shorts to business suits. Kids, who'll enjoy the "Billy The Kid" 6-ounce sirloin, are welcome at this casual dinner restaurant. The bar is known as a great place for older "kids" to scout out new friends after work and on weekends. Lunch, served from 11:30 AM at the restaurant, is available all the time at the bar. Dinner is served from 5 till 10 PM Monday through Thursday, till 11 PM on Saturday and from 4 till 9 PM on Sunday.

Pinellas County

Keystone Club
$$ • 320 Fourth St. N., St. Petersburg • (727) 822-6600

This warm, "uptown" eatery bills itself as a New York-style chop house, a term we so rarely hear. What's even more rare is the quality of steak served at the Keystone Club. Though the claimed specialty is the prime Angus filet, it was the fork-tender New York strip that earned "Best Steak" honors from *Tampa Bay Magazine*. The atmosphere is classy, but the service and patrons anything but snobby, making you realize that quality is truly an attitude and not a price. The Keystone Club serves lunch on weekdays from 11 AM until 2:30 PM and dinner from 4:30 till 10 PM. On Saturday, dinner hours are 4 until 10 PM and on Sunday from 4 until 9 PM.

Jimmy Hall's Steak House & Cypress Lounge
$$, no credit cards • 515 Hendricks St., Clearwater • (727) 446-3151

Just minutes away from the beach, Jimmy Hall's bills itself as downtown Clearwater's oldest and finest steak house. The fact that it's been around since 1959 lets you know Insiders like it here. They know it's the place to go for inexpensive lunches, early-bird specials or tantalizing steak and seafood dinners. From the very first, the menu feature has been Jimmy Hall's original Wunderbar Steak, a 10-ounce center-cut rib steak. The atmosphere takes you back to the days of casual gentlemen's clubs, but don't feel you have to leave the kids behind. The kitchen offers youngster-pleasing choices from a grilled cheese sandwich to a 5-ounce portion of sirloin steak. The restaurant serves lunch from 11 AM till 3 PM Monday through Saturday and dinner from 3 till 9:30 PM, except Friday and Saturday when service continues till 10 PM.

E&E Stakeout Grill
$$ • Belleair Causeway at Indian Rocks Rd., Belleair Bluffs • (727) 585-6399

Southwestern fare is popular here in the Southeast and E&E proves why. The interior's casual decor gives a cool sense of the evening desert, setting a relaxing mood for lunch or dinner. Hearty eaters will particularly take to the 20-ounce porterhouse steak. But there are more unusual choices, too, such as rack of lamb, pastas and chargrilled chicken breast in green pear and apple chutney. Even the familiar entrees on the children's menu receive a special touch, such as the chicken tenders covered by a crunchy almond crust. Meals are served from 11 AM till 10 PM Monday through Thursday and till 10:30 PM on Friday. Saturday the restaurant is open from 4 till 10:30 PM and on Sunday, from 4 till 10 PM.

Sunday Brunch

Hillsborough County

CK's Revolving Restaurant
$$$ • Tampa International Airport, Tampa • (813) 879-5151

What better way to spend a lazy Sunday than taking in the whole Bay area without expending any of your own energy? Every hour, CK's completes one revolution, giving you an ever-changing view of the Tampa, St. Petersburg and Clearwater area. For a prix fixe of $19.95, you'll indulge in eggs Benedict, seafood, omelets to your order, a vast variety of fruits, hot entrees and sweets from 10:30 AM until 2:30 PM. Reservations are strongly recommended.

Oystercatchers
$$$ • Hyatt Regency Westshore, 6200 Courtney Campbell Cswy., Tampa • (813) 281-9116

A panoramic view of Old Tampa Bay and close-up glimpses of native birds give the upscale Oystercatchers its unique ambiance. The brunch selction, served from 10:30 AM until 2:45 PM, is extensive — from hot and cold entrees to pastas, pastries, seafood and desserts. Prix fixe is $26 for adults and $14 for children.

BuddyFreddy's
$ • 134 S. Gornto Lake Rd., Brandon • (813) 661-6005
1101 Goldfinch Dr., Plant City • (813) 754-5120

You say you've got a hankerin' for some real Southern cookin'? You say you're hongry? Well, here's where to head for heaps of good eatin'. BuddyFreddy's has been an extremely popular place in Plant City for years and years, and now that there's a location in Brandon, it's even easier to indulge in hearty, homestyle fare. Insiders know to wear elastic waistbands or a belt with an extra notch, because the buffet includes everything from eggs, grits and gravy to roast chicken, fish, ham and turkey with dressing. Brunch is set up for only one hour — 11 AM till noon.

Pinellas County

Apropos
$ • Bayshore Dr. at Second Ave. N.E., St. Petersburg • (727) 823-8934

This bistro and bar serves up true waterfront dining — just dock the boat and come on in. Eggs tenderloin and eggs Benedict are two of the favorites here, but oh those macadamia waffles are delish! Brunch is available from 8 AM until 2 PM, which delights early-risers and late-sleepers alike.

Maritana Grille
$$$ • 3400 Gulf Blvd., St. Pete Beach • (727) 360-1881

Dining is casual on Sundays at the Don CeSar Beach Resort Hotel, where this restaurant has been voted best brunch for the last couple of years. Why? Just one glance at the buffet will tell you — there are 150 different foods to choose from! The price is $26.95 a person and the brunch is served from 10:30 AM until 2:30 PM.

No matter what your entertainment taste — from boot scootin' boogie to the blues, from comedy to crooners — it's time to slip into a party mood.

Nightlife

You've spent the morning sunning on the beach, relaxing in the gentle offshore breeze. Then, after a delicious grouper sandwich for lunch (puh-leaze make it sans frommage — any respectable Insider knows that cheese does nothing to enhance perfection), it was off to the links, the tennis courts or shopping. You've already decided where to dine this evening. Is there anything you've forgotten?

Yes. Go back to your room, lie down and take a nap. Momma wanted you to do that when you were little so she could take a break. You'll want to do it for a very different reason — so you can stay up late and play!

And to party hearty, you won't have to stray far from your hotel room, no matter where you stay. The beaches are lined with places where the cool libations and the live music flow. But there's a lot more being offered around Tampa Bay than beach-bar-Jimmy Buffett and Melissa Etheridge-wannabees. Don't hesitate to explore them all, because they do provide a good time.

First, you need to know that the great nightlife spots tend to crop up in pockets around Tampa Bay, instead of being spread all over. Most of the places that attract the college crowd, for example, are out toward the University of South Florida. An incredible array of nightlife for all ages and tastes takes place in Ybor City — the Bay area's version of Bourbon Street, where cars are banned on weekend nights and the music explodes onto the sidewalk. Downtown St. Petersburg offers hot spots attracting sophisticated clientele. Clearwater tends to cater to the ca-sual crowd out for a very loose time. But the bottom line remains — a good time waits to be had by all!

So no matter what your entertainment taste — from boot scootin' boogie to the blues, from comedy to crooners — it's time to slip into a party mood. Let's rock out for a night on the towns!

Alternative

Hillsborough County

The Edge
1704 N. 17th Ave., Tampa
• (813) 242-0023

The phrase "belly up to the bar" takes on a whole new meaning here. At 120 feet, this bar has got to be Tampa's longest! And it gives you some idea of the size of this place, where the rooms are dark, the lights explosive and the dance music blares from hip hop to mega-mix. The DJs here have big followings, but occasional live acts such as Run DMC and Redman perform, and satellite sporting events are broadcast over three big-screen TVs. For a break from the dance floor, head up to the balcony or play some Foosball or pool. (One of the tables is black-light reactive; puts a whole new spin on the balls!) There's never a dress code at this 18-and-older club. Most of the time the cover charge is $5 if you're younger than 21 and $3 if you're older than 21. The Edge is closed Tuesdays. Otherwise, doors open at 9 PM and close at 3 AM.

INSIDERS' TIP

Sipped a little too much to be driving? Just call DDA, Designated Drivers of America, and one of their insured and licensed drivers will steer you home in the comfort of your own vehicle. Call (813) 360-0557 for rates and options.

The Masquerade
1902 E. Seventh Ave., Tampa
- **(813) 247-3319**

The old Ritz Theater got a new face and new life as part of the Atlanta chain, and now it's Tampa's top alternative bar. Music ranges from shock rock and hip hop to swing and big band, definitely an odd mix. But it works. This place stays packed from Wednesday through Sunday once the doors open at 10 PM. The cover charge at this 18-and-older spot ranges up to $10 or so, depending on whether the DJ's hot or the acts live.

See this and many other **Insiders' Guide®** destinations online — in their entirety.

The Rubb
1507 E. Seventh Ave., Tampa
- **(813) 247-6234**

From the bathtub full of iced longnecks to the amply stocked humidor, this 14,000-square-foot nightclub is conducive to lounging, drinking, dancing and conversing. Downstairs, the style is colorful murals and neo-industrial ducts. The dance floor is dark, which is perfect for the eclectic, funk and house sounds that permeate. Upstairs, the decor's more warehouse renaissance, with a bright, airy bar and cozy corner nooks. Wednesday through Saturday the doors are open from 10 PM until 3 AM. There's no cover till 11 PM on Wednesday; otherwise it's $3 for those 18 through 21 and $5 for those older than 21.

Pinellas County

Gasoline Alley Cafe
17928 U.S. Hwy. 19 N., Clearwater
- **(727) 532-0265**

While there's plenty of Top-40 rock dished up, Gasoline Alley's a great source for alter-native music in Pinellas County. As one might suspect from the name of this roaring place, all 6,000 feet of it is filled with rock 'n' roll and automotive memorabilia. Open seven days a week from 4 PM until 2 AM, there's live music every night starting at 10. On Mondays there's acoustic jam, and Thursday is swing night with cigar and martini specials. You'll enjoy a full bar plus full menu till 11 PM (midnight on Friday and Saturday) and munchies are served up till 1:30 AM. The game room never charges a cover, but the entertainment cost ranges from $3 to $7.

Blues

Hillsborough County

The Blues Ship Club & Cafe
1910 E. Seventh Ave., Tampa
- **(813) 248-6097**

Everybody's welcome on the Blues Ship … young, old, black, white, lovers of Delta, Chicago, NYC or rockin' blues. A lot of locals perform here — live music is nightly — but so do such national names as Clarence Collins, who blues Insiders know starred with the Imperials back when Frankie Lymon was known as "the boy wonder." While the music fills the hole in your soul, fill the hole in your tummy with mouth-watering, Southern-style food. On weekends, the cover if $3 if you're older than 21and $5 if you're younger. The Blues Ship & Cafe is open from 5 PM until 3 AM.

Skipper's Smokehouse & Oyster Bar
910 Skipper Rd., Tampa • (813) 971-0666

This open-air venue shocked Insiders a

INSIDERS' TIP

How good is the brew from Ybor City Brewing Company? Its signature Ybor Gold beer was honored with the silver medal in the Dortmunder/European-style export category at the 1997 Great American Beer Festival — the nation's largest and longest running beer festival.

couple years ago by putting down a small wooden dance floor. (Some people just have to be coddled!) Everyone knew that a quarter of the fun here was dancing in the sand (or the mud, depending on the season). The other three-quarters of the fun is the music: live local bands and some incredible national headliners, ranging from blues to rock to world beat and reggae. Anybody who's anybody seems to play here at least once. Several nights of the week feature specific styles, such as Thursday when the house band draws Deadheads. Give them a call to check the lineup. And plan on munching a gator-tail sandwich to sustain your energy. Closed Mondays, Skipper's is open 11 AM till 11 PM Tuesday through Saturday and noon until 10 PM on Sunday.

Pinellas County

Dave's Bar & Grille
10820 N. Gandy Blvd., St. Petersburg
• **(727) 576-1091**

This is a primo blues dive, where the bartender's wit only fuels the conversation around the bar. In other words, you ain't a stranger long! Sandwich-type fare is served nights, along with live music. Amateurs are encouraged to drop by for the blues jams on Wednesdays and Sundays. Dave's package store opens at 10 AM and the bar stays open till 2 AM. (Dave's has a special claim of fame among Pinellas residents: since it's just inside the Hillsborough County line, its package store opens an hour before Pinellas stores start selling on Sunday.) There's no cover and no American Express.

Ringside Cafe
2742 Fourth St. N., St. Petersburg
• **(727) 894-8465**

Maybe the Ringside's dedicated to the blues because long ago it was a boarding house and boxing ring, and all those thrown punches musta brought the losers down. Ah, but the best thing about the blues is it brings you up, 'cause you know you're not alone in the miseries of life. This is evidenced by the eclectic crowd that fills the parking lot with everything from pickups to Porsches for live music seven nights a week. Only the best of the local blues talent and occasional national acts make it to the stage here. The best-known blues venue in the Bay area, the Ringside is open 11 AM until 2 AM and serves its more-than-tasty full menu right up till closing.

Comedy Clubs

Hillsborough County

Side Splitters
12938 N. Dale Mabry Hwy., Tampa
• **(813) 960-1197**

This comedy club really features la créme de la créme of the national circuit. Just weeks after being named 1998 Comic of the Year, Mary Ellen Hooper was cutting 'em up here. Shows are held Tuesday, Wednesday, Thursday and Sunday at 8:30 PM; and Friday and Saturday at 8 and 10:30 PM. Prices vary according to night and performer, generally ranging around $10 plus a two-item minimum. Add another $2 for preferred seating in the first two rows. And yes, reservations are strongly recommended.

Pinellas County

Coconut's Comedy Club
6100 Gulf Blvd., St. Pete Beach
• **(727) 360-5653**
24095 U.S. Hwy. 19 N., Clearwater
• **(727) 797-5653**
430 S. Gulfview Blvd., Clearwater Beach
• **(727) 443-5714**

Did you know that little children laugh 400 times a day, but by the time we get to be "grownups" we only laugh 15 times a day? A mighty sad state of affairs for your funny bone! So give it a good workout at one or all of these three clubs. The comedy's first rate, ranging from homegrown national headliner G. David Howard to Tommy Blaze and Happy Cole to Dennis Regan and Dean Haglund. (Now, Scully would probably disavow it, but we think Fox Mulder's Lone Gun buddy Langly does stand-up as a ruse to keep track of the Cigarette Man.) Tickets cost $10 for weeknight shows and $12 on weekends, all with a two-drink minimum. Acts go on Wednesday through Sunday at 9:30 PM on St. Pete Beach, on Friday and Saturday at 8 PM on Clearwater Beach and 9:30 PM in Clearwater. Do call ahead for reservations.

Country-Western

Hillsborough County

The Dallas Bull 301
8222 U.S. Hwy. 301 N., Tampa
• (813) 985-6877

Absolutely the oldest Country-Western bar/ dance hall in the Bay area, the Dallas Bull caters to a sit-down, stand-up crowd. That's because one room has a mellow atmosphere for drinking and swapping tall tales. The other one's where foot-stompin' fools fill the dance floor. Stop on by for free line-dance lessons, and a great time is had by all! Closed Mondays and Tuesdays, the doors are open 4 PM until 3 AM Tuesdays through Saturdays.

Round Up Country & Western Club
13918 W. Hillsborough Ave., Tampa
• (813) 855-1464

Diamond Rio, Doug Supernaw and Rhettt Atkins are just a few of the Nashville names to have packed the 3,000-square-foot dance floor at the Round Up. But even when the music's recorded instead of live, this is a wild place to party. Take free boot scootin' lessons from 7 until 9 every night; beginners at line-dance will want to show up especially on Fridays. Wednesday nights offer mechanical bull riding contests with cash prizes; Thursdays the ladies go for title of sexiest belly in the Naval Battles; Saturdays feature tight jeans contests for the gals, and there are all sorts of drink and food specials all the time. The place starts rocking at 4 PM, and the heel-kicking doesn't end till 3 AM.

Spurs
1915 E. Seventh Ave., Tampa
• (813) 247-7787

Ybor's only honky-tonk, Spurs serves up good drinks, live Country and Western, pool and darts in Southwestern-style surroundings.

Doors open at 5 PM Thursdays though Saturdays, with happy hour running from 6 until 8 PM. If you miss happy hour on Thursday, get more booze for your buck from 9 PM till closing, when it's $5 for all you can drink. On Friday nights there are shot specials every half hour, and there's free line-dancing each night between 7 and 9 PM. There's no cover charge. Everyone 18 and older is welcome, and the doors don't shut till 3 AM.

Pinellas County

Bull Pen Cocktail Lounge
3510 34th St. N., St. Petersburg
• (727) 526-3366

Some '50s, some '60s, all country and a little Chinese! That's what you find at the Bull Pen. The music is live every night of the week ... which is where the '50s, '60s and country styles come from. The Chinese? That's delivered from the restaurant next door when you get a hankering for some finger foods to go with your drinks. This mellow, rustic place attracts everyone from grease monkeys to the wing-tip crowd, and Canadian snowbirds tend to flock back year after year bringing new friends. You've got to be at least 21 to enter, but there's never a cover. The pool games are free on Mondays and Thursdays, which is a good thing since it's so expensive to play other days — a whole 25¢ a game! The doors are open from 11 AM until 2 AM Monday through Saturday, and on Sunday service runs from 1 PM until 2 AM.

Joyland Country Music Night Club
11225 U.S. Hwy. 19 N., Clearwater
• (727) 573-1919

If you swear you've never been to Joyland before, but something about the place seems so familiar, it's not deja vu — probably you've just seen Crazy Heart's first video plenty of times. This is where it was taped, and 500 fans showed up to step in with their own two-steppin'. But there's a lot more than dancing that goes on here, everything from line to swing to country waltz. So whether you're 21 or 71, there's no excuse for not stopping by. The Joyland's restaurant serves up good family food from 5:30 PM Tuesday through Saturday. To enjoy the music that rollicks the Ballroom, there's a $3 cover charge and a one-drink minimum (but it doesn't have to be alcoholic.)

Dance Clubs

Hillsborough County

The Castle
16th St. and Palm Ave., Tampa
• (813) 247-7547

The black granite bar is a moat where water flows through crevices in its top. Adding to the medieval atmosphere are Gothic wall sconces and candle lighting. The Castle gets "best" ratings for two highly divergent reasons. The first is the best jukebox, with music ranging from Arabic to Nat "King" Cole. Second, this is where the Tampa Bay Martini Club meets. Open Wednesday through Saturday,

the cover charge is $4 for folks 18 through 21 and $3 for those 21 and older.

Club 1509
1509 E. Eighth Ave., Tampa
• (813) 247-6606

When Key West came to Tampa, it created Ybor City. When Club 1509 came to Ybor, it re-created South Beach — well, at least on the Patio Bar. Open Wednesday through Sunday from 9 PM until 3 AM, Club 1509 sports three large main rooms plus three VIP rooms, a great cigar selection and some fine martinis. But Thursday night, the big college draw is free beer and wine till midnight. Friday, the music is merengue and salsa. Saturday, it's dance music and chocolate martinis. In case your body's a bit run down from sucking up too much booze, slip in on Sunday night to Oxygen2, and suck up some pure O for a great reviving rush. (This may be the only oxygen bar east of California and south of NYC!) There's a cover charge, which is nominal and fluctuates depending on the night and the promotion.

Photo: Tampa/Hillsborough Convention and Visitors Association

Downtown Tampa's skyline is spectacular at night.

Empire

1902 E. Seventh Ave., Tampa
• **(813) 247-2582**

Claiming the best of all dance music and the biggest sound system in Florida, Empire's been voted "Best Dance Club" two years running by the *Weekly Planet*. Attracting thousands upon thousands nightly, when you're downstairs, you're in the party. When you slip up to the new mezzanine, you're surrounded by so much mahogany you can understand why this wood's scarce! Pool tables, Foosball and darts provide diversion upstairs, or hang out on the largest balcony in Ybor City to watch the masses parade by. Doors open at 10 PM, and the cover charge is $2 on Monday and $5 on Thursday with free well drinks and draft. Friday and Saturday nights the cover charge is $6 for partiers 18 through 21; $5 if you're older than 21. Other nights, which would be Sunday, Tuesday and Wednesday, the staff takes a well-deserved break.

Pleasure Dome

1430 E. Seventh Ave., Tampa
• **(813) 247-2711**

Filling an entire block between 15th and 17th avenues, this building first gained nightclub fame as El Goya, where the most gorgeous and outrageously witty female impersonators drew throngs to the showbar. A bit of that tradition survives, as a female impersonator revue still fills the El Goya Showroom on Tuesday and Saturday at midnight and on Friday at 11 PM and 1 AM. But no matter your age or taste or (ahem) intimate proclivity, you'll find a source of pleasure at the Dome. The dance floor is definitely high-energy house. In the Fluid Lounge, it's a lot more relaxed, with couches, tables, high-end liqueurs, martinis and jazz. Cafe Cohiba's Mediterranean ambiance lends itself to tasting the extensive selection of wines and cigars. If you eat at the Cafe, there's no cover charge to the Dome; otherwise it's $5 on Friday, $6 on Saturday, and on Tuesday's, $3 for those older than 21 and $5 for those 18 to 20. Dress code? Dressed to a T, or wearing T's ... just don't wear a cap. Doors open at 9 PM Tuesday, Thursday, Friday and Saturday, and don't lock up till 3 AM. Leave your plastic behind and pack cash.

Pinellas County

Club Chicago

40349 U.S. Hwy. 19 N., Tarpon Springs
• **(813) 942-1110**

On the truly upscale side of Pinellas nightclub life, this is the place for dining and dancing. After tripping the Electrifying Lights Show

Tampa Theatre

Walking past the mirrored wall on your way into the elaborate lobby, it seems you're being accompanied by ghosts. And maybe you are, because this stately theater has seen it all since opening in 1926 — silent movies, vaudeville acts, music, comedians, foreign films and public forums. In fact, a lot of people swear there's a real ghost: A projectionist who worked here for years and years is said to still stroll around in the night.

And what a beautiful night it always is inside Tampa Theatre. Designed by renowned theater architect John Eberson, this grande dame of nightlife is simply too ornate to fully describe. The Florida/Mediterranean courtyard design combines Italian Renaissance, Greek Revival and Spanish influences. High over the balconied statues float 99 twinkling stars above diaphanous clouds, perfect for staring into and letting yourself drift away at the start of an excursion into fantasy on screen or stage. And when the "Mighty Wurlitzer" white organ — with its 1,000 pipes — makes its occasional rise from the orchestra pit to send its music off to the stars, you're truly transported.

— continued on next page

Photo: George COH/Chroma Inc.

The stately Tampa Theatre, a restored 1926 atmospheric movie theater, features films, concerts, special events and tours.

Tampa Theatre, which was named to the National Register of Historic Places in 1978, has undergone a complete refurbishing during recent years. Seating just more than 1,400 people in orchestra, mezzanine and balcony areas, patrons love its intimacy and the eclectic selection of entertainment that is provided. Most regular are the foreign and classic films, but the acoustics are fantastic for live musicians as well. Nearly 600 different events are held here annually.

Even if you can't make it to the theater for a show, call and see when the next tour is scheduled; they're offered two or three times a month, last about 90 minutes and include a mini-concert on that magnificent "Mighty Wurlitzer." A $1 donation for the tour benefits continuing restoration and operations.

Tampa Theatre is at 711 N. Franklin Street Mall, Tampa, (813) 274-8286. For a schedule of events, call (813) 274-8981.

fantastic, romantic couples can slip away to an intimately elegant nook off the dance floor. Just from that mention you should know this isn't a shorts and T-shirt sort of place. As a manager notes, this is "98 percent upscale, and the other 2 percent usually don't get through the door." Open from 8 PM until 2 AM Wednesdays through Saturdays, a $3 cover is charged only on Fridays and Saturdays.

The Turtle Club
15481 49th St., Clearwater
• (727) 524-8777

What's the draw here? Well, check the calendar: What night of the week is it? Monday, The Turtle Club does Yucatan. Wednesday, it's Biker's Night on the patio and techno on the dance floor. Thursday, ladies, it's all yours for the Male Revue that starts at 9 PM (guys, you can get in after 11). Friday and Saturday, it's simply the huge dance floor that draws the crowd. The nightclub is open 9 PM until 2 AM; cover charges vary from $4 and up. The club's restaurant serves appetizers after 8 PM on Monday, lunch on Tuesday, lunch and dinner Wednesday through Friday, and dinner only on Saturday. But don't show up Sunday … it's all closed.

Eclectic

Hillsborough County

Frankie's Patio
1920 E. Seventh Ave., Tampa
• **(813) 248-3337**
   Three bars and no waiting makes this more upscale spot good for family and friends when you're in the mood for something modern but different. National acts in the past have included George Clinton, Marcia Ball and Leftover Salmon. Closed on Sundays, Frankie's opens at 11 AM weekdays and 5 PM on Saturdays and doesn't close till 3 AM.

The Rare Olive
1601 E. Seventh Ave., Tampa
• **(813) 248-2333**
   Plush carpet and upholstery, fine but not stuffy, The Rare Olive dishes up some of the best entertainment to come through Tampa; not to mention the smoked baby octopus that gets served up in the martinis — 18 from which you may choose, along with fine wines and spirits and premium cigars. Live music Tuesday through Saturday, generally starting at 9:30 PM, runs the gamut from swing to disco. Doors open at 7 on those nights and don't close till 3 AM. Friday, stop in for happy hour and complimentary sushi from 4 until 8 PM. Only on Friday and Saturday is there a cover charge — just $3 — and you must be 21 or older to get in.

Pinellas County

Club More
703 Franklin St., Clearwater
• **(727) 466-6673**
   From the top swing bands of the nation to jazz, acoustic folk, funk, alternative, rock, zydeco, salsa, merengue and rockabilly, this place offers more than you can imagine on the musical scene. You'll find top local entertainment and such national names as Bill Kirchen (yes, of Commander Cody fame), the Blazers — one of L.A.'s hottest groups — and emerging acts like Slobber Bone. The Gallery, which seats about 85 people, is more upscale than the Warehouse, with it's 100-foot deck "set in a lush tropical breezeway," says one of the owners with a touch of satiric ad-speak. Anybody who's ever stood behind a mike will be more than glad to hand over the cover charge, which ranges from $3 up to $10 or $12 for national acts. Why? Club More's the enterprise of a few musicians, and every cent of the cover goes to the bands — very nice. Wednesday through Friday, the place opens at 4:30 PM and on Saturday at 8 PM. The doors close at 2 AM. Sunday the place rocks from noon till midnight.

Jazz/Piano

Hillsborough County

Carmine's Seventh Avenue
1802 E. Seventh Ave., Tampa
• **(813) 248-3834**
   As a top daytime contender for best Cuban sandwich, this place serves up good

---

INSIDERS' TIP

While the Bay area attracts top national entertainment, it also provides some really big names to the nightlife scene. Here's just a partial list of folks you'll probably recognize: Angela Bassett, Ray Charles, Bertie Higgins, Hulk Hogan, Lauren Hutton, Gallagher, Tyrone "Tiny" Johnson, Stephen Stills, Pam Tillis and Lari White.

food, micro-brews and martinis. Carmine's is pretty much upscale, but there's no dress code out on the Polyester Patio, and dress-casual (like, guy's shorts should have cuffs) is OK upstairs at Luna or in the new venue, Zion. You know how beautiful a soft Southern night can be? Luna is the ideal place to experience it. The tin roof retracts over the handcrafted iron furniture wrought by local artists. It's the perfect place to woo love! The Polyester Patio, Luna and Zion are open from 9:30 PM until 3 AM on Fridays and Saturdays. The spin-and-mix DJs here attract a strong regular following for their acid jazz and house music. Carmine's restaurant serves lunch seven days a week and dinner Monday through Saturday nights. Bring cash … they take no plastic.

Club 442
442 W. Kennedy Blvd., Tampa
• **(813) 254-0442**

This is the place to see and be seen among the professional crowd. Martinis, cigars, jazz, and a gorgeous cherry wood bar set the tone, especially before or after a stupendous culinary foray into the highly regarded Mise en Place restaurant next door. And it's Mise en Place that provides the late-night appetizer menu for 442. Closed Sunday through Tuesday, 442 opens at 5 PM on Wednesday and Thursday and at 5:30 PM on Friday and Saturday. Entertainment is provided nightly.

Jazz Cellar
1916 Avenida Republica de Cuba, Tampa
• **(813) 248-1862**

Around the back corner from Ybor Square is where you'll find the intimate elegance of the Jazz Cellar. OK, there's no such thing as a cellar this close to sea level, but you do go down steps to enter. And once you do, you won't want to come back up from the fabulous sounds washing over you. Surrounded by a virtual jazz art museum, this couples-club with a 42-foot bar hosts a fantastic 11-piece house orchestra and draws top-notch national names like Maynard Ferguson, The Count Basie Orchestra and Richie Cole. The cover charge is $3 and the cellar door is open from 8 PM until 2 AM on Friday and Saturday. Special shows are sometimes booked

Another perfect ending to another perfect day.

Photo: St. Petersburg/Clearwater Area Convention & Visitors Bureau

on Thursdays, but even then the cover charge isn't more than $10.

Jellyrolls
1912 N. 17th Ave., Tampa
• **(813) 247-2447**

Not your daddy's piano bar, this place rocks with dueling pianos and crowd-rousing sing-alongs. And they ain't your daddy's crooning snoozers, neither. Who doesn't know the words to *Itsy Bitsy Spider*? For everyone, from those who remember Annette Funicello's first hit to the kiddos raised on Sesame Street songs, this place is tons-o-tune fun. The doors open at 8 PM on Fridays and Saturdays only, and there's a small cover charge.

Pinellas County

C Note Cafe and Night Club
526 Central Ave., St. Petersburg
• **(727) 892-2408**

Once home to a well-known local shoe store, the toes still tap at the C Note. The shoe store started in the "old days" of Florida, long before high-tech hit the scene, and the new decor reflects those more laid-back days:

hunter green colors, dark woods and old-fashioned lighting lend a cool background to the cool jazz that blows here. Almost as rare as jazz in downtown St. Pete is the fact that there's plenty of parking nearby! Lunch and dinner are served, but what this place is really known for is the music, which starts at 9 PM every Thursday through Saturday. There's a cover charge that changes, depending on who's performing.

Pubs

Hillsborough County

Four Green Fields
205 W. Platt St., Tampa • (813) 254-4444
Tucked between Old Hyde Park Village and the Platt Street Bridge, Four Green Fields is fairly upscale during the lunch hour. But nightly crowds are attracted to the warm Irish atmosphere, music, and best Guinness in Florida. Now, you say, Guinness is Guinness. Wrong, according to these folks in the know. There are 10 separate factors, including special handling, temperature and pouring method, that determine the taste — try it here and you'll know the way the gods of Guinness smile down from above upon the thatched roof. And it's an authentic one, too. When the little white building went up, laborers were brought over from the Old Country to work their unique skills. Open at 11 AM seven days a week, doors close at 2 AM, except on Friday and Saturday when they close at 3 AM. Live music runs Wednesday through Saturday nights and on Sunday afternoons.

Yeoman's Road Restaurant & English Pub
226 E. Davis Blvd., Tampa
• (813) 251-2748
For the best English ales and no electronic darts, pubbers truly appreciate the friendly atmosphere, good drinks and good chat here. Yeoman's opens daily (except Sunday) at 11 AM with lunch and serves up the Shepherd's Pie and fish 'n chips till well after midnight. Take the bridge across to Davis Islands, then

follow the main thoroughfare and watch for the old phone booth standing right outside. Sorry, they don't take American Express.

Pinellas County

The Harp & Thistle Pub
650 Corey Ave., St. Pete Beach
• (727) 360-4104
The first Irish pub along the beaches, this family-operated haven still lays claim to the best live Irish music in the Bay area. This isn't just typical Irish braggadocio — the group Seven Nations got its start right here, and now that they've graduated to the national recording scene, this is the only pub they still play. Surrounded by memorabilia from the British Isles, drinkers and diners are treated to continuos music and video scenery of the Old Sod in the afternoons. Along with authentic Irish food, you can chooose from beer, wine, imported drafts — even English hard ciders — and there's always the sound of hearty laughter in the background. Open from 10 AM until 2 AM Monday through Saturday and from 1 PM until 2 AM on Sunday, musicians take the stage at 9 PM Wednesday through Saturday and at 8 PM on Sunday.

Rock, Pop and Top 40

Hillsborough County

Green Iguana Bar & Grille
4029 S. West Shore Blvd., Tampa
• (813) 837-1234
1708 E. Seventh Ave., Tampa
• (813) 248-9555
In South Tampa, this is a tiny place that packs in big crowds looking for large rock sounds, great sandwiches and a gander at Samson, the live iguana who's made his home here for seven years. Although there's no live iguana at the Ybor City place, the 30-foot fake one atop the bar spews smoke out its nostrils, which definitely sparks some fun! The Iguana on West Shore attracts a pretty diverse bunch, while the larger place in Ybor tends to a more upscale crowd. There's no cover charge for the live music seven

nights a week at either place, but you've got to be 21 to get in. Hours are 11 AM until 3 AM daily, except Sunday at West Shore, when the door opens at 1 PM. Insiders know the Green Iguana for gargantuan grouper sandwiches, but their burgers are the greatest in the South, so says *Southern Living* magazine.

Pinellas County

ChaCha Coconuts
800 Second Ave. N.E., St. Petersburg
• (727) 822-6655

The top of The Pier is where ChaCha's tropical antique atmosphere attracts a bit of everybody. This touristy attraction is definitely beach casual, which means you've got to be wearing shoes and a shirt, but other than that, hey ... When it comes to munchies, the wings are the thing, although ChaCha's now also serves steaks, seafood and sautes. "Nine days a week" you find live entertainment: from 7 until 11 PM Monday through Thursday, from 8 PM till midnight on Friday and Saturday, during Friday evening happy hour, and Saturday and Sunday afternoons.

Hurricane Seafood Restaurant
807 Gulf Way, St. Pete Beach
• (727) 360-9558

When it comes to beach stops, the Hurricane is probably the most famous. This is a place to spend a whole evening. Start with some liquid refreshment up on the Hurricane Watch rooftop bar, with its 360-degree view of Pass-A-Grille and the stunning sunsets over the Gulf. Next, time for dinner, but where to dine? Well, walk down one flight to Stormy's for cool Caribbean dining indoors or on the two verandas, then follow it up with dancing under the light show that starts at 10 PM. Feeling even more mellow than that? Take the stairs down another flight, back to street level, to dive into the Key's Club, where tropical fish suspended from the ceiling create an underwater setting and the piano bar is the ideal place to sip a Hurricane from your souvenir glass. Lunch starts at 11 AM daily, and the doors don't close till way after midnight.

Albertsons®

FOOD & DRUG

- 2170 Gulf-To-Bay — Clearwater
- 3700 Fourth Street North — St. Petersburg
- 2770 West Bay Drive — Belleair Bluffs
- 3030 54th Avenue South — St. Petersburg
- 3900 66th Street North — St. Petersburg
- 7880 113th Street — Seminole
- 3825 East Bay Drive — Largo
- 26583 U.S. Hwy. 19 North — Clearwater
- 4701 Park Boulevard — Pinellas Park
- 13031 Walsingham Road — Largo
- 35439 U.S. Hwy. 19 North — Palm Harbor
- 1921 North Belcher Road — Clearwater
- 10500 Ulmerton Road E. #800 — Largo
- 12101 Little Road — Hudson
- 500 East Lake Road — Palm Harbor
- 1075 South Pasadena Avenue — South Pasadena
- 1295 South Missouri Avenue — Clearwater

- 8701 West Hillsborough Avenue — Tampa
- 8411 Dale Mabry Highway — Tampa
- 610 East Brandon Boulevard — Brandon
- 3838 Britton Plaza — Tampa
- 5371 Ehrlich Road — Tampa
- 3610 U.S. 27 North — Sebring
- 3313 Lithia-Pinecrest — Valrico
- 14939 North Florida Avenue — Tampa

Shopping

Hands up! You've been spotted with an AmEx card in your pocket with fingerprints that are more than a day old. Inexcusable. As in all unforgivable cases like this, we will show no leniency. You are sentenced to head for the nearest shopping center for a minimum of three hours of hard shopping. Pronto.

Now we both know that there's not much explanation necessary for a chapter about shopping. Every store gladly welcomes cash, and almost all honor major credit cards and traveler's checks. While operating hours may sometimes vary according to season, especially along the Gulf beaches, most retail shops are open Monday through Saturday from 9 or 10 AM until 5 or 6 PM and Sundays from noon until 5 or 6 PM. Most malls are open 10 AM until 9 PM from Monday through Saturday and noon until 6 PM on Sunday.

No Small Malls

Whatever your mall tastes — sprawling under a skylit roof, strip-type centers, upscale boutiques or factory outlets — you've arrived in shopping mecca. Indeed, as you travel down major highways such as Dale Mabry in Hillsborough County or U.S. 19 in Pinellas County, you shopping addicts may get whiplash from checking the spend-your-money options that serve as the landscape on both sides of the road. As we all know, however, the sign of a true, bona fide shopper is "focus," so here we'll give you the credit card-endorsed tour of our favorite places to snap up all those things we didn't even know we needed before we saw that 50 percent-off sign.

Hillsborough County

Brandon TownCenter
S.R. 60 just east of I-75, Brandon
• (813) 661-6255

They came. They saw. They shopped. But first they had to find a parking place. In the first hour on the first day in February 1995, more than 5,000 parking places were snapped up by frenzied mall-addicts who just couldn't wait one more shopping second to get inside this $200 million showplace. In fact, it only took until day 17 to count a million shoppers scattering through the 974,000 square feet of retail heaven. But, enough with statistics, let's get down to hard facts. Such as the largest Dillard's in all of Florida; a pink, coral and white Palm Beach Gardens-designed Burdine's; a huge Sears sporting a much more "feminine" look; and good old JCPenney with a spiffed-up face. Along with your mall favorites such as Ann Taylor, B. Dalton (look for the huge Barnes & Noble on the perimeter of the mall!), The Limited, Gap and Talbots, there are other stores making their inaugural appearance in the Bay area: The Warner Bros. store, complete with Tweety and Sylvester; Eddie Bauer; Abercrombie & Fitch; Liz Claiborne; The Finish Line; and Guess. If all this shopping makes

INSIDERS' TIP

If you're looking for a gift for that special someone, check out the gift shops in our local museums, where you'll most likely find the unique and unusual at very reasonable prices. Along with the shops at MOSI, Tampa Museum of Art, the USF Contemporary Art Museum and the H.B. Plant Museum, you'll find great gift shops at the Lowry Park Zoo, Florida Aquarium and at the CenterStore at the Tampa Bay Performing Arts Center.

you hungry, not to stomach-grumble. In addition to Mozzarella's and Ruby Tuesday, you can head for the circular food court that has a huge, animated pelican tower at its center and offers everything including pizza, pasta, Cajun and Japanese cuisine.

Brandon TownCenter, nearly a decade in development, is truly a magnificent place to spend an afternoon. Or a week. With courtyards, palms, fig trees and even bamboo, it's almost like the great outdoors, with natural light spilling from ceilings that peak, arch and open to glass domes. There are bubbling fountains, 14 to be exact, and a 1,400-pound bronze manatee. The almost half-mile length of the main corridor gently curves so that you can actually see what stores are ahead of you. And if you must take along a grumpy non-shopaholic, more than 500 seats are available for waiting out your attack. If you're in our area even for a few days, Brandon TownCenter is an architectural and retail marvel you really shouldn't miss.

Prime Outlet at Ellenton
5461 Factory Shops Blvd., Ellenton
• **(941) 723-1150**

If you're not spent physically or spent out financially from your swing through Brandon TownCenter, keep going south on I-75. At Exit 43, do a wheelie into the Prime Outlet at Ellenton and watch the steam start to rise from that MasterCard. Formerly called the Gulf Coast Factory Shops, this sprawling 340,000-square-foot bargain hunters paradise is actually in neighboring Manatee County, but so close to Tampa that we usually just claim it as our own. From Ellen Tracy to Baldwin Brass, JH Collectibles to Sony, these are deep-discount shops bringing you mostly first-quality, just-like-department-store goodies at unbelievable prices. The shops you'll discover here, such as Donna Karan, Carole Little and Adrianne Vittadini, you won't find anywhere else in the Bay area. One note of caution, however: before you buy, do check each individual store's return policy. Some have very liberal return policies, while others are strictly "final sale"; others are somewhere in-between. It will

be a good use of your time to try on anything you're not quite sure about.

Old Hyde Park Village
1509 Swann Ave., Tampa
• **(813) 251-3500**

Now here's a place you'll want to dress up for. It's perhaps the chicest shopping in the area, not only because it features a great Ralph Lauren Polo Shop, Laura Ashley, Ann Taylor, Brooks Brothers, Williams-Sonoma, Pottery Barn and Jacobsons, but darling restaurants (try the Cactus Club!) with outdoor, cafe settings where you can sit and people-watch while people watch you. Nestled in one of Tampa's oldest and most historic neighborhoods, Old Hyde Park Village is a charming enclave in which to spend a leisurely afternoon among the wanna-be rich and famous.

Tampa Bay Center
3302 W. Buffalo Ave., Tampa
• **(813) 870-0876**

Using Raymond James Stadium as your landmark, steer toward Tampa Bay Center, one of the area's biggest and most popular shopping experiences. Along with anchors Burdines (which sadly has announced they will be closing to relocate in the new Citrus Park Town Center in 1999), Sears and Montgomery Ward, you'll also find all your in-the-mall favorites such as The Limited, Lerner New York, Joseph A. Banks, Gap, Waldenbooks and more, totalling 160 check-it-out options. There's a great food court, too, to survey the damage in your shopping bags and to grab some nourishment to continue the hunt.

West Shore Plaza
253 Westshore Blvd., Tampa
• **(813) 286-0790**

It's the hottest mall talk — Saks is coming! As part of a $100 million renovation and expansion, West Shore Plaza has unfurled the red carpet to the ritzy retailer expected to open its 100,000-square-foot store by the 1998 Christmas shopping season. With other retailers in the Plaza committing to another $70

www.insiders.com

See this and many other **Insiders' Guide®** destinations online — in their entirety.

Visit us today!

Photo: St. Petersburg/Clearwater Convention & Visitors Bureau

Shopping for an unusual gift? You may just find it in
"America's Sponge Capital" — Tarpon Springs.

million in renovations and upgrades (including a massive landscaping plan, new four-level parking garage and 18-screen movie theater), West Shore Plaza may just earn a new distinction of being the most upscale of upscale places to shop in the entire Tampa Bay area.

One of the first large shopping centers on Florida's west coast, West Shore Plaza has already spent more than $9 million on a face-lift in the last few years, and being able to snag Saks is its reward. Until Saks opens, however, you can rush from Burdines to Dillard's to JCPenney, stopping in between to check out more than 95 other specialty stores and boutiques, including FAO Schwarz, Ann Taylor, Gap, Brookstone, Casual Corner, The Disney Store and The Bombay Company. Just off I-275 at the corner of Kennedy and Westshore boulevards, it's easy to get to and hard to leave, especially when you settle into the International Food Court for an afternoon treat. A traveler's tip: There's a self-service U.S. post office here, making it foolproof for sending off that postcard to the friends you left at home.

Ybor Square
1901 13th St., Ybor City • (813) 247-4497

Once the world's largest cigar factory, today Ybor Square is a kaleidoscope of more than three dozen specialty shops and boutiques where you'll discover unique and ex-

otic treasures you're not likely to find anyplace else in the area. This is especially true in the Nostalgia Market, where independent antique dealers will be pleased to part with quilts, jewelry, linens and furniture. If you plan to come here, we advise that you start by just strolling through Ybor City first, so you won't have to drag along those heavy bags of purchases.

University Mall
2200 E. Fowler Ave., Tampa
• (813) 971-3465

A quick hop from the University of South Florida campus, this is a lively place to tempt your resistance to great bargains. Anchored by Burdines, JCPenney, Montgomery Ward and Sears, U-Mall's enjoying a $35 million expansion that showcases a greatly enlarged, two-story Dillard's, a 16-screen movie theatre and a new food court. You'll still be able to stuff those shopping bags with goodies from more than 130 of your favorite mall-type stores such as Casual Corner, Victoria's Secret, Gap, J. Riggins, Spencer Gifts and Lerner New York.

Citrus Park Town Center
Sheldon Rd., Tampa

New mall alert! For those of you ever vigilant shoppers always on mall alert, we have good news to report. On the horizon is the much anticipated opening of the largest mall in Tampa Bay — Citrus Park Town Center — scheduled to swing wide its doors in mid-1999. On 140 acres off Sheldon Road just west of Gunn Highway in Hillsborough County, anchors will include Burdines (relocated from Tampa Bay Center), Dillard's, Sears and JC Penney. Also on tap: 120 other shops, a two-story, 20-screen theater (with attached three-story parking garage) and a food court with 10 restaurants.

Yet, even more interesting than the shopping possibilities of this 1.2 million-square-foot, glass-turreted mega-structure is the technology incorporated into the building. Every door will be hooked into a computer that will alert mall operators if any are opened after hours. Plus, the energy management system is so sophisticated, a computer will be able to pinpoint when a particular air conditioner needs a new filter. Not to mention the highly sensitive light meters that will read how much outside light is coming in and then adjust light levels accordingly. All to keep us shoppers happy and comfortable to ensure that we shop till we drop.

Pinellas County

Bay Area Outlet Mall
15579 U.S. Hwy. 19 N., Clearwater
• (727) 535-2337

Now we're smokin', Lucy! Ahead of us sits a humongous four-winged complex, packed with almost 100 outlet stores with the best bargains this side of the Gulf of Mexico. Actually, it's Pinellas County's only outlet mall, so be prepared to fight over that parking space. Inside, start at TJ Maxx, zip into Swim Mart, pop over to Ross Dress for Less, send the menfolk to Johnston and Murphy's and meet in front of our favorite Bookland Book Outlet. Also housed here are Bass, Leggs and so many more off-price merchants vying for your affections. If you love brand names at great, low prices, you'll love it here.

Countryside Mall
U.S. Hwy. 19 at Countryside Blvd.,
Clearwater • (727) 796-1079

Here's the anchor list: Burdines, Dillard's, JCPenney and Sears. Fill in between these mega-

stores with 160 more shops, and you've got Pinellas County's largest shopping center — and at 1,200,000 square feet, the largest mall in the whole Bay area. The highlight for kids sits first-floor center in the mall — Centre Ice, a fabulous ice-skating rink that's always packed with wanna-be Olympic stars and wobbly-ankled fun-seekers. If you can take a break from shopping, you can look down on the rink from the second-level railing and enjoy all the action from a safe and standing distance. There's also a great food court, plus, right across Countryside Boulevard you'll find another shopping complex starring what we consider to be one of the best TJ Maxx's in the area.

Clearwater Mall
U.S. Hwy. 19 and Gulf-to-Bay Blvd.,
Clearwater • (727) 796-2335

If you're traveling from Tampa to the beaches over the Courtney Campbell Causeway, you'll pass this terrific mall on your left. Burdines and Dillard's join Gayfers and Montgomery Ward to anchor this 120-store mall that's a local favorite. For the gals, choose from The Limited, Lerner New York and Victoria's Secret. For manly-types, you'll find Gap, J. Riggings and County Seat. AMC movies are here, too, plus a huge Michael's Arts and Crafts sits out in the perimeter parking lot.

Tyrone Square Mall
6901 22nd Ave. N., St. Petersburg
• (727) 345-0126

One of the granddaddies of local malls, Tyrone Square has just undergone a major facelift, adding more than 50,000 square feet. Situated just northwest of downtown St. Pete, it lures many a shopper to anchors Burdines, Dillard's, Sears and JCPenney. At 150-plus stores strong, you'll also find B. Dalton along with your other mall favorites such as The Limited and Limited Express, Casual Corner, JW, Wet Seal and Bentley's Luggage and Gifts. Be sure to check out the new Gap, Paul Harris and a beautifully remodeled Victoria's Secret, too. Movie buffs can take in the latest release at one of the six movie theaters. You can grab your carbs at the expanded food court, and there's even a tourist information desk. If you're craving some air-conditioned exercise, check into their popular Wellness Walker mall-walker

An extra suitcase might be a necessity after enjoying all the
shopping options in the St. Petersburg/Clearwater area.

Photo: St. Petersburg/Clearwater Area Convention & Visitors Bureau

program, a joint venture with St. Anthony's Hospital that currently has 2,500 registered walkers. Walkers are welcome Monday through Saturday from 9 until 10 AM and Sunday from 11 AM until noon.

The Pier
800 Second Ave. N.E., St. Petersburg
• **(727) 821-6164**

Well, it's not a mall exactly. Or a restaurant complex. Or an entertainment complex. It's, well, The Pier, and nothing in the area even comes close to the electric energy that flows here from early morning until way past when the stars come out. While this is not a place you'd head to for a day of serious shopping, there are almost 20 small specialty boutiques, each with its own unique collection of unusual finds. Test a chapeau at Just Hats, drool over the gems at Gray Jewelers, pick out the perfect gift at Applewood Cottage or snap up a souvenir at the Pier Aquarium shop. Or do as we do, just pack your bag heavy from Just Fudge 'N in the food court.

Pinellas Square Mall
7200 U.S. Hwy. 19 N., Pinellas Park
• **(727) 527-7241**

Yes, another mall! Another $18 million in renovations to get you to slide by and spend, spend, spend! The updated Pinellas Square has more than 90 shopping options, including anchors JCPenney, Dillard's and Montgomery Ward. You'll find a greatly expanded food court and new movie theaters right inside the mall, so you can come early and stay all day if that's your heart's desire. In an effort to see that your stay includes a little exercise, Pinellas Square owners have also installed a $1 million 120-foot oval-shaped ice-skating rink.

Shopping Pockets

We couldn't quite figure out what to call them. They're not malls or your regular flavor of strip center. They're just little pockets of shopping intrigue that include specialty boutiques and galleries that are singularly, tropical Tampa, each with a personality of its own; places you just happen to slide into and wind up spending money on that perfect little gimcrack or gewgaw. Here are just a few of our

favorites that we stumbled into by fortunate accident. All are found on the Gulf beaches.

The Boatyard Village
16100 Fairchild Dr., St. Petersburg
• **(727) 535-4678**

Resting on the shores of Tampa Bay, this Victorian-style shopping center is reminiscent of an old fishing village, but the wares are decidedly 20th century. As we told you in the Attractions chapter, the shops are constructed out of weathered wood and tin, and inside you'll find a marvelous collection of handmade crafts, shells and specialty merchandise. We always complain of shopping fatigue while here so we can be wined and dined at 94th Aero Squadron, one of our favorite restaurants in St. Pete.

Dolphin Village
4615 Gulf Blvd., St. Pete Beach
• **(727) 367-3138**

Smack in the middle of St. Pete Beach on Boca Ciega Bay, you can ride the glass elevator in this two-story art deco shopping pocket and fill your shopping bags with T-shirts, books, shells and a bikini or two. (If you're into windsurfing fashions, make a wake to Aguera Wind 'N Surf Shop.) You'll also find Publix Supermarket, Eckerd Drugs, a liquor store, casual restaurants and haircutting places for both men and ladies in this 35-shop complex. You'll come here, too, if you plan to hop aboard one of the many charter boats that will steer you out into the Gulf.

John's Pass Village and Boardwalk
12901 Gulf Blvd., Madeira Beach
• **(727) 391-7373**

More than 100 shops are squeezed into this converted fishermen's village at the southern tip of Madeira Beach. You'll discover one-of-a-kind crafts, antiques, beach and resort wear, glasswork, woodwork and jewelry. If you're an adoring fan of Red Skelton, head straight to the Bronze Lady — the largest single dealer of Red's artistic endeavors — where you'll discover collector plates, a limited-edition canvas-transfer collection, storybooks, drawings, pastels and paintings. You can even buy a radio cassette to take Red along on your drive home.

The Shoppes at Sand Key
1201 Gulf Blvd., Clearwater Beach
• **(727) 595-5998**

Right next to the Radisson Suite Resort is a strip of the charming, tropical-feeling shops at Sand Key. The deli is delish, but watch that girlish figure so you can zip up some of the most unique (though a trifle expensive) resort wear to be found along the beaches. Cruise the other shops that offer everything from shell and nautical crafts to jewelry and collectibles, then take a leisurely stroll along the harborside boardwalk and watch the boats passing along the Intracoastal Waterway.

Specialty Shops

In an area as large as ours, you can bet your checkbook there's a store filled to the rafters with just one category of goodies — a store known for extensive inventory of the unique and unusual, and staffed by personnel who not only know their stuff, but are anxious to help you locate exactly what you're looking for. Here's our list of the best of the best.

Roaming for Tomes

Bayboro Books
121 Seventh Ave. S., St. Petersburg
• **(727) 821-5477**

Remember that chummy college bookstore that just smelled like straight A's? Well, that's Bayboro and more. Sitting adjacent to the University of South Florida's Bayboro campus, this cozy shop takes the notion of an academic bookstore to a higher level. Its shelves are filled with textbooks, high-quality trade journals, biographies and of course, an overwhelming selection of the great classics of literature. For more than 13 years, students, faculty and the local community have picked Bayboro as the place to browse when the mind cries out for a stimulation hit.

Books and Bagels
119 108th Ave., Treasure Island
• **(727) 367-8029**

Did you say book bargain? Dave and Carolyn Moore heard you. They're the team behind this marvelous little jewel of a shop,

strategically located just behind McDonalds and across form City Hall. We're talking used books; paperbacks and hardbacks priced 50 percent and more off the original cover prices. They've got fiction, nonfiction and a tremendous collection of gently used children's books. Sure, you can pick up that newest bestseller, but we suggest you check out yesterday's thriller at half the price.

Now for the bagel part. The fabulous St. Pete Bagel Company delivers no less than 13 different flavors of its delicious bagels each morning, so you're welcome to slide into a comfy wicker chair with a hot cup of java and a bagel and relax in the shade of a good read.

Books to the Ceiling
15126 Municipal Dr., Madeira Beach
• **(727) 392-3070**

If something here eerily reminds you of Haslam's, you're right on the mark. Judy Fish, proud owner of Books to the Ceiling in the Winn Dixie Shopping Center, is a former Haslam's staffer who can boast of the generosity of the Haslam family. From the fixtures that graced the original store to Mrs. Haslam's hands-on support, this unique bookstore has well earned the title of "Haslam's on the Beach." Of course there are the typical new and used collections, but there's also a well-respected collection of scholarly and collectible books tenderly supervised by Harry Nash. In fact, if natural history is your thing, this is one place you'll find that special book you've been longing for. There's also a remarkable mystery section, and a huge stash of used magazines that are a real steal at two for $1.

Dolphin Book Nook
4667 Gulf Blvd., St. Pete Beach
• **(727) 360-0186**

It's too early for dinner and you've had enough of the surf and sun. This is what we call "Nook" time, the time to slide into this charming, eclectic shop nestled in the Dolphin Village Shopping Center. Jam-packed with books and treasures from all over the world, you can browse the shelves for a bestseller, a juicy paperback, foreign language books and even German and Canadian newspapers. Then, there are the marvelous trinkets, souvenirs and gifts with international flavor that owner Antoinette Parsons loves to stuff into any empty crevice. Do check the collection of Chokin (the high-gloss Japanese porcelain that is so delicately hand-engraved), cassettes and more. For more than 17 years, locals and visitors have discovered that a trip to the Nook is the perfect anecdote for the hot, flaming sun. We suggest you try it, too.

Haslam's
2025 Central Ave., St. Petersburg
• (727) 822-8616

We are not talking bookstore. We're talking BOOKSTORE. Boasting more than 300,000 tomes, new and used, hardcover and soft, Haslam's is a book-lover's pathway to heaven. You'll find Florida's largest book emporium between 20th and 21st streets N. Be prepared to linger. There are bargains to be scavenged on practically any subject in this renowned family-run "library" founded in 1933. It's open Monday through Thursday and Saturday from 9 AM until 5:30 PM and on Friday from 9 AM until 9 PM.

Inkwood Books
216 S. Armenia Ave., Tampa
• (813) 253-2638

While we're flipping pages, we'll also recommend a browse through Inkwood Books. Independently owned and operated, the shop is one of the few places where customer service is spelled with all capital letters. Housed in a charming 1920s Florida-style bungalow, Inkwood really knows the tastes of Tampa Bay readers, and you can often find a special book here that you wouldn't find in a megastore five times its size. It's great about special orders, providing books for business conferences and meetings, offering free delivery to local hospitals and hotels, even gift wrapping. Check them out Monday through Saturday from 10 AM until 6 PM and Sunday from 1 till 5 PM.

Palm Harbor Bookstore
33633 U.S. Hwy. 19 N., Palm Harbor
• (727) 787-0551

It's a well-known fact that owners Rita and Connie are cat nuts. Just ask Hemingway, the real live cat that shows up to work each morning as faithfully as the human proprietors. So,

needless to say, you can find an exceptional collection of books relating to our four-legged friends, along with a great selection of used children's books and both new and used hardcovers and paperbacks. And if you need a gift for a cat-loving friend, you've come to the right place. From kitty bookends to unique greeting cards, if it's cat-related, it's here at Palm Harbor Bookstore in the Steinmart Plaza at U.S. 19 and Nebraska Avenue.

Gifts

The Calico Cat
5101 Busch Blvd., Tampa
• (813) 988-0481
14388 N. Dale Mabry Hwy., Tampa
• (813) 962-3583
716 Lumsden Rd., Brandon
• (813) 684-2072

Anyone looking for that precisely perfect object for the home, whether a small lamp, print, accessory or tableware, must head directly to The Calico Cat. Just chock-a-block with marvelous goodies at quite reasonable prices, this is really the place to come during the holidays when the unique ornaments and so many other holiday exceptionals await your inspection. A crafters note: One whole room in both the Busch Boulevard and Brandon shops is dedicated to the needle arts, including the largest selection of books, fabrics and accessories for the avid cross-stitcher.

if and only if
4336 Fourth St. N., St. Petersburg
• (727) 528-9490

Feeling a little bit droopy? Need a little more spunk in your life? Well, get up, Louise, and steer right over to if and only if, a shop that houses more spirit-lifting, big-city gewgaws and gimcracks than you could ever imagine. How about a deluxe, recycled steel-covered day planner? Or a tiny, dancing, wooden Felix the Cat to perch on your desk? These, plus zillions of other opportunities, exist to bring that certain panache into everyday objects. It's a great place to browse for yourself or for that special gift you promised your wacky sister.

Tres Artsy

Pearl Artist and Craft Supply
3916 Hillsborough Ave., Tampa
• **(813) 354-8555**

No matter whether you're a serious water-colorist, rubber stamper or dollmaker, Pearl is your one-stop shopping center for supplies of every description. Crafty-type people can wander for hours through the narrow aisles that are spilling out with paper, pens, beads and books, plus way too many serious artist and craft necessities to mention. The new location on Hillsborough Avenue just west of Dale Mabry, is a must-visit for anyone into the world of arts and crafts.

Simply Beachy

Wings
6705 Gulf Blvd., St. Pete Beach
• **(727) 367-8876**

This should be a required stop for anyone on the way to the Gulf beaches. Anything and everything that has anything vaguely to do with sand and water — swimsuits, lotions, hats, beach chairs, towels and the obligatory T-shirt cover-up — is here. The shop in St. Pete Beach fills a whole block, and it swings open its doors at 9 AM and keeps them open until 10 PM. You can find other Wings locations at John's Pass Village in Madeira Beach, (727) 392-9211; and in Clearwater Beach at 400 Poinsettia Avenue, (727) 449-2710, and 646 S. Gulfview Boulevard, (727) 441-1042.

Mulligan Madness

One Up
211 N. Dale Mabry Hwy., Tampa
• **(813) 877-7272**

Love the links? We can guarantee you'll be blown away by a visit to these phenomenal golf shops. If you can play through the Burner Bubble-Shafts, you'll go ga-ga over the golf attire — the most complete collections of logos under the flag, all displayed as if in the finest of department stores. We're partial to Ralph, Bobby Jones and Ashworth, but whatever suits your fancy, literally from head to toe, if you can't find it here, you can't find it. Plus, the staff is as welcoming as the atmosphere, a truly nice touch in the mainly impersonal retail world. The Tampa store even comes complete with an elevated putting green. In Clearwater, you'll find its other store on Gulf-to-Bay Boulevard, just an iron-shot away from the end of the Courtney Campbell Causeway.

T&D Golf
4205 W. Waters Ave., Tampa
• **(813) 888-5433**
725 Lumsden Rd. W., Brandon
• **(813) 684-0300**

If you've got to have a dozen Balatas, but cringe at the thought of dropping $30 at the pro shop, just take a swing at T&D. Here you can snap up all the best brand-name golf balls, (reclaimed from your last shot into the woods) cleverly packaged in egg cartons starting at just $7.99. Staff members are also experts at regripping and reshafting, plus they can boast the largest selection of used clubs in the area, not to mention a full collection of new clubs, clothes, shoes and accessories. T&D Golf is open Tuesday through Saturday from 9 AM until 6 PM.

Paper Chase

The Pen Store
2404 Zack St., Tampa • (813) 223-3865

Even if you use a computer eight hours a day, nothing comes closer to the real thing than the mark of a fine pen on paper. If you feel the same, it'll be worth your while to detour to downtown Tampa between the Franklin Street Mall and Florida Avenue to peruse this shop that specializes in the finest pens in the world. It's here, too, that you can find special inks in a zillion colors, and if you have a cherished pen that needs repair, this is one of the few places in the Southeast that can have you writing again. It's open Monday through Friday from 9 AM until 5 PM and Saturday from 10 AM until noon.

Stationary Square
1601 Snow Cir., Tampa • (813) 251-1601

Paper, paper everywhere! Handsome stationary, lavish note cards, albums, sealing wax and so much more. Nestled in Old Hyde Park Village, you can slowly negotiate the narrow aisles that spill over with fine papers, exceptional gifts and the most unusual greeting cards. This is also the place to come to special order that wedding invitation, new-home announcement or calling card for your little prince.

World of Maps
6820 N. Florida Ave., Tampa
• **(813) 237-1711**

Let's say you've got a pen pal halfway around the world. How would you like a map to pinpoint the exact location, even if it's a place you can't get to from here. Well, just call Gil D'Amore at World of Maps and rest assured that he'll be able to find that impossible-to-locate map you've been looking for. With his Rand McNally training, Gil knows his maps. In fact, he imports and exports more maps than anyone could even fathom, from gorgeous wall-size charts perfect for conference-room framing, to handy guides to the backroads of Tahiti. Named Florida's Entrepreneurial Success for 1998 by the U.S. Small Business Administration, World of Maps well earns its distinctive nickname "the Outback Steakhouse of the Map Trade."

¿Qué Pasa?

La Loma
3224 N. Armenia Ave., Tampa
• **(813) 877-1855**

Searching for something with a Hispanic flair? Head straight to La Loma, a center for Hispanic goods for more than 30 years. In addition to meats, veggies, fruits and candies from Latin American countries and Spain (yucca, plantains, black beans, mangoes and the like), here's where you'll find Hispanic magazines

and paperbacks, CDs and tapes by your favorite Hispanic artists, small toys and general merchandise from countries in the Caribbean, Spain, Central America and South America. It's sort of like the old-fashioned general store, with everything packed into this convenient, store-sized market. If you've missed that family-style, friendly, customer service that's all but disappeared today, head on over for a real treat. And do try out a Yerba Mate, a very interesting soft drink direct from Argentina.

Fashion Education

When it's time for Bay area residents to dress up to the nines, they head to designer "fashion alley," also known as the strip of S. Dale Mabry Highway between Plant High School and Henderson Boulevard. Look right! Look left! One phenomenal boutique after another awaits turning your credit card into couture. Be aware that these shops are not for you discount hounds. They are only for those discriminating fashion plates who long for exquisite European and American designer labels with the sort of pampered service that is reserved for those who put style way before the price tag. Not-to-miss shops, all found on S. Dale Mabry Highway, include Deborah Kent's, A'propos, M, Sarah & Grete Clothes Friends, Boulevard Designer Clothing and Seval's European Fashions.

Syms
3251 Hillsborough Ave., Tampa
• **(813) 876-6655**

You know the thrill you get when you discover a classy designer name among the racks at your favorite discount store. Well, at Syms you'll have that thrill at every hanger and display shelf. This is truly a fashion discount shop for the snobbish — we're talking Ralph Lauren, Anne Klein, Bobby Jones, Adrianne Vittadini

---

INSIDERS' TIP

If whodunits are your favorite type of reading, spy on Snoop Sisters, a two-room bookshop that sells only books that have a singular story line: murder. From detective novels to crime mysteries, if it's a bloodcurdling mystery tale, you'll find it here. Snoop Sisters Mystery Book Shoppe & Boutique is at the very end of Antique Alley, just off Indian Rocks Road in Belleair Bluffs.

Photo: St. Petersburg/Clearwater Area Convention & Visitors Bureau

Outdoor art shows are popular shopping stops throughout the year.

and all the others. The stores cater to men, ladies and their pampered kids. The large store on Hillsborough (next to Office Depot) is immaculate, with every garment tenderly placed on evenly spaced hangers. There are no salespeople here, just "educators" who know the merchandise and are obliging to a fault to help you find just what you're looking for. Whether it's that special Gottex bathing suit, exceptional cocktail dress, beautifully tailored suit or casual weekend wear, Syms is definitely a shopping experience in a league of its own.

Tasty Temptations

Orange Blossom Groves
5800 Seminole Blvd., Seminole
• (727) 392-1277, (800) 237-9860
16200 U.S. Hwy. 19 N., Clearwater
• (727) 536-3588, (800) 237-9870
Packed to the rafters with the sweet-smelling elixir of fresh citrus and homegrown veggies, Orange Blossom Groves is a great place to stop for Mother Nature's bounty. Since 1948, this family-owned and -operated market is a combo of growing, packing and shipping the freshest pick of citrus and farm-fresh vegetables. Browse the open-air produce market, slip into the gift shop for some homemade ice cream and even get a complimentary taste of some freshly squeezed orange juice. We know you won't want to go home empty handed, so just snag a beautifully arranged citrus gift, or request shipping. Richard Miller and his crew will be more than happy to oblige. It's open Monday through Saturday from 8 AM until 5:30 PM and on Sunday from 10 AM until 5 PM.

Coarsey Groves
6703 N. Armenia Ave., Tampa
• (813) 933-1709
When Mary Baker's grandfather started tending his orange grove in the early 1920s, he had no idea what a popular spot he was creating from the rich soil. Today, the Gift Shop

at Coarsey Groves welcomes visitors from all over the world. Here you can snap up the tastiest of a variety of oranges, tangerines, grapes and other tart and tangy citrus fruits. Pack your bag heavy with the homemade marmalades and candies, too — they're delish! For those who want to create their own fruit masterpieces, Coarsey Groves is also the perfect place to find that indispensable grapefruit or orange spoon and many other gourmet tools no proud kitchen should be without. And since you can't forget those friends in far-away places, Mary will be delighted to ship your gift selection to the destination of your choice. While it's only open during the season, from November through April, you can get a fully illustrated brochure of all the Coarsey Grove offerings by dialing the off-season answering machine/fax number, (813) 933-4478.

Il Fornaio Italian Gourmet
483 Mandalay Ave., Clearwater
• **(727) 442-7721**

From the moment you get within a few feet of Il Fornaio, your mouth will start watering, your nostrils will come to attention and you'll be overcome with an overwhelming hunger. It's here that you'll pack your basket with everything authentically Italian: homemade brick-oven breads and pastries, imported salamis and hams, freshly made mozzarella and pastas and daily offerings of specialty dinners-to-go such as sausage, peppers and cheese and eggplant or chicken Parmigiana.

There's also a full line of imported, packaged goods such as must-have flavored oils and vinegars, and we dare you to actually give away the divine chocolates as a gift. If you can't decide where to begin, just settle into an outdoor table and sip a frothing cup of cappuccino from the complete espresso bar. And make sure you select a warm-from-the-oven biscotti to complement it. Housed in Pelican Walk Plaza, Il Fornaio will entertain your gourmet pleasures from 9 AM until 7 PM Monday through Saturday and from 9 AM until 4 PM Sunday.

Antiquing We Will Go

Now, maybe you can't get that antique treasure in your suitcase, but we guarantee that you'll discover something you'll have to ship home. We're talking antiques in the Tampa Bay area. From the tip of one county to the next, there are marvelous little pockets of antique heaven, with independent dealers who scrounge the world for furniture, china and decorative items displaying Old World craftsmanship. Start in South Tampa along the 4300 block of El Prado Boulevard where shops line both sides of the street. Head over Tampa Bay to downtown St. Petersburg from Central Avenue and Ninth Street to 16th Avenue N. Then truck north to Belleair Bluffs along the 560 to 590 blocks of Indian Rocks Road. And this is just the beginning! All told, there are more than 100 shops in the Tampa Bay area where you can snap up a cherished memory from the past.

While it's impossible to describe every antique shopping option, we'll attempt to clue you into those areas that offer the most shopping possibilities. You can find furniture, china and glassware in most every one, and we've noted specialty areas where appropriate. For a connoisseur's guide to antiquing in Tampa Bay, grab a copy of *The Antique Press*, available at most antique shops. If you can't find a copy, call (813) 935-7577.

Gaslight Antiques
3616 Henderson Blvd., Tampa
• **(813) 870-0934**

Just two blocks east of S. Dale Mabry Highway, you'll find one of the largest collections of fine antiques in our entire market area. Gaslight Antiques is really three shops in one. The first is Gaslight Antiques Main Gallery with its fine Victorian furniture, clocks, lamps, art glass and Tiffany. Then wander into Gaslight Antiques Office Furnishings, a full 3,000 square feet, complete with a beautiful selection of fine leather upholstery, rolltop and partner's desks, bookcases, conference tables and chairs. Finally, there's the Gaslight Antiques Georgian Furniture Gallery, the newest store featuring fine Revolutionary period Chippendale, Sheraton and Hepplewhite furnishings. The buyers are strewn across the northern states, snapping up the best of the old and shipping it here for your inspection. If you're serious about antiques, this should be your first stop. It's open from 10:30 AM until 5:30 PM Monday through Saturday and from noon until 4 PM Sunday.

The Antique Mall of Tampa
1102 E. Busch Blvd., Tampa
• **(813) 933-5829**

Don't let the dismal exterior of this "warehouse" fool you. Inside are more than 70 dealers who not only are anxious to tell you the story behind every item in the shops, but will also cordially guide you to a neighbor who might just have just what you're looking for. If you're interested in old toys and rare books, this is a great place to explore. If you need a break, there's a large lounge area where you can rest while watching taped antique shows. Unique!

Downtown Antique District
E. Tarpon Ave., Tarpon Springs

All those things from times gone past have landed in Tarpon Springs. Taylor Arcade Antique Mall, 118 E. Tarpon Avenue, has more than 6,000 square feet of old-time treasures. If you're looking for vintage jewelry and elegant glassware, check out Antiques on the Main, 124 E. Tarpon Avenue, and Antiques Forever, 143 E. Tarpon Avenue. Those with a passion for old fishing lures, wrought iron and pottery shouldn't pass up Victorian Ivy, 151 E. Tarpon Avenue. All together, there are seven charming shops in the district. Visit them all.

Downtown Dunedin
Main St., Dunedin

Downtown Dunedin is itself a charming restored antique, so hunting for collectibles here is all the more enjoyable. Start out at Treasures Forever, 1153 Main Street, then head to Cindy Lou's, specializing in Roseville Pottery, at 330 Main Street. Just around the corner on Scotland Street, find The Beehive Antique Emporium, 362 Scotland Street, with its gorgeous brass, silver, clocks and Orientals. Check out P. Kay's Downtown Antiques & More, 359 Scotland Street, for linens, buttons, fishing nostalgia and more.

Cleveland St.
Clearwater

Stroll Cleveland Street in Clearwater and uncover the past. Must-stops include Singletree Antiques, 1413 Cleveland Street, with prints, china, lamps and primitives; The Emporium, 1411 Cleveland Street, with unusual handmade laces and jewelry; Pack Rat Corner, 617 Cleveland Street, with coins, gold and silver, canes and toys; and our favorite, A Blue Moon Books, 1415 Cleveland Street, with old and rare books and collectibles.

The Shoppes in Antique Alley
Indian Rocks Rd., Belleair Bluffs

Get those walking shoes ready! Back-to-back shops vie for your attention here along Indian Rocks Road. In the 560 block, you'll find Posh Pineapple Antiques, with beautiful textiles; Pickering's, with great garden accessories; Merndale Antiques, with beautiful quilts; and The Regal Rooster, with vintage clothing and linens. In the 590 block, you can wander through Dempsey Antiques for pictures and mirrors; Victoria's Parlour Antiques for Oriental rugs; and Elaine's for baskets and dolls. And you haven't even started yet! There are many more shops here, and you don't want to miss any of them. We'd like to suggest that after you're pooped from antique overload, slide right around the corner to The Black Cat Cafe at 2601 Jewel Road, and enjoy the afternoon tea that's served until 4 PM Monday through Saturday.

INSIDERS' TIP

Rated by those in the know as the largest model railroad store in the world, Chester Holley Model Railroad is a frustrated train engineer's paradise. From the parlor with trains displayed from floor to ceiling, stretching across three walls, to the 60-foot-long narrow room that holds mostly O Gauge and S Gauge trains collected over the years, no spot is without a miniature train car or train village decor. The collection numbers more than 6,000 cars, and some are more than 100 years old. To jump aboard, head to 3818 S. Himes Avenue in Tampa, (813) 831-7202.

Central Ave.
St. Petersburg

We don't know exactly why antique shops seem to clump together, but we're glad they do. Here, along the 7200 block of Central Avenue in St. Petersburg, is another yellow-brick antique row. You'll find Ma's Glass Barn, Wedgewood Manor and Hope's and Cappy's Corner. If you're looking for really oddball stuff, try Harpie's Bazaar, and for unusual sterling silver, check out Blue Bear & Burr.

Duck Duck Goose Country Store
4424 Park Blvd., Pinellas Park
• (727) 546-1355

We've singled out Duck Duck because if you're into country decor, this is a place you shouldn't pass up. From teddy bears to Amish cupboards, we are talking good old hometown trinkets and decor. If you see something you like, better snap it up — merchandise really moves quickly here, but new goodies come in daily to fill any blank spaces.

Paris Flea
3115 Bay to Bay Blvd., Tampa
• (813) 837-6556

Locals in Paris shop the world renowned Paris Flea. Now you can uncover the same marvelous bargains right here in Tampa Bay. Ashley Moseley, the former publisher of *Southern Homes Magazine*, and her daughter, Melanie Horwick, offer an amazing collection of exquisite European antiques and classical furnishings at the shop on Bay to Bay. It's an eclectic mix of Italian, French and English pieces, along with a few period antiques — all fabulously priced. And if you don't see exactly what you want, just ask. They might be able to locate the antique of your dreams through their numerous purveyors worldwide. If you happen to be in town during the holiday season,

Paris Flea is a must visit ... its unique ornaments and decorations are truly one-of-a-kind! Visit Tuesday through Saturday from 10 AM until 6 PM.

Consignment and Thrift Shops

So you say things are better the second time around. Then scavenging through Tampa Bay's consignment and thrift shops is you, baby. One Insider we know likes to refer to the fine art of secondhand bargain hunting as "alternative shopping," and she's helped us out with the following list of some of the most popular places to seek out that designer look when your wallet's on empty. Her favorite consignment shops? Triage, 3705 Henderson Boulevard, Tampa, for truly elegant designer fashions for women; A Bon Marche, 2425 S. Dale Mabry Highway, Tampa, with chic clothing for men, ladies and children; and Alexander's Fine Arts Gallery, 3225 S. MacDill Boulevard, for exquisite costume and fine estate jewelry. A note here: When we talk about thrift shops, they're normally associated with a charity. Consignment shops, on the other hand, are independent retailers specializing in "almost new" recycled clothing and accessories.

PWA (People with Aids) Provider Services
2718 S. MacDill Ave., Tampa
• (813) 837-6850

If you're looking for designer labels along with a great deal, here's the place. You can snap up a big-name blouse for 99¢ and even take a Yves Saint Laurent suit home to your finicky spouse for as little as $20. Proceeds from the outlet go to provide services for AIDS victims,

---

INSIDERS' TIP

The word's out ... Insiders have heard that while the paint is drying on Citrus Park Town Center (scheduled to open in mid-1999), another mall will be under construction on 150 acres that is currently the site of the Hall of Fame Golf Course next to Tampa International Airport. This $300 million mall will be called International Plaza and will be anchored by Nordstrom and Lord & Taylor.

and they'll accept practically anything you can donate with the exception of medical supplies.

Salvation Army
Four thrift stores in Tampa, Four in Pinellas County • (813) 972-0471 (for all stores)

You name it, you can find it at one of the Salvation Army Thrift Stores. From furniture to bric-a-brac to clothing for ladies, men and kids, it's all here and bargain-priced. This is a great place to hunt for books and housewares, too.

Goodwill Industries–Suncoast
15 stores throughout Tampa Bay • (813) 223-3701

The granddaddy of thrift shops, Goodwill has a plethora of goodies, including fine china, leather briefcases and like-new furniture. One thing you're not likely to find is old, broken appliances and really old, worn clothing. Because it costs so much to repair items today, those castoffs not worthy of resale are carted off to the dump site. What remains for your inspection are items that are in good shape and ready to start a new life with you. And if you hit it just right, you can even find never-worn clothing still attached to their JCPenney or Burdine's sales tags.

Best Thrift
5016 E. 10th Ave., Tampa • (813) 247-7705

Say you're looking for a Liz Claiborne or Tommy Hilfiger bargain. Try Best Thrift, well-known for its designer-clothing bargains. Proceeds go to the Purple Heart Foundation in support of military veterans. Best Thrift welcomes your designer castoffs, too.

The League of Mercy
2520 W. Hillsborough Ave., Tampa • (813) 874-2229

For antiques such as cabinets, tables and chairs priced at around $100, here's the place. The League of Mercy is a nondenominational religious organization that supports homeless people.

Shops, restaurants and water activities draw visitors to John's Pass Village in Madeira Beach.

Photo: St. Petersburg/Clearwater Area Convention & Visitors Bureau

Photo: St. Petersburg/Clearwater Area Convention & Visitors Bureau

You can satisfy your hunger for watersports adventures at a host of rental and retail shops in the Tampa Bay area.

Sunshine Thrift Store Inc.
4304 S. Dale Mabry Hwy., Tampa
233 34th St. S., St. Petersburg
• (813) 831-4377 (for both stores)

If you hit the 20,000-square-foot Tampa store at the right time, you're in for a real treat, especially if you're looking for designer clothing. The selection of kids' clothes is phenomenal, as is the collection of furniture and housewares. Proceeds benefit the National Kidney Foundation.

Flea Markets

Hitting the fleas isn't shopping — it's a treasure hunt. Stuff we'd never even think to buy retail is suddenly irresistibly alluring. And then there's the entertainment value to be found at the fleas. People-watching is as much fun as scanning the booths and racks for bargains. We do have one rule: we won't shop the indoor fleas. Experience has taught us these are not true flea markets, but low-overhead retail shops. We know a lot of people

value them, though, especially on 90-degree afternoons.

So let's don the sunscreen, a hat and dark glasses, grab a $10 bill and go have some fun.

Big Top Flea Market
9250 E. Fowler Ave., Tampa
• (813) 986-4004

At the center of this market is a huge, circular, enclosed shopping area. Jutting outward are spokes of open-air shops with more than 600 vendors. Rain or shine, the market is open Saturday and Sunday between 9 AM and 4:30 PM.

Oldsmar Flea Market
180 Race Track Rd., Oldsmar
• (813) 855-5306

From old tools and collectibles to new clothes and furniture, you'll find it for sure. More than 1,000 booths are open Saturday and Sunday from 9 AM until 5 PM. From October 1 through March 1, the market also opens on Fridays.

Joe & Jackie's Flea Market
311 W. Dr. Martin Luther King Jr. Blvd., Seffner • (813) 689-6318

Joe says their 20-something countryside flea market "put Seffner on the map." With as many as 200 participating vendors, it's open every day of the week from 8 AM until 4 PM. There's ample parking, even for overnight motorhome stays. Stop by the office and say hi to Joe — he's the guy in the red jump suit. You'll find Jackie out roaming around, chatting folks up. The market is 3 miles east of I-75.

Wagon Wheel Flea Market
7801 Park Blvd., Pinellas Park • (727) 544-5319

From "the old school to the new breed and each point in between" is an accurate description. This one's a biggie — more than 2,000 vendors covering 125 acres. There's even a tram to shuttle you to or from the parking lot or to various spots in the market. The Wagon Wheel is open Saturdays and Sundays year round from 8 AM until 4 PM.

Stadium Flea Market
1400 Central Ave., St. Petersburg • (727) 894-5856

OK, OK, we go back on our word — this is an indoor market with lots and lots of good junk. Excuse me, junque. So the searching is fun. The market is open 9 AM until 5 PM on Friday, Saturday and Sunday, and parking is free.

49er Flea Market
10525 49th St. N., Clearwater • (727) 573-3367

Small but fun, the 150 or so vendors hawk wares ranging from garage-sale variety to collectibles. Open 7 AM until 3 PM on Saturday and Sunday, this is a good one to hit early when you want to do several markets on the same day.

Webster Westside Flea Market
Webster • (800) 832-7396

Webster, a bit more than an hour's drive north of Tampa off I-75, is home to the granddaddy of all flea markets. It's open only on Monday. For an in-depth rundown, check our Daytrips chapter and read all about it.

Get up early, pack
in a hearty breakfast
and slip into your most
comfy shorts and
tennies. We've got
places to go!

Attractions

OK. You've bobbed, surfed, fried, dined and relaxed yourself into oblivion. Now it's time to put a little zip into your day — and do we have the choices for you. If you're saying, "Not today! It's just too beautiful outdoors!" not to fret. Because around Tampa Bay, if you like what's outside today, you'll very likely find the same glorious fiery yellow orb above the beach tomorrow. Today is the day for spontaneous exploration through the places that you'll find nowhere else on earth, from the natural sponge market in Tarpon Springs to the Museum of Science and Industry in Tampa.

Here we'll present you with our attractions, large and small, and we'll also give you a few tips along the way to make your visit most pleasant. The biggest overall tip we can offer is that if you are zoning in on one of the major attractions, such as Busch Gardens, start out early, head for the back of the park and wind your way forward. It's just a little end-run that will often help you avoid gridlock at the most popular rides.

Hours of operation and admission prices are accurate as of this minute, but, depending on the season of your outing, we suggest that you double-check if you're watching your pennies closely. You may also want to pick up several of the numerous brochures available at all major hotels and visitors centers. Many contain coupons for reduced admission, which can come in handy if you're a family of four or more. Also, most all the major attractions accept credit cards for admission, so you can stash your cash for liberal spending at the gift shops. Unless otherwise noted, children younger than 3 are admitted free.

Some of you more astute readers may notice the omission of parks and beaches, both of which would normally be the meat and potatoes of an attractions chapter, especially in Florida. Because there are just so darn many in each of these categories, we cleverly made the decision to include them in chapters where

they seemed to go naturally. Park-seekers should check out our Parks and Recreation chapter, and beach bunnies will have to turn to Beaches and Watersports.

So get up early, pack in a hearty breakfast, and slip into your most comfy shorts and tennies. We've got places to go!

Tampa/ Hillsborough County

Busch Gardens
Intersection of Busch Blvd. and 40th St., Tampa • (813) 987-5082

Actually, we should call this Day One, because you really need a full day to capture all the magic at Busch Gardens. You can be literally overwhelmed with the choices of where to go first in this 335-acre family entertainment park that's packed with thrill rides, live entertainment, animal exhibits, shops, restaurants and games — all in nine distinctively themed sections that capture the spirit of turn-of-the-century Africa.

Busch Gardens, 2 miles east of I-275, is open daily year round from 9:30 AM until 6 PM with extended summer hours. Admission, which includes all rides, shows and attractions, is $33.95 for adults with a 15 percent discount for seniors and $27.95 for children ages 3 to 9. The parking fee is $3. For a real armchair tour of Busch Gardens, just wheel your La-Z-Boy to the Close-up in this chapter.

Adventure Island
4500 Bougainvillea Ave., Tampa • (813) 987-5660

This is no day at the beach, this is exercise! Adventure Island, just a quarter-mile northeast of Busch Gardens, is a 36-acre outdoor water theme park with water play areas, a championship volleyball complex, a games arcade, outdoor cafes, gift shops, picnic spots and sunbathing areas. Kids who would normally scream bloody murder at the suggestion of a bath at home will lunge out of your grasp to hit the River of No Return, Gulf Scream, Everglides, Courageous Falls and, of course, the infamous Tampa Typhoon, where you have the dubious thrill of plummeting seven stories straight downhill. If you're still coherent at this point, go ahead and try out the Aruba Tuba, in which you are twisted and turned through dark and light down a 420-foot tunnel before being unceremoniously plopped into the pool that waits at ride's end. If that's still not enough for you, may we suggest Key West Rapids, where a 60-foot pool welcomes your decline from six full stories of sinister twists, turns and slides. The only saving grace is that for the first time in 16 years, the 1998 Adventure Island season will boast heated slides and pools.

The park has immaculate dressing room facilities, so you and the little folk can play your hearts out and then change to dry clothes before the trip home. Operated by Busch Entertainment Corp., Adventure Island is open 10 AM until 5 PM from mid-February through early September and weekends only mid-September through late October. Admission charges are $19.95 for adults and $17.95 for children ages 3 to 9. You'll be asked to pay $2 for parking. We suggest you just wear your bathing suits, and don't forget to bring along plenty of towels and high-powered sunscreen.

The Florida Aquarium
701 Channelside Dr., Tampa
• **(813) 273-4020**

From aquifer to ocean, it's nothing short of spectacular. It's the state-of-the-art, $84 million Florida Aquarium, tempting you to enter its signature three-story-high, seashell-shaped dome of more than 1,110 thermal glass panels. Rising proudly along the waterfront on the 4½-acre site of the Tampa Port Authority's Garrison Seaport, it is three levels and 152,000 square feet of underwater amazement.

The aquarium, in downtown Tampa, is home to more than 4,300 animals and plants representing 550 native Florida species in more than a million gallons of fresh and salt water. With exhibits exploring everything from Florida wetlands to offshore waters, the aquarium has taken on the monumental task of telling the unique story of Florida's waters from their underground source to the open sea. It tells the story so well, in fact, that it received the Travel Industry Association's 1995 Odyssey Award for outstanding public and community service in protecting the environment. Not to be missed is the million-gallon tank in the Coral Reefs Gallery with its 43-by-14-foot acrylic window offering unobstructed floor-to-ceiling viewing space.

Admission to the Florida Aquarium costs $10.95 for adults, $9.95 for senior adults and $5.95 for children 13 and younger. Annual family memberships that permit unlimited admission are available for $75. Hours are 9 AM until 6 PM daily, with the last tickets sold at 4 PM. Parking costs $3.

Lowry Park Zoo
7530 North Blvd., Tampa
• **(813) 933-3830**

Ranked as one of the top three zoos of its size in North America, this 24-acre zoological garden features exotic creatures from four continents in their natural habitats. Its $3.3 million Manatee and Aquatic Center is only one of three manatee hospitals and rehabilitation centers in Florida. Here, you can get a fish-eye's view of the manatees when you watch them through the 3-inch-thick glass of their 75,000-gallon tank.

Especially exciting is the Florida Wildlife Center, a special sanctuary for native Floridians such as alligators, panthers, bears and red wolves. Here you'll see these zoo residents in their simulated environment as you time-travel from the Florida Keys to Tallahassee. Kids adore the petting zoo, and older kids become spellbound in the free-flight aviary, except, perhaps, when they come toe-to-nose with the humongous green iguanas that freely roam here.

The phenomenal $500,000 Harrell Discovery Center was completed in 1997. What was once the Key West Gift Shop is now a new educational exhibit where practically everything is

www.insiders.com

See this and many other **Insiders' Guide®** destinations online — in their entirety.

Visit us today!

Photo: Florida Aquarium

Get up-close and personal with Florida's sea life, such as this manta ray, at the Florida Aquarium.

designed to be touched and studied, with the exception of some delightfully disgusting small animals and insects that are poisonous. The whole premise of the exhibit is to display for close observation some of the smaller animals of our region. With dramatic full-color blowups of some of our area's most recognizable critters, the center also boasts a huge walk-in globe that could be described as a video kaleidoscope ... visitors are literally surrounded by the sights and sounds of nature. An outdoor amphitheater was also added in 1997 — Saunders Conservation Theater — where performances by two-toed sloths, porcupines, hedgehogs and falcons leave the audience breathless.

To top off your zoo visit, don't miss the Fun Forest at Lowry Park, with rides, an arcade, Fairytale Land and Rainbow Bridge, a grand place for the little ones to drain off any extra energy. The zoo is open every day except Thanksgiving and Christmas from 9:30 AM until 5 PM. Admission costs $6.50 for adults, $5.50 for seniors and $4.50 for children ages 3 through 11.

The Museum of Science and Industry (MOSI)
4801 E. Fowler Ave., Tampa
• (813) 987-6300

The largest science center in the Southeast, MOSI is a simply wondrous facility with more than 450 "hands-on, minds-on" activities. At this scientific playground, kids from ages 1 to 101 learn by doing such things as exploring the universe through space simulators in the Challenger Learning Center, braving the re-created force of 74 mph winds in the Gulf Coast Hurricane exhibit, relaxing in the 6,400-square-foot free-flight butterfly garden that's part of the 3-mile Back Wood Nature Trail and getting starry-eyed in the area's only planetarium. The eight-story IMAX DOME Theater, Florida's first, made its debut in the summer of 1995 — part of MOSI's $35 million expansion that has made it the largest science center in the Southeast, covering acreage that's the equivalent of three and a half football fields. You'll be totally awestruck by the amazing sights and sounds.

Hours are 9 AM until 5 PM Monday through Thursday and 9 AM until 9 PM Friday and Saturday. Admission costs $8 for adults, $7 for seniors and students with valid IDs, and $4 for children ages 2 through 12. MOSIMAX admission is $6 for adults, $5 for seniors, students and children ages 13 through 18, and $4 for children ages 2 through 12. There is no charge for parking.

Seminole Indian Casino
5223 N. Orient Rd., Tampa
• **(813) 621-1302, (800) 282-7016**

You won't find a chapter of Gamblers Anonymous here. This is 24 hours a day, seven days a week of high-stakes bingo, bingo, bingo, with a little poker thrown in for variety. Well, actually, bingo is played from 10 AM until 1 AM, but the poker and gaming machines run nonstop. Nearby on the Seminole Reservation, you'll find the Cultural Center, depicting the colorful history of the Seminoles complete with alligator wrestling matches. It's fascinating to see artisans demonstrating their basket-making and beadwork and carving in their chickees (thatched huts). You can pick up a freshly made trinket in the gift shop. There's no admission charge except for special bingo packages, and parking is free.

Gator Jungle of Plant City
5145 Harvey Tew Rd., Plant City
• **(813) 752-2836**

Slither your way through a self-guided tour of a real Florida swamp with, naturally, alligators and other charming Florida animals living in their natural environment at this alligator

and crocodile farm. We say send Dad with the kids to this one, especially when it means coming face to face with Old Bad Eyes, the world's ugliest alligator, weighing in at 600 pounds and measuring 11 feet long. Admonish the family to strictly adhere to the "No Swimming" signs (no kidding!), and encourage them to take along a camera so they can have a picture taken holding a live alligator. It's open daily from 8:30 AM until 6 PM. Dad pays $5.99, and kids ages 3 through 11, $3.

Historic Ybor City

Designated one of three national landmarks in Florida, the 110-block collection of historic buildings known as Ybor City is literally today's smokin' hot spot of Tampa. Just mix the antique streetlamps, wrought-iron balconies and ornate grillwork of Spanish architecture with jammin' restaurants, cafes and shops, and you've got a magnet that draws visitors and locals alike, seven days and nights of the week. Even if you do nothing more than take a leisurely stroll down La Setima (Seventh Avenue), you can take in as much history and contemporary good times as one body can absorb in a single day. From art galleries to nightclubs blasting everything from blues to reggae, to the famous Columbia Restaurant (check out our Restaurants chapter for all the rich details of this landmark eatery), Ybor City is the place to see — and be seen.

To get the up-to-date info on all the Ybor happenings, contact the Ybor Entertainment and Arts Association (nicknamed YEAA! Don't you love it?) at (813) 247-2144. Walking tours are offered Tuesday, Thursday and Saturday starting at the Information Desk of Ybor Square that's between Eighth and Ninth avenues. Walking tours are offered free of charge, but

INSIDERS' TIP

Can't decide where to go first and don't know how to get there? Call the Swiss Chalet Tampa Bay Visitor Information Center at (813) 985-3601. They'll not only arrange to get you discount tickets (forget waiting in line!), but they have an extensive menu of sightseeing tours, transportation services (buses and rental cars), plus answers to any newcomer question you might possibly dream up to ask. They're across from Busch Gardens at 3601 E. Busch Boulevard in Tampa.

call (813) 223-1111 to confirm the starting time, which is currently 10:30 AM.

Here are just a couple of the many attractions you'll want to put on the top of your Ybor must-see list.

Tampa Rico Cigar Company
1901 N. 13th St., Ybor City
• (813) 247-6738

At this revered landmark of the fabulously popular Ybor Historic District, you'll see cigars being made by hand as they have been since the beginnings of this family-owned and -operated cigar store. It's open Monday through Saturday from 10 AM until 6 PM and Sunday from noon until 5:30 PM, but call ahead for specific cigar-rolling demonstration times. Admission and parking are free of charge.

Ybor City Brewing Company
2205 N. 20th St., Ybor City
• (813) 242-9222

This renovated 100-year-old brick cigar factory is the home of Ybor Gold, Tampa Bay's first handcrafted beer and an award winner in national microbrewery competitions. The microbrewery, which pumps out 60,000 barrels of the elixir every year, is open for tours Monday through Saturday from 7 AM until 6 PM, and you'll be treated to a firsthand view of the brewing process. Afterward, you're invited to the hospitality tasting room for a sip of the Gold. Admission is $2, and parking is free.

Ybor Square
Eighth Ave. and 13th St., Ybor City
• (813) 247-4497

Three enormous historic brick buildings, built in 1886 by Vicente Ybor as a place to make his cigars, and a zillion quaint shops and restaurants — this is Ybor Square, more than just your everyday shopping experience. Ethnic shops and eateries, offering everything from Spanish, Oriental, Cuban and even American cuisine, make this place a true happening. Adding to the charm are the original wooden interiors, hand-blown glass windows and floor-to-ceiling murals. The Nostalgia Market is an especially popular shop, with its individual antiques merchants offering everything from rare magazines to quilts and furniture. The complex, listed on the National Register

of Historic Places, is open Monday through Saturday from 10 AM until 6 PM and from noon until 5:30 PM. There is no charge for admission or parking.

Ybor City State Museum
1818 Ninth Ave., Ybor City
• (813) 247-6323

If you really want to get the full flavor of the history of the cigar industry, here's the place to do it. In the century-old yellow brick building that was once the Ferlita Bakery (circa 1896), the museum features exhibits and displays that bring mid-19th-century cigar making to life, especially when it comes to the impact of the cigar factories on the commerce of Tampa Bay. See these plus the original brick ovens from the bakery for just a $1 admission charge. The museum's hours are 9 AM till noon and 1 till 5 PM Tuesday through Saturday.

Tampa Theatre
711 Franklin St., Tampa • (813) 274-8981

Elaborate is an understatement when describing the Tampa Theatre, a restored 1926 movie palace that sits in the midst of a steel-towered downtown Tampa. Noted for its Florida/Mediterranean architecture, it is the perfect backdrop for numerous films, concerts and special events. Guided tour times vary, so call ahead if you want to do more than just gawk at the phenomenal exterior.

St. Petersburg, Clearwater and Pinellas County

The Pier
800 Second Ave. N.E., St. Petersburg
• (727) 821-6164

It's amazing how $9.7 million can turn an old, rundown landmark into a place with a life of its own. This can only be described as a five-story inverted pyramid structure that proudly sits extended a quarter-mile out over the waters of Tampa Bay. Inside is a whirlwind of activity. There are shops, boutiques and cafes on the first level, an aquarium on the second and meeting space on the third. Up on the fourth level, enjoy a true feast at the Columbia Restaurant, and way at the top, Cha Cha Coconuts serves up the frostiest tropical drinks and meanest black-bean chili — not to mention some ear-shattering live entertainment when the stars come out.

You can catch great views of the public boat docks and Bay waters from the observation deck, and, if fishing is a pastime of yours, bring along your rod and reel. You can rent bicycles, sailboats and in-line skates to add a little excitement to your Pier experience. The Pier is open daily, with most shops operating from 10 AM until 9 PM. No admission fee is charged, even to the aquarium. To rest after your visit, or as a prelude, stroll through Straub Park, which is adjacent to The Pier. It's a 36-acre waterfront park that runs between First and Fifth avenues along Beach Drive, and it's a great place to be a voyeur of all The Pier's activity.

Great Explorations
The Pier, 800 Second Ave. N.E., St. Petersburg • (727) 821-8885

Phenomenal Arts, Explore Galore, Exchange, Think Tank, Touch Tunnel and Body Shop — these are just hints of the exhibits in this wonderful hands-on museum where visitors are encouraged to touch, move and interact with the wild and wacky displays. It's a place where kids can crawl through a long, dark tunnel, measure their strength and flexibility or paint with sunlight, all without getting into a lick of trouble. Rush the kids over Monday through Saturday from 10 AM until 5 PM or Sunday from noon until 5 PM. Admission is $6 for adults, $5.50 for seniors and $5 for children ages 4 through 17.

Sunken Gardens
1825 Fourth St. N., St. Petersburg • (727) 896-3186

Dating back to 1903, this 7-acre tropical garden houses more than 50,000 plants, flowers and trees, all blooming year round. You can wander through this lush paradise, then stroll through the aviary that is home to all types of tropical birds. There are four daily bird shows at 10 AM, noon, 2 and 4 PM. There's also a magnificent Orchid Arbor, boasting thousands of rare, fragrant orchids — an amaz-

ing sight for anyone with a brown thumb. To spice it up a bit, Sunken Gardens puts on exhibitions of gator wrestling, the "Kachunga and the Alligator Show," along with a biblical *King of Kings* wax exhibit, antiques gallery, Flamingo Cafe and the self-described world's largest gift shop. The gardens are open daily from 10 AM until 5 PM. Admission costs $14 for adults and $8 for children. Group rates are available.

Tropicana Field
1 Stadium Dr., St. Petersburg • (727) 825-3100

All hail the "Fruit Dome," home to the spanking-new Devil Rays, the newest Major League Baseball franchise that means joy for thousands of Tampa Bay baseball fanatics. The Tropicana, built to the tune of $110 million in 1990 as the future home to a major-league team, has finally seen its time come as the Devil Rays took to the diamond for their first-ever game in spring 1998. This slant-roofed marvel sits on a 66-acre parcel between 10th Street S. and 16th Street S., and First Avenue S. to Fourth Avenue S. Its cable-supported dome is the first of its kind in the United States and one of the largest in the world. Besides baseball, the stadium hosts all manner of fairs, shows and events, owing its versatility to a series of moveable stands that slide independently on pneumatic tires, then lower into place hydraulically. As many as 60,000 people can be accommodated here. Tours are available on nonevent days, but call ahead to guarantee day and time.

Kopsick Palm Arboretum
901 N. Shore Dr., St. Petersburg • (727) 893-7335

Visitors from the North country are always amazed at the graceful beauty of the palm trees that line our highways and grace our yards. Here at Kopsick you can see them all in one panoramic glance, with more than 200 palms and cycades representing more than 45 species from around the world. Here in this 2-acre park along the Bayfront, you can stroll along the red-brick pathways and marvel at Mother Nature's handiwork. Guided walks are available by appointment, and this brush with nature is free from dawn to dusk.

The *Sea Hogge*, an authentic reproduction of a pirate ship, plies the waters of the Intracoastal Waterway to the Gulf of Mexico.

Photo: St. Petersburg/Clearwater Area Convention & Visitors Bureau

Clearwater Marine Science Center
249 Windward Passage, Clearwater
• (727) 441-1790

A remarkable place with a singular mission — to learn as much as possible about our vast undersea world so as not to destroy the natural delicate balance — the Clearwater Marine Science Museum is the only facility with government permits for the rescue and rehabilitation of marine mammals on the west coast of Florida. Here you can see eye-to-eye with Sunset Sam, an 18-year-old rehabilitated Atlantic bottle-nosed dolphin; Big Mo, a 400-pound loggerhead sea turtle; and Max, an extremely rare Kemp's Ridley sea turtle that was permanently disabled in a boating accident.

You'll see a 200-gallon tank depicting Florida's coral reef plus another 1,200-gallon artificial-reef tank that's home to all sorts of slithery sea creatures. Especially weird is the nocturnal tank, where you'll check out marine animals normally active only at night.

You can also get up-close and personal with a stingray at the new Stingray Beach exhibit. Whether you look on from eye level or from a safer distance on two levels of a pier deck overlooking the 3-foot-deep pool, you'll see all you want to see of the creatures feared for their lashing tails and serrated spines. Just think of the poor starfish, hermit crabs and clams who actually share the water with these devilish creatures. This busy place is open Monday through Friday from 9 AM until 5 PM, Saturday from 9 AM until 4 PM and Sunday from 11 AM until 4 PM. Admission costs $5.25 for adults and $3.50 for children 3 and older.

Boatyard Village
16100 Fairchild Dr., Clearwater
• (727) 535-4678

Right next to the St. Petersburg/Clearwater International Airport, you can be transported back in time to this re-created 1890s fishing village nestled in a cove along

Tampa Bay. Strolling through the boutiques and galleries or relaxing in one of the restaurants (94th Aero Squadron is an Insiders' favorite!) are great escapes from the heat of the beaches. There are special events and entertainment held regularly amidst the charming stores built out of old rustic wood and tin, so you might want to call to plan the best day and time to visit. The stores are open daily from 10 AM until 6 PM, but restaurants and shops close at 5 PM on Sunday. There's no admission charge.

Suncoast Seabird Sanctuary
18328 Gulf Blvd., Indian Shores
• **(727) 391-6211**

More than 6,500 injured and permanently crippled birds find sanctuary at Suncoast each year, a well-known refuge and rehabilitation center for our feathered friends. Known worldwide for its preservation of wild birds, the nonprofit facility is proud to show off its residents, such as brown pelicans, cormorants, white herons, birds of prey and songbirds. Because the birds are so used to spectators, picture-taking is a favorite activity — in fact, a few of the white pelicans really seem to pose for the camera. It's open daily from 9 AM until dark, and there's no charge for admission. You're welcome to wander on your own, or you can call ahead to arrange guided group tours.

Heritage Village
11909 125th St. N., Largo
• **(727) 582-2123**

Twenty-one wooded acres shelter this fascinating collection of restored homes and buildings, the oldest existing structures in Pinellas County. The centerpiece of the park is the historical museum, where the county's pioneer lifestyle is re-created. Special exhibits of spinning, weaving and the like are regularly held, but because of ever-changing schedules, you should call in advance to see what the craft du jour might be. If you plan your visit for the fourth Saturday in October, you'll be just in time for the park's annual Country Jubilee, a gala event that's reminiscent of a century-old faire. There is no charge for admission. The park is open Tuesday through Saturday 10 AM until 4 PM and Sunday from 1 until 4 PM.

John's Pass Village and Boardwalk
12901 Gulf Blvd. E., Madeira Beach
• **(727) 391-7373**

According to legend, John's Pass was created in 1848 by a violent hurricane that destroyed the Egmont Key lighthouse and even washed away a few offshore Gulf islets. Today, it's a thriving, quaint seaside village, complete with the weather-beaten shingled boutiques, art galleries and restaurants that just ooze charm from every door and window. While this is the spot to catch a ride on one of the many charter deep-sea fishing vessels that sail out to Gulf waters, landlubbers can stroll the village and boardwalk in this place that seems almost trapped in history. The biggie event here is the John's Pass Seafood Festival. Usually held the last weekend in October, this festival fills the air with the sweet aroma of every type of fish and shellfish and has events such as oyster-eating contests, alligator wrestling and so much more (see our Annual Events chapter for more details).

Konger Coral Sea Aquarium
852 Dodecanese Blvd., Tarpon Springs
• **(813) 938-5378**

Right in the heart of this town rich in Greek heritage, you'll stumble upon the Konger Coral Sea Aquarium and find yourself mesmerized by the nurse and lemon sharks, stingrays, angelfish and other Gulf of Mexico and Caribbean Sea natives that swim nonchalantly around the coral reef in the 120,000-gallon tank. Smaller tank displays show off marine life from the Pacific Ocean. The aquarium is open daily from 10 AM until 5 PM. Admission costs $4 for adults, $3.25 for seniors 55 and older, and $2 for children older than 3.

Spongeorama
510 Dodecanese Blvd., Tarpon Springs
• **(813) 943-9509**

Here on the site of the original sponge exchange, you'll see more natural sponges than you ever believed could exist in one place. Exhibits at a museum/theater trace the town's Greek settlers and the sponge industry, and a film demonstrates sponge diving. Get totally absorbed in the ambiance of "America's Sponge Capital," and perhaps even plan to hop aboard one of the many excursion boats

Photo: Tampa Bay Magazine

The Pier is one of St. Petersburg's most popular attractions.

where you can watch divers in their heavy dive suits and huge helmets harvest the sponges from the Gulf bottom. Spongeorama is open daily from 11 AM until 6 PM, and admission is free of charge. (We bet you'll buy a sponge to call your own before you leave!)

Historical Museums and Societies

Tampa/ Hillsborough County

Henry B. Plant Museum
Univ. of Tampa, 401 W. Kennedy Blvd., Tampa • (813) 254-1891

The Victorian era of the Tampa Bay Hotel, a National Historic Landmark, and the city is preserved here, as is the hotel's role in the Spanish-American War. In December you can

take a candlelight stroll daily during special hours from 1 until 9 PM. Throughout the rest of the year the museum is open from 10 AM until 4 PM Tuesday through Saturday and from noon to 4 PM on Sunday. The suggested donation is $3 for adults and $1 for children 12 and younger.

Tampa Bay History Center
225 S. Franklin St., Tampa
• (813) 228-0097

History may not change, but Tampa Bay History Center's presentation of it does. Now in digs at the Tampa Convention Center Annex, this "preview" center is designed to operate only until the year 2000, when a permanent Tampa History Museum will be built. Along with 2,400 square feet of exhibits pertaining to the county and Tampa Bay region in its interim mini-museum, the center provides meeting space to history and heritage organizations, archaeology and genealogy societies, writers groups and others. Hours are Tuesday through Saturday from 10 AM until 5 PM, and Sunday from 1 until 5 PM. In summer, the museum is closed on Sundays. There is no charge for admission.

Tampa Historical Society
245 S. Hyde Park Ave., Tampa
• **(813) 259-1111**

Housed in the historic Peter O. Knight house, the Tampa Historical Society provides educational programs, local and regional tours, a cemetery ramble, historical marker placement and an annual banquet with presentation of the D.B. McKay and the Tony Pizzo awards. It's generally open Monday, Wednesday and Friday from 9:30 AM until 1:30 PM, but hours may be subject to change because of programs and events, so it's best to call ahead and check the week's schedule.

Ybor City State Museum
1818 Ninth Ave., Tampa • (813) 247-6323

The museum complex covers about half a city block and includes an ornamental garden, three restored cigar worker houses and the Ferlita Bakery Building. Admission to the museum costs $2, and hours are 9 AM until 5 PM daily, except for major holidays. The cigar worker houses are open for viewing from 10 AM until noon and from 1 until 3 PM Tuesday through Saturday. The museum also gives free, escorted walking tours, starting in front of Ybor Square, Tuesday through Saturday at 10:30 AM.

St. Petersburg,
Clearwater
and Pinellas County

Florida International Museum
100 Second St. S., St. Petersburg
• **(727) 822-3693**

Downtown St. Petersburg's little gem, the Florida International Museum is unlike any museum you've probably ever visited. You'll find spectacular exhibits on display for just six months of the year, usually from November to May. Major collections from Russia, Egypt and Greece have all had their days of glory, and *Titanic: The Exhibition* is the all-time most visited display. Museum hours are daily from 9

AM until 8 PM with the last tour beginning at 6 PM. Admission prices vary with the current exhibit.

Pinellas County Historical Museum
11909 125th St. N., Largo
• **(727) 582-2123**

Take a stroll through the turn of the century at Heritage Village, a 21-acre open-air, living history museum. Two dozen of Pinellas County's oldest structures, two of which date back to the Civil War, are open to visit in a setting of tall pines and palmettos. Admission to the park and museum is free of charge, but donations are welcomed. Docents enhance self-guided tours in various locations, such as the Plant-Sumner house and Seven Gables. Hours are 10 AM until 4 PM Tuesday through Saturday and 1 until 4 PM Sunday.

St. Petersburg Museum of History
335 Second Ave. N.E., St. Petersburg
• **(727) 894-1052**

From prehistory to historic flights, the museum hosts a variety of displays, including a Model B No. 43 Benoist plane like that flown by Tony Jannus on the St. Petersburg-Tampa Airboat Line, interactive exhibits and an intimate gallery for rotating exhibits. You can explore a re-created 1870s country store, and even take a journey on a simulated trolley ride. And don't neglect to give your best regards to the museum's most famous resident, a 5-foot, 3,000-year-old mummy. The museum is open Monday through Saturday from 10 AM until 5 PM and Sunday 1 until 5 PM, except on major holidays. The museum charges $4 for adult admission, $3.50 for senior adults and $1.50 for children ages 7 to 17. Children younger than 6 are admitted free. Situated on the water at the foot of The Pier, the museum is also a great locale for special events such as business parties, birthdays or weddings.

Gulf Beaches Historical Museum
115 10th Ave., St. Pete Beach
• **(727) 360-2491**

This museum traces the history of Pinellas County's barrier islands through photos, news clippings and artifacts dating back to the 1500s. The 1917 building that houses the museum was the first church built on the barrier islands. Donations are accepted in lieu of a set admission price. The museum, near the famous Don CeSar Hotel, is open Thursdays and Saturdays only from 10 AM until 4 PM and Sunday from 1 until 4 PM.

Safety Harbor Museum
329 Bayshore Blvd. S., Safety Harbor
• (727) 726-1668

Safety Harbor's history is rich, beginning with Tocobaga Indian residents who revered the natural spring waters that are found here. This community museum, recognized as one of the best Florida museums of its size in 1996, includes a depiction of archeological digs in the area and a small research library. Adult admission costs $1, and children visit for 50¢. Museum hours are Tuesday through Friday from 10 AM until 4 PM and Saturday and Sunday from 1 till 4 PM.

Dunedin Historical Museum
341 Main St., Dunedin • (727) 736-1176

Dunedin's old train station, built in 1888, houses memorabilia and displays from the area's frontier days to the present. The elaborate HO-gauge model train on display in the train room will thrill railroad buffs of all ages. Docents occasionally present lectures on their areas of historical expertise. The museum is open Tuesday through Saturday, but only from 10 AM till 1 PM. A $1 donation is requested, and larger donations are welcomed.

Sailing into the Sunset, Tampa Bay Style

With water, water everywhere, it sure makes sense to cruise the open seas while you're here. To satisfy that sailor's hunger in you, ships galore await your boarding, from authentic pirate's replicas to catamarans and every species of floating vessel in between.

From forward to stern, you can bet they're ready for you, with scrumptious meals, entertainment and music, even casino-style gambling, but absolutely no one can engineer the breathtaking sunsets you'll likely encounter on a late summer's afternoon on the Gulf.

While you can simply board a sightseeing-only vessel a half-hour prior to departure, reservations for the popular luncheon and dinner cruises are imperative, especially during the busy season. The helpful people at the front desk of your hotel or motel can help you select your sailing experience and make reservations for you, or you can call the ship of your choice directly. Children are always welcome, but we'd advise you to park them in front of a TV with a babysitter for the late-night casino-style excursions. You need a little time to yourself anyway.

Our last bit of advice is on wardrobe. Plan on loose, comfortable clothing and tennies for a daytime trip, and think about bringing along a light sweater or jacket for any sojourn that will take you from daylight into a starry night. Even though the temperatures may be warm, cool Gulf breezes have been known to put the chill into anyone who's had a bit too much midday sun.

Empress Cruise Lines
John's Pass, Treasure Island
Clearwater Beach Marina, Clearwater
• (727) 895-DEAL, (800) 486-8600

We're talking Florida's favorite party ships! Operating twice a day (three times daily Fridays and Saturdays), seven days a week, you can expect a magnificent gourmet buffet, bilevel casino (blackjack, Caribbean stud poker, roulette and craps), live entertainment, bingo, games, contests and more. The *Crown Princess*, three full decks of party, party, party, makes daily six-hour cruises to nowhere, and her sister ship, the *Majestic Empress*, matches her sibling's frenetic

---

INSIDERS' TIP

The most asked question at the Florida Aquarium? "Why don't the big fish eat the little fish?" Well, we know they don't fill up on the divers who clean the tanks, so the answer must be that the big fish are kept well-fed so they're less aggressive. While sometimes they do have a small nibble or two, natural enemies in the same tank are separated by dividers.

activity. Cruises sail Sunday through Thursday from 11 AM until 5 PM and from 7 PM until midnight; and Friday and Saturday from 11 AM until 5 PM, from 7 PM until 1 AM and from 1:30 AM until 6 AM. Prices range from $20 to $38 and include a service fee. There are also popular half-day casino cruises that sail twice daily from John's Pass Village. All aboard for just $9.50 a person, excluding service and port charges. Call for reservations.

The Admiral Tour Boat
Clearwater Beach Marina, Clearwater
• (727) 462-2628

Take your pick: A two-hour narrated sightseeing and bird-feeding cruise, a two-hour luncheon escapade or an evening dinner/dance cruise. It's yours for the boarding on the triple-decker *Admiral Tour Boat*. The two-level dining room is a true feast for the eyes and a fine background for the continental cuisine. The *Admiral* cruises the smooth waters of Clearwater Bay, making it an excellent choice for those prone to seasickness. Board at noon for the 12:30 PM daylight sail Tuesday through Saturday (adults, $7.75, children ages 3 through 12, $4.95, not including optional luncheon). Evening cruises depart at 7 PM daily and cost $9.95 Tuesday through Friday and most Sundays, and $11.50 on Saturday. Dinner is an additional charge and usually costs between $8.95 and $13.95.

Casablanca Cruises
Tarpon Springs • (813) 942-4452

These lunch, dinner and sightseeing cruises depart from the historic sponge docks to the Gulf of Mexico and cruise the scenic Anclote River and surrounding waters. You'll spend $8 for a sightseeing excursion (daily from 2 till 3 PM), and $29.95 for the three-hour dinner cruise on Friday and Saturday evenings starting at 7:30.

The Starlite Princess
St. Pete Beach Cswy., St Pete Beach
• (727) 462-BOAT

Expect a special voyage on the *Starlite Princess*, an authentic paddle wheeler that sails from St. Pete Beach Causeway in St. Petersburg, and sister ship, the *Starlite Majesty*, that boards passengers at Clearwater Beach Marina in Clearwater. Dinner Dance cruises are definitely popular, with full cocktail service, your choice of seven freshly prepared entrees and live music for listening and dancing. More for family fun are the casual daytime cruises, from the two-hour luncheon/sightseeing tour to the two-and-a-half-hour Dixieland Jazz Cruise to the five-hour Sunshine Skyway Tour. Daytime cruise costs begin at $7.05 for adults and $4.70 for children. Dinner Dance cruise admission is $11.75 ($14.10 on Saturday). Food and beverage costs are additional. Call for departure times and to make reservations.

Photo: St. Petersburg/Clearwater Area Convention & Visitors Bureau

The playful antics of bottle-nosed dolphins enthrall visitors and locals, young and old.

Lady Anderson Dining Yacht
St. Pete Beach Cswy., St. Pete Beach
• (727) 367-7804, (800) 533-2288

A sleek vessel, the stately and elegant *Lady Anderson* pampers you with delightful luncheon and dinner cruises along the waters of Boca Ciega Bay and the Gulf of Mexico from her berth at Capt. Anderson Cruise Port on the St. Pete Beach Causeway. Especially popular are the gospel music cruises every Thursday evening. Adult prices for luncheon cruises begin at $14.50, and dinner cruises $19.50, with children's tariffs slightly less. Reservations are a must, and boarding begins a half-hour prior to departure. *Lady Anderson* sails from October through mid-May; call and check current departure times when making your reservations.

Sea Trader Cruises
Harbour Island Marina, Tampa
• (813) 245-SAIL

For custom cruising at its best, your private party of six or less can sail out into Tampa Bay aboard this fine 38-foot sailboat for an afternoon of dolphin-watching or sightseeing. Meals are catered, or you can bring your own. You must call well in advance for rates and reservations.

Captain Memo's Pirate Cruise
Clearwater Beach Marina, Clearwater
• (727) 446-2587

Looking for a bit of high-seas adventure? All aboard the *Sea Hogge*, an authentic reproduction of a pirate ship, decorated to the nines with all the trappings of the real thing. Little girls will talk for days about joining the all-female crew of Captain Memo (alias Bill Wozencraft), as you sail out along the Intracoastal Waterway into the Gulf of Mexico, perhaps sighting dolphins and a few pirates along the way. Adults can walk the plank from $27,

seniors and teens from $20 and mini-mates from $15. The admission price includes complimentary beer, wine or soft drinks (they uncork the bubbly for sunset cruises). Departure times for the two-hour cruises are daily at 10 AM, 2 and 4:30 PM, with a 7 PM sailing from April through September.

Show Queen
Clearwater Beach Marina, Clearwater
• (727) 461-3113

All three riverboat decks and 65 feet of the *Show Queen* make her truly a showboat. All aboard for two- or three-hour sightseeing cruises of the Clearwater area. Choose a lunch cruise ($12.95 for adults and $6.95 for children ages 4 to 10) or summer sunset cruises with a buffet and entertainment ($19.95 for adults and $9.95 for the kids). Departure times vary according to the season and the time of the sunset; call so you won't miss the trip.

Europa Fun Kruz
John's Pass Marina, Madeira Beach
• (727) 393-5110

Pull away from the dock, and start the party! A Fun Kruz means a full meal, Las Vegas-style casino gambling and live entertainment for the party animal in you. Adults can board for an afternoon or evening cruise from $39.95, and if you bring the kiddies on Saturday or Sunday mornings, there's a special children's program to keep those little fingers off the blackjack tables. Again, departure times change with the seasons, so call in advance for your ticket to ride.

Sea Screamer
Kingfish Wharf, Treasure Island
• (727) 447-7200

If you feel the need for speed, this honey is for you. Reputed to be the world's largest speedboat, the *Sea Screamer* is a 73-foot,

---

INSIDERS' TIP

One of the best manatee viewing spots is Tampa Electric's Manatee Viewing Center in Apollo Beach. Open from mid-November through early April each year, you'll likely catch a glimpse of one of the hundreds of West Indian manatees who gather here in search of Tampa Bay's warm inland waters. Both admission and parking are free. For information, call (813) 228-4289.

turbo-charged, twin-engine vessel with a split personality. Once aboard, you go from a white-knuckled, wake-making thrill ride screeching through the Gulf of Mexico to a demure, leisurely narrated tour around Treasure Island. Tighten up that life jacket and hand over $11.85 for adults and $7.59 for children ages 6 to 12. You can get the Screamer experience from Treasure Island Wednesday through Saturday at noon, 2 and 4 PM and from Clearwater Beach Marina Sunday through Tuesday at 11 AM, 2 and 4 PM. From June 1 through September 15, a 6 PM adventure is added to the *Sea Screamer* departure times.

Dolphin Encounter Cruises
W. Drew St. Dock, Clearwater
• **(727) 442-7433**

If watching for dolphins and feeding sea birds is more to your liking, head to downtown Clearwater and take a spin on the 125-passenger, double-deck catamaran *Clearwater Express*. The 90-minute journey out into the

Gulf meanders along the beaches and shoreline for a close-up encounter with dolphins and sea birds. The company provides free food for bird feeding, but you'll have to pay for your own snacks at the snack bar. Grab your binoculars, and expect to pay $9.35 for adults and $5.40 for children. Sailing times vary according to season, so call for current departure times.

St. Nicholas Boat Line
693 Dodecanese Blvd., Tarpon Springs
• **(813) 942-6425**

If you're fascinated by all the sponge activity at Tarpon Springs, this 30-minute boat ride should put the topper on all the sponge trivia you'll ever need to know. Aboard you'll hear all about the history of sponge diving, the different types of sponges and even be witness to a diving and harvesting operation. Soak up the info for $5 for adults, $4 for seniors and $2 for students and kids ages 6 through 12.

Busch Gardens Tampa Bay

It's chills, it's thrills. It's adventure, it's nature. It's Busch Gardens Tampa Bay — the centerpiece attraction for kids of all ages who dare to enter "where wild things go." Sprawling along 335 magical acres, the park is ranked among the premier zoos in the nation. It houses more than 2,800 animals representing almost 320 species in its lush, tropical landscapes, cascading waterfalls and vast, rolling plains.

As theme-meisters go, the Busch organization is at the top of the adventure-to-remember list. Here you'll find it hard to believe that you're not actually in the exotic African villages that have been so painstakingly recreated. Taking our own aforementioned advice, we'll climb aboard the Trans-Veldt Railroad and start our tour at the back of the park so hopefully we can outwit the other fun-seekers and avoid long lines. Hold on to your flip-flops — here we go!

A note: Height determinations are made for children at each ride location, and the pee-wee adventurer must pass the tall test before boarding. For most rides, 42 to 48 inches is the minimum, and children must measure at least 52 inches to ride Kumba.

The Conga

As you step off the train, you're face to face with the meanest, scariest and most popular ride here. Kumba, one of the Southeast's largest and fastest roller coasters, is not for the faint of heart. You'll whip along nearly 4,000 feet of steel track, reaching a height of 143 feet and speeds exceeding 60 mph. You'll twist and turn through three

— continued on next page

first-of-a-kind roller coaster elements: a diving loop, a camelback and the world's largest vertical drop. And, when your voice finally returns from the pit of your stomach back up to your throat, we guarantee you'll "roar" — the translation of "kumba" in the Congo language. If your legs and bravery haven't given out, there's also the Python, a double-spiral corkscrew coaster that goes a mere 50 mph.

After a rush on the Congo River Rapids and the Monstrous Mamba, check out Claw Island, a lush habitat surrounded by water that houses rare white and yellow Bengal tigers. If you're as enamored with these magnificent animals as we are, you might want to slide into the Tiger's Den to pick up a souvenir decorated with these handsome creatures. For those who'd rather remember their ride on Kumba, march them to The Roar Store for a T-shirt.

Stanleyville

Following the railroad tracks, you're deposited at Stanleyville, a charming African village that boasts its own flavor of excitement. At the Tanganyika Tidal Wave, you will tranquilly glide through a lush jungle setting before being demonically plunged over a 55-foot drop that creates a formidable wall of water engulfing the observation bridge. More water thrills are at Stanley Falls, a log flume ride with a final drop of 40 feet for the four-passenger logs. Those with less ambition for self-punishment will thoroughly enjoy the shopping bazaar and live entertainment in the Stanleyville Theatre and Zambezi Pavilion. Animals to note: the orangutans and warthogs trained not to laugh at their drenched visitors. Nature lovers will truly appreciate the gorgeous Orchid Canyon, lush with beautiful plants and exotic animals from the tropics.

Timbukto

Replicating the ancient desert trading center, Timbukto is a great place to grab a bite to eat — that is if your tummy is back in correct position. Das Festhaus is a huge 1,000-seat dining (you must order the giant corned beef sandwich) and entertainment complex, with a little shopping bazaar tossed in for good luck. The Dolphin Theater is also here, featuring the Dolphins of the Deep Show. Take a real close look at the beautiful dolphin statue: It's made entirely out of recycled aluminum cans. If you're feeling a bit frisky, try the Scorpion coaster (with a 360-degree loop in the center!) and the Phoenix boat swing ride. Kids who need a break from physical action can stimulate their minds in either the games or electronic arcade while Mom heads to the West African Trading Company Ltd. for handcrafted gifts of brass, wood, leather, onyx, ceramic and much more.

Nairobi

Come face-to-face with a gorilla or a chimpanzee in the 3-acre Myombe Reserve. If your pleasure is for a smaller animal, visit the Victorian-style Nairobi Field Station animal nursery and see just how cute these critters can be before they eat their Wheaties. A petting zoo, reptile exhibits and elephant and tortoise displays are also here, along with Nocturnal Mountain where you can get a glimpse of animals normally seen only at night. The Show Jumping Hall of Fame is curiously part of the Nairobi experience.

Morocco

On to Morocco, a bustling city with restaurants, shops, authentic craft demonstrations and live entertainment in the Moroccan Palace and Marrakesh Theatres. If you've never seen a real live snake-charmer, this is the place to do so. It's here that you can rent

— continued on next page

Giraffes roam in the Serengeti Plain at Busch Gardens.

strollers and wheelchairs from Jeepers & Creepers. Morocco is also home to one of our favorite shops, The Nature Store, the best place to pick up a very special gift for friends and family back home. Even though this village sits at the very front entry to the park, you're far from done. Head west, young man, to ….

Bird Gardens

Do plan to get here in time for the World of Birds show, a truly feathered spectacular. Handy map guides that you'll pick up when you enter the park will announce current show times. Here you'll also share your space with exotic birds and birds of prey, and have a chance to see the four adorable fuzzy koalas that live with other species from Down

— continued on next page

Under. Catch your breath just for a minute before steering the kiddies to the new Land of the Dragons. Dragons fill this playground, led by the chief dragon named Dumphrey, who helps kids find their way around the three-story playhouse and just-for-kids rides. You can park yourself on a shaded bench while the kids run amock. You deserve it.

Egypt

Now here's one of the areas that keep the bold of heart coming back time after time … the 7-acre adventure called Egypt, the largest addition to the park and completed to the tune of an amazing $20 million. We'll start at the top, literally, with Montu, the largest inverted roller coaster in the whole wide world. Named after an Egyptian warrior god, Montu soars across nearly 4,000 feet of track at speeds of more than 60 mph. You'll swallow hard as you zoom through four elements never before seen on an inverted coaster, such as an inverse diving loop called the "Immelman," and a "Batwing" maneuver with its two 45-degree angled vertical loops.

Not enough for you? How about a 60-foot vertical loop through an underground themed excavation trench and then the world's largest inverted loop at a whopping 104 feet. If you should live through the terrors of Montu, take those shaky legs to check out King Tut's Tomb, a walk-through tour of a replica of the infamous king's burial site. Let the kids try their hands at an archeological sand dig, see the Pylon, a 55-foot wall covered with Egyptian symbols and figures and, lastly, browse the Treasures of the Nile shopping bazaar featuring Egyptian handicrafts and memorabilia.

Crown Colony

Tracking back to the front of the park, you'll find Crown Colony, with the Victorian-style Crown Colony House Restaurant and Hospitality Center. The restaurant is absolutely charming, the service superior and even the food, from chicken dinners and fresh seafood to heaping sandwiches, tastes all the better because of the breathtaking view overlooking the Serengeti Plain. If you're having ride withdrawal, take a twirl on the Questor simulator adventure ride. You must also take time to visit Clydesdale Hamlet, where six of the famous Clydesdale horses are boarded and pampered. From here, on to the last adventure, this time on the Monorail. We're off to the vast wilderness, known as …

The Serengeti Plain

More than 500 wild and wonderful African animals roam freely in herds on this 80-acre natural grassy veldt in the northeast corner of the park. Whether you take the elevated Monorail, or stay at ground level on the Trans-Veldt Railway (also departing from the Crown Colony), you'll most likely spot giraffes, rhinos, zebras, hippos, gazelles, impala, lions and even a Greater Kudus or two. The pristine landscape and tranquil sounds of nature are in complete contrast to the villages packed with thrill rides, but it is the one place to really soak in the enormity — and ingenuity! — of the Busch undertaking here at Busch Gardens Tampa Bay.

Highlighting your visit to the Serengeti Plain is your safari through the new 15-acre Edge of Africa, a so-called immersion experience into the world of the African animal-like lions, hyenas and hippos. In fact, it is as close to these magnificent animals in the recreated natural environs as a piece of glass will allow … lions can even enter the same vehicle you are sitting in, separated only by a pane of glass! The adventurous might actually enjoy crawling through termite mounds, and the more inquisitive will certainly enjoy tracking cave drawings to decode hidden messages. According to Busch representatives, Edge of Africa is the next step in transforming exhibits into more intimate, active and hands-on attractions.

Kids. Whatcha gonna do with 'em? You've run clean out of ideas, and they're running very close to having a temper tantrum that registers 7.8 on the Richter scale.

Kidstuff

You've buried them up to their necks in the sand. You've gotten them that triple scoop with sprinkles that they would absolutely die without ... Now! You bought that hard-to-find Beanie Baby that was immediately swept out in the first tide. You've told them "we're almost there" 47 times. You've run clean out of ideas, and they're running very close to having a temper tantrum that registers 7.8 on the Richter scale.

Kids. Whatcha gonna do with 'em? You're going to head straight to the car and drive them to one of the places all Tampa Bay parents go when they can see the handwriting on the wall (crayon, that is!). We did extensive "mommy and daddy on-the-street interviews," and here are the results of the practically unanimous votes.

Attractions

Busch Gardens
3000 E. Busch Blvd., Tampa
• **(813) 971-8282**

Flip to our Attractions chapter to get the full armchair tour of the excitement that just waits for your ticket. If you're a newcomer, area mommies suggest you sign up immediately for a season ticket; remember, all children younger than 3 get in free. Head for the Land of the Dragons, and let them whirl themselves into a frenzy with lead dragon, Dumphry, as you sit in the shade and chill.

Adventure Island
4500 E. Bougainvillea Ave., Tampa
• **(813) 971-7978**

Ditto on the Attractions chapter, but be prepared to get wet yourself, because you don't want those darn kids to hog all the fun themselves.

Fun Forest at Lowry Park
7525 North Blvd., Tampa
• **(813) 935-5503**

Introduced in its full glory in 1990, Fun Forest is new to your kids, but will remind you of an old-fashioned park with a big Ferris wheel, merry-go-round and bumper cars, along with numerous other little-person-only rides. Once you've led the little ones through the zoo, this is the perfect place to come to show them you really do care. Admission is free, but we know you'll gladly pay 50¢ a ride (or a coupon book for $12) to see the glee on their little faces while you rest your frazzled nerves on a shady bench.

Kid-Friendly Museums

Museum of Science and Industry (MOSI)
4801 E. Fowler Ave., Tampa
• **(813) 987-6300**

Yes, you read all about it in the Attractions chapter, but we can't really begin to tell

---

INSIDERS' TIP

Looking for a special way to make your child's birthday party a real wild time? Just give the Lowry Park Zoo a jingle. For about $75 to $85, the zoo'll supply the party animals, such as cockatoos, parakeets, snakes, unusual giant insects and the like. The uncaged carnivores are deftly monitored by zoo staffers, so they're not likely to take up residence, but partygoers still get an up-close and personal encounter of the slimy or feathered kind. To get the scoop on how to book a baby alligator for your next party, call the zoo at (813) 932-0245.

you how eye-opening this is for kids. Plus, if you plan a visit to the 350-seat MOSIMAX theater (where features are projected with a 180-degree fisheye lens onto an 85-foot high domed screen), we'll wager that you'll fight for the front-row seat yourself.

www.insiders.com

See this and many other **Insiders' Guide®** destinations online — in their entirety.

Visit us today!

crawl through the pitch-black 96-foot tunnel for kids 7 and older and playing firefighter (complete with firefighter coat and boots) on a fire engine with flashing lights for kids younger than 6. If you dare, match your wits against that brainy child in the Think Tank with its computer-ized brain twisters. Admission is $6 for adults, $5.50 for seniors and $5 for children ages 4 through 17. Visit Monday through Saturday from 10 AM until 5 PM and Sunday from noon until 5 PM.

Children's Museum of Tampa
7550 North Blvd., Tampa
• (813) 935-8441

Any people younger than 10 should be rushed immediately to the Children's Museum. Along with the ever-changing exhibits designed for the inquisitive touch (such as blowing giant bubbles!), you can steer them through the kid-sized town of Safety Village, where future drivers can learn the rules of the road in mini pedal cars, "shop" at a Publix/Eckerd store, play teller at the mini-bank, broadcast news as a TV anchorperson and even become a police officer or firefighter for a day. The museum itself serves as the entrance to Safety Village, where there is a kaleidoscope of hands-on exhibits that encourage even the shyest kid to get involved. Children younger than 2 are admitted free, and adults and children older than 2 will pay $3. It's open Monday through Thursday, 9 AM until 4:30 PM, Friday from 9 AM until 3 PM, Saturday from 10 AM until 5 PM and Sunday from 1 until 5 PM.

Great Explorations
The Pier, 800 Second Ave. N.E., St. Petersburg • (727) 821-8885

Featured in our Attractions chapter, Great Explorations is three stories of interactive thrills for kids of all ages. Must-dos include a

Science Center of Pinellas County
7701 22nd St. S., St. Petersburg
• (727) 384-0027

A museum that doubles as a teaching center, the Science Center offers fabulous in-house workshops covering topics such as computers, marine biology, rocketry, photography and more, along with field trips to places such as the Lowry Park Zoo and the Bishop Planetarium in Bradenton. In the Laser Odyssey Theatre, you'll be captivated by the Magical Music Tour and Pink Floyd's *Dark Side of the Moon*. Circling the theater are exhibits that feature electricity and optics, along with precious little iguanas and South American rodents.

Florida Gulf Coast Railroad Museum
U.S. Hwy. 301 and 83rd St., Parrish
• (941) 776-9656

Grab those pint-size engineers and choo-choo them to the Railroad Museum. Here you'll discover railroad cars from the 1920s and 1950s, plus you can all climb aboard for a 70-

INSIDERS' TIP

Little Thespians are certain to delight in the Kid Time Series of performances held at the Tampa Bay Performing Arts Center in Tampa. Five wonderful productions, specifically for children ages 5 through 11, are presented during the year on Sunday afternoons. For subscription information, call (813) 229-STAR. In St. Petersburg, check out the American Stage Children's Theatre. It offers a series of imaginative productions for the entire family. For current production calendar and ticket information, call (727) 822-8814.

Photo: Tampa Museum of Art

The children's art workshop at the Tampa Museum of Art encourages creative expression.

minute train ride through the ghost town of Willow. The train runs Saturdays at 11 AM, 1 PM and 3 PM and Sundays at 1 and 3 PM. An adult ticket to ride costs $8 and for children ages 3 through 11, $5.

Animals and Sea Creatures

Old McMickey's Farm
19215 Crescent Rd., Odessa
• (813) 920-2921

This is an absolutely marvelous escape for kids of all ages. Here you'll plant those children face to face with real-live, not-in-a-zoo animals. This is a complete miniature farm, so be prepared to milk a cow, go inside a chicken coop and, if your timing is right, see a mother pig nurse her young. You'll also ride a mule, pony or horse and even crawl through a hayloft and slide into the haystack that sits outside the two-story barn. If you survive, you're welcomed into Nature's Playground, a quarter-mile-long nature study around two lakes, complete with a fishing dock and a very popular two-story treehouse with fabulous rope swings. General admission costs $6 a person and it's worth every penny.

The Florida Aquarium
300 S. 13th St., Tampa • (813) 273-4020

Even the smallest child will stare in absolute amazement at the variety of animals, reptiles, sea creatures and birds that are housed at the Florida Aquarium along Tampa's downtown waterfront. While you're here, you might want to check out the Aquarium's "Baywalks on Tampa Bay," a real treat for older children. Every week, special guided tours of the coastal plants and animals are held at McKay Bay Nature Park in Tampa and Weedon Island County Preserve in St. Petersburg. Tours rotate between the parks, so call (813) 273-4020 for current times and schedules.

Lowry Park Zoo
7530 North Blvd., Tampa
• **(813) 932-0245**

Check out the stats in the Attractions chapter, but where kids are concerned, steer them right to the manatees. Maybe it's a genetic thing, but kids can stare for hours (well, maybe a half-hour) at these spectacular creatures.

Sunken Gardens
1825 Fourth St. N., St. Petersburg
• **(727) 896-3186**

Back to the Attractions chapter for this kid wonderland, too. The bird shows are the real draw for kids — make sure you go at scheduled times: 10 AM, noon, 2 and 4 PM.

Quiet Time

Barnes & Noble
213 N. Dale Mabry Hwy., Tampa
• **(813) 871-2228**
2501 Tyrone Blvd. N., St. Petersburg
• **(727) 384-5200**
122 Brandon TownCenter, Brandon
• **(813) 661-9883**

Yes, Barnes & Noble. Here, you can have the literary pleasure each Saturday of having someone else read fantastic tales to mesmerized kids. Current regularly scheduled story times are "Toddler Time" at 11 AM, and "Big Stories for Big Kids" at 11:30 AM. Both are free, but do arrive early to secure a front row seat for your little Dickens.

Bookstop
1251-B Fowler Ave., Tampa
• **(813) 977-0404**
2541 Countryside Blvd., Clearwater
• **(727) 791-9430**

Not only does the Bookstop stock one of the area's largest selection of children's books, the staff does a great job of enchanting youngsters ages 3 through 7 with their applauded Children's Story Hour. Check it out in the Tampa location every Saturday at 1 PM and at the Clearwater location every Saturday at noon.

County Libraries

County libraries also offer fabulous story hours for toddlers and older children. To find out current schedules and library locations in Hillsborough call (813) 273-3652; in Pinellas County call (727) 893-7724 for St. Petersburg and (727) 462-6800 for Clearwater. *Tampa Bay Family* magazine also has monthly listings of activities, entertainment and storytelling hours at Tampa Bay libraries.

Toys and Stuff

Once Upon a Child
14839 N. Dale Mabry Hwy., Tampa
• **(813) 264-6119**

Here's a place where kids can shop their baby hearts out and barely put a dent in your adult wallet. You'll find an amazing assortment of "kid's stuff with previous experience," from shorts and T-shirts, swimwear and toys to outdoor play equipment, books, strollers and cribs. Local parents are paid cash on-the-spot for their gently-used "outgrowns," and you and your little mall-shoppers-in-training can walk away with real, practically new bargains. A note for locals: if family or friends come to visit and you need a car seat, crib or other small-size paraphernalia, you can rent it here at a very reasonable price. Once Upon a Child is open Monday through Friday from 10 AM until 7 PM, Saturday from 10 AM until 6 PM and Sunday from noon until 5 PM.

Toys R Us
1235 E. Fowler Ave., Tampa
• **(813) 971-0091**
2486 U.S. Hwy. 19, Clearwater
• **(727) 797-5222**
1900 Tyrone Blvd., St. Petersburg
• **(727) 347-7272**

If your child is old enough to say, "Buy me!," we need not tell you any more about Toys R Us. Suffice it to say that you need not even attempt to enter these toy mega-stores unless you're prepared to spend some serious play money.

Young Editions
14308-B N. Dale Mabry Hwy., Tampa
• **(813) 963-0214**

Toys that do more than break ... they open the imagination. Young Editions is the best place to find the full selection of GeoSafari learning toys, along with Playmobil, Brio and more. Choose puzzles, games, books, toys and more, all with a focus on stimulating young minds under the premise of having lots of fun.

FAO Schwartz
260 Westshore Plaza, Tampa
• **(813) 287-0010**

From the two-story clock tower at its entrance to the waving Kermit the Frog, FAO Schwartz gives kids of all ages the opportunity to interact with dozens of toys and displays of all sizes in this satellite store of the famous New York City emporium. Featured are a miniature train for your miniature engineers and a whole Barbie section for your own little doll. Be there during Westshore Plaza hours: Monday through Saturday from 10 AM until 9 PM and Sunday from noon until 5:30 PM.

Recreation

There's hardly a vacationing family that doesn't jump aboard either a rented or charter vessel during their stay along the Gulf of Mexico. If you fit this category, and especially if you're from a "dry" hometown, here are just a few tips to guarantee your children's safety while sailing into our crystal blue waters.

Every child should wear a life preserver. Check to make sure that the life preserver has a flotation collar and a strongly stitched lifting ring on the back and the front.

Always attach a safety line to a child's life preserver. If the child should fall overboard, they can pull themselves toward the boat. While this is always important, it is absolutely critical if seas become rough.

Children should always be seated in the most stable area of the craft. This is normally near the transom.

If you're on a rented vessel with very young children, check to make certain there are latches and locks on those compartments that may hold toxic substances, including the head.

Companionway stairs should be blocked. Use a plastic gate or nylon netting to prevent any falls by active children.

If you prefer to stay closer to dry ground, there are so many outdoor places and indoor facilities where you and your children can burn off excess energy. Here are a few of our favorites.

City Parks

They're free, they're fun, they're all around you. Here, those mini-bundles of energy can run full out to let off steam, hike along nature trails and roll themselves dizzy in the grass. Favorite parks for local mommies in Pinellas County are Fossil Park (with its foam-padded playground for your clumsy little climbers), Crescent Lake (with a great swimming pool) and Fort DeSoto (with super beaches plus the cherished fort that kids can explore). In Hillsborough County, Lowry Park (right next to the zoo), Al Lopez Park (with its great playground equipment) and Ben T. Davis Beach (with its shallow, calm waters) are moms' favorites. For the details on all our local parks, see the Parks and Recreation Chapter.

Ice-Skating

In Tampa Bay? You betcha! As soon as they're steady on their feet, ice-skating is a wonderful way to get those coordination genes working full time. Actually, many a mom has advised that the younger they are, the less fear they have. Maybe it's because they're so close to the ground, or ice, that they don't have that far to fall. Find places to hit the ice on rented skates at Centre Ice at Countryside, Countryside Mall, (727) 796-0586; and Sun Blades Ice Skating Center, 13940 Icot Boulevard in Clearwater, (727) 536-5843.

In-line and Roller Skating

If your kids feel safer with wheels instead of blades strapped to their feet, rush them to Skate Odyessy, 14210 N. Nebraska Avenue, Tampa, (813) 632-3700; Skateland of Brandon, 750 Robertson W., Brandon, (813) 681-3635; or Southland Roller Palace, 10001 66th Street N., Pinellas Park, (727) 546-0018.

Congo River Golf
20060 U.S. 19 N., Clearwater
• **(727) 797-4222**

Just across from Clearwater Mall, your young explorers can follow in the footsteps of the famous African Congo explorers Henry Stanley and David Livingston as you putt-putt through a lush tropical environment, complete with waterfalls, streams and mountainous terrain. While there are many miniature golf places throughout the area, Congo River, operated by the Golf & Exploration Co., is the hands-down favorite. And when you're too pooped to putt, you can collapse on a shaded bench while your mini-people run amuck in the Family Fun Arcade that's packed with the typical arcade games. It opens daily at 10 AM. You'll also find a cloned Congo River in Tampa across from Busch Gardens at 4011 E. Busch Boulevard, (813) 988-9888.

Create 'n' Play
4212 W. Kennedy Blvd., Tampa
• **(813) 289-PLAY**

Want to see your kid's eyes light up like firecrackers? Just walk them through the door of Create 'n' Play and watch them scatter like hyper mice. They'll discover a bubble room, giant sandbox, dinosaur cave, shadow room, role playing and arts and crafts activities galore. Parents, thankfully, can relax in the parent's cafe and stay out of the bedlam. The price is right, too. For just $4.99, kids can play until they collapse (or it's naptime, whichever comes first). Children younger than 1 and parents are admitted free. Closed on Mondays, the center is open Tuesday and Wednesday from 9:30 AM until 5 PM, Thursday through Saturday from 9:30 AM until 8:30 PM and Sunday from 10:30 AM until 5:30 PM.

Kidscene Imagination Playhouse
3300 Ninth St. N., St. Petersburg
• **(727) 894-2611**

Everything here is kid-sized, from the grocery store and kitchen to the puppet theater and work bench. Parents are requested to play alongside their child as they become stars in the theater, create masterpieces in the arts and crafts studio or celebrate in the special party room. The opportunity for play is almost endless, that is if you can keep the kids out of the enormous 150-square-foot indoor sandbox! Toddlers to preteens will pay $5.35; parents are free. Closed on Sunday, Kidscene is open Monday through Saturday from 9:30 AM until 2:30 PM.

Q-Zar
7807 N. Dale Mabry Hwy., Tampa
• **(813) 933-6995**

Let's see if we can describe this. A smoky arena. Laser-shooting phasers. Techno music. Flashing strobe lights. Up to 40 players

wearing vests with targets creep through swirling smoke; their sole goal is to zap the opponent. This is Laser Tag. Older children can get their hearts beating fast for $7 for each 15-minute game. If virtual reality appeals to your child, $5 will buy them a five-minute experience under the computerized mask that will take them to a three-dimensional computerized world. Q-Zar is looking for you Monday though Thursday from 3 until 11 PM, Friday from 3 PM until 1 AM, Saturday from 10 AM until 1 AM and Sunday from noon until 10 PM.

Malibu Grand Prix
14300 N. Nebraska Ave., Tampa
• **(813) 977-8370**

Send that little hot-rodder wheeling around the tracks in fine Grand Prix form. Or try out a go-cart, 36 holes of miniature golf, batting cages or two state-of-the-art game rooms. It's all here at Malibu Grand Prix, the perfect place to bring the family when everyone's feeling that need for speed. Operating hours and prices vary with the season, so call ahead to check it out. If you're visiting and staying at a local hotel, see the front desk for discount coupons and group rates.

Celebration Station
U.S. Hwy. 60 and I-75, Tampa
• **(813) 661-4557**
U.S. Hwy. 19, Clearwater
• **(727) 791-1799**

This place is to kids as a mall is to mom ... tiny little hearts start beating fast as you pull in the parking lot with the anticipation of the scatter-and-panic glee of not knowing where you want to go first. Go-carts, bumper boats, Playland super-playground, batting cages, miniature golf, miles of arcade games ... and a great pizza restaurant to refuel. You can buy a Pass Play that allows unlimited access to all the outdoor attractions, or a Family Value Pack that includes everthing your entire family needs for a full day of food and fun. The restaurant and arcade are open noon until 9 PM Monday through Thursday, with outdoor activities opening at 4 PM. On Friday, the restaurant and arcade are open from noon until midnight, with outdoor activities again opening at 4 PM. All activities are open 10 AM until midnight on Saturday and 10 AM until 9 PM on Sunday. The Clearwater location is 2.5 miles north of U.S. 60.

Get the hang of what it's like to be an eel at the Florida Aquarium.

Kidz Kastle
16017 Tampa Palms Blvd., Tampa
• (813) 975-9112

Kids rule in this 11,000-square-foot indoor playground in Tampa Palms Shopping Center. Kids can scamper between 22 different play areas, give the video games a try and generally let off steam while you relax in the nifty Quiet Room. Sip on a cup of coffee and watch those kiddies on closed-circuit TV.

Chuck E. Cheese
14308 N. Dale Mabry Hwy., Carrollwood
• (813) 963-7200
1024 58th St. N., St. Petersburg
• (727) 345-3736

You'll find one of these popular national game places in practically every major neigh-

borhood throughout both Hillsborough and Pinellas counties. Charge on over to Chuck E. Cheese and you can be certain that if you come within a football-field distance of one, your kids will be pointing it out.

Balloon Palace
14995 Gulf Blvd., Madeira Beach
• (727) 393-2706

While not really a kids-only place, the Balloon Palace has a very kid-friendly menu, with loads of options for finger foods such as pizza fingers, chicken wings and fish sticks. The real draws are the dozens of miniature hot-air balloons that float across the ceiling, and the loosey-goosey beach-party atmosphere. This is a guaranteed hit for the whole family.

Insiders know that the party to end all Bay area parties takes place in February — Gasparilla! Pirates and maidens and beads, oh my!

Annual Events

There are only two reasons for having nothing to do during your free time around Tampa Bay — either you're a very dull person, or it's August. Actually, you're just a very dull person because even August offers up a few events to take your mind off the heat, the humidity and the height of head-thumping summer.

Most visitors dream of spending long days at the beach, being washed by warm sun and soft sea breezes and rocked by the Gulf's languid sounds of lapping waves. Those of us who live here, and any traveler who picks up a weekend newspaper, know that such a Zen approach to leisure is strongly countered by a desire to party, party, party! — over any excuse at all and preferably outside. With so much glorious weather to make use of, you can be sure that parties, events and festivals abound year round.

Insiders know that the party to end all Bay area parties takes place in February — Gasparilla! Pirates and maidens and beads, oh my! Tampa's version of Mardi Gras draws hundreds of thousands of people from across the nation to Bayshore Boulevard and downtown for this pirate invasion, parade and blowout weekend event. The celebration actually continues over the course of several weeks, so we've devoted a Close-up in this chapter to all the fun that's included in Gasparilla.

Dressing up as pirates is just one of the popular costume events. If you suggest donning a tux or gown, you'll hear a chorus of derisive snorts. Guys here think "dressing up" means wearing socks. But give us a good excuse and in a New York minute we'll garb ourselves in outrageous or ridiculous "finery." From Gasparilla to Guavaween and almost everything in between, some of the best fun you'll have is gasping in delight at what others are (or aren't) wearing. Even the most staid transplant from Lake Wobegon soon discovers that playing dress-up is as much fun at 40 or 80 as it was when you were 4.

There's an incredible array of fun stuff to do every single month around the Tampa Bay area. It would take a book as thick as this entire guide to fully detail all the activities and events. So, what follows is a month-by-month overview of the major happenings. It's a good idea to check *The Tampa Tribune's* "FridayExtra!," the *St. Petersburg Times'* "Weekend" sections included in Friday editions or the alternative *Weekly Planet* for the most comprehensive coverage of what's taking place around town.

In other chapters, we usually list information according to whether it's in Hillsborough or Pinellas county. In this chapter, however, events are listed by month and generally in order of when they occur during that month. Participating in all these events is so much fun that where they're held matters a lot less than when they're held.

Unless otherwise noted, there's no admission fee, but count on having lots of places, such as vendors and food booths, to spend your cash. And keep in mind that all the festivities provide a great time, even on the tightest budget. So, like my mom always says, get up and do something — you'll feel better.

January

Outback Bowl
Raymond James Stadium, 4201 N. Dale Mabry Hwy., Tampa • (813) 874-2695

This nationally televised New Year's Day football game at Raymond James Stadium matches third-ranked teams from the SEC and Big Ten Conference in a post-season showdown. A week-long series of events scheduled around the Bay area lead up to the 11 AM game. Outback Bowl tickets cost $40 and become available through TicketMaster, (813) 287-8844 (or check your local directory), in October. But it's usually later than that before we find out who'll be playing.

Feast of the Epiphany
13 Hibiscus St., Tarpon Springs
• (813) 937-3540

Epiphany, which falls on the Twelfth Day of Christmas and marks Christ's baptism, is both a solemn and joyful occasion for the Greek Orthodox. This day-long celebration in Tarpon Springs begins at St. Nicholas Cathedral. After worship, a processional travels from the church to Spring Bayou. There, a white dove of peace is released, and the Bishop blesses a cross and tosses it into the chilly water. A hoard of young men dive to retrieve it because legend has it that the one who finds it can expect a year of luck and blessings. Blessing of the sponge fleet, plus Greek foods, music and dancing round out the day for more than 40,000 celebrants.

Martin Luther King Jr. Celebration
Downtown St. Petersburg
• (727) 327-0085

A variety of events take place in St. Petersburg throughout the weeks leading up to the anniversary of the late reverend's birth. Annual essay contest awards and presentations are made at the Enoch Davis Center, 1111 18th Avenue S. Kingfest is a celebration of black achievement at the Pinellas Pioneer Settlement, 2900 31st Street S. A commemorative concert with the Florida Orchestra and Florida Gospel Choir is held at Bayfront's Mahaffey Theater. The Southern Christian Leadership Conference hosts the Martin Luther King Jr. Festival of the Bands at Al Lang Stadium. There's a candlelight walk from Straub Park to the Bayfront Center, where another Festival of Bands is held. Then, Dr. King's birthday, honored on the third Monday of the month, is the date for the SCLC's Annual Drum Major For Justice National Parade along Bayshore Drive to Central Avenue, down Martin Luther King Jr. Street to Third Avenue.

For information on the essay contest, call (727) 893-7134; for the gospel concert, (727) 286-2403; and for the candlelight walk, (727) 893-7134.

www.insiders.com

See this and many other **Insiders' Guide®** destinations online — in their entirety.

Visit us today!

Snowbird Extravaganza
Florida State Fairgrounds, U.S. Hwy. 301
at I-4, Tampa • (800) 265-3200

What started out as an annual gathering for the Canadian Snowbird Association now pulls more than 50,000 people from around the United States and our northern neighbor for two days of nationally known entertainment and consumer exhibits. The event is usually held near the end of January. Watch local papers or call for specific dates and detailed information.

February

Gasparilla

There are parades in the day and parades at night, parties, stage events, marathon races, art festivals, sailboat races, equestrian shows and believe it or not — more! These events and festivities are all part of this wonderful, weeks-long celebration in and around downtown Tampa known as Gasparilla. Since there's far too much to tell you about in just a paragraph or two, we're devoting a special Close-up in this chapter to capture all the excitement.

Florida State Fair
Florida State Fairgrounds, U.S. Hwy. 301
at I-4, Tampa • (813) 621-7821

We host the largest major fair in the Southeast, featuring one of the largest midways in the country. For two weeks starting early in the month, more than 86 rides and shows spread over 325 acres at the Florida State Fairgrounds east of Tampa. There's a wide variety of agricultural, educational and arts and crafts exhibits, plus lots of livestock. There's also a glimpse into Florida's Cracker lifestyle at the turn of the century. Concerts feature headline entertainment to please everyone, ranging from comedy to country, rock to rap. Concert ticket prices vary, but usually they're downright cheap! Last year, fairgoers got to see Bill Cosby for a whopping $5! Daily admission to the fair is $7 for adults and $4 for children ages 6 through 11. Group discount rates and advance tickets are available at lower prices, plus special days give you ways to get in for less. Parking is free. The fairgrounds are 7 miles east of Tampa off I-4 exits 4, 5 and 6A. You can plan on heavy traffic since more than a million people attend every year.

Florida Writer's Conference
Univ. of South Florida, 140 Seventh Ave. S., St. Petersburg • (727) 974-1711

Writers of every age, ilk and ability converge on the University of South Florida's St. Petersburg campus for one of the finest conferences in the nation. Starting the first Thursday of February and running through Saturday, dozens of award-winning and highly regarded authors — the likes of John Updike, Peter Mathiessen, Sterling Watson and Garbiel Horn — present seminars on the techniques of fiction, poetry, journalism, playwriting, screenwriting and publishing. Registration is required. The cost is $110 if paid in advance and $135 at the door. Teachers and students qualify for a substantial discount. Call (813) 974-2403 to register in advance.

LPGA Tour
7979 Bayou Club Blvd., Largo • (727) 444-4444 Ext. 8

February may be the shortest month, but it's the longest on golf events around Tampa Bay. And starting the month is the Ladies Pro Golf Association Tournament. A purse of at least $500,000 attracts some of the top women players in the nation to this four-day competition. Call the tournament activity line for up-to-date information on times, tickets and prices.

GTE Suncoast Classic
Van Dyke Rd., Tampa • (813) 265-4653

Three-quarters of a million dollars in prizes will catch anyone's attention, and it sure attracts the Senior PGA Tour. In turn, these outstanding golfers draw nearly 200,000 spectators to Tampa's Tournament Players Club course at Cheval. And millions more are attracted through ESPN's live and taped coverage. Tournament week begins with practice rounds on Monday and Tuesday followed by pro-am tournaments on Wednesday and Thursday. Then from 8 AM until 5 PM on Friday, Saturday and Sunday, the tour players get down to the really serious business of a 54-hole championship. The par 71 course allows spectators to view multiple holes from nearly any vantage point. Admission costs $20 Tuesday through Thursday and $25 Friday through Sunday, and all proceeds benefit local charities. Parking costs $3.

As a non-golfer, this Insider will attest to two things: This really is fun; and Chi Chi Rodriguez is known to smile very brightly at redheads! For an in-depth Insider's view of the GTE Suncoast Classic, check the Golf chapter for our Close-up on this event.

Ebony Fashion Show
Tampa • (813) 229-8117
St. Petersburg • (727) 872-5767

This is one of 190 shows, held in the United States, Canada and the Bahamas, where glamorous models in stunning fashion take to the runway for charity. But there's just as much fashion to drool over in the audience — gorgeous women in gowns, handsome men in tuxes and even children dressed to the nines — that adds to the aura of this event. The multicultural fund-raiser is held in Tampa to benefit the Tampa-Hillsborough Urban League Guild. The following night, the fashion show moves to St. Petersburg's Bayfront Center on behalf of Alpha Kappa Alpha. Tickets are $25 and $30, and reservations are a must.

Florida Grand Prix of St. Petersburg
Downtown St. Petersburg • (727) 894-7749

The world's fastest sports car drivers turn the streets around Tropicana Field into the fast lane at the end of the month. Practice laps in all

INSIDERS' TIP

Paint Your Heart Out Tampa! is a great way to spend a Saturday early in April. Thousands of volunteers converge on more than 100 homes to paint exteriors and do minor repairs for elderly, low-income residents. Call (813) 915-1735 to volunteer — it's an event that will warm your heart as well as someone else's.

Strawberries are one of Tampa Bay's strongest agriculture products, and there's an annual festival in honor of the succulent berry.

six race classes are on Friday. Saturday brings qualifying and practice laps with two World Challenge races on the 1.6-mile, eight-turn course. Sunday brings a variety of other races plus the biggie, the first race of the annual SCAA Pro Racing Trans-Am Championship. Throughout the whole weekend, take in the Sports/Lifestyles Expo and a midway that kids of all ages will love. Friday is "Free Prix Day," which means no gate admission. Two-day (Saturday and Sunday) general admission costs $20 and allows one adult ticket holder to bring in two kids younger than 12 at no extra charge. Reserved grandstand seats are $35 and $45, and three-day Race Car Paddock passes are $20. The venue opens daily at 9 AM and closes at 6 PM.

Strawberry Festival
2200 W. Reynolds St. (S.R. 574), Plant City • (813) 752-9194
    This festival, which marks the height of the strawberry season, typically gets under way

the next to the last day of February. Since the majority of the event's activities are held during the next month, we've included all the "juicy" details there. See the first write-up in March.

March

Strawberry Festival
2200 W. Reynolds St. (S.R. 574), Plant City • (813) 752-9194
    This 11-day festival begins in Plant City on the next to the last day of February and draws hundreds of thousands of visitors from around the nation at the height of fresh strawberry season. Visitors not only indulge in those sweet, bite-sized fruits fixed every which way you can imagine, but also are treated to free, daily concerts by some of the biggest acts in country music. Every year the Strawberry Festival folks seem to outdo the past

by booking Nashville's greatest. And people throng to the stands hours before showtime to grab seats for acts that have included Reba MacEntire, The Judds, Randy Travis, John Anderson, Wayne Newton, Vince Gill, Pam Tillis (who was born in Plant City, she proudly points out), Kathy Matea, Billy Ray Cyrus, Joe Diffie, Charlie Daniels, Kenny Rogers ... how long a list would you like? If you want reservations for the concerts, tickets cost just $8 for ground-level seats and $4 for seats on the west bleachers.

And believe it or not, you'll find more than just berries and music at this old-fashioned country-style fair. You'll enjoy a baby parade and contest, cook-offs, farm animal and agriculture judging, a milking contest, the Queen's Pageant, an art show, a parade through downtown Plant City, plus a huge midway of games and rides and, of course, a strawberry shortcake-eating contest.

Admission costs $6 for anyone older than 10, but discount days can lower that price. The festival grounds are about 24 miles east of Tampa. Follow I-4 east to Exit 10 (Branch Forbes Road) or Exit 11 (Thonotosassa Road). Head south from there and all ways leading to the festival are clearly marked. Parking on the grounds costs $3, and off-property rates are offered at different prices.

Renaissance Festival
Central Park Dr. at E. Bay Dr., Largo
• (727) 586-5423

For six weekends from early March through mid-April, the storybook days of medieval lords, ladies, jesters and jousters come alive behind the Largo Library. Each weekend is given a specific theme, which makes stepping back in time fun over and over again. While living the days of yore is pretend, some things are very, very real, including the armored contact jousting that takes place twice daily. A few years ago, one competitor landed in the hospital after a lance blow to the head. Less dangerous, but just as fascinating, are the human chess matches, hundreds of costumed entertainers and the Children's Realm, with theater and ancient games. More than 125 crafters offer handmade wares, from glass artistry to clothing, and food vendors hawk roast

turkey drumsticks, apple dumplings and more modern delights. At the gate, tickets cost $11.95 for adults and children older than 4 (only $9.95 if you're 55 or older) and $4.95 for children younger than 4. Advance purchase saves a dollar, and remember to check local papers for discount coupons. Parking is free.

Chiselers' Market
Univ. of Tampa, Kennedy Blvd., Tampa
• (813) 253-3333

A volunteer's joshing remark to her friends while working on a fireplace led to this annual fund-raiser for renovations to H.B. Plant Hall at the University of Tampa. Now one of the oldest incorporated volunteer preservation groups in the state, the Chiselers hold an annual sale, usually in early March, with a variety of departments ranging from bargains to gourmet goods. The event date floats a bit, but usually falls on the second Saturday during the university's spring break. Plant Hall is on the east side of Kennedy Boulevard near downtown Tampa — you can't miss it; it's the beautiful red brick building topped by silver minarets.

Winter Equestrian Festival
Florida State Fairgrounds, U.S. Hwy. 301 at I-4, Tampa • (813) 623-5801, (800) 237-8924

Top riders and their mounts, included on the world's richest hunter-jumper horse show circuit, compete at the Bob Thomas Equestrian Center at the Florida State Fairgrounds during this nearly three-week event. Princess Anne showed up one year, attesting to the event's international acclaim. The competition climaxes around the first of April with the $100,000-purse American Invitational that is covered by ESPN.

Admission to events at the fairgrounds costs $6 on weekdays and $8 on weekends. Tickets to the American Invitational, held at Raymond James Stadium, cost between $10 and $20 if purchased in advance and slightly more at the gate. To reach the fairgrounds, take I-4 east to Exit 5 (Orient Road) and follow signs to the Equestrian Center. Raymond James Stadium is on Dale Mabry Highway, north of I-275.

Jose O'Reilly St. Patrick's Day Parade
Seventh Ave., Tampa • (813) 248-3712

It may just be a bunch of blarney, but isn't everybody Irish on St. Patty's Day? Sure, an' begora! More than 100 entries fill a 12-block parade route with floats, bands, bagpipers, a drum corps, horses and motorcycles at this Saturday festival. The parade gets under way at 7 PM.

President's Cup Regatta
Harbour Island, Tampa • (813) 253-6241

Top collegiate rowers from such schools as Yale, Dartmouth and others compete in scores of scull races along Seddon Channel off Tampa's Harbour Island. Other contests take place on the Hillsborough River at the University of Tampa. A corporate challenge for business executives adds a level of mirth to the sporting excitement. Call ahead for details on what's taking place when and who's participating.

Bark In The Park
4810 N. Himes Ave., Tampa
• (813) 274-8615

Pack up the puppy and head out mid-month for a tail-wagging good time at Al Lopez Park. This festival for dogs and their humans includes obedience demonstrations, pet vendors, an obstacle course run, a Frisbee contest, a talent show and K-9 Fun Run. All dogs must be leashed and wearing their rabies vaccination tags. The event lasts from 10 AM until 2 PM.

Country In The Park
Town Square, Pinellas Park
• (727) 541-0700

This event, sponsored by the City of Pinellas Park, the Chamber of Commerce and various public service organizations, promises a fun-filled day of music, exhibits and demonstrations. Always held on the third Saturday of the month, the town square fills with everything from free food to a community blooddrive. You'll enjoy face painting, clowns, a potted tree sale, seedling giveaways and lots of

musical entertainment on two stages. One of the most popular elements is an arts and crafts show that draws 150 vendors. There's also a trade show, so you can get to know at least 100 local businesses. Town Square is bounded by 78th Avenue, 52nd Street, 82nd Avenue and 49th Street.

Tampa Bay Blues Festival
Vinoy Park, St. Petersburg
• (727) 287-8844

Ry Cooder says to "get rhythm when you got the blues." And since blues is a rhythm of its own, you don't have to have the blues to get the blues. You just have to hie yourself down to Vinoy Park where you'll get the best of blues like they're played in Chicago, the Delta and the bayou. Daily and two-day passes may be purchased for this festival, which is usually held during the middle of the month. Prices are slightly higher if bought the day of the show. Vinoy Park is on Bayshore Drive at Fifth Avenue N.E.

International Folk Fair
Vinoy Park, St. Petersburg
• (727) 327-7999

Ethnic foods, arts, crafts, songs and dances represent more than 50 nations during this three-day, mid-March festival. Members of each national group set up a village decorated to reflect a landmark or identifying decor, and present a cultural exhibit of their native country. Along with mini-performances in the villages, continuous entertainment fills the main stage. The audience can get into the performing fun on a showcase stage for dancing, storytelling and other activities. Admission costs $6 for adults, $4 for senior adults, and $3 for children 6 through 14. Kids younger than 6 are admitted free. Group rates are available. Vinoy Park is on Bayshore Drive at Fifth Avenue N.E.

Mardi Gras on Main Street
Downtown Dunedin • (727) 733-3197

Can't make it to the Crescent City? Try Fat Tuesday in Dunedin. A parade, beads, food,

INSIDERS' TIP

Palm Harbor celebrates its 1878 founding with an outdoor festival on the first Saturday in May.

beads, street musicians, beads, palm readers, beads and kids and adults dressed in costumes (and beads) make for a fun night.

Pinellas County Fair
7901 Park Blvd., Pinellas Park
• **(727) 541-6941**

A week of fun kicks off at the end of March when the fair officially opens. Weekday hours are from 1 until 11 PM and on Saturday and Sunday, 10 AM until 11 PM. You'll find about 60 rides on the midway and two stages with continuous entertainment, including nationally known acts. For more homespun fun, watch the judging of livestock, baking, canning and home crafts. Almost every day has a special promotion allowing free admission such as Senior Citizen's Day, Law Enforcement Day or Church Bulletin Day. Discounts are also available with newspaper coupons. But even if you pay full price, you won't go broke — general admission for persons older than 7 usually costs less than $5, and parking costs $1.

Old Hyde Park Village Art Festival
Snow Ave., Tampa • (813) 251-3500

Old Hyde Park Village turns into a pedestrian mall throughout a weekend near the end of the month and then again in late October, filled with exhibits by nearly 150 artists. Strollers browse fine arts in watercolors, photographs and a variety of other mediums from 10 AM until 6 PM during this Friday, Saturday and Sunday event. You'll also enjoy the upscale ambiance of the Village stores and restaurants. Old Hyde Park Village is off Swann Avenue between Bayshore Boulevard and Howard Avenue.

Virginia Slims Legends
Saddlebrook Resort, 5700 Saddlebrook Way, Wesley Chapel • (813) 973-1111

Although Saddlebrook Resort is slightly outside our book's immediate boundaries for the Tampa Bay area, any tennis enthusiast knows some things are worth driving for, and the short distance to Wesley Chapel qualifies. It's especially worth it when it comes to watching the legends of the Women's Tennis Association. Part of a six-stop tour, this exhibition competition has attracted such stellar names

as Chris Evert, Martina Navratilova, Billie Jean King, Tracy Austin and Evonne Goolagong for two days of play. To get to Saddlebrook Resort, follow I-275 north to State Road 54, then head east. Call ahead for ticket prices.

April

Renaissance Festival
Central Park Dr. at E. Bay Dr., Largo
• **(727) 586-5423**

This festival, which began early last month, continues on weekends through mid-April. See our write-up in March for all the details.

Festival of States
Downtown St. Petersburg
• **(727) 898-3654**

What originated in 1896 as a birthday party for Washington, is now the largest civic celebration in the South. More than 500,000 people enjoy 10 days of events that include two parades, a major fireworks display, concerts headlined by stars such as Ray Charles, B.B. King, Belinda Womack and REO Speedwagon, a 5K race, a national high school band competition, art shows and auto and motorcycle shows.

Oldsmar Days & Nights
Downtown Oldsmar • (813) 855-4233

During four days in the first week of April, Oldsmar celebrates community pride with carnival rides, food, costumed characters, a parade and live entertainment. Most of the fun takes place at R.E. Olds Park on Shore Drive at Bayview Boulevard. Just a note for the curious: Olds, the town's namesake, is more famous for the cars he built. The parade starts at 10 AM Saturday in front of the Oldsmar Civic Club on St. Petersburg Drive (Fla. Highway 580) and ends near Buckingham Avenue and Chestnut Street. The Oldsmar Chamber of Commerce, at the number listed, can tell you more.

Pioneer Jamboree
2900 31st St. S., St. Petersburg
• **(727) 866-6401, (727) 894-7519**

Pinellas County gives you a chance early in the month to step back in time with bluegrass and folk music, antique engines, Native American crafts and old-timey children's games. The Jamboree takes place at the Pinellas Pioneer Settlement, which is open year round. General admission costs $2. Hours are Saturday from 9 AM until 5 PM and Sunday from 9 AM until 4 PM.

Tampa/Hillsborough Storytelling Contest
5000 Central Ave., Tampa
• **(813) 273-3648**

A vivid imagination is wonderful, and it comes to life through the spoken word of story spinners whose skills have either been honed through decades of experience or are just developing. Professional storytellers join amateurs early in the month at Hillsborough High School for this Saturday event. For more information, call the Friends of the Library at the number listed.

American Stage in the Park
First Ave. S., St. Petersburg
• **(727) 822-8814**

Demens Landing on downtown St. Petersburg's waterfront is the nightly site from early April till mid-May for Shakespeare as your English teacher never imagined. Each year, the American Stage company reworks one of the bard's masterpieces, adding music and updating costumes, sets and direction. But the words remain the same. It puts a whole new spin on Elizabethan prose to hear *As You Like It* done as a 1920s Chicago guys-and-dolls musical, or *Two Gents* (a.k.a. *The Two Gentlemen of Verona*) set in the 1950s, or *Much Ado About Nothing* filled with the songs of Cole Porter. People hauling blankets and lawn chairs flock to the grounds within minutes of the 6 PM opening. You can plan on buying supper and drinks from one of the local vendors. It's wise to get tickets in advance. You can call the box office for information. Admission costs $7 for persons older than 12, and reserved rental seating is available for $22. Coupons regularly appear in local papers.

Artworks!
Downtown St. Petersburg
• **(727) 821-4069**

This city-wide festival of art, music, theater and dance kicks off with American Stage's Shakespeare in the Park production and runs for two weeks, including three weekends. There are self-guided tours of participating galleries, museum visits, special exhibits, masterworks concerts and more. Call ahead for a brochure chock-full of dates and locations.

Mainsail Sidewalk Art Show
Beach Dr. at Fifth Ave. N., St. Petersburg
• **(727) 893-7734**

Wrapping up the city-wide Artworks! celebration, Mainsail draws hundreds of artists and thousands of art admirers to North Straub Park. Entertainment takes place throughout the event, but the biggest stars of the show are artists from across the country who work in a variety of formats. The event runs from 9 AM until 6 PM on Saturday and 9 AM until 5 PM on Sunday.

Dunedin Highland Games & Festival
Downtown Dunedin • **(727) 733-6240**

Everyone's a Scotsman in Dunedin during this week of mid-month fun. But you needn't wear a kilt, laddie, just join in. The City of Dunedin Pipe Band leads opening and closing ceremonies. Military Tattoo, with spit-and-polish troops, starts the week's festivities. Grand music and drill units are performed at night by torch light in Dunedin High School's Memorial Stadium, 1131 McLean Street. There are also dance exhibitions and contests such as the sheaf toss, hammer throw and tossing the caber — a 15-to-20-foot pole weighing as much as 150 pounds. Festival events take place at Highlander Park off Michigan Boulevard west of Pinehurst Road.

Fun N' Sun Festival
Downtown Clearwater • **(727) 562-4804**

A string of events pulls more than 150,000 people to Clearwater from mid-April through early May. Among the bigger draws are an oldies kickoff concert, a Country-Western dance, a tree sale and Earth Day, a family fun day at Clearwater High School and a celebration at Pier 60. There are more concerts and dances, a 5K run, tennis, golf, softball, fishing, horseshoes, fencing, storytelling, duplicate bridge, a pancake festival and an illuminated night parade. With so much happening, there's something going on at all times for all ages. Small admission fees are charged for some events.

Tarpon Springs Arts & Crafts Festival
Craig Park, Tarpon Springs
• **(813) 937-6109**

Craig Park on Spring Bayou is the beatific setting where more than 200 artists from across the country display their works for sale and judging. A special area is set aside for children's activities, and there's plenty of music, including a free concert on Saturday evening. The art show runs from 9 AM until 6 PM Saturday and from 10 AM until 5 PM Sunday. Admission is $1 for anyone older than 16. Spring Bayou is at the end of Tarpon Avenue west off U.S. Hwy. 19.

Air Fest
MacDill AFB, S. Dale Mabry Hwy., Tampa
• **(813) 828-1110**

On a weekend late in the month, this is the place to be — not only to see the oldest and the latest in air technology, but also to get a closer view of the Blue Angels or Thunderbirds who usually are on hand with their aerial acrobatics. Get started early because more than a half-million visitors start flowing onto the base through four gates when they open at 8 AM. Events last till 5 PM, but count on the gates closing by midday because of the crowd. Head to the base via West Shore Boulevard, S. Dale Mabry Highway, MacDill Avenue or Bayshore Boulevard.

Jose Cuervo Gold Crown
400 Mandalay Ave., Clearwater Beach
• **(727) 461-3222**

Clearwater Beach is popular with volleyball players and never is it more so than during this competition that's part of the Fun N' Sun Festival near the end of April. Two-person teams in ferocious play score with cheering spectators while trying to grab $250,000 in prize money. For more than a decade, this event has attracted the best volleyball rivals in the nation, including many Olympic players. Preliminary rounds usually start at 12:30 PM on Friday and at 9 AM on Saturday, with the championship later that day on the beach in front of the Doubletree Surfside resort.

Hoop-It-Up
8300 N. Nebraska Ave., Tampa
• **(813) 229-7529**

Orlando has the Magic, but the closest we come to NBA-sponsored play is Hoop-It-

Festivalgoers live it up in celebration of ethnic heritage on Fiesta Day.

Photo: Tampa/Hillsborough Convention & Visitors Association

Up. This three-on-three official NBA outdoor basketball festival takes place at the Tampa Greyhound Track at the end of April, and the viewing is as much fun as the playing. Hoop-It-Up is open to players 10 years and older. Last year, nearly 6,000 amateur players signed up. But space is limited, and teams are accepted on a first-come, first-served basis. Registration forms are available at local retail sporting locations. A Hoops Hotline is set up each spring for specifics, or you can call the Tampa Parks and Recreation Department at the number listed.

St. Anthony's Triathlon
Downtown St. Petersburg
• **(727) 825-1271**

As one of the nation's best urban triathlons, this competition attracts more than 1,500 athletes at the end of the month for a 1.5K swim, 40K bike race and 10K run. Divisions based on professional competitor status and age (minimum is 15) and open relay and corporate teams help level the field in this extremely strenuous event. There's also a division for professional racers. Competitors from around the globe don't have to worry if they give out before the races end — the sponsor is St. Anthony's Hospital. To register for this qualifier event to the Gatorade Ironman Triathlon World Championship, or for particulars on public activities, call the triathlon office.

Green Thumb Festival
7891 26th Ave. N., St. Petersburg
• **(727) 893-7335**

Celebrate Mother Earth during this end-of-the-month event sponsored by the St. Petersburg Parks and Recreation Department. You'll find gardening and horticultural exhibits, giveaways and activities for the kids at Walter Fuller Park.

May

American Stage in the Park
First Ave. S., St. Petersburg
• **(727) 822-8814**

The American Stage company performs a Shakespeare masterpiece (with a twist) nightly through mid-May at Demens Landing on downtown St. Petersburg's waterfront. See our write-up in April for more details.

Tampa Greek Food Fest
2418 Swann Ave., Tampa
• **(813) 876-8830**

Dancers garbed in authentic native finery offer Greek folk dancing lessons while goat roasts on a spit nearby, and the sweet aroma of honey on pastry fills the air. This is all just a part of what one Insider claims is Tampa's best Greek restaurant. He also laments that it is, unfortunately, open only one weekend a year. And that's for this festival at St. John Greek Orthodox Church early in the month. Hours are 11 AM until 11 PM on Saturday and 11:30 AM until 7:30 PM on Sunday. Entry costs $1 for those older than 12.

Tropical Heatwave
Ybor City, Tampa • (813) 238-8001

WMNF at 88.5 FM is Tampa Bay's community-supported radio station, offering the most eclectic variety of music you'll ever lay ears on. Tropical Heatwave is its major fundraiser of the year and is backed up by two on-air marathons. And Heatwave is a marathon of its own — an incredible night of music ranging from reggae to rock, world beat to zydeco to acoustic. On the second Saturday of the month, the party rages on four stages in Ybor City's Cuban Club and El Pasaje Plaza and keeps jammin' till well after midnight. Every year there's a different theme for costume dressing, but Insiders know to wear loose, light clothes because in no time flat they'll be soaking wet from the heat, humidity, dancing and all-around exuberance. Call WMNF for information and ticket sales locations.

St. Petersburg Gallery Hop
Downtown St. Petersburg
• **(727) 896-5504**

What better way to soak up the visual pleasures of St. Petersburg's Artworks! festival than to wander through a baker's dozen of galleries all on an evening? Trolley service takes you along the route between 6 and 9 PM, but the galleries are all open from 5 until 10 PM. Nibbles and sips are offered, along with lots of mental creative juices. For all the specifics, call The Gallery at 145 at the number above.

Old Hyde Park Village
Live Music Series
Snow Ave., Tampa • (813) 251-3500

Old Hyde Park Village hosts concerts on the last Wednesday of every month between May and October. Outstanding local groups perform on the common along South Dakota Avenue, and proceeds from food and beverage sales benefit local charities. Nearly 5,000 people show up at each of the monthly events, which start at 6 PM and wrap up around 9.

Seminole Bluegrass Folk
and Art Festival
74th Ave. and Ridge Rd., Seminole
• (727) 391-8345

For more than two decades, the shady oaks at Seminole City Park have provided the setting for this late May musical event that includes arts and crafts plus lots of activities for the kids. The Seminole Junior Woman's Club sponsors the event, and proceeds from the $4 admission fee go to Pinellas County charities. Kids younger than 12 are admitted free. Save yourself the hassle of parking by taking the shuttle from Seminole Mall.

Madeira Gulf Beaches Triathlon
Maderia Beach • (727) 391-7373

From beginners to the well-trained, everyone's invited for "fun on the run" on a Sunday in late May. A .5-mile swim is followed by a 15.5-mile bike race and a 5K run at Madeira Beach Pinellas County Park at 143rd Avenue and Gulf Boulevard. Contestants must register, and entry fees vary.

June

Kid's Week
Downtown Clearwater • (727) 446-4410

This week-long series of events is designed especially as a party for visiting vacationers. There are marine and environmental pro-

grams, plays, magic shows, arts and crafts, beach fun, a fishing tournament, a variety show and a dance. Call ahead to find out where and when everything takes place.

Taste of Pinellas
Straub Park, St. Petersburg
• (727) 892-4193

More than 50 popular restaurants participate in this fund-raiser to benefit All Children's Hospital. Admission is free, with tasty food samples offered at prices from 50¢ to $2.50. Along with restaurant specialties, you'll also enjoy nationally known musical entertainment and other fun at St. Petersburg's Straub Park, on Bayshore Drive between First and Fifth avenues N.E. Call for dates and information.

Juneteenth
601 14th St. S., St. Petersburg
• (727) 821-3833

Although the Emancipation Proclamation was issued in January 1863, Africans enslaved in Florida and many other parts of the South didn't get word of their freedom until June of 1865. In celebration of the Proclamation, Juneteenth is recognized as the nation's oldest African-American holiday. A week of events surrounds this legal state holiday, designated as June 19, and features a fund-raising breakfast, historic workshop, inspirational folk and gospel musical gala and candlelight vigil and dinner. The biggest event of the week is the Saturday Family Fun Fest that includes everything from soul food to gospel, a 5K run and adult basketball games.

Old Hyde Park Village
Live Music Series
Snow Ave., Tampa • (813) 251-3500

Old Hyde Park Village hosts concerts on the last Wednesday of every month between May and October. Outstanding local groups perform on the common along South Dakota Avenue, and proceeds from food and bever-

INSIDERS' TIP

Oldsmar was named for R.E. Olds, a winter visitor to the area who is best remembered for introducing the Oldsmobile. Did you know he also invented the process used to coat bathtubs with porcelain?

age sales benefit local charities. Nearly 5,000 people show up at each of the monthly events, which start at 6 PM and wrap up around 9.

July

Fourth of July Celebrations
All around the Bay area

Anywhere you are in the Tampa Bay area, you'll find birthday parties for the good old U.S. of A. Local newspapers carry all the particulars, so you can find anything from huge fireworks displays to small-town parades and picnics. Curtis Hixon Park, between Ashley Street and the Hillsborough River, is the site of Tampa's Freedom Fest. Live music and entertainment start in the afternoon and end with a spectacular fireworks demonstration choreographed to a musical score. More than 50,000 people turn out, but you can view the fireworks from a variety of nearby spots. Take along a boom box to enjoy the music that is simulcast over a local radio station.

Also, check out the old-town parade in Brandon, starting at the intersection of Parsons and Lumsden roads. There are fireworks after dark over Regency Square Mall on Fla. Highway 60. Or hoof it on out to the Foot Stompin' 4th of July in Temple Terrace, with fireworks at Riverhills Park, along the water next to Lewis Elementary School, 405 Riverhills Drive.

St. Petersburg puts on its party at Straub Park, with a day-long gala of exhibits, entertainment and food followed by fireworks over the waterfront. The park is on Bayshore Drive between First and Fifth avenues N.E. In Clearwater, Celebrate America! brings concerts, an arts and crafts show, a food festival and fireworks to Coachman Park, 301 Drew Street.

Tampa Bay Caribbean Carnival
Downtown St. Petersburg
• (727) 866-0759

Vinoy Park is the site for this festive weekend event featuring steel drum bands, authentic Caribbean food, limbo dancing, pageantry and a host of other activities that pulls in nearly 50,000 revelers. If you've never been to the Islands, you'll be stunned by the fabulous, fan- ciful and colorful costumes that partiers take pride in wearing for the parade and pageantry. Along with the free fun at the park, the festival includes several other events. Call for dates and ticket information.

Gallery Hop Around Tampa
Tampa • (813) 348-4838

Ah, a sultry summer's night of artistry. For more than 10 years, the Tampa Gallery Association has offered tours of prominent galleries and museums on a Saturday night Gallery Hop in the summer. Tour buses, which make getting there part of the fun, start out at the Tampa Museum of Art at 5 PM. Or choose a guided van tour for eight, 10 or 12 people. If your party really wants to go in style, there are even luxury limo tours for six. After the tour ends at 9:30 PM, a Post-Hop Party runs from 10 PM till midnight with hors d'oeuvres, entertainment, live and silent auctions and prizes. All the galleries and museums on the tour are free of charge, but there's a small admission fee to the party. Artsiphartsi gallery's phone number is listed to call for information.

Old Hyde Park Village
Live Music Series
Snow Ave., Tampa • (813) 251-3500

Old Hyde Park Village hosts concerts on the last Wednesday of every month between May and October. Outstanding local groups perform on the common along South Dakota Avenue, and proceeds from food and beverage sales benefit local charities. Nearly 5,000 people show up at each of the monthly events, which start at 6 PM and wrap up around 9.

August

Puerto Rican Cultural
Parade of Tampa
Raymond James Stadium, 4201 N. Dale Mabry Hwy., Tampa • (813) 290-0081

Pride in having Puerto Rican roots flowers into a colorful, musical fiesta that's as hot, hot hot as the August air, and not just for those whose earlier addresses were on the islands. Nearly 100 floats and marching units set a Saturday afternoon ablaze on the streets surrounding Raymond James Stadium with a 2

PM parade that wends into the stadium parking lot. There, from 3 PM till midnight, it's carnival time! The food? Ah, bueno! La música? Jumping! From merengue to mariachi, from Afro-Antillano to rap … there's something to set every age toe to tapping.

India Festival
Univ. of South Florida Sundome, 4202 E. Fowler Ave., Tampa • (813) 526-1228

Independence is a wonderful thing to celebrate, no matter how far away home is from "home." For natives of India, this festival honors their country's break from British rule in 1947 and offers a chance to share their heritage with fellow Americans. The celebration begins Saturday around 1 PM with competitions in folk dance and is followed by partying till 11 PM. On Sunday the festivities pick up again at 3 PM. Food and crafts vendors provide repasts and diversion during both days of the festival. One-day admission costs $7 for adults and $2 for children. Two-day admission costs $10 for adults and $3 for children.

Fishathon
37th St. and 10th Ave. N., St. Petersburg • (727) 893-7734

Here's one last chance for the kids to be kids before school starts. For nearly 50 years, the Civitan Club of St. Petersburg and the St. Petersburg Parks and Recreation Department have hosted this one-day fishing contest for kids younger than 12 and their parents. There are 15 six-minute fishing periods that start at 9:30 AM, but mom and dad have to wait until period 13 for their turns at helping win some great prizes. Don't bother loading up on fancy gear — it's not allowed. Cane poles, as well as bait, are supplied by sponsors. And don't worry about registering either. All you need to do is show up at Lake Jorgensen behind the Main Library.

Hurricane Offshore Classic
Vinoy Park, St. Petersburg • (727) 343-6634

If you think watching boat races means standing on shore and squinting at fast-moving dots along the horizon, think again. Here the racing boats get up-close and personal, and when they are speeding off in the dis-

tance, there's plenty of action on shore to keep you entertained. Trailered boats fill the dry-pit area of Vinoy Park, while Vinoy Basin serves as the wet pit. Music and entertainment flow from the park onto The Pier, so there's plenty of action no matter what your vantage point. The festivities are free, but a small donation to benefit the Pinellas Association of Retarded Citizens gains you entry into the dry pit — and it's well worth it!

Old Hyde Park Village Live Music Series
Snow Ave., Tampa • (813) 251-3500

Old Hyde Park Village hosts concerts on the last Wednesday of every month between May and October. Outstanding local groups perform on the common along South Dakota Avenue, and proceeds from food and beverage sales benefit local charities. Nearly 5,000 people show up at each of the monthly events, which start at 6 PM and wrap up around 9.

September

Tampa Recreation International Festival
Ashley St., Tampa • (813) 931-2106

Every year, this celebration of the Bay area's multicultural heritage is staged at Curtis Hixon Park, along the Hillsborough River in downtown Tampa, from 11 AM until 7 PM on a Saturday. Varied activities include international showcases, children's games from around the world, a crafts and cultural bazaar, kids' arts and crafts, plenty of educational fun and three stages filled with entertainment. The festival's mission is to bring everyone together so we may all understand each other better and discover all sorts of cool stuff about our varied ancestors. Naturally, you'll find a tempting array of international foods to satisfy any taste. Athough the festival is free, the food isn't, so bring along your pesos, drachma, francs, pounds, rubles, rupees or yen — in U.S. currency version, of course.

Run, Rock 'n' Roll
Channelside Dr., Tampa • (813) 230-1361

Two of America's favorite participant sports — running and in-line skating — roll into one fun event near the end of the month. This benefit, sponsored by the Downtown Corps for local charity, includes an 8K rollerblade race for both elite and citizen-class skaters, a 5K run and a 1-mile fun run. Winners get awards, but everyone wins when it comes to the refreshments, free entertainment lineup and vendors with special offers, information and giveaways. Race registration costs $13 in advance and $15 on race day. Since it's still too hot in September to race when the sun's high overhead, the event gets under way at 6:30 PM and lasts till 10 PM. Channelside Drive is along the Garrison Seaport Center and the Florida Aquarium near downtown.

Old Hyde Park Village Live Music Series
Snow Ave., Tampa • (813) 251-3500

Old Hyde Park Village hosts concerts on the last Wednesday of every month between May and October. Outstanding local groups perform on the common along South Dakota Avenue, and proceeds from food and beverage sales benefit local charities. Nearly 5,000 people show up at each of the monthly events, which start at 6 PM and wrap up around 9.

October

Trinkets & Treasures Sale
333 S. Franklin St., Tampa
• (813) 254-1734

Thousands — and we do mean thousands — of bargain hunters flock to the Tampa Convention Center in mid-October for this one-day sale hosted by the Junior League. The doors open at 9 AM, but Insiders know that the first ones in will have arrived about three hours earlier. Why? Because these are the good goods, folks. There's everything from certifiable antiques to designer couture and lots of brand-new merchandise from some of the toniest stores in town. In addition, there are bargains galore, from vacuum cleaners to house plants. It's a garage-sale junkie's dream come true. Smart shoppers come with a satchel and just blitz through, grabbing anything that looks interesting. Then they find a spot to stop and sort through it all to choose what they want to keep. All proceeds support

Junior League of Tampa's charitable endeavors.

Taste of Florida
Ashley St., Tampa • (813) 259-7376

The wide-open space of sparkling Curtis Hixon Park, between Ashley Street and the Hillsborough River, is the setting for sampling delicacies from top restaurants and vendors. Teams also compete for cash and other prizes in the Steve Otto Chili Cookoff. Participants cook up the smoothest, tastiest and hottest chili ever (enough to make your eyelids sweat). Admission is free, but there's a charge for the tickets that are traded for food and beverages. The mid-month weekend event kicks off on a Friday afternoon, running from 3 until 10 PM. Activities resume both mornings at 11 and continue until 9 PM on Saturday and until 6 PM on Sunday.

Latin American Fiesta
Various locations around Tampa
• (813) 248-3712

This fiesta is more than just the largest Latin pageant in the nation. Behind all the merrymaking is the serious purpose of bringing together people of different national backgrounds in a spirit of understanding and goodwill. The first fiesta was held in 1927, and since 1938 the royal queen and her court, crowned annually at a coronation ball, have visited more than 30 countries throughout South and Central America, Europe, Africa, Australia and the Far East. Although the fiesta and coronation ball take place late in the month, there are a host of activities to enjoy, such as a cultural and civic event in Ybor City, bilingual story telling, flamenco dancing and seminars.

OktoberFest
Florida State Fairgrounds, U.S. Hwy. 301 at I-4, Tampa • (813) 621-7121

This event involves three days of hearty eating, drinking and dancing, plus a carnival midway with rides and games. Other festivities include German beer sampling (no kidding?), 35 hours of continuous entertainment on three stages, a variety of food vendors serving traditional German, ethnic and American dishes, and an arts and crafts exhibit. OktoberFest is usually slated late in the month,

Photo: Bob Fiallo

Golf legends participate at the GTE Suncoast Classic, held
in February at Tampa's Tournament Players Club.

getting under way on Friday from 11 AM until midnight and continuing Saturday until midnight or Sunday until 8 PM. Admission costs $5 for anyone older than 12 . The Florida State Fairgrounds are east of Tampa off I-4.

Circus McGurkis
20th St. and 28th Ave. S., St. Petersburg
• (727) 327-6726

A "people's fair" with arts, crafts, dance, storytelling, juggling and music, Circus McGurkis brings together groups from around the Bay area working to promote environmentalism, peace, human rights and other good stuff. Sponsored by the Tampa Bay Peace Education Program and the Religious Society of Friends (Quakers), the event is held on the last Saturday of the month at Lakeview Park.

Clearwater Jazz Holiday
301 Drew St., Clearwater
• (727) 461-5200

This weekend of music late in the month draws jazz musicians and aficionados from across the nation for spectacular performances at Coachman Park. Previous performers have included Acoustic Alchemy, Joshua Redman, Arturo Sandoval, Hiroshima, Herbie Mann and Tito Puente. VIP Pass Packages cost $250 and include seating for two in the VIP area for the entire event, admission to a hospitality tent, two commemorative T-shirts, parking passes and a poster. The hoi polloi are welcome, too, and at much lower prices. Call the Clearwater Jazz Hot Line and leave a message if you want information. A volunteer will get back to you as soon as possible.

Old Hyde Park Village Art Festival
Snow Ave., Tampa • (813) 251-3500

During a weekend near the end of the month, and also during a weekend in late March, Old Hyde Park Village turns into a pe-destrian mall filled with exhibits by nearly 150 artists. From 10 AM until 6 PM on this Friday, Saturday and Sunday, you can browse through fine arts in watercolors, photographs and a variety of other mediums. You'll also enjoy the upscale ambiance of the Village stores and restaurants. Old Hyde Park Village is off Swann Avenue between Bayshore Boulevard and Howard Avenue.

Country Jubilee
11909 125th St. N., Largo
• (727) 582-2123

On the fourth Saturday of the month, the Pinellas County Historical Society invites Heritage Park visitors to step back into pioneer days. More than 125 vendors are on hand with crafts, a petting zoo and clown face-painting. The park is open from 9 AM until 5 PM with entertainment starting at 10 AM.

Guavaween
Ybor City, Tampa • (813) 248-3712

Steve Otto, a columnist for *The Tampa Tribune*, dubbed this city "The Big Guava" years ago. Then one fall day more than a decade ago, a sleazy, trash-talkin' imitation of Carmen Miranda slunk into town, introduced herself as "Mama Guava" and invited Otto and everyone else to one hellacious party in Ybor City. Scheduled for a Saturday night close to Halloween, the raucous celebration starts with the Mama Guava Stumble, a parade of floats and characters far too absurd to ever make it into Gasparilla. (That'll tell you something right there!) Afterward, about 80,000 revelers in various states of costume/uncostume turn the streets into a pretty wild festival. Choose a designated driver, then park downtown and take the shuttle bus to Ybor; it's a wisely spent $5. Watching the parade is free, but admission to the fenced-in street party is $5. It's an incredible night of

INSIDERS' TIP

If you should be so unfortunate as to be a visitor in our region when a hurricane strikes, reach for the GTE Yellow Pages directory. In the front of the book, in the Community Access Pages, you'll find detailed maps indicating evacuation routes, shelter locations and phone numbers for the appropriate emergency services.

Ahoy, mates! It's Gasparilla

There's foulness afloat 'neath the skull and crossbones flapping o'er a vast ship's sails on the Bay! 'Tis the end of January, and maybe the end of Tampa, for the *Jose Gasparilla* lurks off shore! Pirates threaten our fair city! Men and women are crazed! Young children squeal! What should we do? Run and hide?

Heck, no. It's party time!

Long before Spain sent explorers to "La Florida," pirates were sailing the ships that passed our coasts. In fact, it was shipwrecked booty washed ashore that led the Spaniards to mistakenly believe that gold mines filled the land. But like those dreams of gold, the pirates soon vanished.

Or did they? One crew still roams the seas — the dastardly deed-doers of the *Jose Gasparilla*. And near the end of every January, their "assault" begins. Ybor City's "navy" (one tugboat) falls, then Tampa. The fun's just begun, and it lasts for more than a month.

Insiders disagree as to whether Jose Gaspar was man or myth. Legend, now supported by author Kenneth W. Mulder, has it that Gaspar was an 18th-century high-ranking Spanish naval officer gone bad. Dubbed a thief, murderer, seducer and rapist, he supposedly operated out of Gasparilla Island, north of Fort Myers. On nearby Captiva Island, he housed stolen women until ransoms were paid. Useppa Island, which did give up one of the largest pirate treasures ever discovered on the Gulf coast, was another of Gaspar's hiding place. Rumors still abound about treasure hidden underneath the waters off Gasparilla Island, where Gaspar's ship was sunk in 1821 by the USS *Enterprise*.

What is accepted as fact is that in spring 1904, a society writer for the *Tampa Morning Tribune* decided this town was in need of a good party. So, someone was sent to New Orleans to rent costumes and returned with pirate garb from that year's Mardi Gras. And the first invasion of *Ye Mystic Krewe of Gasparilla* — all 40 pirates strong — descended on Tampa's "unsuspecting" May Festival Parade. Although that event is a receding memory, Gasparilla lives on, larger and more spectacular every year.

Festivities were halted only during years of war (once, unfortunately, between local factions). So, pirates continue to invade Tampa each winter and for nearly 50 years have sailed ashore on the world's only fully rigged pirate ship. About 10 years ago, the event was moved from Monday to Saturday. Today, Gasparilla Fest events spread out over Friday night, Saturday and Sunday. The high point of the festival is, however, still the pirate invasion. After the town "surrenders," the 700-plus marauders parade through the streets and prove surprisingly magnanimous by tossing beads and booty to the populace they've just captured.

Gasparilla is so much more than just one parade for the nearly 300,000 people who throng Bayshore Boulevard and downtown streets to greet them. It's an entire series of events. So hoist the *Jolly Roger*, mates! Let's set sail for fun!

Ybor Navy Clears The Way
Seddon Channel, Downtown Tampa • (813) 248-3712

Seems like there's always some U.S. Navy vessel hanging around the Bay, making life difficult for pirates. That is, until the last Sunday afternoon in January, when a ragamuffin, tug-boated crew dubbed the Ybor City Navy "overwhelms" those "Boys In Blue." The mock skirmish along Seddon Channel, between Harbour Island and downtown Tampa, clears the way for an unchallenged assault on the city. We worry ... we wonder ... when will they come?

— continued on next page

Pirate Fest
Downtown Tampa • (813) 353-8070

We've got our kids, we've got our Cuban sandwiches and we've got our sodas and beer. By 10 AM the downtown crowds are thick on the first Saturday in February. Let the marauders arrive!

Since we can't wait till the invasion on Saturday, the fun begins Friday night in the Channelside District, from the Ice Palace to the Florida Aquarium. Free-wheeling musical performances get everyone in the mood for the next day's rowdy parade and party.

Saturday, aboard the *Jose Gasparilla* pirate ship around 1 PM, *Ye Mystic Krewe of Gasparilla* (otherwise known as some of the best, brightest and richest local businessmen) sails from Ballast Point into Hillsborough Bay, surrounded by a flotilla of vessels from skiffs to yachts. The invaders come ashore on Harbour Island, where our mayor accedes the pirates' superiority and surrenders. The town is at their mercy!

But what's this? Instead of pillaging and looting, the pirates create a parade that winds from Rome Avenue down Bayshore Boulevard and through downtown streets. Starting at 2 PM, the parade includes local dignitaries, marching bands, floats galore and crews of every creed. Since everyone loves a winner, by now *Ye Mystic Krewe of Gasparilla* has been joined by the *Krewe of Venus*, the *Krewe of the Knights of Sant' Yago*, the *Krewe of Grace O'Malley* (a famous female pirate, don't you know?), the *Krewe of Bonny-Read*, the *Grand Krewe of Libertalia*, Pinellas County's *Ye Mystic Krewe of Neptune*, the *Rough Riders* and many more.

Downtown, Pirate Fest is a day-long festival from 10 AM till well into the night. Multiple stages feature continuous national and local entertainment, and at Curtis Hixon Park the Pirate's Fest Art Chest shows off original arts and crafts dedicated to Gasparilla (the show continues on Sunday). There are plenty of vendors with everything from food to fake pirate swords, so there's no question there's lots for everyone to do. Capping the day's excitement is a fireworks show over Harbour Island at 10 PM.

Alcoholic beverages are not sold along the parade route, but it is acceptable to bring your own; many partiers tote coolers of libation. What is not acceptable is to imbibe too much and get nasty in your grab for loot or curb space. There is enough candy, cups, doubloons, beads and baubles for everyone to get a bit.

Please do leave the dogs home, and keep babies back from the wildness. And pack earplugs. The pirates' guns (filled with blanks) and cannons on the floats are extremely loud, which can scare the daylights out of animals and really little kids.

Photo: Tampa/Hillsborough Convention and Visitors Bureau

Gasparilla! Tampa's own version of Mardi Gras, draws hundreds of thousands of people from throughout the nation.

Dress accordingly and come out no matter what the weather. Some years it's hot enough for shorts and sunscreen, and other years warm jackets are in order. But the weather never forestalls the invasion, and it shouldn't keep you away, either. When a chill wind blows the meek indoors, it means all the more loot for the hearty!

Now, no matter where you plan to park along the parade route, leave home early so there's lots and lots of time to find a parking place and walk to your destination. An area

— continued on next page

for handicapped drivers is set aside south of Brorein Street, at Franklin Street under the Selmon Parkway. Since streets are closed for the festival, you're wise to research routes in advance. And expect to spend even more time driving away after the parade. Traffic is incredibly heavy, so be patient and enjoy the people-watching.

Ye Mystic AirKrewe/Gasparilla Air Show
Severn Ave., Davis Islands, Tampa • (813) 251-1752

Peter O. Knight Airport on Davis Islands hosts the fly-boys of *Ye Mystic AirKrewe* from 11 AM until 3 PM on parade day. Their aerial display takes place high over Hillsborough Bay as the pirates invade, then flies across Pinellas County and back. The air show is open for all to see or participate in. If you would like to be a pilot in the show, call Neil Cosentino at the Tampa Flyer Service; he'd be pleased to have you join the *AirKrewe*.

Fiesta Day
Ybor City, Tampa • (813) 248-3712

On the Saturday following the invasion and parade, Ybor City is the site of an ethnic celebration that encompasses more than the local Latin heritage. Along with Spanish and Cuban immigrants, the area's Jewish, Italian, German and African-American settlers are recalled in street entertainment, concerts, food and crafts. While it lasts, everyone gets free Spanish bean soup, Cuban bread and a cup of café con leche from the Columbia Restaurant. Fiesta Day fills Ybor's historic district between 13th and 20th streets and Seventh and Ninth avenues from 10 AM until 5 PM.

Gasparilla Regatta
Apollo Beach, Tampa Bay • (813) 645-8377

If you'd rather spend your day on the boat instead of your feet, Fiesta Day Saturday is also the start of the annual Gasparilla Regatta. More than 50 boats from around the state participate, either on an Olympic course or a 7-mile triangular course designed for less serious racers. Class competitions are divided over Saturday and Sunday at Apollo Beach. To register or learn more about the regatta, call the Tampa Sailing Squadron.

Krewe of the Knights of Sant' Yago Illuminated Night Parade
Downtown Tampa • (813) 248-3712

OK, you've had another week to rest up and get ready for another party! And what's a Gasparilla event without a parade? Only for this one, the floats are all lit up and sparkling as brightly as the doubloons, beads and baubles that are tossed to the crowds. Festivities begin at the Florida Aquarium on Channelside Drive — an ideal place for families with young ones — and wends deep into Ybor City, where the bars and restaurants fill with revelers long after the parade has passed by.

Gasparilla Distance Classic
Downtown Tampa • (813) 229-7866

Hope you didn't stay out too late Friday night, because you've got to roll out of bed early this Saturday. Local athletes and some of the world's finest long-distance runners compete in the Gasparilla Distance Classic, ranked as one of the top-10 marathons in the nation according to *Runner's World* magazine. The races start at 8 AM when the 15K wheelchair division takes off, followed 15 minutes later by the 15K runners' field. A 5K run begins at 10:30 AM. Stand on the sidelines along Bayshore Boulevard to cheer these folks on and be thrilled by their endurance. All races finish at the Bayshore Boulevard Marina, south of the Davis Islands Bridge. If you'd like to compete, call for registration information. And here's a really good reason to pump those lungs — foot

— continued on next page

Photo: Tampa Tribune

Gasparilla's Illuminated Night Parade draws kids of all ages to Ybor City.

racers compete for top prizes of $10,000 in the men's and women's divisions, while wheelchair winners split a $15,000 prize.

Junior Distance Classic & Children's Gasparilla Day
Downtown Tampa • (813) 229-7866

The last Saturday in February is a day for family fun. Beginning at 10 AM, young runners at Curtis Hixon Park get to test their endurance over various distances based on age groups. Registration costs $5, which gets everyone a goody-bag and T-shirt. All runners who cross the finish line receive Junior Classic medals. At noon, the Children's Gasparilla Parade fills the Franklin Street Mall. Schools and groups are invited to enter floats, and any kid can march as long as he or she is registered. Just call to do that, but don't worry if your children decide at the last minute that they've just got to march — registration is open until the parade gets under way.

Gasparilla Charity Horse Show
Florida State Fairgrounds, U.S. Hwy. 301 at I-4, Tampa • (813) 839-3476, (813) 626-8454

Starting at the end of February, this marvelous horsy event continues throughout March. Various classes and divisions of American Saddlebreds and Morgans are judged beginning at 7 each evening. Afternoon performances are held on two days. The $3 adult admission and $1.50 fee for children 12 years and younger benefit the Humane Society of North Pinellas. The fairgrounds are east of Tampa, off I-4.

Gasparilla Festival of the Arts
Downtown Tampa • (813) 876-1747

Hundreds of artists in all mediums fill downtown Tampa from Ashley Drive to Curtis Hixon Park for this last event of Gasparilla season. One of the top-25 shows in the country, artists from around the nation compete and display their dazzling, delightful and thought-provoking works at this juried show. Curtis Hixon Park, along the Hillsborough River, fills

— continued on next page

with vendors and musical entertainment of every kind, which means you can fill your tummy and give your feet a break from the browsing. Also, free hands-on arts and crafts projects for kids are offered by the Tampa Museum of Art. On Saturday, the festival runs from 9 AM until 5:30 PM and on Sunday, from 10 AM until 5 PM.

---

fun, but please believe us when we say leave the kids home with a babysitter.

Instead, bring the youngsters down a week earlier to Ybor City from 11 AM until 4 PM for the Family Fun Festival. Admission is free until 3 PM. They'll love the pumpkin giveaway, a scavenger hut, costume parade, mask-making and dozens of other events that lead to toys and prizes. Oooh, and don't miss the scary stories and haunted house at Ybor Square, just in time to put everyone in the Halloween mood!

John's Pass Seafood Festival
Madeira Beach • (727) 391-7373

This festival, held during the last weekend of October, is one of the Southeast's top-20 annual events. The mission is to educate folks on the local fishing industry, but the public perception is an excuse to indulge the palate. The family-oriented festival kicks off Friday afternoon at 5, with a Halloween costume contest and the Dance-O-Ween street party, which is spread out over seven musical locations. The fun ends on Saturday with fireworks shortly after 9 PM. Sunday brings the Arts & Crafts Show, with more than 100 exhibitors. Also featured are a beach season finale volleyball game, a haunted house and other children's activities, environmental sightseeing and exhibits, crab races, a style show, continuous live entertainment and the Seafood Gumbo Cookoff. More stuff and fun takes place on the Treasure Island side of John's Pass, and water shuttle service is available for just $1. On Saturday and Sunday, the John's Pass Seafood Festival fun lasts from 10 AM through 10 PM. If you're wise and want to avoid traffic hassles, park at Madeira Beach Middle School and pay the pittance to ride the shuttle.

Old Hyde Park Village
Live Music Series
Snow Ave., Tampa • (813) 251-3500

Old Hyde Park Village hosts concerts on the last Wednesday of every month between May and October. Outstanding local groups perform on the common along South Dakota Avenue, and proceeds from food and beverage sales benefit local charities. Nearly 5,000 people show up at each of the monthly events, which start at 6 PM and wrap up around 9.

November

Times Festival of Reading
4200 54th Ave. S., St. Petersburg
• (727) 893-8969

Ah, a glorious time for bibliophiles of all ages! On the first Sunday of the month at Eckerd College, some of the nation's most famous names from the pages of books and newspapers converge to read from their works and talk with lovers of the written word. In the past, we've been treated to such names as Tom Robbins, Doris Kearns Goodwin, Ben Bradlee, Robert B. Parker, Winston Groom, Carl Hiaasen, Harry Crews, Connie May Fowler, Molly Ivens, George Plimpton, Ann Rice and P.J. O'Rourke. Whew! The list just goes on! From 10 AM until 5 PM, booksellers and publishers abound, as do food vendors, musical entertainers and famous dead authors. (OK, so they're not ghosts, just actors dressed up as authors who happen to be dead.) There are special activities for kids, including free books for children younger than 12. Since this event may expand its dates and change location, it's a good idea to check by calling either the number listed or the Festival Hotline, (813) 892-2358.

JCPenney Golf Classic
Westin Innisbrook Resort, U.S. Hwy. 19
S., Tarpon Springs • (727) 942-5566

Innisbrook is the site for this PGA- and LPGA-sanctioned tournament slated in early November. First, there are two days of Pro-Am play. Then 52 pro teams compete during a four-day period to win $1.5 million in prize money. But the real winners are local charities that have received more than $8 million from this event during the past two decades. Day tickets cost $18 in advance and $22 at the gate. Seniors who are 65 and older pay only $15 in advance. Or, anyone may buy a $50 badge and get in all week. Parking costs $4.

Ribfest
Bayshore Dr., St. Petersburg
• **(727) 896-2727**
Straub Park is where some of the finest barbecue chefs in the country showcase their special talents during this three-day festival. Along with rib-cooking contests, there's also rib-tickling fun, including hot music and hot rods and classic cars and bikes. No admission is charged if you arrive between 11 AM and 5 PM on Friday; after that, it's $5. On Saturday and Sunday, it costs $3 to get in between 11 AM and 3 PM, then the admission price goes back up to $5. Kids younger than 12 and accompanied by an adult are admitted free.

Ruskin Seafood & Art Festival
Ruskin • (813) 645-3808
Count on the sun shining and plenty of seafood to eat at E.G. Simmons Park, 19th Street N.W., Ruskin, during this mid-month three-day event. In addition to seafood samplings that include shrimp, cracked conch and alligator, you'll find handcrafted goods, commercial exhibits and plenty of musical entertainment. Parking is free, but a small fee is charged to enter the festival. The cost is $2 for adults and $1 for kids between the ages of 5 and 13. Food prices range between $1 and $5, and activities take place between 10 AM and 5 PM. For directions and other information, call the Ruskin Chamber of Commerce at the number listed.

Children's Festival
Univ. of South Florida, 4202 E. Fowler Ave., Tampa • (813) 974-3390
Thousands of kids and their families converge on the USF campus in mid-November to discover that fun is learning and learning is fun. Hands-on activities for children between the ages of 2 and 14 include every-

thing from a bike rodeo to carpentry, all of the arts including literature, music and dance, plus computers, science and math. Kids enjoy the puppetry, story telling and an animal farm, too. When you reach the campus, head to the southeast field near the Sun Dome. Children are charged a $5 entry fee, but the grownups with them are admitted free.

St. Petersburg SnowFest
Downtown St. Petersburg
• **(727) 821-4069**
From Thanksgiving weekend till Christmas, St. Petersburg lights up with an enchanting variety of holiday events. There are candle-light walks and concerts, Chanukah celebrations, a wine tasting, arts and crafts shows, a Snow Ball "creative black tie" party, a lighted boat parade, a parade for Santa early in December and the Jingle Bell Run. Your best bet for information, other than watching the papers, is to call the St. Petersburg Area Chamber of Commerce at the number listed.

December

SantaFest & Holiday Parade
Downtown Tampa • (813) 274-8615
Kids in the know are quick to point out to their buddies that this isn't "real" snow piled up on a downtown Tampa street. But on the first Saturday of December, tons of shaved ice come close enough to the real thing for everyone to enjoy. There's even a special plastic "ice rink" at this family festival. Oh, did we forget something? Why, jolly old St. Nick himself will of course be there, starring in his very own Christmas parade at 5:30 PM. Santa and all the other merrymakers travel down Tampa Street from Tyler to Kennedy Boulevard, then north along Franklin Street to Cass. Entertainers and vendors make this evening a holiday fantasy for the whole family.

Christmas Art Walk
Downtown St. Petersburg
• **(727) 896-5504**
Take an evening's break from the hustle and bustle of holiday fuss to restore your soul. More than a dozen of St. Petersburg's most popular art galleries stay open from 5 until 10 PM on an evening during the first week of the

month and serve up sweet treats to add to the spirit. For all the specifics, call The Gallery at 145 at the number listed.

Brandon Balloon Festival
Brandon • (813) 689-1221

More than 50 colorful hot-air balloons lift off on Saturday and Sunday mornings, competing in races and target contests. Early birds should take note that sunrise is the time to watch the balloons fill and float away. But for a truly spectacular sight, be on hand Friday night for the illuminated Balloon Glow. An arts and crafts show and food and entertainment are offered all day on Saturday. The Brandon Chamber of Commerce can fill you in on dates, details and location.

Lighted Boat Parade
Intracoastal Waterway, St. Pete Beach
• (727) 363-9243

The Intracoastal Waterway at St. Pete Beach fills with beautifully lighted boats in mid-December for this holiday season floating parade. Starting off at Pass-A-Grille Way usually around 5:30 PM, the trek ends at the St. Pete Beach Yacht & Tennis Club around 9 PM. For info on where and when to view the passing boats, call the St. Pete Beach

Parks and Recreation Department at the number listed above.

First Night
Downtown Tampa • (813) 272-1939
Downtown St. Petersburg
• (727) 893-7111

Both downtown Tampa and downtown St. Petersburg celebrate New Year's Eve with alcohol-free, family-oriented First Night. Entertainment in both cities includes musicians of all styles, theater troupes, dancers, jugglers, puppeteers and more.

In Tampa, the party for more than 30,000 begins at 4 PM with special performances for children and a procession through the Franklin Street Mall and surrounding blocks. At 7 PM, more than 30 venues begin simultaneous performances by local artists and musicians. Just before midnight, the entertainment stops so everyone can participate in the Midnight Spectacular climax to the evening. Tickets are available at a variety of local sources.

In St. Petersburg, the occasion is celebrated much the same, with entertainment filling downtown streets and buildings. Call the Chamber of Commerce for complete details on First Night in St. Petersburg.

Everywhere you look there's a font of opportunities — from frugal to flamboyant but always fun — to satisfy every form of artistic soul.

The Arts

No longer is it necessary to travel to New York — or even Atlanta — to see major stage plays, hear excellent musical performances or view international exhibits. It all comes to us, all around the entire Tampa Bay area, and the plethora of arts available to us brings along an incredible economic benefit — far greater than that generated by sports.

The Tampa Bay Performing Arts Center and Clearwater's Ruth Eckerd Hall attract hundreds of thousands of people for theater and orchestral programs that cover the gamut from local symphony to stellar Broadway extravaganzas. Museums on both sides of Tampa Bay garner national and even international praise for the quality of exhibitions. The Florida International Museum of Art in St. Petersburg attracted more than a half-million viewers to the famed *Titanic — The Exhibition* and St. Petersburg is also home to the largest collection of Salvador Dali's works.

In addition, an extensive array of art galleries and shows abound throughout the region and year, so be sure to check our Annual Events chapter to learn when. The largest and most acclaimed arts event is definitely The Gasparilla Festival of the Arts — one of the premier juried shows of the South — held on a March weekend in downtown Tampa. In mid-February and again in mid-July, The Tampa Gallery Association hosts a Gallery Hop with more than 20 members participating. St. Petersburg devotes an entire month to its citywide Artworks! event, which closes with the renowned Mainsail art show. At last count, downtown St. Petersburg alone had 15 art galleries, ranging from the state headquarters for the Florida Craftsmen Inc. to the signature gallery for noted artist P. Buckley Moss. Scores more can be found in every direction around the Bay area.

So everywhere you look, there's a font of opportunities — from frugal to flamboyant but always fun — to satisfy every form of artistic soul.

Performing Arts

Tampa Bay Performing Arts Center
1010 N. MacInnes Pl., Tampa
• (813) 229-7827, (800) 955-1045

In an area where getting dressed up often means just changing into a clean T-shirt and slacks, the Tampa Bay Performing Arts Center presents wonderful excuses to go for the glamour. The center is the largest complex of its kind south of the Kennedy Center in Washington, D.C.

Host to incredible productions ranging from *Master Class* with Faye Dunaway to *Miss Saigon*, complete with its twirling helicopter, such programming spells success for the Tampa Bay Performing Arts Center. No other similarly sized theater in the nation grosses higher revenues than the center's Morsani Hall.

There's much more to the Performing Arts Center, though. It sponsors the Tampa Bay Youth Orchestras, an organization including three regional youth orchestras that regularly rehearse and perform at the center.

It is also home to four theaters. The largest is Morsani Hall, which seats 2,500 people and accommodates major Broadway musicals, operas, ballets and orchestral concerts. The Playhouse, designed with 1,000 seats, provides an intimate, three-tier arena for dance, drama and smaller musical performances. Experimental performances, works-in-progress, television productions, cabarets, recordings and business meetings are all hosted in the 289-seat Jaeb Theater. The Off-Center Theater, which seats 125 people, is a blackbox venue designed for community performances and visual artists. Since it's a nonunion facility, local groups, musicians, poets, dancers and comedians are granted an affordable setting to showcase their talents.

Looking for just the right gift for the stagestruck? The CenterStore, Festival Shoppe and

Playhouse Boutique all offer unique show-related gifts and accessories. The CenterStore is open Wednesday from noon till 2 PM, Saturday from noon till 4 PM and one hour prior to most performances. The Festival Shoppe and Playhouse Boutique are open for one hour prior to shows in their respective halls. Call (813) 222-1019 for more information or to schedule an appointment for personal shopping.

Accessibility is an area of pride at the Performing Arts Center. Special disabled valet parking is available, and wheelchair seating may be purchased in all price locations in all theaters. Infrared Listening System wireless headphones are offered free of charge at the lobbies' information tables. And during designated Sunday evening performances in Morsani Hall, theatrical interpretation is provided by sign-language interpreters for the hearing-impaired.

www.insiders.com

See this and many other **Insiders' Guide®** destinations online — in their entirety.

Visit us today!

The Tampa Bay Performing Arts Center is in downtown Tampa, just off Interstate 275 at the Ashley Street Exit. As you pass by at night watch for the bright yellow shooting stars on its lighted sign. Visitors may tour the $57 million facility free of charge on any Wednesday or Saturday at 10 AM; just meet in front of the box office. Performance times and costs vary, and reservations are de rigueur for most events, so call well in advance for prices and dates. Also, subscribing patrons get first crack at tickets. Although auditory devices are available free of charge to the hearing-impaired, donations are appreciated. The box office is open Monday through Friday from 10 AM until 6 PM, Saturday from noon until 6 PM and on performance dates, 90 minutes prior to curtain. Information is available 24 hours a day on the CenterLine, (813) 222-1049.

Bayfront Center
400 First St. S., St. Petersburg
• **(727) 892-5767**

The Bayfront Arena hosts a range of events from the annual January visit of the Ringling Bros. Barnum & Bailey Circus and the Ice Capades to boat shows and rock concerts. In Mahaffey Theater's more intimate venue of 2,000 seats, year-round performances range

from Broadway productions to the Southern Ballet Theatre, classical orchestra to jazz, and include annual holiday favorites such as *The Nutcracker*. Audio aids for the hearing-impaired are loaned free of charge. A buffet is offered at the Sun Pavilion room before most major performances, and desserts and drinks are available in the lobby during intermission.

Ruth Eckerd Hall
1111 McMullen Booth Rd., Clearwater
• **(727) 791-7400**

Designed by the Frank Lloyd Wright Foundation in Arizona, Ruth Eckerd Hall is the only performing arts center in Florida designated as a Major Cultural Institution. Professional theater, music and dance make up each season's schedule, and there's nonstop entertainment from October through May. Past performers and performances have included a variety ranging from Rosemary Clooney and Victor Borge to the Boston Pops, *Les Misèrables* to *Cats*, Roger Whittaker to Lyle Lovett Jr. Pre-show dining, including specialty-themed menus, full cash bar and wine list, is offered.

The Adults-at-Leisure Series, which hosts a separate slate of performances, will be of particular interest to winter vacationers. Curtain time for these programs, held on Tuesdays or Wednesdays from the end of January through mid-March, is generally 1 PM, and ticket prices are as low as $10. Weekend Family Theater and Adventures in the Arts offer family entertainment, classes and workshops. The box office is open Monday through Saturday between 9 AM and 7 PM, and on Sunday from noon until 5 PM.

Wheelchair locations, designed to include companion seats, are available for all performances, and a new state-of-the-art FM hearing assistance system is available for loan to patrons.

Stageworks
428 W. Kennedy Blvd., Tampa
• **(813) 253-6243**

The professional company of the Stageworks has for more than a decade served the area with a full main-stage theater. Throughout the year, the company offers various programs, such as tours to schools, a cabaret show for senior centers, a development program for Florida playwrights, plus classes and workshops for theater artists. It also presents Rainbow Tribe, a multinational performance troupe.

Stageworks produces six shows at the University of Tampa's Falk Theater from September through June. Tickets cost $15. Students and seniors are admitted for $12.

Spanish Lyric Theatre
Tampa Bay Performing Arts Center, 1010 N. MacInnes Pl., Tampa • (813) 229-7827

When the Spanish Little Theatre first debuted in 1959, its mission was to revive native heritage through performances of turn-of-the-century zarzuelas. During the next 25 years, its focus expanded to include American musical productions with lyrics sung — as its name suggests — in Spanish (as well as in English). Now called the Spanish Lyric Theatre, its summer music series attracts more than 12,000 viewers to shows that have included *Cabaret*, *Kiss Me Kate* and even Viennese operettas. Light concerts are also occasionally offered at the Hillsborough Community College campus in Ybor City.

American Stage
211 Third St. S., St. Petersburg
• (727) 822-8814

The annual American Stage In The Park at Demens Landing, performed on the waterfront in downtown St. Petersburg, is the best know production of the American Stage. Shakespeare is presented nightly from early April through mid-May, and people hauling blankets and lawn chairs fill the grounds within minutes of the 6 PM performances. What appeals to all types and ages is that this is not your English teacher's Shakespeare. Each year, the company reworks one of the Bard's masterpieces, adding music and updating costumes, settings and direction. The words do, however, remain the same. Believe me, it puts a whole new spin on Elizabethan prose to hear *As You Like It* done as a 1920s Chicago guys-and-dolls musical.

During the rest of its year, American Stage performs to a maximum audience of 130 people at its permanent theater. Curtain time is at 7:30 PM on Wednesdays and Thursdays, 8 PM on Fridays and Saturdays, and matinees are offered at 3 PM on Saturdays and Sundays. Ticket prices vary, so be sure to call ahead for reservations.

Photo: St. Petersburg/Clearwater Area Convention & Visitors Bureau

The Salvador Dali Museum in St. Petersburg is the cornerstone of an outstanding mix of cultural offerings in the area.

St. Petersburg Little Theatre
4025 31st St. S., St. Petersburg
• **(727) 866-1973**

For more than 70 years, the St. Petersburg Little Theatre has annually presented six shows in two-week runs between September and May. Performances are slated at 8 PM on Thursdays, Fridays and Saturdays, and Sunday matinees are at 2 PM. Tickets to most productions cost $12, but if the show is a musical, the price is $15.

Musical Arts

Florida Orchestra
101 S. Hoover St., Tampa
• **(813) 286-2403**

Orchestras everywhere have felt the economic pinch during past years, and our excellent group has weathered its share of financial woes. A lust for the arts is a soul-deep thing that burns brightly in both the Florida Orchestra's musicians and passionate supporters around the Bay. The budget has been balanced for three years now, which means the artists are able to concentrate on their music rather than on whether next month's paychecks will clear.

The quality starts right at the top: Internationally acclaimed Jahja Ling has been the group's music director for the past decade; Skitch Henderson provides pops music direction; and Thomas Wilkons is the resident conductor.

A perennial favorite in the area is the annual Bay-Thoven Festival, which includes five symphonies performed during February and March. Throughout the year, the orchestra presents 12 Masterworks programs, seven Super Pops programs and four Coffee programs. Each performance is repeated in Tampa, St. Petersburg and Clearwater. Several free outdoor concerts are also offered, again in each of the three cities. All totaled, the orchestra gives about 100 performances during its season between September and May. The orchestra also provides children's educational programs, from classroom visits to concerts to cable television programming.

Single tickets to Masterworks and Super Pops programs cost from $15 to $35 and tickets to the Coffee concerts cost from $15 to $24. Student discounts are always available.

The Tampa Oratorio Singers
(813) 247-3866

This 60-voice adult choir is one of the area's oldest performing groups, enjoying more than 30 seasons. The Tampa Oratorio Singers appear three to five times a year, usually at the Tampa Bay Performing Arts Center. Repertoire ranges from pop to classical. Membership in the all-volunteer group is determined by audition, and Monday night rehearsals are held at the Ybor Campus of Hillsborough Community College. Tickets cost $10. Call the society or the Tampa Bay Performing Arts Center box office at (813) 229-7827.

Tampa Bay Arts Inc.
1222 S. Dale Mabry Hwy., Ste. 602, Tampa • **(813) 837-4485**

An umbrella organization, Tampa Bay Arts Inc. encompasses the Tampa Bay Men's Chorus, the Tampa Bay Womyn's Chorus and the Tampa International Gay & Lesbian Film Festival. Along with local productions and the annual Pride Concert, the musical talent of Men's Chorus is known around the state and the nation. Each year, both choral groups present six concerts, usually at the Tampa Bay Performing Arts Center, and at a number of special events. Each performance is artistically interpreted for the hearing-impaired. Ticket prices vary according to program.

Dinner Theaters

Early Bird Dinner Theatre
Bill Irle's Banquet Hall, 1411 N. Ft. Harrison Ave., Clearwater
• **(727) 446-5898**

Local actors of the Early Bird Dinner Theatre present popular comedies and dramas following luncheon or dinner buffets. Seating is at 11 AM and 4 PM on Thursdays and Saturdays, with shows following at 1 and 6 PM, respectively. Evening performances only are held on Fridays and Sundays at 6 PM, following a 4 PM dinner. The buffet and show, excluding tax, costs $14.95 a person, cash only.

Reservations should be made by phoning and leaving your name and telephone number for a confirmation return call.

Mystery Dinner Theater
511 Rosary Rd. N.E., Largo
• (727) 584-3490

Like a living game of Clue, audience participation is crucial to Mystery Dinner Theater's productions. On Friday and Saturday evenings, the dinner and play at Clearwater's Belleview Biltmore Resort and at the Doubletree Resort on Clearwater Beach costs $44 a person.

Visual Arts

Tampa Museum of Art
600 N. Ashley Dr., Tampa
• (813) 274-8130

Serious members of the art world have long been aware that the Tampa Museum of Art houses one of the top Greek and Roman antique collections in the nation. More than 5,300 works of art, specializing in classical antiquities and 20th-century American art, comprise the permanent inventory. In addition, 15 to 20 major exhibits of paintings, photography and sculpture are annually presented. More than 100,000 people come through the museum's doors each year to enjoy both the permanent and periodic displays.

Downstairs from the main galleries, visitors get a more hands-on approach to art in the Gallery Experience. The museum offers a variety of activities, such as workshops for children and adults, lectures and classic movie showings. At noon on the first Thursday of every month, brown-baggers "eat up" a little culture at the hour-long Art For Lunch. There's

no charge in addition to the cost of regular museum admission, and beverages and desserts are provided.

The museum's hours are 10 AM until 5 PM Monday through Saturday, except Wednesday, when closing is at 9 PM. Sunday hours are from 1 till 5 PM. Everyone is admitted free of charge from 5 until 9 PM on Wednesdays and between 10 AM and 2 PM on Saturdays. Regular admission costs $5 for adults, $4 for senior adults and students, and $3 for children ages 6 through 18.

University of South Florida Contemporary Art Museum
College of Fine Arts, 4202 E. Fowler Ave., Tampa • (813) 974-2849

The University of Southern Florida's Contemporary Art Museum each year showcases five to seven traveling exhibits by emerging artists in its East and West galleries. There is no charge for admission and hours are Monday through Friday from 10 AM until 5 PM and Saturday from 1 until 4 PM.

Salvador Dali Museum
1000 Third St. S., St. Petersburg
• (727) 823-3767

The Dali Museum is the permanent home of the world's most comprehensive collection of this great Spanish surrealist's works. The collection, assembled by Eleanor and A. Reynolds Morse throughout a 45-year friendship with the artist, spans the years from 1914 to 1980. The museum has recently begun to offer regular exhibits by other highly recognized artists who are continuing Dali's legacy in the field of surrealism.

A permanent retrospective of oil paintings showcases Dali's early works in Impressionist and Cubist styles, his transition to Surrealism

---

INSIDERS' TIP

A teenage girl suffers from clinical depression and her mother is oblivious to the disease. This is certainly the basis for drama — an award-winning drama, in fact. *Dirty Dishes* won Monica Wrobel, a Dunedin High School student, a national award in the younger than 18 division of the 1997 Very Special Arts Playwrights Competition. The one-act play earned Wrobel spending money and a trip to Washington, D.C., to see her play presented at the John F. Kennedy Center for the Performing Arts.

and later works reflecting his preoccupation with science and religion. The collection is comprised of 94 original oils, more than 100 watercolors and drawings, nearly 1,300 graphics, sculptures, objets d'art, photographs and an archival library. Exhibits from the collection are rotated and special exhibits are offered on a regular basis.

The museum is open year round. Hours are Monday through Saturday from 9:30 AM until 5:30 PM and Sunday from noon until 5:30 PM, with extended hours until 8 PM on Thursday. The museum closes on Thanksgiving and Christmas days. General admission costs $8 for adults and $7 for senior adults. Students are admitted for $4 and children 10 and younger are admitted free of charge.

Museum of Fine Arts
255 Beach Dr. N.E., St. Petersburg
• (727) 896-2667

Twenty galleries at the Museum of Fine Arts house a diverse collection from ancient to contemporary works. The museum's strengths are its collection of American and European 18th- and 19th-century art and its large photography collection. Pre-Colombian and Far Eastern art are also highlighted, and period rooms display antique and historical furnishings, a gallery of Steuben crystal and special exhibits of decorative arts. Among the artists represented in the permanent collection are Monet, Renoir, Cézanne, Gauguin, O'Keefe, Rauchenberg and Bellows. Sketching with charcoal and pencil is permitted.

Throughout the year, the museum also presents concerts of classical, modern and jazz music, and educational programs are offered to schools. Adults may enjoy the "Art at Leisure" and "Art a la Carte" lecture programs, which are offered monthly, except in midsummer. To assist the visually impaired, large-print labels have been placed on selected works and large-type notebooks for self-guided tours are available. Special interpreters may also be arranged for the hearing-impaired.

Adult admission costs $6. Seniors 65 and older are charged $5, while children 6 and older pay $2. On Sundays, all visitors are admitted free of charge. The museum is open Tuesday through Saturday from 10 AM until 5 PM and Sunday from 1 until 5 PM. The museum is closed on Thanksgiving, Christmas and New Year's days.

Florida International Museum
100 Second St. S., St. Petersburg
• (727) 821-1448, (800) 777-9882

Since opening in 1995 with an international splash, bringing the *Treasures of the Czars* from the Kremlin Museums in Moscow to sellout crowds in St. Petersburg, the area's newest museum, the Florida International Museum, continues to create smashing seasonal hits.

The 300,000-square-foot building showcases grand-scale traveling exhibitions from the world's most prestigious collections. A recent display, *Titanic — The Exhibition*, broke all previous records for attendance. Starting in October 1998 is *Empires of Mystery — The Incas, The Andes and Lost Civilizations*. With the largest exhibition of Peruvian artifacts ever to visit the United States, the show encompasses thousands of years of history for more than 30 civilizations through rituals, artistry, warfare and daily life.

Although each show runs for several months, interest is always strong, so it's a virtual necessity to reserve tickets in advance, both for date and visiting time. Attendance is limited to enhance the viewers' tours. Tickets for recent exhibitions cost $13.95 for adults, $12.95 for seniors and $5.95 for students. Chil-

INSIDERS' TIP

Keep an eye out for slithering creatures along I-275 near Fifth Avenue N. in St. Petersburg! High atop the Fleet Maintenance Building sits the 30-foot-long *Security Lizard*. It was created by artist Paul Eppling, who used scrap parts from city vehicles to form the reptilian creature. More of his works can be seen at Great Explorations, the hands-on museum at The Pier, and at Boyd Hill Nature Park.

Tampa's Poet Laureate

Most everybody knows there's a poet laureate of the United States. (No, it's not Maya Angelou; it's Robert Pinsky.) What you may not know is that Tampa has its own poet laureate, and we're probably the first city in the nation to bestow such an honor. His name is James Tokley Sr.

An established and well-known writer, Tokley is poet laureate of the National Urban League. His melli-  fluous voice is well recognized by listeners of WMNF, the community radio station, where he's considered poet in-residence. Tokley's also a teacher, motivational speaker, historian, folklorist and lecturer. He operates a private consulting business on cultural diversity and has hosted an urban affairs television program.

"I try to sculpt words to turn them inside out," Tokley told *The Tampa Tribune*, "so I can uncover their mystical powers. I truly believe words have the power to impact, to reveal, to speak."

His words do speak volumes, whether in a poem telling of the crowd at Tampa's Red Top Bar or considering *The Rape of Kuwait*, which was nominated for the Pulitzer Prize in 1994. Tokley's also written an epic poem titled *Genesis: The History of the African Upon the Face of the Earth*, and books, including *Oh, St. Regent*.

"I don't look at this as some great award that you hang around your neck like a racehorse," *The Tribune* quoted him on his acceptance of the city's honor. "I view this as an opportunity to speak with a thousand voices through one pen."

Photo: Paula Stahel

Tampa's James Tokley Sr. may be the only person in the nation touted as a city's official poet laureate.

dren younger than 5 are admitted free of charge. Tickets may be purchased either by phone, at the ticket office or at American Automobiles Association locations. The museum is open daily from 9 AM until 8 PM, and the last tour starts at 6 PM.

Florida Gulf Coast Art Center
222 Ponce De Leon Blvd., Belleair
• (727) 584-8634

The Florida Gulf Coast Art Center is a large facility featuring a diverse exhibition schedule in addition to classes, workshops and educational programs. Its Master Artists workshop series brings in nationally recognized names. "Lunch With An Artist" is offered on the third Friday each month from September through May at the Seminole Community Library, 9199 113th St. N., Seminole. There are several galleries operating on varying schedules. The Pilcher Gallery is open from 10 AM till 4 PM Tuesday through Friday, and The Shillard Smith Gallery is open Tuesday through Saturday from 10 AM until 4 PM and on Sunday from noon until 4 PM. The center is closed on Mondays and throughout the month of August. There is no charge for admission.

Tampa Bay Holocaust Memorial Museum
55 Fifth St. S., St. Petersburg
• (727) 821-8261

From humble beginnings at the St. Petersburg Jewish Community Center in Madeira Beach, the Holocaust Memorial Museum quickly gained international recognition and now has the space worthy of such distinction. The Holocaust Museum recently moved into 27,000 square feet of space, making it the fourth largest Holocaust center in the United States. For the first time, a permanent exhibit is provided, detailing European life from World War I to the creation of Israel. One of its most gripping elements is a 30-foot-long, 15-ton boxcar that transported so many people to Nazi concentration camps. Traveling exhibits are offered to visitors, as well as a library and media center. Museum hours are Monday through Friday from 10 AM until 5 PM, and Saturday and Sunday from noon until 5 PM. Students may visit the museum free of charge, and admission for adults is $6 and seniors, $5.

Dunedin Fine Arts Center
1143 Michigan Blvd., Dunedin
• (727) 738-1892

The focus at the Dunedin Fine Arts Center is to display the contemporary works of Florida artists and to offer a wide range of activities and classes for children and adults. Although there is no charge for admission, donations are welcomed. The center is open 9 AM until 5 PM Monday through Friday and 1 until 4 PM on Sunday.

Medieval Brass Rubbing Centre & Museum
822 Dodecanese Blvd., Tarpon Springs
• (813) 934-6760

Centuries ago, brass engravings attached to cathedrals commemorated the passing of members of the nobility, gentry, merchants and ecclesiastics. Between the 13th and 17th centuries, artisans created hundreds of thousands of these "brasses," but fewer than 2,000 have survived the ravages of time, war and pollution. To preserve the ancient works, most have been replaced by detailed facsimiles. The Medieval Brass Rubbing Centre has a collection of more than 300 facsimiles from the Medieval and Renaissance periods, as well as Celtic, Islamic and religious designs. Another highlight is an illuminated Renaissance alphabet from which rubbings may be made.

In an unusual juxtaposition, the museum also spotlights composers, antique cars and dinosaurs! Although there's no charge to visit the museum, fees between $2 and $18 apply if you want to make a rubbing. The museum provides instruction and all necessary supplies. The museum is open from 10 AM until 7 PM Sunday through Thursday, and from 10 AM until 8 PM on Friday and Saturday. It's closed on major holidays.

Galleries

Alexander's Metro Art Jewelry & Gallery
1517 E. Seventh Ave., Tampa
• (813) 247-6363

All the work at Alexander's Metro Art Jewelry & Gallery is original — no prints, no litho-

Photo: St. Petersburg/Clearwater Area Convention & Visitors Bureau

Downtown St. Petersburg offers six major museums and several art galleries, shops, restaurants and entertainment options, all in a charming waterfront setting.

graphs — so you're sure to get only the unique from sculpture to handcrafted jewelry. The gallery's hours are from 11 AM until 6 PM Monday through Saturday. When hosting special events on Friday and Saturday evenings, the gallery is also open between 8 and 10:30 PM.

Artsiphartsi
2717 W. Kennedy Blvd., Tampa
• **(813) 348-4838**

The pronunciation of this little shop says it all — no stuffy stuff here! Instead, there are outstanding fine American crafts, ranging from 3-D art to jewelry, from 500 artists whose works are seriously whimsical. Special shows are occasionally held to highlight very well-known crafters. Artsiphartsi is open Monday through Saturday from 10 AM until 6 PM and on Sunday from noon till 4 PM.

Brad Cooper Gallery
1712 E. Seventh Ave., Tampa
• **(813) 248-6098**

Original contemporary works of living artists are exhibited at the Brad Cooper Gallery and are directed toward highly individualized museums and collections. This Ybor City gallery also offers museum-quality framing. It's open from 11 AM until 5 PM Wednesdays through Saturdays.

Centre Gallery
4202 E. Fowler Ave., Tampa
• **(813) 974-5464**

At the University of South Florida, Centre Gallery serves as a showcase for contemporary works by students. Shows tend to change every three weeks. The gallery, which is housed in the Marshall Center, also holds an art auction in the fall. Hours vary during the summer, so it's best to call ahead. The gallery is open during the university year — fall through spring — from 11 AM until 4 PM Monday through Friday.

Lee Art Gallery
330 W. Robertson St., Brandon
• **(813) 662-1367**

The works of recognized artists from around the state, as well as the artistic efforts of area students, are represented at the Lee Art Gallery. The gallery is open Monday through Friday from 10:30 AM till 5 PM and on Saturday from 10 AM till 2 PM.

Beaux Arts Society Gallery
2635 Central Ave., St. Petersburg
• **(727) 328-0702**

All types of contemporary works are presented during one-man shows at the Beaux Arts Society Gallery, the oldest gallery in Florida. Two annual competitions are held, one during the spring Festival of States and the second during the July 4th holiday. Poetry, songs and dance are also presented, and there are outdoor-life painting classes. Art movies are shown on Sundays at 2:30 and 8 PM. Annual membership in the gallery is available for $25, or donations between $2 and $5 are accepted at the door. The gallery is open daily from noon until 5 PM.

Fiber Arts Institute
34950 U.S. Hwy. 19 N., Palm Harbor
• **(727) 784-0107**

If it can be done to fabric, it's probably been done at Fiber Arts. The institute works in all forms of fine fabric art, but specializes in tapestry, wearable art, banners and paintings on silk. It's open Mondays and Wednesdays from 9 AM till 5 PM, but appointments for visiting on other days may be scheduled by calling the number listed.

Florida Craftsmen Inc.
501 Central Ave., St. Petersburg
• **(727) 821-7391**

St. Petersburg is the headquarters for Florida Craftsmen Inc., a statewide nonprofit group that promotes fine works by Florida's best contemporary craftspeople. The gallery is open Monday through Friday from 10 AM until 5 PM, or by appointment.

The Glass Canvas
233 Fourth Ave. N.E., St. Petersburg
• **(727) 821-6767**
1609 W. Snow Cir., Tampa
• **(813) 253-0055**

Glass is an art form unto itself, and at The Glass Canvas you'll find works from emerging international artists. The St. Petersburg gallery is open from 10 AM until 6 PM Monday through Friday, from 10 AM until 5 PM on Saturday and from noon until 5 PM on Sunday. The gallery in Old Hyde Park Village is open from 10 AM till 9 PM Monday through Saturday and from noon till 5 PM on Sunday.

P. Buckley Moss Gallery
190 Fourth Ave. N.E., St. Petersburg
• **(727) 894-2899**

P. Buckley Moss is one of the area's most renowned artists and this is where you'll find her original watercolors, etchings, prints and other works. The gallery is open from 10 AM until 6 PM Monday through Friday and from 10 AM until 5 PM on Saturday. From September through May, the gallery also opens on Sunday from noon until 5 PM.

Pass-A-Grille Art Colony
107 Eighth Ave., Pass-A-Grille
• **(727) 367-5654**

Local and Native American original works in traditional Florida themes are offered here. For an art experience that embodies the Gulf Coast, visit Pass-A-Grille Art Colony from 11AM until 4 PM Wednesday through Saturday. It's really a good idea to call ahead since the colony is often open other hours or may be closed on a particular day, depending on the season.

INSIDERS' TIP

The University of South Florida owns one of the nation's largest collections of turn-of-the-century music composed or performed by African Americans. USF received a privately owned, 350-piece collection of the late Sammy Davis Jr.'s musical arrangements. The collection is on loan until the year 2000.

Art in Tampa's Public Places

Ten years ago Tampa took a proactive stance for art by requiring that 1 percent of construction costs on municipal building projects be spent on art at the site. The following is a list of some of the resulting works and where to find them:

Sunshot — a painting by James Rosenquist, in the lobby of the Ashley Tower (Florida National Bank Building) at the southeast corner of Ashley and Whiting streets. It's open during business hours on weekdays;

Solstice — a stainless-steel sculpture by Charles Perry, at Barnett Plaza on Kennedy Boulevard at Tampa Street;

Close-up

Untitled — an opaque fiberglass sculpture by Doris Leeper, in the First Florida Tower on the southwest corner of Tampa and Madison streets;

Solaris — a solar-powered hanging sculpture by William Severson, in the lobby of the TECO Energy Building. Regional artists also have exhibits in this lobby. It's open during business hours on weekdays;

Untitled — a sculpture by George Sugarman in the NCNB Building at the corner of Ashley Drive and Kennedy Boulevard. This work is colloquially dubbed "the exploding chicken;"

Over the Waves — a bronze sculpture by C. Paul Jennewein at the Tampa City Center Esplanade, Franklin and Jackson streets;

Shamayin – Fire & Water — a fountain by Yaacov Agam at the Tampa Convention Center, 333 S. Franklin Street;

Bronzed Immigrant Statue — by Steve Dickey at Centennial Park, Eighth Avenue at 18th Street, Ybor City;

Family of Man — an aluminum sculpture by Geoffery Naylor, on Bayshore Boulevard near Gandy.

Photo: Paula Stahel

Bud Olsen's metal-sculpted horses grace, and graze, Tampa's Bayshore Boulevard.

All our glorious parks are meticulously maintained, and most recreation centers offer the widest spectrum of classes.

Parks and Recreation

If you ever stop to ponder the vast numbers of parks and good old-fashioned outdoor activity alternatives in the Tampa Bay area, it's hard to believe that any of us ever work, let alone find time to write a book about them. In fact, Hillsborough County alone has a network of 34 recreation centers, 19 athletic complexes and almost 150 parks. And we haven't even crossed Tampa Bay to the vast Pinellas County yet.

Needless to say, we'd run out of breath — and ink — trying to detail every park and recreation center in our region. Let it suffice to say that all our glorious parks are meticulously maintained, and most recreation centers offer the widest spectrum of classes, from swimming lessons to arts and crafts, with mind- and body-stimulating experiences for every age group from infants to senior adults.

Our nearly constant glorious weather brings forth a real desire to get out and do something, and all around the Bay area is a plethora of recreation to keep you active on vacation or to dust out the cobwebs after a desk-bound day.

Let's take a quick peek at some of the fun you can join. First, we'll take a look at our wonderful parks. Then we'll introduce you to a few of the recreational activities available in the area. For information about fishing, tennis and golf, see our individual chapters devoted to those sports.

For a complete list of all the recreational, athletic and park complexes in Tampa Bay, we will guide you to these organizations: Hillsborough County Parks and Recreation Department, (813) 975-2160, 1101 Rivercove Drive, Tampa; and Pinellas County Parks and Recreation Department, (727) 462-3347, 631 Chestnut Street, Clearwater.

Parks

Before you rush out into the beauty of our state and regional parks, there are a few rules that you should be aware of. First, all plant and animal life is zealously protected, so it goes without saying that hunting and timber removal are prohibited. While you might be tempted to offer a nibble to an adorable park animal, don't. It's for your own safety as well as that of the animals.

Speaking of animals, leave your own at home — pets are not allowed in camping areas, on bathing beaches and in other restricted areas. Where they are allowed, they must be on a 6-foot, hand-held leash and behave like well-mannered humans. Guide dogs for the handicapped are the exception. They are welcome in all areas of our parks.

Lastly, out-of-town visitors who plan on including a saltwater fishing experience to their park trip are required to obtain a saltwater fishing license and should check at the Ranger Station for seasonal guidelines.

Florida State Parks

Anclote Key State Preserve
Tarpon Springs • (727) 469-5918

Accessible only by private boat, this remote preserve just 3 miles off Tarpon Springs is home to six distinctive biological communities that shelter dozens of species of bird life, including the rare bald eagle. Standing sentinel on the southern tip of the beautiful white powder 4-mile-long beach is a picturesque 1887 federal lighthouse. For swimming, tranquil relaxation and spotting ospreys in the tall pines, Anclote is a perfect escape. You will have to bring everything you think you'll need, however, and that means water, food and a litter bag to remove any signs of urban life when you depart.

Caladesi Island State Park
Dunedin • (727) 469-5918

Just off the Gulf Coast and west of Dunedin, sits one of the few remaining large undeveloped barrier islands on Florida's Gulf Coast. While most nature seekers arrive there by private vessel, there is a scheduled passenger ferry that runs hourly from nearby Honeymoon Island State Recreation Area and from the city of Clearwater. Once you've arrived, you can spend a full day boating, fishing, swimming along the 3 miles of unspoiled beaches, shelling and wandering through the unspoiled island trails in this 600-acre park. Anchorage is fairly easy, because there's a 99-slip Bayside marina waiting to throw you a line. If you wish to overnight (from March through Labor Day), you'll have to register before sundown because overnight slips are limited to the first 20 reservations.

Egmont Key State Park
St. Petersburg • (727) 893-2627

At the mouth of Tampa Bay, southwest of Fort DeSoto Beach, is the unspoiled wonderland of Egmont Key. This 440-acre island is a lush habitat for sea, air and land wildlife. It also boasts the only manned lighthouse in the United States. Managed cooperatively by the Florida Department of Environmental Protection, the U.S. Fish and Wildlife Service and the U.S. Coast Guard, Egmont Key was a camp for captured Seminoles during the Third Seminole War and a Union Navy base during the Civil War. For the pleasure of sharing the spectacular landscape with the protected wildlife and history, you must use the power of your own boat — that's the only way to access the island.

Hillsborough River State Park
15402 U.S. Hwy. 301 N., Thonotosassa
• (813) 987-6771

Eight miles of nature trails, camping, swimming, canoeing and picnicking share top billing in the Hillsborough River State Park, 12 miles north of Tampa along the banks of the Hillsborough River. Opened to the public in 1936, this 2,994-acre park is noted for its massive hammocks of live oaks, sabal palms, magnolias and hickories that cast their huge shadows on the river banks. History buffs will thoroughly enjoy Fort Foster, a re-creation of the site as time froze it in history. You can wander though the fort as personnel carry on their daily duties just as they did more than 100 years ago. Kids are particularly fascinated by this living history program as it unfolds all around them. In addition to picnic facilities, freshwater fishing and nature and hiking trails, you can rent a canoe or take a splash in the half-acre swimming pool. Admission costs $3.25 a vehicle, with a maximum of eight parkgoers, plus a small fee if you plan to use the pool.

Honeymoon Island State Recreation Area
Dunedin • (727) 469-5942

In 1939 a New York developer constructed 50 palm-thatched honeymoon bungalows here as prizes for a contest sponsored by major northern department stores. His ingenuity was rewarded, and Hog Island was affectionately renamed Honeymoon Island as a result. It's still a grand place for romance, with its sun-drenched Gulf beaches, mangrove swamps and tidal flats. You can join the osprey and

www.insiders.com
See this and many other **Insiders' Guide®** destinations online — in their entirety.
Visit us today!

INSIDERS' TIP

Egmont Key has the distinction of being located along the Eastern Flyway, the migratory flight path for birds.

shorebirds by driving to the end of Fla. Highway 586, just north of Dunedin. Admission to the park costs $2 for cars with one occupant and $4 a vehicle with up to eight people.

Regional Parks

Hillsborough County

Hillsborough County operates nine parks that last year alone hosted more than 2.6 million visitors from all over the world. While all share the natural beauty that is so distinctively Florida, each park has its own personality, offering diverse recreational opportunities, from camping to swimming, fishing to canoeing and just wandering aimlessly through trails that make you feel one with the environment.

Upper Tampa Bay Park
8001 Double Branch Rd., Tampa
• (813) 855-1765

From the boardwalk along Tampa Bay to the environmental study center, there is much to do in this 2,144-acre park and preserve. Hiking along its trails is a favorite outing for families, who celebrate their efforts with a picnic under the shady trees.

Lake Park
17306 N. Dale Mabry Hwy., Tampa
• (813) 264-3806

The five beautiful lakes in this 600-acre paradise cleverly give Lake Park its name. There's a lot going on here for all ages including a very popular BMX track, radio-controlled car track and archery range. Naturally you'd expect fishing to be a big sport here, and there's also the Bakas Equestrian Center, (813) 975-2157, which caters to handicapped riders.

Lettuce Lake
6920 Fletcher Ave., Tampa
• (813) 987-6204

Mainly geared to cyclists, walkers and joggers, Lettuce Lake offers trails that meander through the park. One of the area's newest parks, it sprawls across the Hillsborough River and offers picnic tables, a playground and a large field for outdoor sports. An observation tower marks the main center for activity as

well as breathtaking views, with its adjacent nature center and boardwalk. A $1 donation for each vehicle is requested for entry.

E.G. Simmons Park
19th St. N.W., Ruskin • (813) 671-7655

A popular magnet for boaters and anglers, this 469-acre park on Tampa Bay also attracts birders, who can spy on the birdlife that thrives along the shallow waters of the surrounding mangrove swamps. On weekends, you'll have to arrive early to reserve your picnic table because this park is a favorite for family cookouts.

Eureka Springs
6400 Eureka Springs Rd., Tampa
• (813) 744-5536

Master gardeners-to-be rave about this 31-acre botanical garden of rare and unusual plants. The greenhouse and charming trellised walks are known to inspire those trying to cultivate an award-winning green thumb.

Alderman's Ford Park
9625 Canoe Launch Loop, Tampa
• (813) 757-3801

Take a look at the address and see if you can guess the most popular activity at this 1,141-acre park. Yup, it's a favorite launching place for canoers, who put out to the Alafia River for an afternoon of paddling. There's also something for landlubbers to do, with the boardwalk and pedestrian/bicycle trails that converge at the picnic area at river's edge. Admission to the park is free.

Edward Medard Park
5737 Turkey Creek Rd., Tampa
• (813) 757-3802

A popular spot for freshwater anglers, Ed Med Park is also a favorite for company picnics and other large local gatherings. A terrific playground area plus large fields for impromptu flag football games lure many a family to this park on weekends.

Lithia Springs Park
3932 Lithia Springs Rd., Tampa
• (813) 744-5572

You can backstroke here almost any day of the year, thanks to the 72-degree waters of these natural springs. There's a bathhouse for changing into your picnic clothes, and campers also are welcome at the park. There are 40 sites available for rental at $7 a night. Admission to Lithia Springs costs 50¢ a person.

Wilderness Park
Northeast Hillsborough County
• (813) 987-6208

Wilderness is actually comprised of six areas in the northeast quadrant of the county. You'll find fishing, canoeing, hiking, boardwalks and picnic areas at all of them.

Of all of these areas, Morris Bridge has certainly garnered the most recent applause because of the efforts of a group of bike-loving enthusiasts. Off-road bicyclists no longer have to cut through barbed wire to enjoy the wind-on-your-helmet bike tour though the park. Thanks to the efforts of SWAMP (that's SouthWest Association of Mountainbike Pedalers), a Tampa Bay bicycle club, more than 15 miles of sand and single-track trails have been given the checkered flag for biking enthusiasts who relish the trip through palmetto bushes, oak hammocks and lush, rolling meadows. In fact, SWAMP even convinced the Hillsborough County Parks and Recreation Department to build a parking lot so bikers could have easy access to the newly marked pedal pathways. They've also spearheaded the creation of maps and sign-in sheets to make sure visiting bikers get in and out of the park safely.

The only thing missing at this point in time is an increased number of bike patrol volunteers who would be available not only to assist visitors and help maintain trails, but also play a part in the planning process for new trails through other sections of the Wilderness Park region.

You'll find Morris Bridge Park on Morris Bridge Road along the Hillsborough River. The bicycle parking lot is east of I-75, just south of Morris Bridge Road at the Trout Creek Park entrance. To volunteer for the Morris Bridge Park Bicycle Patrol call (813) 975-2160.

The other parks within the Wilderness Park network are:

Flatwoods, Morris Bridge Road, a mile north of the Hillsborough River;

Dead River, U.S. Highway 301 and Dead River Road;

John B. Sargeant Sr. Memorial Park, U.S. 301 and Stacy Road;

Veterans Memorial Park, U.S. 301 and Martin Luther King Jr. Boulevard;

Trout Creek, Morris Bridge Road, a quarter-mile east of I-75.

Pinellas County

From Tarpon Springs at the north to Tierra Verde at the southern tip, Pinellas County operates 18 different parks, each with its own special personality, due primarily to the topography of the land on which they sit. At all of the parks you can find easy parking and restrooms, and the majority have sheltered picnic areas and playgrounds. For more specific information on facilities without direct phone numbers, contact the Pinellas County Parks and Recreation Department at (727) 464-3347.

Of all the parks in Pinellas County, the most unique is the Pinellas Trail, a 47-mile linear park that meanders from St. Petersburg all the way to Tarpon Springs, with an additional 23-mile stretch from Tarpon Springs to Seminole now under construction. When complete, the trail will have the distinction of being the longest one of its kind in the eastern United States. Open to walkers, bicyclists, skaters and nature lovers, the 15-foot-wide path, converted from old rail lines, is a marvel. The stalwart who attempt to travel the full length of this well-marked and well-used trail will find themselves weaving through open, rural land and lush, tropical foliage, winding along the Gulf of Mexico, passing through residential neighborhoods and darting along busy commercial areas.

As all county parks, it is open during daylight hours and is off-limits to any motorized vehicles with the exception of maintenance, law enforcement and emergency vehicles. All along its length at 500-foot intervals are little green signs with white numbers that serve as station, or location, numbers so you can be located quickly if you require any help. Walkers, joggers and wheelchair drivers use the pedestrian lane, while bikers and skaters share the bicycle lane.

To get an armchair tour of the trail, call the

Sand Key Park in Clearwater is rated one of America's top-20 beach parks.

Photo: St. Petersburg/Clearwater Area Convention & Visi

Pinellas County Planning Department at (727) 464-4751. Chip Haynes has created a spiral-bound guidebook that, like the old familiar *Triptik*, takes you down the trail in manageable sections. He and his team walked the entire trail themselves, noting important landmarks and interviewing people, restaurants and services along the route. They included answers to the most asked questions: Where can I get a drink of water or a burger?, Can I come in with in-line skates on?, Where can I get air for my bike tires? and Where am I now? Your own copy is free for the asking.

Fund-raising for trail amenities such as benches, water fountains and markers is always under way, as is the Trees for Trails program, which has provided thousands of dollars for the purchase of landscape materials to beautify the corridor. For more information about donation and volunteer opportunities, call the nonprofit Pinellas Trail Inc. at (727) 441-1466.

If you haven't exhausted your enthusiasm for the great ourdoors, grab the family and head out to one of these popular neighborhood parks in Pinellas County.

A.L. Anderson Park
1095 Tookes Rd., Tarpon Springs
• (813) 937-5410

Slide that boat down the ramp from Lake Tarpon's western shores and enjoy a leisurely day of fishing. Then, after a burnt burger on the grill, you can stroll the nature trail and trade fish stories while the kids hang precariously from the playground equipment.

Belleair Boat Ramp
3900 W. Bay Dr., Belleair Bluffs

Your ticket into the Atlantic Intracoastal Waterway, you'll probably have to wait a bit on a sunny day to get that hull wet at this busy ramp. Find additional ramps operated by the county's parks department at Madeira Beach, Indian Shores, Redington Shores, St. Pete Beach and Treasure Island.

John Chestnut Sr. Park
2200 E. Lake Rd., Palm Harbor
- **(727) 784-4686**

On the eastern shore of Lake Tarpon, vying for your activity attention are the boat ramps that lead to some mighty good fishing, a canoe trail, softball field, nature trail, playgrounds and sheltered picnic areas with grills.

Fort DeSoto
3500 Pinellas Bayway S., Tierra Verde

At what seems to be the edge of the world, Fort DeSoto is famous for its 7-mile stretch of quiet beaches laden with all sorts of shells for the picking. Sprawling though 900 acres on five islands that extend into Tampa Bay, Fort DeSoto makes for a perfect day's outing for local families and visitors alike. On Mullet Key, the largest of the islands, you'll find the site of Fort DeSoto, built in 1898 to protect the Bay in the Spanish-American War, but still under construction at war's end. History buffs will be pleased to know that the fort lays claim to never having fired a shot in anger.

The area also has a boat ramp, fishing piers, picnic shelters, playgrounds and restrooms with showers. They also make a mean chili-dog in the snack bar adjacent to the gift shop, although we doubt this contributed much to Fort DeSoto's inclusion as one of the top-20 beach parks in America. Admission to Fort DeSoto is free, but there is an 85¢ toll to enter the park.

Fred H. Howard Park
1700 Sunset Dr., Tarpon Springs
- **(813) 937-4938**

Swim in the crystal blue Gulf waters, fish and play softball. The park has beach showers, too, so you can clean up before that sunset picnic. It's a great hang-out for the younger generation, always ready for a killer game of beach volleyball.

Lake Seminole Park
10015 74th Ave., Seminole
- **(727) 392-2972**

A 2-mile recreational trail, softball fields, boat ramp and fishing are here to enjoy on the banks of tranquil Lake Seminole.

Seminole City Park
7464 Ridge Rd., Seminole
- **(727) 391-0204**

This is a small park, but it certainly makes a lot of noise! That's because it is home to a boisterous resident population of peacocks and peahens, not to mention roosters and chickens. You'll also find the usual collection of playground equipment, picnic tables and shady trees for an afternoon snooze.

Philippe Park
2355 Bayshore Dr., Safety Harbor
- **(727) 726-2600**

This is a great place to teach the younger set the finer points of launching a fishing boat into Tampa Bay. It's also a great place for the younger set to teach you a thing or two about softball. You can both learn a lot from the park's Indian Burial Mound, which has been designated a national historic site.

Ridgecrest Park
12101 Ulmerton Rd., Largo
- **(727) 585-3736**

Ridgecrest features the traditional sheltered picnic areas with grills plus a softball field and fishing.

INSIDERS' TIP

Children and adults who are wheelchair-dependent, have cerebral palsy, autism and other disabilities, at last have a park to call their own. All People's Park, designed specifically to accommodate the special needs of disabled residents, has just been completed on 20 acres in Tampa east of 56th Street and Sligh Avenue. The $15.5 million facility incorporates necessary equipment such as railings and special walkways as well as a center for disabled senior citizens, a performing arts center, an arts and crafts center, a swimming pool, a gymnasium and several cottages where life skills will be taught.

Sand Key Park
1060 Gulf Blvd., Clearwater Beach
• **(727) 595-7677**

Rated one of America's top-20 beach parks, don't even think about finding a place to park if you sleep late during spring break. This is where it's happenin', dude. The beach is the whitest sand powder you'll find anywhere on earth, the Gulf waters are friendly and the volleyball is fierce. For mini-beach lovers, there's a large playground, plus another multi-themed playground for kids up to 12 years of age.

Walkers will definitely appreciate the measured mile. There's a fishing pier with resident pelicans, and you can rent both chairs and umbrellas. A warning if you decide to grab lunch at a beachside eatery: Watch out for the swooping sea gulls, which have a deeper desire for a bite of your lunch than they have fear of you.

Sawgrass Lake Park
7400 25th St. N., St. Petersburg
• **(727) 527-3814**

In the heart of St. Petersburg, Sawgrass Lake Park is the home of the Environmental Education Center that features very popular outdoor classrooms. A favorite pastime here is strolling along the boardwalks and nature trails cut out of the thick foliage.

John S. Taylor Park
1100 Eighth Ave. S.W., Largo
• **(727) 584-7448**

An exercise trail, a softball field, boat ramps and fishing are the draws to this park just off U.S. Highway Alternate 19 in Largo. Canoeing is also a hot family sport here.

War Veteran's Memorial Park
9600 Bay Pines Blvd. N., Bay Pines
• **(727) 392-9575**

On a tip of land that juts out into Boca Ciega Bay, Memorial Park offers a boat ramp, fishing, a playground and sheltered picnic areas with grills.

Tampa

In this area with a year-round growing season, you can bet that the City of Tampa Parks and Recreation Department never sleeps. They are responsible for eight major parks (five have a resident park ranger) and more than 100 small parks that include more than 400 pieces of playground equipment.

Other landside duties include the maintenance of more than 200 landscape medians down the center of streets throughout the city as well as a 5-acre nursery where the shrubs and ground covers are grown that keep parks and parkways green.

At work on the water, too, the Tampa Parks and Recreation Department operates and maintains two city marinas with more than 100 rented boat slips. For more specific information about any of the parks, and to learn how to become a member of the Park Volunteer Program, call (813) 223-8230.

Here is a brief overview of the eight major Tampa parks.

Al Lopez Park
4810 N. Himes Ave., Tampa

You'll find ball fields, picnic facilities, exercise/jogging trails and fishing. Because of its proximity to Houlihan's Stadium, it's a most popular hangout during football season. It's where happy tailgaters often link up to get the Buc's fever whipped into full frenzy by gametime.

Copeland Park
11001 N. 15th St., Tampa

This park has ball fields, tennis and racquetball courts, a swimming pool and nature and exercise/jogging trails.

INSIDERS' TIP

Fall weather's great for getting outdoors, no matter what your age. If you're older than 55, why not participate in the annual Senior Games, hosted during four days each October by the Temple Terrace Recreation Center. If your abilities run more toward baking, dancing or other talents, there are even events for you! Call (813) 989-7180 for dates and information.

Photo: St. Petersburg/Clearwater Area Convention & Visitors Bureau

Tampa Bay's wetland sanctuaries are home to several species of shorebirds and other migratory waterfowl.

Picnic Island Park
7404 Picnic Island Blvd., Tampa
This pleasant little park has a boat ramp, fishing area and a beach.

Rowlett Park
2401 E. Yukon St., Tampa
Rowlett Park has tennis and racquetball courts, a playground and picnic areas.

MacFarlane Park
1700 N. MacDill Blvd., Tampa
Tennis and racquetball courts, a swimming pool and playground are available here.

Riverfront Park
1111 North Blvd., Tampa
Ball fields, tennis and racquetball courts and a swimming pool provide recreational opportunities.

Ben T. Davis Beach
Courtney Campbell Cswy., Tampa
In addition to a pleasant little sliver of beach plus picnic areas, this is a favorite launch spot for Jet Skis. On any given sunny day, anytime of year, you'll have to arrive early to stake out your little patch of beach along old Tampa Bay, and your parking space as well.

Lowry Park
7525 North Blvd., Tampa

Fishing, a beach, concessions and boat ramps join the nature, exercise and jogging trails as attractions here. The park is home to the popular Lowry Park Zoo.

St. Petersburg/Clearwater

Parks dot the landscape throughout the St. Petersburg/Clearwater area — 108 in all, covering more than 2,400 acres. The City of St. Petersburg also stands guard over five beaches, eight swimming pools and the 610-slip Municipal Marina with a 500-foot transient dock for visiting boaters. We've highlighted just a few of the most popular recreational destinations here. For a full menu of all the alternatives, you can contact one of the area's parks and recreation departments:

St. Petersburg, (727) 893-7441;
Clearwater; (727) 462-6531;
Dunedin, (727) 738-1888:
Largo, (727) 587-6720;
Pinellas Park, (727) 541-0770;
Seminole, (727) 391-8345;
Tarpon Springs, (813) 942-5610;
Palm Harbor, (727) 785-9862.

Bartlet Park
2000 Seventh St. S., St. Petersburg
• (727) 893-7731

The St. Petersburg Tennis Center is here, along with ball fields (one lighted for night play), basketball courts, a community center and a sidewalk fitness trail.

Boyd Hill Nature Park
1101 Country Club Way S.,
St. Petersburg • (727) 893-7326

An Insiders' favorite! Sitting at the end of Lake Maggiore, Boyd Hill sprawls over 245 acres of unspoiled land that features more than 3 miles of nature trails and boardwalks. It also boasts an education center, environmental studies area and a library. Bicyclists are welcome, and grills are available to those who hanker to strike up the coals for their picnic supper. Especially popular here are the regularly scheduled night walks, as well as daytime bird, wildflower and ecology walks. Admission costs 50¢ for children and $1 for adults.

Campbell Park
601 14th St. S., St. Petersburg

This park is a sport enthusiast's dream: baseball/softball fields (one lighted), football and soccer fields, adapted play equipment, tennis and racquetball/handball courts, a community center and swimming pool.

Countryside Community Park
2640 Sabal Spring Dr., Clearwater

You'll find these 20 acres a busy place. The park has baseball/softball fields, basketball courts, fishing areas, a multipurpose field and a fitness trail.

Highlander Park
903 Michigan Blvd., Dunedin

This park has baseball/softball fields, a rec center, a swimming pool and a fitness trail.

Lake Vista Park
1401 62nd Ave. S., St. Petersburg
• (727) 893-7744

Lake Vista has baseball/softball fields (one lighted), tennis courts, adapted play equipment, shuffleboard courts, a swimming pool and a fitness trail.

Long Center
1501 N. Belcher Rd., Clearwater
• (727) 462-6028

This complex features 15 acres for a rec center, basketball courts, an indoor swimming pool, a game room, a multipurpose field and playgrounds.

Northwest Park
5801 22nd Ave. N., St. Petersburg

This park includes baseball/softball fields (four lighted), tennis and basketball courts, a sidewalk fitness trail, a community center and a swimming pool.

Ross Norton Recreational Complex
1425 S. Greenwood Ave., Clearwater
• (727) 462-6025

Facilities for baseball, softball, basketball and fishing are part of this complex, as are three swimming pools, tennis courts, a fitness trail and a recreation center with game room.

Sparkle Lake
4501 84th Ave. N., Pinellas Park

This spring-fed lake is complemented by picnic pavilions, multipurpose courts and exercise equipment for the handicapped.

Walter Fuller Park
7891 26th Ave. N., St. Petersburg
• **(727) 893-7443**

This park includes a Busch Major League Complex (where the St. Louis Cardinals hold spring training), a BMX bicycle complex, baseball/softball/soccer/football fields, adapted play equipment, a swimming pool, tennis courts, a community center and an exercise trail.

Recreation

Tampa, St. Petersburg and Clearwater all have city recreation departments with activities from art to yoga for people of all ages and abililites. Each city produces a highly informative booklet describing all of their programs. To get complete information on what's available near you, contact the following:

Tampa Recreation Department, 1420 N. Tampa Street, Tampa, (813) 274-8615;

St. Petersburg Parks and Recreation Department, 1400 19th Street N., St. Petersburg, (727) 893-7441;

Clearwater Parks and Recreation Department, 10 S. Missouri Avenue, Clearwater, (727) 562-4800.

Ballooning

Hillsborough County

Fantasy Flights Inc.
16302 E. Course Dr., Tampa
• **(813) 969-1518**

For the big red balloons, the sky's the limit in sightseeing adventure. You'll cruise over the Tampa Bay area for a panoramic view of the lakes, diverse wildlife and landscape. The three-and-a-half-hour event includes the balloon's inflation, an hour of flight and a catered champagne picnic brunch with a brief

history of ballooning. All pilots are FAA certified. There's also a full training program if you'd like to be a pilot yourself. Flights take place daily, but you've got to make reservations at least a week ahead. The cost is $150 a person, including tax, and all major credit cards are accepted.

Baseball

Hillsborough County

City of Tampa
Recreation Department
1420 N. Tampa St., Tampa
• **(813) 231-5270**

Nineteen recreational and upper level division teams break out in three age categories: 18 through 29; 30 through 39; and 40 and older. Tryouts are required. You can either register as a team or sign up for the player draft. During the spring/summer season, teams play 18 to 28 games. In the fall, teams play 16 games at eight baseball diamonds around town. The two-out-of-three championship playoff is broadcast live on the local government access cable channel. Games are limited to three hours, with play starting at 7:30 PM on Wednesdays and between 10 AM and 6 PM on Sundays. An $80 fee covers the cost of baseballs and paid umpires. You supply the rest.

Pinellas County

Clearwater Parks and
Recreation Department
10 S. Missouri Ave., Clearwater
• **(727) 562-4800**

If Cal Ripken Jr. played recreational ball, this league for players older than 30 is where he'd be. This is a strong coalition of former high school, college and even pro players who still want to be Boys of Summer. The season starts off with a manager's meeting in mid-March. This is serious stuff — the team fee is $1,225. Practices are on Saturdays, with games played at 7:15 PM on Tuesdays and Thursdays and at 10 AM and 4 PM on Sundays.

Basketball

Hillsborough County

City of Tampa
Recreation Department
1420 N. Tampa St., Tampa
• (813) 231-5270

Boys and girls ages 10 through 15 can join weekend or after-school youth basketball leagues that play at local school gymnasiums. League sign-ups take place during several Saturdays prior to seasonal play. There are no tryouts — the purpose here is to introduce kids to the sport and let them enjoy the fun as they learn techniques and skills. The $15 registration fee includes a league T-shirt.

Pinellas County

City of St. Petersburg
Athletics Department
1320 Fifth St. N., St. Petersburg
• (727) 893-7298

Men older than 18 form their own basketball teams to participate in one or all of the four seasonal schedules hosted by St. Petersburg. Based on ability, teams are placed in A, B, C or D leagues. The cost is $275 a team. Sorry, there aren't any provisions to get you signed up with a team if you can't put your own together.

Clearwater Parks and
Recreation Department
10 S. Missouri Ave., Clearwater
• (727) 562-4800

League play for kids ages 8 through 15 is co-sponsored with the Clearwater-for-Youth Organization. Separate leagues are set up for girls and boys. Tryouts take place in November, and play dates start in December and end in February. Games are held Tuesday, Wednesday and Thursday evenings plus Saturday morning at the Long Center, 1501 N. Belcher Road, Clearwater, (727) 462-6425. League registration is $35 and includes a T-shirt.

Clearwater Parks and
Recreation Department
10 S. Missouri Ave., Clearwater
• (727) 562-4800

Men's adult basketball is designed as competitive fun for all those hoopsters who enjoy recreational play. Practice games begin the first week of December to prep for league play between January and March. Team registration is $295.

Biking and Skating — Rentals

Hillsborough County

Blades & Bikes Bayshore
201 W. Platt St., Tampa • (813) 251-0178

Near the Platt Street Bridge into downtown Tampa, Blades & Bikes is the hot spot to start on a leg-driven cruise along the Bayshore. As the name suggests, both in-line skates and bicycles are available. Prices are discounted when you take a spin with a buddy. One hour on in-line skates costs $13 for two people. If there are more, it's an additional $1 a person. All-day rental costs $14 for one person and $24 for two. Two-day rental costs $52 for two, and three-day rental for two costs $62. Bike rental costs $8 an hour for one person. Each additional rental costs only $5. Cash and major credit cards are accepted. This is a great sporting place to make new friends by joining in the ongoing calendar of activities. Not sure if you've got what it takes to skate? Call in advance and reserve a free instruction period.

INSIDERS' TIP

Want to go camping but don't have a tent? The Play It Again Sports store at 13238 N. Dale Mabry Highway in Tampa rents a variety of sizes at $10 to $15 a night. Call (813) 969-0855 to reserve one. You can also snag a pair of rollerblades while you're there.

In the winter season, Blades & Bikes is open weekdays from 10 AM until 7 PM, Saturdays from 9 AM until 7 PM and Sundays from 10 AM until 5 PM. Hours are extended during the summer season. Be sure to ask about the Sunday morning trail skates that meet out at Morris Bridge Park.

Play It Again Sports
13238 N. Dale Mabry Hwy., Tampa
- **(813) 969-0855**

3914 S. Dale Mabry Hwy., Tampa
- **(813) 837-8771**

744 W. Lumsden Rd., Brandon
- **(813) 661-4141**

There are a number of Play It Again Sports stores around the Bay area, but at these three you'll definitely find in-line skates to rent. Along with unisex skates in sizes 5 through 13, you get knee, elbow and wrist protectors. The N. Dale Mabry store charges $10 a day and $15 overnight; or for $25 you get the equipment for three days and two nights. The S. Dale Mabry store at Britton Plaza charges $10 for a 24-hour rental. In Brandon, the fee is $15 for a day or less. A deposit is required, and payment can be made by check, cash or credit card. All three stores are open Monday through Saturday from 10 AM until 8 PM and Sunday from noon until 6 PM.

Skate 2000
2367 E. Fowler Ave., Tampa
- **(813) 977-1677**

2832 S. MacDill Ave., Tampa
- **(813) 831-1936**

217 Brandon TownCenter Dr., Brandon
- **(813) 653-4430**

349A Main St., Dunedin • (727) 234-7849

Think you might like to try in-line skating, but aren't ready to rent or buy? Every Skate 2000 store offers free lessons at 10 AM on Sunday morning, and all equipment is included. Rental costs $5 an hour, $10 for four

hours or $15 for 24 hours, and all protective gear comes with the quality skates. The East Fowler store is a great location for college students and hours are 10 AM until 8 PM Monday through Saturday and 10 AM until 6 PM on Sunday. Down in south Tampa, the store is only two short blocks off Bayshore Boulevard. Hours there are 10 AM until 8 PM Monday through Friday, 9 AM until 8 PM on Saturday and 9 AM to 6 PM on Sunday.

Pinellas County

The Beach Cyclist Sports Center
7517 Blind Pass Rd., St. Pete Beach
- **(727) 367-5001**

The Beach Cyclist is just where its name says it is, right on the beach. Several bike styles are available for rent, along with baby seats and helmets. For $15 you get the bike overnight, or you can rent one for three days at $30, a week at $45 or a month at $75. All rentals include a lock and cable. A major credit card is required for the security deposit, but payment can be made by cash or check. Open Monday through Saturday from 7 AM until 6 PM and Sunday from 10 AM until 3 PM, the same rates apply to in-line skate rentals.

Transportation Station
652 Gulfview Blvd., Clearwater Beach
- **(727) 443-3188**

Bikes, blades and scooters are all for rent here and what's more, you get a free tank of gas and free mileage with the scooter. One- and two-passenger scooters go for $13 and $18 for an hour or can be rented for up to a month. Bikers choose from beach cruisers, one-speeds, tandems, road bikes, mountain bikes and three-wheelers, at a range of rates including hourly, overnight, multi-day or multi-week. The rental prices start as low as $5. Day use of in-line skates is a flat $5 an hour, but deals go from overnight at $20 to multi-day,

---

INSIDERS' TIP

More than 300 area off-road bikers are members of SWAMP (Southwest Association of Mountain-bike Peddlers) and they take to area trails throughout Hillsborough and Pinellas counties. To get involved in the club's active calendar, call (813) 985-5021.

At Weedon Island Preserve, a 4-mile canoe trail and 9-mile hiking trail allow outdoor enthusiasts to study and enjoy Mother Nature. Three bald eagle nests have been spotted among the 1,500 scenic acres.

Photo: St. Petersburg/Clearwater Area Convention & Visitors Bureau

weekly and monthly. Baby seat, helmet and car rack rentals also are available for those renting bikes. No refunds are offered, but rain checks are. Between the HoJo and Quality inns near the bridge to Sand Key, Transportation Station is open 365 days a year from 9 AM until dusk.

Bowling

Hillsborough County

AMF Florida Lanes
10400 N. Florida Ave., Tampa
• **(813) 932-6161**

With just 32 wooden lanes, this place is popular with a lot of regulars. Its psychedelic decor is especially fitting during the Moonlight Bowl on Saturdays at 9 PM. A $10 entry fee allows you to bowl in the dark with colored, lighted pins and affords you a chance to win prizes ranging from $200 to $1,500. Daytime is great for open bowling, but there are a lot of specials offered during the week, such as $1 games daily during Happy Hour (3:30 until 5:30

PM) and the Monday Night Football special at $1.25 a game. Regular rates for adults are $2.35 during the day and $2.60 in the evening; kids pay $1.75 at all times. The Conbow Cafe and Bill's Sports Bar & Grill provide a range of snacks and drinks. Florida Lanes opens at 9 AM every day. Closing is at midnight Sunday through Thursday and at 3 AM on Friday and Saturday. Parking lot security is provided.

AMF University Bowl
13109 N. 56th St., Tampa
• **(813) 985-4468**

Lanes one through six are synthetic and the rest of the 50 lanes are wood, giving bowlers a choice of play. The game room is a big hit with the kiddies, as is the old-fashioned photo booth — you remember the kind where you pull the curtain, feed in quarters ($2.50 worth now) and make funny faces that get captured on strips of black-and-white prints. Near the lounge is a pool table, and the clean snack bar offers everything from grilled sandwiches to salads. League play is heavy on weeknights (a free nursery is available) from 6 to 9:30 PM, so the best time for open bowling is before or after those hours. The cost for adults is $2.95 a game after 6 PM or $2.35 before, with various specials offered. Games for kids always cost $1.90. AMF University Bowl is open Sunday through Thursday from 9 AM until 1 AM and Friday and Saturday from 9 AM until 3 AM. The parking lot is patrolled by security after dark.

Crown Bowling Lanes
5555 W. Hillsborough Ave., Tampa
• **(813) 884-1475**

This 40-lane center is always hopping since it's a block east of the Veterans Expressway and easily accessible from northern Pinellas County. Leagues play every night, all year long. Bumper bowling is a great place to start off the little ones, or sign up older youngsters for the kids' leagues. Video games and pool tables fill the game room. Sandwiches, salads and chicken wings can be munched at the snack bar, or there's the full-service bar for relaxing.

Security guards cover the parking lot at night, and on weekends an off-duty member of the sheriff's department keeps an eagle eye on things. The price of a game during the day is $2.20, and at night it goes up to $2.60. Crown opens at 8:30 AM on Sunday, Tuesday, Wednesday and Thursday and 11 AM on Monday, with closing on all those days at midnight. On Friday the center opens at 11 AM and on Saturday at 8:30 AM. Closing time on these two nights is "whenever," which loosely translates as sometime between 2 and 3 AM.

Brandon Crossroads Bowl
609 Crater Ln., Brandon • (813) 621-2363

This place seems to have it all, and its popularity attracts folks from all over. Being easy to get to helps. It's just off I-75, U.S. Highway 301 and the Lee Roy Selmon (Crosstown) Expressway. All 40 lanes are synthetic, which helps Crossroads' claim of being the highest-scoring bowling center around the Bay.

From 6 PM until midnight every night, there's so much league bowling it's not even funny. If you're looking for open play, the best bet is weekdays, Saturday afternoons, after 9 PM on Friday and Saturday or during the day on Sunday. Prices vary, so you might want to call ahead and check. Seniors get a discount. A large video room carries all the latest games, and eight full-size billiards tables attract an-

other style of gamesmanship. The restaurant and lounge attract a lot of locals, especially to the weekday business lunch specials between 11 AM and 2 PM. Former pro champ Tom Milton operates the pro shop, so you can count on quality in both advice and products. To make sure everyone stays safe, video security keeps surveillance indoors and out. Brandon Crossroads is open seven days a week from 9 AM until 1 AM.

Pinellas County

Sunrise Lanes
6393 Ninth St. N., St. Petersburg
• **(727) 522-2174**

With 32 lanes, Sunrise prides itself on being a cozy, homey sort of place — it's a popular morning coffee stop for folks from the Snell Isle and Shore Acres neighborhoods. There's a regular Junior League for kids from ages 5 through 19, and on Saturdays during the summer, the Handicap Youth/Adult League, a social club for folks with disabilities, bowls here. Friday and Saturday nights offer something special for everyone — Galactic Bowling at $3 a game.

For additional entertainment, the game room pays out tokens redeemable for prizes, or pretend you're Minnesota Fats at one of the five pool tables. Short-order service is available in the snack bar, and the lounge offers televised satellite programming. The Sunshine Pro Shop carries supplies, and there's a nursery for kids 7 years and younger during league play. The best time for open bowling is all day Sunday, business hours during the weekday, evenings after 9 PM or Saturday after 2 PM. If you're the sort who likes to mix housework and play, take your clothes to the next-door laundromat and bowl between wash and dry cycles. The Sunrise Resource Center, a neighborhood information center manned by volunteers and police, is also in the same strip shop area.

Day price for a game is $2.50; games on nights and weekends cost $2.80; seniors always pay $1.80. All games cost only $1 Sunday from 9 AM until noon. Sunday through Thursday, Sunrise Lanes is open from 9 AM until 2 AM.

AMF Clearwater Bowl
1850 N. Hercules Ave., Clearwater
• (727) 461-2511

This bowling center is a popular place for tournaments. It has 50 wood lanes, a nursery for children younger than 7, a good pro shop, a lounge and a short-order snack bar. The arcade offers a variety of games, and there's a pool table. The regular day price is $2.19; from 5 until 9 PM it's $2.79; and after 9 PM the price drops to $1.99. And all day Sunday, from 9 AM until 5 PM, the cost is only $1.29. While there's usually some open bowling all the time, from 3 to 6:30 PM is best because night leagues start at 6:30 and senior leagues play mornings and early afternoons. AMF Clearwater opens at 9 AM every day. Closing is at 11:30 PM Sunday through Thursday and at 2 AM on Friday and Saturday.

Countryside Lanes
27867 U.S. Hwy. 19 N., Clearwater
• (727) 796-8100

Just north of Countryside Mall, this place has some unique features: first, a beauty parlor; second, its own radio station; and third, a fancy nightclub for dinner and dancing. The folks here pride themselves on the family atmosphere, from bumper bowling for the littlest ones to a popular gameroom that attracts lots of local teens who know rowdy behavior is not tolerated. The pro shop offers the most modern in equipment, and you'll find a restaurant-style snack bar and a sports bar. Open 9 AM until 11:30 PM Sunday through Thursday and until 12:30 AM on Friday and Saturday, Countryside keeps a security guard on the premises. Daytime games cost $1.95 for adults and $1.75 for seniors and "juniors" (kids). At night, games cost $2.40 across the board.

AMF Kenneth City Lanes
5890 54th Ave. N., Kenneth City
• (727) 541-3539

All 40 lanes here are synthetic, making this a jazzy place to put a spin on a ball. There's a large arcade with a wide variety of games, including some that pay out tokens to redeem for prizes. Two pool tables are next to the game room. The nursery cares for kids from 6 months

through 8 years for league players, and a short-order grill and a full bar are available. Parking is ample and well-lit but there's no on-property security. As the manager says, "We don't need it." That's because Kenneth City is 3 miles wide by 3 miles long and has nine police officers, so three cruisers are on the prowl in this hamlet 24 hours a day. Day game price for adults is $2.40, and kids and seniors pay $1.75; at night it costs $2.75. On Sunday mornings, you can play three games for $3.75. Lanes may be reserved for any time, but the best open bowling is between 9 AM and 6 PM or after 9 PM on weekdays; Saturday from noon to close; and all day on Sunday. Crossroads opens at 9 AM seven days a week and closes at midnight Sunday through Thursday and at 1 AM on Friday and Saturday.

Camping and RVs

Hillsborough County

Tampa East KOA Kampground
12870 U.S. Hwy. 92, Dover
• (813) 659-2202

Go ahead, rough it — even if your idea of roughing it is in a fully-equipped RV. Shady and sunny sites abound for pull-through or tenting. Lots of activities give you plenty to do, such as swimming in the pool or playing shuffleboard, horseshoes, volleyball and badminton. The kids have their own playground. Low-pressure gas and RV supplies are available, and there's a convenience store for whatever you forgot or may run out of. Weekly and monthly rates are offered, but prices change during the seasons, so call ahead for specifics.

Pinellas County

St. Petersburg Resort
KOA Kampground
5400 95th St. N., St. Petersburg
• (727) 392-2233, (800) 562-7714

Tucked away on a mangrove-lined bayou along the Pinellas Trail, this award-winning KOA boasts a full array of facilities and amenities. So if your partner wants to get back to nature, but you, like Fran Leibowitz, would rather get back to the hotel, this should please you both. There are more than 300 deluxe waterfront or oak-shaded campsites, an RV camp and, for ultimate convenience, air-conditioned one- and two-room "Kamping Kabins."

To occupy your leisure time, there's a huge, heated pool, three hot tubs and a string of white sand beaches. You can rent bikes for trail rides and canoes for bayou exploration. Volleyball, shuffleboard and boccie ball courts are also available. Canadian visitors can have the fun of sharing the finer points of the popular game Pétanque. Kids have a video game room, playground and miniature golf course, and adults can take part in planned activities during the season.

An on-site convenience store and laundry facilities are offered, and all restrooms have hot showers. Basic rates cover two adults. If there are children or more than two adults, the cost is a bit more. Site rates range from a base of $24.95 up to $32.95, excluding tax, and are based on whether you request water, electric and sewer hookup or waterfront location. Cabins cost from $49.95 to $59.95 a night in season, with rates ranging from $31.95 to $47.95 out of season.

Holiday Campground
10000 Park Blvd., Seminole
• **(727) 391-4960**

Just off Park Boulevard near the bridge to Redington Shores, you've got a choice of more than 600 sunny and shaded sites with water and electric hookups. Cable TV is also available. Reservations can be made for stays of a week or more. For short-term visits during peak season, full hookup sites are subject to availability. Minimum reservation rates range from $20 a day to $420 a month, but prices vary during different seasons, so be sure to call in advance for current information. Off-site storage, required for extra vehicles, boats and such, is provided at an additional charge.

About 3 miles from the Gulf beaches, the camp has a heated pool, spa, a kid's playground, shuffleboard courts, boccie ball, horseshoes, an exercise room and saltwater fishing pier. Across the road is Lake Seminole Park, with freshwater fishing and miles of bike trails.

During the winter season, vacationers have no excuse for boredom as there's a full roster of planned activities. Euchre, cribbage, pinochle and bridge are regular card games. Also offered are bingo, billiards, sing-alongs, choir and line dancing. For those whose RVs are a bit crowded with unused stuff, periodic Saturday morning flea markets give you a chance to sell and buy goodies. Also at Holiday Campground you'll, of course, find a camp store and RV supplies, mail facilities, coin laundries and phone hookups.

Palm Harbor Resort
2119 Alt. U.S. Hwy. 19 N., Palm Harbor
• **(727) 785-3402**

Next to the Pinellas Trail on a protected bayou leading to the Gulf, both novice and pro fishermen find its grass flats at the mouth of the Bay excellent for catching trout, reds, snook, flounder and tarpon. Artificial offshore reefs are within easy boating distance. Efficiency cottages rent at rates of $35 a day, $170 a week or $600 a month. Park your own RV for only $21 a day, $125 a week or $295 a month (if you stay 6 months or more, the rate's only $275), plus a small electric fee. Dock your own boat or rent one. In fact, you can even rent rods, tackle and equipment. When you're back from the open water, rinse off under the shower, scrub your clothes at the laundry, relax at the resort's heated pool or take off for a bike ride or walk along the trail.

Canoeing

Hillsborough County

Canoe Escape
9335 E. Fowler Ave., Tampa
• **(813) 986-2067**

A lazy day is just what you need to drift out of life's hectic jet stream. And with Canoe Escape's help, you can actually drift, and paddle, all the way back to Florida's "lifestyle" of 2000 years ago! The gathering place to start your trip is at the store on Fowler Avenue. From there, you're transported to Wilderness Park, a 16,000-acre preserve. Your canoe is launched for you — the only thing you have to touch is your paddle — and you're off for a laid-back journey downstream on the upper section of the Hillsborough River.

This area is simply outstanding for viewing native wildlife, from turtles and birds to alligators. That's lots and lots and lots of alligators. Swim at your own risk, shall we say? Basic trips last either two, four or six hours, but as long as you're at the pick-up site by 5 PM, how long you meander is up to you. Rates start at $28 for two adults in a canoe and there's no charge for kids younger than 12. Call ahead for specifics and to reserve your date. (Experienced canoers, take note: ask about the Crystal River trips.)

Alafia River Canoe Rentals
4419 River Dr., Valrico • (813) 689-8645

Only an hour from downtown Tampa, the Alafia River is a narrow, twisting water trail that begins at Alderman's Ford Park. From the drop-off point at the head of the state canoe trail, it's a 12-mile trip back (with the current) along the Alafia, draped under a canopy of oak, cypress and cedar. That's only about half the length of this blackwater river, which means it's clear but has been turned tea-brown by tree roots (so why isn't it called "brownwater," pray tell?). Plan paddling time of about four hours on this fairly swift stretch of river. The Alafia is very changeable, and the degree of canoeing difficulty depends on water level, so the time you spend will depend on that and your own desire for leisure. The set rate is $25 a canoe, which holds up to three adults or two adults and two children. This is a popular place for days off, so you'll want to make reservations.

Flag Football

Pinellas County

City of St. Petersburg Athletics Department
1320 Fifth St. N., St. Petersburg
• (727) 893-7298

Fall may be the season for pro football, but here the game gets played year round.

Men older than 18 can sign up their teams to compete in A, B, C or D leagues. Competition is so tight there are always playoffs to determine the champs. In summer, fall and winter, games are played at Woodlawn Community Center, 1450 16th Street and in spring, at Azalea Community Center, 1400 72nd Street N. If you're a free agent looking for a team, call to see if you can get introduced to some of the captains — that's the best they can do. Team cost is $330 plus a $20 annual registration fee that gets you the FRPA rule book and information on state-ranked tournaments in this state-sanctioned recreational sport.

Clearwater Parks and Recreation Department
10 S. Missouri Ave., Clearwater
• (727) 562-4800

This league is similar to the program offered through the City of St. Petersburg. You and your friends form a team and sign up at the winter flag football organizational meeting in mid-December and then take to the field for eight weeks of competition. Team registration is $290.

Horseback Riding

Turkey Creek Stables
5534 Turkey Creek Rd., Plant City
• (813) 737-1312

Fifty easy-to-control quarter horses make for fun riding times at Turkey Creek Stables. But there's plenty else to enjoy, too, from a petting zoo to riding lessons, hay rides, barrel racing, cow penning contests and summer day camp. The hourly rate for horseback riding is $10, or $30 for a four-hour ride through 1,200 acres of trails. Guides will even go along at no extra cost. Be sure to call ahead to reserve your mount and let them know your level of expertise so they can choose a horse that's comfortable for you. Big groups should call well ahead of time, but individual riders can call just a day or two

---

INSIDERS' TIP

To get the latest recreation news in St. Petersburg, call the Leisure Line at (727) 893-7500. It's a three-minute recorded calendar of events to guarantee you won't miss a thing.

ahead. To reach the stables, take U.S. Highway 60 east through Brandon and on out to Turkey Creek Road. Turn south and go about a half-mile. The stables will be on your left. They're open year round from 8 AM until 6 PM seven days a week, except for Thanksgiving and Christmas.

Horseshoes

Hillsborough County

Tampa Horseshoe Club

This club, the only one in Hillsborough County, is so new it's just getting a permanent court and hopes to introduce the pleasures of pitching to a whole new generation of players. Anywhere from six to 30 people show up at the North Lakes Recreation Center at 2640 N. Lakeview Drive in Tampa on the first and third Saturdays of the month at 9 AM (rain dates are Sundays) for two to three hours of this challenging leisure activity. Annual membership dues are $20, but anyone's welcome to show up and participate. (This Insider will make a pitch, too — be nice and ante up a buck or two if you go.) Right now, the best way to learn more is to call club founder Mike Savidge at (813) 264-6960.

Pinellas County

Clearwater Parks and Recreation Department
10 S. Missouri Ave., Clearwater
• (727) 562-4800

The Clearwater Horseshoe Club has one of the finest facilities in the southeast, if not in the entire country. This 25-year-old club meets at Ed Wright Park on the corner of Lakeview Road and Greenwood Avenue. Home of the Florida Hall of Fame and host to at least seven sanctioned national tournaments each year, this is also the place to find open horseshoe pits. League play is year round, but anyone interested in the sport is welcome to meet on Tuesdays and Thursdays from 11 AM until 4 PM. Between

November and March, the club also offers play on Wednesdays from 6 until 9 PM. Call in advance for price information.

Ice-Skating — Figure and Hockey

Hillsborough County

Ice Sports Forum
10222 Elizabeth Place, Brandon
• (813) 684-7825

A fabulous new addition to our professional hockey presence, the Ice Sports Forum serves as a training camp and facility for the Tampa Bay Lightning — but it's much, much more. There's plenty of ice for recreational skaters, an academy affiliated with USA Hockey, and learn-to-skate programs. Public skating sessions go on seven days a week under two rate schedules: either A, $7 plus $3 skate rental; or B, where the session fee is $5.50 and skates cost $2.

There are really too many different session schedules to detail here, so give a call and listen to the menu to find a time convenient for you or your family. Generally, they run between 7:30 AM and midnight. But you don't have to be a skater to enjoy the offerings here. Spectators are always admitted free, and each of the two present rinks has room for up to 800 people! The Ice Sports Forum includes a camp and pro shop, a concession cafe area and spacious concourse, plus rooms for parties and events. Intended to become the area hub for both youth and adult hockey and figure skating, two future rinks are already in the plans.

Pinellas County

SunBlades
13940 Icot Blvd., Clearwater
• (727) 536-5843

SunBlades is home to the Florida SunCoast Figure Skating Club. Founded in 1979, this is one of the oldest, largest and most active ice-skating clubs in the south-

Canoeing is a popular pastime at Weedon Island Wildlife Preserve.

eastern United States. A full lesson program is available for serious students of ice hockey or figure skating, or just come out for the fun of it. Recreational skating is offered between 1 and 3:30 PM Sunday; noon till 2 PM Monday; 10:30 AM till noon Tuesday; noon till 2 PM and 7:30 till 9:30 PM Wednesday; 10:30 AM till noon Thursday; noon till 2 PM and 8 to 10:30 PM Friday; and from 1:30 to 3:30 PM and 8 to 10:30 PM Saturday. Rates, depending on times, vary from $3.75 to $5.50, but skate rental is always $2. On Sunday (Family Day) groups of up to six can skate for just $9.

Tampa Bay Skating Academy
251 Lakeview Dr., Oldsmar
• (813) 854-4010

Whether you're a snowbird who misses slipping into the skates or the parent of a Gretzgy-wannabe, Tampa Bay Skating Academy meets your needs. There are lessons from beginners to intensive, or just come out for the fun of it. Public skating sessions run seven days a week at various two-hour periods — check the phone menu to find one convenient to you. It will cost $6 to skate on weekends

and $5 on weekdays. Skate rental costs an additional $2.

Mountain Climbing

Hillsborough County

Vertical Ventures
5402 E. Pioneer Park Blvd., Tampa
• (813) 884-7625

Mountain climbing in flat Florida? Well, why not, even if the "mountain" is artificial. Vertical Ventures is Central Florida's only indoor rock climbing gym and provides a training environment for climbers of all skill levels. There are more than 6,000 square feet in the professionally designed climbing surface and the largest bouldering cave in the Southeast, plus a fully stocked pro shop. Rates are $11 on weekdays and $12.50 on weekends and holidays. Memberships are available starting at $65 for one month. College students and seniors get a 10 percent discount, and daily classes are held for beginners.

Climbing time and rental charges for shoes, harnesses and belay devices are included in the $30 course fee. And if you're looking for a unique place to host an event, Vertical Venture has a large observation deck that is ideal for private parties. The site is open Tuesday through Friday from 3 until 10 PM and Saturday and Sunday from 9 AM until 5 PM.

Roller Hockey

Hillsborough County

12th Street Park
209 S. 12th St., Tampa • (813) 227-9543
Ice hockey may be a great winter pastime up North, but down here in-line skates take the place of blades and the game goes on year round; especially since 12th Street Park opened in Tampa's Channel District this past year with an outstanding facility and wide array of roller activities. These include a Hockey Camp, Skate Dance Camp, tournaments, public skating, one-on-one hockey, pick-up games, leagues and coaching for everyone from "mites" ages 8 and younger to "seniors" older than 30 (ouch — if the action doesn't make you feel old, this designation sure will!). Pick-up games and public skating costs $5 a person, and skate rental is extra. Call to get the various schedules. The park is usually open Monday, Wednesday, Friday, Saturday and Sunday after 3 PM.

Brandon Indoor Arena
930 Lithia Pinecrest Rd., Brandon • (813) 654-5400
This full-sized roller hockey facility is a primo choice for blade enthusiasts who enjoy air-conditioned comfort when they sweat. The professional play area is 190 feet by 85 feet with 30-foot ceilings. There's league play for adults and youth, plus pick-up hockey clinics. Skate and shoot play is offered Monday through Friday from 4 until 6 PM at a cost of $4. Hours vary during the day, so call ahead for more information.

Running

Runners in the Bay area are loosely organized into a few clubs. Here's a list of numbers to contact if you want the camaraderie of companions:

Hillsborough County

The Bayshore Runners Club, Tampa, (813) 831-9381;

Tampa Bay Runners Club, Tampa, (813) 661-3790;

Pinellas County

Forerunners Florida Track Club, Tampa, (727) 864-4058;

Suncoast Runners Club, St. Petersburg, (727) 544-3856;

Sunshine Running Team, Clearwater, (727) 462-9094;

West Florida Y Runners Club, Clearwater, (727) 581-2676.

Shuffleboard

Pinellas County

Clearwater Parks and Recreation Department
10 S. Missouri Ave., Clearwater • (727) 562-4800
Open shuffleboard courts for drop-in play are at Morningside Recreation Complex, 2400 Harn Avenue, (727) 462-6983; Martin Luther

---

INSIDERS' TIP

Want to learn to play old-timey music? The Sunshine State Acoustic Music Camp welcomes all ages every October for a weekend of instruction at the Boyd Hill Environmental Studies Area in St. Petersburg. Expect the tuition fee to be around $180. Call (727) 784-1771 to learn more.

King Jr. Recreation Center, 1201 Martin Luther King Jr. Avenue, (727) 462-6119; and Ed Wright Park, 1326 S. Greenwood Avenue, (727) 462-6141. The Clearwater Shuffleboard Club provides play for adults on a leisure level and for those who enjoy tournament competition. The club maintains 52 courts and provides exercise, good sportsmanship and social interaction. Games are played daily Sunday through Friday from 1 until 3 PM, and doubles are played Thursdays and Sundays from 1 until 3 PM. Call ahead for rate information.

Softball

Hillsborough County

City of Tampa
Recreation Department
1420 N. Tampa St., Tampa
• (813) 231-5270

League softball is one of the most popular athletic programs offered by the city — more than 1,300 teams play during three seasons at 16 lighted fields around the city. The usual setup is that friends put teams together and then register, but newcomers are encouraged to sign up. The staff will help you find a team — it's a great way to meet people. Men's, women's and coed teams are divided according to skill. Games start at 7, 8 and 9 PM, with a 65-minute play time limit. Plan to supply your own gloves, shoes, softballs and bats. (Easton aluminum softball bats are recommended). Helmets aren't required, but they certainly are a good idea — your skull's not as thick as some people might think. Don't worry about uniforms; dress code is whatever's comfortable. Cost is $205 a team.

Pinellas County

City of St. Petersburg
Athletics Department
1450 16th St. N., St. Petersburg
• (727) 893-7294

Adults can join men's, women's and coed organized slow-pitch softball leagues and play year round at various fields throughout the city. Teams are sanctioned by the American Softball Association, and games are held Monday through Friday nights. Call ahead for information on registration dates, times and costs.

Track and Field

Hillsborough County

City of Tampa
Recreation Department
1420 N. Tampa St., Tampa
• (813) 231-5270

The All-Comer Track and Field Meets are open to anyone regardless of age, sex or ability. In fact, beginners are encouraged to attend because the emphasis is on fun. Open divisions mean you'll be competing against all levels of skill and talent. Track includes the 110-meter high hurdle, 100-meter dash, 1,500-meter challenge, 60-meter dash, 400-meter run, four by 100-meter relay, 800-meter run, 200-meter dash, 1,600-meter relay and 5K run. Field events include long jump, triple jump, shot put, discus, high jump and pole vault. Meets usually take place monthly at the University of South Florida campus track, a regulation eight-lane outdoor facility. Call to get the specific dates. Registration is at 8 AM, and starting times for field events and the 5K are at 8:30 AM. Running events get under way at 9 AM. Now, hold your breath — here comes the expensive part. If you're younger than 18 you'll have to pay 50¢ an event; if you're 18 or older it'll cost you a whole dollar for an event. The 5K race fee is $1 for all ages.

You need some
vigorous exercise,
and around Tampa Bay,
that's spelled tennis
with a capital T. Come
on, it's your serve.

Tennis

It's a tennis toss-up question. Does watching our hometown boys Pete Sampras and Jim Courier make you want to (A) hit the courts with a new, oversized titanium racket and renewed fervor, (B) give up the game and switch to shuffleboard, or (C) just buy the right wardrobe, throw some water beads on your sweatband and walk through the grocery store looking like it was an easy game-set-match?

No matter which direction you drive, you're likely to find a tennis court every few blocks — at our schools, in our parks, at our hotels and within our communities. If any little bit of extra land has not been chiseled into a bunker and a green, you can bet it's covered with Har-Tru. Every day in every county, there are hundreds of togged up players taking a swing at the sport, some even with an eye on making it all the way to the pros.

Davis Cup in Tampa Bay

Summer 1954. Ike was in the White House, the silver screen flashed Marlon Brando in *The Wild One* and the heavyweights were ruled by Rocky Marciano. And the Davis Cup, the international competition where world-class tennis players compete in venues around the globe for the honor of their country, came to be played in the state of Florida for the very first time.

You can play today on the red-clay courts of St. Petersburg's Bartlett Park Tennis Center, where the United States, led by Ham Richardson and Straight Clark, took the crown from Cuba and the "Flying Garrido Brothers," Orlando and Reynaldo. Temporary bleachers were brought in for the event, which drew 400 to 500 spectators each day. While the Cubans fared poorly on the court, they were treated like visiting dignitaries when the matches were over — entertained with a huge party thrown by the Tampa Cuban Club and even on an outing to see the Sunshine Skyway Bridge

that at the time was about a month away from completion.

St. Petersburg last rolled out the tennis carpet in 1990; this time at Florida Suncoast Dome (now Tropicana Field), matching the United States against Australia. On a red-clay surface trucked in from a Plant City brick company, the Americans reclaimed the Cup for the first time since 1982. Andre Agassi and Michael Chang showed the winning American spirit, but Agassi showed less than winning form when he quit during his last match claiming injury.

While no plans have been set for the return of Davis Cup play to the Tampa Bay area, Tropicana Field, spruced up for the Devil Rays major league baseball team, might just convince Davis Cup officials to bring this world-class event back for another love-match in our own backyard.

So, even if you're never going to make it to the big leagues with your power serve, you've got to admit that you've probably had enough of that lolly-gagging mindlessly on the beach. You need some vigorous exercise, and around Tampa Bay, that's spelled tennis with a capital T. Come on, it's your serve.

Hillsborough County

City of Tampa Tennis Complex
4001 Tampa Bay Blvd., Tampa
• **(813) 870-2383**

On the campus of Hillsborough Community College, you'll find the largest public tennis complex in Tampa, boasting 16 hard courts and a dozen clay courts. There are also racquetball courts, along with a pro shop and locker rooms and, of course, primo lessons for beginners and aces alike. Reservations are recommended if you want to take the court at this facility, which was awarded the U.S. Tennis Association's national facility award.

Marjorie Park
59 Columbia Dr., Davis Islands
• (813) 253-3997

Overlooking Harbour Island, you can try to perfect your backhand on any one of eight clay courts or on the practice wall. With its grand waterfront view, it may be hard to keep your concentration between the lines. But give it a go — it's the only other local tennis complex awarded the national facility award by the U.S. Tennis Association.

www.insiders.com

See this and many other **Insiders' Guide®** destinations online — in their entirety.

Visit us today!

Riverfront Park
900 North Blvd., Tampa • (813) 223-8602

At the north end of the University of Tampa and right across the river from the Tampa Bay Performing Arts Center, you can try out a standing-ovation performance of your own on one of the 11 courts. Courts are lit until 10 for night play and, although the rule is first come, first served (no pun intended), you really should make reservations in advance for this popular complex.

County Courts

Other backhand opportunities await behind practically every junior and senior high school in the county as well as in parks operated by the City of Tampa Parks and Recreation Department. To find your love-match on any of the 20 public courts in Tampa or to find out which ones are currently lighted for night play call (813) 870-2383. Those parks serving up tennis courts for swingers like you and me are:

Cal Dixon Tennis Complex, 4000 Watrous Avenue, Tampa.

Copeland Park, 11001 N. 15th Street, Tampa.

Cuscaden Park Playground, 2900 15th Street, Tampa.

Eighteenth Avenue Playground, 2901 32nd Avenue, Tampa.

Forest Hills Playground, 4700 S. Clark Avenue, Tampa.

Highland Pines Playground, 4505 E. 21st Street, Tampa.

Himes Avenue Sports Complex, 4500 S. Himes Avenue, Tampa.

MacFarlane Park, 1700 N. McDill Avenue, Tampa.

Perry Harvey Sr. Park, 1201 Orange Av-enue, Tampa.

Rowlett Park, 2401 E. Yukon Street, Tampa.

Williams Park, 4362 E. Osborne Avenue, Tampa.

Pinellas County

St. Petersburg's claim to tennis fame rests at the $93 million Renaissance Vinoy Resort, a 16-court tennis complex and world headquarters of the Women's Tennis Association. Here, the WTA hosts tournaments, clinics and year-rounds visits from the world's top-ranked professional women players. For the latest scoop on upcoming celeb visits and clinics, call (727) 895-5000.

For us normal weekend swingers, you'll find chances to self-improve your backhand on courts at almost every major resort hotel, high school or county park. In fact, there are more than 200 private and public tennis courts in Pinellas County. Pump those Nikes to the following major complexes, followed by a list of favorite places (along with hallowed courts reserved for only the most serious players among us) to swing in the Pinellas parks system.

St. Petersburg Tennis Center
650 18th Ave. S., St. Petersburg
• (727) 894-4378

Nestled in Bartlett Park, the St. Petersburg Tennis Center offers 15 Har-Tru courts with drill sergeants ready to put you through your

---

INSIDERS' TIP

Too hot to exercise? Check out your nearest mall. Many open their concourses early for walkers — take your constitutional in a comfortable climate, and maybe make some new friends while you're at it.

Photo: St. Petersburg/Clearwater Area Convention & Visitors Bureau

All one's cares seem to disappear after enjoying a beautiful Gulf of Mexico sunset.

paces on an individual or clinic basis. After play, you can clean up in the locker rooms equipped with showers, grab a bite in the snack bar and then pursue love in other territory.

McMullen Tennis Complex
1000 Edenville Ave., Clearwater
• **(727) 462-6144**

Seventeen lighted courts, a pro shop and a locker room are all here off U.S. Highway 19 between Gulf-to-Bay Boulevard and Belleair Drive. Open at 8 AM every day of the week, it's a pretty popular spot, so reservations are definitely recommended.

Nick Bollettieri Tennis Academy
Westin Innisbrook Resort, Tarpon Springs • (813) 942-2000, (800) 456-2000

Using the teaching methods of renowned tennis coach Nick Bollettieri, the pros at the $1 million Tennis and Fitness Center are poised to put both adult and junior players through the paces. We're not talking pickup games here. At the 11 Har-Tru and four Laykold courts (seven illuminated for night play, for those who have to stay after school), we are talking the strategies of the game taught by the best in the biz under the direction of Clint Lolley. Private instruction and clinics are offered along with weekend and midweek programs. Costs vary with the intensity of the instruction. Call the center for the most current rate schedule.

Bardmoor Tennis & Fitness Club
800 Cumberland Rd., Largo
• **(727) 391-2205**

Even an ace server would be hard pressed to hit a ball from one end of the line of tennis courts to the other here at Bardmoor. A private facility (seasonal memberships are available), the campus is touted as the area's most complete tennis and fitness facility, boasting 16 Har-Tru courts, two natural grass courts, two red-clay courts and eight hard courts. Home of the Billy Stearns International Tennis School, ATP and WTA professionals are always on hand for individual and group instruction. It's also here that Wimbledon wanna-bees can try their backhand at the Grassroots Challenge, a ladies' amateur doubles tournament program sponsored by Virginia Slims. Winners get the opportunity to advance to regional play during a Virginia Slims Legends tournament stop and then on to the national championships. For information about the Grassroots Challenge program, call (800) 544-7171.

County Courts

The following courts in the Pinellas parks system all offer from two to eight tennis courts on a first-come, first-served basis. If a phone number isn't listed, you can get all the info by calling St. Petersburg Leisure Services at (727) 893-7441 or the Clearwater Parks and Recreation Department at (727) 462-6531.

Azalea Park, 1400 72nd Street N., St. Petersburg, (727) 893-7731.

Brown Park, Harbor Drive, Indian Rocks Beach.

Campbell Park, 601 14th Street S., St. Petersburg, (727) 893-7733.

Childs Park, 4301 13th Avenue S., St. Petersburg.

Clearwater Beach Recreation Center, 69 Bay Esplanade, Clearwater Beach, (727) 462-6138.

Coachman Ridge Park, 1400 Old Coachman Road, Clearwater

Coquina Rey Park, 3595 Locust Street S.E., St. Petersburg.

Country Hollow Park, 2724 Brattle Lane, Clearwater.

Crescent Lake Park, between 13th and 22nd avenues N., St. Petersburg.

Davis Field Ballfield Complex, 6050 76th Avenue N., Pinellas Park.

Del Oro Park, 401 McMullen-Booth Road, Clearwater.

Fossil Park, 6635 Dr. Martin Luther King Jr. Street N., St. Petersburg,

---

INSIDERS' TIP

The average temperature here is 73. Tampa's mean temperature in January is 60; in August it's 82. Our annual rainfall averages 47 inches, 30 of which come in summer.

Forest Run Park, 3450 Landmark Drive, Clearwater.

Highlander Park, 903 Michigan Road, Dunedin.

Kolb Park, 1507 Bay Palm Boulevard, Indian Rocks Beach.

Lake Vista Park, 1401 62nd Avenue S., St. Petersburg, (727) 893-7744.

Martin Luther King Jr. Complex, 1201 Martin Luther King Jr. Avenue, Clearwater, (727) 462-6119.

McLaughlin Park, Paradise Boulevard, Treasure Island.

Morningside Recreation Complex, 2400 Harn Boulevard, Clearwater, (727) 462-6983.

North Shore Park, 901 North Shore Dr. N.E., St. Petersburg, (727) 893-7727.

Northwest Park, 5801 22nd Avenue N., St. Petersburg.

Ross Norton Recreational Complex, 1425 S. Greenwood Avenue, Clearwater, (727) 462-6025.

Puryear Park, 5701 Lee Street N.E., St. Petersburg.

Valencia Park, Hercules Avenue at Montclair Street, Clearwater.

Walter Fuller Park, 7891 26th Avenue N., St. Petersburg, (727) 893-7443.

Wildwood Park, 2650 10th Avenue S., St. Petersburg, (727) 893-7750.

Wood Valley Recreation Center, 2116 Park Trail Lane, Clearwater, (727) 462-6125.

Woodgate Park, 2495 Countryside Boulevard, Clearwater.

Worth the Drive

Harry Hopman/Saddlebrook International Tennis School
100 Saddlebrook Way, Wesley Chapel • (813) 973-1111, (800) 729-8383

We are talking serious tennis here. Founded by the late Harry Hopman, one of the most successful coaches in Davis Cup history, this is the place for those with grand slam in their hearts and minds. The resort is headquarters of the U.S. Professional Tennis Association and the first designated regional training center of the U.S. Tennis Association for its Player Development Program. You might spy tennis celebs such as Jim Courier, Jennifer Capriati and Mary Joe Fernadez sharpening their skills here. The school welcomes beginners and advanced players to its 45 courts and offers a hard-hitting five-day, six-night package to those who are truly focused on improving their game. Count on paying from around $650 a person for the dubious pleasure of being drilled on everything from fitness and agility to backhands and footwork. The fee includes accommodations at the magnificent Saddlebrook Resort. Strap on a wristband and go for it.

Come. Play a round
or two with us. Pack
your bag heavy, and
prepare yourself for
excruciating ecstasy.

Golf

If you watch a game, it's fun. If you play it, it's recreation. If you work at it, it's golf. It is simply incredible how the same folks who can't wash off a dinner dish can polish an iron (that actually survived a 3-foot divot-making experience) so shiny you can see your reflection in it. Yes, the same people who can't remember your anniversary, but have instant recall of every shot on every hole of the last 1,000 courses they've played. And yes, the same ones who track untraceable boat shoe mud through the kitchen, but have golf shoe spikes so clean you could use them as aperitif forks.

This can only be attributed to the incurable addiction to the honorable game of golf, played to the extreme of cult worship around Tampa Bay. We live it. We breathe it. We dress for it. And lastly, we work all week (or at least until Tuesday) to get another whack at it. We're hooked, and there's no turning back.

Welcome to golf heaven. From tip to tip, more than 100 glorious opportunities for total frustration await you, from simple, executive courses to the most magnificent PGA pro links.

Any day of the week, 52 weeks a year, the golf monster awaits in water, bunkers and rough. All that matters is your four-hour battle with Mother Nature, contorted by fiends such as Ron Garl and Tom Fazio, who are obviously in cahoots with the devil, or at least with those cool guys with the tungstun titanium shafts in the Pro Shop.

Come. Play a round or two with us. Pack your bag heavy, and prepare yourself for excruciating ecstasy. As Lawrence Packard, designer of all three courses at Innisbrook, is known to say, "You're supposed to have 71 shots. By golly, we want you to take them."

Here's a quick note about our course listings. While many magnificent private courses are tucked into our landscape, only members and guests have the privilege of using a sand wedge in their pristine bunkers. Therefore we will only profile semiprivate and public courses

where mere mortals such as you and I can simply pick up the phone to reserve a tee time.

The greens fees we list include the cart rental and represent a general range between summer and winter seasons. It is always advisable to check with your course of choice for current rates, understanding that there will be a difference between weekdays and weekends and before or after a specific time, say 11 AM or noon. Plus, if you do just a little homework, many of the courses place coupon savings ads in visitor and local golf magazines as well as local newspapers. Let her rip!

Hillsborough County

Babe Zaharias Golf Club
11412 Forest Hills Dr., Tampa
• **(813) 631-4374**

Operated by the Tampa Sports Authority, the Babe is not necessarily kind to those who fear tight fairways and small greens. The shortest of the city's courses, it's a par 70, 6142-yard public course that welcomes golfers of every handicap. The thrill is to be found in the 453-yard, par 4 16th, a dogleg right with a brace of tall trees to the left of the fairway. Better fade on this one to keep your score in double digits. Greens fees are quite reasonable, ranging from $25 to $34 for 18.

Bloomingdale Golfers Club
1802 Nature's Way Blvd., Valrico
• **(813) 685-4105**

It's been written that Ron Garl was in a Pete Dye state of mind when he designed this course in 1983, a course that's been rated No. 1 in the area by *Golfweek* magazine. Most of the holes are shaped to dictate your shot. If you don't just take a deep breath and go for it, you're likely to make it to the green with only one shot left to make par. The semiprivate par 72 course, with water coming into play on 14 holes, measures a terrifying 7165 undulating yards from the back tees. Greens fees will range from $36 to $60 from low to high season.

Countryway Golf Club
11111 Waters Ave., Tampa
• (813) 854-1182

One of the area's most affordable courses, Countryway winds through the Countryway community that borders Westchase in northwest Tampa. A semiprivate executive course best suited to an irons game, it measures 3556 yards and is a par 61. Play any day from just $12.

Diamond Hill Golf & Country Club
11315 Sidney Rd., Valrico
• (813) 689-7219

If you're a levelheaded duffer, this is not your course. Hilly and demanding, you won't often find your ball on a level lie at Diamond Hill, so practicing how to hit from a stance above or below your ball is a marvy warm-up. The par 5, dogleg-left 13th is a real doozie — it measures a full 567 yards from tee to green. You'll pay $20 to $35 for the pleasure of covering the par 72's 6306 yards.

Eagles Golf Club
16101 Nine Eagles Dr., Odessa
• (813) 920-6681

Thirty-six holes of the most frustrating golf in the area await your tee time at the Eagles — a golfer's nirvana sprawling over 1,000 wooded acres punctured by more than 30 lakes, ponds and canals. Ron Garl was at it again when he designed the original three nine-hole courses with 17 holes playing into water. The Oaks and Lakes courses both feature large, elevated greens along with more water, bunkers and humongous oak trees. Most golfers we know like to play the Forest Course as the back nine, even with the par 4, 435-yard 14th hole. Not only will you have to drive onto a tight fairway, but there's a formidable big lake smack in the center.

The newest nine-hole drama can be played out on The Islands course (a Robbin/Koch design) with its signature 6th hole with true island green. You can select the two nine-hole courses you wish to play for an average $35 for 18, but expect to pay a premium if The Islands course is one of your choices.

Golf and Sea Club
801 Golf and Sea Blvd., Apollo Beach
• (813) 645-6212

Get a good night's sleep, and prepare for what is rumored to be the hardest hole in Hillsborough County — the dogleg-right No. 5. It's a par 5, 447-yard monster that puts both water and trees on the right side, not to mention the five fairway bunkers and out-of-bounds on the left. You can never relax here because the entire course plays to water, including your shot over the Bay on both the 13th and 14th. Snap up a tee time with greens fees ranging from $20 to $38 on this public Robert Trent Jones course that measures a scary 7026 white-knuckle yards from the back tees.

www.insiders.com

See this and many other **Insiders' Guide®** destinations online — in their entirety.

Visit us today!

Haii of Fame Golf Club
2222 N. Westshore Blvd., Tampa
• (813) 876-4913

A simple, straightforward course, Hall of Fame is forgiving with its wide fairways and large greens, many recently upgraded to present a more pleasing, and challenging, environment. The 5th hole of this par 72, 6263-yard course presents the hardest test, measuring 408 yards with water and trees on both right and left. If your approach shot is good, you'll have to deal with a long and narrow green that can be difficult, especially if a jet screeching from the adjacent airport causes a lapse in your concentration. Call for current rates.

Links of Lake Bernadette
5430 Links Ln., Zephyrhills
• (813) 788-4653

The challenge awaits just 25 minutes from downtown Tampa on what many have rated the No. 1 course in Pasco County. Here, water, sand and pampas grass share the spotlight at this well-manicured 6044-yard, par 71

Photo: Bob Fiallo

Whether you're playing or watching, welcome to golf heaven.

course in one of Tampa's newest residential hotspots. The unusual thing about this course is the lack of cart paths ... you are free to go after your ball no matter where it lands. The downside is the danger of landing in player-made trenches after a hard rain. If you dare, pay from $20 to $35, and see if you can beat the course record: 61!

Northdale Golf Club
4417 Northdale Blvd., Tampa
• **(813) 962-0428**

If your ball always seems to gravitate toward water, this might not be the course you'll want to see in your dreams. Course architect Ron Garl not only put bunkers, trees, rolling terrain and contoured greens in your path to the flag, but he also integrated water into 11 out of 18 holes. Even the best will be tested by the double-dogleg par 5 with water bordering both sides of the fairway, along with that infamous four-level green that creates devilish pin placements. It's a 6791-yard, par 72 play-

ground designed for every caliber of player. Expect greens fees that run from $25 in the summer months to a high of $45 in season.

Pebble Creek Golf & Country Club
10550 Regents Park Dr., Tampa
• **(813) 973-3870**

You're standing on the 5th tee. There's water in front of you and a high, elevated green 365 yards away. This is fun? Sure is, and it stays that way through all 6410 yards of more water, woods, heavy bunkers and more elevated greens. Pebble Creek is a frustrating par 71, and you'll pay from $16 to $49 for the privilege.

Plant City Golf and Country Club
3102 Coronet Rd., Plant City
• **(813) 752-1524**

Originally built by Consolidated Mineral Company in 1928 and modified in 1973, this cherished course is one of the oldest in the region. If you have a rough day with your graphite shafts and Balatas, just think about how you'd score with the hickory-shafted clubs and round rubber balls that were used when then course was first opened. Greens fees range from $20 to $25 on this par 72 with 5663 yards to challenge every club in your bag.

River Hills Country Club
3943 New River Hills Pkwy., Valrico
• **(813) 653-1554**

One of the regional homes of the renowned Roland Stafford Golf School, River Hills' multiple tees and sculpted greens challenge your accuracy. Fairways with a mix of sand, large oaks and water also come into play on your quest for that par 72 on this 7004-yard monster. Better bring your TI II driver to the par 3 No. 14. You'll have to drive 200 yards over marshland from the back tees. Rates swing from a low of about $20 to a high of $70, so it's a good idea to call for current greens fees when you're ready to play.

Rocky Point Golf Club
4151 Dana Shores Dr., Tampa
• **(813) 673-4316**

A member course of the Tampa Sports Authority, this public course is a mixed bag of open holes and tree-lined fairways, with water coming into play on 12 holes. A cherished antique, it dates back to 1918 and was used as an Army base during World War II. Well-maintained and well-played, the par 71, 5936-yard course is near the Tampa International Airport, so you can blame that last takeoff for your three-putt. Greens fees range from $16 to $32 for 18.

Rogers Park Golf Club
7910 N. 30th St., Tampa
• **(813) 673-4396**

Rolling along the Hillsborough River, Rogers Park is a picturesque 6855-yard course with enough lakes, sand and trees to challenge your

game. It's a par 72 championship course, designed by the infamous Ron Garl, and kept in tip-top shape by the Tampa Sports Authority. Let's hear how you play the par 3 12th, where you have to hit your ball between two towering pines that are only 15 yards apart and known to frequently hide the pin from view. Plan on paying from $25 to $34 to navigate through 18.

Silver Dollar Trap and Golf Club
17000 Patterson Rd., Odessa
• **(813) 920-3884**

A public course that is every bit as well-maintained as a private club, Silver Dollar has been carved out of the open countryside in rural Odessa. Opened in 1990, there are three nine-hole courses: the Gator, Bobcat and Panther. Its 27 holes present a challenge to golfers of every ability (and a true thrill to those dogleg lovers) throughout its 6481 yards. Plan on dropping $18 to $30, not counting greenies.

Summerfield Golf Club
13050 Summerfield Blvd., Riverview
• **(813) 671-3311**

A Scottish links course that truly captures the ambiance of Scotland, Summerfield is a 6883-yard championship course designed by Ron Garl. It is unique in its use of pot bunkers, vast waste areas and small, undulating greens. Watch the wind here. It's known to swirl from 10 to 15 mph, taking your ball for a ride in the wrong direction. This par 71 course also offers a two-tiered driving range, putting and chipping greens, practice bunker, full-service bar and golfer's grill. Call for current greens fees.

Tournament Players Club of Tampa Bay
5100 Terraine de Golf, Lutz
• **(813) 949-0090**

Throughout Tampa Bay, even non-golfers can tell you about TPC. It's here that the GTE

INSIDERS' TIP

If you're planning a whirlwind Florida golf adventure, let Tee Times USA give you a hand. It offers a free, statewide Central Reservation Network that makes it idiot-proof to set up the perfect holiday for your foursome. To receive a free guide to the best golf in the state and a special 20-page guide that focuses exclusively on Tampa Bay, call (800) 374-8633.

Suncoast Classic is played each February — the only Senior PGA Tour event in the area and won by such well-known champions as Jack Nicklaus. Designed by Bobby Weed, with Chi Chi Rodriguez serving as player consultant, this course's "Stadium Golf" design is unique to the region. What that means is, if you often miss the fairway, there's plenty of high gallery sidelines to help keep your ball in play. If you can come up with $58 to $96, we dare you to play the 6898 yards from the TPC tees.

University of South Florida Golf Club
4202 Fowler Ave., Tampa
• (813) 632-6893

Unlike many Tampa Bay courses that weave through country club communities, you won't see homes along the USF course (nicknamed "the Claw"). It's just peaceful, natural forest. If you're above a 10 handicap, stick with the middle tees so you don't completely ruin your day. This 6971-yard beauty is a true challenge. Play where future champions train for a low-high range of $22 to $33.

Walden Lakes Golf and Country Club
2001 Clubhouse Dr., Plant City
• (813) 754-8575

With the shine still on a $1.8 million renovation, the 36 holes of championship golf at Walden Lakes are a shot-maker's paradise. Here you'll find trees, water and undulating, elevated greens (18 have recently been upgraded) designed by Jack Nicklaus and Ron Garl. The Hills Course measures 6698 yards from the gold tees; the Lakes Course measures 6531. Both are par 72 and cost from $18 to $45 for the privilege.

Westchase Golf Club
10307 Radcliffe Dr., Tampa
• (813) 854-2331

When Westchase Golf Club opened in 1992, *Golf Digest* called it Florida's best new course. Westchase demands accuracy off the tee with its tree-lined fairways, but the gently contoured greens are large, averaging more than 5,000 square feet. Par is tough on the signature par 3 No. 3. You'll face 212 yards

from the back tees that require a long carry over water to the wide green framed with bunkers. A diagonal bulkhead that fronts the green can mean a longer shot to clear the water, so beware the sliced shot. You might also heed the warnings of the staff and be alert when approaching the wetlands on the 5th hole. It's here that a rather unpleasant 7-foot alligator makes his home — one who doesn't always appreciate unexpected company.

All along the course, fairway sprinklerheads do double duty, clearly marking the yardage to the center of the green — a huge help for club selection that also speeds up play on this par 72, 6233-yard beauty. Completed late in 1995, the spectacular 9,500-square-foot clubhouse is a welcome sight to players who have survived the 50-yard-wide carry over wetlands to putt out on 18. If your foursome craves country club attention and first-class service, it's well worth the average $37 to $55 to take the Westchase challenge.

Pinellas County

Airco Golf Club
3650 Roosevelt Blvd., Clearwater
• (727) 573-4653

If you haven't played a round in six months or so, start here at Airco, a simple public course that will help you get your swing, and confidence, back. Measuring 6635 yards from the back tees, this par 72 course may give you trouble on the 17th, where you might find the pin hidden behind both a tree and a large-mouth bunker. Even a bogey here won't diminish the ego boost you're certain to get at this course that's adjacent to the St. Petersburg-Clearwater airport. You'll also find a turf driving range, restaurant and bar plus a complete pro shop with name-brand goodies at discount prices. Call for current rates.

Bardmoor North Country Club
8000 Bardmoor Blvd., Largo
• (727) 392-1234

If you're the type who appreciates your clubs cleaned after your round, Bardmoor is for you. With a length of 6960 yards and 18 contoured and elevated greens, this par 72 course may not pamper you with easy birdies, but you might consider that a trade-off with the beverage cart and halfway house where you can snag a sandwich and a cool drink. You might just need it after you've saved par through the 3rd green that's surrounded by a 3-acre lake — one of the most challenging holes in the Tampa Bay area.

If your score just won't fit on the scorecard, better head on over to the new practice bunker and green on the south end of the Tom Fazio-designed practice range. Actually, maybe you'd better sign up for the Weekend Golf School or one of its daily clinics. If you'd just rather talk golf, check out the brand-new clubhouse, completed in March 1998, where you can relax in the gorgeous new grill and then stroll over to the 1,300-square-foot pro shop that's stocked to the rafters with the latest in golf and tennis equipment and apparel. Call the pro shop for current rates.

Baypointe Golf Club
9399 Commodore Dr., Seminole
• **(727) 595-2095**

Among locals, this is considered a "fun" course … maybe just what you're looking for. It's a par 61, 3167-yard course, and if you live until the 15th, you can gaze out on the Gulf of Mexico and wonder why you're standing in the rough with spikes on your shoes. There are seven par 4 and 11 par 3 holes, just enough to send you to the driving range … or the lounge. You know what we mean. A round of 18 will only set you back an average of $14 if you choose to walk; add another $14 for two to ride.

Belleview Biltmore Country Club
1501 Indian Rocks Rd., Belleair
• **(727) 442-6171**

At the closest championship golf course to the Gulf beaches, you can take your Greatest Big Bertha on a historic swing of the Donald Ross-designed, 6655-yard challenge, originally opened in 1926. With a full complement of driving range and putting and chipping greens, this par 72 beauty boasts a new $2.5 million clubhouse with restaurant, lounge and phenomenal pro shop.

While most of the holes are as long and straight as a Kansas highway, beware the 5th hole, which doglegs so sharply you'd need X-ray vision to have any idea where it falls. Likewise, be sharp on the 17th, one of the few holes with water. If you're a long hitter, take a power swing over the huge pond that's smack in the center of the fairway. Otherwise that Balata is destined for the drink.

To enjoy the full splendors of this magnificent course, plan on greens fees that range from $38 to $65. You might also want to check out the Frank Reynolds Golf School, the ultimate golf school/resort experience. With no more than a 4-to-1 student-to-PGA professional ratio, you're certain to improve every aspect of your game.

Chi Chi Rodriguez Golf Club
3030 McMullen Booth Rd., Clearwater
• **(727) 726-4673**

Opened in 1989, this par 69 public course measures 5689 yards from the back tees and presents just enough obstacles for an invigorating and affordable round of 18. With greens fees that range from a mere $4 to $16 if you choose to walk, it's a great course to take all the young "Tigers" in your family.

Clearwater Country Club
525 N. Betty Ln., Clearwater
• **(727) 443-5078**

If you can hit your approach shots high and soft to the greens, you might just have a good day at the Clearwater Country Club. Designed by Donald Ross, the No. 2 hole is the real stinger, a par 3, 210-yard challenge with its elevated green that not only is undulating, but also well-bunkered. Plan to spend $18 to

INSIDERS' TIP

Seniors have a league of their own in Tampa Bay: the Senior Golf Association. Open to both men and women, the association schedules four to six events each month. For membership information, call its Clearwater headquarters at (727) 791-1499.

Photo: St. Petersburg/Clearwater Area Convention & Visitors Bureau

From tip to tip more than 100 glorious golfing opportunities await you in the Tampa Bay area.

$48 for a bump-and-run-type round on this par 72, 6300-yard beauty.

Clearwater Golf Park
1875 Airport Dr., Clearwater
• (727) 447-5272

Adjacent to the Clearwater Executive Airport off Hercules Avenue, you can pop off your private jet for a quick round of 18 on this par 63, 4350-yard course. There's an even split between par 3 and par 4 holes, and the greens are always in immaculate shape. Call for current rates.

Countryside Executive Golf Club
2506 Countryside Blvd., Clearwater
• (727) 796-1555

"One of the finest executive courses I've played." So sayeth Sam Snead ... and who are we to say otherwise? The large greens are forgiving, and fairways lined with native Florida trees and foliage make for a beautiful, if sometimes frustrating, round on this 3362-yard, par 58 executive course. See if you agree with Snead for a greens fee range of $12 to $20.

Dunedin Country Club
1050 Palm Blvd., Dunedin
• (727) 733-7836

Whether you're a scratch player or a beginner, this Donald Ross course will present you with a great opportunity to enjoy what golf's all about. The 2nd hole (par 4, 439 yards) is the hardest on this classic, 6565-yard course. From the tee, there's a dogleg left playing uphill, with a giant oak guarding the left side of the small green on your approach shot. Plan on greens fees that range from $24 to $41 to play this par 72 beauty.

East Bay Country Club
702 Country Club Dr., Largo
• (727) 581-3333

In the heart of Pinellas County, East Bay tests your nerves with water on 14 of its 18 championship holes. The sometimes severe bunkers can explode your score — not to mention the menacing rough. Stretching 5983 yards, this par 71 is just minutes from the Gulf beaches, where you'll probably need to head once you've survived this beautiful course.

Maybe you can win back the $25 to $38 you'll pay in greenies.

Fox Hollow Golf Club
Robert Trent Jones Pkwy., New Port Richey • (727) 376-6333

This is the course where the Senior PGA pros qualify to play the TPC for the GTE Suncoast Classic purse. With a good mix of woods, water and bunkers, this 7138-yard, par 71 course is proud to boast some of the finest greens in the entire state. They are huge, but they do have humps, ridges and "hollows" to make certain that you don't get too cocky about your putting stroke. And, if you need to work through the yips, check out the 18-hole putting green that's complete with a pitching and bunker area. Or just give it up and head for a great meal in the clubhouse or a whole new outfit at the well-stocked pro shop. You'll pay from $33 to $60 for a round of 18, but you can choose from any of six sets of tees so that you can aim for any course length from 4454 yards to the full 7138 yards.

Glen Oaks Country Club
1345 Court St., Clearwater • (727) 446-5821

The second of Chi Chi's courses, this 18-hole, par 54 small course is perfect for a quick round to practice for the big guys. Standing sentinel all along the course are majestic oaks, adding their own formula of natural beauty and obstacles to par. This is another super course for beginners who can easily afford the $4 to $10 a round greens fees while they practice for the Tour.

Isla Del Sol Yacht and Country Club
6000 Sun Blvd., St. Petersburg • (727) 864-2417

This semiprivate 6349-yard course, built in 1976, is the last one you'll find as you travel south along the Gulf beaches to the Gulf of Mexico. Water plays a starring role here, and take care not to let the breathtaking vistas deter you from concentrating on the par 72 you know you can shoot. Our die-hard golfing buddies report that this course is one of the most beautiful in the area, a must for those who appreciate the natural environment as much as the difficulties of the course. You'll have to call the pro shop for current rates.

Lansbrook Golf Club
2500 Village Center Dr., Palm Harbor • (727) 784-7333

Imagine a 6714-yard course with no parallel fairways and water on 16 of 18 holes. Welcome to Lansbrook, where your score will probably look the best if you visualize how you'll play when practicing on the area's finest driving ranges with target greens, manicured teeing ground and a complete chipping/bunker/putting complex. For those who know that the Masters is not in their future, come play the 11th at Lansbrook. Its green is a replica of the notorious 16th at Augusta. And, if you should birdie it, you just may want to share the good news with Clyde, the club's mascot. Keep your distance, though. Clyde happens to be an 11-foot alligator who's not exactly a supportive golf groupie. The pro shop can quote current rates and set up your tee time.

Largo Municipal Golf Club
12500 131st St. N., Largo • (727) 587-6724

A par 62 executive course, Largo holds its secret challenges for the uninitiated. With eight par 4 and 10 par 3 holes, you'll likely meet us at the large practice green, wondering what happened to that birdie that got away. A $920,000 face-lift has just been completed on the course, including the addition of a 7,300-square-foot clubhouse and new tees and greens for several of the holes. Even with this investment, you'll pay only $14 for a brisk 18.

Mainlands Golf Club
9445 Mainlands Blvd. W., Pinellas Park • (727) 577-4847

A par 63 semiprivate course, Mainlands offers its own set of challenges on its 18 holes that stretch 4300 yards. One of the Mainland's top attractions is its pro shop, which offers unbeatable discounts on name brands such as Ping Zing, Mizuno, Hogan and Maruman. Greens fees are quite reasonable, ranging from just $9 to $23.

The GTE Suncoast Classic

The tension becomes thick. He's walking straight toward you with the long, purposeful strides of a man who will not be diverted from his mission. You can sense the crowd closing in around you, but you cannot move. You are transfixed to the image that comes closer, ever closer to where you seem to have grown roots deep into the earth. His arms swing easily as his gait quickens. Then, suddenly, he's right there 2 inches from you. His brilliant blue eyes squint from the glare of the sun, and his tanned face breaks out into a smile that reveals a flash of Rembrandt-white teeth. He lifts his right arm and his hand missiles out to shake yours. He says, "Thank you for your support," and briskly moves on. You are numb with awe and respect. You have just met Arnold Palmer.

Like more than a few of the golf fans who crowd the Tournament Players Club of Tampa Bay for the GTE Suncoast Classic, I don't know a 7-iron from a pitching wedge. But I do know Arnold Palmer. And Lee Trevino, Raymond Floyd, J.C. Snead, Tom Weiskopf. And Jack Nicklaus, the Golden Bear. That's the thing about a golf tournament like this, the only area stop for the Senior PGA Tour. You may not play the game, but being able to watch these pros, truly up-close and personal, is what the tour is all about. You can sit just inches from the fringe of a green, stand alongside a tee box, even spread a beach towel and picnic lunch along a fairway. And watch the best in the business do what they do best: Play golf.

Before the first of the senior pros steps up to the first tee, there's much work to be done. A literal battalion of tournament planners, backed by more than 1,700 volunteers, must make ready for the more than 200,000 golf fans who swarm over the 125-acre TPC during the weeklong tournament event. It seems that the entire Tampa Bay region goes golf nuts in the weeks leading up to the event (ESPN broadcasts the final three days), watching to see not only which of the top Senior players have signed up to compete,

— continued on next page

Photo: Bob Fiallo

Jack Nicklaus watches his putt on the 18th green during the GTE Suncoast Classic.

but also the weather reports. Corporate sponsors make preparations for their hospitality tents. Food and beverage concessionaires gear up for the hungry crowd. Ticket orders are fulfilled, and appropriate badges are issued to sponsors and the press. Buses are readied to shuttle visitors from parking fields to tournament site. And the final touches are made to the 12-foot-high amphitheater surrounding the 18th green, created in late 1995 specifically to offer a large, grass-covered seating platform for spectators destined to polka-dot the plateaued area east of the green. Arching 50 feet in width, this grassy area rises 1 foot for every 6 feet in width, providing great views of the drama to be played out on the finishing hole.

Also preparing for the annual event are sign makers, caterers, tent suppliers and scores of other businesses that provide goods and services to tournament organizers. In fact, on average, $1.7 million is spent to put on the event. Sounds like a lot of money, but consider that the weeklong hoopla generates more than $32 million to the local economy through revenues to restaurants, hotels, retailers and local attractions.

The real beneficiary of the Classic is not the pros, not the golf fans, not local businesses. It is the charities that receive the profits from the event. During the first decade of the tournament, more than $2.7 million has been donated to charities in the Tampa Bay area.

Whether you opt to attend during Pro-Am or Shoot-Out days, when personal cameras are allowed and the players are more relaxed, or hold back until the actual $1,000,000 purse tournament begins on Friday, the GTE Suncoast Classic can promise a magic that no other spectator sport can deliver. There are no halftimes. No cheerleaders. No public-address system. No reserved seating (although a corporate hospitality tent can certainly masquerade as a skybox). The bottom line is this: If you really want to get the full pleasure out of the tournament, you've got to work at it. Sure, you can just stake out a spot at a particularly beautiful hole, like the popular 17th, and watch the golfers go by. Or you can study the pairing sheet, pick out your favorite pro, slip into a comfy pair of shoes and walk the course with him. Either way is proper golf spectator etiquette. And, either way, the GTE Suncoast Classic is one of the best ways to spend a February day in Tampa Bay.

For information on the GTE Suncoast Classic, including benefiting charities, ticket sales, sponsorship and volunteer opportunities, call the Classic's office in Tampa at (813) 265-GOLF.

Mangrove Bay Golf Club
875 62nd St. N.E., St. Petersburg
• **(727) 893-7797**

The City of St. Petersburg dares you to try this 6113-yard, par 72 championship course, where you'll pay from $16 to $33 to play 18. While the fairways are open and greens are large, keep your eye on the water that comes into play on five holes. On the dogleg-left 12th hole, you'll have an approach shot over water that guards the front of the green. If you need to better your play, you can grab a bucket of balls even at night. The lighted driving range is open until 9 PM. See you there.

Treasure Island Golf, Tennis & Rec Club
10315 Paradise Blvd., Treasure Island
• **(727) 547-4575**

If you just need a quick game tune-up, head to Treasure Island, a nine-hole, par 27 course just off the Treasure Island Causeway. For just $5 to $11 you can get out the kinks from a hectic day, or practice your bunker shots on this relatively simple and quiet course.

St. Andrews Links
620 Palm Blvd., Dunedin
• **(727) 733-5061**

Enjoy this small but challenging 18-hole,

par 54 course that is an excellent place for high-handicapper success. Heavily wooded, St. Andrews Links features a great driving range, and lessons are available to get your form in pro shape. Plan on $14 to $20 to play the full 4600 yards this course has to offer.

Tarpon Woods Golf and Tennis Club
1100 Tarpon Woods Blvd., Palm Harbor
• **(727) 784-7606**

If you miss the North country, come to Tarpon Woods with its pine tree-lined fairways. An 18-hole, 6692-yard, par 72 course, it has all the amenities you'll need to soothe your golf-soul — practice facilities, a restaurant and bar and a very tempting pro shop. On the course, you'll face a pond or a creek on every hole, but it's that tall, solitary cypress tree that guards the fairway some 210 yards to the green on signature No. 3 that's the real killer. Tarpon Woods also boasts the best 18th hole in the Tampa Bay area. It is a difficult dogleg right with out-of-bounds on the left and trees along the right, and you must negotiate a creek to reach the green. Check with the pro shop for current rates.

Tides Country Club
11832 66th Ave. N., Seminole
• **(727) 392-5345**

Grab those birdies on the front nine, because it's downhill from there. Take the 13th, for example. It's a dogleg-right, par 4 that stretches 415 yards from tee to green, with a fairway guarded by trees on both right and left. The semiprivate, par 72 course measures 6329 yards from the back tees, and greens fees range from $25 to $50.

Twin Brooks Municipal Golf Course
3800 22nd Ave. S., St. Petersburg
• **(727) 893-7445**

If you're a beginner, here's the place to generate that stamina you'll need for the big guys. Twin Brooks is a par 54, 2016-yard course that has its own set of challenges. The tees, greens and driving range have been completely renovated, and even the pro shop sports a brand-new look to get you in fashion for the PGA instruction. Best of all, you can afford it; greens fees range from just $8 to $11.

Worth the Drive

Saddlebrook Golf and Tennis Resort
5700 Saddlebrook Way, Wesley Chapel
• **(813) 973-1111**

If you're a links type of golfer, 36 holes at Saddlebrook should satisfy the craving. The centerpieces of this highly rated resort, the two 18-hole courses designed by Arnold Palmer, feature all the elements critical to an exceptional links course: rolling hills, large mounds, numerous bunkers and, of course, small greens. Check the winds, however, because the open architecture inherent in a links course gives Mother Nature a free hand to play with your ball in the air. It is here you'll find the world headquarters for the Arnold Palmer Golf Academy, with a maximum 5-to-1 student-teacher ratio for beginner, intermedi-

---

INSIDERS' TIP

When you're not playing golf, why not shop it? The Tampa Bay area is bursting with golf shops that offer every imaginable name brand that will make you look better on the course, even if they can't improve your handicap. Although we hate to play favorites, don't miss a trip to One Up Golf and Sportswear in Tampa at 211 N. Dale Mabry Highway, (813) 877-7272, and on Gulf-to-Bay Boulevard in Clearwater, (727) 725-2114. A smooth swing with your American Express card can outfit you in Ralph Lauren, Bobby Jones, Nicklaus or Ashworth — the most complete collections you'll find anywhere. The store also carries the largest selection of golf equipment in the area, and the staff is personable to a fault.

Photo: St. Petersburg/Clearwater Area Convention & Visitors Bureau

Many magnificent golf courses are tucked into Tampa Bay's landscape.

ate and advanced players. Whether you choose to challenge the Saddlebrook or the Palmer course, please call the pro shop for current rates.

Silver Oaks Golf and Country Club
36841 Clubhouse Dr., Zephyrhills
• (813) 788-1225

Host of the Zephyrhills Open, here's a course where your driver can become your best friend, especially on the front nine with its wide fairways. Get the rhythm quick, because the back nine not only has narrower fairways, but also features mammoth oaks on both sides to keep you accurate. One of the best public

courses in north Tampa, Silver Oaks is a par 72 that measures 6609 yards from the back tees. Plan on investing $10 to $35 in your game for the day.

Timber Greens
6333 Timber Greens Blvd., New Port Richey • (727) 372-8633

You should know this up front: If you're long off the tee, but just can't seem to stay out of the rough, forget Timber Greens. Built in, around and through intimidating conservation areas, there are, shall we say, large critters in them thar woods that are not worth fighting for your golf ball. In fact, you are advised that if your shot goes astray, consider it non-re-trievable. Just take a drop and go on from there. This par 71, 6133-yard course has just celebrated its second birthday and, even with the possibility of coming face to face with an 8-pound snake or two, has become quite a popular spot for a weekend 18. The last hole is the toughest, the No. 1 handicap hole. If your approach shot to the green is long, you're in conservation (read "critters"). If your ap-proach shot is short, you're in, you guessed it, conservation. So play it safe ... and enjoy liv-ing to tell all about it. Plan on greens fees that average an affordable $26.

World Woods Golf Club
17590 Ponce de Leon Blvd., Brooksville • (352) 796-5500

The course that everyone's buzzing about these days is a 36-hole gem just about 45 minutes north of Tampa. It's literally a golf heaven in the middle of nowhere, ex-cept in the minds of the brave linksters who set out to conquer the Tom Fazio-designed nightmare. Comprised of two award-winning championship courses, one short nine course and three practice holes, World Woods even boasts a 2-acre undulating

practice green and a driving range where you'd be smart to warm up.

If you dream "green jacket" but have no way to make it to the Masters, the Rolling Oaks course is for you. This 6985-yard, par 72 beauty mimics Augusta National with remarkable ac-curacy, especially the par 3 16th hole that is a masterful blend of Augusta's famous numbers 12 and 16. With its flourishing azaleas, ice-slick greens and manicured fairways, this course pre-sents a challenge to every handicap at every single hole. That's probably why it earned *Golf Digest*'s 1996 rating of No. 73 in the U.S. Top 100 among upscale daily-fee facilities. Pine Bar-rens, the second 18, is a par 71 that diabolically slams sandy waste areas up against brilliant green fairways throughout its 6902 yards, and it was rated No. 9 in the U.S. Top 100 and 66th in the world by *Golf Digest* in 1996. Fazio bor-rowed from Pine Valley in this design, making it a little tighter than Rolling Oaks and a decided test of accuracy off the tee.

If you don't mind hitting the Interstate for a day on the links, head to World Woods. It's well worth the trip. The World Woods pro shop will be pleased to take your reservation. Plan on paying from $50 to $85 for 18; $80 to $120 for 36.

Now ... slide
those cute, little worm
wigglers, beetle spins,
slimy slugs, Power
Grubs and Love's Lures
in your tackle box. We
is goin' fishin'!

Fishing

Take a long stick. Attach a very, very long string. At the end of the string, attach a sharp hook decorated with something dead and fuzzy or alive and slimy. Cast that string out into the water. We are now fishing. And, hey, are we having fun!

OK. So this could be considered heresy, especially in Tampa Bay, where fishing is next to godliness, and it's not only great sport but also really big business. From our waters you have a chance to snag more than 300 varieties of fish, and there are almost as many charter boats waiting to give you that opportunity.

For saltwater anglers, the Gulf shoreline and beyond offers up grouper, snapper, trout, flounder and pompano, along with sea bass, tarpon, sailfish, snook, redfish, kingfish and mackerel. Freshwater anglers pray to the fishgods for bass, speckled perch and an unwary catfish or two.

Licenses and Limits

The next paragraph is very, very important. Read it.

The most critical piece of equipment to carry in your tackle box is a fishing license, whether you fish from land, pier or sea. Saltwater licenses for non-residents cost $5 for three days, $15 for seven days and $30 for a full year, and you'll pay an extra $2 each for a stamp permitting you to land crayfish or snook. If you opt to go aboard one of the charter vessels, they will provide the license for you. But if you're out on your own, head to the nearest county tax collector's office or one of the many bait and tackle shops. If freshwater fishing is your fancy, you'll likewise need a license, costing the same as saltwater fees.

If you think you'll try to get away with not taking the few minutes it takes to obtain a valid license, be prepared for the $500 fine that might just be your biggest catch of the day. For more information on licenses, con-

tact the Florida Game and Freshwater Fish Commission, (904) 488-4676, or the Saltwater Fish Commission, (904) 488-7326.

Also note that Florida's fishing regulations are constantly changing to protect various species of endangered fish such as redfish, sea trout, snapper and tarpon. The snook is a prime example of how well these regulations actually work. Because of recreational anglers, pollution, loss of habitat due to construction and freezes, thousands of these linesiders were killed. Today, thanks to the closed seasons imposed several years ago, snook are making a dramatic comeback. (Snook closed seasons are January and February when cold weather makes them sluggish and during their spawning season from June through August.)

Bag, possession and size limits are also fervently enforced. Whether measured in fork size (nose tip to rear center of the tail) or overall length (nose tip to tail tip), you should be aware of the limits for each variety before you drag your catch back to the dock. A full listing of species and respective limits, along with other Florida fishing rules and regulations, is available in the brochure called *Know Your Limits*, published by the Florida Marine Patrol. These brochures are available at all bait and tackle shops, or you can order your copy by calling the Tampa district office, (813) 272-2516.

A tip here: Those non-boater freshwater anglers with tiny little attention spans and fear of wading beyond the vegetation that hugs the shoreline can bag 'em like the big guys right around the boat ramps at practically every lake in the Tampa Bay area. This is because not only are many catches released from boats right at the ramp, but also the turbulence caused by power-loading stirs up lots of fish-food goodies, which tempts those critters to hang around for a snack. If you do plan to fish near a boat ramp, the best time is right before daybreak or at sundown, when the fish aren't scared away by the sounds of roaring boats.

Watch the Skies

You've rented a boat and you're pulling those babies in right and left. Suddenly you realize there's a dark ominous cloud way out there on the horizon. Don't ignore it. Florida has more thunderstorms and lightning-strike deaths and injuries than any other state in the nation. With more than 90 thunderstorm days annually, the danger of lightning is a fact to take very seriously, especially on the open sea. Because thunderstorms are so unpredictable and can pop up at any time, we implore you to investigate the lightning protection available on your vessel prior to leaving the dock or ramp. Some basic rules to remember as soon as you hear even the faintest rumble:

1. Stay in the center cabin. If your boat has no cabin, stay low in the boat;

2. Immediately stop fishing. Lightning can precede the storm cloud by 10 miles;

3. Disconnect electronic equipment, including the radio, and do not attempt to use it during the storm;

4. Lower, remove or tie down the radio antenna and any other protruding devices if they are not part of the lightning protection system;

5. If possible, avoid contact with any two components of the system at the same time, say, for instance, the gear levers and the spotlight. This will avoid the possible deadly path of electrical current.

The Wendy's Hydra-Sports Fishing Team

We thought we'd just slip in a word or two about the Tampa Bay area's most popular fishing team. A legend in their own line, the acclaimed Hydra-Sports Fishing Team makes the rounds at all Tampa Bay's tournaments and sports shows all over the Southeast. The team of nine custom-rigged crafts, and those who are talented enough to captain them, are local folk heroes — not only because of their professional know-how, but also because they are always willing to share a hot tip or two with their admiring fans.

The major goal of this goodwill team is not just to display the logos of the companies that sponsor them. The team's mission is to cast for funds to support their primary beneficiary, the Children's Home Society, the favorite charity of Wendy's Restaurant founder, Dave Thomas. In fact, the monies start flowing as the team raffles off Hydra-Sports boats at major sports shows. If you have the opportunity to see them at a local show, try out their infamous mechanized fighting chair that will give you the virtual reality of being hooked up to a 1,000-pound marlin, all the way to your rod bending back on itself as your electronic target takes off on a long run. If fish with less of a mean streak are more your fancy, you'll pick up invaluable instruction on bait-rigging, fishing knots, tackle selection and cast-netting. And, while they may share many a tip, there must be a few that they keep to themselves. Team members have won eight major tournaments in the last couple of years, along with 41 top-20 finishes. And that ain't no fish story, Bubba.

www.insiders.com

See this and many other **Insiders' Guide®** destinations online — in their entirety.

Visit us today!

Of Pelicans and Piers

Every year when fisher-folk get into a wild frenzy, there is one species other than the targeted fish that often suffers dire consequences. They are our pelican residents, and many of them reside at Pier 60 at Clearwater Beach. Pier 60, one of the most popular fishing spots on the Gulf, was recently rebuilt at a cost of nearly $2 million, providing quite extravagant lodging for the many pelicans and gulls that call it home.

Many an angler has found one of these birds at the other end of the hook, attempting to steal bait as it's cast out to the Gulf or swooping down to catch your fish before it's reeled in. If you should snag one of these mischievous thieves, the Suncoast Seabird Sanctuary urges you not to cut the line, a certain death sentence for the bird since it can be strangled or maimed in the line. Instead, follow these timely tips for release:

1. Slowly reel the bird to you;

2. Put a towel or other cloth over its head

(darkness calms the bird) and hold its beak. Don't shut the beak completely because that's how the bird breathes;

3. Push the hook through the skin until you see the barb;

4. Cut the barb with wire cutters and remove the hook and line before letting the bird go. The Pier 60 bait shop has wire cutters to help you. They also can take a badly injured bird in a pet cage to the Seabird Sanctuary for recovery. If you should spot an injured bird, call the sanctuary at (727) 391-6211 or Wildlife Rescue at (813) 238-0341.

Now … slide those cute little worm wigglers, beetle spins, slimy slugs, Power Grubs and Love's Lures in your tackle box. We is goin' fishin'!

Hillsborough County

You won't find a lineup of charter boats in Tampa, but you will find rivers, lakes and bays chockablock with targets for your line. Tampa is for lazy fishing, drifting without a care in the world in a freshwater lake environment, or hanging off a pier starting interesting conversations with opening lines such as "What's biting?" or "Whatcha usin' for bait?"

Here are some pier fishing tips from the experts. First, all you need is some live bait, cut bait, jigs or spoons along with a popping rod (a stiff casting rod with a long grip) and a turning spool reel.

Second, because many of the fish caught from our piers can slice right through a light monofilament line with ease, it's best to go for a heavy monofilament leader tied to your small monofilament line. If this all seems like gibberish to you, you've already shown your fishing naivete, but not to worry. Not only will your pier du jour be lined with experts ready to help you out (and share a tall tale or two), but you can also rent all the equipment and buy the necessary slimy bait at all the piers we've listed here:

Ballast Point Park, 5300 Interbay Boulevard, Hillsborough Bay, Tampa, (813) 831-9585;

Gandy Bait & Tackle, End of the Gandy Bridge, Tampa, (813) 839-555;

Oak Haven Fish Camp, 12143 River Hills Drive, Hillsborough River, Tampa, (813) 988-4580;

Denny B's Quality Bait & Tackle, 9735 W. Hillsborough Avenue, Upper Tampa Bay, Tampa, (813) 885-9811;

Interbay Marina and Bait, 5200 W. Tyson Avenue, Lower Tampa Bay, Tampa, (813) 839-3577.

Pinellas County

We are heading out into the Gulf, and we are not coming back until we catch the big one! This is fishing heaven, where you can trek to a pier, rent a boat or jump on board the zillions of charters just waiting to steer you to where they're biting. Along with your equipment, make certain you pack heavy with sunscreen, hat, jacket and T-shirt. Even if you land a fish, you're also likely to bring back an overdose of the tropical sun.

Pier Fishing

You'll find small piers and boat launches at the majority of parks in Pinellas County (please scan our Parks and Recreation chapter). But according to the old-timers, if you plan to do some serious pier fishing here, these are the best three places to aim your shiners and spinners.

Redington Long Pier
17490 Gulf Blvd., Redington Shores • (727) 391-9398

It is long — 1,021 feet into the Gulf of Mexico. Although it's open 24 hours a day, the best times to cast a line are before dawn until about daybreak (especially when the tide is coming in) and from about an hour before sunset until midnight (again, with an incoming tide). You can rent all the equipment you'll need, including the appropriate bait, and you'll find a snack bar, restrooms and even a place to clean those fish you've caught. To fish, adults will pay $6 and children, $5. If you just want to walk out and check the action, the fee is 50¢.

Pier 60
West end of Fla. Hwy. 60, Clearwater Beach • (727) 462-6466

For almost a half-century, inshore anglers have parked their gear on Pier 60, in the center of the Clearwater Beach strip. With the shine still on a $2 million-renovation, it's open 24 hours a day with rod rentals, a bait and tackle shop, a snack bar, restrooms and an observation deck with telescopes to spy on the beautiful bodies strewn across the beach. You can walk out for 50¢ or fish for $5.35 a person.

Sunshine Skyway Fishing Pier
Sunshine Skyway, St. Petersburg
• **(727) 823-8804**

Three million dollars for a place to fish? Yep, that's what the State of Florida has spent on renovations to this new pier, just to give anglers a casting alternative. Reputed to stand ready to take its place as the most productive pier in the state, its most important features are the artificial reefs made from the rubble of the old Sunshine Skyway Bridge, partly destroyed by a ship in 1980. These reefs, about 10 yards apart, attract all sorts of marine life to the barren, sandy bottom. The Skyway is the only pier in the area that you can drive out on,

so you won't have that far to lug your stuff. It's also a wheelchair-friendly pier, so it's a favorite of our disabled angler community. You'll pay the $1 bridge toll, $3 to park your car and $2 an angler to fish.

Fishing Charters

Capt. Hubbard's Marina
150 128th Ave., Madeira Beach
• **(727) 392-0167**

Since 1929, Capt. Wilson Hubbard, who passed away in 1995, had been the king of this "fish famous" spot, the focal point of John's Pass. Here you can have a swing at all types of fishing, from the docks to the fleet of ships that offer everything from half-day to full-day to deep-water "long" fishing trips far out into the Gulf of Mexico. If you're after a big one, the John's Pass Fishing boats are a good choice — they claim to catch more fish than

Photo: St. Petersburg/Clearwater Area Convention & Visitors Bureau

Deep-sea fishing is plentiful and very popular on both party boats and private charters.

any other boat on Florida's West Coast nine out of 10 days! Capt. Hubbard's sons will supply a fishing license, bait and parking, so just head off and ship out. If you have a good strike, take advantage of their "you catch, we cook, you eat" policy. For just $3.95 a person, your catch will be cooked at the Friendly Fisherman Restaurant and served with fries, slaw and corn fritters. The cost of your fishing adventure will range from around $20 for a half-day to $100 for an overnight trip.

Double Eagle's Deep Sea Fishing Center
Clearwater Beach Marina, Clearwater
• **(727) 446-1653**

Fishing with a twist. Here you'll fish from either an 83-foot or 63-foot catamaran bobbing 25 miles offshore in the Gulf. Bait is provided on the half-day or full-day excursions, with the tab running from $20 for adults and $16 for mini-anglers. You can rent all the tackle you'll need for $4.

Captain Kidd
4737 Gulf Blvd., St. Pete Beach
• **(727) 360-2263**

If you're a novice, you can learn all the tricks of the trade aboard the *Captain Kidd*, a 63-foot twin diesel-powered beauty that makes wake from behind the Dolphin Village Shopping Center. It's like one-stop shopping, because your ticket will include a parking pass, Florida fishing license, rod, reel, bait and even a fish stringer. If you get the hungries, they've got a fully equipped galley offering soft drinks and beer along with breakfast and lunch. Sign on for half-day or all-day Gulf fishing trips from $24 for adults and $21 for seniors and children.

Devil Ray Deep Sea Fishing
801 Pass-A-Grille Way, St. Pete Beach
• **(727) 360-6606**

No drawbridges or slow-speed areas slow down the 46-foot twin turbo-diesel *Devil Ray* on your way to snag a big one in the Gulf of Mexico. Self-proclaimed as the fastest party-fishing boat on the beach, this handsome vessel under the steerage of Capt. George Roux is also beamy enough to offer great stability and comfort on the high seas. Bait, tackle and fishing licenses are included in the fare, and they even offer taxidermy services. Half-day and full-day trips are offered, from $28 for adults and $22 for children. The *Devil Ray* departs from Merry Pier in St. Pete Beach.

Miss Pass-A-Grille
1 Corey Ave., St. Pete Beach
• **(727) 360-2082**

"Quit wishing. Go fishing!" That's what they say about the *Miss Pass-A-Grille* that's berthed at the Corey Landing Marina, right across the street from Leverock's restaurant. Whether you opt for a half-day or full-day fishing frenzy, the crew of this 51-foot party vessel is always available with tips to improve your skill. They'll provide all the basics: parking, fishing license, rod, tackle and bait. Plus, you can buy beer aboard or bring your own. Head to the deep sea from $25 a person.

Florida Sportfishing Center
13201 Gulf Blvd., Madeira Beach
• **(727) 393-0407**

Barracuda? Shark? Marlin in a shade of white or blue? Go deep-sea fishing for the monsters seven days a week on one of the fleet of sportfishing boats docked here, about three blocks north of John's Pass Bridge. From about $20 a person, you can select a half-day, three-quarter day or full day of monster-tracking in the Gulf of Mexico.

Capt. Dave Spaulding's Queen Fleet
Clearwater Beach Marina, Clearwater
• **(727) 446-7666**

One of the largest fishing fleets in the Clearwater area, good old Capt. Dave can send you out for the big ones for a half-day, three-quarter day or a full-day's adventure. Sign up (from $20 an angler) at Slip 50 at the

---

INSIDERS' TIP

For the 24-hour marine forecast, call the NOAA Weather Service Broadcast at (813) 645-2506.

Clearwater Beach Marina. Your fishing license and bait are included in the price, but you'll pay extra if you need to rent a rod and reel.

Far Horizons Deep Sea Fishing Charters
9610 Gulf Blvd., Treasure Island • (727) 367-7252

"You hook 'em, we cook 'em." Your captain and mate will also clean, bag and ice your catch if you prefer. On this 42-foot vessel with its twin Caterpillar diesel engines, you'll whisk out to the Gulf for a half-day, three-quarter day or full day of chasing sailfish, cobia, amberjack, swordfish, barracuda and the like. For longer trips, catering can be arranged, or you can opt to bring along your own food and drinks. Like most charter fleets, Far Horizons includes fishing license, instructions, bait and tackle in its fees, which start around $20 for adults.

S.S. Miss Bellmar
Kingfish Wharf, John's Pass • (727) 360-6886

If you really want to fish, but want something a little more stable under your fighting chair, try the S.S. Miss Bellmar, a 121-foot-long, 31-foot-wide fishing/party boat with more than 60 years of experience under her stern. Aboard this family-owned and -operated boat, you'll enjoy a full galley, separate restrooms for ladies and gents and a comfortable, air-conditioned lounge to take a break from the action. Half-day trips leave every morning at 8 and cost $20 for anglers and $10 for children and those who just want to ride along and watch.

Annual Tournaments

The bustling blue waters of the Gulf bring out the competitive spirit in local anglers as they gas up the engines and head out to bring home the winning specimen. While tournaments of every size and duration are a normal, everyday occurrence around these parts, here are a few tournaments that are certain to supply the best fish stories to be told — and retold — all year long. Even if you don't go to fish, you should really check out the action on the shore. As Captain

Hubbard used to say, "If you're too busy to go fishin', you're just too busy."

The Tampa Pro Bass Spring Series
Cory Lake Isles, Morris Bridge Rd., Tampa • (800) 789-0525

Talk about a fishing spectacular! This two-day event held in April not only brings out the best of the regional bass anglers, but the poor fish also have to compete with internationally known fishing professionals such as Jimmy Rogers, Roland Martin, Hank Parker, Larry Nixon and Orlando Wilson. This is not just a fishing tournament, but a true event, complete with water-ski shows, a dinner/dance and an awards ceremony. The entry fee is a bit hefty — $1,500 for the amateur entry package — but rewards are high. You get to fish with a pro, plus take a cast at big prizes like a new, fully rigged bass boat and motor valued at more than $5,000. If you just want to go watch the action, daily spectator passes cost $10 for adults and $3 for children.

The Suncoast Tarpon Open
Gulf of Mexico • (727) 964-2232

Head out for the big ones from May through July during the annual Suncoast Tarpon Open. If you should happen to land the biggest of the big, there's a $5,000 award check waiting for you; weekly prizes are awarded for the biggest tarpon landed by both adult and junior anglers. Entry fees for the event are $60 for the regular division and $10 for the junior division. For details and entry forms, check your favorite bait shop or the nearest sporting goods store.

Budweiser Suncoast Kingfish Classic
Kingfish Wharf, Treasure Island • (727) 363-0071

For more than five years, kingfish anglers have headed to Treasure Island to reel in the big one for the big prize. The entry fee for the early April event is $300 a boat. Other kingfish tournaments include: The King of the Beach Kingfish Tournament (Hamlin's Landing, Indian Rocks Beach, (727) 547-8421, $100 entry fee); and the Wahoo/Mercury Suncoast Kingfish Classic (Sarasota Quay, Sarasota, (800) 243-7659, $300 entry fee).

West Coast Blue Water Tournament
Gulf of Mexico • (727) 360-5539

During September, anglers head way out into the Gulf to catch the species rarely seen in inshore waters, including blue marlin, yellowfin tuna and wahoo. This popular tournament marked its 15th year in 1998. Boats fish as far as 100 miles offshore at the edge of the continental shelf. Entry fees and prizes vary, so call to check on the details of the tourney.

Alafia River Catfish Tournament
Williams Park, Gibsonton
• (813) 671-6144

Here's a freshwater tournament for river boaters that's gotten more and more popular during its seven-year history. The one-day event takes place in September, with anglers pushing off from the ramp at Williams Park. To get in the middle of the catfish action, adults pay $7, juniors enter for $5 and children 5 and younger pay $2. To enter, just show up with your trusty rod and reel between 7 and 10 AM.

It's not just birds that find the fishing prospects excellent in the St. Petersburg/Clearwater Area.

Photo: St. Petersburg/Clearwater Area Convention & Visitors Bureau

Fishing Clubs

No matter what your fishing passion, there's probably a group in the area that shares your love of sea spray and tangled monofilament. The more organized clubs have specific meeting places and dates, offer a variety of seminars on a variety of subjects and always welcome a new face into the fold. Here are a few of the most active clubs in Tampa Bay.

Tampa Bay Fly Fishing Club
(813) 961-0097

Tie one on the first Wednesday of every month at Interbay Community Center at Ballast Point Park in Tampa. Meetings and seminars begin at 7 PM, but come at 6:30 PM for fly tying and casting lessons.

Suncoast Fly Fishers
(727) 726-3835

Pinellas County fly-fisher people gather round on the third Thursday of every month at the Wyoming Antelope Club at 3700 126th Avenue N. in Clearwater. Meetings and seminars begin at 7:30 PM.

Old Salt Fishing Club
(727) 393-2428

Check out the free seminars on the second Tuesday of each month at the American Legion Hall at 660 American Legion Drive in Madeira Beach. Meeting times vary so call ahead.

Golden Triangle Fishing Club
(813) 935-3293

The fourth Wednesday of every month at 7:30 PM is the time to take in a free seminar offered by the Golden Triangle Fishing Club. Club members meet at the Days Inn, 7627 Courtney Campbell Causeway on Rocky Point.

Hurricane Pass Anglers Club
(727) 785-3018

Motor on down to the Homeport Marina on Orange Street in Dunedin, and pick up a tip or two from these avid anglers. They meet at 7:30 PM on the first Tuesday of every month.

The sand here
is what you come to
Florida for, all silky
white powder that
seems to stretch forever
… a perfect place to
bring that float to
drift along under
the rays.

Beaches and Watersports

There it is! The beach is easy to recognize because it's covered with the most glorious white powder sand that goes all the way down to the water. The beach is why you came here. The beach is where you want to be.

Something about the everyday life. Like building a multilevel castle with no blueprints, knowing full well that it will wash away in the next tide. Like throwing a Frisbee. Like laying comatose on a blanket with no connections to a computer or a fax and actually relaxing. Like holding hands, tightly, with your partner as you stroll into the sunrise along the water's edge.

Yet, while you're literally soaking up the delirious pleasures of our Gulf beaches, you're also probably soaking up too much of what makes the beach the beach. That old Mr. Sun, just hanging around all day with potentially dangerous rays with your name written all over them. We will stifle the urge to lecture you about how your body will be turned into a bright red, painful, untouchable crisp under the tropical sunlight. We will just say, "You have been warned." Even a high-test SPF 1,382 will be no protection if you insist on flinging yourself with mindless abandon onto the beach for a full eight-hour spin-and-turn cycle. Be sensible. Start exposure slowly. Wear that sunscreen, and a hat and a T-shirt if your shoulders feel tingly. Drink lots of water. Protect your eyes with good sunglasses. End of lecture.

Thus warned, and tempted, grab your flip-flops, superstrength sun protection and that brand-new beach towel with the gaudy pink flamingo ... let's speedo to the beach!

The Beaches

Hillsborough County

Ben T. Davis Beach
Courtney Campbell Cswy., Tampa
We hate to admit it, but this will be the only entry in the Hillsborough County beach section ... this is the only real beach you'll find within its jurisdiction. You can just wheel off the causeway and plant yourself along the narrow beach that slides down into Tampa Bay, or you can keep driving toward the "real" beach along the Gulf of Mexico. At the prospect of being traitors to the Tampa Visitors and Convention Bureau, we say keep driving. You may have to pay to stash your car at a meter or a lot, but you'll see why Florida beaches are so highly rated by sand-bucket connoisseurs.

Pinellas County

Northern Pinellas

Caladesi Island State Park
3 miles off Dunedin Beach
• **(727) 734-5263**
A beach with a little Bali Hai flavor, you ask? It's here at Caladesi Island with some of the most luscious, white powder sand to be found anywhere along the Gulf coast. Caladesi Island is consistently rated by *Conde Nast Traveler* magazine as one of the

very best beaches in the entire country. If you can pry yourself off the beach, you'll find a playground for the kiddies, a large concession stand, bathrooms, showers, changing rooms and a shady picnic area all set up with grills.

You will have to work a bit to get here, though, because the island sits about 3 miles off Dunedin Beach and can be reached only by boat or a mile-long trek along a closed pass. You'll be asked for a $3.25 entry fee, but that covers up to eight people in your vessel.

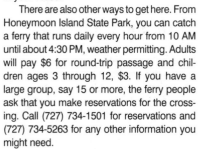

www.insiders.com

See this and many other **Insiders' Guide®** destinations online — in their entirety.

Visit us today!

There are also other ways to get here. From Honeymoon Island State Park, you can catch a ferry that runs daily every hour from 10 AM until about 4:30 PM, weather permitting. Adults will pay $6 for round-trip passage and children ages 3 through 12, $3. If you have a large group, say 15 or more, the ferry people ask that you make reservations for the crossing. Call (727) 734-1501 for reservations and (727) 734-5263 for any other information you might need.

If you're coming from downtown Clearwater, the Harbor Hopper is your ticket to Caladesi. The Hopper leaves from the west end of Drew Street from 9:30 AM until 1:30 PM at 70-minute intervals, with return trips in the afternoon at 12:25, 2 and 4 PM. The 25-minute ride will cost $6.05 for adults and $4.20 for kids, but that includes park admission.

If you want to combine a trip to the island with a little jaunt around the Gulf, give Dolphin Encounters a ring at (727) 442-7433. On Wednesdays and Fridays, this ferry leaves at 10:30 AM from the Clearwater Beach Marina for the trip to Caladesi. You can spend the day relaxing on the island and then board for the ride back to the marina at 4 PM. Cost for adults, including lunch, is $24.30 and for children, $20.55.

Honeymoon Island State Recreation Area
End of Fla. Hwy. 586 • (727) 469-5918

For the longest time, Honeymoon Beach was in desperately sad shape, long neglected from its original shining beauty as the vacation getaway prize for a northern department store contest. Finally the state moved in and bought the park and has lovingly restored it to its former romantic self. You'll find Honeymoon Beach at the end of Fla. 586 (that's Curlew Road). As at most state-operated beaches, there are bathrooms, cooking facilities and a concession stand. It's one of the few places where leashed pets are allowed, and it's on only one part of the beach. You can choose to park yourself on the Gulf side, where the beach has coarse sand and occasional rocks and the water is moderately deep, or on the causeway side of Hurricane Pass, where the sand is considerably more "Florida" and the water shallow. There is an entrance fee to take advantage of the unspoiled beach and nature trails. It will cost $4 a car or $3.25 a boat, up to eight people. If you should choose to drive alone, the fee drops to just $2.

Clearwater Beach

Here's where the action is, dude! We are talking beautiful bronzed bodies (that's men and women, both!), spontaneous beach volleyball battles, weathered, active seniors and family groups ... all sharing this little bit of paradise. The sand here is what you come to Florida for, all silky white powder that seems to stretch forever. The water is relatively shallow and pleasantly calm, so it's a perfect place to bring that float to drift along under the rays.

For nibbles, there's a whole complex of concession stands (watch for hungry, swoop-

---

INSIDERS' TIP

All boats, regardless of size, must have a wearable U.S. Coast Guard regulation life jacket for each person on board. And remember, having a life vest on board won't do any good unless you wear it.

Photo: St. Petersburg/Clearwater Area Convention & Visitors Bureau

With more than 35 miles of beaches and almost 400 miles of shoreline, there's always an open space to try out that Boogie Board.

ing sea gulls!), plus the Pier Pavilion and the South Pavilion that serve the main beach. About a mile north is the North Pavilion, where you can order a brew. You must, however, drink it there since alcoholic beverages are not allowed on the beach. If you want something frosty and a little more tropical, you can order an umbrella-garnished beverage from nearby hotels where open decks welcome beachgoers. Our favorite is the Adam's Mark Caribbean Gulf Resort (with a live Jimmy Buffet-like band that plays daily). Wander a little off the beach to Baymont Street, Eastshore Drive or Rockaway Drive and you'll find almost too many choices for your favorite beverage and a snack.

A favorite landmark here is Pier 60, a quarter-mile-long pier that dominates the Clearwater Beach skyline. You can stroll out as far as the bait house for nothing, but you'll pay 50¢ to go all the way to the end. If fishing is your thing, you can spend a full 24 hours swinging that rod for $5.35. If you need to rent equipment and miscellaneous gear, $14 will cover a whole day of frustration casting for the big one.

Mid-Pinellas

Treasure Island

This municipal beach is our newest, so you can count on squeaky clean restrooms. It claims the whitest beach on the west coast, and it really is amazing. Parking here is free, which can be a real benefit if you plan to stay the whole day long. If you do stay, don't miss the sunset. It's one of the primo activities for locals and visitors alike.

St. Pete Municipal Beach

St. Pete Municipal Beach is really at Treasure Island, but it's owned by the larger county to the east. This is probably the widest beach in the county, stretching football fields from the concession stand (with showers and restrooms) to the water, but it's also one of the most crowded. The sand here is also fairly shelly, so unless you have feet of steel, it's a good idea to wear sand shoes or flip-flops.

A note about alcohol: Beer is permitted on city-operated beaches, but glass containers are prohibited. You're not allowed to bring beer down to the beach from the beach bars, either.

Madeira Beach

Just north over the John's Pass Bridge you'll hit Madeira Beach. It stretches north and south, and you can reach it through about 20 access walks from Gulf Boulevard, the main road. The beach is narrower here than Clearwater to the north and Pass-A-Grille to the south, but it is also a lot less crowded. One exception is Archibald Beach because it boasts a large concession stand and a real parking lot, too. You can drink alcohol on these beaches, but, again, no glass containers are allowed.

All the towns along this stretch of mid-Pinellas, including Redington Beach, Redington Shores, Indian Shores and Indian Rocks, likewise have public access walks to reach the beach and Gulf. There are small parking lots scattered to the right and left of Gulf Boulevard to stash your car, but read signs carefully. Many of these lots are reserved strictly for motel or restaurant guests. We advise you to park only in designated spots, and watch traffic very, very carefully if you must cross Gulf Boulevard. Remember Mom saying "Look both ways!"? There will never be a better time to relearn that practice if you want your vacation to stay on track. All along Gulf Boulevard, there's a scarcity of stoplights to slow anxious drivers, so give yourself ample leeway before trying to dash across the asphalt while laden with coolers, chairs, beach bags and assorted kid people.

South Pinellas

Pass-A-Grille

The best way to reach the southern Pinellas beaches is to take I-275 to the Pinellas Bayway, which will cost a 50¢ toll. Pass-A-Grille, on the south end of St. Pete Beach, has that same lovely powder sand that's on Caladesi Island. This is a great place to haul out that huge old blanket, because lounging in the dunes by the sea oats is the chic way to relax at Pass-A-Grille. Activity is brisk here on a sunny day (which is really

almost any day!), and there are restaurants and concession stands galore to help quench that thirst or hunger. One of our favorites is the Hurricane Seafood Restaurant just across the street. If you're not in a hurry to get back home or to your hotel, linger long enough to toast the sunset ... it's a truly spectacular watercolor of lavenders, pinks and yellows that are almost impossible to believe. Make sure you climb all the way to the top floor for a breathtaking panorama of the beaches to the north and deserted Shell Island and Egmont Key to the south. Even the photographs you take won't accurately duplicate our sunset's breathtaking beauty.

Fort DeSoto

Nothing but you and the sun and the sea. That's Fort DeSoto, a barrier island and 900-acre park off south St. Petersburg, with 7 glorious miles of waterfront and two beaches that are perfect for swimming. There is a small charge (less than a dollar) to enter the park, but once inside, you can just pull your car up off the road and head for the beach ... you'll know where that is because someone is always there ahead of you. Just watch for a group of cars along the dune-laden roadway. The beaches here are fairly desolate and pretty coarse and shelly, so wear shoes while staking out your territory. If the kids get bored splashing in the calm waters, have them dig for sand dollars in the shallow waters close to shore. Just wiggle your toes in the sandy bottom until you feel one, whip down and scoop him up. It's also wise to put them right into a bucket of seawater, otherwise the aroma can be fierce. It's also a good idea to toss the whole batch back to their nesting grounds before you leave. Our attempts to dry them to the beautiful white specimens you can buy at gift shops have never yet worked.

Speaking of gift shops, and food, you can find them here at Fort DeSoto. There's a large concession stand/gift shop complex with plenty of outdoor, beachside benches, and the food is quite reasonably priced. A fishing pier, a boat ramp that's open 24 hours a day and campgrounds are also available. To find out more about camping here, call (727) 866-2662.

Watersports

WaveRunners, windsurfers, canoes and inner tubes. If you can float on it in the water, you can find it here in Tampa Bay. Watercraft are just waiting for your rental, whether you're a novice and want to just give an Aqua-Ray a spin or prefer to be taken on a scuba diving experience.

Here, we'll skim the waves of just a temptation of the varied rental opportunities waiting for your boarding, but not without first giving you a few important words of advice. In the past 10 years, Florida has led the nation in the number of boating deaths and accidents, and personal watercraft have played an increasingly dramatic role in these grim statistics. Those who study this distressing situation can point to the fact that many novice watercraft operators are not prepared to handle the problems that might occur while on the water. When you rent a personal watercraft in the Tampa Bay area, you will be given a checklist to familiarize you with the vessel's operation. Pay attention. This vital information could save your life, or someone else's.

In brief, here are just a few of the precautions you should keep in mind when heading out on Tampa Bay waters in a personal watercraft:

• Wear your life vest at all times;

• Keep a whistle around your neck in case you have to summon help;

• Steering is jet-propelled, so allow additional turning and stopping room;

• Check under your seat for a fire extinguisher. You may need it in time of emergency;

• Obey no-wake signs. Know the difference between speeds on the waterway — "normal," "slow" and "idle;"

• Stay in a minimum of waist-deep water;

• Stay at least 50 to 100 feet away from other personal watercraft or boats;

• Beware of tunnel vision. Don't neglect to continually check behind and beside you for other boat activity. Always look over your shoulder before turning;

• Keep out of swim zones and avoid parasail boats, water-skiers and windsurfers;

• Do not under any circumstance ride under the influence of drugs or alcohol.

Canoeing

Alafia River Canoe Rentals
4419 River Dr., Valrico • (813) 689-8645

To get away from all the hubbub and encounter Florida nature nose to snoot, flop that body into a canoe for a four-hour lazy drift down the breezy Alafia River. You'll most likely glide by a zillion species of birds, some unconcerned turtles and even a nosy gator or two. Alafia River Canoe Rentals is right on the river. See our Parks and Recreation chapter for more about canoeing on the Alafia.

Canoe Escape
9335 E. Fowler Ave., Thonotosassa • (813) 986-2067

Two in a canoe ... how lovely. And it truly is as you paddle the peaceful Hillsborough River through Hillsborough County's Wilderness Park System (see our Parks and Recreation chapter). Depending on the time you want to spend with oar in hand, you can choose from seven different cruises, differing from point to point and with varying approximate paddle times. You can opt to canoe solo, or join in an interpretive guided tour. Reservations are required. The cost ranges from $24 to $30 a canoe with two persons. There's no charge for kids younger than 12. See more about canoeing in our Parks and Recreation chapter.

Parasailing

Capt. Mike's Watersports
6300 Gulf Blvd., St. Pete Beach • (727) 360-1998
4900 Gulf Blvd., St. Pete Beach • (727) 360-1053

This is reputed to be a real thrill. One minute you're comfortably seated on a large carpeted deck, the next minute, you're soaring 500 feet over St. Pete Beach. For more than 18 years, Captain Mike and his crew have shown 60,000 people an aerial view of the Gulf of Mexico ... in fact, they are the only U.S. Coast Guard-inspected Parasail operation in Florida. If you're so charged up you can't wait, you can save $5 on the $35-ride of a lifetime if you take your soar before 10 AM. Capt. Mike can also outfit you with pontoon boats, snorkeling equipment, boat rentals and water-ski equipment and lessons. Find them on the beach behind the Colonial Gateway Inn and the Dolphin Beach Hotel.

Fly-N-High Parasail Inc.
208 John's Pass Boardwalk, Madeira Beach • (727) 397-1050

Oh, so 500 feet isn't high enough for you? Head on down to John's Pass and hitch a ride with Fly-N-High. They promise the highest flight on the beach ... 700 feet if you dare. All take-offs and landings are directly from the towing vessel, so you can get mammoth butterflies in your stomach and not even worry about getting wet. You can also rent WaveRunners here from the location on the East End Docks.

Parasail City
Slip 2, Clearwater Beach Marina, Clearwater Beach • (727) 449-0566

How high do you dare to go? When you rent from Parasail City, you get to choose between three different heights which translate to three different prices. You can also choose to stay dry or get wet and, if you're really in a crazy kind of mood, ask to experience a free-fall which simulates a parachute drop. They'll be happy to accommodate at no additional cost. Find Parasail City just across the street from Clearwater Beach. They're open from 9 AM until dusk. If you want to rent a WaveRunner or jet boat, ask about their free shuttle service to Pierside Waterworks at The Pier in St. Pete.

Powerboats and Paddleboats

Club Nautico
Waterwalk at Harbour Island, Tampa • (813) 223-2107

Boats of every flavor, from ski boats to pontoon boats to boats that are fishing-ready,

are here for the steering at Club Nautico. You can be the skipper of your own fate from $99 to $179 for a half-day of powerboat rental or pay slightly more for the pontoon variety.

Boating Zone
Clearwater Beach Marina, Clearwater Beach • (727) 446-5503

Exactly what is your need for speed? If you can handle a boat on your own, Boating Zone can put you in a water-worthy vessel equipped with motors that range from 70hp all the way to 175hp. If you'd rather just poke along, go for the 8-foot mini-boat with a passable 6hp motor, just right for two people to embark on a leisurely cruise. Sign on at Slips 5 and 6 at the Clearwater Beach Marina.

Fun Rentals
555½ 150th Ave., Madeira Beach • (727) 397-0276

If weaving along the Intracoastal Waterway is just your speed, Fun Rentals behind Leverock's restaurant is where you should head. Here, you can stow your family of 10 in a 22-foot pontoon boat and head out for fishing, sightseeeing or just drifting along. You'll shell out $150 for a full day of pontoon pleasure.

Ocean Adventures
John's Pass Marina, Treasure Island • (727) 363-1131

Pop into a new Grady White boat with that zippy Mercury motor and you are headed for fun. These boats are fully equipped with built-in coolers, depth finders and swim ladders, so once you've stowed your crew aboard, you're ready to fly. If you need equipment to fulfill your dream of fishing, water-skiing or snorkeling, Ocean Adventures has a rental package to tack right on to your tab.

Sheraton Sand Key Resort
1160 Gulf Blvd., Clearwater Beach • (727) 393-1611

You'll find this largest of watersports cen-

INSIDERS' TIP

Tampa Bay is an estuary, a body of water partially surrounded by land. It is Florida's largest open-water estuary with about 398 square miles and an average depth of 12 feet.

Photo: St. Petersburg/Clearwater Area Convention & Visitors Bureau

Windsurfing is another of the many popular water activities in the Tampa Bay area. Rentals and lessons are available at many locations.

ters at the northern tip of Sand Key Island next to Sand Key Park. If you pass on the windsurfing lessons, you can go straight for a glass-bottomed paddleboat, Hobie Cat or catboat. Prices range from $12 to $35, depending on your boat selection.

Suncoast Boat Rentals
545 150th Ave., Madeira Beach
• (727) 391-5266

Another rental haven behind Leverock's restaurant, Suncoast can slide you into a 16- to 24-foot powerboat that will whisk you out for a day of fishing, water-skiing or cruising. A two-hour jaunt will cost from $49 to $89, depending on the size of the boat you need for your adventuring party.

Sailing

Annapolis Sailing School
6800 34th St. S., St. Petersburg
• (727) 867-8102

Hoist the sails, matey! No powerboats for us, we're doing it the old-fashioned way at this branch of the world-famous Maryland-headquartered sailing school. This is a place to seriously learn the techniques of sailing; not for a half-day jaunt. For information about the two-, five- or eight-day courses, call the school's staff at the number above.

Kai Lanai
Clearwater Beach Marina, Clearwater Beach • (727) 446-6778

This is not a do-it-yourselfer, but a lovely two-hour cruise aboard a magnificent 50-foot catamaran you couldn't handle by yourself anyway. Set sail in the morning, afternoon or for a sunset cruise, from $20 for adults and $12 for children. Reservations are definitely recommended for this popular adventure.

Southern Romance
Clearwater Beach Marina, Clearwater Beach • (727) 461-6148

Another fantastic sailboat cruise opportunity, you'll come aboard the Southern Romance at Slip 16 at the Clearwater Marina. It's a 40-foot ocean-racing/cruising yacht that

holds passengers to a maximum of 12 for a two-hour cruise of the Clearwater harbor and Gulf waters. Reserve your $16-sail in advance to be assured passage.

Suncoast Sailing Center
Clearwater Beach Marina, Clearwater Beach • (727) 581-4462

Be steered on-board a 65-foot Windjammer or a 38-foot racing yacht. Or, take the helm yourself on a small sloop. The choice is yours at Suncoast Sailing Center. They're even prepared to give you a lesson or two if you make reservations in advance.

Scuba Diving

Blue Adventure
12665 Seminole Blvd., Largo
• (727) 585-7997, (800) 536-DIVE

Go for it, baby! You could hang around Blue Adventure for a week and do something new and daring every day. Why not start with a scuba adventure, offered to even the uninitiated? Or, you can elect to snorkel. In either case, it's likely you'll come nose-to-nose with a manatee from October through March. Certified divers can opt for a spring dive in one of our clear spring-fed rivers, or head out to the Gulf to get up-close and personal with large game fish, sponges and coral. Lastly, for sheer relaxation, put your bottom in your own personal inner tube and join the troop as it meanders down the pristine Crystal River, landing on shore long enough to picnic at lunchtime. For all the details and a current price list for all these adventures, call the big Blue at the numbers listed above.

WaveRunners and Jet Skis

Captain Dave's Watersports
9540 Blind Pass Rd., St. Pete Beach
• (727) 367-4336

Satisfy your water adventure hunger here at Captain Dave's, right beside the Blind Pass Bridge in the Lighthouse Point Shopping Center. Thirty minutes on a WaveRunner will set you back $35, or go for a full hour for $60. The good captain can also get you a Parasail ride or rent you a powerboat. Snorkel, sailing and shelling trips are on the menu, too.

Blue Water WaveRunners
545 150th Ave., Madeira Beach
• (727) 393-4566

From the Holiday Isles Marina, you can screech off into the horizon on a WaveRunner that fits your size. They're right next to Leverock's restaurant at the end of the Tom Stewart Causeway. We'll just go there and watch you from the delish glass-walled restaurant. WaveRunner rentals cost from $35 to $45 an hour, depending on size.

Florida International Jet School
9555 Blind Pass Rd., St. Pete Beach
• (727) 360-8669

Sea-Doos are the star of the show here at the Florida International Jet School that's at the marina behind Sidekicks Restaurant. In addition to watercraft rentals that start at $45 an hour, you're also offered guided two-hour pleasure cruises for $69 and four-hour touring cruises from St. Pete to Clearwater for $125. If you're hot to really learn how to race a personal watercraft, you can sign on for lessons with French runabout champion Betrand Ollier for $69 an hour.

Island Marine
11045 Gulf Blvd., Treasure Island
• (727) 367-2132

Rent a WaveRunner from $30 for 30 minutes, or opt for a more sophisticated journey on a 17- to 19-foot powerboat or maybe a 24-foot catamaran. Or, maybe you'd rather stick to terra firma and rent some beach cruiser bikes, or rods and reels for fishing. This is a one-stop watersports-type place that opens at 8 AM for you get-up-and-goers.

Jack's at John's Pass
John's Pass Village and Boardwalk,
Madeira Beach • (727) 392-6912

If you're ready to hit the waves before 11 AM, you'll save 20 percent off a WaveRunner rental at Jack's. After that, rental rates for one hour cost just under $50. Matter of fact, if it's a bit nippy, they'll even let you use a form-fitting wetsuit free of charge. If you're more of a powerboat-type person, you can rent them, too, from 14 feet and longer.

Rick's Jet Ski Rental
St. Pete Beach • (727) 360-7670

If a tandem Kawasaki WaveRunner blows your trunks up, head on over to Rick's and snag one for $35 for a half hour. You and your partner can crash through the waves in the wide-open water and then cruise back to John's Pass to take a snooze on the beautiful beach or grab a beer and snack at one of the bars, pubs or restaurants waiting to accommodate you.

Waterworks Rentals
The Pier, St. Petersburg • (727) 363-0000
200-D 150th Ave., Madeira Beach
• (727) 363-0000

Got the urge to explore the Bay? Waterworks can get you the water flotation vessel you need, whether it be a WaveRunner (starting at $25 for 30 minutes) or a powerboat from 12 to 22 feet.

Since days before most people's memories, spring around the Tampa Bay region hasn't been defined by a change in weather. Instead, it's defined by the arrival of the Boys of Summer.

Spectator Sports

Excuse me, but do we really need ESPN? OK, OK. We'd miss out on those hilariously bizarre commercials no one else carries. And we wouldn't want to give up watching NASCAR or Indy racing (which some silly folk refuse to recognize as true sport). Still, even if all the sports-coverage satellite dishes up there in space blew at once, there'd be no need for sports withdrawal anywhere around Tampa Bay.

How do we serve up sports? Let us count the ways ....
Spring training, our Devil Rays, a Yank's farm team;
Ah! Pewter Power Bucs of our dreams;
A Storm in the arena, Lightning on ice;
Basketball Magic nearby for spice.
The blistering speed of Thoroughbreds,
Greyhounds, Tennis, Golf and Polo
Racquets, irons and mallets fly high.
Soccer, where everyone gets their kicks;
And softballs fast-pitched by fem FireStix.
The annual college Outback Bowl;
Soon, we'll host a third Super Bowl;
And next year, play-offs of the NCAA;
Plus a bid for Olympics is well under way.
To the whole nation pro sports we deliver,
And in year-round delight do all our fans shiver!

Sorry, Elizabeth Browning. We promise not to trade our season tickets for the poet's podium.

Baseball

Spring Training

Since days before most people's memories, spring around the Tampa Bay region hasn't been defined by a change in weather. Instead, it's defined by the arrival of the Boys of Summer. We don't care what anyone out in Arizona says about their share of the Grapefruit League — we know all the greats come here to train! St. Petersburg has its own boys, the Devil Rays; Clearwater gets the Philadelphia Phillies; and the Toronto Blue Jays call Dunedin home. Tampa has long been the training center for a New York Yankees' farm team, and now the Yanks themselves train here, at Legends Field, a replica of The House That Ruth Built.

All totaled, there are nearly a dozen Grapefruit League baseball clubs warming up within a two-hour drive from Tampa Bay. In addition to the the teams that train regionally, you'll find the Detroit Tigers in Lakeland and, a little farther to the east, the Cleveland Indians in Winter Haven; the Kansas City Royals go to Baseball City, and the Atlanta Braves are at Disney's Sports Complex. To the south, Sarasota is the training camp for the Cincinatti Reds, while Bradenton hosts the Pittsburgh Pirates.

So, here's where to enjoy watching your favorite teams warm up for the season. The

---

INSIDERS' TIP

Guys aren't the only ones who grow up around Tampa Bay and go off to play in the big leagues. On June 4, 1996, Pam Davis, a pre-med student and former pitcher for the University of Florida's softball team, made baseball history as the first woman to pitch for a major league affiliate. Her pitching fame was in a Class AA Jacksonville Rays game against the Australian National Team.

listed phone numbers may change since many ticket offices open only during training weeks. The sports sections of the local papers are your best source of complete information on game schedules and ticket prices.

New York Yankees, Legends Field, 4200 block of N. Dale Mabry Highway, Tampa, (813) 879-2244.

Tampa Bay Devil Rays, Al Lang Field, St. Petersburg, (727) 893-7490.

Philadelphia Phillies, Jack Russell Stadium, 800 Phillies Drive, Clearwater, (727) 442-8496.

Toronto Blue Jays, Dunedin Stadium, 311 Douglas Avenue, Dunedin, (727) 733-9302.

Pittsburgh Pirates, McKechnie Field, 17th Avenue W. and Ninth Street W., Bradenton, (941) 748-4610.

Cincinatti Reds, Ed Smith Sports Complex, 12th Street and Tuttle Avenue, Sarasota, (941) 954-7699.

www.insiders.com

See this and many other **Insiders' Guide®** destinations online — in their entirety.

Visit us today!

Detroit Tigers, Joker Marchant Stadium, 3201 Lakeland Hills Boulevard, Lakeland, (941) 603-6278.

Cleveland Indians, Chain O'Lakes Park, Cypress Gardens Boulevard, Winter Haven, (941) 293-3900.

Kansas City Royals, Baseball City Stadium, Haines City, (941) 424-2424.

Atlanta Braves, Disney Sports Complex, Lake Buena Vista, (407) 939-1500.

Major League

Tampa Bay Devil Rays
Tropicana Field, 1 Tropicana Dr., St. Petersburg • (727) 825-3127

Team loyalty has a long history around the Tampa Bay area. Even though the Devil Rays have played their very first season in Major League Baseball, the people of this region backed "their" team for nearly 20 years before actually getting one. Some of the behind-the-scenes players working to bring a team died or went broke, but never would we give up hope. Every time expansion was talked, word came we'd get a team. And every time the league owners held a vote, we didn't. Ev-

ery time an existing team talked of moving, we made a bid. We lured the Minnesota Twins, the Oakland A's, Chicago's White Sox and the Texas Rangers. Deals with the Seattle Mariners and San Francisco Giants were, we just knew, sure bets. But always, always, we fouled out.

Then ... finally ... the ball came our way. On March 9, 1995, the 13th expansion team in major league history was named: The Tampa Bay Devil Rays. Could the local paper headlines have been any bigger when man set foot on the moon?

With only three years before the first pitch, the local owners, headed by president and chief officer Vince Namoli, swung into immediate action to ready the team and its home field. By summer, Chuck Lamar was building the team, leaving the Atlanta Braves to become the Rays general manager. By the following summer, a farm team was in place in the Gulf Coast League. In 1997, team acquisitions speeded and the team was placed in the AL East. Ace-pitcher Rolando Arrojo defected Cuba and was signed. Along came Tampa homeboys Wade Boggs, after five seasons with the Yankees, and Fred McGriff, "The Dawg"-ed first baseman on the Braves, Quinton McCracken from the Rockies, Tony Saunders from the Marlins ... and 36 other seasoned and promising players.

Speaking of the Florida Marlins, it's interesting to note that the team fire-sale after taking last year's pennant allowed the Rays to snag Larry Rothschild as team manager. A Florida State grad, Rothschild was the Marlin's pitching coach and also had a World Series championship as bullpen coach for the Cincinnati Reds in 1980.

And speaking of World Series champs, the Rays played all six of the last winners during their first season. While hopes ride high that having so many seasoned leaders and talented vets on our team will produce winning results, we're tempering our expectations based on the history of first-year expansion teams. But guess what? All we want to do is be taken out to the ballpark. No matter how

Photo: Selbypic

Raymond James Stadium is home to the Tampa Bay Buccaneers.

the season standings end, the Tampa Bay Devil Rays are winners. So are we all.

To see a game, contact the box office at Tropicana Field or TicketMaster. To order tickets by phone, call (813) 282-RAYS from Hillsborough or (727) 898-RAYS in Pinellas. Single-ticket prices run the gamut from $3 in the "Fan Fare" section up to $195 behind home plate.

Tropicana Field

"Build it," they said, "and we will come." So build it we did — spending $30 million to create the "baseball ready" ThunderDome.

They came. Eventually. They looked. They said, "Well, we want something nicer. Build it some more. Maybe we'll come."

By that time, Tampa and St. Petersburg had been spurned by Major League Baseball more often than Liz Taylor's dumped husbands. But deeper into our pockets we dug, begrudging every penny of the extra $62 mil, to renovate and expand the dome. And son of a gun, we won a team, and every single fan won a wonderful place to watch them play — Tropicana Field.

Walking up to the entrance rotunda at Tropicana Field, fans pass over the largest ceramic tile mosaic in the state — a 900-foot image of a floating devil ray. Inside the main entrance rotunda, pedestrians follow "streets" leading around the ballpark and to seven escalators and 10 elevators.

Center Field Street features a food court, plenty of shops and a sports bar and grill that's open every day of the year. But there's no confusing this place with any typical mall — literally "leaping" through the ball field wall is an 18-foot "player," glove in hand, foiling a fabulous home run. Fans themselves can get into plenty of games with interactive baseball, football and basketball, plus traditional pool, Foosball and more in the game room.

A major area of focus is "The Taste of Tampa Bay," where local restaurants serve up their specialties — everything from the Outback's Bloomin' Onion to deviled crab

Our Great Sporting Neighbors

The Tampa Bay area proudly claims some of the greatest names in sports. Not surprisingly, most of our homegrown athletic stars show up on baseball rosters. But take a look at this "who's who" and you'll find names recognizable in almost every sport. Although most of these folks grew up here, some of them just came to play and several now have homes in the area. Some of our sporting neighbors include:

Close-up

Baseball: Richie Ashburn, Nelson Beleno, Derrick Bell, Wade Boggs, Darren Daulton, Lenny Dykstra, Carl Everett, Steve Garvey, Luis Gomez, Dwight Gooden, Ty Griffin, Sterling Hitchcock, John Hudek, Howard Johnson, Tony Larussa, Hall of Famer Al Lopez, Dave Magadan, Tino Martinez, Fred McGriff, Sam Militello, Rich Monteleone, Jim Morrison, Lou Piniella, Frank Pulli (umpire), Brad Radke, John Ramos, Kenny Rogers, Gary Sheffield and Ozzie Timmons.

Negro League Baseball: Clifford Brown, Billy Felder, John Ray Gibbons, Walter Lee "Dirk" Gibbons and Bo "Lefty" Maddox.

Basketball: Tommy "Cochise" Brown, Katrina Colleton and Matt Geiger.

Bodybuilding: Diane Giordan.

Bowling: Tom Milton.

Boxing: Dr. Ferdie Pacheco.

Football: Forest Blue, Rick Casares, Jim Del Gaizo, Wayne Fontes, Ernest Gibbons, Henry Larence, William Lloyd, John Matuzak, Lee Roy Selmon, Barry Smith and Freddie Soloman.

Golf: Woody Austin, Jill Briles-Hinton, Dawn Coe-Jones, Dale Eggeling, Rufus Lewis, ChiChi Rodriguez, Roberta Albers Speer and Colleen Walker.

Ice-Skating: Dianna-lynne Webster and Jim Millns.

Indy Car Racing: Eddie Cheever.

Hockey: Terry Crisp and Phil and Tony Esposito.

Kickboxing: Dean Cochran.

Running: Peter Maher.

Sailing: Ed Baird.

Swimming: Brooke Bennett and Nicole Haislett.

Tennis: Jennifer Capriati, Jim Courier and Jared Palmer.

Track: Colin Jackson and Mark McKoy.

Volleyball: Gabriella Reese.

Wrestling: Hulk Hogan.

Photo: New York Yankees

Tino Martinez

cakes from the Columbia Restaurant, to Cuban sandwiches and seafood. All told, there are 16 restaurants, plus one that offers just a kids' menu.

Through some odd quirk of baseball mysticism, the actual playing field is an almost exact replica of the legendary, asymmetrical old home of the Brooklyn Dodgers. Everyone swears it wasn't intended, but once this coincidence was realized, it was capitalized on by redesigning the east-side entry of the stadium to mimic the entrance behind home plate at Ebbets Field. But under the world's largest cable-supported domed roof there's not a single other thing that's "old-fashioned" about the home of the new Rays.

Tropicana Field sports a dirt infield and base paths, making it the first synthetic turf field with this feature in more than 20 years, and players like it a lot. What fans like most is how close they can get to the action. Foul territory was reduced to add more seats, placing some just 50 feet behind home plate. The deepest part of the park is 415 feet, slightly to left center, but fans who want to stay on top of every ball can get seats equipped with computers. From these "Scout Seats," the viewer can call up all of the camera angles in the dome, the radar speed of the last pitch and even a special menu for seat-side waiter service.

Parking is always a challenge at major sporting events, and the Rays have attempted to address that problem in several different ways. The on-site lot holds nearly 7,000 cars (parking costs $10 here), but the immediate surrounding area doesn't offer much extra space. In fact, parking is verboten on many of the nearby streets during games (residents are required to display a special window decal so they don't get towed or ticketed). The best bet is to keep an eye out for private parking lots which the city has approved — they sport signage with three palm trees and a circle that reads "Event Parking." There are more than 20,000 parking spots for cars in public, private and metered street spaces. The majority are within walking distance of the field, and others offer free shuttle service to and from the dome.

The most direct route to Tropicana Field is to follow I-275 to Exit 9, the downtown St. Petersburg feeder exit. However, a range of alternate routes encourage drivers (via electronic message boards) to use other routes.

Minor League

Tampa Yankees
Legends Field, 4200 block of N. Dale Mabry Hwy., Tampa • (813) 879-2244

The Florida State League's Tampa Yankees — the "T-Yanks" — now play minor league ball at the new Yankee stadium in Tampa. Games generally begin at 7 PM on weekdays and 1 PM on Sunday, with the season running from April through September. Reserved seats cost $5 and general admission is $3; seniors, students and military personnel get in for a dollar less. Plus, a lot of discount promotions help make games even more affordable.

Football

Tampa Bay Buccaneers
Raymond James Stadium, 4200 block of N. Dale Mabry Hwy., Tampa • (813) 879-2827, (800) 282-0683

"Touchdown! Tampa Bay!"

Oh, how sweet to hear those words! After an eternity as the doormat of the National Football League, our brawny, brash Bucs brandished their way to the playoffs! No more nasty cracks about Buccaneer Bruce. We've got Pewter Power, and we are darned proud of it!

And for so long, we didn't even know if we'd keep the team in Tampa. Truth be told, a lot of us got to the point we didn't care, what with all the bickering over stadium funding, plus a perception that owner Malcolm Glazer played by rules he'd often change. Well, everything worked out just fine. Glazer got his team a new stadium — it opened with the first home game of the 1998 season — and Tampa Bay fans have been assured that the team will stick around at least 30 years.

Now, some Insiders wonder if that's what we really wanted ("Be careful what you ask for; you might get it!"). But we'll admit that our hearts swelled with pride the first time Terry

Bradshaw said something about the Bucs that was actually complimentary. By the end of the season, our grins were greater than the Cheshire Cat's because all the sportscasters were fawning over "our boys," and famous players were actually asking how they could get on the team!

As any good player knows, there's no "I" in "Team," and turning the Bucs from crummy to contenders took the effort of every single player. But the one man who set the tone, who believed in his players before they believed in themselves, is the one and only Tony Dungy. A deeply spiritual, soft-spoken gentleman devoted to his family, Dungy is to role modeling what the Dallas Cowboys are to bail bondsmen. The foundation of that strength is a belief every good parent works to instill in a child, the same belief that connects every good coach: your talent is unique, give all of yourself; do your very best; never give up.

And give up, they didn't, even the few times that "SOB" line (Same Old Bucs) surfaced after lost games or blown plays. This was because the season was what mattered and the Bucs moved from the NFL's laughingstock to laudable. Finishing 10-6, the Bucs made a valiant play for the division championship before losing out to the Green Bay Packers.

Dungy's belief in developing talent finally became apparent to the fans this year — NFL fans voted him Coach of the Year. Trent Dilfer's growing confidence and skill took him to the Pro Bowl, accompanied by seven other Bucs — Mike Alstott, Derrick Brooks, John Lynch, Tony Mayberry, Hardy Nickerson, Warren Sapp and Warrick Dunn, who was named the NFL Offensive Rookie of the Year. It was the most massive show of players sent by any one team to the Pro Bowl.

But the Bucs put on a show in every game played during the season. Dilfer passed for 2,555 yards and 21 touchdowns — one of which he made himself! Alstott displayed the stoppability of a Sherman tank, literally pushing piles of tacklers before him at times like he used to shove his Jeep Wrangler in 100-yard sprints at Purdue. Lynch proved team loyalty came above family when, in a game against Buffalo, he smacked his own brother-in-law so hard it knocked him out. Mention Brooks and Dunn around town and people don't even

think of the country-western duo. Derrick Brooks is one of the NFL's top linebackers, and Dunn — once considered too little to play pro ball — is the Artful Dodger when it comes to scooting through line openings only he can find. Sapp recorded a career-high 10½ sacks and 68 tackles during the season and won a new six-year contract worth $36 million.

Such a team turnaround also earned Tony Dungy hearty approval from his boss. After only two years of a six-year contract, Glazer tore it up and signed Dungy to a new six-year term at double his previous salary. Yet it was never a demand Dungy had considered. He's the kind of man who sticks by his word while also giving back to the community.

And the team players have followed suit. Warrick Dunn gave a spectacular Christmas gift to four low-income families, making down payments on homes for each of them. Mike Alstott hosts and personally leads a football camp for kids between the ages of 8 and 19. Mike Husted is active with the Tampa Children's Home, Big Brothers/Big Sisters, and also hosts Kick for Kids events to raise money for local charities. Trent Dilfer participates in the Fellowship of Christian Athletes, the United Way, the Police Athletic League and other groups. Hardy Nickerson, who went to the Pro Bowl two years in a row, created a foundation to assist at-risk youth and leads Hardy's Huddle, a program that provides tuition assistance for kids with learning and/or behavioral problems.

Bay area kids are also getting a boost from a new program started by the team owner. For each Bucs victory, the Glazers donate funds — to top out at $3 million — to the Tampa Bay Sports Commission, established last fall to support amateur youth sports activities.

So even off the field, this team's made up of winners. The 1998-99 season is shaping up to be even better than last, with a strong team building more strength. The signings of veteran fullback Lorenzo Neal from the Jets and wide receivers Bert Emanuel from the Falcons and Jacquez Green, fresh from winning seasons at the University of Florida, have definitely helped the cause.

It used to be that in the days of the SOBs, anyone who was interested could walk up to the ticket window on game day and get a good seat. Needless to point out, that's all changed. If tickets remain on game day, they go up for grabs at 9 AM. But smart players know to get their seats well in advance. Tickets (single-game prices range from $26 to $48 last season and may change) can be purchased by phoning or visiting the stadium box office or through TicketMaster nationwide.

Raymond James Stadium

When founding owner Hugh Culverhouse died and the Buccaneers were purchased by Malcom Glazer, a big sticking point in keeping the team here was his demand for a new stadium. Coughing up the construction cash stuck in the craws of many Tampa Bay residents ... and a lot of the reason was the Bucs were (simply) lousy. After a lot of legal wrangling and lawsuits and counter-efforts and squabbling, the matter finally went to a vote and taxpayers grudgingly approved a "community investment tax" that funded the stadium while also supporting schools and fire and law enforcement.

Now that the Bucs head into this season fresh from playoff-contention, the mood's changed a lot. A move's afoot to save the old stadium, formally known as Houlihan's Stadium but affectionately dubbed "The Big Sombrero" for its design, as a possible venue for the Olympics bid the area's making. But all prideful eyes are on the new Raymond James Stadium going up right next door, which MUST be completed before the Bucs' first home game on September 20, 1998. (MUST is an underemphasis ... if it isn't ready, the area has to pay Glazer $437,000 for every game that can't be held there!)

While sentiment may be on the side of the old stadium (constructed in 1966 for $4 mil-

lion), it's a fact that the new one (costing $168.5 million) is true venue gem for the area. Displaying brightly designed architecture and festive landscape end-zone plazas, the design allows for greater technology to be added in the future, features wider concourses for fan comfort and 65 percent of seating on the sidelines.

With 66,321 armchair spectator seats (with cup holders, no less) the new stadium can expand seating to accommodate 75,000 when necessary. At max capacity, that's only a few hundred seats more than the old stadium permanently provided. Though actual seating is less, the changes make for greater fan viewing pleasure. For example, general seating is armchair style, meaning no more crummy aluminum benches; disabled seating has increased by more than 400 percent; the number of air-conditioned luxury suites nearly tripled and are placed a maximum of 78 feet from the field (instead of the old 118-foot minimum). Plus, there are two 65,000-square-foot, air-conditioned lounges, four sports bars and two specialty restaurants, as well as scads more concession areas. Twenty escalators (the old stadium had none) and five elevators make getting around a lot easier and faster. And female fans, you'll love this ... the ratio of "fixtures" in the stadium is 1-to-81, while the guys' ration is 1-to-129.

Like the old stadium, the new one will host far more than sporting events. The first scheduled event was a ministry crusade by Dr. Billy Graham on October 22-25, 1998. It's the third crusade — and the first in 19 years — that he's held in the town where he attended Bible College and got his start as an evangelist.

We hope it isn't blasphemous to suggest that the blessings his crusade bestowed on the area might include the win-loss record of

---

INSIDERS' TIP

Not only can we boast about having some of the top sports teams, Tampa Bay can boast its ranking as a sports center. The *Sporting News* says that Tampa Bay is No. 23 on its list of 238 sports cities around the United States and Canada. (The fact that Tampa Bay is not a city is an issue we'll overlook in this honor.) The survey scored every North American city with at least one team in MLB, the NFL, NBA or NHL, or an NCAA Division I football or basketball team.

the Bucs ... if they don't get into the 1999 Super Bowl, we can always hope to see them at Super Bowl XXXV, right here at home, in 2001!

Tampa Bay Storm
401 Channelside Dr., Tampa
• **(813) 276-7300**

After you've spent a few autumn afternoons baking under the sun or sitting through a fast-moving rain watching the Bucs, you can appreciate the popularity of arena football, played indoors at Tampa's climate-controlled Ice Palace. But this is more than football under a roof. In fact, it's so different it's actually patented. Scoring remains the same, but the field is a padded surface 85 feet wide and 50 yards long. Goal posts are narrower and higher than NFL regulation. Instead of 11 players, only eight take the field under arena rules. Kickoffs are made from the goal line, and punting is illegal. So while many of the aspects are the same, minor changes make the game's finer points a fun challenge to follow.

The Tampa Bay Storm are four-time world champs, so this team's a real winner for those

who suffer withdrawal after the NFL season. Games are played between April and August. Single-game ticket prices range from $7 to $50 and are available at the box office and other locations. You can also catch play on WTOG (Channel 44) TV or listen to it on WHNZ 540 AM.

Outback Bowl
Raymond James Stadium, 4200 block of N. Dale Mabry Hwy., Tampa
• **(813) 874-2695, (800) 282-0683**

On New Year's Day, Raymond James Stadium fills with the sounds of fans cheering their favorite college teams. The third-ranked teams in the SEC and the Big Ten are in town for the Outback Bowl (formerly known as the Hall of Fame Bowl), and the playoff draws crowds from around the nation. The 11 AM game is broadcast on ESPN, but it's a lot more fun to watch in person — especially since it's too-often blacked out locally! Tickets cost $35 and are available beginning in October at the stadium box office and through TicketMaster. For more information about activities leading up to game day, check out our Annual Events chapter.

A Legendary Field of Dreams

The old legends of baseball never fade, they only get larger during the years. And many of the legendary Boys of Summer took part in spring training around Tampa Bay.

A little more than a year ago, all those mythic places and players became a permanent part of our landscape with the opening of Legends Field. The newest, and largest, training facility in the nation, Legends Field is home to the New York Yankees during the rites of spring. And the stadium truly must feel like home — it's an exact replica of the House That Ruth Built in the Bronx, right down to copies of the monuments at Yankee Stadium and the signs directing fans to their seats.

Two levels with a combined 10,000 seats create a V-shape along right and left fields and there's not an obstructed view in the house. While vendors certainly ply the stands with popcorn and peanuts and hot dogs, food courts offer a variety of fare from basic to gourmet. In case you missed a big play, catch it on the video replay scoreboard. Outfit yourself as a true fan at the novelty store, patterned after the Yankee Clubhouse, or in one of two other small shops at each end of the stadium. A covered walkway rises high over the heavy automobile traffic on N. Dale Mabry Highway, so fans can easily, and safely, cross that busy highway to nearby parking.

The location of Legends Field provides another community perk. It's adjacent to the

— continued on next page

Tampa's Legends Field is the spring training home for the New York Yankees.

main campus of Hillsborough Community College. Between the Field and the school, the Yankees built a Community Use Field, where the HCC Hawks play. Of course, the proximity is probably as much a benefit for scouts as it is for the players , particularly since the Hawks, who've sent four players to the major leagues since 1994, is one of only three Florida school teams to win a national championship. Both the Community Use Field and Legends Field also host high school, college and amateur tournaments.

After spring training season ends, the ballpark is home to the T-Yanks, the Yankees farm team that plays 72 home games during its April to September season.

But more than baseball is served up here. Legends Field has turned out to be a terrific venue for outdoor concerts. Within the first few months, music fans were treated to such stars as Rod Stewart, Sting and the Moody Blues (backed by the Florida Orchestra, no less) on a night with wild lightning as a spectacular special effect. Or maybe it wasn't just lightning. Do you suppose it was The Mick, blasting fast-balls across the universe, in celebration of all the legends Legends Field honors?

Hockey

Tampa Bay Lightning
401 Channelside Dr., Tampa
• **(813) 229-2658**

Phil Esposito is famous for two reasons: as one of the NHL's most prolific goal-scorers and for bringing ice hockey to the Tampa Bay region. The first recorded date of his launching this idea was in March 1990; nine months later, the National Hockey League granted an expansion to the Tampa Bay area. And during its first years, the team was so hot that fans everywhere were fired up.

Alas, just as the Bucs emerged from their eternity of ennui, all the crackle went out of our Lightning. Last season was not a good one.

What's been so frustrating is that no one seems to know why, and nothing seems to help. After taking the team into the playoff in only its fourth season, beloved coach Terry Crisp was signed to a new contract that earned him a place in NHL record books; no other coach had ever stayed as long with one team.

Unfortunately, coach Crisp didn't get to live out the contract. He was first to feel the blade, sliced from the team mid-season with no replacement coach on board. But hopes ran high when Jacques Demers stepped behind the bench. The Stanley Cup winner and two-time NHL Coach of the Year quickly showed the team who was boss, declaring that players could forget about their golf balls until their puck power improved. That didn't happen before the end of the season, which the team finished out in last place.

Part of the blame had to be laid on team management. While folks at the helm in Tampa had a role in the problem, their efforts were governed by the guys up above them, or at least far east of them — the majority owner, Okubo International, in Japan. Then, in spring 1998, after 18 months up for sale, the team was acquired by retired insurance tycoon Arthur L. Williams. A well-known motivational speaker, Williams promises big changes in Lightning attitude.

While fan pride has wavered, team dedication to this community remains strong. Since arriving in the area in 1992, the team and players have supported nearly two dozen local charities. Kids are the biggest winners, with financial support going to such groups as the Children's Cancer Center and Toys for Tots. But the team's also active in bringing up future players of the sport, by donating equipment to more than 7,000 youngsters playing at 41 area youth centers and recreational facilities. The team also supports The Tampa Bay Junior Lightning Youth Hockey Program in Clearwater and the Greater Tampa Youth Hockey Association in Oldsmar, which serves another 400 aspiring puck-chasers.

The Tampa Bay Lightning season runs October through April. General admission starts at $16 and ranges up to $72 for reserved seating. Sofa-bound netminders can view games on WTOG-TV Channel 44 and cable's Sunshine Network, or listen in on WFNS 910 AM radio.

Ice Palace

Unlike our efforts with baseball, the NHL gave us the Lightning four years before the team had a permanent place to play. And when the magnificent Ice Palace opened in 1996, fan and team patience was well rewarded.

Every one of the 19,500 seats was filled for that first game. But the crowds turn out for many more events than just hockey. Designed as a multi-purpose venue, the 660,000-square-foot Ice Palace can accommodate even larger crowds — up to 20,500 people for basketball or 21,500 for stage events.

Along with the Lightning, the Palace serves as home to the Tampa Bay Storm arena football team. Working around the two teams' schedules, about 100 other events are hosted here each year. Brightest on this year's horizon is the NHL's 1999 All-Star Game slated for Sunday, January 24.

With seven levels of seating, there's not an obstructed sight line in the house, whether fans turn out for sports or other events. So far, those have included concerts by top music acts, the circus, rodeo, gymnastics, wrestling and spectacular ice shows with Olympic champions. There are also two meeting rooms that may be utilized by business groups.

Plaza suites on Level 3 put viewers just 60 feet from the event. Up two more levels, seating at the Terrace Club is about 90 feet from the action. On Level 4, the Palace Club offers 3,000 club seats and a private concourse including a restaurant and bar. A second restaurant on Level 4, Ventanas Caribbean Bistro, is open to the public, though. Nearly two dozen concessions are scattered throughout all three concourses, and stay open till the third period of games. And since the sound system pipes the action onto the concourse areas, you won't miss any of the action out on the floor while grabbing a bite. (Same holds true for the restrooms!)

Knowing that all types of fans come with all types of abilities, construction of the Ice Palace included close attention to needs of the disabled. Nearly $2.5 million went into ensuring that the facility and services meet or surpass requirements of the Americans with Disabilities Act. Physically handicapped patrons have 365 seats available, arena workers are trained in sign language for the hearing impaired, and braille menus are offered at the concessions. While pets aren't allowed, service dogs are welcomed.

Plenty of parking surrounds the Ice Palace, including 1,500 primo spaces in the adjacent garage. Another 10,000 slots are available within easy walking distance throughout the downtown area.

Polo

Tampa Bay Polo Club
Walden Lake, Plant City • (813) 752-8731

It may be the sport of kings, but it doesn't take a king's ransom to enjoy watching the fast-paced action of this game. The Tampa Bay Polo Club started about a dozen years ago when the Walden Lake residential community began development. Now the club is the fifth largest in the country and has 40 members. Every Sunday at 2 PM between November and April (except for Easter), players saddle up and take to the field for six chukkers (that's what periods of play are called). Polo requires a great deal of skill and athletic ability, but the horses work a lot harder than the riders, so each horse plays only one chukker. That means each player uses six different mounts in a game. As many as 1,000 people turn out to watch the matches, especially when charity events and jazz concerts are included. So, on some lazy Sunday afternoon, fill the cooler, grab a lawn chair or blanket, and see what all the fun's about.

Admission is $4 for anyone older than age 10. For a little extra, there are some reserved seats under the shade of a tent. To reach the Walden Lake community, take Exit 11 off I-4 E. Head south to Baker Street and turn left, then turn right on Alexander Street and follow it to the main entrance. There's good signage along the way.

Racetracks

Tampa Bay Downs
Race Track Rd., Oldsmar
• (813) 855-4401

The only Thoroughbred track on Florida's west coast, Tampa Bay Downs has strengthened its fame as "The Santa Anita of the South" since its renovation and reopening in the early 1980s. Originally opened as Tampa Downs in 1926, its name was changed to Sunshine Park in 1947. During the '50s, the race course was a popular spot for many sportscasters who covered area spring training baseball games. Such legendary names as Grantland Rice, Red Smith and Arthur Daley became regulars during racing season. And contemporary fans find the present-day track combines old-time charm with up-to-the minute amenities.

Newest on the turf is a real turf course, completed in time for the 1998 season. Insiders predict the installation of the .875-mile course with a .25-mile chute will be a hit with both horse people and bettors.

Every year attendance and purses continue to increase, which attracts more and better horses and riders. Back in 1992, Hollywood Wildcat finished second in the Florida Oaks race here before winning the Breeders' Cup for fillies. The following year, Not So Surprising ran in the Oaks and went on to win other national races.

Thoroughbred season runs from December through early May. But the really-big day of the year comes at the end of March, when both the $150,000 Tampa Bay Derby and the $100,000 Grade III Florida Oaks are showcased on the same Sunday.

Admission to the Downs costs a paltry $1.50, but adults are encouraged … er, invited, to bring betting cash. Race Track Road runs north off Tampa Road, next to the Oldsmar Flea

INSIDERS' TIP

Make those sports vacation plans now! Here's what's on the line-up for the future: the NHL All-Star Weekend at Tampa's Ice Palace January 23 and 24, 1999; NCAA Men's Final Four basketball tournament at St. Petersburg's Tropicana Field March 27, 28 and 29, 1999; and Super Bowl XXXV at Tampa's Raymond James Stadium January 28, 2001.

Market. Tampa Bay Downs is also open year round for simulcast racing. Call the track office for specific route directions from your particular starting gate.

Tampa Greyhound Track
8300 N. Nebraska Ave., Tampa
• **(813) 932-4313**

Tampa Greyhound Track offers parimutuel wagering on live greyhound racing from July through December. From January through June, patrons can bet on simulcast races from various horse and dog tracks around the state. Matinees play Monday, Wednesday and Saturday at 12:30 PM and Sunday at 1 PM. Races take place nightly except Sunday at 7:30. And new this year is a card room, just opened in July and specifically designed to attract poker players. Clubhouse admission costs $2.50 and grandstand admission, $1. To reach the track, take I-275 N. to the Bird Street Exit. The track is closed on Tuesdays.

Derby Lane
10490 Gandy Blvd., St. Petersburg
• **(727) 576-1361**

As the world's oldest continuously operating greyhound racetrack, Derby Lane has opened its season every January since 1925. The live races end in June, but year-round full-card simulcast wagering is offered on Thoroughbreds, Harness, Greyhound and Miami Jai-Alai.

Derby Lane is the home of the two top dogs recognized by the National Greyhound Association: 1998 Rural Rube (best sprinter) Scott Free and Flashy Sir (best distance) Racer Winsome Doe. And don't pass up a chance to have some fun simply because you've never read a race form. The track offers an easy to read guide called *How To Speak Greyhound*. You'll learn everything from the layout of the grandstands to what "OOP" means (out of the picture).

There's also plenty of action at the tables in T.L.'s Card Room, where six days a week you can play your kind of poker — including seven-, five- and three-card stud, hold-em and Omaha. T.L.'s is open from 10:30 AM until 1 AM on Monday, Wednesday and Saturday and from 5:30 PM until 1 AM on Tuesday, Thursday an Friday.

Race matinees run at 12:30 PM on Monday, Wednesday and Saturday, with evening races starting at 7:30 Monday through Saturday. Sunday offerings are strictly simulcast. Derby Lane, on Gandy Boulevard just west of the Gandy Bridge, is closed Tuesdays.

Soccer

Tampa Bay Mutiny
Raymond James Stadium, 4200 block of N. Dale Mabry Hwy., Tampa
• **(813) 289-6811**

Back when every kid in town knew the words to the jingle "Hey, Hey, We're the Rowdies," we all knew the team could really kick grass. Sadly, the game went into a decline, the Rowdies faded, and soccer disappeared from the scene for a while ... but only until players refused to roll away without an uprising. Then came a grass-roots return to soccer power; a mutiny against the disbanded leagues. And the Tampa Bay Mutiny arose!

That was 1996, and attendance at Mutiny soccer games more than tripled by the team's third season. Why? 'Cause this is one fun group of guys to watch. They display everything from the World Cup talent of goalkeeper Thomas Ravelli to Carlos Valdarrema, who's also known for a hairdo any Komondor breed of dog would be proud to sport.

Ravelli is one of 11 new faces on the field. With the addition of former U.S. National Team player Dominic Kinnear and Swedish star Jan Eriksson to Valdarrema and his teammates, including 1997 All-Star Steve Ralston, 1997 Rookie of the Year Mike Duhaney and current U.S. National Team player Roy Lassiter, these guys have some serious play-off plans.

With the second-best overall record through the first two seasons of Major League Soccer, which runs April to September, the team gives fans more for their money than just fun on the field. This spring, the hot sounds of the Neville Brothers were just one of the national music acts to deliver a free concert after the game, and the Fourth of July fireworks display is one of the area's most blazing extravaganzas. If all that isn't bargain enough, wait'll you purchase a ticket — just $3.

Photo: St. Petersburg/Clearwater Area Convention & Visitors Bureau

The Tampa Bay Devil Rays finally brought Major League Baseball
to St. Petersburg's Tropicana Field in April 1998.

Softball

Tampa Bay FireStix
5202 E. Fowler Ave., Tampa
• (813) 980-3278

When the Women's Professional Fastpitch softball league started last year, Tampa added another feather in its ball cap by being named one of only six league cities in the nation. And the Tampa Bay FireStix did a mighty good job, ending the second half of the season as the second-best team in the WPF. Plus, after a slow and losing start to the inaugural season, the FireStix took league honors with the longest winning streak — 13 games.

In addition, the team earned a couple of other "firsts" in the WPF: it was the first team to score 10 runs in a game, and first-year player Meghan Murray was the first WPF player to hit a home run in a nationally televised game.

The WPF was created to provide elite female fastpitch athletes a professional venue to showcase their skills. And with the constantly growing attention to women's pro sports, the Firestix are second to none when it comes to showing girls what it really means to "throw like a girl" while whipping up a good and affordable time for the whole family. General seating costs $5 and reserved seating, $6. The season runs from late May through August. All games start at 7:30 PM at the University of South Florida's Red McEwen Field.

**By understanding
the Tampa Bay climate
and ecological system,
we can all do our
part to ensure its
lasting beauty.**

The Natural World

Wonderful weather and incredible expanses of water are the two biggest reasons for Tampa Bay's popularity. We easily (well, OK, not so easily) ignore the heat and humidity that may make us slaves to air conditioning for months at a time, because it absolutely beats running a furnace most of the year. Snowbirds and transplanted Insiders delight in wearing shorts when friends and family "back home" are dressed for polar expeditions.

Our part of Florida presents such intriguing contrasts. We periodically decry the land's flatness, but during the summer rainy season we marvel at the mountainous panorama that towering clouds paint on our sky. This subtropical climate means soft, fine-leafed lawns are unachievable, yet it provides a lush bounty of plants and flowers so different from most parts of the country. And, of course, the same weather patterns which make this flora possible also tend to place us on the path of dangerous tropical storms and hurricanes. But it still beats snow, earthquakes, mud slides, dry wind and Biblical plagues of locust.

Bugs — now they're another story. Fleas constantly irritate pets and their owners with year-round proliferation. Summer mosquitoes aren't quite as huge as their Canadian counterparts, but they still bite and often carry the threat of encephalitis. Then there's our ubiquitous cockroach. Everybody's got them, even the cleanest homes and facilities with the most rigorous pest-control programs (in those places, the roaches just use their best manners and politely remain out of sight — most of the time). But on the positive side, we have a variety of natural bug predators helping out, like those darling little lizards that populate our yards.

The enormous population growth we've experienced in the last two decades does strain our environment, from usable land to potable water. Unlike our almost ever-present sunshine, our natural surroundings need care and nurturing. That means from you, and me, because by understanding the Tampa Bay climate and ecological system, we can all do our part to ensure its lasting beauty.

Weather

While many people claim there are no seasons here, we really do have them. They just don't necessarily follow the same timetable set out elsewhere according to the calendar. Instead, seasons here are often denoted symbolically. For example, through fashion — darker colors are worn in autumn and winter, while lighter shades and shorter sleeves mean spring and summer. For us, seasons are a state of mind.

Spring is when temperatures are balmy all day, cool at night and the humidity stays below 50 percent. The lovely interlude of "Spring" usually lasts about three weeks, coming some time in late March or April. Hot on its heels is the unrelenting heat of summer. This means humidity levels are as high or higher than the temperatures, and massive thunderstorms arrive just about the same time people get off work. Fall has nothing whatsoever to do with cooler temperatures or falling leaves; it's when football games start. Winter comes and goes, usually in three-day spasms. Locals know that when the Alberta Express or another frigid front dips from the north, we'll turn on the heater and bundle up for a day, feel a bit warmer the next day and then the next again, after which we'll stay comfortably warm until another arctic blast surges south. While Insiders shiver when temperatures fall into the 40s, photos of Northern visitors sunbathing on the beaches make all the daily papers. Those escapees from subzero temps think we're the silly ones for complaining about the cold.

While there's certainly no scientific evidence supporting the theory of "thin blood,"

Insiders swear it's true. The first full winter you spend here, you're wearing tank tops and shorts while the locals crawl into their woollies. Within three winters, though, you too are bundled up like Nanook of the North when the temperature drops below 60. It's not about thin blood, it's about vessels. There are lots of little muscles controlling how close blood comes to the surface of your skin. Those muscles get good workouts in areas with big temperature swings throughout the year. But in the constant warmth of our climate, those muscles get as lazy as you'll feel on an August afternoon. And the closer your blood stays to the outside of your skin, the more it's cooled by the temperature.

The trouble is, a winter day that starts out at 40 degrees can warm up into the mid-70s. Even then, the wind can be cutting-cold when you're in it, but when it's blocked by a wall the sun can actually feel hot. And once the sun sets, the temperatures again plunge. The trick to winter comfort is to dress in layers, so top coverings can be slipped on or off as temperatures fluctuate.

For those tempted around Tampa Bay to paraphrase Miss Scarlet and proclaim, "Ah'll nevah be cold ah-gayne!" keep this in mind: We really do get some truly cold weather at times, so don't throw out the gloves and scarves when you move here. The record low was 18 degrees in Tampa one December day in 1962. In January 1985, it fell to 21. The following June, we hit a record low of 53. OK, so we didn't all fall prey to hypothermia, but for June that was cold.

Now, during peak summer sun and humidity, you'll only think it's hotter than Hades. Never in history has the temperature broken 100 in the Tampa Bay area. The record high, set in June 1985, stands at 99. Close, but still no cigar.

On a monthly average, daily temperatures range from 59 in January to 82 in July and August. April and May are generally the most comfortable months, with relative humidity ranging between 51 and 87 percent. Prevailing offshore winds help the comfort factor. But come summer, all the water surrounding Florida combines with the intense sun so close to the equator, and the heat index can be as miserable as its winter northern opposite, the wind chill.

Fitness freaks, please note. You will see people jogging at high noon during summer months. Although these people are not mad dogs nor necessarily Englishmen, they are crazy. They are not professionals. Do not try this yourself. Heatstroke is a serious risk, for both humans and animals. So plan those workouts for early morning or after sunset, the most comfortable times to intentionally work up a sweat.

Thunderstorms and Lightning

Summer rains are one way nature cools things off for us. Well, a little bit anyway. In late afternoon along the Gulf Coast, it's marvelous to watch billowing thunderheads fill the sky, turn asphalt gray and unleash a torrent of rain. Sometimes, the drama builds for hours. Other times, storms erupt so suddenly the sky seems to darken from a solar eclipse. Often, the rains splash past as quickly as they arose.

While beautiful to watch, these storms can be extremely dangerous, producing tornadoes, waterspouts and, most of all, lightning. In fact, the Tampa Bay area is considered the nation's lightning capital. And once the storm's leading edge comes within 10 miles of where you happen to be, lightning poses a true threat to safety, so take cover. If you're in or on the water, get out as fast as your legs or boat can carry you. If you're on the beach, pack up belongings and loved ones and leave immediately. And if you're on the golf course, speed that cart to the 19th Hole pronto! Don't ever expect the storm to blow off in another direction or think you can safely sit it out. Those chances aren't worth taking.

Convertibles are popular rental cars in balmy Florida, but they're not safe during an electrical storm. Unlike hardtop cars, convertibles leave you exposed to the danger of lightning strikes. Besides, summer afternoons are

www.insiders.com

See this and many other **Insiders' Guide®** destinations online — in their entirety.

Visit us today!

too hot to be riding around with the top down anyway, so save the convertible rental for another season.

Safety precautions are also important even when you're indoors. Stay away from open windows or doors — lightning does zap inside through them. Stay out of the shower, and delay doing chores involving contact with water. And stay off the telephone — people do get hurt when lightning strikes the lines.

Tornadoes

Because of Dorothy and Toto, we usually associate twisters with the Central Plains and Midwest. Wrong. Tampa Bay is actually a hotbed for tornadoes, especially during our tropical storms or hurricanes. Unlike other geographic areas where weather patterns tend to develop more slowly and make advance tornado prediction possible, storms here often build so rapidly that funnel clouds can appear and disappear before weather alerts can be sounded. Waterspouts are common. This form of weak tornadoes usually remains harmless over water, but can move inland to cause damage and injury.

Cable TV's Weather Channel provides a constant source of weather information, and local network television and radio weather coverage is outstanding during storm season. When tropical depressions form in the Caribbean or Atlantic, you're wise to monitor the weather news.

Hurricanes

While the rest of the nation has four seasons, we claim five — winter, spring, summer, fall and hurricane, which lasts the longest, from June 1 to November 30.

Hurricanes start out as tropical disturbances, meaning there's a concentrated area of thunderstorms in the tropics that lasts more than 24 hours. When the storm's surface rotation builds and the highest constant windspeed reaches 34 mph, the storm becomes a tropical depression. If the winds increase to more than 39 mph, the depression is upgraded to a tropical storm.

At this point, the storm is given a name by the National Oceanic and Atmospheric Administration (NOAA), which has been monitoring

Photo: St. Petersburg/Clearwater Area Convention & Visitors Bureau

I'm for the Birds

The Suncoast Seabird Sanctuary is the busiest wild bird hospital in the United States.

the situation since first noting subtle changes. Naming the storm alerts everyone to the potential danger developing and means it's time to prepare for some very intense weather. Specially modified aircraft operated by the NOAA and the U.S. Air Force Reserve fly into the storm at regular intervals to gauge its growth and intensity.

As the storm moves across the open waters, "watch" and "warning" areas are outlined based on predictions of where it will make landfall. Insiders know this is the time to prepare for personal and material protection. Public emergency preparedness teams ready evacuation plans and shelters. Once wind speeds reach 74 mph, the storm is officially classified as a hurricane. Depending on the wind's intensity, NOAA ranks hurricanes in five categories:

• Category 1 — Winds 74 to 95 mph, causes minimal damage;

• Category 2 — Winds 96 to 110 mph, causes moderate damage;

• Category 3 — Winds 111 to 130 mph, causes extensive damage;

• Category 4 — Winds 131 to 155 mph, causes extreme damage;

• Category 5 — Winds more than 155 mph, damage is catastrophic.

Hurricane Andrew, which ravaged south Florida in 1992, was "only" a Category 4 storm. With sustained winds of 145 mph and gusts more than 175 mph, Andrew left more than 200,000 people homeless. Only two stronger hurricanes have ever hit the United States: the 1935 Labor Day hurricane that struck the Keys; and 1969's Camille, which slammed Mississippi and Louisiana. No one can even guess what the toll to property and lives will be if a Category 5 storm blasts Florida. The closest hurricane-call the Tampa Bay area has had in several years was Elena in 1985. The hurricane stalled over the Gulf for several days, only 80 miles to our west. Damage in Pinellas County alone exceeded $100 million, plus there were four deaths and 471 injuries as a result of high tides. And Elena was far from a direct hit. The last hurricane to strike Tampa Bay came in 1921. Before that, the last direct hit was in 1848. So in all probability, we're due.

Our low-lying coast, shallow bay waters and extremely dense population combine for a situation that could be devastating in a major storm. Evacuation routes are clearly posted throughout the area, but it will be impossible to effectively evacuate everyone in time if we're ever threatened. Landfall predictions still cannot be accurately projected far enough in advance for roadways to accommodate evacuating traffic.

At greatest risk are people on the barrier islands. Once uninhabited protectors of the Gulf shores, most are now connected to the mainland by bridges and are filled with expensive homes and high-rises. These properties will take the first impact of storm surges and winds. If you are in an area where evacuation is suggested, do it — do not wait until ordered to leave. Hurricane preparation guides are published every June and distributed through both *The Tampa Tribune* and the *St. Petersburg Times*. They also are available at a variety of retail stores. Residents and long-term visitors should keep them handy and be familiar with precautions.

Animal owners need to be aware that Red Cross evacuation shelters do not allow pets. Make arrangements with family or friends living on higher ground to care for your pets, or contact a veterinary office to learn where animals can be boarded in emergency weather situations.

The devastation caused by Andrew and its 1989 predecessor, Hugo, did bring about some beneficial changes — regional emergency preparations improved dramatically, and Insiders clearly realized the potential for danger. But with the 1993 "No Name Storm," we learned that even the best weather watchers can be caught off-guard. A tropical storm developed so suddenly that we had almost no warning whatsoever — we literally awoke to it one Saturday morning in March. Temperatures dropped into the low 40s, hurricane-force winds tore down power lines and spawned dozens of tornadoes. Icy rain lashed us all day and some of us swear we saw snow. Storm surges swamped coastal areas and caused millions of dollars in damages up and down Florida's Gulf coast.

Does this sound scary? Good. Summer thunder-boomers may be a refreshing change from intense heat and sunlight, but tropical storms and hurricanes are not an excuse for parties or surfing. Stay alert to intense weather

INSIDERS' TIP

Looking to save the earth and your money? Check out the Swap Shop and Household Chemical Collection Center at 28th Street and 110th Avenue N., St. Petersburg. What someone else didn't want or couldn't use is yours for the taking. You'll find freebies from paints to brake fluid, and you're welcome to take as much or as little as you need. The center is open Mondays from 9 AM until 5 PM, Thursdays from 10 AM until 6 PM and the third Saturday of every month from 9 AM until 4 PM. Call (727) 464-7565 to obtain more information.

conditions, and do as the emergency officials ask. Your life may depend on it.

Water

With the nearby Gulf waters and our summer rains, you'd think water wouldn't be such a precious commodity in the Tampa Bay area. Unfortunately, the Ancient Mariner fairly well describes our region: "Water, water everywhere, nor any drop to drink." OK, so it's not quite that bad, but our water resources are limited and literally restricted in many cases.

Between 1988 and 1993, our region received far less rainfall than average. Drought conditions were declared. Things improved in 1994. In 1995, it got even better. And in 1997, everything was screwy. First, our normal summer rainy patterns didn't fully materialize. Then, beginning in September — usually the start of drier weather — we wondered if the rain would ever stop. During the last weekend of that month, some places got as much as a foot of rain. And December's rainfall of 15.5 inches set an all-time record. Then, in June 1998, rainfall was so scarce we actually reached desert-like conditions.

As a result, both Hillsborough and Pinellas counties continue restrictions on lawn watering. No watering is allowed at all between 9 AM and 5 PM. (Exceptions are made for new sod and plants.) Residents whose addresses end in even numbers or letters A through M may water on Tuesdays and Saturdays. Residents whose addresses end in odd numbers or letters N through Z may water on Wednesdays and Sundays. Boats may be flushed 10 minutes a day.

A variety of other regulations apply to water use. The Southwest Florida Water Management District (known as Swiftmud) is in charge and will provide details. If you've got any questions, call their hotline, (800) 848-0499, weekdays from 8 AM until 5 PM. For local regulations, here are other numbers to call:

Tampa Water Department,
(813) 274-8121;
Hillsborough County Public Utilities,
(813) 272-5977;
St. Petersburg Public Utilities,
(727) 893-7261;
Clearwater Water Department,
(727) 462-6848.

Water control is a major political issue in the area. Florida's freshwater source is an underground aquifer holding more water than all of the Great Lakes. Population growth has, however, pushed up demand and led to water disputes about who gets to use how much from where. Water management is something each of us needs to exercise. Here are 10 simple things every one of us can do to conserve:

• Empty pets' water bowls or unused drinking water onto plants instead of down the drain;

• Dump ice from to-go drinks outside before trashing the cups;

• Turn off the water while brushing your teeth and shaving;

• Make long, luxurious showers a rare treat, not a daily routine;

• Don't run the cold water tap waiting for the water to cool — it won't, except in dead of winter. Chill water in the refrigerator instead;

• While waiting for the tap to run hot, catch water in a clean, empty milk jug for plants or pets;

• Wash vegetables and fruit over a basin, saving runoff for plants;

• Retain and cool cooking water for watering plants or for soup;

• Run the washing machine and dishwasher only when they are full;

• Flush less often: If it's brown, flush it down. If it's yellow, let it mellow.

For more water conservation tips, call Swiftmud, (800) 423-1476, and ask for the free brochure *50 Ways to Do Your Part*.

INSIDERS' TIP

Bird and Sunken islands on Hillsborough County's Alafia River are nesting colonies to 21 species of waterbirds — more than 14,000 pairs of birds — making these islands the most divergent breeding areas on the North American Continent.

Wetlands and Wildlife

Wetlands are a lot like kids when they're having the most fun — messy. This is what makes them ideal homes for native birds and other wildlife.

Those nearby "woods" or "fields" that stay boggy during rainy weather are marvelous wetland sanctuaries for birds, amphibians and mammals. By attracting birds, they help control both mosquitoes and gnats. In summer, the wetlands release cool breezes. In winter, water-warmed air helps moderate temperatures.

Until about 20 years ago, developers spent the century thinking of wetlands as "problem areas" and filled or drained them. What we learned the hard way was that we lost valuable plants, birds, animals and water-cleansing processes. Today, wetland management is strictly controlled and any clearing, filling or excavating requires special permits.

Wetlands are freshwater areas. Salt marshes, or estuaries, are coastal wetland filters where fresh water mixes with sea water, such as in bays, bayous and sounds. From Florida's Panhandle south to Tampa Bay, these marshes are the primary coastal vegetation. In their shallow waters grow seagrass beds, which stabilize marine sediments. Serving as nursery areas for more than 70 percent of the commercially harvested fish and shellfish species in Florida, salt marshes also are home to birds and small mammals. Sea turtles and manatees forage on the grasses and algae that bloom there.

One distinctive tree that grows along salt marshes is the mangrove, which helps protect shorelines from erosion. With roots standing well above the water at low tide, in evening light these smooth-barked trees look like ghostly stalkers along the shore. Because mangroves shelter our coastlines, they've had to compete with residential developers for waterfront property. Today, this fast-dwindling natural resource is protected by law, although restrictions now allow limited trimming in residential areas. The oleander plant also is protected. Again, as salt-marsh vegetation, it provides a protective buffer along coasts. Oleander is highly poisonous, and it's illegal to cut or burn because of its toxicity.

Along with area freshwater lakes, the Hillsborough River that flows through the northeast section of the county is extremely important. Besides being a geographic boundary, a natural wildlife habitat and a recreational site, the river provides much of the county's drinkable water. A special watchdog board monitors and protects the river. Conscientious care during the past decade recently resulted in three of the river's major tributaries and all of the river north of Fletcher Avenue being designated as Outstanding Florida Waterways.

Marine Life

When it comes to water, be it fresh or salt, most people immediately think of fish. And we have plenty of 'em! Tampa Bay and the Gulf are home to more than 300 varieties. Among the tastiest are grouper, snook, snapper, mullet, tarpon, kingfish and sea bass, plus those delectable shrimp and crab.

Our region is home to many tropical fish breeding companies. Between 80 and 90 percent of all the tropical fish grown in Florida are farmed in southern Hillsborough County. In fact, the county grows more tropical fish than any other place in the nation. At a tropical fish research center in Ruskin, where most of those farmed fish are raised, six scientists from the University of Florida Institute of Food and Agriculture Sciences study fish health, reproduction and genetics, plus water quality and marine aquaculture.

One form of marine reproduction that sets everyone to grumbling almost every spring is red tide. This toxic algae blooms in the Gulf and kills fish by the hundreds. They wash ashore and give off an incredible stink. The algae itself emits a gas that, in concentration, can cause irritation to people's eyes, noses and throats. Generally, airborne red tide particles create only a minor inconvenience, but people with respiratory problems may experience more discomfort.

Of greater concern to beachgoers are other forms of aquatic life. Jellyfish and stingrays can cause excruciating pain if stepped on. The best way to avoid an accidental meeting is simple: just shuffle your feet through the sand as you wade. This disturbs the creatures in advance and allows them to shuttle off. It's also wise to buy a pair of inexpensive water shoes — you'll find them every place from the Sports Authority to Kmart. They also protect tender soles from sharp shells.

What about sharks? Well, they're really delicious, especially blackened. Oh, you mean, as in *Jaws*? Out of 50 to 75 yearly attacks around the world, Florida records 10 to 15. So, yes, there are sharks in the Gulf, but they're most often sighted along the Atlantic Coast.

Why does Florida have the highest concentration of shark attacks? Probably because more people swim along our coasts than anywhere else in the world. But still, not to worry — odds are one in 300 million that a shark will ever look at you as lunch. (Guess what? The odds of winning our state lottery are a whole lot better!) According to George Burgess, director of the International Shark Attack File, the risk of injury or death by shark is far lower than any other type of injury or death encountered in the water. If you want to be extra cau-

Protect Your Pets

• Use the same caution you would use with children when it comes to letting your dog swim. Rivers, lakes and ponds often harbor alligators, and they do find pet animals quite tasty.

• Keep your pet's rabies vaccinations up to date. This deadly disease is on the increase in Florida, and portions of the state are regularly put under rabies quarantine. The rabies virus is most often spread

Close-up

through raccoons, feral cats and other typical neighborhood wildlife. Exercise caution for both yourself and your pets around unfamiliar animals.

Photo: Paula Stahel

• Fleas can literally kill. Small dogs have been known to die due to blood loss resulting from the insects' constant feeding. Unlike colder regions where winter temperatures slow flea reproduction, they thrive here all year round. There is no known eradicator, but keep things under control with pet baths, dips, medication and home and yard treatments.

• Exotic pets can be attractive and charming, especially when you live in such tropical surroundings. Just be sure you know what you're getting into before adding an iguana, snake or parrot to your household. With proper care, reptiles and birds live wonderfully long lives, but require far more care than the average cat or dog. The Tampa Bay area has the nation's greatest concentration of veterinarians certified as avian specialists and a large number of other practitioners who treat exotic pets. Talk to them and breeders before you make such an investment in the future.

Dr. Margaret Wissman is one of six certified avian specialists in the Tampa Bay area. No other area of the country boasts such a large concentration of bird specialists.

tious, don't swim where birds are diving, fish are jumping or people are fishing. Also, remove glittery jewelry that sharks may mistake as food because the light bouncing off shiny objects in water resembles fish scales. And definitely don't swim at night: more species are active then and come near shore to feed.

When swimming, keep an eye on the water's surface for fins — the dark, curved ones you see belong to friendly dolphins, not sharks. The two don't get along well and when dolphins are nearby, sharks usually stay away. Maybe this is one reason for the international belief that dolphins symbolize good luck.

Residents and visitors should note that May through October is the most active nesting season for turtles. Florida has strict laws designed to protect endangered species such as loggerheads and Kemp's Ridley, the rarest of all sea turtles. Identified nests are cordoned off with stakes and yellow plastic tape. Please don't disturb these areas. Beach restoration and artificial lighting also are tightly controlled in order to protect the nests and babies as they make their way to the Gulf.

Other Animals

Out of the water, it's not unusual to encounter raccoons or opossums in neighborhood yards. You may occasionally spot an armadillo, but in all probability it'll be as road kill. Please exercise caution when you're behind the wheel. Creatures' itty-bitty legs are no match for your auto's speed.

Cruising overhead and nesting along Tampa Bay shores are some 25 species of colonial waterbirds, totaling about 40,000 breeding pair. The easiest to spot are pelicans, which nest in large groups. Brown pelicans, once an endangered species, are now only "threatened," as their numbers have increased during the past few years. The white ibis and snowy egret are two other noticeable birds in the area. Ibis counts show the popula-

tion growing during the past 10 years; unfortunately, this is only a small turnaround in the 75 percent decline which began in the 1940s. The snowy egret is not faring as well. One of the more common herons, its numbers continue to decline due to wetland destruction. Wetland protection and excellent corporate management, such as that of the Hyatt Hotel on the Courtney Campbell Causeway, are helping the situation, and some species are again returning to the area.

The roseate spoonbill, with its bright orange-red beak shaped like an upside-down spoon, is one to watch for. Watch for the laughing gulls, too. It may seem they're everywhere, but populations have dropped dramatically in the past 15 years. Please do not feed these birds your beach picnic food. Yes, it's fun to see a flock swoop and dive for airborne potato chips and bread, but it feels more like a scene from an Alfred Hitchcock movie when the birds become brazen enough to assume rights to your meal. Plenty of fish are in the Gulf — let 'em find their own food.

Vying with the waterbirds for fish-food are our beautiful, majestic Southern bald eagles. Federally classified as an endangered species, the eagles are listed only as threatened in our state. Between 300 and 400 mated pairs nest in Florida every year, giving us about 86 percent of the entire Southern population. Many of the birds head north for cooler temperatures during summer, but return to their traditional nests, most of which are 4 to 5 feet across and can be as large as 9 feet and weigh up to 2 tons.

Bugs!

Think bugs in Florida and what comes to mind? Yup, cockroaches. La cucaracha. Palmetto bugs. By any name, they're disgusting. And they're everywhere. Like war, what are they good for? Well, finally, someone has an answer.

INSIDERS' TIP

Think it would be fun to experience a hurricane? It can be — at Tampa's Museum of Science and Industry. MOSI lets you experience the intensity of hurricane winds without the fear of devastation. It's fun and teaches you respect for the real thing.

University of Cincinnati researchers discovered that proteins produced by cockroaches kill certain bacterial species. At a time when more bacteria are becoming resistant to antibiotics, the cockroach's sophisticated immune system may actually hold the key to more effective cures.

That's wonderful. Truly. We're glad to hear it. But that doesn't mean they're welcome in our houses!

Still, they're going to be there, no matter how clean you keep your house. But vigilance does help. Store food in tightly covered containers — don't even think about leaving that plate of cookies or cake on the counter overnight. Keep kitchen waste out of the room if at all possible, and take garbage out nightly. Rinsing cans or other containers before throwing them away also helps. Many pest-control products are available, or for a more natural barrier against these pests, sprinkle boric acid powder along floor and counter cracks. (Be careful children and pets can't get to the powder, though.) It also helps to eliminate water sources, such as dirty dishes, dripping faucets or wet dish-cloths that attract roaches to moisture. Paper grocery bags also attract the bugs, so store them away from the kitchen.

Fire ants are another common nasty. So named because their bite seems to set the skin on fire, their sting can prove deadly to some people who are allergic to bee and wasp venom. The ants build sandy mounds that can grow truly huge, and they're very difficult to eradicate. But one way to combat them is with that great old staple of Southern breakfast tables -- grits. Spread the uncooked grits around the mound. The worker ants then carry them back to the queen to eat, who literally explodes when she follows her meal with a refreshing drink of water. Not being too bright, the worker ants follow her lead.

A lot of arachnids, such as the really, really big wood spider, help control other pests and should be treated kindly. One spider to be extremely careful of, however, is the brown recluse. Also called the brown widow, it's one of five venomous species in Florida. Like the black widow, it has an hourglass design on its underside. Unlike the black widow, its color is light gray to light brown. Its web is stronger than those of other spiders', and its tan egg

sacs have tiny spikes. The brown recluse isn't aggressive, but likes to live in dark places you're likely to touch, such as the underside of garbage can lids, among gardening tools and along the bottom side of yard furniture.

Most of the bugs we contend with are year-round fixtures. Twice a year we are treated to another pesky visitor — lovebugs. For several weeks each May and September these little black bugs take to the air to perform their mating ritual on the wing. They don't bite, so they're really just an annoying nuisance. With the incredible number squished to death on the fronts of cars and trucks, it's amazing they continue to flourish. During lovebug season, your car's grill and windshield will be littered daily with their bodies But lovebug juice is highly caustic to vehicle paint and it's important to wash the bug residue off each day.

Pest control is a continuous aspect of Florida life. Thankfully, we have a good bit of help from Mother Nature herself. Toads are rife wherever there's dark cover for them to enjoy during the day. At night they come out to eat and they're not at all picky about their meals — bugs of all types, cutworms, slugs, snails and all sorts of crawly creatures are enjoyed. Anoles, little lizards that are usually the color of twigs, dart around yards and up buildings and particularly relish cockroaches. The brown Anole originally came from the Caribbean, but the green Anole, better known as the chameleon, is a native.

Plants and Landscape

Until early this century, Florida's natural landscape was primarily pine flatwood-palmettos, grasses, herbs and pines. Today, it's easy to believe that the predominant landscape is concrete, asphalt and glass. On the positive side, though, backyards still serve as home to citrus, avocado and loquat trees, plus other edibles and plants that simply are a feast for the eye.

In cold northern climes, crocus is a harbinger of spring. Here, banks of azaleas lining homes and flats of strawberries for sale along roadways serve that purpose. During late January and early February landscapes begin the blaze of color that continues well into late fall. Tall bougainvillea bushes maintain the bright

Photo: St. Petersburg/Clearwater Area Convention & Visitors Bureau

Nature trails traverse many of the city, county and state parks in Tampa Bay.

pink season. Jasmine next pops tiny flowers out of vines wrapped over fences and up telephone poles. Wildflowers in every shade carpet the shoulders and median strips of otherwise boring stretches of highway. Jacaranda trees shower their purple petals on sidewalks and driveways. Waxy, white magnolia blossoms the size of dinner plates stand out against deep-green tree leaves. As early summer days turn hot, crape myrtle trees send out delicate cones of purple, pink or white. And with fall comes false foxglove, deer tongue and a lyrical litany of other wildflower wonders.

Though most colorful in spring and early summer, the changing of flowering plants continues throughout the year. Even in winter, our subtropical temperatures coax delicate rose buds into bloom. Conditions so hospitable to native plants don't, unfortunately, discriminate against exotic intruders. The majestic Australian pine, which intermingles with palms at Fort DeSoto Beach, is one. Another Australian import, and highly reviled, is the messy punk tree with its papery bark and a proclivity for spreading rapidly. Brazilian pepper's aggressive nature drives out other plants wherever it roots, and it now covers more than 70,000 acres of Florida. With no natural predators, exotics such as these pose multiple menaces. They displace native plants, cross-pollinate, produce hybrids and increase competition for soil nutrients and light, all of which decrease diversity.

The increased importance of water conservation and awareness of pollution from stormwater runoff has led to a heightened interest in xeriscaping. This landscaping method, pronounced "zeer-ah-scaping," relies on native plants selected for energy savings and grouped according to their water needs. While lush, green lawns still carpet neighborhoods, more attention is being focused on natural pest control methods and grasses requiring lower year-round water usage.

If you'd like to learn more about native flora, here are several knowledgeable sources to contact:

Hillsborough County Extension Service, (813) 744-5519;

Pinellas County Horticulture Hotline, (727) 582-2110;

Florida Native Plant Society, Suncoast Chapter, (813) 949-2412;

Florida Native Plant Society, Pinellas Chapter, (727) 544-7341;

University of South Florida Botanical Garden, (813) 974-2329.

Indulge in the theme parks around Orlando. Explore country roads and revel in the citrus scent out in Cracker country. Step into Florida history where it was made.

Daytrips

If it's just another day in paradise, why in the world would you want to leave? Well, eventually the question of just how much sun and sand one person can stand will be asked. Or, heaven forbid, you thought that SPF 3 suntan lotion from home would do just fine under our subtropical sun, and now you're decked out in a color more appropriate to lobster accompanied by drawn butter. And sometimes we actually do get cloudy days or — believe it or not! — cold days here. This tends to make beach outings popular only among those hardy visitors who find sunbathing in 40-degree weather a treat compared to what they left behind.

So what's the alternative? Daytime TV? Nah, you can do that at home. Besides, you didn't come here to stay inside. All around Central Florida are pursuits to delight every interest and budget. Indulge in the theme parks around Orlando. Explore country roads and revel in the citrus scent out in Cracker country. Step into Florida history where it was made. Meander through antiques shops just off the beaten path. Let your heart race with the splendid horses being raised at renowned farms barely north of here. Delve into the spiritual and have your future told or meditate while a carillon concert calms your soul.

Within easy driving distance of less than three hours are an abundance of sights and sites. From the natural to the man-made, cultural to the historical, a multitude of choices is yours to enjoy. All you need for these quick escapes is a little imagination, a sense of adventure and a day to spare.

Orlando

OK, let's do the "Goofy" stuff first. If you've got kids or just are a kid at heart, there's no question you'll do Disney sometime. It really is possible to spend as much as a week seeing all of Disney World, but few budgets or

brain cells can withstand such an unrelenting expedition into fantasy. Marvelously, each of the Disney World theme parks makes for an ideal daytrip, as do Sea World, Universal Studios, Splendid China and dozens of other fun places to visit in Orlando, all about two hours east of the Tampa Bay area.

Daytrips to the theme parks aren't inexpensive, but the fun is definitely worth it. If you're a member of AAA, check with them about specials. Disney never offers discounts (well, Florida residents do get a break at certain times of the year), but other theme parks occasionally do. More information is available by calling AAA in Tampa, (813) 289-5000; St. Petersburg, (727) 892-8000; or Clearwater, (727) 448-2600. All the parks take all the major credit cards, which makes spending a bit less painful (at least till the bill comes in).

When visiting the theme parks, put people-watching on your list of fun. There's no sense being impatient; waiting to get on rides and into attractions is a given, especially on weekends and during holiday breaks. As an Insider, I have a tip for non-NFL addicts: Super Bowl Sunday is one of the least crowded days of the year!

The Magic Kingdom
Exit off I-4, Lake Buena Vista
• (407) 824-4321

Magic Kingdom's 100 acres are divided into seven lands filled with 41 major adventures, fantasy, dozens of attractions, restaurants and shops based on favorite Disney themes. Travelers with visual handicaps will be enchanted by the helpful Braille/large-print guidebooks available on loan at the Guest Services office. The Lion King is still a popular attraction with its "animateered" performance that creates a mystical jungle where animators' drawings are brought to life in an advanced form of puppeteering and special effects. You can ramble through the Old West in

Frontierland and then blast into space on one the world's longest flumes — Splash Mountain. It boasts a five-story, 47-degree plunge. You can also hurtle through the dark aboard Space Mountain's miniature shuttles.

The Magic Kingdom is open daily year round, and hours vary by season. Admission, including tax, costs $36.04 for children ages 3 through 9 and $44.52 for anyone 10 and older. Toddlers younger than 3 are admitted free of charge.

EPCOT Center
Exit off I-4, Lake Buena Vista
• (407) 824-4321

Greeted by Spaceship Earth just inside the gates of Epcot (Experimental Prototype Community of Tomorrow), visitors of Future World experience today's scientific achievements and tomorrow's technologies. Be sure to grab a copy of *The Epcot Insider* at the entrance. This free daily newsletter lists times for the don't-miss shows, including IllumiNations, a nightly fireworks, light and laser display.

www.insiders.com

See this and many other **Insiders' Guide®** destinations online — in their entirety.

Visit us today!

The Universe of Energy re-creates the primal start of our world, complete with life-size dinosaurs. At The Land, plants are grown hydroponically, which means without soil. Ride the thrilling Body Wars flight-simulator in Wonders of Life. Peek into futuristic scientific visions at Horizons before speeding off on the Test Track. Here, you're behind the scenes of automobile testing, with all its acceleration, braking, hill climbs, curves, straightaways and the extremes of heat and cold. When you Journey into Imagination, a playland for all ages, be sure to see the high-tech 3-D misadventure, Honey, I Shrunk the Audience. Definitely plan to devote lots of time to The Living Seas — this massive aquarium gets you up-close and personal with hundreds of saltwater species, including Florida's darlings, the manatee.

Eateries abound throughout Epcot, but for a special treat plan a leisurely meal at the Coral Seas restaurant. Built beneath The Living Seas, it offers a view of a wall of the aquarium with its ever-changing scenery of sea life. It's a good idea to zip into the restaurant and make reservations so you'll have a comfortable rest to

look forward to; otherwise you'll have to wait. The delicious seafood meals are a bit pricey, but then so are sandwiches and salads in the other restaurants and, hey, this is a treat, right?

Across the lagoon from Future World is the World Showcase, where 11 nations offer distinctive wares, ethnic cuisine, shows, entertainment and architecture representing their cultures. Each village hosts holiday events and festivals, giving guests a chance to get caught up in the international celebrations. And once a month, special Kids' Days celebrations let children interact with ambassadors in games from different regions of the world.

Admission to Epcot costs the same as for the Magic Kingdom — $36.04 for children ages 3 through 9 and $44.52 for anyone 10 and older. Toddlers younger than 3 are admitted free of charge. Epcot is open 365 days a year, but hours vary. Future World opens early morning and closes mid-evening, while World Showcase opens late morning and stays open until IllumiNations begins after dark.

Disney-MGM Studios
Exit off I-4, Lake Buena Vista
• (407) 824-4321

Go glamour — go Hollywood! Not Hollywood, Florida, but La-La Land. From the Siskel & Ebert Academy Awards Special to The Disney Channel's Emerald Cove, Disney-MGM Studios combines motion-picture and television production with attractions and shows based on the glamour of movie making. Watch for visiting celebs — the actors aren't look-alikes here. If you think you saw Bette Midler, you did!

The Disney-MGM Studios are open year round, but hours change with the seasons. One-day admission costs $44.52 for visitors 10 years and older and $36.04 for kids between 3 and 9.

Disney's Animal Kingdom
Exit off I-4, Lake Buena Vista
• (407) 397-6397

This newest and fourth major theme park at Walt Disney World Resort opened in spring 1998 and offers high adventures with real exotic animals, close encounters with prehistoric giants and the warm, fuzzy moments expected with Disney characters.

Sprawled across more than 500 acres, Disney's Animal Kingdom reconfigures Central Florida into deep green jungles, forests and a vast savanna reminiscent of African or Asian animal reserves. There's also a dinosaur dig, recreated in a "primeval forest" of 65 million years ago, where human visitors can experience a real "Honey, I shrunk us all" sensation as they encounter towering dinosaurs.

From the cool, natural flowering glades and falling waters of the Oasis entry, visitors plan their own journeys through a wildlife reserve and coastal village in Africa; the Caravan Stage featuring the Flights of Wonder bird show in Asia; Camp Minnie-Mickey, a character greeting and show area featuring animals from such films as *The Lion King*, *Pocohantas* and other animated classics; DinoLand U.S.A., an open-air paleontological dig; and Safari Village, where the 3-D special effects film *It's Tough To Be A Bug* is drawing incredible rave reviews.

As with other Disney parks, toddlers younger than 3 are admitted free, but admission costs $36.04 for kids between ages 3 and 9 and $44.52 for everyone older than 10. The park is open year round, and hours vary according to the season.

Pleasure Island
Adjacent to The Disney Village, Lake Buena Vista • (407) 824-4321

A playground for really big kids (as in, older than age 18), Pleasure Island is Disney World's 6-acre nightclub theme park featuring seven nightspots and restaurants galore. You'll find Planet Hollywood plus a 10-screen theater complex. An evening pass is $19.03, including tax, but it is possible to dine at a few of the park's restaurants without paying the cover charge. Plan to make reservations!

Sea World
I-4 and the Bee Line Expy., Orlando • (407) 351-3600

The world's most popular marine-life park, Sea World of Florida is best known as the home of Shamu and his family of performing killer whales. In the 1.7 million-gallon natural-

istic habitat, visitors can come face-to-face with these powerful, playful creatures. Every element of the park combines entertainment with hands-on attractions, education, research and conservation to let you share the mysteries of the sea.

Quiz: What is the sea when it's too cold to flow? Icebergs! And what lives on icebergs? Why, polar bears, of course, and now they live at Sea World's Wild Arctic attraction. Probably the most famous residents are Klondike and Snow, the brother and sister bears whose fight for survival after birth was chronicled by PBS. The Arctic adventure also delivers a thrilling "flight" over the frozen North to encounter animals such as waddling penguins, slippery seals and … what's that, a white whale? Moby Dick? No, but it is his cousin, the beluga.

After you've chilled out at the cold, cold North, warm up with a "visit" to the southernmost city in the United States — Key West at Sea World. This lighthearted, 5-acre family festival offers three animal habitats. They are called Dolphin Cove, Stingray Lagoon and Sea Turtle Point. Shop and dine along a replica of Duval Street and watch the kind of eclectic acts that create a street-party atmosphere before the sunsets at the real Key West's Mallory Square.

From Key West to Atlantis — or at least in the days when men from ancient Greece sailed the seas — comes a new thrill ride unveiled in spring 1998. Guests embark on the Journey to Atlantis only to find themselves trapped in the midst of a battle between a mythical sea horse and an evil siren. Speeding along at 45 mph, riders twice fall 60 feet as the seven-minute coaster/flume ride hurdles them through a 6-acre tour of the legendary lost city in the sea.

Hours at Sea World change during the summer and holidays, but the park is generally open year round from 9 AM to at least 7 PM. Admission, excluding tax, costs $39.75 for people 10 and older and $32 for kids between ages 3 and 9. Children 2 and younger are admitted free. If you're a AAA member, handicapped, a senior adult or in the military, be sure to ask for your 10 percent discount. Parking costs $5 for cars and $7 for RVs or campers.

Ca' d'Zan, the former winter home of John and Mable Ringling, is an architectural masterpiece along Sarasota's bayfront.

Universal Studios Florida
Near I-4 and the Florida Tpk., Orlando
• (407) 363-8000

Not content to just jump *Back To The Future*, or shake you up in *Earthquake*, Universal Studios is out to blow you away, or at least make you think it's gonna happen! Some of the new rides and attractions are definitely not for the faint of heart, but everyone will love the fun and adventure of being up on the screen.

OK, let's start out with info for Type-T personalities — those of you who love to safely face danger. You will not want to miss the three new rollercoasters —TWISTER, Dueling Dragons and The Hulk — that are part of Universal's spanking new Islands of Adventure located adjacent to the studios. There are five islands within Islands of Adventure, and each has its own theme and personality. Their names certainly provide good clues to their personalities — Suess Landing, Lost Continent, Toon Lagoon, Marvel Super Hero Island and Jurassic Park.

Now, here's the scoop on the coasters. TWISTER literally pits Mother Nature against humans. An ominous funnel rapidly builds to a five-story-tall cyclone circulating more than 2 million cubic feet of air per minute and gains speed until it suddenly disappears a mere 20 feet away from the crowd. Whew! Anyone who's ever lived through a real tornado will find this just too real. The Hulk catapults riders up a 150-foot tunnel at G-force speed (remember the last time you were in a F-16 fighter jet?), immediately spins into a weightless, zero-G roll upside down more than 110 feet above the ground and dives at 60 mph to skim the waves of the lagoon and head back up again. No sweat? Then climb aboard Dueling Dragons and see if you're scared. This is the world's first pair of coasters deliberately designed so they furiously speed toward each other. Their tracks twist into a knotted mass of metal where the coasters narrowly miss colliding at the last second by camelback, double-helix and compound inversion action. Hey, wanna go again? Love to!

The littlest kiddies certainly love Barney, the purple dinosaur. At Universal Studios, enjoy A Day In The Park With Barney, a make-believe preschool world brought to life in an imaginative, interactive musical show and hands-on playground. Each of seven play areas stimulates creative thinking through sensory exercises that encourage kids to touch, see, smell and listen. What certainly sets the little ones to clambering is Barney's Treehouse, with its beckoning slides and tunnels.

Older kids will insist on visiting another new attraction — Hercules & Xena: Wizards of the Screen. Audiences go behind-the-scenes and do battle with the blockbuster TV stars in an interactive episode that features exotic location footage filmed in New Zealand, home of both television series.

Universal is a real working studio — the largest outside of Hollywood — with more than 40 full-scale re-creations of scenes from the most famous movies ever made. Since the sets are often in use, watch out for crashing helicopters, high-speed boat chases and unexpected explosions.

The studio's back lot presents locales from the sidewalks of New York to the streets of San Francisco and from a New England village to the Garden of Allah. To make your mark among the visiting cast of millions, take along a marking pen; you get to add your own bit of graffiti to the subway walls on your way into a Kongfrontation.

When your tummy is hungry, rub elbows with working actors at the Studio Stars Restaurant, or grab some be-bop and a burger at *American Graffiti*'s own Mel's Diner. True rock 'n' roll purists won't miss Hard Rock Cafe; try the pulled pig sandwich and your tongue will thank you for the memories.

Plan a really long daytrip to do Universal since it takes a good 14 hours just to see everything at the studios. If time isn't on your side, you'll want to be selective about your electives. Tickets cost $44.52, including tax, for visitors 10 years and older and $36.04 for youngsters 3 through 9. Children 2 and younger get in free of charge. Parking costs $6 for autos and $7 for RVs and trailers. If you're feeling very rich and glamorous, a valet will park your Porsche (or pickup) for a $12 fee. Universal's parks are open every day of the year, but some sections may be closed because of film production, and hours vary according to the season and special events.

Splendid China
3000 Splendid China Blvd., Kissimmee
• (407) 397-8800, (800) 244-6226

Anyone curious about the country that is host to the world's largest population will want to visit this near-duplicate of the original. It was created several years ago near Hong Kong and more than 60 of China's best-known scenic, historic and cultural sites are depicted. There's a half-mile-long miniature of the Great Wall in addition to reproductions of the Forbidden City and the Imperial Palace, the Leshan Buddha and the Lushan Stone Forest where the Terra Cotta Warriors were unearthed. Performances at the park run the gamut from Chinese ballet to martial arts. Oriental art collectors should note that authentic artifacts, as well as reproductions, are available.

Daily admission, excluding tax, costs $26.99 for visitors ages 13 and older and $16.99 for children 5 through 12. Children 4 and younger are admitted free of charge. The park opens at 9:30 AM every day of the year, and the closing hour varies by season. To get to Splendid China, take I-4 east to Exit 25-B and head west 3 miles.

Winter Haven

There's a lot more to Central Florida than Orlando, so let's set out in other directions.

Cypress Gardens
Cypress Gardens Blvd., Winter Haven
• (941) 324-2111

This botanical paradise, edged by sparkling lakes and ancient cypress swamps, covers more than 200 acres and is home to more

---

INSIDERS' TIP

The Guinness Book of World Records cites St. Petersburg as having the longest continual string of sunny days — 768 — from February 9, 1967, to March 17, 1969. The Tampa Bay area enjoys an average of 361 sunny days a year (meaning predominantly sunny days that could include just a short rain shower).

than 8,000 varieties of plants and flowers from more than 90 countries. Debuting in 1936, Cypress Gardens quickly became popular as the host for gala performances of water-skiers forming human pyramids and demonstrating uncanny feats on their feet — and other body parts! For this Insider, though, the best part of Cypress Gardens is Wings of Wonder, The Butterfly Conservatory. More than 1,000 butterflies in free flight, exotic waterfowl and iguanas reside in a 5,500-square-foot educational conservatory. When you step inside, you actually step outside into an enclosed jungle of rain forest and waterfalls that shelter and nourish the delicate creatures. Move slowly. The butterflies are everywhere, often hidden by their natural camouflage, and sometimes startlingly brilliant in their colorings. Just stop and watch, and don't be surprised if a butterfly chooses to alight on you.

Each season brings a varied decor of flora to Cypress Gardens, which is open 365 days a year from 9:30 AM until at least 5:30 PM. General admission, excluding tax, costs $30.95 for adults, $20.95 for children between ages 6 and 12 and $25.95 for seniors. Be sure to check on group rates and special offers. During 1998, one teenager is admitted free if accompanied by someone who is paying the regular daily admission fee. This offer, however, doesn't apply to annual passes or other special offers. Parking is free, and preferred parking is available for a small fee. Kennel facilities are also available.

Webster

History buffs will want to visit nearby Dade Battlefield State Historic Site. As far as this Insider's concerned, though, there's only one reason to go to Webster, and there's only one day of the week for making the trip — Monday, early Monday. That's the only day of the week, 52 weeks a year, that the Sumter County Farmers Market is open. No one ever calls it that, though. It's commonly known as just the Webster Flea Market. Gosh, where to begin describing this 40-acre must-junket for junk junkies? It certainly isn't fair to call the finds "junk," since they're anything but, including fresh produce, baked goods and incredible collectibles.

First, be alert to the fact that early means early! Many of the vendors set up before 6 AM

and, especially during hot weather, pack it in by early afternoon. Parking is available in nearby yards for a bit more than the $2 fee for the flea market lot, and you have a little better chance of parking in shade. Be sure to wear shoes that are comfortable for walking in the loose, sandy soil, and take a hat and sunscreen.

What you're interested in should determine where you begin your rounds here. Newer merchandise and produce sold by "permanent" vendors tends to be housed under the covered shopping area east of the main drive. There's also an enclosed building of antiques and other stuff on this side. On the west side, covered stalls on the north end of the market are also filled with regular vendors, but their wares run the gamut from old tools and used golf clubs to new gadgets and old collectibles. We recommend that you start traipsing past the vendors who set up in and around the parking lot. This is for two reasons: It's here you'll find some truly unusual real flea market stuff; and these folks are the first to fold up shop when the sun gets too intense. We made our best finds in this area, including a pitcher to match the blue Shirley Temple bowl from grandma, baby-face milk bottles and antique fishing lures.

There really is no specific address to give you for the Webster market, but it's easy to find. Follow I-75 north to Webster Exit 61 (about 12 miles past U.S. Highway 98). Turn left at the exit ramp stop sign onto Fla. Highway 50. Keep driving a few miles through really pretty countryside until you come to another stop at busy Fla. Highway 471. Turn left again. Just a very short ways down, you'll turn right and soon be part of a long line of cars snaking toward the parking lots way up ahead. The flea market is on the left.

These country directions may seem awfully general but, believe us, there'll be so many other cars that all you'll have to do is fall in line and follow.

Bushnell

Dade Battlefield State Historic Site
7200 C.R. 603, Bushnell • (352) 793-4781

As with other Florida parks, the Dade Battlefield is maintained as close as possible to the condition it was in when the first

Europeans arrived. One of the darker chapters in our nation's history is the treatment of Native Americans. Because of continuing minor clashes between Florida's white settlers and the Seminoles, the United States government enacted a policy to remove the tribe to Oklahoma reservations beginning January 1, 1836. Military authorities, aware there would be resistance, ordered Maj. Francis L. Dade to move 107 troops from Fort Brooke (now Tampa) to Fort King (now Ocala) in December. Seminole Chief Osceola and his allies had no intention of accepting their fate. They watched Dade's command move north, patiently waiting as the column passed the most dangerous ambush points. Then, on a cold, rainy morning and on open terrain, 180 Seminoles attacked, killing Dade and Capt. Upton S. Fraser and wounding three of the other six officers. The troops managed to force the Seminoles back, but the attack lasted until early afternoon when the troops surrendered. Most of the command was dead. Only three wounded soldiers managed to escape. Two returned safely to Fort Brooke. The third, Dade's African-American interpreter, was captured. Only three Seminole warriors had been killed and only five were wounded.

Except for the troops' bodies, the scene of the ambush was deserted for seven weeks before an expedition arrived and buried the 98 enlisted men in two graves. The command's cannon was retrieved from a pond and mounted, muzzle down, at the officers' graves. And so, the Second Seminole War was begun.

The major annual event at Dade Battlefield is a weekend re-enactment of the ambush. It is held late in December and is staged at 2 PM on Saturday and Sunday, with day-long festivities that include Native American dance demonstrations, soldier drills and vendors selling period items, Seminole crafts and clothing. The historic site is open 365 days a year from 8 AM till sunset, and admission costs $2 a vehicle or $1 for pedestrians and bikes. The visitors' center is open between 9 AM and 5 PM. Follow I-75 north to Exit 63 at Bushnell, and follow the signs to the park, about 2 miles east of the interstate.

Ocala

Though seemingly near extinction, the Sunday drive — no matter what day of the week it's taken on — is still a pleasant way to spend a day, especially when you forsake the bland interstate for roads less traveled. Point the wheels north on U.S. Highway 41 to Ocala. Once past Lutz (that's "loots," not "luhts"), your drive takes you through small towns and the countryside. The land undergoes subtle changes, from subtropical flatness to rolling beauty, with deciduous foliage that's scarce around Tampa Bay.

Racing Horses

If an aimless drive goes against your Type-A nature or leaves the kids less than enthusiastic, turn the steering wheel toward Ocala's prestigious horse farms. Ocala has had a national reputation for purse-winning thoroughbreds since Bonnie Heath Farm turned out Needles, winner of both the Preakness and the Kentucky Derby in 1956. Ocala is also known for Gate Dancer, winner of the 1984 Preakness. In Marion County, the area boasts more than 450 thoroughbred farms plus another 300 where Arabians, Paso finos, harness, miniatures, draft, quarter horses and more are bred and raised.

If you follow U.S. 41 N. to Fla. Highway 200, Bonnie Heath Farm is situated three-quarters of a mile west of I-75. Unfortunately, growth has turned this once-leisurely country road into a major thoroughfare, so you'll only get a glimpse of the farm. Proceed east on Fla. 200, and then turn right on S.W. 27th Avenue to reach the Ocala Stud Farm. While Bonnie Heath Farm bred Needles, this is where he was broken and trained. Carryback, the 1961 Derby winner, was also broken and trained here. The Ocala Stud Farm is one of the state's oldest and was the first farm in Florida to breed and sell an eventual Horse of the Year — 1965's Roman Brother. The farm houses between 300 and 400 horses depending on the time of year. Visitors are welcome as long as they call in advance, (352) 237-2171.

County Road 326 and Fla. Highway 475, both off I-75, make for especially scenic drives for horse-farm viewing. A number of farms are open for driving through, but for an up-close and personally guided tour, call Lorna Hagemeyer, (352) 351-5524. She takes tourists to see morning workouts and on farm visits on Tuesdays and Fridays starting at 9 AM. The charge is just $5 a person and is by appointment only. Large coaches are also accommodated during the week at group rates. Call ahead of time to set up a tour.

You might also want to check out the Ocala Breeders Sales Company on N.W. 60th Avenue, directly across from the airport. It's west of I-75, off U.S. Highway 27. Real horse trading goes on here several times a year, including mid-January, late in March and April, early June, toward the end of August and early in October. The March sale is the biggest, a two-day affair called the Weekend of Champions. Call (352) 237-2154 for specific dates and information.

"Big Daddy" Don Garlits Museum of Drag Racing
13700 S.W. 16th Ave., Ocala
• (352) 245-8661

If racing of another sort piques your interest, check out "Big Daddy" Don Garlits' place just south of Ocala. His collection of Swamp Rat dragsters is definitely the highlight, but you'll also view cars once driven by such historic names as Shirley "ChaCha" Muldowney, Tom "Mongoose" McEwen, the "Golden Greek" Chris Karamesines and Dwight D. "Ike" Eisenhower. The 33rd president's personal '56 Chrysler sedan isn't a racer, but it's in "Big Daddy's" vintage Antique Car Museum collection along with a broad array of other classic cars. The special focus here is on the Ford V-8s built between 1932 and 1953.

Christmas is the only day of the year the museums are closed. Otherwise, they're open daily from 9 AM until 5 PM. Admission to both museums costs $10. You can visit just the drag racing museum for $7.50 (seniors 55 and older, $6) or just the antique car museum for $5. The museum sits right next to I-75 at Exit 67.

Marjorie Kinnan Rawlings State Site
S.R. 325, Cross Creek • (352) 466-3672

Remember *The Yearling*? This is where Marjorie Kinnan Rawlings lived the experience she turned into her most famous novel. It was an unusual experience for any woman of her day — she left New York City in 1928 to live alone in the wilds of Florida and work the land and write. The site is open seven days a week, but tours through the house are given Thursday through Sunday at 10 and 11 AM and again at 1, 2, 3 and 4 PM. Donations are requested — $3 from adults and $2 from children ages 6 through 12. Tours are limited to 10 people. Visitors may tour the grove, barn and grounds around the house free of charge. After your visit, swing into nearby Micanopy on U.S. Highway 441 for some antique hunting.

Silver Springs
I-75 at Exit 69, Silver Springs
• (800) 274-7458

The famous glass-bottom boats of Silver Springs are known for giving visitors a glimpse beneath the surface of the world's largest artesian spring. The water is so clear that the sun's light actually reaches 83 feet deep. Above and out of the water there's also plenty else to do, including a jungle cruise, jeep safari and animal shows. On the Lost River cruise you get a glimpse into Florida as it was thousands of years ago and see why the Seminoles called this place "Suaille-aha," meaning sunglinting water.

Silver Springs, just 1 mile east of Ocala, tries to host a different event every weekend in conjunction with 16 concerts, ranging from classic to country, to enjoy throughout the year. This national landmark is open daily from 9 AM until 5:30 PM. For a couple of months during the summer, hours are extended just a bit later. Admission, including tax, costs $29.95. Children between the ages of 3 and 19 are admitted for $20.95. Parking costs $3, and kennels, picnic grounds, camper parking and handicap facilities are available.

Mt. Dora

Serious antiques hounds may swear they've found nirvana in Mt. Dora, which is 25 miles north of Ocala. Shoot up I-75 or follow U.S. 301, and then head east on Fla. Highway 40 to U.S. Highway 441. You'll find nearly two dozen antiques shops in the center of this Victorian-era town. The rolling landscape originally attracted New Englanders, who brought along the furnishings that became the base for the market.

For those who love to hunt treasure in more of a flea-market setting, Renninger's is a must. In more than 150 air-conditioned shops there's more than 35,000 square feet of antique furniture, collectibles, jewelry, glass, china, dolls, oriental rugs and more. Whatever you're into, you'll find it here. This largest gathering of antiques and collectible dealers in the state hosts three extravaganzas and eight fairs during the year. January, February and November are when you'll find the weekend-long extravaganzas. The enclosed displays open at 8 AM while the outdoor area is ready at 10 AM. Both stay open till 5 PM. The entrance fee is $10 on Friday and $5 on Saturday and Sunday. Call (352) 383-8393 Thursday through Sunday for specific dates. From March through October, on the third full weekend of each month, the fairs attract from 350 to 500 dealers. Hours are the same, but there's no charge for admission. There's plenty of unpaved free parking available.

Citrus County

Ted Williams Museum & Hitters Hall of Fame
2455 N. Citrus Hills Blvd., Hernando • (352) 527-6566

This shrine should be subtitled Cooperstown of the South. The museum is a showcase of the Splendid Splinter's life and career as well as a tribute to the past 55 years of baseball. Williams was the last major-leaguer to hit .400. The museum highlights his achievements with statues, photos and memorabilia from his sandlot beginnings in San Diego to his retirement in Citrus County, where he's also known for his hunting and fishing skills. (Betcha didn't know he was John Glenn's wing-man during the Korean War!)

The museum is closed on Mondays and on Easter, Thanksgiving, Christmas and New Year's days. Hours are from 10 AM until 4 PM Tuesday through Sunday, and admission costs $3 for adults and $1 for kids. To get there, follow I-75 north past the Florida Turnpike junction and head west at Exit 66. Swing north on Fla. Highway 41 into Hernando.

Brooksville

In Hernando County, one of the nation's fast-growing regions, Brooksville offers a variety of pleasures ranging from the mermaids at Weeki Wachee Spring and upscale shopping to river canoe history trips. To get there, head north on U.S. 19 through Pinellas County or follow I-75 north from Tampa to Fla. Highway 50 W. After the congested highway traffic you'll find it a relaxing drive into a bit of old Florida mixed with the new.

The Hernando County Tourist Information Center, (904) 796-4580 or (800) 601-4580, will send you a whole packet of informative brochures about the area. Here's one of the special highlights to get you started.

Weeki Wachee Spring
U.S. Hwy. 19 at S.R. 50, Weeki Wachee • (352) 596-2062, (800) 678-9335 in Fla.

For years, Weeki Wachee's beautiful mermaids have captivated audiences with their legendary performances in the world's only underwater spring theater. It's fascinating to watch them glide, seemingly without need of a refreshing breath, through the deep spring (so deep that some depths have never been reached). There's plenty to do and see above water, too. Colorful exhibitions of macaws, cockatoos and other parrots perform exotic bird shows daily. Overhead, winged wonders such as eagles, hawks, falcons and owls swoop and dive on command in a display of beauty, speed and power during the free-flying Birds of the World show. Since it's more on the cuddly side, kids will enjoy the animal forest petting zoo, where the touchable critters include a llama, a pygmy deer and an emu. For a peek at some of the native animals of Florida, you might want to take the Wilderness River cruise. One highlight here is the pelican preserve, where disabled or injured birds are nursed back to health and then released back to the wild or given a home for life.

The spring opens every day of the year at 9:30 AM, but closing hours vary. Admission, excluding tax, costs $16.95 for people 11 and older. Children 3 through 10 get in for $12.95; kids younger than 3 (and your car) are allowed in free of charge.

Lake Wales

Little more than an hour's drive from Tampa Bay, Lake Wales is a place to soothe your soul. After getting through the traffic on Fla. Highway 60 through Brandon, you slip into rural Florida — flat, almost desolate-looking in stretches — and your mind has a chance to slip out of the fast lane. Stay alert though, and please don't try to pass everything in front of you, especially around the phosphate mines near Mulberry. There's a lot of truck traffic along this stretch, and impatience can be life-threatening. Shortly past Mulberry, the pace picks up through Bartow and then turns rural once again.

Soon you're entering Lake Wales, with the scent of citrus in the air, mysterious Spook Hill and magnificent Bok Tower (set on Florida's highest point). Get out and stretch your legs on the historic architectural tour and at the Depot Museum. Indulge your palate at Chalet Suzanne, which *Gourmet* magazine calls "glorious." Keep an eye out for Hillcrest Elementary School on the north side of Fla. 60, east of Fla. Highway Alternate 27. There's almost always a delightful paper sign on the front of the school, certain to give you a smile.

Bok Tower Gardens
Off Burns Ave., Fla. Hwy. 17A, Lake Wales • (941) 676-9412

If angels have favorite vacation places on earth, this surely must be one of them. The 128-acre gardens 3 miles north of Lake Wales have a serenity that naturally makes people speak softly and move slowly. Squirrels tamely approach you on the paths. Ducks glide on the reflecting pool. Cardinals nestle in bushes caressed by butterflies. Thousands of azaleas, camellias, magnolias and other flowering plants deliver seasonal vistas of color against a background of ferns, palms, oaks and pines. Everywhere is the scent of the sweet land and a sense of refreshment, even on the hottest, most humid Florida days.

Dedicated in 1929, Bok Tower Gardens was the gift of publisher and author Edward W. Bok. A Dutch immigrant, Bok wanted to make America more beautiful because this country had been so good to him. These gardens and bell tower became his final resting place too soon after his dream was realized.

The historic bell tower houses one of the world's great carillons, made up of a mechanical keyboard and 57 bronze bells ranging in weight from 17 pounds to nearly 12 tons. Recitals are offered daily at 3 PM, and clock music plays on the half-hour every day beginning at 10 AM. There are moonlight recitals, an Easter Sunrise service, Christmas programs and the International Carillon Festival to enjoy at various times during the year at this National Historic Landmark. It's a bargain, too. Adult admission costs $4, and children ages 5 to 12 are admitted for $1. Members and toddlers are admitted free. You can enter the gardens from 9 AM until 4:45 PM, and lunch is served at the Garden Cafe until 3 PM. Call (941) 676-1408 for information on memberships, tours and group rates.

Spook Hill
East on North Ave. off Fla. Hwy. Alt. 27 N., Lake Wales

Cars don't really roll up hill, do they? Maybe they do, at Spook Hill.

Circuit riders carrying mail between Florida's coasts first gave it this name, when the old trail around Lake Ticowa made their horses labor while going downhill. About 40 years later, as the hills around the lake filled with citrus groves, workers driving wagons were startled when their mule teams struggled, again downhill. Years later, the road was paved and residents scratched their heads as their cars would roll uphill by themselves. How does it happen? Stop by — there's no charge to visit — and try to figure out this mystery for yourself.

Black Hills Passion Play
Off Fla. Hwy. 27A, Lake Wales
• (941) 638-1508, (800) 622-8383

Vivid with the pageantry and splendor of Biblical times, the *Black Hills Passion Play* reconstructs dramatic events in the last week of Christ's life. The eloquent portrayal depicts the love and fury of 2,000 years ago, when the Roman domination of Judea clashed with the devotion of Jesus, his disciples and friends and led to the supreme sacrifice of the Son of Man.

Outdoor performances take place at the Lake Wales Amphitheater starting about six weeks before Easter. Evening shows are on Sunday, Tuesday, Friday and Saturday at 7 PM (except on Easter Sunday, when the performance is at 3 PM). Regular matinees are offered at 3 PM every Wednesday. Ticket prices range from $10 to $16. Children 11 and younger are admitted for half-price. Seating begins an hour before the performance.

Cassadega

Spirituality of a different sort is the focus in Cassadega, about 45 minutes northeast of Orlando off I-4. Taking the exit near Deland, you plunge into rolling hills and vegetation reminiscent of upstate New York, which just happens to be the locale of the spiritualist camp that spawned this village. The camp's center is open Monday through Saturday from 9 AM until 5 PM and on Sundays from noon until 4 PM. The center sells books, meditation tapes, crystals and healing stones. The staff will direct you to respected readers if you're interested in hearing what the future may hold. Many of the camp's spiritual readers are so popular that they book reservations weeks in advance. You can call the camp bookstore, (904) 228-2880, if you'd like more information before you visit.

Sarasota/Manatee

Sarasota is a marvelous destination in itself for a weekend visit or full-length vacation. Pick up *The Insiders' Guide® to Sarasota & Bradenton* to discover everything to do here, including small art galleries, beach walks, shopping on St. Armands Circle and more. Hardly an hour south of Tampa Bay across the Sunshine Skyway Bridge, Sarasota is not to be missed.

Anna Maria must have been an incredibly alluring woman because this island, whoever it was named for, certainly is. The sand on

Photo: Bradenton Herald

Anna Maria Island and Longboat Key are perfect daytrip destinations.

Anna Maria Island is silky and the water inviting. Off in the distance from Bean Point — one of the best beaches in the area — you can see the Sunshine Skyway Bridge and Egmont Key. Holmes Beach and Bradenton Beach in Manatee County are popular with families. Longboat Key's beaches do exist, although you'd do well to stop and ask an Insider for directions on how to easily reach them. North Lido Beach is a haven for privacy purists, while Lido Beach and South Lido Park are great family destinations.

Siesta Key is renowned for its white powdery sand and has been judged tops among 25 beaches around the world. If you're looking for a beach with more bite, head south of Sarasota to Casey Key, known as the sharks' teeth capital of the world. Kids love this place, especially its treasure hunt souvenirs. Shelling is the attraction at Casperson Beach, which offers both a developed beach area and a wonderfully long stretch of sand untouched by pavilions or other amenities. You could also slip away to Boca Grande, a daytrip in itself, with 7 miles of beach plus a bike path, shady spots to rest and lighthouses to remind you of days of yore.

For glimpses into other forms of the past and present, Sarasota and Bradenton offer lots more. Let's take a quick look.

The Ringling Museum
5401 Bayshore Rd., Sarasota
• **(941) 359-5723**

This legacy of circus magnate and art collector John Ringling and his wife, Mable, is certainly the crown jewel of Sarasota's attractions. The state's official art museum offers 18 galleries with one of the world's most important collections of 17th-century Baroque art intermingled with a 500-year pageant of European and American works. The museum's courtyard is reminiscent of a European formal garden, including reproductions of renowned sculptures. Adjacent to the gallery grounds is Ca' d'Zan, the "House of John." The Ringlings built this 30-room palace as their winter home in 1926 for $1.5 million and filled it with marble, tapestry and elaborate furnishings.

Making an almost surrealistic departure from the grandeur of the art galleries and Ca' d'Zan is the The John and Mable Ringling

Museum of Art. This is a special favorite of kids — and anyone else who's ever marveled at the attractions of The Big Top. Take in the displays of rare drawings, vividly colored posters, gilded wagons, calliopes and costumes; you'll leave with a hankering for cotton candy and popcorn. For added circus pleasure, the museum is hosting *The History of the Ringling Family Circus* exhibit from November 1998 through September 1999.

Regular admission costs $9. Senior adults pay $8, and children 12 and younger are admitted free. In groups of 10 or more, admission is only $6.50 a person. On Saturdays (except during the annual Medieval Fair in March) anyone can tour the Art Galleries free of charge. Any resident school teacher or student with an ID can also visit free of charge. The museums are open daily from 10 AM until 5:30 PM, except on Thanksgiving, Christmas and New Year's days.

Gamble Plantation
3708 Patten Ave., Ellenton
• **(941) 723-4536**

Unlike other Southern states, Florida — especially west central Florida — isn't long on antebellum history. The Gamble Plantation, a state historic site, is the only memorial to the Confederacy in the state. The 1890s farmhouse is filled with era furnishings. Six tours are offered daily Thursdays through Mondays. The times are 9:30 and 10:30 AM and 1, 2, 3 and 4 PM. The Plantation is situated a mile west of I-75 at Exit 43. Adult admission costs $3, and children 6 through 12, $1.50.

Selby Gardens
811 S. Palm Ave., Sarasota
• **(941) 366-5730**

This 11-acre open-air and under-glass museum houses more than 20,000 plants, including many collected on expeditions into tropical rain forests by the gardens' researchers. On the grounds of the internationally recognized Selby estate are 15 gardens ranging from the spectacular Banyon Grove to the tranquil Waterfall Garden. The Gardens' Museum of Botany and the Arts is housed in the former Christy Payne Mansion, a unique example of eclectic Southern Colonial architecture. Selby Gardens is best known for its collection of more than 6,000 living orchids. The museum is open from 10 AM until 5 PM every day except Christmas. Admission costs $8 for adults and $4 for children ages 6 through 11.

Sarasota Jungle Gardens
Two blocks west of U.S. Hwy. 41 at the end of Myrtle St., Sarasota
• **(941) 355-5305**

Cool, shaded trails make this a peaceful retreat any time of the year. Banana trees, palms, hibiscus and roses only hint at the depth of this jungle. And birds — hundreds of them, from flamingos to peacocks to ducks — roam freely presenting great photo opportunities. Reptiles and birds strut their stuff at several performances throughout the day. If you want to pack a picnic lunch, Swan Lake is the place to enjoy it, and then let the kids act like little monkeys in their own jungle playground. Admission costs $9 for adults, $7 for seniors and $5 for children 3 through 12. Anyone younger than 17 must be accompanied by an adult. The jungle is open from 9 AM until 5 PM every day except Christmas.

Herrmann's Lipizzan Ranch
Singletary Rd., Myakka City
• **(941) 322-2539**

Those gorgeous, enormous, snow white stallions ... where do they vacation? Right here! Actually, this is more of a training camp before their annual national show tour begins. The Royal Lipizzaner stallions are internationally famous show horses with ancestry dating back to 1580. Starting the first of November, you're invited to come wander the ranch grounds. From the last weekend in December and continuing through the first weekend in April, everyone is welcome to attend free shows. These are generally held at 3 PM on Thursdays and Fridays and at 10 AM on Saturdays, but are definitely subject to change. Be sure to call ahead for performance dates and directions.

Myakka River State Park
S.R. 72, Sarasota Co. • (941) 361-6511

Step back into Florida circa A.D. 1500, but bring your binoculars, camera, sketchpad or notebook. This park is our state's largest, encompassing 28,865 acres and 7,500 acres of wilderness preserve. The alligator population is far too healthy to permit swimming in the two lakes and 12 miles of river, but canoes are available, as are airboat and tram rides. The freshwater fish almost always bite here (better have a license, though!). You can explore the park on a rented bike or take a walking tour and join in a free birding program. Since nature's critters live by Ben Franklin's words — early to bed and early to rise — the best times to see their activity are early morning and near dusk.

The park is about 11 miles east of Sarasota. Hours are from 8 AM until sunset, and the only day it's closed is Christmas. Admission costs $2 a person or $4 a carload (maximum of eight people), and additional charges apply to airboat rides and canoe rentals.

Yankeetown

Though well within daytrip drive-time, a visit here takes you so much further back in time, to when Florida was true South — not the southern North. You'll want a weekend to unwind here, as this is a place to just relax. The most stressful thing you're likely to battle is a fish on the end of your line, and about the most confusion you'll encounter is trying to sort out the osprey, egrets, herons and anhinga (also known as snakebirds, because only their heads and long necks are visible above water when they're swimming).

Yankeetown got its name for being just that — a place that attracted Yankees. It's also popular with Floridians too, whether natives or transplants, who want to enjoy boating on the Gulf, canoeing on the Withlacoochee River or walking under umbrella oaks. The town's main area is all of three blocks wide and 6 miles long, so walking and biking are attractive pursuits. Many of the 650 residents live in small Florida Cracker-style cottages built on stilts, a necessity during times of flood.

The Izaak Walton Lodge on 63rd Street and Riverside Drive is Yankeetown's favored inn. The lodge was named for the 17th-century author who wrote *The Compleat Angler*. The lodge has two restaurants — the Compleat Angler serves dinner while the Little Angler provides breakfast and lunch fare.

Yankeetown is about 100 miles up the Gulf

coast in Levy County, and the drive takes only a couple of hours from Tampa. Follow U.S. 19 N. to Inglis, and then take County Road 40 W. For information about the Izaak Walton Lodge, call proprietors Linda and Wayne Harrington, (352) 447-2311.

Cedar Key

Up the coast from Yankeetown are the islands of Cedar Key, part of a national wildlife refuge. This is one of the state's oldest fishing ports, but a variety of natural and man-made situations has just about wiped out that industry. The town is best known now as an artist's colony. Shops abound and are filled with local work including everything from sculpture to jewelry. March brings an annual art festival, and October offers a seafood festival. Both attract thousands and thousands of visitors during those weekends. If you plan to stay overnight, which you should, you'd best call ahead for reservations, even if nothing special is planned in the town. Try the popular Cedar Key Bed & Breakfast, (352) 543-9000. Unless it's summer, take a jacket, sweatshirt or heavy sweater; the wind off the Gulf can be downright cold, and you'd probably have to go to Gainesville to buy warm clothes. Cedar Key is at the end of Fla. Highway 24, west of U.S. 19. If you're leaving from Tampa, plan on a three-hour drive.

Daytona Beach and the Space Coast

Although still within our time confines for a daytrip, a jaunt to Daytona or the Kennedy Space Center really deserves a weekend to fully enjoy. Any time of the year is perfect along the world's most famous beach. Almost 500 feet wide and spanning nearly 23 miles — 18 of which are open to auto traffic — Daytona Beach is lined with beautiful bodies, flashy cars and cycles, gift shops and nightspots. And

possibly more famous than the white-sand beaches is the Daytona 500. This annual "Super Bowl" of auto racing takes place in mid-February. Bike Week is another event that attracts throngs to the area.

If you're more interested in what's above the beach, visit Kennedy Space Center's Visitor Center. You can view the history of America's space travel in three IMAX films with footage shot by NASA astronauts. Double-decker buses offer two different guided tours of the center; the red buses visit the shuttle launch pad while the blue buses tour Cape Canaveral Air Station. The tours costs $7 for adults and $4 for kids ages 3 to 11. There is no charge to tour the Visitor Center, which opens daily, except Christmas, at 9 AM. Hours are subject to change because of space shuttle launches and landing operations. If you'd like more information prior to visiting, call (407) 452-2121 or (800) KSC-INFO in Florida.

St. Augustine

While too far for a single daytrip, St. Augustine makes a wonderful weekend destination. As Insiders, let us forewarn you: If you want exciting nightlife, look elsewhere. There's little to do but enjoy the Atlantic beaches and historic sites.

Since it's the oldest city in the United States, we all learned lots about St. Augustine and the Spanish settlers back in our elementary school days. But it seems history is never complete, and this city continues to slowly divulge bits of its past. For instance, palmetto posts that made up part of an ancient city wall are being uncovered at the Cubo Defensive Line Project. In south St. Augustine, at a site known as Lincolnville, local archaeology association volunteers and Flagler College interns are unearthing a rare glimpse into a little-known chapter of African-American history.

African-born slaves who risked their lives to escape from slavery more than 250 years ago

INSIDERS' TIP

The name Tampa was originally the Native American word "tanpa" first ascribed to a Spaniard named Fountaneda who lived with the Indians in the late 1570s. Tanpa is often defined as "sticks of fire," but some translate it as "city by the bay."

didn't always head north. Spanish colonists promised sanctuary to runaways who came to Florida and converted to Catholicism. In 1738, the Spaniards established Fort Mose as the first legally sanctioned free black community in what is now the United States. All male residents of Fort Mose were members of the Spanish Militia, and the fort served as Florida's first line of defense against the British to the north. Although this black militia was not unique — Africans were regularly enlisted in Colonial militias throughout the Spanish colonies — the Fort Mose militia served in a number of significant battles before the post was abandoned in 1763 after Spain ceded Florida to England. The entire colony then moved to Cuba.

After the end of the Civil War, freed slaves returned to the area where Fort Mose had stood. These settlers called their community Lincolnville in honor of the assassinated president. Lincolnville was eventually absorbed by the city of St. Augustine as remnants of Fort Mose all but disappeared.

Historians and archeologists are now bringing to light an even older chapter of frontier history. In January 1996, archaeologists revealed that they'd discovered a fort presumably settled in 1565. It's believed to be the first site built by Pedro Menendez de Aviles, who established Spain's toehold in the New World.

More information on the area's historical interests is available by calling the St. Augustine/St. Johns County Chamber of Commerce, (800) 653-2489. They'll also be able to provide information on other places to visit as well as available accommodations.

You will quickly
see why living in the
Tampa Bay area is like a
vacation in paradise —
except you never have
to check out.

Real Estate

High-rise, low-rise, three floors or one, city mouse, country mouse, mermaid or land-lubber, Tampa Bay beckons with as many lifestyle choices as there are families to embrace them. From the new master-planned communities in North Hillsborough County to the last tip of land along the Gulf beaches, we venture to bet that making your final neighborhood choice will not only be overwhelmingly bewildering, but also wildly exciting.

Whether you choose to unpack in Pinellas or Hillsborough county, you may be assured of one thing: value for your housing dollar. Indeed, transplants from the north and far west are astounded at the remarkably reasonable sales prices in both the new construction and resale marketplaces. In Hillsborough County, the average sales price for existing single-family homes is $99,992; in Pinellas County, $150,376. Prices shoot upward and moderately down depending on the neighborhood and amenities, so you will pay considerably more for a Gulf beach or prestigious golf-course view. After all, life's little luxuries do have their price.

Before you go delirious with all the housing alternatives that await you, we will attempt to give you just a bit of guidance. First, there's the logical approach, to seek out a neighborhood that's close to your place of work and also matches your lifestyle choice and pocketbook. Second, there's the grass-is-always-greener approach, stretching your commute for a real Florida home that brings you into a hub of activity or separates you far from the crowds. Lastly, there's the psychological approach to Tampa Bay housing — our personal favorite. Satisfy that inner yearning by surrounding yourself with luscious palm trees, a crystal-clear backyard pool and floor-to-ceiling windows that drench your home in natural sunlight — no matter where you may find it. After all, with our well-planned network of interstates and highways, you can easily get anywhere you need to be from a home you truly love.

A note here about a few quirks we've discovered in the Tampa Bay real estate picture. We love our walls. Yes, build a beautiful new community and slap a 12-foot-high wall around it. In many communities — Carrollwood, for example — we build walls within walls to further stake out our territory. With a few exceptions, these walls are not so much for security as they are to define the turf and buffer any street noise. And as you may surmise, the more elaborate the wall, the more expensive the home it safeguards.

Next is the total absence of signs of life in many new communities. Read that: Put your car in the garage and hermetically seal it in. We would venture to say that Tampa Bay has the highest proportion of garage-door openers to population in the entire nation. The obvious reason, of course, is that there's easy access from garage to kitchen in all new construction, plus, keeping your car out of the hot Florida sun keeps it cool for you and protects the finish.

INSIDERS' TIP

When you're involved in the drama of house hunting, do yourself a favor: Stay someplace that feels almost like home. Here in Tampa Bay, there are several extended-stay facilities that offer generously sized suites with amenities such as kitchens to make your stay more comfortable. Most are clustered in the Rocky Point and Westshore areas and include Guest Quarters Suite Hotels, Marriott Residence Inn and Courtyard by Marriott.

Lastly, if you're moving here from northern climates, we'd advise a mega-garage sale prior to stuffing the U-Haul. Since most homes, old and new, have no basements or expansive attics for hiding all the former essentials, we all must make do with the skimpy closets available to us. If this fact caused the hair on your neck to stand up, our suggestion is to contact one of the many local closet-organizer companies that can transform your limited storage space into a clutter-hound's utopia.

The most important task you have before you buy is to do your homework. There are a zillion free real estate publications available throughout both counties, including *Homes & Land*, *Harmon Homes*, *New Homes* and *Real Estate Showcase*, that you can use as your textbooks. By studying home exteriors, sale prices by neighborhood and new construction/resale options, you may be able to narrow your search considerably. It's then time to call on a Realtor who can take you for a tour through those communities you've selected (more about our real estate companies later in this chapter). Your agent will be able to thoroughly explain the advantages of each neighborhood, from schools to shopping to nearby recreational, medical and professional facilities. Zero in, make your offer and whammo! Kick off your shoes — home at last!

Once you and your family are happily ensconced in your new Tampa Bay home, thoughts turn to … taxes. When it comes to savings on your real estate taxes, we've got you covered. Under the provisions of the Homestead Exemption Statute, your home is exempt from the first $25,000 of the assessed value. This also applies to duplexes, but only to that portion occupied by the owner.

A homeowner must meet four requirements in order to qualify for homestead exemption: 1) You must have the title of record to the property as of January 1 of that year and reside in the property as well; 2) You must be a legal, permanent resident of Florida; 3) You must make application of the Homestead Exemption with the county property appraiser between January 1 and March 1; and 4) You must take with you the deed or tax statement, Florida driver's license and vehicle registration or voter registration to the property appraiser's office when filing. While it may sound complicated, it really is a quite simple process and probably the easiest money you've ever saved.

Come with us now on our own whirlwind tour of Tampa Bay real estate, through the neighborhoods and communities that give our region the diversity to indulge any homeowner's fantasy. You will quickly see why living in the Tampa Bay area is like a vacation in paradise — except you never have to check out.

Hillsborough County

South Tampa

Hyde Park

Let's start posh. If you're going to live SOK (south of Kennedy), it might as well be here. The oldest residential area in Tampa, this historic district was the result of the building boom of the 1920s, when O.H. Platt named the area after his hometown of Hyde Park, Illinois. Immediately across the Hillsborough River to the west of the downtown business and cultural core, Hyde Park has been a magnet for industrious souls who have vigorously renovated the area's charming bungalows, Colonial Revival homes and Victorian mansions.

Breaking the sedate civility of the neighborhood is Old Hyde Park Village, a hub of activity with its collection of upscale retail shops and restaurants that swirl around the village's circular green. A step away, along Bayshore Boulevard, rise cloud-touching condos and gorgeous estates on rolling lawns. They all take advantage of the view of the sea-walled Hillsborough River and the longest sidewalk in the world.

Davis Islands

Born from the vision of inspired developer and entrepreneur David P. Davis, Davis Islands

www.insiders.com

See this and many other **Insiders' Guide®** destinations online — in their entirety.

Visit us today!

It's just another busy day on the Bay.

is a picture book of the most elegant architectural styles of the early 20th century. The three islands at the mouth of the Hillsborough River were declared the "Eighth Wonder of the World" by Davis in the 1920s, and inspired the creation of the Mediterranean-style home, a resplendent combination of stucco and tile. Connected to downtown Tampa by the Davis Islands Bridge, the islands today are home to Tampa General Hospital, Peter O'Knight Airport, golf, tennis and yacht clubs, and 4,600 very lucky homeowners.

Harbour Island

Let the elevated monorail People Mover whisk you from downtown Tampa to Harbour Island, South Tampa's only master-planned community. This 177-acre pocket of paradise features five distinctive upscale neighborhoods with a generous mix of single and multifamily residences. For all to enjoy is the true heart of Harbour Island, a handsome waterfront facility that has an athletic club, office space and a luxury hotel.

Culbreath Isles

A truly enviable address, Culbreath Isles was one of Tampa's first totally secured neighborhoods and remains one of the most exclusive. The Isles, developed in the 1960s near the popular Westshore area, are laced with canals, thus increasing waterfront access. Here you'll discover one imposing home after another, most in the time-honored traditional style, with the indulgent addition of swimming pools and boat docks tethering elegant yachts.

Beach Park

Fully developed during the 1960s, Beach Park was one of the first neighborhoods to take advantage of environmental planning. A spirited community graced with 200- to 300-year-old oaks and towering palms, some 30 large Mediterranean-style homes formed the nucleus for the neighborhood when they were built for upper-crust families during the '20s boom. Today the winding streets offer a variety of architectural styles from traditional to contemporary.

Palma Ceia

Nestled within Tampa's Interbay Peninsula, Palma Ceia dutifully serves as anchor for Tampa's elite. With its antique, red-brick roads, renowned Palma Ceia Golf Course and mix of upscale homes shaded from the Florida sun by enormous oaks, Palma Ceia has come from the 1920s into today's world as a matriarch of neighborhoods. Close to downtown, the Selmon Expressway and all points west, Palma Ceia continues its tradition of appeal to Tampa Bay residents with discriminating tastes.

Northwest Tampa

Westchase

A premier master-planned community, Westchase has emerged as Tampa's fastest growing neighborhood, according to local real estate watchers. It sprawls over hundreds of acres with nature preserves, lakes and a championship golf course. New construction is the watchword, and beautiful, affordable new construction it is. Westchase residents are surrounded by parks, playing fields, school sites and nature trails. A spectacular clubhouse, outfitted with tennis courts, a swimming pool and marvelous restaurants, serves as a meeting hub for Westchase residents. Here you have the environmentally correct option of using natural gas and reclaimed water, which protects our natural resources and lowers monthly bills. Another unique program, the Tree Planting Program, has added thousands of trees to homesites, parks and common areas. You may visit model homes of several of the region's most respected builders, all beautifully decorated to really get you in the mood to buy.

Countryway

A Westchase neighbor, Countryway is a wonderful family-oriented community comprised of small neighborhoods. Almost 50 percent of this 750-acre planned community has been set aside for a golf course, tot lots (playgrounds), two recreation parks, nature preserves and numerous lakes. Single-family homes are surprisingly affordable, and you can check out a variety of attractive, new model homes.

Bayside

Through the walled and landscaped entrance to this San Marino development, you enter the private world of Bayside, where every home is as beautiful as the next, and most perch on the winding waterways that finger through this community bordering Old Tampa Bay. Homes in Bayside are what you think about when you think "new Florida home," with soaring glass, two-story entries and barrel tile roofs. It is a true mystery why so many of these handsome properties are always available for sale, usually hovering around the $300,000 mark on the price tag. All have the convenience of shopping and dining in this "Town 'N Country" area of Tampa.

North Tampa

Carrollwood

As you zoom north along Dale Mabry Highway, you'll enter the pleasure zone called Carrollwood, almost a little city unto itself, and certainly one of the most honorable NOK (north of Kennedy) neighborhoods. Into the plethora of shopping strips, restaurants and office complexes spill the residents of this North Hillsborough County community, well-known for its quality schools and old-fashioned neighborly atmosphere. Off to its fashionable start when Matt Jetton purchased 200 acres of orange groves in 1957, Carrollwood has become an established mecca for young families seeking a stable environment in which raise children, for senior adults seeking a casual lifestyle and for all those in-between folk who just want to enjoy the best of Florida living at an affordable price.

To the east of Dale Mabry sits Original Carrollwood, with homes standing sentry over its namesake Lake Carroll. Architecture here is truly a mixed bag of comfy ranchers and imposing lakeside mansions, and home prices vary as wildly, from the low $90,000s way up to a half-million dollars and more. All residents, regardless of their property's value, share exclusive privileges for use of Lake Carroll and its recreational facilities.

To the west of Dale Mabry is Carrollwood Village, one of Tampa's first comprehensively planned developments, created by Jetton in 1971. Single-family homes, midrise condominiums, townhouses and cluster homes line the lush 27-hole golf course, and numerous small ponds and creeks provide upscale housing for resident geese, herons and wayward alligators. Because Carrollwood Village is a deed-restricted community, the common areas and roadways are lush and impeccably maintained, and with the much applauded Reclaimed Water Program, homeowners are free to lavish their own landscaped lawns with water courtesy of Mother Nature. While the housing styles come in many different flavors, Insiders do joke about the common thread: a predominance of exterior facades painted in what is lovingly known as Carrollwood brown. To move into your own Carrollwood home, expect to pay from the $130,000s on up to $400,000, depending on square footage and location within the village.

Northdale

Just a bit north of Carrollwood is the affordable golf-course community of Northdale, a neighborhood of country homes built by a collection of builders. Families are big here, as evidenced by the recent remodeling of one of Hillsborough County's largest YMCA's. Northdale offers recreational amenities to keep the little ones off the streets, and shopping and schools are nearby. Resale home prices range from the high $80,000s to mid $100,000s, and those well-kept beauties along the golf course or conservation areas do seem to get snapped up as quickly as they appear on the market.

Avila

This isn't heaven, this is Avila. But don't even think you're going to drive up to this walled community in the northern lake region of Hillsborough County for a little look-see. Pleasant but steadfast guards at the single, main security gate give entry only to homeowners or perhaps those fortunate enough to be invited to play 18 on the private golf course. Homes here can only be described as palatial, sitting proudly on sweeping pinperfect grounds, and each a unique architec-tural reflection of the family that resides within. Avila is self-proclaimed as "an extraordinary community of refined affluence and uncompromised elegance," and those who propose to build here must submit their plans to the scrutiny of a special committee of fellow property owners for approval. A nice round number to begin your dream of living in this exceptional community would be $450,000.

Cheval

The way to describe Cheval is 1,748 glorious acres of lushness and high living. This elite community is home to the Tournament Players Club of Tampa Bay that each February takes its turn on the PGA Senior Tour circuit. The intimate villages that comprise the whole of Cheval offer a variety of lifestyle housing, from patio and single-family homes to townhomes and breathtaking custom estates. All visitors are pre-screened at the 24-hour manned gatehouse, but you can slide into the impressive sales center to receive a pass. Besides the TPC, you'll find another 18-hole golf course, a 45-acre equestrian and polo complex, a health and tennis center with nine Har-Tru courts, a private gourmet restaurant and an elegant clubhouse. Hidden away from the bustle of the county, Cheval is a remarkably quiet, tranquil retreat, yet just minutes from Westshore and downtown via the Veterans Expressway, which ends almost at Cheval's front door. If you're home-shopping here, plan on spending from the $170,000s to $1 million for the luxury of a Cheval address.

New Tampa

Springing out of the north hinterlands of Hillsborough County is the future of Tampa: master-planned golf-course communities that tease and beckon with sparkling new homes and townhomes, groomed golf courses, tennis complexes, new schools and the friendship of pioneer families just like yours. Tampa Palms leads the way with its separate villages of distinctive homes, a golf and country club, Tampa Palms Elementary School and a convenient shopping plaza. Named the nation's finest master-planned community by the National Association of Homebuilders, about half the community has been reserved for parks, a golf course, open green space and protected woodland areas. A favorite haven for corporate transferees, you'll find a mind-boggling choice of resale properties, many barely warm from the original owners. Pack from $90,000 to $1.5 million in your back pocket before being lured by Tampa Palms' charms.

Hunter's Green likewise greets you with an impressive landscaped entry into the privileged world of golf-course living. Sprawling over 1,940 acres, it was voted the Top Master-Planned Community in the Southeast by the National Association of Homebuilders. Here, you can start out in a luxury apartment, and move yourself all the way up through a $100,000 townhome to a $700,000 masterpiece. The Tom Fazio-designed golf course — recognized by *Golfweek* magazine as one of Florida's top-15 golf courses — is a local favorite, along with the Tennis and Athletic Center with 17 Har-Tru courts, a fitness center, a junior Olympic-size, heated pool and the Courtside Cafe. The focus here is on the active, healthy lifestyle, with environmental concerns reflected in the more than 800 acres of nature preserves. That's one for every 3 acres in the entire community. That is also why Hunter's Green has also been honored with a Florida Quality Development Award, recognizing the achievements of developers that exceed environmental guidelines. Because of the area's growing popularity, brand-new schools that have just swung open their doors to students are already busting at the seams.

By far the newest star on the New Tampa horizon is Arbor Greene, the offspring of Hunter's Green. Even though it sports its own separate gated entrance, Arbor Greene's 596 acres remain inside the original golf-course community. Claiming the distinction of a master-planned community for "the new genera-tion," the community is truly dedicated to preserving the natural beauty of the site. In fact, because only 974 homes are planned for an area that could have accommodated 2,400, a full 70 percent of the homesites have views of nature preserves and parks. To head the moving van in the direction of Arbor Greene, see your friendly mortgage banker for a minimum of $150,000.

To get more home for your homebuying dollar, you can head even farther north. Here you'll stumble into more new home communities such as River Park, Kensington, Pebble Creek and Meadow Pointe. All offer exceptional value in new construction, considering the small price you will pay for the longer commute into the hub of Tampa activity.

Still north and to the east of I-75 is what is billed as the last great waterfront community, Cory Lake Isles. With homes perched on fingers of land that protrude into Cory Lake — the largest lake in Tampa, with more than 10 miles of shoreline — you'll need a minimum of $200,000 to find your place on the water, but in return you'll enjoy the protection of 24-hour, manned security. Entry to this exclusive community with hand-laid brick streets is currently via Morris Bridge Road. There is an additional entry with direct access to Bruce B. Downs Boulevard.

Temple Terrace

Pluck a juicy Temple orange off the tree in your backyard; that's about the speed of life in Temple Terrace. In 1925 it was incorporated, the last city to do so in Hillsborough County. The former hunting reserve of the early 1900s has given way to the Temple Terrace Golf & Country Club and the Mediterranean-style homes that are so popular in Tampa Bay. Even homes on the meandering Hillsborough River are quite reasonably priced and, therefore, a great magnet

INSIDERS' TIP

Spring is the season when plant lovers have lots of sales to choose from in selecting new additions for the yard. Tampa Bay's largest plant sale is in mid-April, benefiting the University of South Florida Botanical Garden. The nonprofit "museum for plants" is open year round. Call (813) 974-2329 for hours and directions.

Photo: St. Petersburg/Clearwater Area Convention & Visitors Bureau

Tarpon Springs is one of the most unique communities in America and is the center for the world's natural sponge industry.

for young, growing families who appreciate the easy lifestyle just minutes from the University area of town.

Brandon

Now we are talking growth. This unincorporated town continues to experience explosive growth, not to mention the inclusion of Brandon TownCenter, the mother of all mega-malls. Once a relatively isolated community, Brandon has been "discovered," and its many master-planned golf-course communities are hot properties for homebuyers in today's market. The gently rolling landscape with massive oaks and numerous creeks, lakes and rivers make it a favorite refuge for those seeking old-country charm a quick jaunt from big-city life. In south Brandon, you'll find Bloomingdale, with modestly priced housing tucked into heavily wooded natural surroundings. A popular place for young families, Bloomingdale boasts a championship golf course, tennis courts galore and huge sports fields for a variety of leisure sports and activities.

In Valrico, Brandon's neighbor, is River Hills, a gated community that rightfully brags about its Joe Lee-designed golf course, eight lighted Har-Tru tennis courts and fantastic Aquatic Center with competition-size pool (where Brooke Shields trains). Bordering the Alafia River, River Hills offers you the choice of either the 230-acre nature preserve or the golf course as your backyard neighbor. River Hills covers 1,053 miles of master-planned utopia developed by Arvida, which promises to include about 1,000 single-family homes when it is complete. Homes ranging from $90,000 to more than $600,000 await your moving van.

Pinellas County

North St. Petersburg

Bayou Club Estates

A manned and gated entrance, numerous lakes, a Tom Fazio-designed golf course and natural bayou define this sophisticated community, landmarked by a handsome clubhouse with 16 tennis courts, a swimming pool and an accommodating staff. If you plan to build here, expect to adhere to prudent architectural guidelines that were adopted to preserve the community's integrity and value. In return, you will have at your disposal a private, secured retreat where you can leisurely walk to the club-house for a quiet supper with friends. A new, single-family home on a third- to half-acre lot can be yours for $300,000 to $1 million; a smaller, maintenance-free abode will set you back $250,000.

Feather Sound

Just a short hop to the Howard Frankland Bridge, Feather Sound hugs the western shore of Old Tampa Bay and is another highly popular self-contained golf-course community. Here, you can choose from luxurious single-family homes ($130,000 to $600,000) and townhomes ($130,000 to $250,000) or opt for a brand-new home in Feather Sound's last section, Eagle Pointe. Waterfront or golf-course lots, sans home, will drain a minimum of $135,000 from your bank account.

Florida Living Lingo

"Carrollwood — 4/2/2 split plan on conservation. Huge FR w/ plant shelves and pocket sliders opens to screened lanai, open pool w/spa and pool ba. Master w/wi closets and Roman tub. CHA, 3-car garage, sec sys, ti roof, deed restricted community. Hurry!"

Huh? If you're from them Northern states, reading a real estate ad in Tampa Bay can seem like Greek mixed in with a little upper-Mongolian. Here's a down-and-dirty primer to help you sort through a few of those abbreviations and off-the-wall terms used oh-so frequently in our marketplace.

Close-up

Split plan — This means that the master bedroom is on one side of the home, secondary bedrooms are on the other, and they're separated by the main living areas. When you see 4/2/2, that will tell you the home has four bedrooms, two full baths and two half-baths. You can assume that the master bedroom is on one side of the home and the other three bedrooms on the other.

Conservation — Conservation lots. This references the fact that behind the home there are not, and will probably never be, any other structures, just protected woods or greenbelts. A home on a conservation lot is a prized possession, especially since you know you can go skinny-dipping in your pool with no one to watch but the wildlife in the woods behind you.

FR, LR, DR. — FR = Family Room, LR = Living Room, DR = Dining Room. If the ad reads Great Room, you may assume that there is no separate (read formal) living room.

Plant shelves — A marvy invention by new-home builders, plant shelves are literally shelves that are built into the walls, way above any normal human being's reach. Most Insiders we know use them for placing odd baskets and fake plants — there's no way you'd want to consider getting up to that level to regularly water the real thing.

— continued on next page

Pocket sliders — Most Florida homes have one thing in common — sliding glass doors. In better homes, there are allowances made for the open doors — tracks that run along the adjoining solid wall to accommodate the glass sliding door so that the door opening is totally unobstructed when fully open. Believe us, this is a good thing and shows quality workmanship and attention to detail.

Lanai — Lanai is a Hawaiian term for a roofed-over exterior area exposed on two or more sides to the outdoors. Because you'd be eaten alive by the native Florida bug population if left exposed relaxing on your open Lanai, we have wisely chosen to enclose most of our Lanais with screening. What this really means is, if you have sliding glass doors that lead to your Lanai, you can slide those doors way open and comfortably expand your living space to the great outdoors during much of our temperate year.

Real Florida living . . . an enclosed pool and lanai.

Photo: Cindy Sper, Prudential Florida Realty

Open pool, screened pool — Some swimming pools will be open to the outdoors with no covering. The majority of pools, however, will be encased by the same screened enclosure that will extend from the Lanai. Bottom line: If you have a screened pool, it means you almost have a swimming pool "inside" your home for most of the year. Not bad at all.

Pool bath — No, this is not a shower in the pool. It refers to a bathroom accessible from the pool area and, normally, is the bathroom that serves a secondary bedroom as well.

Roman tub — This is an oversized, usually raised bathtub, often equipped with whirlpool jets, that is a dramatic feature in many of the new homes being built in the Tampa Bay area today. We figure they're called Roman tubs because it would take a true gladiator to attempt to clean the enormous bathtub ring after just one use.

WI closets — Walk-in closets. This is a very, very good thing. In homes that seem to pride themselves on being stingy with closet and storage space, a walk-in closet is truly something to boast about.

CHA — Central heat and air conditioning. You want these things. Trust us.

Sec Sys — Security system. Security systems are big business here. We especially like those that are tied into an intercom system so that you can detect a possible intruder through any conceivable entry point in your home.

Ti roof — Tile roof. This is a big deal. Not only does it look real Florida, but it's also the most expensive roofing you can cap your home with. In most cases, when you see "ti roof," you can immediately translate that into "more expensive."

Deed restricted community — It is the name of the game for most master-planned communities in the Tampa Bay market. This means that each home must comply with certain specifications and/or architectural guidelines, be it size, set-back from the street, etc. It assures you that no one will be able to frivolously build a nuclear reactor in their backyard or erect a humongous fence with parapets that would detract from the overall appearance of an otherwise civilized neighborhood.

Northeast St. Petersburg

Snell Isle

When you're ready to move on up, head northeast, just like C. Perry Snell, who built a replica of a Venice bridge to his island in 1925. For a most exclusive address to engrave on your personal stationery, may we suggest Snell Isle, a posh peninsula of luxury residences including traditional Mediterranean-style mansions on walled and gated waterfront mini-estates, priced from a mere $500,000 when they are available. You may find other housing alternatives more to your liking (and your pocketbook's liking) in the modern ranchers on inland lots, or in condominium and apartment complexes. All are complemented by a golf and country club, a marina, and office and retail establishments.

Allendale

Charming and stately homes nestle among mammoth mature trees in this neighborhood developed in the 1940s. Because of its proximity to downtown St. Petersburg, many homeowners adept with power tools are moving to this established area to renovate the period homes that are usually priced from $175,000 to more than $1 million.

Also in the northeast section of the city, you'll find a variety of other communities that take full advantage of their proximity to the waters of Tampa Bay. You can be a resident of Patrician Point or Placido Bayou starting from around $200,000; Coffee Pot Bayou from $230,000; or go all the way to the top at North Shore, with its $1 million-plus beauties. For those with more moderate tastes, try the inland neighborhoods of Woodlawn ($100,000) or Barkley Estates ($150,000 and up).

South St. Petersburg

Pinellas Point

Homes in south St. Petersburg are so popular that buyers snap them up as soon as the sign is placed in the front yard. Pinellas Point with its pink streets is one such neighborhood where homes with price tags around $500,000 offer a panoramic view of the water and the Skyway Bridge.

With lots of luck — and $300,000 — you might find a home in Bahama Shores, a community known for family homes passed from one generation to the next. Many historical homes, circa 1920s, can be found in Driftwood and, along with the 1950s ranch-style homes in Tropical Shores and Coquina Key, are becoming very popular remodeling targets for energetic homebuyers.

Southwest St. Petersburg

Pasadena Yacht & Country Club

Anchoring the southwest part of the city is the gated enclave of Pasadena Yacht & Country Club. Orginally designed by Walter Hagan, it boasts historic links as well as a marina that offers access to Boca Ciega Bay, gateway to the Gulf of Mexico and beyond. The community has gone through many phases of development since the 1920s, and the last phases are selling now, with new homes beginning in the $200,000 range and topping off at $1 million for waterfront or golf-course settings.

Dolphin Cay

There's been feverish activity in Dolphin Cay since it opened its gates a few years ago. With condominiums from $123,000 and single-family homes along the Maximo Channel from $279,000, sales have definitely been brisk.

Other popular southwest stomping grounds include the new, gated community of Bayway Isles, the condominium heaven of Isla Del Sol and Maximo Moorings with its single-family homes built in the early 1960s.

Countryside

People laughed back in the 1960s when visionary developers journeyed into east Clearwater to create an area called Countryside. Today, just stand in line and take a number to order up a home in one of the many thriving neighborhoods that comprise Countryside. There are endless options for affordable housing, miles of shopping and dining alternatives, and of course, Countryside Mall with its indoor ice-skating rink. The development also has a golf course, a country club, tennis courts, a swimming pool and an always-busy community center.

East Lake

If you're into "power living," East Lake is the Pinellas home of choice. From a waterfront home on Lake Tarpon to one that borders a fairway or green, you'll find it here. Within East Lake, there are many communities at various stages of development, including Landsbrook and East Lake Woodlands. Pocket at least $150,000 on up to $1 million, and you're home free.

Oldsmar

The oil wells that used to dot this area have given way to a quaint town called Oldsmar, named after the original property owner and father of the Oldsmobile, Ransom E. Olds. The original subdivision fans out like spokes of a wheel from Tampa Bay, and housing alternatives are as varied as the people who reside here. Residents enjoy wide-open spaces, along with a progressive city government that has eyes on the future. Of special interest is the 30-acre Oldsmar Flea Market, which causes major gridlock every weekend as thousands pour into the city from every compass point.

Safety Harbor

If you stroll along Main Street in Safety Harbor, you'll immediately understand its mystique. An old-fashioned, small-town feeling coupled with beautiful new Florida-style homes share the quaint atmosphere of this small, caring community. It's the former residence of the aboriginal Tocobaga Indians, who greeted Hernando de Soto in 1539. The landmark is the world-famous Safety Harbor Resort, luring celebs to partake of the legendary secrets of its therapeutic natural springs.

Dunedin

The sister city to Sterling, Scotland, Dunedin is a charming little town that borders the Gulf of Mexico north of Clearwater. Vintage homes, meticulously preserved by ardent residents, line Victoria Drive along St. Joseph's Sound. Other established neighborhoods such as Fairway Estates, Spanish Trails and Country Woods all share the same cozy, small-town feeling. The quaint downtown area is a rehabilitated hub of activity, with marvelous shops, galleries and delightful restaurants.

Palm Harbor

Stretching from Dunedin north to Tarpon Springs, Palm Harbor is a community of sparkling new neighborhoods that share the area's history with the old downtown area and its 100-year-old, moss-covered oaks. To its west is the Gulf of Mexico and the communities of Crystal Beach and Ozona. To its east are Lake Tarpon and the sprawling developments along E. Lake Road. Actually, Insiders will tell you that Palm Harbor is wherever Oldsmar, Tarpon Springs or Safety Harbor are not. They'll also tell you that it is home to the world-renowned Innisbrook Golf and Country Club.

Tarpon Springs

Enriched by the Mediterranean heritage brought here by Greek sponge divers, Tarpon Springs remains true to the customs and practices of the earliest settlers. The modern world hasn't bothered to mess with this quaint community, but locals seeking out natural sponges flood the charming marketplace every weekend.

Belleair

Watch eyebrows lift if you casually mention you live in Belleair, trapped by the Intracoastal Waterway on one side and the Gulf of Mexico on the other. One lovely neighborhood piggybacks another in this distinctive community, and all seem to begin with the word "Belle" or "Harbor." There's Belleair Bluffs and Belle Isle, Harbor Oaks and Harbor Hills ... even Bel-Harbor. No matter how you connect the names, you're certain to find a great place to hang your flip-flops.

The Gulf Beaches

Driving along Gulf Boulevard, you'll find it hard to discern one beach community from the next. They slam one to another, and if you miss the small markers, you won't know exactly which town you're in. It doesn't matter, though, since they all share the white-powder beaches and warm, friendly waters of the Gulf of Mexico.

Condominiums are the residences of choice from Sand Key to Indian Rocks and Indian Shores, selling between $40,000 and $400,000. You may be able to find a single-family home at Redington Shores, Redington Beach or Madeira Beach, priced from $80,000 inland to $900,000 on the Gulf of Mexico.

New and hot in North Redington Shores is The Tides Beach Club. On the quarter-mile, Gulf-front site of the former Tides, one of Florida's first luxury beach resorts, The Club will boast a 6,000-square-foot clubhouse with swimming pool and veranda, not to mention private beach cabanas with concierge service for the residents. Six Mediterranean-style buildings are planned, with prices from $190,000 to more than $500,000. Perhaps not quite as new and posh, but always a hotbed of activity, check out Clearwater Beach or Treasure Island, where homes start around $200,000 and can top out as high as $1.5 million.

St. Pete Beach

This 7-mile beach is now officially known as St. Pete Beach, having shortened its name from the original St. Petersburg Beach. An ever-popular tourist destination, it is landmarked by the gorgeous "pink palace," the Don CeSar Beach Resort & Spa. Tiny Pass-A-Grille at the southern tip is one of the most popular beach destinations. With true nostalgic Key West ambiance, it is only a few blocks wide in most places and is embraced by the Gulf of Mexico to the west and Boca Ciega Bay to the east. For the pleasure of residency, a small duplex will start at around $130,000. For that same price and on up to about $300,000, you may choose to live on the adjacent Intracoastal island of Vina Del Mar.

Tierra Verde

Not until the sands were dredged from Boca Ciega Bay and bridges were linked did Tierra Verde make its mark as a primo residential community. Home to luxury dwelling aficionados from as far away as Holland, Germany, England and Malaysia, the island is the foundation for elegant waterfront mansions, many with European architectural flavor. When homes are available for resale, your piggybank should be stuffed with about a half-million before you plan your move.

Who's Selling

Real Estate Companies

Here's the scenario. If you lived in Tampa Bay and had your home on the market in the past year, your front yard might have suffered from a whirlwind of ever-changing sign displays. You confidently listed your home with the oldline firm of Marie Powell & Associates/Better Homes and Gardens. Before you could say "open house," Marie Powell was bought by the huge South Florida firm of Gimelstob Realty Inc. Then, before you could learn to spell Gimelstob, men were yanking up your still shiny For Sale sign and replacing it with the Coldwell Banker banner. If you thought you were safe listing your home with Tam-Bay Realty, the oldest independent real estate firm in the region, ha! Even Tam-Bay fell to Coldwell Banker's charms, surrendering all 10 offices and more than 300 agents to the hungry real estate giant. Even Bobby Byrd Real Estate, the venerable beach property guru, could not resist acquisition overtures. And no one will dare predict whether Coldwell Banker's feeding frenzy is over.

With all that is happening, we obviously can't play favorites here. There are still so many competent real estate companies with so many knowledgable sales associates that it would be lunacy to steer you in one direction or an-

INSIDERS' TIP

Splish-splash! Nothing cools the spirit like a dip in your own backyard pool. At last count, Pinellas County had 40,000 residential in-ground swimming pools, and Hillsborough had 33,000.

Photo: Bradenton Herald

The calm Gulf waters delight watersports enthusiasts of all ages.

other. If you're relocating from another area of the country, a good, safe start would be to ask for a referral from your hometown Realtor, who should be able to advise you on an affiliate or member of their relocation network in the Tampa Bay region.

It is wise to remember that, while most local real estate professionals do have an excellent grasp of the entire community (not to mention Multiple Listing Services), most specialize in specific areas such as Carrollwood or South Tampa, Gulf Beach properties or Countryside in the Pinellas. Most of the larger companies have satellite offices in each neighborhood, so if you're driving around an area that looks particularly inviting to you, just look over your shoulder for a real estate office.

With that said, here is an abbreviated directory of the major local firms serving the Tampa Bay area, with main office/relocation phone numbers only. For complete listings of the offices of these and all the national companies — ERA, Century 21 and RE/MAX, for instance — we humbly suggest the GTE Yellow Pages of the appropriate county.

Coldwell Banker
Hillsborough/Pinellas • (800) 624-5292

As we just explained, the real estate world let out a collective gasp in late1997 and early 1998 when NRT Inc., the corporate giant that owns Coldwell Banker, went on a buying spree and purchased Bobby Byrd Real Estate, Gimelstob Realty Inc./Better Home and Gardens (which had just acquired Marie Powell & Associates) and Tam-Bay Realty, the area's oldest independent firm. While no one is exactly sure whether the dust has completely settled, it is certain that Coldwell Banker, which specializes in residential real estate, has zoomed to the No. 1 spot on our real estate landscape. At last count, the combined troops numbered more than 1,600 agents manning more than 48 offices scattered throughout the West Central Florida region. To understand exactly how big this new and improved Coldwell Banker is, consider a combined sales volume of more than $1.8 billion.

Plumlee Gulf Beach Realty
417 First St., Indian Rocks Beach
• (727) 595-7586, (800) 521-7586

Take three generations of real estate bro-

INSIDERS' TIP

The U.S. Census Bureau predicts newcomers to Florida will make the state the third largest in the United States by the year 2015.

kers, plant them on the Gulf and you've got the inside track for the people who really know the scoop on beach properties. Specializing in sales and rentals of condominiums, Pat Plumlee and her son, Todd, are following in her parents' footsteps, finding that perfect second home for clients and then managing the rental of the property when the owners head back north. As active in the community as in her profession, Pat keeps a sharp eye over her team of a dozen agents, all who live right here on the beach from Sand Key to Madeira Beach. A favorite vacation resource for European visitors, you can call toll-free from Germany, ASIT 013816782, and from the United Kingdom and Scotland, 0-800-96-8094, to reserve your place in the sun.

Prudential Florida Realty
Hillsborough • (813) 689-8102
Pinellas • (727) 442-4111

Going by the numbers, Prudential Florida Realty is Tampa Bay's second largest Realtor presence, with 23 offices throughout both Hillsborough and Pinellas counties. With more than 600 full-time agents and a 1996 sales volume of an astounding $932 million, there's no doubt that the "rock" can deliver the homes of your dreams.

Smith & Associates Investment Co., Realtors
Hillsborough • (813) 839-3800

While it has only two offices in the Tampa Bay area, the power of Smith & Associates and its 75 agents is not to be underestimated. It's supported by a 1996 sales volume of $180 million and is the exclusive affiliate of Sotheby's International Realty in the Tampa Bay market. Legend has it that when the company was founded, different colors were painted on the "for sale" signs to test their endurance against the blazing Florida sun. Orange won, and it's still the firm's flagship color.

ERA–The Polo Group
Hillsborough County • (813) 962-1177

No, we are not talking designer real estate. We're talking about a legion of more than 85 proven sales associates under the watch-

ful eye of Mario Polo, president of this ERA affiliate. Operating out of refurbished offices in the Carrollwood area of Tampa (the old offices were extensively damaged by fire in late 1994), the organization serves the entire Bay area with great professionalism and Polo pride.

Barbara Realty
Hillsborough • (813) 933-1761

Sales associates affiliated with Barbara Realty are part of an elite group of career professionals hand-selected by former broker/owner Barbara Wilcox, a well-known civic leader. Now under the leadership of Jeanette Yates, the 30-plus agents proudly represent properties in Hillsborough, eastern Pinellas and south Pasco counties.

The Toni Everett Company
Hillsborough • (813) 839-5000

If you can't live another day without a posh south Tampa address, throw yourself on the steps of The Toni Everett Company. Respected for their representation of some of the most exclusive upscale properties, the 30-plus agents who carry out President Toni Everett's mission of superior service are well-known for their industry expertise and area knowledge.

Murphy–Matthews & Associates
Hillsborough • (813) 931-5300
Pinellas • (727) 343-1230

Biggest is not always the best, and that's certainly the case with Murphy-Matthews, a venerable, old-line force in fine properties throughout the region. Because of its exceptional property management division, this is the firm to contact if you'd rather lease a fine property before you buy.

The Rental Scene

The Tampa Bay area is a renter's delight. Not only will you be able to find everything from townhomes and condominiums to waterfront estates on the rental roles, but you'll also have no difficulty in seeking out an apartment. Wherever you decide to rent, a security deposit of one or two month's rent is usually required, whether you lease seasonally or for a full year.

If you're of the pioneer spirit and are dead set on doing the search on your own, be sure to pick up the free publication called *The Greater Bay Area Apartment Guide* at any Circle K or 7-Eleven. It will give you a complete description of the multitude of choices available in the region.

For assistance in locating an apartment complex that fits the bill, give the following services a buzz.

The Apartment Store
(813) 960-7000

The Apartment Store is like a shopping mecca for those in search of the perfect fit in apartment living. The service is free, and they can supply you with maps, brochures and other detailed info to help you make your decision.

Real Estate Review Inc.
Apartment Locator
(813) 289-9794

Representing 500 communities throughout the greater Tampa Bay area, Apartment Locator can help steer you to the complex that best matches your criteria for size, location and amenities.

The National Accessible
Apartment Clearinghouse
(800) 421-1221

For those residents who require accessible housing, there's also help at the other end of the line. The National Accessible Apartment Clearinghouse is a valuable information service that has identified more than 65 local communities that offer accessible housing for the physically challenged.

In the Tampa Bay area, strong teacher commitment and parental involvement are the cornerstones to the schools' successes.

Education

With more than a million and a half people in the Tampa Bay metropolitan area, it's not surprising that the public school system is augmented by hundreds of private schools. And it's not surprising that universities, colleges and junior colleges make their homes here. What is surprising is the vast range of educational pursuits available in the area.

Florida is often listed as a state where the public education system needs improvement, but when you take a look at the Hillsborough and Pinellas schools, you understand why companies often cite quality of education as a factor in choosing to locate here. In higher learning, adults have an incredible array of choices — from a top-notch medical school at the University of South Florida to the alternative Chinese medical arts, from outstanding liberal arts programs at the University of Tampa to a "distant learning" theological school and the United States campus of an international university.

In Pinellas County alone there are nearly 90 private and parochial schools. It would take a book as thick as this to completely describe all the public and private schools, continuing education and specialty programs available around the Bay area. So what we've tried to provide here is a comprehensive overview of educational offerings.

Public Schools

Hillsborough County

The Hillsborough County School Board operates 150 regular public schools. Total enrollment of more than 152,000 makes this the third largest school system in the state and 12th largest in the nation. But as this Insider's old choir teacher used to say, it's quality, not quantity, that counts. And Hillsborough County knows quality — ACT and SAT scores for the county beat both the state and national averages.

The downside of these statistics is that county growth has outstripped capacity at many schools. New facilities are going up as fast as the local budget allows, but not nearly fast enough. The upside is that those new facilities are state of the educational arts.

The newest is Orange Grove Middle School for the Arts, a magnet school in Ybor City focused toward visual and performing arts as well as communications technology. It's assumed that many Orange Grove students will move onto Howard Blake High School, a magnet school for the performing arts now in its second year. While a large number of the high school's students are drawn from its neighborhood near downtown Tampa, thousands of students vie for special placement in the arts program. Tryouts as rigorous as for any Broadway production are required, and you can bet these kids have excellent performing abilities in addition to academic skills. For those students interested in pursuing the written arts, Tampa Bay Tech has added a journalism program to its current curriculum that also includes health professions and engineering technologies.

A much older school, H.B. Plant High School on Himes Avenue, is possibly the most highly recognized for its students' academic achievements. Ninety-seven percent of Plant's students pass both the math and communications sections of the High School Competency Test, considerably higher than both district and state percentages. Excellence is evident in extracurricular activities as well: Plant's varsity cheerleaders recently made history when they won their third consecutive national division title at the Western Conference Championship, and the girls' cross-country coach is one of the tops in the state. Plant was named in June 1998 as a Blue Ribbon School of Excellence by the U.S. Department of Education; this was the second time it's been awarded that distinction (the first was in 1990).

But the list of educational brain-power is long. Broward Elementary, in one of Tampa's poorer neighborhoods, proves that money isn't the most important factor behind good education. Broward, which made *Redbook*'s fourth annual list of best schools is the nation, has also been named a U.S. Department of Education Blue Ribbon School and is Florida's only National Global Education Pilot School. Forest Hills Elementary teacher Lynn McDaniel is the only teacher in the country who's won the Time Warner Inc. Crystal Apple award for two consecutive years. At the middle school level, Woodrow Wilson Middle School, which is also the oldest junior high in Tampa, is the only school serving 6th through 8th graders in the state to be named a national Blue Ribbon School by the U.S. Department of Education.

Strong teacher commitment and parental involvement are the cornerstones of such successes. There's also a challenge to be innovative, as indicated by Durant High School, which opened at the start of the 1995-96 academic year. It was one of the first high schools in the nation to use the Copernican Plan of class scheduling. Here, students have four 90-minute classes each day, rather than six 60-minute classes. So instead of accruing six credits during a school year, Durant's students can earn eight credits. And this means they can qualify for graduation in just three years. Results from the plan's first year were encouraging enough that Brandon and Robinson high schools adopted the format the following year.

Magnet schools offer a different focus on learning, with six such specialized programs in Hillsborough County and more planned for next year. Presently, students can enroll at magnet centers oriented toward technology

www.insiders.com

See this and many other **Insiders' Guide®** destinations online — in their entirety.

Visit us today!

and computers, the International Baccalaureate program and a health academy.

And five charter schools, which are publicly financed but privately operated, are now open to students. The first to open was The Richardson Academy at 3807 Swann Avenue, South Tampa, (813) 879-5088. Using Montessori methods, the school serves a small group of children in kindergarten and 1st grade, plus a handful of preschoolers.

The Hillsborough County Public School offices are at 901 E. Kennedy Boulevard in Tampa. Here are special numbers to note:

Information Switchboard, (813) 272-4000;
Superintendent's Office, (813) 272-4050;
Boundaries, (813) 272-4096;
Athletics, (813) 272-4587;
Exceptional Student Education,
(813) 273-7000;
Early Childhood Learning Center,
 (813) 805-6180;
Head Start, (813) 805-6073;
Magnet Programs, (813) 272-4818;
Technical/Career and Adult Education,
(813) 276-5654.

Pinellas County

When you combine overall reading, writing and math scores, Pinellas elementary and middle schools come up tops in the Tampa Bay area. All of the county's schools received the Florida Golden School Award in the same year for outstanding community involvement programs. Plus, college-bound students score higher than the national average on both verbal and math portions of the SAT.

To serve more than 106,000 students in grades K through 12, the Pinellas system operates 158 schools — 82 elementary, 23 middle and 16 high schools plus five exceptional education centers, two disciplinary cen-

---

INSIDERS' TIP

Within the next 10 years, the number of Florida high school graduates enrolling in college is expected to increase by 40 percent.

ters, 29 alternative programs and one charter school. This is the Academy DaVinci in Dunedin, where elementary education in the performing arts serves students in grades 1 through 5. In addition, there are three community schools, one adult-education center, a secondary vocational center and two technical education centers, plus two evening adult high schools.

Pinellas teachers and students have taken on and succeeded in such a variety of challenges that we can name only a few. At Bardmoor Elementary, one teacher was chosen as a United States citizen-ambassador to Russia, and another was selected to visit the People's Republic of China. Safety Harbor Elementary students earned state and national recognition for a recycling project. The math team from Skycrest Elementary placed in the top-20 percent during a recent National Math Olympiad against 33 countries. Tarpon Springs Elementary is one of 25 designated butterfly sanctuaries in the state. Westgate Elementary is a state model school for math, science and technology. And students at Bay Point and Perkins elementary schools are able to study a foreign language — these are the only two county elementary schools to include the study of a second language in the curriculum.

At Boca Ciega High, students can accelerate their high school career and attend year round to graduate in three years, rather than four. Countryside's English and journalism teacher was one of four in the nation named as a Distinguished Adviser by the Dow Jones Newspaper Fund. Osceola High was named to the *Redbook* magazine Outstanding High School Programs, while Lakewood High was recognized earlier by *Redbook* in its America's Best Schools Project.

With more than a dozen different magnet programs, Pinellas students have a range of studies to pursue. Among them are Lakewood's Center for Advanced Technologies, which earned third-place honors at a recent Department of Energy Science Bowl, and Pinellas Park High Criminal Justice Academy, which works hand-in-hand with Stetson University College of Law and the Criminal Justice Institute at St. Petersburg Junior College.

The Pinellas County Schools offices are at 301 Fourth Street S.W., Largo 34640. Here are telephone numbers to note:

Information Switchboard, (727) 588-6297;
Superintendent's Office, (727) 588-6011;
Boundaries, (727) 588-6210;
Magnet Programs, (727) 588-6432;
Exceptional Student Education,
(727) 588-6042;
Technical/Career and Adult Education,
(727) 588-6009;
Homework Helpline, (727) 442-3226 or
(727) 547-7223.

Private Schools

Hillsborough County

Academy of the Holy Names
3319 Bayshore Blvd., Tampa
• **(813) 839-5371**

At this Blue Ribbon School, classes for grades 1 through 8 are coed, while the high school is the area's only Catholic all-girl educational program. Primary, middle and high school classes are held on separate but co-joined campuses with common recreational areas, which foster interaction between kids of all ages. Family participation is a strong focus at the Academy, with such annual activities as a family canoe trip, father-daughter luncheon, father-son picnic and Grandparents Mass. Acceptance is based on screening or testing results.

Bayshore Christian School
3909 S. MacDill Ave., Tampa
• **(813) 839-4297**

An interdenominational school founded in 1971 as a ministry of Bayshore United Methodist Church, this school attracts students in grades K through 12 from Hillsborough, Pinellas and Polk counties. The largest percentage of its students come from Methodist, Baptist and Catholic homes, and daily Bible classes and weekly chapel services are provided. Its top-quality educational offering is reflected in the fact that the 1997 graduating class of 32 students was offered $500,000 in college scholarships. Extended care for younger students is available year round from 7 AM until 6 PM.

Berkeley Preparatory School
4811 Kelly Rd., Tampa • (813) 885-1673

This coed, Episcopalian, independent day school has an enrollment of more than 900 students in pre-kindergarten through 12th grades. Computer skills are important here, with training starting in kindergarten. Foreign language is also emphasized — Spanish classes start in pre-kindergarten, and all 6th graders study both French and Latin. Recent classes have included a Presidential Scholar, a member of the U.S. Physics Team, All-American volleyball players and award-winning actors and actresses. On the faculty are a published poet, an actress, a lawyer, an Olympic swimmer, several university professors, former military officers and a conductor for the Tampa Bay Opera.

The Hebrew Academy
14908 Pennington Rd., Tampa
• (813) 963-0706

The Hebrew Academy provides classes for toddlers and elementary-age children, with a 6-to-1 ratio of students-to-teacher. The day school curriculum combines a modified Montessori program with both secular and Judaic studies. An extended-care program is available, offering music, art, creative movement, dramatics and storytelling as well as unstructured play.

Hillel School
2020 W. Fletcher Ave., Tampa
• (813) 963-2242

For nearly three decades, Hillel has served the area with a strong academic curriculum complemented by comprehensive Judaic studies. With nearly 200 children in kindergarten through 8th grade, the earliest program is a transitional kindergarten, which helps prepare 4- and 5-year-olds for elementary education. Hebrew language study begins in pre-kindergarten, with Spanish added in 5th grade. Students in 6th, 7th and 8th grades attend class at the Wuliger Middle School on the main campus in Carrollwood.

Jesuit High School
4701 N. Himes Ave., Tampa
• (813) 877-5344

Established in 1899 as Sacred Heart College, Jesuit is a private Catholic school for young men in 9th through 12th grades. Students are required to volunteer service to the community, which may be one reason so many Jesuit grads mature into local business and political leaders. All students are encouraged to participate in at least one of the 10 interscholastic sports. *Baseball America* magazine ranked the school's team No. 1 after it won the Class 4A state championship last year, and the football team is known as a powerhouse. While theology is part of the curriculum, Jesuit attracts students of all religions and races with its reputation for excellent education. The school has a financial assistance program that offers limited support to a significant number of the students. Classes start in mid-August and finish at the end of May.

St. John's Parish Day School
906 S. Orleans Ave., Tampa
• (813) 259-1091

"A parish school is not a private school. It must be as public as the parish church that operates it." So states the student/parent handbook of this school operated by St. John's Episcopal Church in Tampa's Hyde Park. Children ages 4 through 14 attend "forms," which correspond to grades from pre-kindergarten through 8th. Limited enrollment makes early application an absolute necessity — the school keeps two waiting lists, one for siblings of present students and parishioners' children, a second for all other children. Some financial aid is available, but the school strives to keep tuition affordable to encourage a fairly wide socioeconomic cross-section of the community.

St. Mary's Episcopal Day School
2101 S. Hubert Ave., Tampa
• (813) 258-5508

Low student-to-teacher ratios ensure individual attention for 400 students in pre-kindergarten through 8th grades. St. Mary's is known for a strong academic curriculum, which includes computers and Spanish for all students. Students in 6th, 7th and 8th grades contribute to the community by volunteering with such diverse groups as the American Heart Association and Meals On Wheels. Parents get into the act, too — they're invited to attend weekly chapel with their children and regularly assist teachers with enrichment activities.

St. Peter Claver
1401 Governor St., Tampa
• (813) 224-0865

Since 1894, St. Peter Claver's purpose has been to educate Tampa's African-American Catholic children. But the majority of the 115 students in kindergarten through 5th grade are drawn from all religions, because the school is highly regarded by parents for its emphasis on personal morality and discipline as well as education. Students wear uniforms, and the school year runs concurrent with the public school schedule. Extended-care hours begin at 7 AM, and an after-school program is available from 3 until 6 PM. During the summer, a six-week program is offered.

Tampa Baptist Academy
300 E. Sligh Ave., Tampa
• (813) 238-3229

As a ministry of the Tampa Baptist Church, the staff and faculty of the Baptist Academy see their responsibility as providing a balance of experiences — spiritual, intellectual, social, emotional and physical — to children. The school is accredited by the Association of Christian Schools International, which requires member schools to meet rigorous academic and Christian standards. It is the only Christian organization to which the National Honors Society will grant new charters. Day care and preschool is available for children between the ages of 6 weeks and 4 years. There's also an after-school program for students through the 8th grade. Elementary, middle and high school classes include Bible study as well as an integration of the Bible within all subject areas. Registration fees are based on four different dates, so the earlier a child is registered, the more the fee is discounted.

Tampa Catholic High School
4630 N. Rome Ave., Tampa
• (813) 870-0860

Tampa's only coeducational, diocesan high school is administered by the Congregation of Christian Brothers, which holds a highly regarded, 200-year reputation for education. Fully accredited by the Congregation of Christian Brothers, three integrated academic programs are offered. Honors, college prep and general programs are available to the approximately

600 students, as are more than 20 religious, service and social extracurricular clubs, organizations and sports (including one bruiser of a football team). And, yes, uniforms are the rule.

Tampa Preparatory School
625 North Blvd., Tampa • (813) 251-8481

This nondenominational, coed, independent day school for students in 7th through 12th grades is actually on the grounds of the University of Tampa. Classes for the 450 students are taught as seminars, labs and lectures with 12 to 16 students in each class. Sports are a major component of the school — more than 90 percent of the students play on at least one of the 42 teams offered. Tampa Prep has won nine Girls Volleyball State Championships, and the 1994 Boys Basketball team was the state's Team of the Year. This is also the only area school with an interscholastic crew team. The administration stresses that no student should hesitate to apply because of limited finances because aid is available.

Pinellas County

Admiral Farragut Academy
501 Park St. N., St. Petersburg
• (727) 384-5500

Uniforms are a usual part of the private school experience, but instead of plaid and navy blue, here it's Navy — and education on the water is as much a part of the curriculum as academics. Dual enrollment courses allow students to earn college credits while working on their high school diplomas, and the school boasts that 100 percent of its graduates are accepted to colleges and universities. Both girls and boys between 5th and 12th grades are admitted to this boarding and day school. Summer cruises aboard U.S. Navy vessels are offered to students older than 14, and an off-campus flight instruction program is available as a special activity. Among the academy's graduates are two of the 12 men who have walked on the moon.

Shorecrest Preparatory School
5101 First St. N.E., St. Petersburg
• (727) 522-2111

Founded in 1923, this college-prep program for 870 students is the state's oldest coed independent day school. On the 28-acre campus is an early childhood center, a lower school for students in kindergarten through 6th grade, middle school for grades 7 and 8 and upper school for grades 9 through 12. After-school programs and a month-long summer camp program are available for children ages 3 through 12.

Brighton Preparatory School
5330 Central Ave., St. Petersburg
• (727) 327-1454

This oak-shaded school in the heart of downtown provides a coed program for students in elementary and middle school grades. Along with the fundamentals and foreign languages, the school takes advantage of its location to expose students to museums and stage productions. The versatile physical education program includes such activities as bowling, tennis, horseback riding and sailing.

Central Christian School
4824 Second Ave. S., St. Petersburg
• (727) 321-3700

No need to buy "Hooked on Phonics" when your kids are enrolled here. Central Christian's reading/language program sticks to the basics, as do the math, science and social studies courses, with hands-on programs intended to teach children to think. The detailed registration form gets down to such specifics as the child's individual interests, eating habits and how well he or she sleeps. In addition to the registration and tuition fees, something called a "consumable" fee is charged. Preschoolers may be enrolled for half-days or full days on a two-day, three-day or five-day schedule. An after-school program is also offered.

St. Paul's Catholic School
1900 12th St. N., St. Petersburg
• (727) 823-6144

Opened in 1930, St. Paul's is staffed by the Franciscan Sisters of Allegheny, New York, and is accredited by the Committee of the Florida Catholic Conference. Its 300 students in kindergarten through 8th grades include children of all races and religions. A half-day, pre-kindergarten program is available. Children bring their lunches, but on Monday,

Wednesday and Friday the noon meal may be purchased. Each student's family provides 25 hours of volunteer service to the school during the year.

St. Cecelia Interparochial School
400 Hillcrest Ave., Clearwater
• (727) 461-1200

Fully accredited by the Florida Catholic Conference, St. Cecelia's recently celebrated its 50th anniversary. More than 770 students attend grades kindergarten through 8 for a strong program of academics and extracurricular activities, including sports teams for both boys and girls during middle school. One-way and round-trip bus service is available, so transportation shouldn't be a deterrent to attending.

Clearwater Central Catholic High School
2750 Haines Bayshore Blvd., Clearwater
• (727) 530-1513

This nationally recognized school of excellence has more than 600 students in grades 9 through 12. With programs running the gamut from the basics to special needs, from foreign language to computer technology, the focus here is on developing the whole human being — both physically and spiritually. A textbook buy-back program gives students discounts during each succeeding year of attendance.

Colleges and Universities

Hillsborough County

University of South Florida
4202 E. Fowler Ave., Tampa
• (813) 974-2011

Once known as "Suntan U," the University of South Florida (USF) is putting that sobriquet to rest as one of the country's 20 largest universities. USF has five campuses throughout West Central Florida serving more than 35,000 students — the main campus is in Tampa, with auxiliary campuses in St. Petersburg, Sarasota, Fort Myers and Lakeland. Still think commuting or attending lectures isn't convenient? Then plug into university lectures cybercast over the Internet.

More than 70 Fulbright Scholars are members of USF faculty, and many others are internationally recognized for their work. To name just a couple, Jacob Neusner, a graduate research professor, is an internationally known Judaic scholar, and Hank Hine is an art publisher and scholar who came from Stanford University to direct USF's highly regarded Graphicstudio. Graphicstudio produces the work of artists such as Robert Rauschenberg, William Burroughs, Roy Lichtenstein and James Rosenquist, and more than 300 of its editions are permanently archived at the National Gallery of Art in Washington, D.C.

The Sun Dome, home to the USF Bulls nationally ranked basketball team, is also a popular venue for shows ranging from adopted son Jimmy Buffett to heavy-metal bands. And for the very first time ever, the 1998 class had its own football team to cheer.

One of USF's newest programs is a satellite office for students pursuing their MBAs. Evening classes meet at the MetLife Insurance building on Boy Scout Boulevard, eliminating a long cross-town drive for a lot of folks after a full day at the office.

University of Tampa
401 W. Kennedy Blvd., Tampa
• (813) 253-3333

The 13 silver minarets of the old Tampa Bay Hotel, which first housed international multi-millionaires and even Teddy Roosevelt and his Rough Riders, are now the campus centerpiece of this private college which boasts enrollment of nearly 3,000. The school's semi-annual literary magazine, *Tampa Review*, is a national leader in its field and received the 1995 Phoenix Award for "significant editorial achievement."

On the sciences side, more than 80 percent of the premed students are accepted to medical school, while 97 percent of the school's graduates in chemistry, biology and marine science/chemistry are accepted to grad programs and granted stipends. Other study choices include a College of Business, a School of Continuing Studies, Military Science and a Graduate Program. Though football is

only a fond memory, baseball is still mighty hot at the site where Babe Ruth signed his very first contract — UT's Spartans started its 1997 season ranked No. 1 in the *Baseball America* national poll.

Embry-Riddle Aeronautical University
MacDill AFB, Tampa • (813) 840-0111

Embry-Riddle is the only fully accredited, nonprofit university in the world that is totally oriented to the aviation/aerospace profession. Military and civilian students pursue associate, bachelor's and master's degrees in classes meeting once a week, usually in the evening, for nine-week terms. Admission to the degree programs requires a high school diploma, evidence of specialized aviation skills and knowledge gained from experience and training in an eligible aviation occupation. As many as 36 semester hours of credit may be granted for previous technical and nontechnical learning. This is one of more than 100 campus locations throughout the United States and Europe.

Faith Theological Seminary & Christian College
7302 Sheldon Rd., Tampa
• (813) 886-8492

Here, the concentration for undergraduates and postgraduates is on disciplines pertaining to the ministry. Four schools comprise the college: Theology and Bible Studies, Christian Counseling, Music Ministry and Church Business Administration. Students who have not graduated high school or earned an equivalency certificate, and those who audit courses at a discounted cost, may earn certificates of completion.

Florida College
119 N. Glen Arven Ave., Temple Terrace
• (813) 988-5131

For more than 50 years, this accredited school has provided two-year degree programs. Associate of Arts degrees can be earned in areas ranging from art and drama to teacher training, prelaw and premed. Bible courses are required for the approximately 400 students, and on-campus housing is mandatory for all unmarried students younger than 21 who do not live locally with a close relative.

Hillsborough Community College

39 Columbia Dr., Tampa
• (813) 253-7000

The largest of its campuses is on Dale Mabry Highway in Tampa, but Hillsborough Community College (HCC) makes education convenient for nearly 50,000 students with campuses in Ybor City, Plant City and Brandon, plus telecourses on WEDU-PBS and cable's Educational Channel.

The college's associate in science degree programs cover more than 40 fields. The nursing program here is consistently ranked as one of the best in the Southeast.

HCC is one of the few community colleges in Florida to feature more women's sports teams than men's. Women can go out for tennis, basketball, volleyball and softball, but guys can only choose between basketball and baseball. The New York Yankees new spring training complex adjacent to the Dale Mabry campus includes a community-use field that's also the home ballpark of the HCC Hawks.

Pinellas County

Eckerd College

4200 54th Ave. S., St. Petersburg
• (727) 867-1166

Eckerd is a private, coed, four-year school for liberal arts and sciences, in covenant to the Presbyterian Church. Founded in 1958, the school has more than 1,400 students from around the United States and 55 foreign countries. A degree course for adults requiring scheduling flexibility is offered through the Program for Experienced Learners.

Possibly the most unique aspect of Eckerd College is the Academy of Senior Professionals, in which retired professionals volunteer as mentors, career advisers and lecturers. In fact, this program was cited as the main reason Eckerd college was ranked by *U.S. News & World Report* as one of the five most innovative colleges in the country. There is also a highly regarded marine science program, which draws nearly 40 percent of incoming freshmen who have identified it as their major. Students are offered opportunities to study in Europe, Asia, Central America and many other locations

around the world. The college also is an approved Elderhostel site.

Florida Institute of Technology

9549 Koger Blvd., Ste. 109, St. Petersburg • (727) 576-4474

Postgraduate business courses are offered in a format allowing students to work around employment schedules while advancing their education at this fully accredited, independent university. Several of the institute's programs, including contracts, human resources management and health administration, are unique in the area. Today, more than 40 areas of study are offered in 23 degree programs. Also, noncredit courses are available to students seeking professional development.

St. Petersburg Junior College

8580 66th St. N., Pinellas Park
• (727) 341-3600

St. Petersburg Junior College offers more than 40 associate of science degree programs in a variety of subjects ranging from aviation technology to respiratory care. Founded in 1927, the school has grown to several campus locations in St. Petersburg plus one in Clearwater and another in Tarpon Springs.

St. Petersburg Theological Seminary

6550 Mango Ave. S., St. Petersburg
• (727) 399-0276

This interdenominational college prepares men and women for leadership and lay roles in Christian churches and schools. Both undergraduate and postgraduate courses are offered in theology, Bible, apologetics, Hebrew, Greek, Judaic studies, church history, Biblical counseling, religious education and sacred music. An extension campus is at 3909 S. MacDill Avenue in Tampa, (813) 835-1311.

Stetson University College of Law

1401 61st St. S., St. Petersburg
• (727) 562-7800

Good lawyers know not to ask a question they don't already have the answer to. And Stetson, Florida's first law school, is the answer to this: What's the best trial and appellate advocacy school in the nation? *U.S. News & World Report* studied 177 law colleges and

Photo: Bradenton Herald

Even youngsters quickly learn the rewards of fishing in the Gulf waters.

decided that Stetson University makes a better case for quality than even Temple or Georgetown (ranked as second and third). Stetson's undergraduate program is on the state's East Coast, but the Pinellas campus serves more than 600 law students. The 21-acre campus was built in the 1920s as a luxury hotel resort, and the roof tiles, originally from monasteries and other structures in Spain, are estimated to be 400 years old.

Clearwater Christian College
3400 Gulf-to-Bay Blvd., Clearwater
• **(727) 726-1153**

Evangelism, patriotism and scholarship have been the cornerstone here for more than 30 years. Clearwater Christian is a four-year, fundamental, liberal arts, coed college with areas of study in the church, business, education and the arts.

Schiller International University
452 Edgewater Dr., Dunedin
• **(727) 736-5082**

Eight campuses in six nations comprise this truly international university. First founded in Germany as an American college, the Dunedin campus is the only one in the United States. The emphasis here is on business and international relations. All students are required to have a second language and are encouraged to take courses at other school campuses while pursuing their four-year degrees.

Alternative Education

Baywinds Learning Centres
722 E. Fletcher Ave., Tampa
• **(813) 977-0996**

This isn't so much a school as it is a place where people who have something to share meet with people who want to learn it. Don't expect college or continuing education credits — just sign up for the fun of expanding your mind and social connections. The "education"

is definitely eclectic. You can take an intro course on fly-fish casting or enjoy a two-day canoe trip through Florida's 10,000 Islands. Learn to fence, take line-dancing or in-line skating lessons. Study Buddhist philosophy or blackjack, craps and roulette. Brush up on your grammar. Learn to write grants. Find 101 fun and exciting things to do in the Bay area. Study investment strategy. Discover alternative careers for nurses. Take computer classes. Weave a shawl. Delve into the father-daughter relationship. These aren't ongoing courses — most are one-shot classes that are held a few times each quarter. Give the school a call and ask for a copy of its free, quarterly catalog.

International Academy of Merchandising & Design
5225 Memorial Hwy., Tampa
• **(813) 881-0007**

With campuses in Chicago, Montreal, Toronto and Tampa, this school offers associate's degrees in fashion design, merchandising management and advertising design, and communications, plus a bachelor of fine arts in interior design. Tampa's interior design program is accredited by The Foundation for Interior Design Education Research, and the academy is accredited as a senior college.

Annapolis Sailing School
6800 34th St. S., St. Petersburg
• **(727) 867-8102, (800) 237-0795**

This is the Florida branch of the nation's first — and still the biggest — sailing school. With the largest fleet of instructional boats in the world, this is the only sailing school able to conduct live-aboard cruise courses. A broad spectrum of courses suit the needs of beginners and advanced sailors. On-board classes in the basic courses are limited to a maximum of four students per boat. Advanced auxiliary courses cover sailing techniques of handling larger craft. Students as young as 12 years old are accepted into beginner's

INSIDERS' TIP

For more than a decade, Hillsborough County schools have graduated more students identified as Florida Academic Scholars than any other county in the state.

courses, with 16 the recommended age for advanced classes.

Center For The Arts
100 Seventh St. S., St. Petersburg
• **(727) 822-7872**

What started out in 1964 as a place for local artists to gather, collaborate and share techniques has grown into a city- and state-funded organization that includes children's classes and weekend workshops. Courses also provide college credit through Eckerd College's Program for Experienced Learners. Along with drawing and painting, classes include mixed media, clay and jewelry. Members of the Arts Center receive discounted tuition and the opportunity to exhibit their works.

Florida Institute of Tradition. Chinese Medicine
5355 66th St. N., St. Petersburg
• **(813) 546-6565**

Westerners are finally paying more attention to the very different but highly effective medical treatments developed during 5,000 years of Chinese practice. The goal here is to integrate the methods of both Far Eastern and Western disciplines in a three-year educational program. The school was founded in 1986 by Su Liang Ku, who was one of the first acupuncturists to practice in the United States and who has held a number of high positions in state and national professional organizations. Applicants must have a minimum of two years of college or post-secondary education.

As far as independently operated child-care facilities go, one flip through the Yellow Pages can bring you to total confusion about where to start your search.

Child Care

There is nothing more precious to the future of a community than the nurturing of its children. Here around Tampa Bay, we take that responsibility very seriously and have exceptional watchdogs for our children's safety and protection in both the public and private sectors.

In today's economy, it is rare to find a household with a full-time mom. The same holds true for the Tampa Bay area, where you're more likely to see mom in early morning gridlock on the way to the office than wheeling the kiddies to the playground. And, while we must be vigilant in selecting the people who will care for our children while we work, it's comforting to know that there are professionals equally as vigilant watching out for our children, too. Indeed, child care is one of the most highly regulated small businesses in the state of Florida.

Pinellas County leads the state in its steadfast commitment to children. In 1961, the county was one of the first in the entire state to pass a law requiring child-care regulations, the purpose of which is to protect the health, safety and mental development of children cared for in children's centers and family day-care homes. Since that year, Pinellas County has been a national model in establishing new and tougher standards for child care. In fact, the state child-care law enacted in Florida in 1974 used the Pinellas law as its model. Today, the Pinellas County License Board oversees the actions of 390 child-care centers and about 1,100 licensed family day-care homes.

In Hillsborough County, Hillsborough County Child Care Licensing monitors the guardians charged with the care of our children. Like Pinellas, Hillsborough licensing requirements are stricter than those of the State of Florida, with regulations that cover no less than 85 different areas, including health and safety, personnel background, accommodations and facility practices. And as of July 1,

1995, for every 20 children in a licensed child-care facility, one caregiver in the facility must have a Child Development Associate (CDA) credential or a Child Care Professional credential. To earn a CDA, a nationally recognized credential in early childhood education, a candidate must go through rigorous training, including 120 hours of classroom training and 480 on-the-job hours.

The corporate world also is attuned to the child-care needs of Tampa Bay residents. Many major employers in our area have developed corporate child-care centers to attract new employees and to boost productivity. Salomon Brothers, Honeywell, Barnett Bank, Moffit Cancer Center, Martin Marietta, Bayfront Medical Center, Tampa General Hospital and University Hospital are among the many leaders in providing on-site child care. Office complex developers and property managers see a child-care facility as a lure to attract and keep large tenants. The Wilson Company is the innovator in this area, having recruited a daycare center for the Carillon Office Park more than nine years ago. The Gingerbread School at Carillon serves as the daytime home for children of tenant companies such as Raymond James & Associates, Allstate and Xerox Corporation, all of whom are given priority and discounted rates at this independently owned and operated office park facility.

When neither the corporate or development sector are there to help, businesses sometimes find ways of their own to provide for daily child care. Take, for instance the Westshore Alliance Partnership School, an ambitious partnering of the Westshore Alliance (an organization of Westshore area businesses), the City of Tampa and Hillsborough County Schools. In a facility purchased by the Alliance, children of the more than 70,000 Westshore area employees are cared for close to their parent's place of business, with a teacher and aide from the school district on board to direct the on-site kindergarten. The project, which began in 1992, has grown in stature, reputation and enrollment, today serving 240 youngsters in its day-care and school programs. It has been so successful, the school district has recently proposed the reopening of a former educational facility as a new elementary school to accommodate the long waiting list of young students.

And finally, the education community has seen the light — Hillsborough Community College has introduced an innovative child-care proposition for students hailing from Tampa's "Enterprise" zone in and around Ybor City. In exchange for 20 hours of free parenting training, HCC agrees to have Creative World School haul the little tykes away for fun and games while mommy or daddy works toward a degree.

As far as independently operated child-care facilities go, one flip through the Yellow Pages can bring you to total confusion about where to start your search. Along with the well-known chains such as Kinder-Care, Montessori schools and La Petite Academy, there's page after page of smaller day-care facilities, church-sponsored centers and private home care options — with as many options and services offered, including bilingual curriculum, computer training, gymnastics and even horseback riding.

To help you with your search, here are the agencies and organizations that can streamline your first journey into Tampa Bay's child-care arena. Take advantage of their knowledge and willingness to assist you in finding a safe, stimulating environment for your child. The sooner you start, the sooner you'll have a response to the age-old question, "Are we there yet?"

Resources

Hillsborough County Child Care Licensing Program

County Center, 24th Floor, 601 Kennedy Blvd., Tampa • (813) 272-6487

Working in partnership with the early childcare and education community, the Child Care Licensing Program oversees a broad spectrum of activities that serve to support the highest quality child-care programs. It sponsors training programs, offers technical assistance to providers, produces quarterly newsletters and enforces uniform child-care standards throughout Hillsborough County. Of special interest to parents just entering the wild and wonderful world of child care are the files the office maintains on every licensed center and private home in the county. They are readily available for your review from 8 AM until 5 PM Monday through Friday at the Child Care Licensing Office.

Pinellas County License Board for Children's Centers and Family Day Care Homes

6698 68th Ave. N., Pinellas Park
• (727) 547-5800
2451 Enterprise Rd., Clearwater
• (727) 725-9778

Like its sister agency in Hillsborough County, the Pinellas County License Board is your major referral source for all your childcare questions in Pinellas County. Whether you need background information on the providers you are considering, have a special-needs child or want assistance in obtaining

www.insiders.com
See this and many other Insiders' Guide® destinations online — in their entirety.
Visit us today!

INSIDERS' TIP

If your child is home alone in the afternoon and needs something — help with homework, an idea for an activity to pass the time or advice about a problem or concern — there's a friend waiting on the end of the line at PhoneFriend, a free service sponsored by Northside Mental Hospital in Tampa. Volunteers are on duty from 2:30 until 5:30 PM and are specially trained to deal with children's concerns. Post the number, (813) 681-6543, by the phone for your child.

before- or after-school care, preschool or infant care, a child-care specialist is as close as your phone. If you are very early in your search, the board can even mail or fax you a list of licensed centers that meet your specifications within a certain zip code, say near your home or workplace. It is also charged with the responsibility of providing training and technical assistance for day-care providers and monitoring the USDA Child Care Food Program for family day-care homes.

PITCH Child and Family Center
Nova Southeastern Univ., 1408 Westshore Blvd., Tampa
• **(813) 288-9547**

Founded in Ft. Lauderdale in 1969 by Dr. Marilyn Segal, The Family Center at Nova Southeastern University opened its Tampa Bay satellite in 1991. The Family Center offers a variety of parent-child classes, focusing on infant awareness (birth to 12 months), toddlers (12 to 24 months) and explorers (2 to 3 years of age). The center's training team includes early childhood and family support specialists with advanced degrees and decades of experience serving young families. They serve caregivers, too, through training classes and their H.E.L.P. line, which offers both phone and on-site assistance to the directors of child-care facilities on subjects ranging from room arrangements to developing positive parent relationships. The H.E.L.P. line can be reached through the number listed above.

Partners In Care
Children's Services Center, 707 E. Columbus Dr., Tampa • (813) 805-6210, (888) FL-CHILD

Child Care Resource and Referral–Partners In Care is a service for parents, caregivers and the community at large. Counselors are there to provide valuable information on child-care centers, family child-care homes, preschool centers, before- and after-school programs, camps and babysitting. Parents can receive information on funding for child-care and tax credits for child care, as well as current legislative issues and child-care organizations. Caregivers are assisted with a Toy/Resource Lending Library and training and technical assistance, and businesses can consult with the organization

concerning child-care options or speakers for meetings and programs.

Latch Key Kid Assist
The Legend Group
4111 Helena St. N.E., St. Petersburg
• **(727) 527-2464**

If your children are old enough to be left at home for a short while before you get home from work, but just not old enough for you not to worry about their safety, the Latch Key Kid Assist program is your security blanket. Its message/response service works like this: Prerecorded messages (by you or Latch Key Kids personnel) are phoned to your child at preset times, as many as three times a day. The child is instructed to press "1" if everything's OK or "0" if they need help. Prerecorded reminders such as "It's 4 PM — time for homework" can also be placed. Your message can be changed as often as you wish, and the small monthly cost is negligible in context of the peace of mind it can offer.

The Ultimate Child Care Solution: Nannies and Au Pairs

Just imagine: No more worries about before- or after-school care; someone there to help watch your scattering brood on the beach or at the mall; help with the mounting diaper pile and scrubbing behind the ears at bath time. All this may sound too good to be true, but it's a reality in many Tampa Bay homes. It's called a "nanny."

Nannies are not just glorified babysitters. They're trained professionals who, for about $200 to $225 a week, will move right into your home and assume total responsibility for the loving care and feeding of your children. Through A Choice Nanny, a Tampa-based agency that matches American nannies and parents, both prospective nannies and their potential employers are rigorously interviewed to ensure compatibility. Credit and criminal background checks are handled by the agency, which also requires first aid and CPR training of its placement participants. While the up-front fee for this service is hefty — from $1,000 to $1,500 — it brings the peace of mind of knowing that the person responsible for the nurturing of your children has squeaky-clean references and unblemished experience.

A Choice Nanny also acts as the local representative for the Au Pair Programme USA, one of eight agencies authorized by the federal government to bring caregivers into the States from other countries. Young women, from countries such as England, Denmark, Ireland, Spain and Greenland, who join the au pair program, are usually between 18 and 26 years old and are allowed to enter and stay in the United States for only one year on a student visa. While they perform basically the same duties as a nanny, their work week is limited to 45 hours versus a 50- to 60-hour work week for a nanny.

Although all the paperwork is handled out of the au pair agency in Salt Lake City, A Choice Nanny is there to greet the au pair on arrival in Tampa Bay, familiarize her with the region and introduce her to other au pairs in the area. All au pairs are required to speak fluent English, be in good health and have prior child-care experience. Prospective employers are responsible for paying the au pair's airfare and visa, as well as providing healthcare and weekly pocket money of $115. The family must also supply a separate bedroom for the au pair's accommodations. The initial cost, including all referral fees, can average $3,000.

So, if your household could use a little order, and you have a bedroom to spare, consider bringing an American nanny or au pair into your family unit. For all the tempting details, call A Choice Nanny, a franchise of the International Nanny Association, (813) 254-8687.

Day Care When Your Child is Sick

If your child is sick and can't attend the regular day-care center, the following places are there to fill in.

While in a hospital environment, they do look like normal day-care facilities with toys, books and other mind-stimulating activities. They have limited spaces, so you must call ahead, and remember to bring up-to-date immunization records with you. All are staffed and supervised by licensed nurses and pro-

fessional caregivers, and meals and snacks are provided.

KIDCare
Tampa General Hospital, 2 Columbia Dr., Tampa • (813) 251-7192

Thirty-five spaces are available and the center operates from 5:30 AM until 7 PM Monday through Friday. They will not accept children with communicable diseases such as chicken pox, measles or mumps. Fees are $2.50 to $3.50 an hour on a sliding scale based on income.

Rainbow Recovery
Morton Plant Hospital, 323 Jeffords St., Clearwater • (727) 462-7831

Operating Monday through Friday from 6 AM until 6 PM, Rainbow Recovery has spaces for 18 children. It will accept children with chicken pox and other communicable diseases including colds and gastro illnesses. Hourly cost is $3.

Caring For Your Special Child

Parents of kids with special needs, whether with a physical or mental disability, will be relieved to know that there are the widest variety of facilities, organizations and support groups to help you provide the finest in treatment and care for your child. The following are the first places you should turn to discover exceptional people who understand the challenges facing parents raising special children. If you need special assistance to locate specific services that might be available to your child and your family, you can call Children's Medical Services at (813) 805-6210 or the Parent Resource Organization (PRO) at (813) 949-5898.

All Children's Hospital
801 Sixth St. S., St. Petersburg • (727) 892-6726

All Children's Hospital is responsible for early identification of at-risk children in Pinellas and Pasco counties. In addition to its pediatric cancer program, which is one of the largest in the Southeast, the hospital offers the Developmental Evaluation and Intervention Program (DEI), a federal- and state-funded program that ensures early diagnosis of developmental delays in children from birth to 3 years of age. Its much applauded Family Support Plan Process is a program that includes the entire family in a multidisciplinary evaluation.

All Children's Specialty Care of Tampa
12220 Bruce B. Downs Blvd., Tampa
• **(813) 631-5000**

An outreach of All Children's Hospital, this clinical facility offers outpatient services for youngsters with speech, language and hearing difficulties who need occupational or physical therapy and those who have learning, emotional and behavior problems. Operating in cooperation with the USF College of Medicine and the Moffit Cancer Center and Research Institute, the center is open Monday through Friday by appointment.

Tampa General Rehabilitation Center Pediatric Team Davis Islands
2 Columbia Dr., Tampa • **(813) 253-4415**

The TGH Pediatric Therapy Team operates an outpatient clinic devoted to the treatment of children requiring speech/language therapy, and occupational and physical therapy for fine, perceptual and gross motor development. There are also special teams for Cleft Lip and Palate and Cranial-Facial problems. TGH has a Children's Daycare Center (CDC) funded by the Easter Seal program, which serves primarily as a developmental pre-school for employees of Tampa General, along with special-needs kids. The center was a 1997 recipient of the National Easter Seal Society Excellence in Programs Innovations Award.

Julianne Rock Early Intervention Center
2401 E. Henry Ave., Tampa
• **(813) 236-5589**

Children with conditions such as spina bifida, Down's syndrome, cerebral palsy, cystic fibrosis, birth defects, hearing impairments, developmental delays and victims of accidents or abuse find loving care at this center operated by the Easter Seal Society. The program offers full-day developmental training for these children, including physical, speech and occupation therapy provided on an individual basis. Family support and counseling services are also offered.

Easter Seals was recently tapped by the Hillsborough County School Board to provide day care for potentially at-risk children of teenage mothers. In January 1997, Teen Parent/Infant Centers were opened at both MacFarlane Park School in Tampa and Burney Simmons School in Plant City to provide high quality day care so teen mothers could stay in school while learning important parenting skills.

Lean on Me ... Parent Support Groups

Tampa Bay is really a big bunch of groupies ... support groupies, that is. Here's a basic, streamlined list of some of the most active parents' support groups that meet around the area. Please feel free to contact the group that meets your special needs to confirm meeting locations, specific days and times.

Parents Network, Hillsborough County
St. Joseph's Hospital, 3003 W. Dr. Martin Luther King Jr. Blvd., Tampa
• **(813) 870-4666**

Parents of newborns to 4-year-olds meet bimonthly in Classroom 1 at St. Joseph's Hospital Medical Arts Building. The network sponsors special events and weekly play groups. If you call ahead, arrangements will be made for child care during the meetings.

Parents Network, Pinellas County
Step Ahead, 7754 66th St. N., Pinellas Park • **(727) 531-2091**
Grace Lutheran Church, 1812 N. Highland Ave., Clearwater
• **(727) 531-2091**

Parents can share their child-rearing concerns with other parents on Mondays in Pinellas Park and Tuesdays in Clearwater. The Network also maintains a 24-hour Parent Helpline, (800) 352-5683.

Sick children are treated with special care at Tampa Bay area day-care centers.

St. Petersburg Parents of Twins and Supertwins
Church of Christ Annex, 6045 Park Blvd., Pinellas Park • (727) 527-0721, (727) 381-6706

Multiple births can mean multiple joy — and headaches. Share your tips and solutions the fourth Monday of every month with parents who can truly understand your situation.

Upper Pinellas Parents of Twins and Triplets
Mease Hospital, 601 Main St., Dunedin • (727) 538-2750

Commiserate with other parents of twins and triplets on the fourth Monday of every month. Also enjoy other activities, in addition to playgroups scheduled throughout the month.

Parents Anonymous/ Parents Network
Various churches in Tampa and Plant City • (813) 251-8080

Parents concerned about losing control while dealing with their children find support and guidance every Monday at various churches in both Tampa and Plant City. Child care is provided. To find out the meeting location nearest you, call the Child Abuse Council at the number listed above.

After Baby: Transition to Parenthood
Morton Plant Hospital's Women's Center, Bay Ave. and Pinellas St., Clearwater • (727) 462-7504

This group for postpartum adjustment for new parents meets the second and fourth Tuesdays of each month.

La Leche League
This nationally known organization that recognizes the needs of nursing mothers meets monthly throughout both Hillsborough and Pinellas counties. Nursing babies are welcome at all meetings and activities sponsored by the League. Find the most active groups in:

Tampa, Temple Terrace, Brandon, various locations, (813) 932-3664;

Clearwater East Library, 2251 Drew Street, Clearwater, (727) 585-6666;

Palm Harbor Library, 2330 Nebraska Avenue, Palm Harbor, (727) 937-1569;

St. Bartholemew's Episcopal Church, 3747 34th Street S., St. Petersburg, (727) 398-6956;

Pinellas Square Mall Community Room, 7200 U.S. Highway 19 N., Pinellas Park, (727) 321-3342.

Windmills
All Children's Hospital, 33 Sixth St. S., St. Petersburg • (727) 892-4403

Parents with children who have special needs meet the third Thursday of each month at All Children's Hospital Center for Child Development. Group meetings are held on the third floor of the center.

Young Mothers' League Inc.

Young mothers unite monthly to share common concerns and highlights and sponsor play groups in Pinellas County. Call the League nearest you for specific information:

St. Petersburg, various locations, (727) 528-1632;

First Church of the Nazarene, 1875 Nursery Road, Clearwater, (727) 797-0056;

Seminole Hospital and Women's Center, 9675 Seminole Boulevard, Seminole, (727) 398-6871.

MOMS Club of North Pinellas
North City Park, 2075 Swan Ln., Safety Harbor • (727) 725-4679
St. Alfred's Church, 1601 Curlew Rd., Palm Harbor • (727) 725-4679

This very active support group is for stay-at-home moms. The Safety Harbor group meets every second Wednesday, and the Palm Harbor group meets on the second and fourth Tuesdays of every month. Special play groups and activities are sponsored throughout the year.

Rest assured, the medical services available here in the Tampa Bay area are among the best in the country.

Healthcare

If you or a loved one is bleeding profusely, swelled up with bug bites or infection, suffering heat stroke or heart attack, put this book down right now and dial 911. Within a few swift moments, you'll be in the caring hands of outstanding emergency medical services personnel and receiving top-notch medical care.

OK, now that we're sure no one's near dying, you'd just like to know where to go and who to call in case a problem does arise, right? Rest assured, the medical services available here in the Tampa Bay area are among the best in the country.

In fact, Tampa General Hospital is nationally recognized for its regional burn unit and Level 1 Trauma Center, which is staffed by trauma specialists certified to handle the most difficult life-threatening injuries. With more than 50 hospitals in the region, there's one near you, where you can count on receiving TLC along with the latest technology and treatment.

Hospitals

Hillsborough County

Cancer Care Center
2715 W. Virginia Ave., Tampa
• (813) 877-2273
The medical staff and radiation specialists at the Cancer Care Center are committed to combining advanced technological resources with emotional support and sensitivity. As a freestanding, outpatient radiation-therapy facility, the center focuses on providing comfortable surroundings to help alleviate the tension and intimidation usually associated with oncological treatment.

H. Lee Moffitt Cancer Center
12902 Magnolia Dr., Tampa
• (813) 972-4673
The mission here is to contribute to the prevention and cure of cancer — and the work is so highly respected that the center received a prestigious National Cancer Institute research grant. Since it is one of only 57 hospitals in the nation to receive such a grant, it makes Tampa one of only two places in the state offering outpatients the newest radiation pellet treatment for prostate cancer. The Moffitt campus, on the grounds of the University of South Florida, is supported by the teaching and research activities of the USF Health Sciences Center. The six-level hospital houses both patient-care services and clinical research. With 162 beds, it includes two special-care units and a bone marrow transplant unit. The Moffitt Research Center also is a site for future basic science research and a comprehensive screening program.

James A. Haley Veterans' Hospital
13000 Bruce B. Downs Blvd., Tampa
• (813) 972-2000
Military veterans in Central Florida receive outstanding care here, as evidenced by the

INSIDERS' TIP

Tampa General Hospital made news in 1996 that had a national effect on healthcare for new moms. The hospital's then-president Fred Karl grabbed some control back from health insurance companies with a program that allowed any new mother to stay up to an additional 48 hours at absolutely no charge. This was the impetus which led the federal government to require insurance companies pay for longer maternity hospital stays.

hospital's earning the Robert W. Carey Quality Award in recognition of staff accomplishments. Services at this 581-bed teaching hospital with 240 nursing home care beds include spinal cord injury services, comprehensive rehabilitation and radiation therapy. The hospital is responsible for two satellite outpatient clinics in the region plus readjustment counseling centers in Tampa and Orlando. The USF College of Medicine is affiliated with the hospital.

Memorial Hospital
2901 Swann Ave., Tampa
• (813) 873-6400

Sister to Town 'N Country Hospital on Webb Road, Memorial provides diagnostic, medical, surgical, psychiatric and home healthcare services. The emergency room is open 24 hours a day. The Women's Imaging Center offers mammography and ultrasound imaging, and the Memorial Rehab Center focuses on intensive care for those in cardiac or pulmonary rehabilitation programs. Other specialty services include clinics for sleep and memory disorders.

St. Joseph's Hospital
3001 W. Dr. Martin Luther King Jr. Blvd.,
Tampa • (813) 870-4000

Opened in 1934 by the Franciscan Sisters, St. Joseph's is a private, nonprofit healthcare provider. A 649-bed acute-care center, its Heart Institute is a national leader in preventing and treating heart disease in adults and children, while the Cancer Institute provides treatment, research, education and community screenings. Diagnosis, treatment and support programs for neurological injuries and disorders are handled through the Neuroscience Institute.

St. Joseph's Women's Hospital
3030 W. Dr. Martin Luther King Jr. Blvd.,
Tampa • (813) 879-4730

Across the street from St. Joseph's main medical complex is its Women's Hospital. As the Bay area's largest provider of healthcare services exclusively for women, the 234-bed specialty facility offers obstetrical, perinatal, gynecological and women's educational services. About 6,000 babies are born here every year, but what really put this place on the map was the birth of Elvis Presley's first grandbaby, born to the King's daughter, Lisa Marie.

Tampa Children's Hospital
3001 W. Dr. Martin Luther King Jr. Blvd.,
Tampa • (813) 870-4000

In March 1998, only 18 months after the children of Tampa's Children's Hospital at St. Joseph's broke ground on a "hospital of their own," the new facility opened its doors.

The 50,000-square-foot building, constructed on the east side of St. Joseph's Hospital campus, was designed with special features to meet the unique needs of Hillsborough County children and their families. The 76-bed hospital includes 50 private medical/surgical rooms in clusters with decentralized nursing stations, a 16-bed Level I Pediatric Intensive Care Unit and a 10-bed, day hospital for short-term observation.

The facility was designed to alleviate stress associated with a hospital stay for both child and parent. For example, children can enjoy many of the amenities of home, including computers, televisions and VCRs in their private rooms, and recreational opportunities are also scheduled. Parents are given full-length beds and allowed to sleep in the child's suite, and the Family Resource Center offers information to parents so they can learn more about their child's illness.

Shriners Hospital for Crippled Children
12502 N. Pine Dr., Tampa
• (813) 972-2250

The Tampa unit of this national network of 22 hospitals and burn units is a pediatric orthopedic facility serving children primarily from Florida, southern Georgia and the Caribbean. Since opening in 1985, more than 14,000 youngsters between infancy and age 18 have been treated at this 60-bed facility. The mission of the Shriners organization, whose international headquarters is at 2900 Rocky Point

www.insiders.com

See this and many other **Insiders' Guide®** destinations online — in their entirety.

Visit us today!

Drive in Tampa, is to provide free, expert medical care for children and emotional support for their families.

Tampa General Hospital
2 Columbia Dr., Davis Islands, Tampa
• (813) 251-7000

Beginning in 1929 as a county-operated hospital, Tampa General now serves as a regional medical center with advanced cardiac care, rehabilitation services, oncology care, an acute burn center, a children's medical center and Level 1 Trauma Center plus two aeromed helicopters. Now a private, nonprofit facility, this 1,000-bed medical center and teaching hospital, affiliated with the USF College of Medicine, is considered the most comprehensive on Florida's west coast. Its burn center is one of four in the state, serving patients from the Caribbean and South America as well as the United States. The Rehabilitation Center is nationally known, especially among disabled athletes, for its wheelchair sports program.

Town 'N Country Hospital
6001 Webb Rd., Tampa • (813) 885-6666

Sister to Memorial Hospital on Swann Avenue, Town 'N Country Hospital offers a pediatric unit specially designed for children's comfort. The hospital's Florida Laser Center is a leader in minimally invasive surgery. This facility also boasts the area's only acute and chronic Hemodialysis Unit.

University Community Hospital
3100 E. Fletcher Ave., Tampa
• (813) 971-6000

An independent, nonprofit hospital, UCH includes the Pepin Heart Centre for treatment of cardiovascular disease and a Chest Pain ER (a specialty aspect of its 24-hour emergency room services), a Women's Center with advanced reproductive technologies programs and a pediatric care center decorated as a child-friendly "jungle land" designed by Busch Gardens. The hospital hosts a Senior Celebration event each spring and also operates Health Source, which provides community health education, wellness information, physician referral and screening services, at University Mall on E. Fowler Avenue.

University Community Hospital at Carrollwood
7171 N. Dale Mabry Hwy., Tampa
• (813) 932-2222

This 120-bed facility delivers general, surgical and medical care. Its Chest Pain ER (a special aspect of the 24-hour emergency room services) allows physicians to quickly diagnose if a person is having a heart attack.

U.S. Air Force 6th Medical Group
MacDill AFB, Tampa • (813) 828-5393

Full medical care here is for active-duty military personnel plus retired members of the armed services and their families. Surviving family members of deceased active or retired military personnel also qualify for treatment. The base hospital includes ob/gyn, internal medicine, orthopedics, surgery and physical therapy among its programs.

Columbia Brandon Hospital
119 Oakfield Dr., Brandon
• (813) 681-5551

Best known for its obstetrics services, this 255-bed, full-service hospital includes a massive Family Center. This is one of only three hospitals in the county that provides Level I, II and III Neonatal Intensive Care services. Columbia Brandon was one of the hospitals named in the *Top 100 Hospitals Benchmarks for Success* study.

South Florida Baptist Hospital
301 N. Alexander St., Plant City
• (813) 757-1200

This 132-bed acute-care facility offers a full range of medical, surgical and rehabilitative services. It also has a skilled nursing unit to care for patients in the transition phase between illness and recovery.

Columbia South Bay Medical Center
4016 S.R. 675, Sun City Center
• (813) 634-3301

With 112 beds, this is the only hospital serving a 25-mile radius in south Hillsborough and north Manatee counties. Services include family practice, internal medicine, gerontology, cardiology, oncology, orthopedics, gastroenterology, gynecology, general and thoracic surgery and pediatrics. A transitional-care unit provides rehabilitative services.

Pinellas County

All Children's Hospital
801 Sixth St. S., St. Petersburg
• **(727) 898-7451**

A wide range of specialized services makes All Children's a pediatric referral center for children from all over the nation and many foreign lands. From the most sophisticated medical equipment to the simple smiley-faced bandages, kids' special needs are kept in mind at this 216-bed hospital where more than 80,000 patients are treated each year. Parents are cared for, too; patient rooms have fold-out beds so they can spend the night. For extended-care needs of the family, the Suncoast Ronald McDonald House is right next door. As part of the Children's Miracle Network, All Children's holds a weekend telethon each June and has raised millions of dollars to expand facilities and maintain its leading edge in researching children's diseases. The hospital also operates a Speech, Language and Hearing Services facility and outpatient cancer care in space leased from the Moffitt Institute on the USF grounds.

Bayfront Medical Center
701 Sixth St. S., St. Petersburg
• **(727) 823-1234**

A private, nonprofit hospital, Bayfront is Pinellas County's oldest hospital and serves more than 150,000 patients each year; nearly 5,000 of them taking their first breath of life. With the county's only Trauma Center, Bayfront is equipped to handle even the most serious emergencies. Specially trained nurses and paramedics man Bayflite helicopter medical emergency flights. Family practice, obstetrics and gynecology, and pathology are affiliated with the USF College of Medicine. Bayfront is one of a handful of institutions advancing neuroscience from a solely diagnostic discipline to that of treatment and rehabilitation.

Bay Pines VA Medical Center
10,000 Bay Pines Blvd., St. Petersburg
• **(727) 398-6661**

With nearly 250,000 military veterans living in Hillsborough and Pinellas counties, the proximity of two veterans hospitals is important. Bay Pines provides acute medical and surgical services, neurologic and psychiatric care, a post-traumatic stress recovery unit, substance abuse treatment, nursing home care and long-term rehabilitation. Ongoing research programs in endocrinology and nephrology are unique to this center. Bay Pines VAMC is affiliated with the USF College of Medicine, the University of Florida College of Dentistry, the University of Houston College of Optometry, numerous other colleges and universities around the nation and five military reserve units. To reach the center, follow Tyrone Boulevard west; the road eventually changes names to Bay Pines Boulevard, and the facility is just before the bridge to Madeira Beach.

Columbia Edward White Hospital
2323 Ninth Ave. N., St. Petersburg
• **(727) 323-1111**

This facility bears the name of a man St. Petersburg is proud to claim as a native son — Lt. Col. Edward White, the first man to walk in space. Along with a fully staffed emergency room, the hospital offers an express care center for nonemergency medical attention without an appointment. Several centers of excellence are supported at the hospital. The Company Care Workers' Compensation Managed Care Arrangement includes a musculoskeletal

---

INSIDERS' TIP

It's the middle of the night and the baby is sick. What to do — wake the doctor? Rush to the ER? "All Children's On-Call" will help your peace of mind when urgent health problems arise with your kids. Call your pediatrician's answering service. A pediatric nurse specialist will call you right back and give you the advice you need.

clinic, occupational therapy and psychological services. The Chronic Pain Treatment Center is dedicated to providing relief for people who suffer from continuous pain. Special programs in the Rehabilitation Institute include hand therapy, swallow studies and stress-reduction training.

St. Anthony's Hospital
1200 Seventh Ave. N., St. Petersburg
• **(727) 825-1100**
Like Tampa's St. Joseph's, this 434-bed general and acute care, nonprofit facility was founded by the Franciscan Sisters. It delivers such programs and services as behavioral medicine, cancer care, cardiology (including a chest pain center in the hospital's emergency room), diabetes, fitness, home care and health promotion. St. Anthony's vascular rehabilitation program was the first in the Southeast to provide an education and exercise program for people suffering from peripheral vascular diseases. A full-service treatment center for HIV patients is operated in conjuction with the Pinellas County Health Department.

Columbia Largo Medical Center
201 14th St. S.W., Largo
• **(727) 588-5200**
Largo Medical Center, which has been nationally recognized for outstanding care, provides such services as the Center for Heart and Circulatory Care, a cancer treatment center, occupational health services and home care. Columbia Largo also operates two outpatient surgery centers and four walk-in Family Care Centers in Clearwater, Largo and Seminole.

Columbia Northside Medical Center
6000 49th St. N., St. Petersburg
• **(727) 521-4411**
This hospital handles specialties such as critical, intensive and neurointensive care, car-

diology, orthopedics, pain management, rehabilitative services and programs specifically designed for the needs of senior adults.

Columbia Clearwater Community Hospital
1521 E. Druid Rd., Clearwater
• **(727) 447-4571**
This Columbia facility offers a free program called Canadian Advantage for winter visitors from the northernmost part of our continent. Just present your Canadian health card along with traveling or private insurance. Also, a Seniors Club Medical program is free for year-round residents. A range of medical and surgical services is available, including 24-hour emergency care, same-day and laser surgery, home health, skilled nursing, home infusion and respiratory care.

Palms of Pasadena Hospital
1501 Pasadena Ave. S., St. Petersburg
• **(727) 381-1000**
Palms of Pasadena offers care and treatment in a wide range of medical specialties, including critical care, orthopedics, cardiology, general and laser surgery, gynecology, sports medicine, ostomy surgery and pulmonary medicine. Palms also operates the Florida Fatigue Center. The emergency center is staffed around the clock.

Columbia St. Petersburg Medical Center
6500 38th Ave. N., St. Petersburg
• **(727) 384-1414**
This 219-bed acute-care hospital provides services in a wide array of specialties. The 24-hour emergency department includes pediatric emergency care. An incontinence diagnostic clinic, chronic pain management, a skilled nursing unit and a geriatric psychiatry center are also on premises. Unique to the area is the hospital's Wound Care Center, dedicated

---

INSIDERS' TIP

Bayfront Medical Center researchers are first in the nation to conduct tests on a new drug which may help prevent heart attacks. Called xemilofiban, doctors hope it will prevent a first heart attack in much the same way a daily dose of aspirin helps prevent a second one.

to caring for people whose wounds resist healing due to diabetes, poor circulation, surgery or an accident.

Morton Plant Mease Hospitals
323 Jeffords St., Clearwater
• (727) 462-7000
3231 McMullen Booth Rd., Safety Harbor
• (727) 725-6111
U.S. Hwy. 19 N., Palm Harbor
• (727) 462-7000
601 Main St., Dunedin • (727) 733-1111

Mease and Morton Plant hospitals entered into an unusual partnership a few years ago after state and federal regulators turned down a request for complete consolidation. While both facilities retain independence, some of the operations, as well as the name, are combined. The entire range of services is too extensive to detail, but of special note is that Morton Plant Hospital is one of only 20 cardiac-care specialty units in the nation. Its Women's Center was nationally honored as an Outstanding Comprehensive Women's Center. The Neuroscience Orthopedic Center is among the top in the nation in joint replacement surgery for people older than 65. A Bed & Breakfast program is available for patients' families, such as those at the women's center, the Joslin Center for Diabetes, the heart and vascular center and the psychiatric center.

Healthsouth Rehabilitation Hospital
901 Clearwater Largo Rd., Largo
• (727) 586-2999

Devoted exclusively to rehab programs, both inpatient and outpatient services are offered, ranging from medical intervention to family counseling, nutrition and behavior therapy. Physician referral is required.

Columbia University General Hospital
10200 Seminole Blvd., Seminole
• (727) 397-5511

This 140-bed teaching hospital provides complete general medical and surgical care. Free transportation is available for physician office visits, hospital admission and discharge, outpatient services and spouse visits. The hospital also has a bloodless medicine and surgery program, especially to serve Jehovah's Witnesses and others whose religious or medical preferences eschew transfusions.

Helen Ellis Memorial Hospital
1395 S. Pinellas Ave., Tarpon Springs
• (813) 942-5000

A patient services tower stands eight stories high, and the birthcenter is at the pinnacle. What an astounding first view newborns must enjoy here! The tower also houses inpatient facilities for general medical and surgical care, plus an outpatient center. The Watermark Center for Pain Treatment is a dedicated facility within the hospital for treatment of chronic pain. A walk-in care unit serves as an alternative to the hospital emergency room when immediate treatment is required but not critical.

Mental Health Centers

Charter Behavioral Health System of Tampa Bay
4004 N. Riverside Dr., Tampa
• (813) 238-8671
12891 Seminole Blvd., Largo
• (727) 587-6000
12895 Seminole Blvd., Largo
• (727) 587-1010

Now with three hospitals and nine clinics in the area, plus two other hospitals in the greater region, Charter delivers outpatient programs and counseling, partial hospitalization (a treatment plan allowing some patients to leave the hospital during certain periods of the day, such as to attend school), 24-hour assessment and referral and emphasis on prevention of mental illnesses through education and early treatment. Specialized programs target care and treatment of children, adolescents, adults and senior adults.

Northside Mental Health Hospital
12512 Bruce B. Downs Blvd., Tampa
• (813) 977-8700

Outpatient counseling is available here for individuals and families. There is an alternative residential treatment program for adults, as well as hospitalization for adolescents and adults. Alternatives to hospitalization through social and vocational rehabilitation programs are offered in addition to in-home crisis intervention and stabilization programs. Family seminars on such

Photo: St. Petersburg/Clearwater Area Convention & Visitors Bureau

Wonderful weather year round helps support a healthy,
active lifestyle in the Tampa Bay area.

subjects as parenting infants and toddlers, single parenting, life after separation or divorce and successful step-parenting are offered in evening programs throughout the year.

Fairwinds Treatment Center
1569 Ft. Harrison Ave. S., Clearwater
• (727) 449-0300

This is a multifaceted center for individuals needing treatment for emotional, psychological or interpersonal troubles or chemical dependency. Adolescent and adult care is offered on three levels at the 30-bed residential facility. Intensive outpatient service and an aftercare program also are provided.

Boley Centers for Behavioral Health Care
1236 Dr. Martin Luther King Jr. St. N., St. Petersburg • (727) 821-4819

For more than a quarter-century, Boley Centers has developed a multifaceted program encompassing supervised residential living, medication management and activities to improve skills. Residents of Pinellas and Pasco counties who are older than age 18, and have a mental illness or significant emotional problems, may qualify. A Youth Employability Program, an alternative school and job training and placement program, is available for young adults between ages 16 and 21 who have

INSIDERS' TIP

Nontraditional practices can often enhance Western medical treatment. The clinic at the Florida Institute of Traditional Chinese Medicine, 5335 66th Street N., St. Petersburg, (727) 544-0987, provides treatments for a wide variety of illnesses and injuries through herbal and acupuncture care.

dropped out of school or are at risk of doing so. Overall services include continuous day treatment, intensive psychiatric rehabilitation, independent living, a drop-in center, partial hospitalization and outpatient psychiatric care.

Special Services

Florida Spine Institute
2250 Drew St., Clearwater
• **(727) 797-7463**

Here at the nation's largest spine center, specialists range from orthopedic spine surgeons to physiatrists who help people get relief from neck and back problems.

Hospice of the Florida Suncoast
300 E. Bay Dr., Largo • (727) 586-4432

Working to meet the needs and desires of both patients and families, Hospice offers a variety of programs for Pinellas County patients. Among them are children's support, counseling and support groups for the bereaved, a caregiver program and a nursing home program. Jewish patients and families are assured that rituals specifically prescribed by religious tradition are followed, and the hospice will assist in locating a rabbi if the family doesn't have one during a time of crisis.

LifePath Hospice
3010 W. Azeele St., Tampa
• **(813) 877-2200**
1501 La Jolla Ave., Sun City Center
• **(813) 634-7621**

Patients and their families who are dealing with life-limiting diseases can turn to this nonprofit organization for supportive care. With help from Hospice, patients are able to live their lives out comfortably at home rather than in an institution. This fully accredited group provides physical, emotional and spiritual services for people of all ages who live with a variety of diagnoses, including cancer, heart, lung and liver disease, kidney failure, AIDS, Alzheimer's and other illnesses.

Transitional Hospital of Tampa
4801 N. Howard Ave., Tampa
• **(813) 874-7575**

This 102-bed specialty hospital provides intensive, long-term critical care for patients suffering from catastrophic illnesses or acute-level chronic diseases. Patients are referred when the severity and complexity of their conditions precludes acceptance at a rehabilitation hospital, subacute unit or skilled nursing facility.

Vencor Hospital
4555 S. Manhattan Ave., Tampa
• **(813) 839-6341**

This small facility is devoted exclusively to people dealing with catastrophic illnesses and complex body system failures. Patients here are more acutely ill than average ICU patients and require long-term care and treatment.

Physician Referral Services

If you're seeking a new doctor, every hospital in both Hillsborough and Pinellas counties provides a physician referral service. Just call a nearby hospital's main number and they'll connect you to someone who'll help. Or, if you prefer, call one of these numbers:

Hillsborough County Medical Association, (813) 253-0471

Pinellas Medical Society, (727) 541-1159

If you'd like to find a chiropractor, here's who to call:

Hillsborough County Chiropractic Society, (813) 881-1400

INSIDERS' TIP

Good Housekeeping **magazine's 1997 list of "401 Best Doctors for Women" included three Tampa practitioners — doctors Ronald Chez, William Spellacy and Denis Cavanaugh. Dr. Cavanaugh specializes in gynecologic oncology, while Dr. Chez and Dr. Spellacy are both specialists in maternal and fetal medicine. All are affiliated with Tampa General Hospital.**

Medical and Emergency Numbers

Hillsborough County

Alcoholics Anonymous, (813) 933-9123
Al-Anon/Al-Ateen, (813) 889-4544
Ask A Nurse, (813) 870-4444
Abuse Hotline, (800) 962-2873
AIDS Hotline, (800) 352-AIDS
Alzheimer's Helpline, (813) 578-2558
American Cancer Society, (813) 254-3630
American Red Cross, (813) 251-0921
Child Abuse Council Inc., (813) 673-4646
Crisis Center of Hillsborough County Inc.,
(813) 238-8411; 24-hour Hotline,
(813) 234-1234
Dental Society, (813) 931-3018
Eldermed Clinic, (813) 237-6988
Hillsborough County Medical Assoc.,
(813) 253-0471
Hotline of Hillsborough County Inc.,
(813) 234-1234
Narcotics Anonymous, (800) 234-0420
Poison Control, (813) 253-4444

Project Recovery, (813) 251-8437
Spousal Abuse Hotline, (813) 247-7233

Pinellas County

Abuse Hotline, (727) 464-4878
AIDS Community Project of Tampa Bay,
(727) 898-3705
Alcoholics Anonymous, (727) 530-0415
Al-Anon/Al-Ateen, (727) 786-0120
American Red Cross Tampa Bay
Suncoast Chapter, (727) 898-3111
Alzheimer's Hotline, (800) 229-2872
Crisis Center, (727) 344-5555
Dental Association, (727) 321-4850
Family Resources Inc. Helpline,
(727) 344-5555
Family Service Center Inc., (727) 535-9811
Narcotics Anonymous, (727) 547-0444
Neighborly Senior Services,
(727) 573-9444
Operation PAR Inc., (727) 570-5080
Pinellas Emergency Mental Health
Services, (727) 541-4628
Pinellas County Medical Society,
(727) 541-1159
Poison Control, (800) 282-3171

Hidden in the millions of bona fide tourists is a hearty variety of migratory population that arrives not just for a week's worth of fun in the sun, but for a stay of up to six months.

Retirement

Picture this. You wake up at the crack of dawn, hustle into your tennies and head out for an invigorating morning walk. The whole day lies ahead — no deadlines, no bosses, no meetings, no racing the clock. So, you're off to tennis, to slip in 18 holes of golf, to stroll through the newest museum opening or perhaps to join your volunteer group for a planning session. You have a light dinner, take in a stimulating concert or theater performance and then settle in for a grand night's sleep. No, honey, this isn't paradise. It's retirement in Tampa Bay.

From 1985 to 1990, 320,000 senior adults saw the writing on the wall, and it spelled "Florida!" Nearly 70,000 of those numbers found their way to our own Gulf Coast communities, with Pinellas County as the promised land of choice. Our wonderful climate definitely has much claim to the magnetism, but credit must be given to the affordable housing, agreeable tax rate and exceptional network of services that await those empty-nesters seeking new lives along our beaches and within our vibrant neighborhoods.

We're ready for you, too, offering opportunities to spread your wings and learn new sports, new languages and new ways to become involved with the community. The Florida Chamber of Commerce reports that there are more than 600,000 adults enrolled in adult education and college courses across the state. If you want to go to college here in Florida, there is nothing to stop you but your own fear of cafeteria food. That's because anyone age 60 years and older can attend any state university class free of charge(if it has room) through the state's tuition waiver program. Locally, there are two institutions that offer special courses for seniors. In Tampa, call The Learning in Retirement Institute at the University of South Florida at (813) 974-2403; in Pinellas, call The Academy of Senior Professionals at Eckerd College in St. Petersburg at (727) 864-8834.

The picture is just as rosy on the volunteer side of your new take-it-easy lifestyle. A study by the state Department of Elder Affairs revealed that between July 1994 and June 1995, about 36,640 people donated more than 4 million hours helping older people, with the vast majority of those volunteers being older people. Statistics also show that local charitable organizations are more likely to find themselves flush with volunteers during the months of October through April or May. While this may seem strange to newcomers, longtime Insiders know the reason … the elusive senior species tagged "snowbirds."

For decades, the Tampa Bay region has found a swelling population during those months when northern weather motivates an escape to a more pleasant climate like ours. Hidden in the millions of bona fide tourists is a hearty variety of migratory population that arrives not just for a week's worth of fun in the sun, but for a stay of up to six months. A study recently completed by the University of Florida's Bureau of Economic and Business Research reveals some amazing statistics about these elusive snowbirds. They are 92 percent white, 66.7 percent married, 71 percent retired, 66.4 percent age 55 or older and, because they can afford to maintain a home up north as well as a residence here in the Bay area, have financial nests that are obviously very well-feathered. While we locals tolerate the snowbird's affinity for slow driving, mall flocking and swarming over every golf course in town, we certainly appreciate the contributions they make in their annual southern flight. It is the snowbirds who swell the ranks of our senior volunteer community and contribute heartily to our retail economic base.

So, whether you're here for a half-year escape or a newcomer just about to enter retirement paradise, Tampa Bay welcomes you. If you choose to embrace an active, fully independent routine, require continuing care or seek any level of senior care in between, you'll not have to look far to find the housing, services or support group that matches your needs. From AARP to the Elder Helpline in both Pinellas and Hillsborough counties, referrals for services and programs are as close as your phone.

www.insiders.com

See this and many other **Insiders' Guide®** destinations online — in their entirety.

Visit us today!

Community Care for the Elderly, (813) 272-5242, provides support services in the home for frail or functionally impaired residents ages 60 and older; Elder Helpline, (813) 273-3779, is a central telephone number to gain assistance in locating services available throughout Hillsborough County, and calls are answered by friendly operators familiar with programs specific to senior adults. If a caller to this free helpline should need multiple services, a case manager is always there for personalized attention. Homemaker Services, (813) 272-5934, provides housekeeping services to frail, low-income seniors ages 60 and older. Participants are chosen according to need and income qualifications.

Senior Services and Agencies

What do you need to know? Need tips on nutrition or a good direction for volunteer work? How about employment opportunities or where to take a class on improving your golf game? When it's answers you're after, the first place to start is your telephone. Standing by on the other end of the line are truly helpful professionals and volunteers who can steer you on the right path.

American Association of Retired Persons (AARP)
6500 34th St., Pinellas Park
• **(727) 522-0531, (800) 456-2277**
The leading advocate for senior adults, AARP is a national nonprofit association dedicated to men and women ages 50 and older. It is a magnificent resource for publications and information about senior issues and programs in the Tampa Bay market.

Hillsborough County

The Department of Aging Services
601 E. Kennedy Blvd., Tampa
• **(813) 273-3779**
The Department of Aging Services offers a number of special programs designed to meet the needs of senior adults in our community.

Retired and Senior Volunteer Program (RSVP)
(813) 272-5031
This is the central clearinghouse for people ages 55 and older who wish to serve in nonprofit agencies such as hospitals, schools, libraries, nursing homes, museums and community centers. With more than 1,000 volunteers currently enlisted, this program helps match the volunteer's special talents and abilities to the organization that can best use them.

Senior Adult Day Care/ Senior Centers
(813) 272-6261
Adult day care is provided at six centers throughout Hillsborough County. These centers are open Monday through Friday from 8 AM until 5 PM. A hot midday meal is served, and many activities are offered, including arts and crafts lessons, exercise classes, lectures, field trips, parties and current events discussions. Also offered in the day-care setting are three special programs: the Alzheimer's Dis-

INSIDERS' TIP

Confused on who to call for help? Call the Eldercare Locator, a national toll-free number designed to help identify community resources for senior adults anywhere in the United States. Funded by the U.S. Administration on Aging, the number is (800) 677-1116.

Photo: St. Petersburg/Clearwater Area Convention & Visitors Bureau

If you're ready for retirement paradise, Tampa Bay welcomes you.

ease Initiative, which offers relief for those caring for an Alzheimer's patient; Adult Day Health, providing adult day care and therapeutic services to functionally impaired adults ages 60 and older; and the Community Care for Disabled Adults, providing adult day care and therapeutic services for disabled participants between the ages of 18 and 59. The six centers and their locations are:

Brandon Senior Adult Day Care Center, 204 Morgan Street, Brandon, (813) 744-5592;

Lutz Senior Center, 112 First Avenue N.W., Lutz, (813) 264-3803;

New Orleans Adult Day Care Center, 1109 Obsorne Avenue E., Tampa, (813) 272-7108;

Plant City Senior Center, 1205 Waller Avenue, Plant City, (813) 757-3824;

South Hillsborough County Adult Day Care Center, 815 College Avenue, Ruskin, (813) 671-7665;

Westshore Adult Day Care Center, 305 Manhattan Avenue N., Tampa, (813) 554-5059.

The Life Enrichment Senior Center
9704 North Blvd., Tampa
• (813) 932-0241

Dedicated to ensuring that older residents live active and independent lives, the center does not charge for any of its services and activities, which are offered on a space-available basis. The Life Enrichment Senior Center is a private, nonprofit corporation funded by tax-deductible contributions from private citizens, charitable foundations, businesses, service groups, churches and fund-raising events.

Senior Citizens Nutrition and Activity Program
(813) 272-5160

This program provides midday meals for people ages 60 and older at 25 locations throughout Hillsborough County. There are also lectures, films and demonstrations on nutrition education as well as recreational activities. Home-delivered meals are provided to senior and disabled adults who are unable to leave their residences. While contributions are welcomed, no one will be denied service because of an inability to pay.

Working Seniors
(813) 272-5321

Offering employment assistance to seniors ages 55 and older, Working Seniors provides Employability Skills Training and on-the-job training leading to permanent employment for residents who meet the program's income guidelines. Seniors learn basic skills including interviewing techniques, job application completion, resume writing and job networking.

ElderNet/Telephone Lifeline Program
(813) 238-8411

The Crisis Center of Hillsborough County Inc. has designed this three-part program to alleviate the isolation and feelings of loneliness experienced by the elderly who are living alone without nearby family or friends. Caring, trained volunteers make daily reassurance phone calls, plan weekly companionship visits and arrange for registration in Carrier Alert, in which letter carriers watch for signs of distress. If emergency service is required, volunteers are trained to alert the appropriate parties. There is no charge for this program, and service begins as soon as intake procedures are completed.

Alzheimer's Association/Tampa Bay Chapter
9365 U.S. Hwy. 19 N., Pinellas Park
• (727) 578-2558

An advocate for Alzheimer's patients and their families, this association provides a myriad of support services and educational opportunities for the community. Educational information, basic programs and family support groups are available. The association

serves families in both Hillsborough and Pinellas counties.

American Cancer Society
1001 S. MacDill Ave., Tampa
• (813) 254-3630
407 N. Parson Ave., Brandon
• (813) 685-0670
303 N. Alexander St., Plant City
• (813) 719-1089

The American Cancer Society is the primary resource for information and support for cancer patients and their families. Screenings, support groups and educational materials for the treatment and prevention of the disease are provided. In addition, transportation is offered to ambulatory cancer victims for treatment appointments. Reservations must be made two days in advance by calling (813) 289-6225.

Jewish Community Center
2713 Bayshore Blvd, Tampa
• (813) 835-6614
13009 Community Campus Dr., Tampa
• (813) 264-9000

The Jewish Community Centers offer a wide variety of programs, classes and activities for senior adults. Schedules and activities vary, so place a call to the center nearest you.

OASIS (Older Adult Services Inc.)
1 Tampa City Center, Tampa
• (813) 248-5200

A nonprofit organization, OASIS provides a broad spectrum of services to senior adults, including a housing referral service called Select-A-Home and transportation services for ambulatory or "collapsible-walker" individuals. A newly instituted program targeted at providing the funds for necessary home repair for low income seniors has been a much applauded success. This program, a joint effort with the City of Tampa,

INSIDERS' TIP

St. Petersburg is consistently given top priority as a retirement community in the widely read book, *50 Fabulous Places to Retire in America*. The reasons noted for the city's high rankings included sunshine, outdoor activity, affordable housing, low taxes and abundant senior programs.

provides a deferred payment, no-interest loan which does not require repayment until the home is sold. To date, more than $1 million has been distributed for these home repairs.

Pinellas County

The Office on Aging
330 Fifth St. N., St. Petersburg
• **(727) 893-7101**

Through The Office on Aging in downtown St. Petersburg, seniors can access information on various agencies, clubs, volunteer opportunities and specialized services in St. Petersburg and Clearwater.

Elder Helpline
(727) 576-1533

Seniors can access instant information on the full spectrum of services and programs available in the area, including transportation, respite and home healthcare services.

Neighborly Senior Services Inc.
13650 Stoneybrook Dr., Clearwater
• **(727) 573-9444**

Neighborly Senior Services provides a continuum of 26 essential services to more than 14,000 seniors each year. Along with the following services that compose the nucleus of the Neighborly Program, seniors may use the service for the Alzheimer's Disease Initiative, which provides caregiver relief; Significant Others Support (SOS), for resource information; Telephone Reassurance, which provides daily phone calls; and Housing Referral Service, which maintains a computerized listing of housing alternatives that match senior profiles with appropriate housing opportunities.

Neighborly In-Home Care helps seniors remain independent and avoid institutional care by providing assistance to manage daily tasks and meet medical needs. A personalized care plan is developed for each client.

Neighborly Transportation is available throughout the county and provides seniors with safe, comfortable rides to essential services, doctor's appointments, other Neighborly services and even the grocery store. Call (727) 573-3773, 48 hours in advance, to schedule a ride.

Neighborly Adult Day Care was the first adult day-care program offered in the United States and was developed to provide a stimulating environment for seniors who would otherwise be isolated from the community. Programs are operated in six convenient adult day-care centers, all of which are licensed by the Department of Health and Rehabilitative Services and are certified as Adult Day Care Centers.

Neighborly Meals & More brings hot, nutritious midday meals to adults ages 60 and older through Neighborly Group Dining and Neighborly Meals on Wheels. Seniors who meet at convenient dining sites throughout the county enjoy the social opportunities, varied activities and get nutritious meals at the same time; homebound seniors enjoy the company of the volunteer who delivers the daily meal.

Retired and Senior Volunteer Program (RSVP)
St. Petersburg • (727) 327-8690
Clearwater • (727) 443-1916

This nonprofit organization matches people ages 60 and older with volunteer assignments best suited to their experience, talents and interests. More than 80 nonprofit and public organizations throughout Pinellas County are served by RSVP volunteers.

Better Living For Seniors Helpline
St. Petersburg • (727) 653-7709

Through this helpline sponsored by Family Resources, senior adults can access free information on such topics as transportation services, dining facilities, home-delivered meals and finding doctors and nursing homes. Call Monday through Friday from 8 AM until 5 PM.

Gulf Coast Community Care
14041 Icot Blvd., Clearwater
• **(727) 538-7460**

Gulf Coast Community Care is a resource for homemaker services for senior adults. Eligible clients receive the services of a trained homemaker, under professional supervision, to accomplish specific home-management duties that the senior is no longer physically able to do.

Pinellas Opportunity Council
4039 Eighth Ave. S., St. Petersburg
• **(727) 327-3091**

When senior adults do not have the ability to do simple household chores, such as yard work, seasonal cleaning, lifting and moving or simple repairs, the Pinellas Opportunity Council provides the someone who can. Volunteers also will run essential errands for eligible seniors.

Pinellas Center for the Visually Impaired
6925 112th Circle N., Largo
• **(727) 544-4433**

Since the 1960s, PCVI has been serving people with significant vision impairment. A private, nonprofit organization, the center offers rehabilitation services, classes, social activities and peer support for those who are dealing with serious vision loss.

Retirement Housing

The variety of housing options is as varied as the people who come here to enjoy their retirement years. If you choose not to live among the younger folk in one of our exceptional golf-course communities, you may opt for a specially designed retirement community, called an adult congregate living facility (ACLF), sometimes referred to as assisted-living centers. These are usually master-planned communities or complexes that offer apartment or villa-style residences for independent living along with a variety of amenities that include housekeeping, social events, recreational facilities and a dining room. If a health services package is required, a continuing care retirement community (CCRC) is the answer. These normally charge a fee that incorporates a prepaid healthcare package, allowing for assisted-living or skilled-nursing care. A life-care facility, on the other hand, charges a large, up-front membership or entrance fee to cover the expense of long-term care for the life of the resident.

If you would like a free list of housing opportunities that match your health profile and budget, call OASIS Select-A Home, (813) 248-5200. The service maintains a comprehensive list of all licensed housing options available in the Tampa Bay area and its staff will be happy to provide you with any information.

Hillsborough County

Sun City Center
Sun City Center, Sun City
• **(813) 634-8457**

A whole town for and about packing the most life into retirement years, Sun City Center is just off I-75, about 25 miles south of Tampa. A country club atmosphere embraces this community, which offers 108 holes of championship and executive golf plus one of the fastest growing tennis associations in the entire region, sporting membership ages 55 and older. Residents live in single-family homes and condominiums along meticulously maintained grounds and are just steps away from the typical town amenities such as supermarkets, banks, restaurants and fine shopping. More than 200 organizations are ready to help you explore your favorite passion, be it bridge, dancing, painting, pottery or swimming. In Sun City Center's main clubhouse, you can create a masterpiece in separate rooms dedicated to specific arts and crafts, or enjoy live shows, concerts and special performances in the community's two large entertainment halls.

Bayshore Heights
4902 Bayshore Blvd., Tampa
• **(813) 835-4475**

One of Tampa's premier rental retirement communities, Bayshore Heights is classified as an adult congregate living facility (ACLF), which means that there are no entrance fees required for residency in the 165 apartments for independent living. The facility rises 12 stories above the waterfront on prestigious Bayshore Boulevard. A full-time activities director organizes everything from shuffleboard tournaments to trips; an elegant restaurant-style dining room offers daily meals and lounges; a library, beauty parlor, barber shop and banking services are all onsite; and 24-hour security along with laundry, maid and personal-care services enhance the catered lifestyle. An Alzheimer's wing and special apartments for the physically challenged are also available, along with an Independent Plus option that includes three meals a day, daily housekeeping and assistance with medications and bathing.

Canterbury Tower
3501 Bayshore Blvd., Tampa
• **(813) 837-1083**

Just up the waterfront along Bayshore Boulevard is another popular retirement destination, Canterbury Tower. Residents at this full-service, life-care retirement facility enjoy their own apartment homes with large private balconies that offer spectacular views of Tampa's city skyline or Hillsborough Bay. Just a few of the amenities include a Bayfront dining room, diverse activities organized by the facility's social director, swimming pool, woodworking shop and a private security force. The Canterbury Tower Health Center, a licensed skilled-nursing facility, is on site and has a direct-call system to every apartment should the need arise.

Lakeshore Villas
16001 Lakeshore Villa Dr., Tampa
• **(813) 968-5093**

A popular Tampa retirement community built among fishing lakes and garden-filled courtyards, Lakeshore offers a variety of lifestyle options. Single-family homes are available in either a wooded or garden setting, and The Inn features apartment-style living overlooking a lake with a dock and a gazebo. Neither option requires an endowment fee or large down payment. Monthly rental includes maid and linen services, 24-hour security and transportation in the community's own bus. A dining room, beauty salon, barber shop, library, billiard and card rooms, heated indoor pool and an activities center are all on site. Adult day care is also available.

Tampa Bay Retirement Center
11722 N. 17th St., Tampa
• **(813) 971-8072**

A nonprofit organization, the Tampa Retirement Center is an adult congregate living facility (ACLF) providing 24-hour care for its ambulatory residents. The facility offers private and semiprivate rooms, planned activities and recreation, daily meals and medication supervision. Adult day care is available.

St. Joseph's John Knox Village
4100 E. Fletcher Ave., Tampa
• **(813) 977-6361**

Adjacent to the University of South Florida campus, St. Joseph's John Knox Village is the Tampa Bay area's largest and most established full-service retirement community. Complete with its own grocery stores, a branch bank, pharmacy, chapel and two libraries, the 14-acre village offers a variety of apartment styles and residency plans, including life care. With the recent completion of its five-year, $7 million renovation project, the village now boasts a 75-foot long lap pool, refurbished apartments, billiards room and new barber and beauty shops. They have also recently increased the number of skilled nursing beds, with an emphasis on rehabilitation, allowing residents to receive intensive care services after being discharged from the hospital.

Rocky Creek Village
8606 Boulder Ct., Tampa
• **(813) 884-3388**

From independent living to personal care, Rocky Creek Village is the residence of choice for more than 700 senior adults. Housing and accompanying services are available for purchase or rent, and the on-site amenities include a swimming pool and spa, 24-hour security, a beauty parlor and barber shop and

INSIDERS' TIP

Think only young folks explore Cyberspace? Check out SeniorNet through America Online, where seniors can post messages on bulletin boards or chat in real time on dozens of subjects. Local SeniorNet groupies even meet for barbecues, dances and cruises! To feel more secure on your "net" feet, you can even take SeniorNet classes at the University of South Florida. More information is available by calling (813) 974-2403.

three complete meals each day. Planned activities and a medic-alert call system are also available in this adult congregate living facility (ACLF).

Hudson Manor
115 Davis Blvd., Davis Island
• (813) 254-8399

On lovely Davis Island you'll find Hudson Manor, a gracious retirement residence licensed as an adult congregate living facility (ACLF). All daily meals, housekeeping and laundry services, as well as health services and planned activity programs are offered to its residents.

The Courtyard at Lowry Place
1508 W. Sligh Ave., Tampa
• (813) 935-3600

Specializing in dementia and Alzheimer's, The Courtyard at Lowry Place enjoys an excellent reputation for compassionate care in its secure, homelike atmosphere. A caring staff is on duty 24 hours a day to help with bathing, dressing, meals and medication. Private and semiprivate rooms are available, with a licensed nurse on duty every day of the week.

University Village
12401 N. 22nd St., Tampa
• (813) 975-5009

If you define transportation as a chauffeured Lincoln Town Car, perhaps you should check out University Village. That's just one mode of getting around for residents in this independent and assisted-living facility, which offers a full activities menu including clubs, organizations and interest groups of every flavor. You'll also find an indoor swimming pool, exercise room, bank, woodworking shop, library, arts and crafts room, putting green and even health and nature walk trails. Breakfast, lunch and dinner are served in the U-Village's

dining room, or you can order room service if you want to be alone.

Pinellas County

Sunset Bay
7401 Central Ave., St. Petersburg
• (727) 381-1860

Serving seniors for more than 40 years, Sunset Bay is housed in a historic building, a former hotel that overlooks Boca Ciega Bay. Residents here are likely to be found chatting in comfortable chairs on the property's sweeping lawns or enjoying an evening breeze on one of the welcoming verandas. A gracious active lifestyle is the norm, including field trips to theaters, restaurants and nearby attractions, exercise classes, seminars and dances. The focus at Sunset Bay is on companionship. Whether pampered residents elect month-to-month or year-round residency, the monthly fee includes maid service, daily meals, a courtesy van, entertainment, recreation and social activities.

Palms of Largo
400 Lake Ave. N.E., Largo
• (727) 584-7595

Calling itself an intergenerational living community, the Palms of Largo really is like a small hometown with a diverse mix of people of all ages. It is indeed unique, with its apartment residences for families and independent seniors, healthcare facilities, educational centers, including a children's experimental learning preschool, recreational grounds, gardens and lakes. Making up the campus alternatives are Able Palms, (727) 525-8777, for home and healthcare services; Imperial Palms, (727) 585-3723, for independent living and supported living; Silver Palms, (727) 584-3103, family-

---

INSIDERS' TIP

A team of medical researchers at the University of South Florida unlocked another clue to the mystery of Alzheimer's disease. Early in 1996, several USF neuroscientists turned their attention to the brain's blood vessels instead of its neurons. What they learned is expected to lead to new ways of delivering drugs to those neurons in efforts to control or cure this debilitating disease.

living apartments; Sabal Palms, (727) 586-4211, a healthcare center which includes the Children's Center for subacute pediatrics, Sunshine Palms Memory Disorder Center and rehabilitation and outpatient services; the Wellness Center, (727) 584-7595, for holistic healthcare and outpatient rehabilitation; the Learning Center, (727) 588-1579, an experimental preschool; Cypress Palms, (727) 596-4211, an assisted-living facility and extended-care center; and Royal Palms, (727) 585-8003, an independent and assisted-living residence.

The Princess Martha
411 First Ave. N., St. Petersburg
• **(727) 894-6788**

In the heart of St. Petersburg, The Princess Martha offers residents a wide choice of apartment sizes and features, with no entrance or maintenance fees. Included in the affordable monthly rental plan are daily dinners, weekly housekeeping, a 24-hour emergency response program and all utilities. A multitude of activity rooms offers a diversity of recreational opportunities including game rooms, a sewing room, a library, a pool, lounges and even an ice cream shop. Private dining rooms are available for special entertaining of family or friends.

Palm Shores
830 N. Shore Dr., St. Petersburg
• **(727) 894-2102**

Only steps from Tampa Bay, Palm Shores is a planned-community complex of distinctive buildings, including a 14-story high-rise, in a campus-like setting. Studio, one- and two-bedroom apartments are available, and all include 24-hour security, a 24-hour emergency call system, restaurant-style dining and weekly linen and housekeeping services. Common areas include two libraries, lounges, a billiard room, a hobby and craft shop and the Skyview Deck offering a panoramic view of Tampa Bay and the St. Petersburg skyline. An entrance fee is required.

Coral Oaks Retirement Community
2650 W. Lake Rd., Palm Harbor
• **(727) 786-3136**

Each of the apartments at Coral Oaks features a fully equipped kitchen, washer and dryer and a private, screened patio or bal-cony. Caring staff members are always available to assist residents, and the common grounds and recreational rooms are beautifully maintained. Two meals are provided daily, along with 24-hour security and transportation. Assisted living is also available. No entrance or endowment fees are required.

Majestic Towers
1255 Pasadena Ave. S., St. Petersburg
• **(727) 347-2169**

On a 14-acre campus overlooking Boca Ceiga Bay, Majestic Towers has been serving the retirement community since 1973. Twin towers offer spacious apartments and are connected by the community building and 150-bed Health Center. A heated swimming pool, a fishing pier, shuffleboard courts and a putting green are available for more active residents, while others enjoy cards, bingo and arts and crafts classes. A five-course main meal is served daily.

Freedom Square Retirement Center
7800 Liberty Ln., Seminole
• **(727) 398-0244**

On a beautifully landscaped 15-acre campus just minutes from Seminole Mall is Freedom Square, a Freedom Group Retirement Community offering independent living and a special life-care guarantee for senior adults. Also on the campus is The Inn at Freedom Square, (727) 398-0379, providing assisted-living services tailored to the residents' specific needs, and Freedom Square Nursing Center and Seminole Nursing Pavilion, (727) 398-0123, which offers 24-hour skilled nursing care along with two special, secured units for Alzheimer's care.

Bayview Gardens
2855 Gulf-to-Bay Blvd., Clearwater
• **(727) 797-7400**

A Morton Plant Life Services retirement community, Bayview Gardens offers apartments for both independent and assisted living. Efficiency, one- and two-bedroom garden apartments are available for active senior adults, and studio apartments in the facility's high-rise tower are reserved for those who require assisted-living services. Opened in July 1996, a 120-bed long-term care nursing home gives Bayview the distinction of providing all levels of care on one campus. Planned activities, transportation for shopping and appointments, and a caring staff are all part of Bayview's lifestyle. No entry fee is required.

The Fountain Inn
250 Sixth Ave. S., St. Petersburg
• **(727) 895-5771**

Fully furnished spacious rooms welcome residents of The Fountain Inn, a supervised residential-care community with 24-hour security. Personal assistance, including medication supervision, daily meals and snacks, daily housekeeping and laundry services, is offered. Residents are provided transportation for appointments and activities and can enjoy the facility's own activities and social events.

Pasadena Manor
1430 Pasadena Ave. S., St. Petersburg
• **(727) 347-1257**

Pasadena Manor is one of 130 centers operated throughout the country by Health Care and Retirement Corporation, a leading provider of long-term healthcare, subacute care and rehabilitation services. It is a comprehensive healthcare center that specializes in skilled nursing care and intensive rehabilitation, with specialized care for senior adults with Alzheimer's and dementia. The rehabilitative services include intensive physical and cognitive therapy in a program designed to help patients reach their highest level of independence as quickly as possible. Respiratory therapy, pulmonary rehabilitation and hospice care are also offered at the facility under the Circle of Care program.

The Inn at Sun Care
9381 U.S. Hwy. 19 N., Pinellas Park
• **(727) 576-1234**

Specially staffed with certified nursing assistants, The Inn at Sun Care is designed for senior adults with Alzheimer's disease or other limited-memory disorders. Licensed nurses are always on duty and advise with medical decisions. The Inn offers innovative services such as the five-meal program and hydration conditioning, music therapy, arts and crafts, picnics and scenic drives to ensure the highest quality of life for its residents. Custom programs are created to address each resident's individual needs.

Suncoast Manor
6909 Ninth St. S., St. Petersburg
• **(727) 864-7242**

On an award-winning 30-acre campus in Pinellas Point sprawls Suncoast Manor, founded by the Episcopal Church more than 30 years ago as a caring community for people of all faiths. You'll have grand views of Tampa Bay from the apartments in the multi-story Manor Center, or tropical landscaping surrounding your garden apartment. There's a varied calendar of recreational and educational activities for residents of both the independent and assisted-living programs, along with a heated pool, a large library, a putting green and beauty and barber shops. There is also a skilled nursing center for temporary healthcare available to residents at no additional cost for unlimited 60-day periods.

Crystal Oaks of Pinellas
6767 86th Ave. N., Pinellas Park
• **(727) 548-5566**

Just opened in Pinellas Park is one of the most unique retirement homes in the area, and, in fact, only one of two in the entire nation. It is a brand-new facility conceived, designed and constructed exclusively for the deaf. Administrators, doctors, nurses and staff are all proficient in American Sign Language, and built in to the facility are subtle, yet vital, accommodations for the deaf residents. Fire alarms are bright strobes, a button outside each resident's door flashes to announce visitors, televisions are all close-captioned and throughout are text telephones called TDDs. Crystal Oaks, owned by a private company, offers 60 beds and accepts Medicare and Medicaid. But most importantly, it offers a lifestyle of dignity and security for our deaf and hard-of-hearing seniors.

Transportation Services

Seniors who do not have transportation to take them to necessary services such as doctor's appointments, banking and grocery shopping, can call on one of the following organizations who are standing by to help out. Because they are all staffed by volunteers, there are no charges for transportation services. Donatons are, however, always welcomed. All the services require advance reservations, so please contact your choice in ample time to ensure your trip.

Hillsborough County

American Red Cross "Angel Wings"
(813) 251-0921

Angel Wings provides transportation services specifically for medical appointments, including dentist visits and therapies. The service operates Monday through Friday, and you should call at least one to two weeks in advance to make your reservation. Similar services operate in St. Petersburg/Southern Pinellas, (727) 898-3111, and in Clearwater, (727) 446-2358.

OASIS Senior ExpressLine
(727) 229-5553

OASIS provides free transportation services to seniors age 65 and older who are unable to use public transportation because they need extra help in getting around. If qualified for the service, a senior is allowed three trips per month, which can be used for necessary trips such as medical appointments, banking or grocery shopping. Reservations should be made at least two weeks in advance.

Pinellas County

Neighborly Senior Services Inc.
(727) 573-3373

Neighborly Senior Services offers Neighborly Transportation to seniors throughout Pinellas County. These trips are available at no charge for essential services, medical appointments, other Neighborly services such as adult day care and even the grocery store. Rides should be scheduled at least 48 hours in advance.

**The Tampa Bay
area is a hot spot for
new product launches
and heavy national
advertising.**

Media

The Tampa Bay area ranks as the 15th-largest television market in the nation. This makes us a hot spot for new product launches and heavy national advertising. (About the only national commercials we don't see — and wish we could — are the ones that sell Florida to friends and family up north.)

Of course, the major television networks all have affiliates here. ABC, NBC and Fox studios are in Tampa, while CBS has its studio in St. Petersburg near the Gandy Bridge. A varied scope of radio stations also compete for the air waves, including community-supported, noncommercial radio to all the top national talk shows.

Both Tampa and St. Petersburg boast award-winning daily newspapers. *The Tampa Tribune* constantly garners recognition among its writers. *Time* magazine's recent list again included the *St. Petersburg Times* among the nation's 10-best newspapers. And a survey conducted by *American Journalism Review* recently concluded that "the venerable *St. Petersburg Times* may be the best independent newspaper in America ...." Plus, there's an extensive variety of alternative publications and monthly magazines to keep visitors and Insiders up to date on what's going on, where it's happening and who's doing it.

So, let's take a major media tour — starting on the front page.

Newspapers

Dailies

The Tampa Tribune
202 S. Parker St., Tampa
• (813) 259-7711

Certainly the most famous writer on *The Tampa Tribune*'s staff is Tom McEwen, who has garnered a lot of respect throughout the sports world. McEwen, a member of the NFL Hall of Fame committee, is supposedly semi-retired, but you wouldn't know it from the frequency of his byline.

Two of the newspaper's regular columnists are also very popular. Steve Otto, who's Otto-graphic spin on family, politics, the area and life at the "Type and Gripe Factory" provides thought-provoking fodder for readers. And "provoking furor" could best be used to describe Dan Ruth. PC? Fuhgedaboudit. This guy pulls no punches when it comes to lambasting the local politicos, and his barbs are spiked with a sharp wit. The overall tone of *The Tribune* is definitely Republican and is reflected in the work of Wayne Stayskal, ultraconservative editorial cartoonist. Stayskal's cartoons are syndicated and featured in more than 50 papers around the nation.

Daily circulation is nearing 228,000 and Sunday's is about 320,000. Weekday issues carry a section devoted to neighborhood news and two tabloid sections are of particular interest: "Business & Finance," a pullout in Monday editions that includes extensive technological coverage along with news of local interest; and "FridayExtra!," the weekend entertainment tabloid that arrives on (you guessed it) Fridays.

St. Petersburg Times
490 First Ave. S., St. Petersburg
• (727) 893-8111

With circulation closing in on a half-million and readership numbers nearly doubling that, the *St. Petersburg Times* is the nation's 23rd-largest paper and widely hailed as one of the 10 best. Its most recent Pulitzer Prize for journalistic excellence was earned in 1998, and its sports section has won more awards from the Florida Sports Writers Association than any other major newspaper in the state.

When it comes to writers, Paul Wilborn covers anything that grabs him, and always with sass and spirit. Political editor Howard Troxler never fails to address provocative issues, and editorial writers Bill Maxwell and Martin Dyckman deliver columns that regularly raise ire from either the left or the right — and often simultaneously!

The paper is also known for the foresight and ethics of its late publisher Nelson Poynter, who created the Poynter Institute for Media Studies more than 20 years ago. The Institute provides a range of educational services for the news industry, from sophisticated courses for professional journalists to basic programs for area elementary schools.

The *St. Petersburg Times* tends toward a slightly more liberal position than its cross-Bay rival, *The Tribune*. Like that paper, Monday's issue includes business coverage in a tabloid called "Business Times." The *Times'* main feature section takes a different focus each day, with substantial material directed to young readers. The "Taste" (food) section appears on Thursday, while Friday brings the "Weekend" tabloid, covering local art and music events, plus movie listings and restaurant reviews.

The *Times* also caters to those who prefer their news by voice. The TimesLine is a free, 24-hour service providing national and local news and information by touch-tone phone. This is particularly valuable to print-handicapped residents and visitors. Information on the TimesLine, which is accessed by different phone numbers in different area communities, appears in each issue of the daily paper. Circulation numbers rank more than 320,000 on weekdays and close to 415,000 on Sundays.

www.insiders.com

See this and many other **Insiders' Guide®** destinations online — in their entirety.

Visit us today!

Other Papers — Weekly, Semiweekly, Semimonthly and Monthly

Weekly Planet
1310 E. Ninth Ave., Tampa
• (813) 248-8888

Directed primarily at entertainment-minded readers between the ages of 25 and 44, the *Weekly Planet* gives extensive coverage to films, dining, live and recorded music, theater, dance and art. If you want the listings of what's taking place where, pick up this free tabloid. The paper also delivers well-written, hard-hitting investigative pieces — "kickin' some butt," as they say — on people and issues affecting local life. Published on Thursdays, it's available at more than 1,700 boxes and racks around the Tampa Bay area, especially at office complexes, restaurants, nightclubs and retail stores.

Tampa Bay Business Journal
4350 W. Cypress St., Ste. 400, Tampa
• (813) 873-8225

TBBJ, as it's dubbed by Insiders, is a weekly business-to-business newspaper. It covers local industry, companies, business trends, events and people in Hillsborough, Pinellas, Polk, Pasco, Manatee and Sarasota counties. Each edition carries a special report focusing on specific businesses and industries, as well as current topics related to that sector. Regular Top-25 lists provide facts and figures on top local businesses in a variety of fields. These lists are compiled annually into *The Book of Lists*, an indispensable resource sent to subscribers and available for purchase

INSIDERS' TIP

Webheads, take note: *The Tampa Tribune*'s on-line version was named Best Media Page of 1996 by *Windows* magazine. In addition, *Editor & Publisher* magazine has dubbed it "one of the world's best." These are quite a couple of kudos that the paper's rightly proud of.

by nonsubscribers. The paper's annual subscription rate is $63, and the newsstand price is $1.50.

La Gaceta
3210 E. Seventh Ave., Tampa
• **(813) 248-3921**
This is the nation's only trilingual newspaper. Its stories appear in English, Spanish and Italian, giving testimony to the area's community heritage. Publisher Roland Manteiga's voice is clear throughout each edition of this respected weekly, which comes out on Fridays.

Florida Sentinel Bulletin
2207 E. 21st Ave., Tampa
• **(813) 248-1921**
Published on Tuesdays and Fridays, the *Florida Sentinel Bulletin* covers issues of particular interest to the African-American community. It also provides a place for readers and columnists to voice opinions that don't necessarily reflect the editorial stance of the paper or its publisher. As a result, it's both informative and entertaining. Subscribers can choose to receive either one or both issues of this semiweekly paper.

The Weekly Challenger
2500 Ninth St. S., St. Petersburg
• **(727) 896-2922**
The Weekly Challenger is the seventh most circulated publication in the Tampa Bay area. With community news and wire service reports, it keeps readers current on issues affecting African Americans in the area and around the state. Available only by mail, an annual subscription costs $30.

The Sun Times of Canada
The Canada News
701 E. Jackson St., Tampa
• **(800) 535-6788**
Proudly serving Canadian "snowbird," these sister publications come out weekly between early November and April. Pulling news from Canadian satellite services, the papers keep about 25,000 visitors abreast of what's happening back home. The subscription price is $1.25 (U.S.) a week for each publication. The papers can also be found at newsstands throughout West Central Florida.

Magazines

Tampa Bay Magazine
2531 Landmark Dr., Ste. 101, Clearwater
• **(727) 791-4800**
Tampa Bay Magazine is the closest thing we have to a "city magazine." It's published every other month and offers a variety of features focused on local people and places, travel, home and garden, health and business. The magazine is designed for readers whose median income is $97,000. The newsstand price is $3.95.

Florida Trend
490 First Ave. S., St. Petersburg
• **(727) 821-5800**
Anyone who wants to keep up with the state's business climate subscribes to this magazine. *Florida Trend* is known for exceptionally in-depth and detailed coverage of topics, and analysis of how political issues will impact the state's economy. The cover price is $2.95, and an annual subscription costs $29.95. Trend Publications, publisher of this monthly, also produces a number of state-oriented books on business.

The Maddux Report
1 Progress Plaza, St. Petersburg
• **(727) 823-4394**
The Maddux Report covers "the business of Tampa Bay" on a monthly basis. Its regional coverage area extends to Polk, Sarasota, Manatee, Pasco and Hernando counties as well as Hillsborough and Pinellas. Each four-color issue includes a survey on such topics as retail, office or business park space in the area. The annual subscription rate is $45 and the newsstand price is $4.95. Maddux Publishing also produces *The New Homes Guide* five times a year. It's a residential housing report that goes out to subscribers, but anyone can get a copy by just calling the office.

Tampa Bay Family Magazine
5440 Mariner St., Ste. 312, Tampa
• **(813) 289-4060**
From topics such as "Secrets to Parenting Adopted Children" to information on family-friendly attractions and area schools, this

The Poynter Institute for Media Studies

Nelson Poynter, late publisher of the *St. Petersburg Times* and founder of the *Congressional Quarterly*, created the Poynter Institute for Media Studies in 1975 to promote his personal goals and values in a journalistic education setting. In addition, it was a means of assuring independence for his newspaper after his death.

The nonprofit Institute works to elevate journalistic standards through training and research. While writing for print and broadcast is integral, seminars and programs extend to such areas as ethical decision-making, ethics in photojournalism, graphics design, management leadership at all levels and more.

The Institute's faculty is supplemented by visiting instructors from around the world. Past instructors have included NPR correspondents Howard Berkes and Martha Raddatz; Joann Byrd, ombudsman of *The Washington Post*; consultant and journalist Hodding Carter; *New York Daily News* managing editor Martin Gottlieb; Stanford University professor Shirley Heath; *New York Times* copy editor Charles Klaveness; and Rod Prince and Ira Silverman, senior producers for NBC News.

The Poynter Institute for Media Studies is at 801 Third Street S. in St. Petersburg, (727) 821-9494.

Photo: Poynter Institute

The Poynter Institute for Media Studies was created to elevate standards of journalism through training and research.

monthly magazine is designed to foster ties between the business, family and educational communities. Subscriptions cost $18 a year and the magazine can be found at major bookstores and many retail shops. It's also distributed through child-care centers, elementary schools, libraries, doctors' offices and a number of local businesses and organizations.

Another monthly magazine from this publisher is *Curiocity for Kids*, giving 8-to-12-year-olds the inside scoop on cool things to do around town. In addition, it carries lots of entertaining, educational information. The subscription price is $18.

Women's Fitness
8085 38th Ave. N., St. Petersburg
• **(727) 347-4444**

This upbeat bimonthly is a national magazine showcasing female athletes who represent the cutting edge of fitness. Each issue offers effective exercise tips and routines plus "real gyms, real workouts, and real women!" The cover price is $3.99 and a year's subscription is $18.

duPont Registry Buyers Guide to Fine Homes
duPont Registry Buyers Guide to Fine Autos
duPont Registry Buyers Guide to Fine Boats
2325 Ulmerton Rd., Ste. 16, Clearwater
• **(727) 573-9339**

These three internationally circulated magazines are definitely aimed at the upper-income reader. The guides to Fine Homes and Fine Autos are both published monthly, while the Guide to Fine Boats is issued six times a year. Call for subscription information and sales locations.

Television

Normally, we would provide specific channel numbers for local TV stations. Several stations in Hillsborough and Pinellas counties are, however, assigned different channel numbers based on service areas, especially when it comes to cable. *The Tampa Tribune* and The *St. Petersburg Times* feature daily TV sections in addition to their respective TV magazines that are inserted in Sunday editions. Refer to these sections when searching for the right channel selection in your area.

WFTS-ABC
4045 N. Himes Ave., Tampa
• **(813) 354-2828**

With 73,000-square-feet of space across from Raymond James Stadium, this is the only local station not in a flood zone. This can be mighty important during hurricane season! The public is invited to watch the newsroom in action from the second-floor balcony of this new $20 million studio.

WTSP-CBS
11450 Gandy Blvd. N., St. Petersburg
• **(727) 577-1010**

This channel is easy to keep track of — it's the only network affiliate with the same number, Channel 10, on all the local cable companies. It's also the only station to start its news broadcast at 4 PM.

Veteran news anchor Sue Zelenko shares the six o'clock newsdesk with Reginald Roundtree, and Dick Fletcher's weather report is fun to watch just to see how well he did with yesterday's forecast. He offers a "three-degree guarantee." If he doesn't predict the day's high temperature within three degrees, he sends a viewer a coffee mug. And if he hits the mark all week long, he sends out another mug. His accuracy rate is best in summer when the forecast never really changes: "High in the low 90s, 70 percent chance of rain, Bay and inland waters — light chop." After just one summer here, everyone knows that forecast by heart.

WTVT-Fox
3213 W. Kennedy Blvd., Tampa
• **(813) 876-1313**

WTVT is renowned for its incredible array of weather reporting technology. This station owns the tallest, most powerful private Doppler radar system in the nation. It has a 450-mile range, 175 miles farther than even the National Weather Service system. Rather than broadcasting the usual half-hour of national news, the station produces its own version. The show's hosts are respected co-anchors John Wilson and Kelly Ring. If your day starts too early for you to stay up for the 11 PM news, this is the station to turn to at 10 PM.

WFLA-NBC
901 E. Jackson St., Tampa
• (813) 228-8888

WFLA was the only local affiliate to escape the round of network shifting caused a couple of years ago by Fox's buyout of CBS stations across the country. Since then, WFLA's local news department has continued to win big in the area ratings game. Bob Hite, namesake of his famous newscaster father, often employs his skills as a sailor and diver to deliver some outstanding news stories. Teamed with him at the anchor desk is Gail Sierens, who started out as a sportscaster and in 1987 was the first woman to do network play-by-play for the NFL.

WEDU-PBS
1300 North Blvd., Tampa
• (813) 254-9338

Oooh, are we proud of WEDU! Guess who is its most famous studio star? Here's a hint: He lives in the Treasure House and hangs around with Mr. Green Jeans, Mr. Bunny Rabbit, Grandfather Clock and Mr. Moose. You got it — Captain Kangaroo! Now, the funny thing is, while the national program's first season was taped here (and at Busch Gardens), *The All-New Captain Kangaroo* is not a PBS show, but airs on the Fox Family Channel. During the past few years, WEDU has become a national leader in creating children's programming for public television. From *Mister Rogers' Neighborhood* to *The Newshour with Jim Lehrer*, WEDU is our link to public broadcast.

WUSF-PBS
4202 E. Fowler Ave., Tampa
• (813) 974-4000

The University of South Florida operates WUSF-TV, which carries an eclectic selection of PBS programming between 6 and 12:50 AM. You'll find everything from *t'ai chi* to *This Old House*, as well as lots of cooking and art shows and mind-stimulating lectures.

Bay News 9
7901 66th St. N., Pinellas Park
• (727) 437-2001

The newest station on the TV dial, Bay News 9 is a venture of Time Warner Cable company, so it's logical that it's on channel 9 and available only to Time Warner subscribers. Consider this a local version of CNN; it's the area's first around-the-clock news station. News junkies get regularly updated reports in a half-hour rotating format, and sports nuts can play armchair manager during former NFL player Dave Logan's nightly call-in show.

WCLF-Independent
6922 142nd Ave. N., Largo
• (727) 535-5622

WCLF provides religious programming for the Tampa Bay area. One of its most highly received programs is *Ever Increasing Faith* with Frederick K. Price on Sunday mornings. A variety of well-produced local shows and paid programming rounds out the schedule.

WRMD-Telemundo
2700 W. Dr. Martin Luther King Jr. Blvd., Tampa • (813) 879-5757

A member of the Miami-based Telemundo network, WRMD broadcasts news and entertainment in Spanish.

WTOG-UPN
365 105th Terrace N.E., St. Petersburg
• (727) 223-7471

As a charter member station in the United Paramount network, TOG boasts *Star Trek: Deep Space Nine* and *Star Trek: Voyager*, along with new network shows such as *Moiesha* and *Clueless*.

INSIDERS' TIP

Country music fans, turn that TV dial to WWWB. Its *AM With Haywood Henson* program recently landed the Live Television Show of the Year award from the Country Music Organization of America.

WTTA-Independent
5510 W. Gray St., Tampa
• **(813) 289-3838**

There's lots of variety here, from infomercials and Ernest Angley to *Buffy the Vampire Slayer* and *Baywatch*.

WWWB-Warner Bros.
7201 E. Hillsborough Ave., Tampa
• **(813) 626-3232**

This Hearst Corporation station is the local heavy-hitter of this year's baseball season! Why? Because WWWB landed the rights to carry 50 of the Tampa Bay Devil Ray's games during the team's inaugural 1998 season. This is also where to turn to catch the *Animaniacs* cartoon show.

WVEA-Univision
2942 W. Columbus Dr., Tampa
• **(813) 879-8861**

This station provides viewers with a wide range of Spanish programming, including movies, musicals and soap operas.

Cable Companies

Hillsborough
Time Warner Communications
• (813) 684-6400

Pinellas
Time Warner Communications
• (727) 562-5015
TCI Cablevision of Pinellas County
• (727) 736-1436
GTE Presents Americast
• (800) GTE-VIDEO

Radio

Round and round and round she goes ... and where she stops, nobody knows. Wherever you stop on the FM or AM dial, you'll find something different. As in any major market, the spectrum ranges from classic to contemporary, and from all-talk to "All Things Considered." A complete listing of area radio stations appears here, but a few stations deserve additional comments to help you find your favorite programming or discover a truly unique station.

In Tampa Bay, WMNF-88.5 FM would definitely fit the latter category. About 16 years ago, an odd lot of people came together with the still-odder idea that they could make a success of a commercial-free station broadcasting alternative public affairs programming and music you don't hear on "real" radio. There's no Top-40 playlist. Instead, you'll hear everything including folk, free form, alternative rock, Big Band, jazz, Jewish music and issues, Celtic, Latin, Brazilian, reggae, and rhythm and blues. In addition to its unusual programing, WMNF has a "mighty" political impact.

This is one of the most successful listener-sponsored radio stations in the nation, due in large part to creative fund-raising that includes the annual May music bash, Tropical Heatwave (see our Annual Events chapter), along with other benefit concerts and two week-long on-air marathons. The tiny paid staff is abetted by an enormous cadre of supporters who host shows, answer phones and write monthly listeners' guides. Call the station at (813) 238-8001 and ask for a free copy.

WUSF-89.7 FM, our NPR affiliate, is also the region's Radio Reading Network. People with print handicaps can get the special receiver required to hear the programming by calling (813) 974-4193.

Farther along the FM dial is WQYK-99.5. It's unique in Florida simply because it's had the same call letters and format for 26 years. This station believed Country was cool while Barbara Mandrell was still in school. It consistently ranks as No. 1 in area Arbitron ratings, and WQYK's DJs regularly earn top national honors from groups such as the Country Music Association. This is also where to tune in (along with its AM station at 1010) to hear Buccaneer games during football season.

WFLA-970 is the local AM station of choice for several reasons. First, there's "Cracker" Jack Harris and his cohort in bad jokes, Tedd Webb. Jack has been famous in this market since Hector was a pup, even though he's not really that old. Tedd's also a big name on the sports-coverage scene. And, Dr. Laura fans, take note. This is her local station. She's on weekday afternoons right after Rush Limbaugh, *except* during baseball season, when afternoon games of the Tampa Bay Devil Rays take over whatever time slots they need and *nobody* complains 'cause we finally got our own baseball team!

Tampa Bay Area Radio Stations

Adult Contemporary
WFLZ 93.3 FM (Hits)

Big Band
WRZN 720 AM

Classical
WUSF 89.7 FM (NPR)

Community Radio
WMNF 88.5 FM (Eclectic, Public Affairs)

Country
WQYK 99.5 FM
WRBQ 104.7 FM

Ethnic
WRMD 680 AM (Spanish)
WBDN 760 AM (Spanish)
WQBN 1300 AM (Spanish)
WLVU 1470 AM
WPSO 1500 FM (Greek)
WAMA 1550 AM (Spanish)

Family
WFTI 91.7 FM

Soft Jazz/Pop
WSJT 94.1 FM
WWRM 94.9 FM
WISP 98.7 FM
WILV 101.5 FM

News/Talk/Sports
WHNZ 570 AM (CBS)
WSUN 620 AM (ABC)
WZTM 820 AM (CBS)

WKXY 930 AM (Talk)
WFLA 970 AM (ABC)
WQYK 1010 AM (Talk)
WDAE 1250 AM (Sports)
WAMR 1320 AM (CNN)
WTAN 1340 AM
WCDF 1350 AM (Sports)
WSPB 1450 AM
WUSF 89.7 FM (Radio Reading Network)

Oldies
WYUU 92.5 FM

Religious
WWBA 1040 AM (Talk)
WTIS 1110 AM
WBRD 1420 AM
WYFE 88.9 FM
WBVM 90.5 FM (and Classical)
WKES 91.1 FM
WLPJ 91.5 FM

Rhythm and Blues
WFNS 910 AM
WTMP 1150 AM

Rock
WSSR 95.7 FM
WXTB 97.9 FM (Hard rock)
WAKS 100.7 FM
WHPT 102.5 FM (Eclectic)
WTBT 105.5 FM (Classic)
WCOF 107.3 FM ('70s)
WYNF 107.9 FM (Album)

Standards
WGUL 860 AM
WZHR 1400 AM
WWPR 1490 AM
WGUL 96.1 FM
WDUV 103.5 FM
WLVU 106.3 FM

Urban
WRBQ 1380 AM
WRXB 1590 AM

Even on a Lousy Day, It Can See Forever.

You're zipping down Kennedy Boulevard away from downtown Tampa — OK, traffic and lights make it more of a crawl. At the intersection of Henderson Avenue, you first notice two stuffed gorillas in Bucs gear standing outside a store. Next you see the well-designed and beautifully landscaped building that houses WTVT, Channel 13. But what really draws your eye is a huge, triangular-shaped, monolithic structure just west of the studio. Up, up, up it soars. And sitting atop the structure, like a Times Square New Year's Eve ball designed by Buckminster Fuller, sits this humongous, really weird geodesic sphere.

What in the world is it? Some artist's idea of combining a beachball with a baseball with a soccer ball? And whatever it is, it looks poised to roll off the tower in the first good wind.

Close-up

Not to worry — this 200-foot-high baby is built to stay. The tower's 18-inch-thick steel and concrete walls are formed from a continuous concrete pour seated 75 feet down in bedrock. Now, if we get hit by a Category III hurricane (wind speeds more than 130 mph) the radome is hurricane history — but then, so is everything else..

Pronounced "ray-dome," the air-conditioned dome houses WTVT's electronic equipment and a radar dish that scans 450 miles. This state-of-the-art equipment is unequaled in the nation; the radar range of the National Weather Service reaches only 275 miles.

A radio transmitter unit constantly cycles 360 degrees, capturing radar information and feeding it into the IBM mainframe housed in the studio. From the collected data, the station's staff develops and interprets maps and information. Other stations then purchase these from what are called value-added companies, which is why the maps you see on CNN and on the Weather Channel look alike.

So what's in the tower itself? Just a clunky chain-driven elevator large enough to carry two maintenance engineers up to the satellite dish to keep the equipment fine tuned. And, one would suppose, a few lights so they don't feel like they're on Disney World's Space Mountain.

WTVT respresentatives claim people call all the time asking if they can ride up the tower and see what's up there. Sorry, folks, it's not open for public tours. But you do get to see what the radar dish sees every time you tune in for the weather report.

Besides, isn't what you imagined was up there more intriguing than the facts?

Photo: Paula Stahel

WTVT's radar tower scans 450 miles.

The rich weave of our region's religious tapestry includes the bright threads of Hinduism, Islam, Baha'i, Zen Buddhism, Taoism, spiritualism and many more faiths.

Worship

With its extensive ethnic base deeply drawn from Spanish, Italian and Cuban heritage, it's no surprise that Catholicism in the Tampa Bay area, with more than 2 million followers, is a predominant religion. Nowhere near as large, but of great historical importance, the Southern Baptist church counts nearly 100,000 members around the Bay.

Judaism thrives, of course, but the incredible population and cultural growth we've experienced during the past few decades is excitingly reflected in the wide variety of spiritual pursuits available. The rich weave of our region's religious tapestry includes the bright threads of the Hinduism, Islam, Baha'i, Zen Buddhism, Taoism, spiritualism and many more faiths.

If you glance through the yellow pages of the phone books for Tampa, St. Petersburg and Clearwater, you can easily see there's no comprehensible way for us to detail all the religious leadership or services in our area. (The Religion section in Saturday editions of *The Tampa Tribune* includes an extensive information directory of local services.) What we can provide here is a historic overview of how religion has helped shape us and how our people today are helping shape religion.

Tampa

Many churches were already thriving when Tampa received its initial city charter. On July 26, 1846, a gathering of 17 worshippers convened to form the First Methodist Church. Organized by Rev. John Ley, who'd been assigned as a circuit preacher to the area in 1834, the small group worshipped in a primitive structure built out of driftwood on property owned by the Fort Brooke Garrison. Known as the Church-By-The-Sea, the little building fell to the force of an 1848 hurricane. It took two years for the congregation to raise funds for construction of a new building at the bustling intersection of Lafayette and Morgan streets. Donations came from around the country, including a $5 gold coin sent by General T.J. "Stonewall" Jackson. The First Methodist Episcopal Church, otherwise known as The Little White Church, finally opened its doors in 1853 as the first church building in Tampa — two years before the city charter was awarded.

Records from that early period were later destroyed by fire, but the church and its congregation continued to grow, and in 1968 the current sanctuary went up at 1001 N. Florida Avenue. Only two years later, the church began another construction project: Methodist Place, a 14-story retirement facility for the elderly. The church also opened its doors to Tampa's Korean population during the 1970s, providing a place for the immigrants to conduct worship. During the 1980s, First Methodist continued to reach out to the community by revitalizing its educational building and programs in addition to creating a new home for the Network Ministry agency. To learn more about services provided by First United Methodist, call the church office at (813) 229-6511.

The year the nation plunged into civil war was also the year the Sacred Heart Parish began in Tampa. Two decades later, in 1881, four Sisters of the Holy Names began the Academy of the Holy Names to instruct children of the local parish. Today, its home is on Bayshore Boulevard and it is one of the most highly regarded private schools in the city. Jesuit High School, an all-boys academy, traces its origins to 1899, when the first class was held in what was then known as Sacred Heart College. In 1939, the school gained its present name, and in 1958 the campus on Himes Avenue was dedicated.

Sacred Heart Church, on the corner of Florida Avenue and Twiggs Street, was formally dedicated by the congregation in 1905, the same year it became mother house of all Jesuit missions in South Florida. The magnificent Romanesque sanctuary still serves worshippers today. A variety of services are offered, from the simplicity of the open chapel for daytime prayer and meditation to dances for young adults and retreats for personal spiritual growth. More information about these services is available by calling the church, (813) 229-1595.

While Catholic devotion is based on traditions and pronouncements from the pope, modern challenges have led many to question the church's edicts while wanting to continue practicing their faith. The American Catholic Church, incorporated in 1993, welcomes all Catholics, but differs from its Roman source by ordaining homosexuals as well as married men and women. The American Catholic Church first established its presence in Tampa in 1996. Claiming to be "radically committed to the unconditional acceptance of all those who suffer and are ignored by society and the Church," the area's only congregation meets at 7813 Nebraska Avenue and can be reached at (813) 238-6000.

Today, the Baptist faith operates more than 175 churches and missions in the Tampa Bay area and serves about 100,000 worshippers. The oldest of these congregations gathers at First Baptist Church, 302 W. Kennedy Boulevard, across from the University of Tampa. The church's first house of worship went up in 1859, under the direction of Rev. Jeremiah Hayman, at the corner of Tampa and Twiggs streets. Moving through several locations as it grew, the church settled into its present site in the early 1920s. Five pastors now shepherd a congregation of nearly 3,000 and offer a wide variety of community programs, including a midweek, noon-hour Bible study program for business people. First Baptist is well-known for its children's day-care facility and for Tampa Bap-

tist Manor, a 242-unit high-rise for the elderly. The church's office number is (813) 251-2425

Presbyterian worship services were itinerant, at best, until Mrs. Ida M. Hale offered use of her home as a Sunday school in 1878, six years after moving to Tampa. Her little picket-fenced home on Marion Street soon became so popular and crowded that the school moved to the county courthouse. After four years, prayer meetings were added, although formal establishment of a church was difficult for the group. An early history of the church notes, "At that time there were only Methodists and Baptists among the Protestants (in Tampa), and some were very curious about Presbyterians, asking what kind of folks they were." Curiosity gave way to comfort, and growth at First Presbyterian attracted a regular minister in 1885. In the early 1920s, the church erected the home it maintains today. The Spanish mission-style building at 412 Zack Street also houses the One World Gift Shop. Handicrafts and art works from Central and South America, Mexico, India and Asia are featured. Profits from the two-room shop, open weekdays from 11 AM until 2 PM, go to local charities. Call (813) 229-0679 for more information.

Much earlier than the Presbyterian presence was the establishment of churches serving the African American community. In 1865, Beulah Baptist Church was founded, and it remains one of the most active congregations in the area. Five years later came the founding of St. James Episcopal, another strong organization that continues to this day. Beulah Baptist congregants meet at 1006 W. Cypress, (813) 251-5591. The grand brick cathedral of St. Paul African Methodist Episcopal is downtown at 506 E. Harrison Street, (813) 223-9753.

While many of the city's churches began more than a century ago, one new church in

www.insiders.com

See this and many other **Insiders' Guide®** destinations online — in their entirety.

Visit us today!

INSIDERS' TIP

Belinda Womack is one of the Bay area's hottest jazz/blues singers. She's also music director of Tampa's Hyde Park United Methodist Church. You can enjoy her inspirational addition to the services at 9:30 AM on Sundays.

Our Miracle on Drew Street

Christians have been drawn to such far-flung places as Fatima in hope of seeing her vision. Although miracles can be contemplated in exotic places, how do you explain it when a vision of the Virgin Mary appears in your own town?

Just before Christmas 1996, something happened that's still inexplicable, even to those who do not consider it a miracle. On the glass exterior of a small office building

in Clearwater appeared the likeness of the Virgin Mother. Several people claimed the multicolored shape on the glass had been there for years, but once word spread, hundreds of thousands of people flocked to see the 60-by-20-foot image. Though now in smaller numbers, they still come to see the apparition at the corner of Drew Street and U.S. Highway 19.

Scoffers immediately discounted the image as nothing but discoloration caused by years of the sprinkler system splashing water on the glass. Coincidentally — or maybe just as miraculously — an international gathering of glass experts convened in Clearwater only weeks after the image was first noted. Taking two days away from their long-planned agenda, more than 100 scientists and manufacturers swarmed about the stained glass, pondering the possibilities. They easily concluded the rainbow discoloration was caused by

years of corrosion from elements in the glass. What was impossible for them to determine is exactly what caused the image to so clearly portray the Madonna. "We can try to explain it," Carlo Pantano, Penn State University professor of materials science and engineering told the *St. Petersburg Times*, "but not who controlled it or why it happened here at this time."

The mystery only deepened six months later when vandals attacked the mirrored glass with a corrosive chemical in May 1997, defacing several of the nine panels that make up the image. There was no known way to clean away the corrosion and repair the damaged image, but people continued to travel out of their way to ponder and pray.

Two weeks later, heavy rains drenched the area for two days. When the sun, and the devoted, returned, so had the image of the Blessed Mother — as pristine and perfectly defined as before the desecration.

Whether or not one believes in divine intervention, the mystery of the miracle on Drew Street remains.

Photo: Paula Stahel

Crowds gather to ponder the mystery on Drew Street.

particular is having a great impact on the community. The Without Walls International Church, 2511 N. Grady Avenue, (813) 879-4673, started in July 1991 as the South Tampa Christian Center. Calling itself "the perfect church for people who are not," the ministry's theme is evangelism and restoration. Foremost among the many distinctions it has achieved is that it's the third-fastest growing church in the nation. Among its ministries are support groups offering help in areas from health to homelessness, corporate outreach programs that host lunches and take Bible study to downtown executives, and Operation Explosion's rolling sanctuaries for inner-city residents. Underprivileged children receive school supplies, and massive truckloads of toys go out to the needy at Christmas. On another upbeat note, the church holds the record in *The Guinness Book of World Records* for sponsoring the world's largest Easter egg hunt — nearly a half-million eggs! Through its numerous community programs, services are held in various locations nearly every night of the week. This active church has nearly 3,000 members and serves another 8,000 outside its walls.

Although some may call them "alternative religions," those outside the Judeo-Christian perspective are alive and growing. Eleven mosques now serve the Islamic community; the newest is the Alhamdulilah Islamic Dawah Center at 1936 Dr. Martin Luther King Jr. Boulevard, (813) 354-9539. The area's second Hindu temple opened in Tampa the same year, in 1996, after more than a decade of work and saving by the nearly 4,000 people who follow the faith. At 5501 Lynn Road in Carrollwood, the Hindu Temple of Florida can be reached at (813) 962-6890; a second temple is the Vishnu Mandir at 311 E. Palm Avenue, near downtown Tampa, (813) 221-4482.

Since the city's earliest land boom in the 1880s, the Jewish faith has been well-represented in Tampa. Several families, most notably European *émigrés*, came here and many settled in Ybor City, possibly because of the Spanish Sephardic Jews who had gravitated there earlier. By the early 1900s, two synagogues were thriving: Schaari-Zedek, now at 3303 W. Swann Avenue, (813) 876-2377; and Rodeph Sholom, 2713 Bayshore Boulevard, (813) 837-1911. And by the end of World War I, Tampa's Jewish population was the second largest in the state. Today, the Tampa Jewish Foundation, 6617 Gunn Highway, (813) 960-1840, operates a variety of programs and services, including private schools and retirement centers.

St. Petersburg

Judaism took much longer to become established in Pinellas County. In fact, it was as late as 1911 before the first permanent Jewish resident moved to Clearwater, and not until the late 1930s did other Jewish families join his. Now, the Jewish population in Pinellas County has more than 25,000 full-time residents. Its largest synagogue is Temple B'nai Israel, 1685 S. Belcher Road in Clearwater, (727) 531-5829. For more information about synagogues and community programs, call the Pinellas Jewish Federation at 13191 Starkey Road, Largo, (727) 530-3223.

Centuries earlier, in 1539, the first Catholic Mass was said in the area that became St. Petersburg. Today, the city is the seat of the diocese, which includes Pinellas and Hillsborough counties, in addition to three other counties. St. Jude Church, 5815 Fifth Avenue N., is the diocese cathedral and was formed in June 1968.

Before the turn of the century, Tampa's Sacred Heart parish serviced Mass centers in Tarpon Springs, Pinellas Park and St. Petersburg. In 1892, St. Mary Our Lady of Grace was the first church begun by the beloved Father J.J. O'Riordan, who envisioned and built several churches reflecting different styles. St.

INSIDERS' TIP

Jacob Neusner, one of the world's leading experts in the classical period of rabbinical studies, is a distinguished research professor of religious studies at Tampa's University of South Florida campus. Dr. Neusner is credited with writing about 700 books. During 1995 alone, he wrote 48 books in only 48 weeks.

Paul, (727) 822-3481, the oldest structure, is designed in Romanesque style and was completed in 1920 on a 10-acre site at 1800 12th Street N. Mary's Byzantine structure, 515 Fourth Street S., (727) 896-2191, was built in 1929 and still is one of the most lovely architectural elements in downtown St. Petersburg. Farther north in Pinellas County, the Espiritu Santo Church, 2405 Phillipe Parkway, (727) 726-8477, honors the Safety Harbor site where Hernando de Soto first set foot on the shores of Tampa Bay.

At the northermost tip of the county is Tarpon Springs' St. Ignatius, tracing its roots back to a small mission chapel erected in 1888. Today, several thousand families are served by the parish, which meets in a stunningly modern facility on Orange Street. Call (813) 937-4050 for more information.

Tarpon Springs is also known for the ornate St. Nicholas Greek Orthodox Church. Greeks began emigrating to the Tarpon Springs' sponge industry in 1905, and with them came their faith. In three years, St. Nicholas was incorporated, holding services in a wood frame building for 250 parishioners. The incredible marble structure where worshippers now gather, 13 Hibiscus Street, (813) 937-3540, began construction in 1935, when the congregation had grown to 2,700. Finally, in 1943, at a cost of more than $200,000, the church was completed and dedicated. It is a complete replica of Istanbul's St. Sophia Church, which was constructed between 532 and 537 A.D. as one of the first great, formal Christian cathedrals.

The first church on the area's barrier islands began in 1917, but not until 1941 was the Union Church of Pass-A-Grille formally incorporated as the Pass-A-Grille Community Church. For the first several years, worshippers met at the home of Evangeline Joan Haley, 115 10th Avenue. Today, that "old church" still serves residents and visitors as the Gulf Beaches Historical Museum, while parishioners meet at 107 16th Avenue, St. Pete Beach, (727) 360-5508.

Clearwater

It's this little Gulf-side beach city that is international home to a church with tens of thousands of adherents, and possibly just as many detractors: The Church of Scientology. More than 40 years ago, the late L. Ron Hubbard founded the church, headquartered at 210 S. Fort Harrison, (727) 461-1282. Although founded on spiritually sound principles of self-understanding and study, the church is often embroiled in legal difficulties and accusations that it operates more as a profit-structured cult than a religion. Still, the church's course of study has attracted followers from every walk of life, and it's been credited by many as providing the guidance they needed to improve their lives. The church has two missions in the Bay area: 100 N. Belcher Road in Clearwater, (727) 443-4111; and 3617 Henderson Boulevard, Tampa, (813) 872-0722. There are also many storefront locations.

Index

M

Index of Advertisers

Notes

Notes

Notes

Notes

Notes

FALCONGUIDES® **leading** the **way**

Travel the great outdoors with
*A***FALCON**GUIDE®

- Comprehensive information on essential outdoor skills, trails, trips, and the best places to go in each state.

- Detailed descriptions, maps, access information, photos, and safety tips.

- Easy-to-use, written by expert, and regularly updated and revised.

To locate your nearest bookseller or to order call
1-800-582-2665.

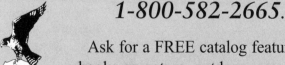

Ask for a FREE catalog featuring books on nature, outdoor recreation, travel, and the legendary American West.

FALCON®

Going Somewhere?

Insiders' Publishing presents these current and upcoming titles to popular destinations all over the country — and we're planning on adding many more. To order a title, go to your local bookstore or call (800) 582-2665 and we'll direct you to one.

Adirondacks

Atlanta, GA

Baltimore

Bend

Bermuda

Boca Raton and the Palm Beaches, FL

Boise

Boulder, CO, and
Rocky Mountain National Park

Bradenton/Sarasota, FL

Branson, MO, and the

Ozark Mountains

California's Wine Country

Cape Cod, Nantucket and
Martha's Vineyard, MA

Charleston, SC

Cincinnati, OH

Civil War Sites in the Eastern Theater

Civil War Sites in the Southern Theater

Colorado's Mountains

Denver, CO

Florida Keys and Key West

Florida's Great Northwest

Golf in the Carolinas

Indianapolis, IN

The Lake Superior Region

Las Vegas

Lexington, KY

Louisville, KY

Madison, WI

Maine's Mid-Coast

Maine's Southern Coast

Michigan's Traverse Bay Region

Minneapolis/St. Paul, MN

Mississippi

Monterey Peninsula

Myrtle Beach, SC

Nashville, TN

New Hampshire

New Orleans

North Carolina's Central Coast
and New Bern

North Carolina's Mountains

Outer Banks of North Carolina

Phoenix

The Pocono Mountains

Relocation

Richmond, VA

Salt Lake City

San Diego

Santa Barbara

Santa Fe

Savannah

Southwestern Utah

Tampa/St. Petersburg, FL

Texas Coastal Bend

Tucson

Virginia's Blue Ridge

Virginia's Chesapeake Bay

Washington, D.C.

Wichita, KS

Williamsburg, VA

Wilmington, NC

Yellowstone

THE INSIDERS'® GUIDE

Insiders' Publishing · P.O. Box 2057 · Manteo, NC 27954
Phone (252) 473-6100 · Fax (252) 473-5869 · www.insiders.com